To the memory of Frederick Rhodewalt, my professor and friend. His scholarship continues to inspire me.

Seventh Edition

Global Edition

The Art and Science of Leadership

Afsaneh Nahavandi

University of San Diego

BPP Professional Education
32-34 Colmore Circus
Birmingham B4 6BN
Phone: 0121 345 9843

Boston   Columbus   Indianapolis   New York   San Francisco   Upper Saddle River
Amsterdam   Cape Town   Dubai   London   Madrid   Milan   Munich   Paris   Montréal   Toronto
Delhi   Mexico City   São Paulo   Sydney   Hong Kong   Seoul   Singapore   Taipei   Tokyo

Editor in Chief: Stephanie Wall
Head of Learning Asset Acquisition, Global Editions: Laura Dent
Senior Editor: Kris Ellis-Levy
Program Management Lead: Ashley Santora
Program Manager: Sarah Holle
Editorial Assistant: Bernard Ollila
Assistant Acquisitions Editor, Global Editions: Debapriya Mukherjee
Senior Project Editor, Global Editions: Vaijyanti

Director of Marketing: Maggie Moylan
Marketing Manager: Erin Gardner
Project Management Lead: Judy Leale
Procurement Specialist: Michelle Klein
Project Manager: Meghan DeMaio
Creative Art Director: Jayne Conte
Cover Designer: Lumina Datamatics
Cover Art: © Taras Kushnir / Shutterstock
Media Project Manager: Lisa Rinaldi
Full-Service Project Management/Composition: Allan Rayer/Integra Software Services, Ltd.

Credits and acknowledgments borrowed from other sources and reproduced, with permission, in this textbook appear on appropriate page within text.

Pearson Education Limited
Edinburgh Gate Harlow
Essex CM20 2JE
England

and Associated Companies throughout the world

Visit us on the World Wide Web at:
www.pearsonglobaleditions.com

© Pearson Education Limited 2015

British Library Cataloguing-in-Publication Data
A catalogue record for this book is available from the British Library

10 9 8 7 6 5 4 3 2 1
15 14

ISBN 10:   1-292-06018-2
ISBN 13: 978-1-292-06018-7

Typeset in 10/12 Times by Integra Software Services, Ltd.

Printed by Courier Westford in the United States of America

BRIEF CONTENTS

PART I   Building Blocks

Chapter 1   Definition and Significance of Leadership   24

Chapter 2   The Global and Cultural Contexts   50

Chapter 3   The Foundations of Modern Leadership   86

Chapter 4   Individual Differences and Traits   126

Chapter 5   Power   164

PART II   Contemporary Concepts

Chapter 6   Current Era in Leadership: Inspiration and Connection to Followers   200

Chapter 7   Other Leadership Perspectives: Upper Echelon and Leadership of Nonprofits   233

PART III   Leading

Chapter 8   Leading Teams   268

Chapter 9   Leading Change   300

Chapter 10   Developing Leaders   332

References   360
Author Index   399
Subject Index   407

CONTENTS

Preface   15
Acknowledgments   19
About the Author   21

PART I   Building Blocks

Chapter 1   **Definition and Significance of Leadership   24**

Effective Leadership   24
Who Is a Leader?   25
When Is a Leader Effective?   25
Effectiveness versus Success   26
An Integrative Definition   27
Why Do We Need Leaders?   28
Research on Significance of Leadership   28
■ **LEADING CHANGE** The Container Store   29

Obstacles to Effective Leadership   30

Leadership and Management   31

Roles and Functions of Leaders   32
Managerial Roles   33
Functions of the Leader: Creation and Maintenance of an Organizational Culture   34
■ **APPLYING WHAT YOU LEARN** Leadership Basics   36

Changes in Organizations and in Expectations of Leaders   36
New Roles for Leaders   37
Factors Fueling Changes   38
Barriers to Change   41

Summary and Conclusions   42   •   Review and Discussion Questions   43   •   Leadership Challenge: Moving to Leadership   43   •   Exercise 1-1: More than Meets the Eye—Characteristics of Leaders   44   •   Exercise 1-2: What Is Leadership?   45   •   Exercise 1-3: Images of Leadership   46   •   Exercise 1-4: Understanding the Leadership Context   47

▶ **LEADERSHIP IN ACTION** David Neeleman Reinvents Airlines   48

Chapter 2   **The Global and Cultural Contexts   50**

Defintion and Levels of Culture   51
Definition and Characteristics   51
Levels of Culture   51

Models of National Culture   53

Hall's Cultural Context Framework   53

Hofstede's Cultural Dimensions   54

Trompenaars' Dimensions of Culture   56

GLOBE—Global Leadership and Organizational Behavior Effectiveness Research   58

■ **APPLYING WHAT YOU LEARN** Using Culture to be Effective   61

Group Culture: Gender and Leadership   61

Current State of Women in Organizations   62

Causes of Inequality   63

■ **LEADING CHANGE** Deloitte Supports All Its Employees   66

Developing a Cultural Mindset   67

Characteristics of a Cultural Mindset   67

The Multicultural Organization   69

Summary and Conclusions   71   •   Review and Discussion Questions   72   •   Leadership Challenge: Juggling Cultures   72   •   Exercise 2-1: World Map   73   •   Exercise 2-2: Proverbs as a Window to Leadership   74   •   Exercise 2-3: Narian Bridges   75   •   Exercise 2-4: Leadership and Gender   77   •   Exercise 2-5: Is This Sexual Harassment?   78   •   Self-Assessment 2-1: What Is Your Primary Cultural Background?   81   •   Self-Assessment 2-2: Do You Have a Cultural Mindset?   82   •   Self-Assessment 2-3: Exploring Views of Women   83

▶ **LEADERSHIP IN ACTION** Leadership Based On Ancient Principles   84

Chapter 3   **The Foundations of Modern Leadership   86**

A History of Modern Leadership Theory: Three Eras   87

The Trait Era: Late 1800s to Mid-1940s   87

The Behavior Era: Mid-1940s to Early 1970s   88

The Contingency Era: Early 1960s to Present   89

Early Theories   89

Fiedler's Contingency Model   90

■ **APPLYING WHAT YOU LEARN** Putting the Contingency Model to Work   95

The Normative Decision Model   95

Path–Goal Theory   99

Substitutes for Leadership   100

■ **LEADING CHANGE** Jim Goodnight of SAS   101

Leader–Member Exchange   104

Summary and Conclusions   109   •   Review and Discussion Questions   111   •   Leadership Challenge: The In-Group Applicant   111   •   Exercise 3-1 The Toy Factory   112   •   Exercise 3-2 Using the Normative Decision Model   113   •   Self-Assessment 3-1: Determining Your LPC   117   •   Self-Assessment 3-2: Assessing

*a Leadership Situation   118   •   Self-Assessment 3-3: Identifying
Your In-Group and Out-Group   122*

▶ **LEADERSHIP IN ACTION** The Caring Dictator   124

Chapter 4 Individual Differences and Traits   126

Elements and Impact of Individual Difference
Characteristics   127

Individual Characteristics Provide a Range   128

Demographic Characteristics of Leaders   129

Values   130

National Culture and Values   130

Generational Differences in Values   131

Values and Ethics   133

Abilities and Skills   134

Intelligence   134

Practical and Emotional Intelligence   134

Creativity   137

Skills   138

Personality Traits That Contribute to Leadership   138

The Big Five Personality Dimensions   140

Proactive Personality   142

Type A   143

■ **LEADING CHANGE** Jeffrey Katzenberg's Transformation   145

Self-Monitoring   146

The Dark Triad: Machiavellian, Narcissistic, and Psychopathic
Personality   147

■ **APPLYING WHAT YOU LEARN** Dealing with Abusive Bosses   149

Using Individual Characteristics   150

*Summary and Conclusions   150   •   Review and Discussion
Questions   151   •   Leadership Challenge: Using Psychological
Testing   151   •   Exercise 4-1 Your Ideal Organization   152   •   Self-
Assessment 4-1: Value Systems   154   •   Self-Assessment
4-2: Emotional Intelligence   155   •   Self-Assessment 4-3:
Proactivity   157   •   Self-Assessment 4-4: Type A   158   •   Self-
Assessment 4-5: Self-Monitoring   159   •   Self-Assessment 4-6:
Narcissism   160*

▶ **LEADERSHIP IN ACTION** Zhang Xin: The Humble Chinese Billionaire   162

Chapter 5 Power   164

Definitions and Consequences   165

Consequences of Using Power   165

Distribution of Power   167

Power and Culture   167

Sources of Power   169

Sources of Power Related to Individuals   169

Organizational Sources of Power: Power for Teams   172

Special Power Sources of Top Executives   174

■ **APPLYING WHAT YOU LEARN** Managing Power When You Are a New Manager 175

The Dark Side of Power: Abuse, Corruption, and Destructive Leadership   176

Causes and Processes   177

The Cycle of Abuse, Corruption, and Destruction   179

Consequences of Abuse and Corruption   180

Solutions   181

Empowerment: The Changing Face of Power   183

Requirements of Empowerment   183

Impact of Empowerment   185

■ **LEADING CHANGE** Sharing Power and Reaping Profits   186

Summary and Conclusions   187 • Review and Discussion Questions   188 • Leadership Challenge: How Much Is Enough   188 • Exercise 5-1 Words of Wisdom   189 • Exercise 5-2 Who Holds Power in Your Team/Organization?   191 • Self-Assessment 5-1: Understanding Your Sources of Power and Influence   192 • Self-Assessment 5-2: Views of Power   194

Self-Assessment 5-3: Recognizing Blocks to Empowerment   195

▶ **LEADERSHIP IN ACTION** The Last CEO of Lehman Brothers: Richard Fuld   196

PART II Contemporary Concepts

Chapter 6 **Current Era in Leadership   200**

New Era in Leadership Research   201

Charismatic Leadership: A Relationship between Leaders and Followers   201

Characteristics of Charismatic Leaders   202

Characteristics of Followers   204

The Charismatic Situation   205

Culture and Charisma   206

The Dark Side of Charisma   207

Evaluation and Application   209

Transactional and Transformational Leadership   210

Transactional Leadership   210

Transformational Leadership   211

Evaluation and Application   213

■ **LEADING CHANGE** The Unconventional Sir Richard Branson   214

Value-Based Leadership: Servant, Authentic, and Positive
Approaches   215

Servant Leadership   216

Authentic Leadership   217

Positive Leadership   219

■ **APPLYING WHAT YOU LEARN** Balancing a Positive Approach
with Realism   221

Evaluation and Application   221

A Critical Look at Value-Based Models   222

*Summary and Conclusions   200   •   Review and Discussion
Questions   223   •   Leadership Challenge: Standing Up to
a Charismatic but Unethical Leader   223   •   Exercise 6-1:
Do You Know a Charismatic Leader?   224   •   Exercise
6-2: Charismatic Speech   226   •   Exercise 6-3: Analyzing a
Charismatic Speech   227   •   Self-Assessment 6-1: Authentic
Leadership   229   •   Self-Assessment 6-2: Positive Leadership   230*

▶ **LEADERSHIP IN ACTION** Andrea Jung's Rise and Fall at Avon   231

Chapter 7 **Other Leadership Perspectives   233**

Definition and Role of Upper-Echelon Leaders   234

Strategic Forces   235

Role of Strategic Leaders   237

Factors That Moderate the Power of Leaders   237

■ **APPLYING WHAT YOU LEARN** Managing in Times of Crisis   240

Characteristics of Upper-Echelon Leaders   241

Demographic and Personality Traits   241

Strategic Leadership Types   242

Culture and Gender   246

How Do Executives Affect Their Organization?   248

Direct Decisions   249

Allocation of Resources and Control over the Reward System   249

Setting the Norms and Modeling   250

Strategic Leaders' Accountability   251

Unique Case of Nonprofit Organizations   253

Characteristics of Nonprofit Organizations   253

■ **LEADING CHANGE** Public Allies: Building Leadership in the Community   254

Leadership Challenges of Nonprofits   255

*Summary and Conclusions   235   •   Review and Discussion
Questions   258   •   Leadership Challenge: The Board of Directors
(BOD) and CEOs   258   •   Exercise 7-1: Understanding Strategic
Forces   259   •   Exercise 7-2: Your Organization   261   •   Exercise 7-3:*

Influence Processes 262 • *Self-Assessment 7-1: What Is Your Strategic Leadership Type? 263*

▶ **LEADERSHIP IN ACTION** Leadership Musical Chairs at P&G 264

PART III   Leading

Chapter 8   **Leading Teams   268**

Participation and Teams: Benefits and Criteria for Use   269

Benefits of Participation and Teams   269

Criteria for Participation   271

The Role of Culture   272

The Issue of Delegation   273

Benefits of Delegation   274

Guidelines for Good Delegation   274

Why Do Leaders Fail to Delegate?   276

Evolution of Participative Management: Teams and Self-Leadership   277

■ **LEADING CHANGE** Google: The Happiest Workplace on Earth?   277

Characteristics of Teams   278

Self-Managed Teams   279

■ **APPLYING WHAT YOU LEARN** Using a Sports Team Model in Management   280

Self-Leadership   281

Leading Teams Effectively   282

Size of the Team   282

Composition of the Team   283

Role of Leaders in a Team Environment   283

Managing Dysfunction in Teams   285

Helping Teams Become Effective   287

Summary and Conclusions 266 • *Review and Discussion Questions 289* • *Leadership Challenge: Who Gets the Project? 289* • *Exercise 8-1: To Delegate or Not to Delegate? 290* • *Exercise 8-2: Strategies for Becoming a Self-Leader 292* • *Self-Assessment 8-1: Delegation Scale 296* • *Self-Assessment 8-2: Are You a Team Leader? 297*

▶ **LEADERSHIP IN ACTION** John Mackey of Whole Foods   298

Chapter 9   **Leading Change   300**

Forces For Change   301

Internal and External Forces   301

Culture and Change   302

Types and Process of Change   303

Types of Change   303

Lewin's Model for Change   304

Process of Planned Change   306

Dealing with Unplanned Change   308

Resistance to Change and Solutions   308

Causes of Resistance   309

Solutions   309

Leading Change: Creativity, Vision, Organizational Learning, and Organizational Culture   311

Creativity   311

Improvisation   312

■ **LEADING CHANGE** Mulally Takes on Ford   313

Vision and Inspiration   314

Learning Organizations   317

Positive Approach   319

Changing Organizational Culture   320

■ **APPLYING WHAT YOU LEARN** Change Agents and Peer Pressure   321

Summary and Conclusions   299   •   Review and Discussion Questions   322   •   Leadership Challenge: Implementing Unpopular Change   322   •   Exercise 9-1: Analyzing and Planning for Change   323   •   Exercise 9-2: Creativity and Parallel Thinking— The Six Hats Method   326   •   Self-Assessment 9-1: Building Credibility   328   •   Self-Assessment 9-2: Creativity   329

▶ **LEADERSHIP IN ACTION** Best Buy's Almost Transformation   330

Chapter 10 Developing Leaders   332

Basic Elements of Leader Development   333

Factors in Learning   333

What Is Developed: The Content   336

Required Elements of Effective Development Programs   337

Methods of Leader Development   339

Self-Awareness   339

Experience   341

Developmental Relationships: Coaching and Mentoring   342

Feedback-Intensive Programs   345

Classroom Education   347

Outdoor Challenges   347

■ **LEADING CHANGE** Howard Schultz Stirs Up Starbucks   348

Development and Culture   349

Gender and Diversity   350

Effectiveness of Development   351

Organizational and Personal Factors in Development   352

■ **APPLYING WHAT YOU LEARN** Personal Development 353

*Summary and Conclusions 331 • Review and Discussion
Questions 354 • Leadership Challenge: Finding the Right
Fit 354 • Exercise 10-1: Identifying Your Mentoring Needs and
Potential Mentors 355 • Self-Assessment 10-1: My Personal
Mission Statement 357*

▶ **LEADERSHIP IN ACTION** Developing Leaders at Southwest Airlines 358

References 360
Author Index 399
Subject Index 407

PREFACE

Leading people effectively is a tremendous challenge, a great opportunity, and a serious responsibility. Since the first edition of *The Art and Science of Leadership* was published, the call for leadership has been growing. Our organizations and institutions, more than ever, need effective leaders who understand the complexities of our dynamic global environment, who have the intelligence to deal with complex problems, and who have the sensitivity and ability to empathize with their followers to motivate them to strive for excellence. Every civilization has focused on its leaders, revering or reviling them. Throughout history, the fate of millions has depended on the leadership qualities of emperors, kings, queens, and other leaders and on their power struggles and succession battles. Children all over the world learn early, through the fairy tales they hear and read, the art they see, and the advice they get, that leaders matter and that the happiness and misery of people depend on the goodness or evilness of leaders.

It is no wonder, then, that we are fascinated by those who lead us. Some consider leadership to be a magical process. Indeed, when we reflect on historical figures or meet some of the leaders of our times, we can be transfixed by their seemingly magical exploits. They move armies, create new countries, and destroy whole civilizations through what often appears to be the sheer strength of their will. The actions of some business leaders during the recent financial crisis is further indication of the power of good and bad leadership. At every level, leaders can affect our very existence on this planet.

Although leaders are the ones who dazzle us, we often fail to consider that they alone can accomplish nothing. It is the strength of their followers that moves history. It is the army of foot soldiers that achieves victory. It is the hard work of employees that turns a profit in a faltering company. It is the initiative of volunteers that achieves an institution's goals. It is the dedication of public servants that makes government work. We also must remember that many extraordinary leaders found themselves shunned and rejected by the people who once admired them. President Charles de Gaulle's road to the leadership of France was long, tortuous, and fraught with failure. After coming to office as a hero after World War II, he was forced out of office twice. Winston Churchill of Great Britain was removed from office on two occasions and faced long periods in his life during which his leadership was neither valued nor wanted. More recently, Benazir Bhutto of Pakistan moved from national hero to national villain and back to hero several times before her assassination. George Watson Jr. was booted out of office after successfully leading IBM for many years. Jack Welch, former CEO of General Electric and considered by many to be one of the most successful U.S. CEOs, was nicknamed Neutron Jack in his early days at GE for decimating the company workforce through layoffs. Many elected leaders around the world face similar challenges. Their magic does not work all the time and with everyone.

If a leader's powers are truly magical, why do they wax and wane? Why are they not effective all the time? Why are they effective with some followers and not others? These questions, along with many others, will be addressed in this book.

For our organizations to be effective and for society to function successfully, we must be able to select, develop, and train the right leaders and know how to help them succeed. Because the processes of leading others to achieve organizational goals are applicable in any institutional settings, this book presents a broad review and analysis of the field of leadership with application to business, public, and other organizations. Current research goes far in demystifying leadership and teaching it to the rest of us mortals. Although we still come across some leaders whose performance and behavior escape the bounds of scientific explanation, by and large, we know a good deal about leadership and how to train people to be leaders. The cornerstone of our new knowledge is that *leaders are made, not born;* most of us can learn to become better leaders. Maybe only a few of us will someday shape human civilization, but to a great extent, we all can improve our leadership skills, connect with our followers, and engage them to shape our organizations and communities.

SOME BASIC ASSUMPTIONS

The seventh edition builds on the strengths of the previous six editions while updating theories and examples. The many debates and controversies within the field of leadership are presented in this edition as they were in the first six. I continue to emphasize integration of the concepts and distill useful and practical concepts from each theory while taking a strong cross-cultural perspective. The guiding philosophy, assumptions, and methods remain the same.

- *Leadership is about others.* Leaders exist to help others achieve their goals. While we tend to focus on the person of the leader, effective leadership is and should be about others, not the leader.
- *Leadership is a complex process* that cannot be explained by one word, one concept, or through a simple definition or action.
- *We all can learn to become better leaders.* For some of us, the learning is easier in certain areas than in others, but with motivation, practice and support from our organizations, we all can improve our leadership skills. While it is not easy to move teams, departments, and organizations toward higher levels of effectiveness and efficiency, there is no magic involved in achieving these goals. We can use the many existing leadership theories to achieve them.
- *A cross-cultural perspective is essential to understanding leadership.* Leadership is not a culture-free process. The book includes extensive cross-cultural and gender-based analyses of leadership as a major part of the discourse about leadership effectiveness.
- *Theories are useful tools.* While they sometimes appear esoteric, complicated, and even contradictory, theories are useful tools that help clarify the complex process of leadership. No one theory alone explains that complex process, but many of them together (even the old ones!) can provide a relatively complete picture of what it takes to lead effectively.
- *Application and practice are essential to learning.* You cannot learn to lead from a book or in a classroom alone. Knowledge is essential; the concepts and theories presented cover that aspect. But to learn to lead, you have to practice. The many examples, cases, and the various pedagogical features such as the *Leadership Challenges* as well as end-of-chapter exercises and self-assessments offer opportunities for engagement and are a starting point for practice to complete the theoretical knowledge.

NEW TO THE SEVENTH EDITION

Research in the field of leadership is dynamic, extensive, and multidisciplinary. As has been the case with every edition, extensive research has gone into this edition. Additionally, I had the opportunity to teach several large undergraduate leadership classes for the past couple of years and my students' feedback has shaped many of the revisions that you will see in this edition. Although the overall structure remains the same, the outline in many chapters has been changed and I have added several new features to ensure that students can learn more easily and apply what they learn more readily. Specific changes include the following:

- Close to two hundred new references have been added throughout the chapters, almost all dating from 2010 forward.
- Close to 150 references were removed because newer more current research was available, the examples no longer fit, or leaders had left or retired.
- Updated and revised learning outcomes for each chapter.
- Two new pedagogical features in all the chapters:
  - Each chapter starts with a "*The Leadership Question*" that focuses the student on the theoretical or practical issues covered in the chapter. The question is specifically addressed at some point in the chapter in "*The Leadership Question—Revisited*" segment.
  - Each chapter includes a "*What Do You Do?*" feature that presents a brief action-oriented scenario to help students connect the material with hands-on applications.

In addition to general updates of research and examples in all the chapters, six of the ten chapters have been substantially revised. Changes include the following:

- In Chapter 2:
  - A substantial revision of the presentation of the GLOBE research
  - Substantial revision and of the material on gender and diversity
  - New exercise added—*World Map*
  - *Cultural Mindset* self-assessment revised
- In Chapter 4:
  - New material and new self-assessment on proactive personality
  - New material on the Dark Triad replaces separate coverage of Machiavellianism and Narcissism
  - Extensive revision on the section on leaders who fail
  - New case about Zhang Xi of Soho-China
- In Chapter 6:
  - Chapter is retitled to address the new era in leadership research
  - Extensively revised presentation of value-based leadership including servant, authentic, and positive leadership
  - New "*Applying what you learn: Balancing a positive approach with realism*"
  - Revised self-assessment on Authentic Leadership
  - Extensive revision of the Avon-Andrea Jung case to reflect her leaving the company
- In Chapter 7:
  - New "*Leading change: Public Allies*"
  - Extensive revision of the *Leadership in Action* case to reflect changes in leadership at P&G
- In Chapter 8:
  - New "*Leading Change: Google*"
  - New material on helping teams become effective
- In Chapter 9:
  - Structure of the chapter has been revised
  - New "*Leading Change: Ford's Alan Mulally*"
  - New exercise – *The Six Hats*
  - Extensively revised *Leadership in Action* that reflects Best Buy's change in policy

INSTRUCTOR'S RESOURCE CENTER

At www.pearsonglobaleditions.com/Nahavandi, instructors can access a variety of media and presentation resources available with this text in downloadable, digital format. Once you register, you will not have additional forms to fill out, or multiple usernames and passwords to remember to access new titles and/or editions. As a registered faculty member, you can log in directly to download resource files and receive immediate access and instructions for installing course management content on your campus server.

Our dedicated Technical Support team is ready to assist instructors with questions about the media supplements that accompany this text. Visit http://247pearsoned.custhelp.com for answers to frequently asked questions and toll-free user support phone numbers.

To download the supplements available with this text, please visit: www.pearsonglobaleditions.com/Nahavandi

- *Instructor's Manual*
- *Test Item File*
- *Test Generator*
- *PowerPoints*

COURSESMART TEXTBOOKS ONLINE*

CourseSmart is an exciting new choice for students looking to save money. As an alternative to purchasing the print textbook, students can purchase an electronic version of the same content for less than the suggested list price of the print text. With a CourseSmart e-textbook, students can search the text, make notes online, print out reading assignments that incorporate lecture notes, and bookmark important passages for later review.

WHO SHOULD READ THIS BOOK?

The Art and Science of Leadership is targeted to students of leadership—whether they are advanced undergraduate and graduate students or managers with a desire to learn and grow. It is written for those who want not only to understand the various theories and research in the field but also to apply that knowledge to become better leaders and to improve the leadership of their organizations. The examples and cases are from different types of industries and from the private and public sectors. Although the theories often are developed and tested by psychology and management researchers, they have broad applicability to all organizations and their leadership.

---

*This product may not be available in all markets. For more details, please visit www.coursesmart.co.uk or contact your local Pearson representative.

ACKNOWLEDGMENTS

Years after leaving graduate school, I continue to be grateful for the faculty with whom I worked. I would like to thank Marty Chemers for putting the leadership bug in my ear when I was a graduate student and Irv Altman, who taught me to look at any issue from many different perspectives. I owe Carol Werner many thanks for teaching me to organize my thoughts.

Many thanks go also to my partners at Pearson: Stephanie Wall, Editor in Chief; Kris Ellis-Levy, Senior Editor; Ashley Santora, Program Lead; Sarah Holle Program Manager; Judy Leale, Project Lead; Meghan DeMaio, Project Manager; and Bernard Ollila, Editorial Assistant. I would also like to acknowledge the reviewers for their thoughtful comments in reviewing the book:

Ray Oman
  Webster University

Carrie Blair Messal
  College of Charleston

Abe Qastin
  Lakeland College

Rusty Juban
  Southeastern Louisiana University

Kelly Gillerlain
  Tidewater Community College—Chesapeake

Brenda Fellows
  University of California - Berkeley

Alan Boss
  University of Washington—Bothell

Lisa Chandler
  Quinnipiac

Gary Kohut
  University of North Carolina

Kathleen Montesarchio
  Broward College

Karen Middleton
  Texas A&M—Corpus Christi

And last, but not least, as always, I sincerely appreciate my family's encouragement and support.

Pearson would like to thank and acknowledge the following people for their work on the Global Edition. For his contribution: Roger Fullwood. And for their reviews: Kim-Yin Chan, Nanyang Business School—Singapore; Robin Cheng, Taylor's University—Malaysia; Jacques N. Couvas, Bilkent University—Turkey; Kate Mottram, Coventry University—United Kingdom.

ABOUT THE AUTHOR

Afsaneh Nahavandi is professor and department chair of Leadership Studies at the University of San Diego and professor Emerita at Arizona State University. She earned a Bachelor of Arts degree in Psychology and French from the University of Denver and holds an MA and PhD in Social Psychology from University of Utah. Her areas of specialty are leadership, culture, ethics, and teams. She has published articles and contributed chapters on these topics in journals such as the *Academy of Management Review,* the *Journal of Management Studies,* the *Academy of Management Executive*, and the *Journal of Business Ethics*. Her article about teams won the *Academy of Management Executive*'s 1994 Best Article of the Year award. Her other books include *Organizational Behavior* (with Robert Denhardt, Janet Denhardt, and Maria Aristigueta, 2014), *Ancient Leadership Wisdom* (2012), *Organizational Behavior: The Person–Organization Fit* (with Ali Malekzadeh, 1999), and *Organizational Culture in the Management of Mergers* (with Ali Malekzadeh,1993). She joined the department of Leadership Studies at the University of San Diego in 2013 after teaching at Arizona State University for twenty six years in both the Business School and in the School of Public Affairs. She also taught in the Business School at Northeastern University in Boston. She has held several administrative positions, including associate dean of ASU's College of Public Programs, Associate Dean of ASU's University College, and director of the ASU West School of Management MBA program. She is the recipient of several teaching awards, including the Arizona State University Parents Association Professor of the Year in 2004.

I

Building Blocks

Part I lays the foundation for understanding the processes of leadership. After studying Part I, you will be able to define the basic elements of leadership and be ready to integrate them to understand more complex leadership processes. Leadership involves interaction among several key elements: a leader, followers, and the situation. Since its beginnings in the West in the late nineteenth century, the formal study of leadership has generated many definitions of the concept. As with any social phenomenon, culture strongly influences not only our definitions of leadership but also how we actually lead and what we expect of our leaders. Tracing the history of the field can help us understand how our current views of leadership have developed and enable us to become aware of how the process of leadership and our images and expectations of effective leaders change with organizational, social, and cultural evolutions.

Chapter 1 provides a working definition of leadership and effectiveness, explores the reasons why we need leadership, describes the roles and functions of leaders, and discusses their impact. Chapter 2 focuses on understanding the role of culture in leadership. Several models for describing culture are presented, and the roles of gender and diversity in leadership are explored. Chapter 3 presents a history of the field of leadership and reviews the theories that provide the foundation for current approaches. Individual differences that affect leadership are discussed in Chapter 4. They include demographic differences, values, abilities, skills, and several personality traits. Chapter 5 reviews the concept of power and its importance to leadership.

1

Definition and Significance of Leadership

After studying this chapter, you will be able to:

1. Define leadership and leadership effectiveness.
2. Discuss the major obstacles to effective leadership.
3. Compare and contrast leadership and management.
4. List the roles and functions of leaders and managers.
5. Explain the changes in organizations and how they affect leaders.
6. Summarize the debate over the role and impact of leadership in organizations.

THE LEADERSHIP QUESTION

Some leaders are focused on getting things done while others put taking care of their followers first. Some look at the big picture, and others hone in on the details. Is one approach better than the other? Which one do you prefer?

Who is a leader? When are leaders effective? These age-old questions appear simple, but their answers have kept philosophers, social scientists, scholars from many disciplines, and business practitioners busy for many years. We recognize bad leadership. Bad leaders are dishonest, self-centered, arrogant, disorganized, and uncommunicative. However, being honest, selfless, organized and communicative are necessary, but not sufficient to be a good leader. This chapter defines leadership and its many aspects, roles, and functions.

EFFECTIVE LEADERSHIP

We recognize effective leaders when we work with them or observe them. However, leadership is a complex process, and there are many different definitions of leadership and leadership effectiveness.

Who Is a Leader?

Dictionaries define *leading* as "guiding and directing on a course" and as "serving as a channel." A leader is someone with commanding authority or influence. Researchers have developed many working definitions of leadership. Although these definitions share several elements, they each consider different aspects of leadership. Some define leadership as an integral part of the group process (Green, 2002; Krech and Crutchfield, 1948). Others define it primarily as an influence process (Bass, 1960; Cartwright, 1965; Katz and Kahn, 1966). Still others see leadership as the initiation of structure (Homans, 1950) and the instrument of goal achievement. Several even consider leaders to be servants of their followers (Greenleaf, 1998). Despite the differences, the various definitions of leadership share four common elements:

- First, leadership is a *group and social phenomenon*; there can be no leaders without followers. Leadership is about others.
- Second, leadership necessarily involves interpersonal *influence* or persuasion. Leaders move others toward goals and actions.
- Third, leadership is *goal directed* and *action oriented*; leaders play an active role in groups and organizations. They use influence to guide others through a certain course of action or toward the achievement of certain goals.
- Fourth, the presence of leaders assumes some form of *hierarchy within a group*. In some cases, the hierarchy is formal and well defined, with the leader at the top; in other cases, it is informal and flexible.

Combining these four elements, we can define *a leader as any person who influences individuals and groups within an organization, helps them establish goals, and guides them toward achievement of those goals, thereby allowing them to be effective*. Being a leader is about getting things done for, through, and with others. Notice that the definition does not include a formal title and does not define leadership in terms of certain traits or personal characteristics. Neither is necessary to leadership.

This broad and general definition includes those who have formal leadership titles and many who do not. For Jonas Falk, CEO of OrganicLife, a start-up company that provide nutritious school lunches, leadership is taking "an average team of individuals and transform(ing) them into superstars" (Mielach, 2012). For consultant Kendra Coleman, leadership is about taking a stand (Mielach, 2012). Bill Gates, founder of Microsoft, considers empowerment to be an essential part of leadership (Kruse, 2013). For the CEO of the Container Store, "leadership and communication are the same thing. Communication is leadership" (Bryant, 2010). In all these examples, the leader moves followers to action and helps them achieve goals, but each focuses on a different element that constitutes leadership.

When Is a Leader Effective?

What does it mean to be an effective leader? As is the case with the definition of leadership, effectiveness can be defined in various ways. Some researchers, such as Fred Fiedler, whose Contingency Model is discussed in Chapter 3, define leadership effectiveness in terms of group performance. According to this view, leaders are effective when their group performs well. Other models—for example, Robert House's Path-Goal Theory presented in Chapter 3—consider follower satisfaction as a primary factor in determining leadership effectiveness; leaders are effective when their followers are satisfied. Still others, namely researchers working on the transformational and visionary leadership models described in Chapters 6 and 9, define effectiveness as the successful implementation of change in an organization.

The definitions of leadership effectiveness are as diverse as the definitions of organizational effectiveness. The choice of a certain definition depends mostly on the point of view of the person trying to determine effectiveness and on the constituents who are being considered. For cardiologist Stephen Oesterle, senior vice president for medicine and technology at Medtronic, one of the world's biggest manufacturers of medical devices and pacemakers, restoring lives is both a personal and an organizational goal (Tuggle, 2007). Barbara Waugh, a 1960s civil rights and antidiscrimination activist and once personnel director and worldwide change manager of Hewlett-Packard Laboratories (often known as the "World's Best Industrial Research Laboratory"—WBIRL), defines effectiveness as finding a story that is worth living: "You decide what you want your life to be about and go after it" (Marshall, 2009: 3). John Hickenlooper, Colorado governor and former mayor of Denver, focuses on an inclusive style, cooperation, aligning people's self-interest, and getting buy-in from the people who are affected by his decisions (Goldsmith, 2008).

Effectiveness versus Success

Clearly, no one way best defines what it means to be an effective leader. Fred Luthans (1989) proposes an interesting twist on the concept of leadership effectiveness by distinguishing between effective and successful managers. According to Luthans, effective managers are those with satisfied and productive employees, whereas successful managers are those who are promoted quickly. After studying a group of managers, Luthans suggests that successful managers and effective managers engage in different types of activities. Whereas effective managers spend their time communicating with subordinates, managing conflict, and training, developing, and motivating employees, the primary focus of successful managers is not on employees. Instead, they concentrate on networking activities such as interacting with outsiders, socializing, and politicking.

The internal and external activities that effective and successful managers undertake are important to allowing leaders to achieve their goals. Luthans, however, finds that only 10 percent of the managers in his study are effective *and* successful. The results of his study present some grave implications for how we might measure our leaders' effectiveness and reward them. To encourage and reward performance, organizations need to reward the leadership activities that will lead to effectiveness rather than those that lead to quick promotion. If an organization cannot achieve balance, it quickly might find itself with flashy but incompetent leaders who reached the top primarily through networking rather than through taking care of their employees and achieving goals. Barbara Waugh, mentioned earlier, considers the focus on what she calls the "vocal visionary" at the expense of the "quiet implementer" one of the reasons many organizations do not achieve their full potential (Marshall, 2009). Joe Torre, the famed Los Angeles Dodgers baseball coach, believes that solid, quiet, and steady managers who do not brag are the ones who get things done (Hollon, 2009).

Ideally, any definition of leadership effectiveness should consider all the different roles and functions that a leader performs. Few organizations, however, perform such a thorough analysis, and they often fall back on simplistic measures. For example, stockholders and financial analysts consider the CEO of a company to be effective if company stock prices keep increasing, regardless of how satisfied the company's employees are. Politicians are effective if the polls indicate their popularity is high and if they are reelected. A football coach is effective when his team is winning. Students' scores on standardized tests determine a school principal's effectiveness. In all cases, the factors that make the leader effective are highly complex and multifaceted.

Consider the challenge faced by the executives of the *New York Times*, one of the world's most respected newspapers. In 2002, the paper won a record seven Pulitzer prizes, a clear measure of success. A year later, however, the same executive editor team that had led the company in that success was forced to step down because of plagiarism scandals (Bennis, 2003). The executive team's hierarchical structure, autocratic leadership style, and an organizational culture that focused on winning and hustling were partly blamed for the scandals (McGregor, 2005). By one measure, the *Times* was highly effective; by another, it failed a basic tenet of the journalistic profession. Politics further provide examples of the complexity of defining leadership effectiveness. Consider former U.S. president Clinton, who, despite being impeached in the U.S. Senate, maintained his popularity at the polls in 1998 and 1999; many voters continued to consider him effective. Hugo Chavez, the late president of Venezuela, was adored by his supporters for his advocacy for the poor and despised by his opponents for his dictatorial style. Whether any of these leaders is considered effective or not depends on one's perspective. General Motors' recent troubles further illustrate the need for a broad definition of effectiveness.

An Integrative Definition

The common thread in all these examples of effectiveness is the focus on outcome. To judge their effectiveness, we look at the results of what leaders accomplish. Process issues, such as employee satisfaction, are important but are rarely the primary indicator of effectiveness. Nancy McKintry, CEO of Wolters Kluwer, an information services company, states, "At the end of the day, no matter how much somebody respects your intellect or your capabilities or how much they like you, in the end it is all about results in the business context" (Bryant, 2009a). The executive editorial team at the *New York Times* delivered the awards despite creating a difficult and sometimes hostile culture. Voters in the United States liked President Clinton because the economy flourished under his administration. Hugo Chavez survived many challenges because he pointed to specific accomplishments.

One way to take a broad view of effectiveness is to consider leaders effective when their group is successful in maintaining internal stability and external adaptability while achieving goals. Overall, *leaders are effective when their followers achieve their goals, can function well together, and can adapt to changing demands from external forces*. The definition of leadership effectiveness, therefore, contains three elements:

1. *Goal achievement*, which includes meeting financial goals, producing quality products or services, addressing the needs of customers, and so forth
2. *Smooth internal processes*, including group cohesion, follower satisfaction, and efficient operations
3. *External adaptability*, which refers to a group's ability to change and evolve successfully

---

THE LEADERSHIP QUESTION—REVISITED

So focusing on the task, on people, on the big picture, on the details, and so forth can all be part of leadership. What works depends on the leader, the followers, and the situation. While some things generally don't work, for example using fear and threats in all situations, there are many different styles and approaches to leading that can be effective. Understanding the situation is key.

Why Do We Need Leaders?

Leadership is a universal phenomenon across cultures. Why is leadership necessary? What needs does it fulfill? Do we really need leaders? In the business world, new leaders can influence a firm's credit rating by affecting the confidence of the financial community. For example, while Xerox weathered considerable financial and leadership problems in 2000 and 2001, the selection of Anne Mulcahy, a company veteran, as CEO helped ease stakeholders' concerns. In other sectors, a city or nation might feel a sense of revival and optimism or considerable concern when a new leader comes to power, as was the case in the 2008 U.S. presidential elections with the win of Barack Obama. We believe that leadership matters. The reasons why we need leaders closely fall in line with the functions and roles that leaders play and are related to the need or desire to be in collectives. Overall, we need leaders for following reasons:

- *To keep groups orderly and focused.* Human beings have formed groups and societies for close to 50,000 years. Whether the formation of groups itself is an instinct or whether it is based on the need to accomplish complex tasks too difficult for individuals to undertake, the existence of groups requires some form of organization and hierarchy. Whereas individual group members may have common goals, they also have individual needs and aspirations. Leaders are needed to pull the individuals together, organize, and coordinate their efforts.
- *To accomplish tasks.* Groups allow us to accomplish tasks that individuals alone could not undertake or complete. Leaders are needed to facilitate that accomplishment, and to provide goals and directions and coordinate activities.
- *To make sense of the world.* Groups and their leaders provide individuals with a perceptual check. Leaders help us make sense of the world, establish social reality, and assign meaning to events and situations that may be ambiguous.
- *To be romantic ideals.* Finally, as some researchers have suggested (e.g., Meindl and Ehrlick, 1987), leadership is needed to fulfill our desire for mythical or romantic figures who represent us and symbolize our own and our culture's ideals and accomplishments.

Research on Significance of Leadership

Despite the common belief that leaders matter, considerable debate among leadership scholars addresses whether leadership actually affects organizations. Some researchers suggest that environmental, social, industrial, and economic conditions determine organizational direction and performance to a much higher degree than does leadership (Brown, 1982; Cyert and March, 1963; Hannan and Freeman, 1977; Salancik and Pfeffer, 1977a). External factors, along with organizational elements such as structure and strategy, are assumed to limit the leader's decision-making options, reducing the leader's discretion. For example, Salancik and Pfeffer (1977a), in a study of the performance of mayors, found that leadership accounted for only 7 to 15 percent of changes in city budgets. Similarly, Lieberson and O'Connor (1972) found that whereas leadership has minimal effects on the performance of large corporations (accounting for only 7 to 14 percent of the performance), company size and economic factors show considerable links to firm performance. Additionally research about managerial discretion indicates that managers have less influence on organizations than environmental and internal organizational factors (Finkelstein and Hambrick, 1996; Hambrick and Finkelstein, 1987).

Other research findings suggest that leadership does indeed have an impact. For example, in reevaluating Lieberson and O'Connor's 1972 study, Weiner and Mahoney (1981) find that a change in leadership accounts for 44 percent of the profitability of the firms studied. Other researchers (Day and Lord, 1988; Thomas, 1988) indicate that the early results were not as strong as originally believed, and recent studies suggest that leadership can have an impact by looking at the disruption that can come from changes in leadership (Ballinger and Schoorman, 2007) and find a strong effect of CEOs on company performance (Mackey, 2008). Additionally, research continues to indicate that leadership has a positive impact on a

LEADING CHANGE

The Container Store

"You can build a much more wonderful company on love than you can on fear," says Kip Tindell, the CEO of the highly successful Container Store chain (Klein, 2013). He has put that principle to work in all aspects of his business. Chances are that if you have engaged in a home or office organization project, you have heard of the Container Store. The privately held company offers creative, practical, and innovative solutions to a multitude of storage problems and has established an enviable track record of success and growth of 26 percent growth per year (Container Store's secret growth story, 2013). The company has been consistently ranked as one of the best places to work in, and it considers its employees its greatest asset. Its unique culture and treating its employees well are other areas in which it claims leadership (Container Store Web site, 2013). One of the principles that the company espouses is that "one great person equals three good people" (Bliss, 2011).

Kip Tindell says, "We talk about getting the customer to dance...every time she goes into the closet...because the product has been designed and sold to her so carefully" (Birchall, 2006). Achieving this level of service takes a dedicated and, the company believes, happy employees that the company carefully recruits (often mostly through its existing employees) and trains. Whereas in comparable companies, the average salesperson gets about eight hours of training during the first year on the job, it is not unusual for Container Store salespeople to get over 200 hours of training before a new store opens (Birchall, 2006). In addition to a family-friendly work environment, the company covers close to 70 percent of its employees' health-care insurance costs, pays 50 to 100 percent higher wages than its competitors' pay, and provides flexible shifts to accommodate its employees' work–life balance.

The investment in employees has paid off. The Container Store has an annual turnover of about 10 percent, compared with 90 percent for most retail stores. Its founders, Kip Tindell and Garrett Boone, believe that the unique culture and the success of the company are inseparable.

Sources: Birchall, J. 2006. "Training improves shelf life," *Financial Times*, March 8. http://search.ft.com/ft Article?queryText=Kip+Tindell&y=0&aje=true&x=0&id=060307009431 (accessed July 8, 2007); Bliss, J. 2011. "Container store—Flames of trust," *SatMetrix*. http://www.netpromoter.com/netpromoter_ community/blogs/jeanne_bliss/2011/10/24/the-container-store—flames-of-trust (accessed May 30, 2013); Container Store's secret growth story, 2013. http://www.youtube.com/watch?v=uDmfbrcGxSk (accessed May 30, 2013); Container store website, 2013. http://standfor.containerstore.com/putting-our-employees-first/ (accessed October 6, 2013); Containing Culture, 2007. *Chain Store Age* (April): 23–24; Klein, J. 2013. "Put people first," *Under 30 CEOs*. http://under30ceo.com/put-people-first-reflections-from-kip-tindell-ceo-the-container-store/ (accessed May 30, 2013).

TABLE 1-1	Significance of Leadership

- Leadership is one of many factors that affect the performance of organizations.
- Leadership can indirectly impact other performance factors.
- Leadership is essential in providing vision and direction.
- Identifying the situations in which leadership matters is essential.
- The combination of leaders with followers and other organizational factors makes an impact.

variety of organizational effectiveness factors including climate and work group performance (McMurray et al., 2012) in both business and public organizations (e.g., Vashdi, Vigoda-Gadot, and Shlomi, 2013).

In trying to reconcile the different arguments regarding the need for and impact of leadership, it is important to recognize that leadership is one of many factors that influence the performance of a group or an organization (see Table 1-1 for a summary). Additionally, the leader's contribution, although not always tangible, is significant in providing a vision and direction for followers and in integrating their activities. The key is to identify situations in which the leader's power and discretion over the group and the organization are limited. These situations are discussed as part of the concept of leadership substitutes in Chapter 3 and in presentations of the role of upper-echelon leaders in Chapter 7. Finally, the potential lack of impact of leaders in some situations further emphasizes the importance of followers in the success of leadership and the need to understand organizations as broad systems.

OBSTACLES TO EFFECTIVE LEADERSHIP

In any setting, being an effective leader is a challenging task. Even with a clear definition of leadership and what makes a leader effective, being effective is not easy. Meanwhile, organizations pay a heavy price for ineffective, incompetent, or unethical leadership (Bedeian and Armenakis, 1998; Kellerman, 2004). The keys to becoming an effective leader are knowledge, experience, practice, and learning from one's mistakes. Unfortunately, many organizations do not provide an environment in which leaders can practice new skills, try out new behaviors, and observe their impact. In most cases, the price for making mistakes is so high that new leaders and managers opt for routine actions.

Without such practice and without failure, it is difficult for leaders to learn how to be effective. The experience of failure, in some cases, may be a defining moment in the development of a leader (George, 2009). The question is, therefore, what are the obstacles to becoming an effective leader? Aside from different levels of skills and aptitudes that might prevent a leader from being effective, several other obstacles to effective leadership exist:

- First, organizations face considerable *uncertainty* that creates pressure for quick responses and solutions. External forces, such as voters and investors, demand immediate attention. In an atmosphere of crisis, there is no time or patience for learning. Ironically, implementing new methods of leadership, if they are allowed, would make dealing with complexity and uncertainty easier in the long run. Therefore, a vicious cycle that allows no time for the learning that would help current crises continues. The lack of learning and experimentation in turn causes the continuation of the crises, which makes the time needed to learn and practice innovative behaviors unavailable.

- Second, organizations are often *rigid and unforgiving*. In their push for short-term and immediate performance, they do not allow any room for mistakes and experimentation. A few organizations, such as Virgin Group Ltd., 3M, and Apple Computers that encourage taking risks and making mistakes, are the exception. The rigidity and rewards systems of many institutions discourage such endeavors.
- Third, organizations fall back on *old ideas* about what effective leadership is and, therefore, rely on *simplistic solutions* that do not fit new and complex problems. The use of simple ideas, such as those proposed in many popular books, provides only temporary solutions.
- Fourth, over time, all organizations develop a particular *culture* that strongly influences how things are done and what is considered acceptable behavior. As leaders try to implement new ideas and experiment with new methods, they may face resistance generated by the established culture.
- Finally, another factor that can pose an obstacle to effective leadership is the difficulty involved in understanding and applying the findings of *academic research*. In the laudable search for precision and scientific rigor, academic researchers sometimes do not clarify the application of their research, making the research inaccessible to practitioners.

The complex and never-ending learning process of becoming an effective leader requires experimentation and organizational support. The inaccessibility of academic research to many practitioners and the short-term orientation of the organizations in which most managers operate provide challenging obstacles to effective leadership. Except for the few individuals who are talented and learn quickly and easily or those rare leaders who have the luxury of time, these obstacles are not easily surmounted. Organizations that allow their leaders at all levels to make mistakes, learn, and develop new skills are training effective leaders.

LEADERSHIP AND MANAGEMENT

What is the difference between a leader and a manager? Are the two basically the same, or are there sharp distinctions between them? These questions have been at the forefront of the discussion of leadership for many years. Kevin Kruse, bestselling author and entrepreneur, believes that organizations need good management to plan, measure, hire, fire, coordinate activities, and so forth. However, he states that leadership is about people (Kruse, 2013). Table 1-2 presents the major distinctions between managers and leaders. Whereas leaders have long-term and future-oriented perspectives and provide a vision for their followers to look beyond their immediate surroundings, managers take short-term perspectives and focus on routine issues within their own immediate departments or groups. Zaleznik (1990) further suggests that leaders, but not managers, are charismatic and can create a sense of excitement and purpose in their followers. Kotter (1990; 1996) takes a historical perspective in the debate and proposes that leadership is an age-old concept, but the concept of management developed in the past 100 years as a result of the complex organizations created after the Industrial Revolution. A manager's role is to bring order and consistency through planning, budgeting, and controlling. Leadership, on the other hand, is aimed at producing movement and change.

TABLE 1-2 Managers and Leaders	
Managers	**Leaders**
Focus on the present	Focus on the future
Maintain status quo and stability	Create change
Implement policies and procedures	Initiate goals and strategies
Maintain existing structure	Create a culture based on shared values
Remain aloof to maintain objectivity	Establish an emotional link with followers
Use position power	Use personal power

The debates suggest that for those who draw a distinction between leaders and managers, leaders demonstrate attributes that allow them to energize their followers, whereas managers simply take care of the mundane and routine details. Both are necessary for organizations to function, and one cannot replace the other. By considering the issue of effectiveness, many of the arguments regarding the differences between leadership and management can be clarified. For example are managers who motivate their followers and whose departments achieve all their goals simply effective managers, or are they leaders as well? Being an effective manager often involves performing many of the functions that are attributed to leaders with or without some degree of charisma. The distinctions drawn between leadership and management may be more related to effectiveness than to the difference between the two concepts. An effective manager of people provides a mission and sense of purpose with future-oriented goals, initiates goals and actions, and builds a sense of shared values that allows followers to be focused and motivated, all actions that are attributed to leaders. Therefore, effective managers can often be considered leaders. Management professor Henry Mintzberg further suggests that good leaders must manage their team and organizations as well. By focusing too much on leadership, at the expense of management, much of the hard work needed to make organizations effective may be left unattended. He states: "Being an engaged leader means you must be reflective while staying in the fray-the hectic, fragmented, never-ending world of managing" (Mintzberg, 2009).

Thus, any manager who guides a group toward goal accomplishment can be considered a leader, and any good leader must perform many management functions. Much of the distinction between management and leadership comes from the fact that the title *leader* assumes competence. Consequently, an effective and successful manager can be considered a leader, but a less-competent manager is not a leader. Overall, the debate over the difference between the two concepts does not add much to our understanding of what constitutes good leadership or good management and how to achieve these goals. It does, however, point to the need felt by many people and organizations for effective, competent, and visionary leadership/management. This book does not dwell on the distinction between the two concepts and uses the terms interchangeably.

ROLES AND FUNCTIONS OF LEADERS

Although leaders in different organizations and different cultures perform dissimilar functions and play unique roles, researchers have identified a number of managerial roles and functions that cut across most settings.

Managerial Roles

To be effective, leaders perform a number of roles. The roles are sets of expected behaviors ascribed to them by virtue of their leadership position. Along with the basic managerial functions of planning, organizing, staffing, directing, and controlling, leaders are ascribed a number of strategic and external roles, as well, which are discussed in detail in Chapter 7. Furthermore, one of the major functions of leaders is to provide their group or organization with a sense of vision and mission. For example, department managers need to plan and organize their department's activities and assign various people to perform tasks. They also monitor their employees' performance and correct employees' actions when needed. Aside from these internal functions, managers negotiate with their boss and other department managers for resources and coordinate decisions and activities with them. Additionally, many department managers must participate in strategic planning and the development of their organization's mission beyond the immediate focus on their own department or team.

One of the most cited taxonomies of managerial activities is proposed by Henry Mintzberg (1973), who added the 10 executive roles of figurehead, leader, liaison, monitor, disseminator, spokesperson, entrepreneur, disturbance handler, resource allocator, and negotiator to an already long list of what leaders do. Mintzberg's research further suggests that few, if any, managers perform these roles in an organized, compartmentalized, and coherent fashion. Instead, a typical manager's days are characterized by a wide variety of tasks, frequent interruptions, and little time to think or to connect with their subordinates. Mintzberg's findings are an integral part of many definitions of leadership and management. The roles he defines are typically considered the major roles and functions of leaders.

Interestingly, research suggests that male and female managers may perform their roles differently. In her book, *The Female Advantage: Women's Way of Leadership*, Sally Helgesen (1995) questions many myths about the universality of management behaviors. Through case studies of five female executives, Helgesen faithfully replicated the methodology used 20 years earlier by Mintzberg in his study of seven male managers. Mintzberg had found that his managers often worked at an unrelenting pace, with many interruptions and few nonwork-related activities. The men felt that their identity was tied directly to their job and often reported feeling isolated, with no time to reflect, plan, and share information with others. They also reported having a complex network of colleagues outside work and preferring face-to-face interaction to all other means of communication.

Helgesen's findings of female managers matched Mintzberg's only in the last two categories. Her female managers also were part of a complex network and preferred face-to-face communication. The other findings, however, were surprisingly different. The women reported working at a calm, steady pace with frequent breaks. They did not consider unscheduled events to be interruptions; they instead viewed them as a normal part of their work. All of them reported working at a number of nonwork-related activities. They each cultivated multifaceted identities and, therefore, did not feel isolated. They found themselves with time to read and reflect on the big picture. Additionally, the female executives scheduled time to share information with their colleagues and subordinates.

The gender differences found between the two studies can be attributed partly to the 20-year time difference. However, Helgesen's suggestions about a different female leadership style, which she calls "the web," are supported by a number of other research and anecdotal studies. Helgesen's web is compared to a circle with the manager in the center and interconnected to all other parts of the department or organization. This view differs sharply from the traditional pyramid structure common in many organizations. Chapter 2 further explores the gender differences in leadership.

Functions of the Leader: Creation and Maintenance of an Organizational Culture

One of the major functions of leaders is the creation and development of a culture and climate for their group or organization (Nahavandi and Malekzadeh, 1993a; Schein, 2010). Leaders, particularly founders, leave an almost-indelible mark on the assumptions that are passed down from one generation to the next. In fact, organizations often come to mirror their founders' personalities. Consider, for example, how Starbucks, the worldwide provider of gourmet coffee, reflects the dreams and fears of its founder, Howard Schultz (see Leading Change case in Chapter 10). The company is known for its generous benefit package and its focus on taking care of its employees. Schultz often repeats the story of his father losing his job after breaking his leg and the devastating and long-lasting effect this event had on him and his family (George, 2007). As is the case in many other organizations, the founder's style, or in the case of Starbucks, the founder's family history, has an impact on the culture of an organization.

If the founder is workaholic and control oriented, the organization is likely to push for fast-paced decision making and be centralized. If the founder is participative and team oriented, the organization will be decentralized and open. Norm Brodsky, a veteran entrepreneur who created several businesses, realized how much his hard-driving personality affected the culture of his company. He also realized that his wife and partner's more caring style was having a positive impact on employees, so he worked on softening his own style and supporting her initiatives (Brodsky, 2006). The leader's passion often translates into the mission or one of the primary goals of the organization, as is the case of Howard Schultz for Starbucks. Similarly, David Neeleman's passion for customers and high-quality service (see Section "Leadership in Action" at the end of this chapter) has shaped the management of all the companies Neeleman has founded. The leaders set the vision and direction and make most, if not all, of the decisions regarding the various factors that will shape the culture (Figure 1-1).

Leaders are role models for other organizational members. They establish and grant the status symbols that are the main artifacts of organizational culture. Followers take their cues from the leaders on what behaviors are and are not acceptable. For example, Stephen Oesterle, senior vice president at Medtronics leads by example in two ways. As the leader in charge of

FIGURE 1-1 Leader's Functions in Shaping Organizational Culture

medicine, one of his key roles is to look for new technology that can advance the company's mission. He is considered an international technology scout who scours the globe in search of technological innovation to assure his company's future success (Walsh, 2012). As a marathon runner, he promotes a healthy lifestyle and its role in restoring lives, which is the mission of his company (Tuggle, 2007). Another example is Tyler Winkler, the senior vice president of sales and business development for Secure Works, who is obsessed with improving sales numbers. One of his first statements to his employees was, "Make your numbers in three months or you're out" (Cummings, 2004). He measures everything, observes employees closely, and provides detailed feedback and training, all to improve sales. His methods became the norm in the organization and created a legion of loyal employees.

Research about the importance of empathy in leadership suggests another function for leaders, related to cultural factors. Researchers argue that a key function of leaders is to manage the emotions of group members (Humphrey, 2002). Even though attention to internal process issues, such as the emotional state of followers, has always been considered a factor in leadership, it is increasingly seen not as a peripheral task, but rather as one of the main functions. This function is particularly critical to maintaining followers' positive outlook in uncertain and ambiguous situations. Followers observe their leaders' emotional reactions and take their cue from them to determine appropriate reactions (Pescosolido, 2002). An unlikely example of the emotion management role of leaders is Bob Ladouceur, the legendary La Salle, California, high school football coach and the man behind a great dynasty of 20 undefeated seasons and 399 wins (Sankin, 2013). Ladouceur, who retired as head coach after 34 years in 2013, focuses on shaping the lives of his students, rather than simply winning. His players are not generally considered to be the most talented or the strongest. Ladouceur, however, gets extraordinary performance from them through hard training and character building. He states, "If a team has no soul, you're just wasting your time" (Wallace, 2003: 100–104). He wants his players to get in touch with their emotions and develop "love" for their teammates. For Ladouceur, managing these emotions is the key to his teams' winning streaks. He considers his relationships with his followers and coworkers, rather than his winning record, to be the highlight of his career (Hammon, 2013).

Other means through which the leader shapes culture are by decisions regarding the reward system (Kerr and Slocum, 1987) and by controlling decision standards. In one organization, rewards (financial and nonfinancial) go to only the highest contributors to the bottom line. In another, accomplishments such as contribution to cultural diversity or the degree of social responsibility are also valued and rewarded. Additionally, leaders are in charge of selecting other leaders and managers for the organization. Those selected are likely to fit the existing leader's ideal model and, therefore, fit the culture. Other influential members of the organization provide leaders with yet another opportunity to shape the culture. Many firms, for example, establish a nominating committee of the board of directors. In such committees, top managers nominate and select their successors. Therefore, they not only control the current culture but also exert a strong influence on the future of their organization. To select his successor before he left in 2001, General Electric's (GE) Jack Welch carefully observed, interacted with, and interviewed many of the company's executives. He sought feedback from top company leaders, and after selecting Jeff Immelt, Welch orchestrated the transition of power. This carefully orchestrated succession ensured that the new leader, although bringing about some new ideas, fit the existing culture of the organization (Useem, 2001). A similar careful process took place at Procter & Gamble in 2009 and again in 2013 (see Section "Leadership in Action" case in Chapter 7).

APPLYING WHAT YOU LEARN

Leadership Basics

Leadership is a complex process that is a journey rather than a destination. All effective leaders continue to grow and improve, learning from each situation they face and from their mistakes. Here are some basic points that we will revisit throughout the book:

- *Find your passion:* We can be at our best when we lead others into something for which we have passion.
- *Learn about yourself:* Self-awareness of your values, strengths, and weaknesses is an essential starting point for leaders.
- *Experiment with new behaviors and situations:* Learning and growth occur when we are exposed to new situations that challenge us; seek them out.
- *Get comfortable with failure:* All leaders fail; good leaders learn from their mistakes and consider them learning opportunities.

Mistakes are more likely to happen when you are placed in new challenging situations that provide you with opportunities to learn.

- *Pay attention to your environment:* Understanding all the elements of a leadership situation, and particularly followers, is essential to effectiveness. Ask questions, listen carefully, and observe intently so that you can understand the people and the situations around you.
- *Remember that it's about others:* Leadership is not about you and your personal agenda. It's about getting things done for, through and with others.
- *Don't take yourself too seriously:* A good sense of humor and keeping a perspective on priorities will help you. You are not as good as your most fervent supporters believe and not as flawed as your reticent detractors think, so lighten up!

The power of the leader to make decisions for the organization about its structure and strategy is another effective means of shaping culture. By determining the hierarchy, span of control, reporting relationship, and degree of formalization and specialization, the leader molds culture. A highly decentralized and organic structure is likely to be the result of an open and participative culture, whereas a highly centralized structure will go hand in hand with a mechanistic/bureaucratic culture. The structure of an organization limits or encourages interaction and by doing so affects, as well as is affected by, the assumptions shared by members of the organization. Similarly, the strategy selected by the leader or the top management team will be determined by, as well as help shape, the culture of the organization. Therefore, a leader who adopts a proactive growth strategy that requires innovation and risk taking will have to create a culture different from a leader who selects a strategy of retrenchment.

CHANGES IN ORGANIZATIONS AND IN EXPECTATIONS OF LEADERS

To some, a leader is someone who takes charge and jumps in to make decisions whenever the situation requires. This view is particularly dominant in traditional organizations with a clear hierarchy in which employees and managers carry out narrowly defined responsibilities. To others, a leader is a facilitator who simply channels the group's desires. The extent to which a leader is attributed power and knowledge varies by culture and will be discussed in Chapter 2. Even though the U.S. mainstream culture is not as authority oriented as some other cultures, a large number of our leadership theories are implicitly or explicitly based on the assumptions that leaders have to take charge and provide others with instructions. For example, the initiation-of-structure concept provides that effective leadership involves giving direction, assigning tasks to followers, and setting deadlines. These activities are considered an inherent part of an effective leader's behaviors. Similarly, the widely used concept of motivation to manage (Miner and Smith, 1982) includes desire for power and control over others as an essential component.

WHAT DO YOU DO?

You have started on a new job, and based on the interview and discussion with people prior to accepting the job you were led to believe that the company strongly believes in employee participation, engagement, and flexibility. A couple of months of working with your new boss, however, all you see is command and control, with little opportunity for you to provide any input. What do you do?

New Roles for Leaders

With the constant need for innovation, intense global competition, economic pressures, and changing demographics, organizations are changing drastically. As a result, many of the traditional leadership functions and roles are changing as well. Figure 1-2 presents the traditional control-oriented model and the new result-oriented model for leaders in organizations. The changing environment for organizations has forced us to reconsider our expectations and requirements for leadership. Effective leaders of diverse and global teams are not necessarily in control of the group. They might need facilitation and participation skills much more than initiation-of-structure skills. For example, employees in traditional organizations are responsible only for production; the planning, leading, and controlling functions, as well as the responsibility for results, fall on the manager (see Figure 1-2). An increasing number of organizations, however, are shifting the activities and responsibilities typically associated with managers to employees. Managers are expected to provide the vision, get the needed resources to employees, act as support persons, and get out of employees' way. The employees, in turn, learn about the strategic and financial issues related to their job, plan their own activities, set production goals, and take responsibility for their results.

Many executives have adopted new management techniques to help them with the challenges inherent in the new roles for leaders. A recent article in *Entrepreneur* featured several

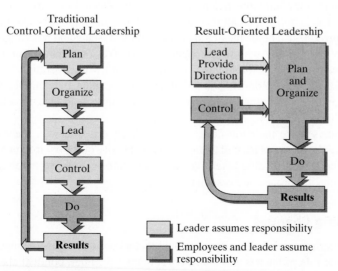

FIGURE 1-2 Control Versus Results-Oriented Leadership

business leaders and their ideas about how leadership is changing. When thinking about what defines leadership, Ted Devine, CEO of a specialized online business insurance company, states: "No walls, no barriers, no hierarchy. Everybody can talk to everybody. Everybody can participate in a decision. We work together" (5 influential CEOs, 2013). Similarly, Scott Abel, CEO of Spice Works, a network management company, believes that the role of leader is to capture the energy of his employees. The idea of cooperation and ownership of the organization are also something that Sheila Johnson, cofounder of BET network embraces. Curtis Symond, who works at BET, says: "Above all else, Sheila leads by example through her passion. It's difficult to work with her, be around all of her excitement and energy, and not want to join in and get involved" (5 influential CEOs, 2013).

Harnessing employees' ideas and engaging them in the goals of the organization is increasingly a key role for leaders. When Rick Sapio was the CEO of the 37-employee New York City Mutual.com, a mutual fund advisory company, he knew that his business was high pressure with little time to stay in touch with his employees (Buchanan, 2001). Recognizing the importance of involving employees, however, Sapio created "Hassles," an electronic mailbox through which employees could express their concerns and ideas with a guarantee from the CEO that they will be addressed within a week. For those who preferred to see the boss in person, Sapio scheduled one hour each week in a conference room (rather than his office, which seemed inaccessible) where anyone could drop in to give him input. Jeffrey Immelt, CEO of General Electric, has made learning and getting to hear everybody's ideas one of his priorities. His predecessor, Jack Welch, notes that a great leader needs to "get under the skin of every person who works for the company" (Hammonds, 2004: 32). Leaders at large companies such as Procter & Gamble, Whole Foods, and Toyota, as well as small start-ups such as Evernote, practice being egalitarian and cooperative. Their priorities are fast decision making, training, and innovation.

The new leadership styles are not limited to business organizations; they can also be seen in government and other not-for-profit organizations. Harry Baxter, chairman and CEO of Baxter Healthcare in Deerfield, Illinois, likes to focus on doing the right thing instead of being right. He suggests, "I have very few definitive answers, but I have a lot of opinions" (Kraemer, 2003: 16). Philip Diehl, former director of the U.S. Mint, and his leadership team transformed the stodgy government bureaucracy into an efficient and customer-centered organization by asking questions, listening to stakeholders, creating a sense of urgency in employees, and involving them in the change (Muio, 1999). These changes also occur in local, state, and federal government agencies. For example, Ron Sims, who was recognized in 2006 as one of the most innovative public officials, is known for always looking for common ground while operating from a clear set of principles (Walters, 2006). Ron Sims is also known for leading by example. When he talked about county employees adopting a healthier lifestyle, he started eating better and biking and lost 40 pounds (Walters, 2006).

These leaders leave their top-floor offices to keep in touch with the members of their organizations. Given the rapid pace of change and complexity of the environment in which many organizations operate, cultivating extensive sources of information and involving many people in the decision-making process are essential.

Factors Fueling Changes

A number of external and internal organizational factors are driving the changes in our organizations and in the role of leaders and managers (Figure 1-3). First, political changes worldwide are leading to more openness and democracy. These political changes shape and are shaped by

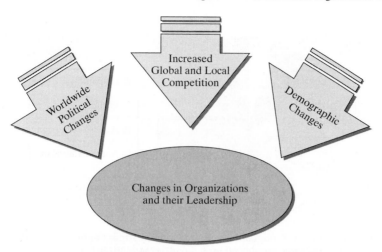

FIGURE 1-3 Factors Fueling Changes in Organizations and Their Leadership

images of what is considered to be appropriate leadership. With the fall of the Soviet Union at the end of the twentieth century, the world has seen a spread in democratic principles aimed at power sharing. Uprising in North Africa and the Middle East and the Arab Spring movement demonstrated the desire of many for more openness and democracy. In the United States, the public continues to expect transparency in both the private and the public sectors. Politicians are forced to share details of their past and their personal life and justify to the public many, if not all, of their decisions. Communities increasingly demand participation in the decisions regarding their schools, health-care systems, and environment.

Second, with the worldwide economic downturn, increasing global and local competition, and complex and fast-changing technologies, numerous organizations struggle for survival and to justify their existence. Many are forced to reconsider how they provide goods and services to their customers and to the public and to reevaluate the assumptions they held as basic truths. For example, while Unions in the United States are struggling for both membership and a new identity, in some cases, their leadership has succeeded by focusing on cooperation with management, something that would have been unimaginable a few years back. Monty Newcomb, a shop steward at a chemical plant in Calvert City Kentucky, worked with his union and with management to integrate trust and team building between union and management with the traditional collective bargaining process (Davidson, 2013). This new collaboration took a while to take hold but eventually resulted in both groups accomplishing their goals, increasing efficiency and quality, and preventing the company from shipping jobs overseas.

Another key factor fueling changes in leadership is the diversity in the United States and many other countries (Figure 1-4). Demographic changes that lead to increased diversity in the various groups and organizations push leaders to consider this diversity when making decisions. Many countries include similar or even greater cultural diversity. For example, Malaysia's population is highly diverse and consists of Malays, Chinese, Indians, Arabs, Sinhalese, Eurasians, and Europeans, with the Muslim, Buddhist, Daoist, Hindu, Christian, Sikh, and Shamanistic religions all practiced (*World Fact Book: Malaysia*, 2013). Although the majority of Singapore's population of more than 4 million is Chinese, it also includes Malays, Indians, and Eurasians. As a result, the country has four official languages: English, Malay, Mandarin, and Tamil (*World*

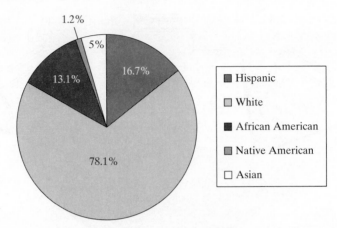

FIGURE 1-4 Diversity in the U.S. Population *Source:* United States Census Bureau, 2013. http://quickfacts.census.gov/qfd/states/00000.html (accessed May 30, 2013).

Fact Book: Singapore, 2013). Table 1-3 highlights some of the ethnic and demographic changes and trends in the United States.

Some of the diversity that leaders must manage is related to age. Roxann Hewertson, CEO of the Highland Consulting Group, an organization that focuses on leadership issues and a faculty at Cornell University, says the younger workers do not respond to traditional hierarchies easily. As a result she believes,"There's a real hunger out there for finding a better way. The old way is broken. It doesn't serve us" (5 influential CEOs, 2013). Nick Petrie, senior faculty member of the Center for Creative Leadership, an influential leadership organization, strongly believes, "There is a transition occurring from the old paradigm in which leadership resided in a person or role, to a new one in which leadership is a collective process that is spread throughout networks of people" (5 influential CEOs, 2013). Other demographic

TABLE 1-3	U.S. Demographic Highlights and Trends

- In 2007, 20.3 percent of the U.S population spoke a language other than English at home compared to 13 percent in 2000.
- More than half of the U.S. workforce consists of women and minorities.
- By 2016, minorities will make up one-third of the U.S. population.
- By 2025, the percentage of European Americans in the population will drop from 72 percent in 2000 to 62 percent.
- By 2025, Hispanics are estimated to be 21 percent of the population, outnumbering African Americans, who will make up 13 percent of the population.
- By 2050, the Hispanic population of the United States will grow to 30.25 percent.
- By 2025, the *average* age will be close to 40, as opposed to under 35 in 2000.
- By 2025, more than 50 percent of the population of Hawaii, California, New Mexico, and Texas will be from a minority group.
- By 2050, the average U.S. resident will be from a non-European background.
- By 2050, only about 62 percent of the entrants into the labor force will be white, with half that number being women.

Source: U.S. Census Bureau, Census, 2010. http://www.census.gov/population; and Bureau of Labor Statistics, 2013. http://www.bls.gov/emp/ep_table_303.htm.

trends in the United States include the largest percentage of the population being older baby boomers (born between the late 1940s and the 1960s) at the top, and the millennial generation (born after the mid-1980s) at the bottom, with the generation Xers (born between the 1970s and 1980s) pinched in the middle. This suggests that many organizational leaders are managing employees from generations other than their own and therefore must take cultural and generational factors into account. We will discuss the impact of generational differences on individuals in Chapters 2 and 4.

The increasing number of women in the workforce is another factor that has an impact on leadership. Although women currently hold only 10 percent of the executive positions in the United States, they make up over 47 percent of the general workforce with a clear majority of women being part of the labor force (Women in the Labor Force, 2010). Similar trends exist all over the world. For example, women make up almost 47 percent of the labor force in Canada, close to 45 percent in China, over 50 percent in Russia (Labor force, 2009). Scandinavian countries are leading the way with the number of women in top management and leadership positions in the executive offices and boardrooms. In Sweden, women hold 23 percent of the board seats (Amble, 2006). As a result, the old ways that were designed for a gender and ethnically homogeneous population do not always work with employees and customers from varied backgrounds and cultures. Much of the burden for devising and implementing the needed changes falls on the leadership of our organizations. The demand to listen to and address the needs of nonhomogeneous groups requires skills that go beyond controlling and monitoring.

Because of the pressures for change, many organizations find themselves rewriting their policies to address the needs of a diverse community and consumer base. Consultant Ted Childs, who used to be IBM's president of global workforce diversity states, "Business is at its core about relationships. I think diversity work takes away barriers that interfere with relationship building" (Child, 2013). He adds: "You're going to have to sell to people who are different from you, and buy from people who are different from you, and manage people who are different from you…. This is how we do business. If it's not your destination, you should get off the plane now" (Swan, 2000: 260). He views getting people to respect those who are different from them as the biggest challenge in managing diversity.

Barriers to Change

Despite the factors that fuel the need for change, few organizations and individuals have adopted new models for leadership painlessly. In part because of perceived financial pressures and attempts to find a quick way out of them, organizations turn to tough autocratic leaders whose goals are clearly not employee motivation and loyalty. For example, John Grundhofer, nicknamed "Jack the Ripper," specialized in implementing massive layoffs and found his skills in high demand. Similarly, Al Dunlap, with nicknames such as "Ming the Merciless" and "Chainsaw Al," for a long time moved successfully from the top position of one organization to another before being fired from Sunbeam Corporation in 1998. For many years, the financial community applauded him for his drastic cost-cutting strategies that involved widespread layoffs. Bill George, the highly respected former CEO of Medtronic, states that this focus on short-term and quick results cannot create the motivation necessary for the innovation and superior service that are essential to leadership and organizational effectiveness (George, 2003).

Another obstacle to implementing new models of leadership is that even though teams are fairly common in lower and middle levels of organizations, top management still remains a one-person show. The hierarchical structure of many organizations makes change difficult. Old cultures resist change. Few organizations truly reward enterprising employees and managers for crossing the traditional hierarchical barriers. Instead, most organizations continue to reward their leaders for tried-and-true approaches or sometimes for nonperformance- and nonproductivity-related behaviors, despite the lack of success (Luthans, 1989). Marcus Buckingham, a researcher at the Gallup Organization, has studied global leadership practice for 15 years. According to Buckingham, "The corporate world is appallingly bad at capitalizing on the strengths of its people" (LaBarre, 2001: 90). Gallup's extensive surveys show that employee engagement can have a considerable positive impact on an organization's performance. Recent surveys of employees in the United States by the Conference Board indicate the low level of overall satisfaction with jobs, at 47 percent (Conference Board, 2012). Other research indicates that job satisfaction is lower in larger companies with more bureaucracy, lower autonomy, and low responsibility (*Wall Street Journal*, 2006). Few organizations take full advantage of their employees' input. Tom Peters, the well-known management consultant, suggests that while business leaders focus on strategy, they often "skip over the incredibly boring part called people," thereby failing to take advantage of one of the most important aspects of their organization (Reingold, 2003: 94). In addition, changing the established behaviors of managers is very difficult. John Kotter, Harvard Business School professor and noted authority on change, suggests, "The central issue is never strategy, structure, culture, or systems. The core of the matter is always about changing the behavior of people" (Deutschman, 2005).

In addition, although they might spend a great deal of time working in teams, employees are still rewarded for individual performance. In other words, our reward structures fail to keep up with our attempts to increase cooperation among employees and managers. Furthermore, many employees are not willing or able to accept their new roles as partners and decision makers, even when such roles are offered to them. Their training and previous experiences make them balk at taking on what they might consider to be their leader's job. Even when organizations encourage change, many leaders find giving up control difficult. Many receive training in the benefits of empowerment, teams, and softer images of leadership, but they simply continue to repeat what seemingly worked in the past, engaging in what researcher Pfeffer calls substituting memory for thinking (1998). With all that training on how to be in charge and in control, allowing employees to do more might appear to be a personal failure. Either because of years of traditional training or because of personality characteristics that make them more comfortable with control and hierarchy, managers' styles often create an obstacle to implementing necessary changes. Research about children's images of leadership indicates that the belief that leaders need to be in control develops early in life. Children, particularly boys, continue to perceive a sex-typed schema of leaders: Leaders are supposed to have male characteristics, including dominance and aggression (Ayman-Nolley, Ayman, and Becker, 1993).

Summary and Conclusions

A leader is any person who influences individuals and groups within an organization, helps them in the establishment of goals, and guides them toward achievement of those goals, thereby allowing them to be effective. Leaders are needed because they create order and organization in groups, allowing them to achieve their goals; they help people make sense of the world and can serve as ideal and romantic symbols for their followers. To be effective, leaders must help the organization maintain internal health and external adaptability. Despite the apparent simplicity of the definitions of leadership and effectiveness, both are difficult concepts to implement.

Various studies propose separate definitions for leadership and management. The activities performed by leaders, however, are similar to those typically considered the domain of effective managers. Although some view the roles of leaders and managers as being different, effective, and competent, managers are often also leaders within their groups and organizations. In addition to performing the traditional managerial roles and duties, leaders also play a special role in the creation of a culture for their organizations. They can affect culture by setting the vision and direction, making direct decisions regarding reward systems, hiring other managers and employees, and being role models for others in the organization. The role of leaders is changing with our shifting expectations and global and organizational pressures. Leaders find themselves providing more vision and direction and focusing on results rather than command and control. While new roles take hold slowly, political, economic, demographic, and social changes drive the need for change. However, leaders find use of traditional models, lack of involvement of followers, and falling back on old practices hard obstacles to overcome.

Review and Discussion Questions

1. What are the essential components of the definition of leadership?
2. Why do we need leaders?
3. How could structure and strategy limit leadership decision-making?
4. Provide one example each of an effective leader and a successful leader. Consider how they differ and what you can learn from each.
5. What are the obstacles to effective leadership?
6. Based on your knowledge of the field of management and your personal definition of leadership, how are management and leadership similar or different? How can the differences be reconciled? How do these differences add to our understanding of leadership?
7. How are many of the traditional leadership functions and roles changing in today's world?
8. How are political changes affecting the role of leaders?
9. Why is job satisfaction lower in companies with a greater degree of bureaucracy, lower autonomy, and low responsibility?

Leadership Challenge: Moving to Leadership

You have been a member of a cohesive and productive department for the past three years. Your department manager has accepted a job in another organization, and you have been moved into her position. You are not one of most senior members, but you have the most education, have been volunteering for many training programs, and have been an outstanding individual contributor. Over the past three years, you have developed close relationships with several of your department members who are around your age. You often go out to lunch together, have drinks after work, and get together on weekends. There are also a couple of "old-timers" who were very helpful in training you when you first came in. They have much more experience than you, but little education. Although you get along with them, you feel a bit awkward about being promoted to be their boss.

1. What are the challenges you are likely to face as the new leader?
2. What are some actions you should take to help smooth the transition?
3. What are some things you should avoid?

Exercise 1-1: More than Meets the Eye—Characteristics of Leaders

This exercise demonstrates the complexity of leadership by identifying the various characteristics, traits, and behaviors that are associated with good leadership. List as many of the characteristics, traits, and behaviors that you think are key. Include behaviors (e.g., taking care of followers, assigning task), personality styles and traits (e.g., honesty, warmth), as well as skills and abilities (e.g., organized, good communicator), and even physical characteristics (e.g., tall). It may help to think of leaders you admire and consider the characteristics they possess.

1. **Characteristics Essential to Leadership**
   Good leaders must/should…

2. **Essentials**
   In your group, review your list and pare it down to 7 to 10 characteristics that you think are essential. These should be characteristics that make or break leadership.

3. **How do you match up?**
   In your group, discuss the following:
   - How many of the characteristics do you personally have?
   - Can you ever match up to the list you just developed?
   - If you do not, how does that affect your ability to lead?
   - Do you know any effective leader who lacks one or more of the characteristics?
   - Do you think the characteristics are essential to that person's effectiveness?

4. **Complexity of Leadership**
   Chances are that you have had some trouble agreeing on the list and that more than one of you is finding yourself lacking one or more of the characteristics you listed. While you may be discouraged, consider that leadership is much more complex than a set of characteristics a person has. Having a set of traits does not guarantee leadership. By the same token, while not having certain traits or abilities may make leadership challenging, it will not necessarily prevent a person from being an effective leader. Additionally, as you will learn throughout the book, effective leadership is not just about the leader. Followers and the situation also play a key role.

Exercise 1-2: What Is Leadership?

This exercise is designed to help you develop a personal definition of leadership and clarify your assumptions and expectations about leadership and effectiveness.

1. **Describe your ideal leader**

   Individually list five desirable and five undesirable characteristics of your ideal leader.

Desirable	Undesirable
1.	1.
2.	2.
3.	3.
4.	4.
5.	5.

2. **Develop group definition:** In groups of four or five, discuss your list and your reasons and draw up a common definition.

3. **Present and defend definition:** Each group will make a five-minute presentation of its definition.

4. **Common themes**
   a. What are the common themes?

   b. Which views of leadership are presented?

   c. What are the assumptions about the role of the leader?

Exercise 1-3: Images of Leadership

One way you can clarify your assumptions about leadership is to use images to describe your ideal leader. Through the use of such images, you can understand your views of the role of leaders in organizations and your expectations of leaders. These images are your personal theories of leadership. For example, viewing leaders as facilitators presents a considerably different image from viewing them as parents.

1. **Select your image:** List the characteristics of that image.

2. **Share and clarify:** In groups of three or four, share your leadership image and discuss its implications for your own leadership style.

3. **Class discussion**
   Groups will share two of their individual members' images of leadership. Discuss implications of various images for the following aspects:
   a. A person's leadership style

   b. Impact on organizational culture and structure

   c. Compatibility with current or past leaders

   d. Potential shortcomings of each image

Exercise 1-4: Understanding the Leadership Context

This exercise is designed to highlight the importance and role of the context in the leadership process.

1. **Individual/group work**
   Select a leader and identify the contextual factors that affect his/her leadership. Consider various elements that may be relevant, such as the following:
   a. Long-term historical, political, and economic factors or forces

   b. Current contemporary forces, including social values, changes, and cultural factors

   c. The immediate context, including organizational characteristics, the task, and followers

2. **Discussion**
   How do all these factors affect the leader? Do they hinder or help the leader achieve his/her goals?

LEADERSHIP IN ACTION

DAVID NEELEMAN REINVENTS AIRLINES

David Neeleman is a legend in the airline industry and given credit for some of the major innovations in the airlines industry, including ticketless travel (Bloomberg TV, 2011). In 1984, he cofounded Morris Air and sold it to Southwest Airlines to join the leadership of that airline. He only survived five months before he was fired for being difficult to work with and being disruptive (Bloomberg TV, 2011). He had to wait five years because of a noncompete clause, and in 2000, he launched the highly successful JetBlue Airways before he left in 2007. He is now engaged in a new venture as CEO of the new Brazilian domestic airline Azul (blue in Portuguese), founded in 2008.

His vision for what an airline should be and his leadership style set him apart from most other leaders in the industry. Neeleman says: "I have this huge goal that I want everyone that works for Azul to say that this is the best job they ever had because I think that is central to customer service and then I want every customer who gets off of every flight to say wow that was a great flight probably the best I have ever had" (Bloomberg TV, 2011). He describes himself as: "I'm not a lofty perch guy; I'm a day-to-day guy" (Elite interview, 2013). He believes that success comes from changing people's lives and contributing to society rather than simply making money.

Neeleman was ousted in 2007 from JetBlue after the airline was caught in a wave of negative publicity after it kept passengers in planes on the tarmac for seven hours during a storm. Neeleman provided a very public and sincere apology (posted on the Web at http://www.jet blue.com/about/ourcompany/apology/index.html), and JetBlue instituted a much-publicized Passenger Bill of Rights to ensure that its much-valued customers continue to remain loyal. JetBlue still has daily flights to more than 50 destinations in the United States and Central America. Continuing to rely on the principles of its founder, the airline emphasizes teamwork and quick decisions and implementation. Top executives and managers consistently interact with employees and customers to listen and get feedback from them to keep addressing their concerns (Salter, 2004a), a practice Neeleman has also instituted at Azul (Mount, 2009). The attention to employees and customers has earned JetBlue high ratings and its former CEO awards for being a visionary (www.jetblueairways.com). Programs such as generous profit sharing, excellent benefits, open communication, and extensive training all get the right employees in the company and retain them.

Neeleman not only provides the vision, but also knows to listen to people who, on occasion, veto his decisions. He says: "The way I channel the risk is that I surround myself with people who are really smart and have a spine and can speak up and can challenge you" (Bloomberg TV, 2011). He believes that "If you treat people well, the company's philosophy goes, they'll treat the customer well." Azul is made of much of the same mold as JetBlue: simple reservations systems, low prices, more leg room, online Internet, and a TV in every seat (Scanlon, 2008). Neeleman is obsessive about staying in touch with both customers and employees. He stops by the call center at Azul regularly, talks to the trainees, and reminds his executives to talk to customers and those closest to them because "we think we know what happens. But they really know" (Mount, 2009). He strongly believes that "it is the people that make it happen" (Ford, 2004: 140). Neeleman's leadership style and magic seems to be continuing to work. Azul is growing fast, with 11,000 passengers when it started up to 45,000 in January 2009 (Azul, 2009), and is flying 70 percent full, which is close to 20 percent better than Brazil's biggest airline (Moura, 2009).

Questions

1. What are the key elements of JetBlue and Azul's culture?
2. Would you to like to work for Azul airlines? If so, please give your reasons.

Sources: Bloomberg TV, 2011. "David Neeleman Profiled: Bloomberg Risk takers." http://www.bloomberg. com/video/72535922-david-neeleman-profiled-bloomberg-risk-takers.html (accessed May 30, 2013); Airways Customer Bill of Rights. 2007. http://www.jetblue.com/p/about/ourcompany/promise/Bill_Of_Rights.pdf (accessed June 16, 2007); Elite Interviews David Neeleman, 2013. *Elite.com*, April 1 http://www.youtube.com/ watch?v=QybWxHdiSpk on May 30, 2013; Judge, P. 2001. "How will your company adapt?" *Fast Company*, 54; Ford, 2004. "David Neeleman, CEO of JetBlue Airways, on people + strategy = growth," *Academy of Management Executive* 18(2): 139–143; Salter, C. 2004a. "And now the hard part," *Fast Company* 82. http:// pf.fastcompany.com/magazine/82/jetblue.html (accessed October 1, 2004); Brazil's Azul airlines to expand this year. 2008. http://www.usatoday.com/travel/flights/2009-02-11-azul-expansion_N.htm (accessed January 7, 2010); Moura, F. 2009. Neeleman expects profit as Brazil's Azul Air flies 70 percent full. http://www.bloomberg.com/ apps/news?pid=20601086&sid= aJl8vaK49DMQ (accessed January 7, 2010); Mount, I. 2009. "JetBlue founder's revenge: A new airline," *CNN Money,* March 20. http://money.cnn.com/2009/03/19/smallbusiness/jetblue_founder_ flies_again.fsb/ (accessed October 6, 2013; and Scanlon. J. 2008. Braving Brazil's "airline graveyard," http://www. businessweek.com/innovate/content/may2008/id2008056_561046.htm (accessed January 7, 2010).

Chapter 2

The Global and Cultural Contexts

After studying this chapter, you will be able to:

1. Define culture and its three levels and explain the role it plays in leadership.
2. Apply the following models of national culture to leadership situations:
   - Hall's cultural context
   - Hofstede's dimensions
   - Trompenaars model
   - GLOBE
3. Identify the impact of gender on leadership.
4. Address how leaders can develop a cultural mindset.
5. Present the steps organizations can take to become more multicultural.

THE LEADERSHIP QUESTION

What is considered effective leadership depends on the cultural context. However, do you think there are some leadership "gold-standards," some characteristics and behaviors that leaders in all cultures must demonstrate? If so, what do think they are?

Leadership is a social and an interpersonal process. As is the case with any such process, the impact of culture is undeniable. Different cultures define leadership differently and consider different types of leaders effective. A leader who is considered effective in Singapore might seem too authoritarian in Sweden. The charisma of an Egyptian political leader may be lost on the French or the Japanese. The exuberant Brazilian leader will appear unnecessarily emotional to German employees. In addition, gender and other cultural differences among groups affect how leaders behave and how their followers perceive them. Understanding leadership, therefore, requires an understanding of the cultural context in which it takes place.

TABLE 2-1	Characteristics of Culture

- Shared by group members
- Transferred from one member to another
- Affects thinking and behavior
- Stable and dynamic

DEFINTION AND LEVELS OF CULTURE

Culture gives each group its uniqueness and differentiates it from other groups. Our culture strongly influences us; it determines how we think and what we consider right and wrong, and it influences what and whom we value, what we pay attention to, and how we behave.

Definition and Characteristics

Culture consists of the commonly held values within a group of people. It is a set of norms, customs, values, and assumptions that guides the behavior of a group. It includes people's life-style and their collective programming. Culture has permanence; it does not change easily and is passed down from one generation to another. Group members learn about their culture through their parents and family, schools, and other social institutions and consciously and unconsciously transfer it to the young and new members. In spite of this permanence, culture is also dynamic and changes over time as members adapt to new events and their environment (see Table 2-1).

Levels of Culture

Culture exists at three levels (Figure 2-1). The first is national culture, defined as a set of values and beliefs shared by people within a nation. Second, in addition to an overall national culture, different ethnic and other cultural groups within a nation might share a culture. Gender,

FIGURE 2-1 The Three Levels of Culture

religious, and racial differences, for example, fit into this second level of culture differences. Although these groups share national cultural values, they develop their own unique cultural traits. Some countries, such as the United States, Canada, and Indonesia, include many such subcultures. Different cultural, ethnic, and religious groups are part of the overall culture of these countries, which leads to cultural diversity. *Diversity*, then, refers to the variety of human structures, beliefs systems, and strategies for adapting to situations that exist within different groups. It is typically used to refer to the variety in the second level of culture. For example, widely held gender stereotypes affect our views of leadership and create significant differences in power and authority between men and women (Eagly and Carli, 2004). Many traditional male traits, such as aggression and independence, often are associated with leaders, whereas traditional female traits of submissiveness and cooperation are not.

The third level of culture is organizational culture (sometimes referred to as corporate culture)—the set of values, norms, and beliefs shared by members of an organization. Given time, all organizations develop a unique culture or character whereby employees share common values and beliefs about work-related issues. These organizational values typically include beliefs about leadership (Schein, 2004). In many cases, leaders, and particularly founders, are instrumental in creating and encouraging the culture. Legendary Apple founder, Steve Jobs, was known for pushing his employees hard and being highly demanding (Love, 2013). His attention to detail and focus on design became everyone's obsession at Apple and is part of the company's culture. The much-talked-about bank, Goldman Sachs, is known as a highly competitive organization that some say puts profit ahead of client interests (Why I left Goldman Sachs, 2012). One of the company's chief accountants, Sarah Smith, says, "It's a 24/7 culture. When you're needed, you're here. And if you're needed and you're not answering your phone, you won't be needed very long" (Alridge, 2009). Another former employee describes the culture as "completely money-obsessed. I was like a donkey driven forward by the biggest, juiciest carrot I could imagine. Money is the way you define your success" (Alridge, 2009).

A very different culture is that of office furniture manufacturer Herman Miller. The company wants employees to bring their "whole person" to work, and it believes that openness breeds loyalty. D.J. Dupree, the company founder, was known for his focus on employees (Pattison, 2010). As a result, the company offers onsite daycare, full benefits, and various work options such as flexible time and telecommuting. Similarly, Google's much-celebrated culture is based on working as a caring family (Boies, 2013). Company cofounder, Larry Page, says: "My job as a leader is to make sure everybody in the company has great opportunities, and that they feel they're having a meaningful impact and are contributing to the good of society" (Chatterjee, 2012). With many benefits and perks, and a focus on collaboration and fun, Google considers its culture as one of its keys to success. These organizations are all effective, but they have different organizational cultures with different models of leadership effectiveness. At Herman Miller and Google, employee satisfaction is key to effectiveness; the leaders are focused on the followers. At the Apple and Goldman, the leader pushes for performance and outcomes.

Because national culture addresses many different aspects of life, it exerts a strong and pervasive influence on people's behavior in everyday activities and in organizations. The influence of organizational culture is, generally, limited to work-related values and behaviors. All three levels of culture shape our views and expectations of our leaders. Whereas people in the United States do not expect leaders to be infallible, in many other cultures, leaders' admission of mistakes would be intolerable and a deadly blow to their authority and ability to lead. For example, several U.S. presidents—most recently President Clinton—when faced with no other option, recognized their mistakes openly and professed to have learned from them. Many in the United States expected President Bush to admit mistakes in the war against Iraq, although no apologies have been forthcoming. Such admissions are rarely expected or happen in other countries, and if they do, they are interpreted as signs of weakness. Former president Vincente Fox of Mexico steadfastly refused to admit any error or to change course in the handling of his country's economy in 2001. When, in 1998, Indonesian president Suharto apparently admitted mistakes that contributed to his country's economic crisis, he was seen as weak. Indonesians did not forgive him, and he eventually resigned.

Each country and region in the world develops a particular organizational and management style based largely on its national culture. This style is called the *national organizational heritage* (Bartlett and Ghoshal, 1992). Although differences distinguish one organization from another and one manager from another, research indicates that national heritage is noticeable and distinct. French companies, for instance, share some characteristics that make them different from companies in other countries. When compared with their Swedish counterparts, they are more hierarchical and status oriented.

MODELS OF NATIONAL CULTURE

Because understanding and handling cultural differences effectively are key to organizational effectiveness in increasingly global organizations, researchers have developed several models for understanding national cultures. These models provide descriptions of different cultural values and help us group people into broad categories by proposing what some have called *sophisticated stereotypes* (Osland et. al., 2000). Just like regular stereotypes, these are generalizations about people. However, they are based on reliable and valid research, rather than on personal experience or opinion. While they have validity and can be used to make better decisions, you should be aware that culture is just one factor among many that impact how people behave. This section reviews four models of national culture with direct application to understanding leadership.

Hall's Cultural Context Framework

One of the simplest models for understanding culture, Edward Hall's model, divides communication styles within cultures into two groups: high context and low context (Hall, 1976; Hall and Hall, 1990). In Hall's model, context refers to the environment and the information that provide the background for interaction and communication. Leaders from *high-context cultures* rely heavily on the context, including nonverbal cues such as tone of voice and body posture and contextual factors such as title and status, to communicate with others and understand the world around them. They use personal relationships to establish communication. Leaders from *low-context cultures* focus on explicit, specific verbal and written messages to understand people and situations and communicate with others (see Figure 2-2). In high-context cultures, communication does not always need to be explicit and specific, and trust is viewed as more important than written communication or legal contracts. In contrast, in low-context cultures, people pay attention to the verbal message. What is said or written is more important than non-verbal messages or the situation. People are, therefore, specific and clear in their communication with others.

High and low context fall within a continuum. As such Asian cultures such as Japan, China and Korea are higher context that many African, Latin American, or Middle Eastern countries

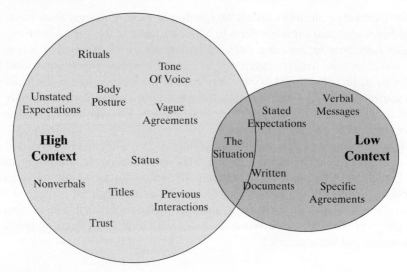

FIGURE 2-2 High- and Low-Context Cultures

that are still higher context than Northern Europeans and Americans. The difference between high and low context can explain many cross-cultural communication problems that leaders face when they interact with those of a culture different from their own. The lower-context European and North American leaders might get frustrated working with followers from higher-context Asian or Middle Eastern cultures because the low-context leaders focus on specific instructions while the high-context followers aim at developing relationships. Similarly, high-context leaders might be offended by their low-context followers' directness, which they may interpret as rudeness, lack of respect, or a challenge to their authority.

The communication context, as presented by Hall, is one of the ways culture impacts our views and expectations of leaders.

Hofstede's Cultural Dimensions

Researcher Geert Hofstede developed one of the often-cited classifications of culture, known as Hofstede's dimensions (Hofstede, 1992; Hofstede, 2001; Hofstede, Hofstede, and Minkov, 2010). He originally conducted more than 100,000 surveys of IBM employees in over 40 countries, supplemented by another series of surveys that led to the inclusion of yet another dimension. He used the results to develop five basic cultural dimensions along which cultures differ: individualism, power distance, uncertainty avoidance, masculinity, and time orientation (Table 2-2). According to Hofstede, the combination of these five dimensions lends each national culture its distinctiveness and unique character.

When compared with other nations, the United States is highest in individualism (closely followed by Australia), is below average on power distance and uncertainty avoidance, is above average on masculinity, and has a moderate to short-term time orientation. These scores indicate that the United States is a somewhat egalitarian culture in which uncertainty and ambiguity are well tolerated; a high value is placed on individual achievements, assertiveness, performance, and independence; sex roles are relatively well defined; and organizations look for quick results with a focus on the present. Japan, on the other hand, tends to be considerably

TABLE 2-2	Hofstede's Five Cultural Dimensions
Individualism	The extent to which individuals, or a closely knit social structure, such as the extended family, is the basis for social systems. Individualism leads to reliance on self and focus on individual achievement.
Power distance	The extent to which people accept unequal distribution of power. In higher-power distance cultures, there is a wider gap between the powerful and the powerless.
Uncertainty avoidance	The extent to which the culture tolerates ambiguity and uncertainty. High uncertainty avoidance leads to low tolerance for uncertainty and a search for absolute truths.
Masculinity	The extent to which assertiveness and independence from others is valued. High masculinity leads to high sex-role differentiation, focus on independence, ambition, and material goods.
Time orientation	The extent to which people focus on past, present, or future. Present orientation leads to a focus on short-term performance.

lower in individualism than the United States, higher in power distance, masculinity (one of the highest scores), and uncertainty avoidance, and with a long-term orientation. These rankings are consistent with the popular image of Japan as a country in which social structures, such as family and organizations are important, their power and obedience to them tend to be absolute, risk and uncertainty are averted, gender roles are highly differentiated, and high value is placed on achievement.

Harry Triandis, a cross-cultural psychologist, expanded on some of Hofstede's cultural dimensions by introducing the concepts of tight and loose, and vertical and horizontal cultures. Triandis (2004) suggests that uncertainty avoidance can be better understood by further classifying cultures into either tight or loose categories. In tight cultures, such as Japan, members follow rules, norms, and standards closely. Behaviors are, therefore, closely regulated; those who do not abide by the rules are criticized, isolated, or even ostracized, depending on the severity of the offense. Loose cultures, such as Thailand, show much tolerance for behaviors that are considered acceptable, and although rules exist, violating them is often overlooked. Triandis (2004) places the United States in the moderate tight–loose category and suggests that the U.S. culture has moved toward becoming looser and more tolerant over the past 50 years.

Triandis further refined the concept of individualism/collectivism by arguing that there are different types of collectivist and individualist cultures (1995). He proposes that by adding the concept of vertical and horizontal, we can gain a much richer understanding of cultural values (Table 2-3). Vertical cultures focus on hierarchy; horizontal cultures emphasize equality (Triandis et al., 2001). For example, although Sweden and the United States are both individualist cultures, the Swedes are horizontal individualists (HV) and see individuals as unique but equal to others. In the United States, which is more vertical individualist (VI), the individual is viewed as not only unique but also superior to others. Similarly, in a horizontal collectivistic (HC) culture, such as Israel, all members of the group are seen as equal. In vertical collectivistic (VC) cultures, such as Japan and Korea, authority is important and individuals must sacrifice themselves for the good of the group. The horizontal–vertical dimension, because it affects views of hierarchy and equality, is likely to affect leadership.

TABLE 2-3	Vertical and Horizontal Dimensions of Individualism and Collectivism	
	Vertical (Emphasis on Hierarchy)	**Horizontal (Emphasis on Equality)**
Individualistic	Focus on the individual where each person is considered unique and superior to others, often based on accomplishments and performance, or material wealth. Example: United States	Although the focus is on each individual being unique, individuals are considered equal to others without a strong hierarchy. Example: Sweden
Collectivistic	Strong group feeling with clear rank and status differentiation among group members; members feel obligation to obey authority and sacrifice self for good of the group if needed. Example: Japan	All group members are considered equal; the group has little hierarchy, and there is strong focus on democratic and egalitarian processes. Example: Israel

Source: Based on Triandis et al., 2001.

Hofstede's cultural values model along with Triandis' concepts provide a strong basis for explaining cultural differences. Hoftsede continues to be used as the basis for research on cross-cultural differences as well as for training leaders to work across cultures. Other researchers have provided additional means of understanding culture.

Trompenaars' Dimensions of Culture

Trompenaars and Hampden-Turner provide a complex model that helps leaders understand national culture and its effect on organizational and corporate cultures (Trompenaars and Hampden-Turner, 2012). They developed a model based on 80,000 participants in organizations in close to 50 cultures and further tested it by adding data and anecdotes from the many training programs they conducted with 60,000 people in 25 countries. Based on their research and experience, Trompenaars and Hampden-Turner have found that there clearly is no one best way to manage organizations and that universal principles of management are not so universal and do not work well across all cultures (2012). More significantly, they suggest that while behaviors many appear the same across cultures, their meaning is often different. They propose that although understanding national culture requires many different dimensions, cross-cultural organizational cultures can be classified more efficiently based on two dimensions: egalitarian-hierarchical and orientation to the person or the task. When combined, they yield four general cross-cultural organizational cultures: incubator, guided missile, family, and Eiffel Tower (Figure 2-3). The four general types combine national and organizational cultures. The leader's role in each type differs, as do methods of employee motivation and evaluation.

Incubator cultures are egalitarian and focus on taking care of individual needs. Examples of incubator cultures can be found in many start-up, high-technology firms in the United States and Great Britain (Trompenaars and Hampden-Turner, 2012). In these typically individualist cultures, professionals are given considerable latitude to do their jobs. Leaders in such organizations emerge from the group rather than being assigned. Therefore, leadership is based

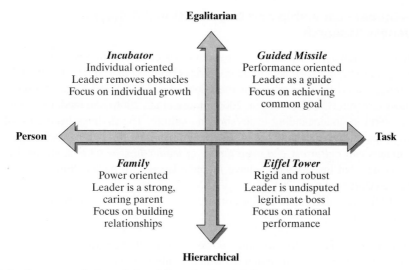

FIGURE 2-3   Trompenaar's Cross-Cultural Organizational Cultures

on competence and expertise, and the leader's responsibility is to provide resources, manage conflict, and remove obstacles.

The *guided missile* is also an egalitarian culture, but the focus is on task completion rather than individual needs. As a result, the organizational culture is impersonal and, as indicated by its name, directed toward accomplishing the job. Trompenaars uses the U.S. National Aeronautics and Space Administration (NASA) as an example of the guided missile. In NASA and other guided-missile organizations, leadership is based on expertise, and follower participation is expected. People work in teams of professionals who have equal status, with performance being the primary criterion for effectiveness.

The *family* and *Eiffel Tower* cultures both are hierarchical. Whereas the Eiffel Tower is focused on the task, the family takes care of individuals. As its name indicates, the family culture functions like a traditional family. The leader's role is that of a powerful father figure, who is responsible for the welfare of all members. Trompenaars suggests that family organizational cultures are found in Greece, Italy, Singapore, South Korea, and Japan. The Eiffel Tower is hierarchical and task focused. Consistent with the name—the Eiffel Tower—many French organizations have such a culture, characterized by a steep, stable, and rigid organization. The focus is on performance through order and obedience of legal and legitimate authority. The leader is the undisputed head of the organization and has full responsibility for all that occurs.

Trompenaars' dimensions and focus on culture in organizations provides a rich model for understanding culture within an organizational context. The most recent approach to explaining cultural differences will be presented next.

WHAT DO YOU DO?

You lead a team made up of people from several different countries. They are all very well qualified and experts in their fields. However, they have trouble working together. They constantly argue over work processes and their arguments are getting increasingly personal. They blame their different personalities, but you think culture has something to do with the problems. What do you do?

GLOBE—Global Leadership and Organizational Behavior Effectiveness Research

One of the most extensive research projects about cross-cultural differences and leadership was conducted by a group of researchers in 62 countries (House et al., 2004). Despite debates about the methodology used by researchers of the Global Leadership and Organizational Behavior Effectiveness research (GLOBE; Graen, 2006; House et al., 2006), the model is comprehensive and highly useful in understanding leadership and culture. The findings from GLOBE suggest that culture impacts, but does not predict, leadership behavior through people's expectations—what researchers call *culturally endorsed theory of leadership, or CLT*. Additionally, GLOBE research indicates that leaders who behave in accordance with their cultures' CLT tend to be most effective (Dorfman et al., 2012).

The GLOBE research suggests nine cultural values, some of which are similar to Hoftstede (House et al., 2002):

- *Power distance:* The degree to which power is distributed equally
- *Uncertainty avoidance:* The extent to which a culture relies on social norms and rules to reduce unpredictability (high score indicates high tolerance for uncertainty)
- *Humane orientation:* The degree to which a culture values fairness, generosity, caring and kindness
- *Collectivism I—Institutional:* The degree to which a culture values and practices collective action and collective distribution of resources
- *Collectivism II—In group:* The degree to which individuals express pride in and cohesion with their family or organizations
- *Assertiveness:* The degree to which individuals are assertive, direct, and confrontational
- *Gender-egalitarianism:* The extent of gender differentiation (high score indicates more differentiation)
- *Future orientation:* The extent to which a culture invests in the future rather than in the present or past
- *Performance orientation:* The degree to which a culture values and encourages performance

Based on their findings, GLOBE researchers defined 10 country clusters. These, along with the key high and low cultural values associated with each of the clusters, are depicted in Figure 2-4.

In reviewing Figure 2-4, you can see for example that countries in the Anglo cluster such as the United States, Canada, and England place a high value on performance orientation and low value on in-group collectivism. Those in the Confucian cluster, for example China and South Korea, value performance and both types of collectivism and are not low on any of the other cultural values. Similarly, people in the African cluster, when compared to other cultures, only rank humane orientation high. The Latin American cluster is high on in-group collectivism, but low on institutional collectivism, performance, and future orientation, and has a low tolerance for uncertainty. Further clarification of the clusters and the countries within them provides more details. For instance, in countries with high power distance, such as Thailand and Russia, communication is often directed one way, from the leader to followers, with little expectation of feedback. Finally, in cultures that value kindness and generosity, such as the Philippines or Egypt, leaders are likely to avoid conflict and act in a caring but paternalistic manner (Javidan and House, 2001).

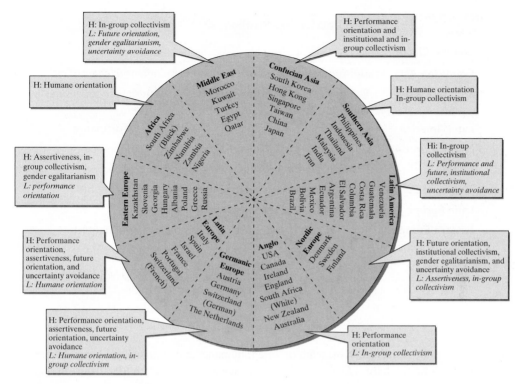

FIGURE 2-4 Country Clusters Based on GLOBE   *Source:* Based on information in House et al. *Culture, leadership and organizations: The GLOBE study of 62 countries* (Thousand Oaks, CA: Sage, 2004).

Although some of the dimensions proposed by GLOBE are similar to those in the other models we have presented, others are unique and refine our understanding of culture. Additionally, GLOBE's unique contribution is the development of six CLTs. These are as follows:

- *Charismatic and value-based:* Leadership based on the ability to inspire and motivate followers through core values and high-performance expectations
- *Team oriented:* Leadership focused on team building and developing a common goal
- *Participative:* Leadership based on involving followers in decision making
- *Humane orientated:* Leadership based on consideration for followers through compassion and generosity
- *Autonomous:* Leadership based on independence and individualism
- *Self-protective:* Leadership focused on safety and security of individual and group through self-enhancement and face saving

Using cultural values, country clusters, and CLTs, the GLOBE research identifies leadership profiles for each country clusters. Table 2-4 summarizes these cultural leadership profiles; for each country cluster, the CLTs are presented in order of importance (i.e., the first one is the most significant). It is important to note that the cultural values presented in Figure 2-4 indicate cultural practices as *they are*, whereas those in Table 2-4 are the ideals, the Culturally endorsed Leadership Theories (CLTs), and represent what people in that culture think ideal leadership *should be*. For instance, people in the Confucian Asian cluster consider

TABLE 2-4	Cultural Leadership Profiles
Cultural Cluster	**CLT**
Confucian Asia	Self-protective; team oriented; humane oriented; charismatic
Southern Asia	Self-protective; charismatic; humane oriented; team oriented; autonomous
Latin America	Charismatic; team- oriented; self-protective; participative
Nordic Europe	Charismatic; participative; team oriented; autonomous
Anglo	Charismatic; participative; humane oriented; team oriented
Germanic Europe	Autonomous; charismatic; participative; humane oriented
Latin Europe	Charismatic; team oriented; participative; self-protective
Eastern Europe	Autonomous; self-protective; charismatic; team-oriented
Africa	Humane oriented; charismatic; team oriented; participative
Middle East	Self-protective; humane oriented; autonomous; charismatic

Source: Based on information in House et al., 2004; Dorfman et al., 2012.

ideal leaders to be self-protective, team oriented, humane, and charismatic; Latin Americans place charisma first, whereas Germanic European see autonomy as an ideal characteristic of leaders.

GLOBE further identifies several categories of leader behavior that are either universally desirable or undesirable or whose desirability is contingent on the culture (Dorfman et al., 2012; House et al., 2004). For example, being trustworthy, just, and honest tend to have universal appeal. Similarly, charismatic/value-based leadership is generally desirable across most cultures and team-based leadership is believed to contribute to outstanding leadership in many cultures. Although participative leadership is seen generally as positive, its effectiveness depends, or is contingent on, the culture. Autonomous leaders are desirable in some cultures but not in all, and being self-protective is seen as hindering effective leadership in most cultures. Even some behaviors that appear somewhat universal reflect cultural differences. For example, Americans and the British highly value charisma, whereas Middle Easterners place less importance on this behavior from their leader. Nordic cultures are less favorable toward self-protective leadership behaviors, whereas Southern Asians accept it more readily (House et al., 2004). Not surprisingly, being malevolent, irritable, and ruthless are universally undesirable, whereas being ambitious, elitist, and humanistic are culturally contingent, meaning desirable in some cultures, but not all cultures (Dorfman et al., 2012).

Because of the large number of countries included in the studies and the extensive research that are conducted, GLOBE provides a comprehensive model for understanding cultural differences in leadership. Knowing the cultural values within each cluster and those held by people in each country, and being aware of their leadership ideals, can be of considerable value when working across cultures. The information provides a starting point for interaction and can assist leaders in understanding what their followers may expect and value, how to relate to them most successfully, what may motivate them, and generally, how to manage them more effectively.

APPLYING WHAT YOU LEARN

Using Culture to Be Effective

Culture at all levels can have a powerful impact on both leaders and followers. The following are some things to keep in mind to manage culture effectively:

- Be aware and conscious of your own culture and its various components. What are your values? How important are they to you? What are the conflicts you experience?
- Understand the culture of your organization. Is cooperation or competition valued? How formal is the environment? How much is performance valued? How about citizenship? What is rewarded?
- Be clear about any areas of agreement and disagreement between your culture and value system and that of your organization.

- Build on the agreements; they are likely to provide you with opportunities to shine. For example, if you value competition and high performance and so does the organization, you are likely to feel right at home.
- Carefully evaluate the disagreements. For example, you value competition and individual achievements, whereas the organization is highly team oriented. Can you adapt? Can you change the organization? A high degree of ongoing conflict among primary values is likely to lead to frustration and dissatisfaction.

The models of culture presented in this section provide different ways of understanding national and organizational culture. Each model is useful, but can also be misapplied if used to stereotype national or organizational cultures. Whereas Hall and Hofstede focus primarily on national culture, Trompenaars provides a model that combines national and organizational cultural and has a strong practitioner focus. GLOBE has one of the most comprehensive models available with a strong focus on leadership characteristics across cultures. All four are used throughout the book to provide a cross-cultural perspective on leadership.

GROUP CULTURE: GENDER AND LEADERSHIP

Anne Marie Slaughter, dean of Princeton's Woodrow Wilson School of Public and International Affairs, who quit her job as director of policy planning in the State Department recently reignited an on-going debate about whether women can achieve the same success as men and how they can balance their personal and work life in the article "*Why women still can't have it all.*" Slaughter states: "I still strongly believe that women can have it all (and that men can too). I believe that we can have it all at the same time. But not today, not with the way America's economy and society are currently structured" (Slaughter, 2012). While many disagree with first part of her assertions (women can't have it all), there is strong consensus about the second part that suggests that women's experiences in the workplace are different than men's.

Talking about the 2008 financial crisis and how the lack of diversity in the financial industry may have contributed to it, Christine Laguarde, former French finance minister and head of the International Monetary Fund (IMF), said: "If Lehman Brothers had been 'Lehman Sisters,' today's economic crisis clearly would look quite different"(LaGuarde, 2010). Are there substantial and significant differences between how men and women lead and what they experience at work? There are no easy or simple answers.

Stephanie Shirley, the British businesswomen who was one of the first women to start a software company in the 1960s, focused on creating opportunities for other women, partly because she faced considerable discrimination in her own career. When describing the business climate she faced, she says: "All the talk was about money, profits, cash flow, whereas I was much more interested in team work, innovation, excellence, quality assurance—some things that people consider the softer things of management" (Martin, 2013). Leaders such as Francis Hesselbein, president and CEO of the Leader to Leader institute, and former chief executive of the Girl Scouts, Nancy Bador, former executive director of Ford Motor Company, and Barbara Grogan, founder of Western Industrial Contractors, chair of the Volunteer Board of America and the first female chair of the Board of the greater Denver Chamber of Commerce, use an inclusive management style that they consider a female style of leadership. They shun the hierarchical structures for flat webs in which they are at the center rather than at the top. Carol Smith, vice president for Conde Nast's Bon Appetit and Gourmet Group, strongly believes that women are better managers, "In my experience, female bosses tend to be better managers, better advisers, mentors, rational thinkers. Men love to hear themselves talk." She further believes that men are better at letting things roll off their back while women rethink and replay events (Bryant, 2009m). Meg Whitman, CEO of Hewlett Packard, former CEO of EBay, and rated by *Forbes* #18 "Power Women" in 2012, is known for her unconventional, noncommand and control use of power. She believes that having power means that you must be willing to not have any (Sellers, 2004). Gerry Laybourne, founder and former CEO of Oxygen Media, the executive who built the top-rated children's television network Nickelodeon, considers competition to be "nonfemale." When she found out that *Fortune* magazine was ranking women in business, she declared, "That's a nonfemale thing to do. Ranking is the opposite of what women are all about" (Sellers, 1998: 80). She contends women lead and manage differently and are better than men at making connections among ideas and building partnerships and joint ventures (Sellers, 2009).

Many other successful female business leaders, however, do not see their leadership styles as drastically different from that of their male counterparts. Cherri Musser, chief information officer at EDS and formerly at GM, recommends, "You don't focus on being female—you focus on getting the job done. If you draw too much attention to your gender, you're not a member of the team" (Overholt, 2001: 66). Darla Moore, chief executive officer of the investment company Rainwater, Inc., and the first woman to be on the cover of *Fortune* magazine and have a business school named after her, argues that women's worse sin is to think, " 'You should be a nice girl. You ought to fit in. You should find a female mentor.' What a colossal waste of time" (Sellers, 1998: 92). She contends, "There are only glass ceilings and closed doors for those who allow such impediments" (Darla Moore Speech, 2007).

Whether women and men lead differently or not, there are differences between them in terms of the presence and power each group has in organizations around the world.

Current State of Women in Organizations

In the United States, women make up almost 50 percent of the workforce and 58 percent of women are working outside the home (Women in the Labor Force, 2013). However, they only hold 10 percent of the executive positions in business (Statistical overview of women in the workplace, 2013). In the United States, women's income continues to lag behind that of men at about 77 percent of men's income (Drum, 2012). In 2011, women held only 15.2 percent of corporate officer positions (Fulfilling the promise, 2012). As of 2013, there were only 20 female CEOs in the *Fortune* 500 (4 percent) in the United States and another 25 in the next 500 companies

(5 percent; Women CEOs, 2013). It is estimated that if the current trends continue, by 2016 maybe 6 percent of top leadership positions will be held by women (Helfat, Harris, and Wolfson, 2006). The salary gap between men and women is further evidence of the challenges women face. According to Forbes, only 2 of the 100 highest paid executives in United States in 2012 were women, ranking number 40 and 88 (America's highest paid executives, 2012). Similar trends exist all over the world. For example, in Canada 62 percent of women work, 68 percent in China, and 56 percent in Russia; with approximately around 50 percent in most Western European countries (Labor participation rate, 2013). In many Western countries, women constitute close to, or over, 50 of the workforce (Labor force, 2009). The number of women in leadership positions is highest in Scandinavian countries where women hold 23 percent of the board seats, in Sweden for example (Amble, 2006). In spite of the growing number of women in organizations, there still are considerable challenges.

An even more disturbing issue is that even when women are in leadership positions, they have less decision-making power, less authority, and less access to the highly responsible and challenging assignments than their male counterparts (Smith, 2002). Another alarming development for women is that despite consistent gains in achieving equality with men in the workplace, a series of surveys conducted since 1972 indicate that overall women are unhappier than they were previously, and they get less happy as they age, a finding that is reversed for men (Buckingham, 2009). The primary explanation provided is that women feel rushed and stressed much more than before and more than men, and that they feel drained rather than fulfilled. All the progress that women have made was assumed to make them happier; it has not.

Causes of Inequality

What obstacles do women face and what explains the challenges they face? Many factors have been considered and researched (for a review, see Eagly and Carli, 2004). Table 2-5 presents the various reasons that have been suggested.

In spite of the fact that women have a strong presence in organizations, including in managerial positions, traditional gender views and stereotypes continue to create obstacles to the their success in organizations. Cinta Putra, CEO of National Notification Network, believes: "The greatest challenge has been balancing all the demand of being a woman, a parent, a wife, a sister, a daughter, a friend *and* a CEO" (Bisoux, 2008a). Similarly, Sheryl Sandberg, COO of Facebook, believes that the disequilibrium in household responsibilities is one of the reasons for women's lack of progress (Sandberg, 2013). Although there have been some changes over the past few years, research indicates that women still continue to carry most of the burden for child care and household work and that, as a result, mothers are less employed than other women, whereas fathers work more than other men (Bianchi, 2000; Kaufman and Uhlenberg, 2000).

In spite of this, women are highly committed to both their education and their work. They are earning 59 percent of the undergraduate college degrees, 61 percent of the master's degrees, and 51 percent of MBAs (Eagly and Carli, 2004; Buckingham, 2009). Research indicates that although more professional women than men do take a break from work when they start a family (16 percent for women vs. 2 percent for men), over 90 percent of them try to get back into the workforce after about two years, further contradicting the idea that women have less commitment to their careers than men (Search for women. 2006; Hewlett, S. A. 2007). Some women executives have even suggested that motherhood provides women with skills that can be helpful in taking on organizational leadership roles. Gerry Laybourne, founder of Oxygen, states, "You learn about customer service from your 2-year-old (they are more demanding than any customer

TABLE 2-5 Suggested Reasons for Gender Inequality	
Issue	**Do they contribute to inequality?**
Gender differences in style and effectiveness	*Not likely* There are some gender differences, but if anything, women appear to have a style that is recommended in today's organizations
Challenges in balancing work life	*Likely* Women still carry a heavy burden of child care and household work
Women are less committed to their career	*Not likely* Women leave more often to have a family and have a nonlinear career, but they come back after a short break
Women have less education and experience	*Not likely* Equal or higher percentage of women compared to men have been getting education in all but the sciences and they have been in various positions in organizations for over 50 years
Persistent stereotypes	*Likely* Continued gender stereotypes held by organizational leaders and structural barriers due to traditional practices negatively impacts women's success in organizations
Discrimination	*Likely* Either intentionally or unwittingly, women face discrimination in the workplace

can be). You also learn patience, management skills, diversionary tactics, and 5-year planning" (Grzelakowski, M. 2005).

In regards to style differences, women have been found to be more cooperative, team-oriented, and more change oriented (Eagly, Johannesen-Schmidt, and van Engen, 2003). Management guru Tom Peters believes that the success of the new economy depends on the collaborative style that women leaders use instead of the command and control style that male leaders have traditionally used (Reingold, 2003). Addtionally, where there are some differences in management and leadership styles between men and women, such differences, if anything, should help women rather than hurt women leaders (see Amanatullah and Morris, 2010; Tannen, 1993; Su, Rounds, and Armstrong, 2009).

That leaves one major explanation for the challenges women face. Continued stereotypes and the resulting discrimination prevent them from achieving their potential. Both men and women continue to hold traditional stereotypes about what roles women should and can play in organizations. Facebook's Sandberg has garnered much attention with her recent book, "Lean in: Women, Work, and the Will to lead," where she suggests that women sometimes sabotage their own career (Sandberg, 2013). She finds that many of the young women she targets for challenging positions take themselves out of the running because they think having a family, which is in their future plans, will not allow them to continue working as hard, so they slow down too early. Women are not alone in this type of stereotypical thinking. Research suggests that bosses' perception of potential conflict between family and work affects their decision to promote women (Hoobler, Wayne, and Lemmon. 2009). Cases from organizations and academic research consistently show that women are still subject to negative stereotypes. They are caught in the double bind of having to fulfill two contradictory roles and expectations: those of being a woman and those of being a leader (Eagly and Karau, 2002). Gender stereotypes that equate leadership with being male persist (de Pillis et. al., 2008), and conventional gender stereotypes help men (Judge and Livingston, 2008). In many traditional settings, being a leader requires forceful behaviors that are more masculine (e.g., being proactive and decisive) than feminine (being kind and not appearing too competent). Women who are masculine, however, are often not liked and not considered effective (Powell, Butterfield, and Parent, 2002). Men particularly expect women to act in ways that are stereotypically feminine and evaluate them poorly when they show the more masculine characteristics typically associated with leadership. In some cases, evidence suggests that women do not support other women in getting leadership positions (Dana and Barisaw, 2006). Further, women who actively seek leadership and show a desire to direct others are not well accepted (Carli, 1999). These stereotypes and contradictory expectations limit the range of behaviors women are "allowed" to use when leading others, further hampering their ability to be effective. As we discussed in Chapter 1, becoming an effective leader requires considerable practice and experimentation. If they want to be easily accepted, women leaders are restricted to a set of feminine behaviors characterized by interpersonal warmth as their primary, if not only, means of influence (Carli, 2001). Because of existing stereotypes, women, and in many cases minorities, are not able to fully practice to perfect their craft. Stereotypes of women and minorities not being as competent or able to handle challenging leadership situations as well as men still persist, making blatant or subtle discrimination a continuing problem.

Stereotypes and tradition then lead to intentional and unintentional discriminatory practices that are difficult to change (Diversity and Inclusion, 2012). Women face a *glass ceiling*—invisible barriers and obstacles that prevent them from moving to the highest levels of organizations (Arfken, Bellar, and Helms, 2004). Some have suggested that men are fast-tracked to leadership position through a "glass elevator," and a recent review suggests the presence of a "glass cliff," whereby successful women are appointed to precarious leadership positions with little chance of success, thereby exposing them to yet another form of discrimination (Maune, 1999; Ryan and Haslam, 2007). *Sexual harassment*, defined as unwelcome sexual advances, requests for sexual favors, and other verbal or physical conduct of a sexual nature that tends to create a hostile or offensive work environment, is considered workplace discrimination. According to the U.S. Equal Employment Opportunity Commission (EEOC), sexual harassment claims were by far the largest portion of sex discrimination claims in 2012 (EEOC Press release, 2013). Other more subtle forms of discrimination include the fact that women and minorities are often not mentored by the right people and at the right time, a factor that is critical to success in any organization. Men are also made team leaders more often than women are (46 vs. 34 percent), they get more budgetary authority (44 vs. 31 percent), and they have increased responsibilities faster (89 vs. 83 percent; Search for women, 2009). Furthermore, women and minorities are often not exposed to the type of positions or experiences that are essential to achieving high-level leadership. For example, women and minorities may not be encouraged to take on international assignments or kept in staff rather than line positions and therefore may lack essential operational experience. Finally, subtle social and organizational culture factors, such as going to lunch with the "right" group, playing sports, being members of certain clubs, and exclusion from informal socializing and the "good old boys" network, can contribute to the lack of proportional representation of women and minorities in leadership ranks.

LEADING CHANGE
Deloitte Supports All Its Employees

Deloitte, one of the Big Four accounting firms with global reach, has 4,500 partners and other top executives. While the large majority is still white, the company is getting considerable recognition for its diversity and inclusion initiatives. The focus on diversity starts at the top. CEO Barry Salzberg believes that "...an organization that is diverse is stronger. It can draw on countless skills. It can innovate better. It can reach a greater number of markets. It can team more effectively" (Diversity and Inclusion, 2012: 16). He is focused on making his company a more diverse place and on opening doors for the talent that Deloitte needs to recruit and retain to succeed. One of the steps the company has taken is to recruit from community colleges rather than only from top-notch universities, a practice that is typical for large global companies. Salzberg states: "Targeting these schools offers us a unique opportunity to reach another distinct population of diverse top talent" (Crockett, 2009). In addition, Deloitte has implemented an innovative program called Mass Career Customization, which provides every employee, not just women and minorities, the opportunity to develop their own unique path. The program grew out of a women's initiative within the company but now applies to all employees. "Mass career customization provides a framework in which every employee, in conjunction with his or her manager, can tailor his or her respective career path within Deloitte over time" (Deloitte, 2010). The program allows employees to create a better fit between their life and career and provides multiple paths to the top of the organization, thereby addressing one of the primary challenges that women face in balancing work and life.

Deloitte's efforts have not gone unnoticed. The company was named by *Business Week* as the number one company for starting a career (Gerdes and Lavelle, 2009) and by a diversity report from Forbes (Diversity and Inclusion, 2012). It also got high marks in the Shriver Report, which describes the status of women in the United States, as a model employer (Shriver Report, 2009). The report gives Deloitte high marks for being "an excellent example of an employer that has taken an aggressive leadership position in protean career approaches, providing career-life integration programs that allow both the organization and its workforce—women and men—to reach their goals" (Deloitte—Shriver Report, 2009). Cathy Benko, vice chairman and chief talent officer at Deloitte, believes that "through our own journey to retain and advance women, we know that what is good for women is good for all our people" (Model employer, 2009).

Sources: Crockett, R. O. 2009. "Deloitte's diversity push," *Business Week*, October 2, http://www.business week.com/managing/content/oct2009/ca2009102_173180.htm (accessed January 18, 2010); Deloitte, 2010. http://careers.deloitte.com/united-states/students/culture_benefits.aspx?CountryContentID=13709 (accessed January 18, 2010); Deloitte—Shriver Report. 2009. Deloitte recognized for its strategies to adapt to the evolving workforce, http://www.deloitte.com/view/en_US/us/press/Press-Releases/press release/5e6c7475aa4 55210VgnVCM200000bb42f00aRCRD.htm (accessed January 18, 2010).

Diversity and Inclusion: Unlocking global potential. 2012. *Forbes Insight,* January. http://www.forbes.com/ forbesinsights/diversity_2012_pdf_download/ (accessed June 24, 2013); Gerdes, L. and L. Lavelle. 2009. "Best place to launch a career," *Business Week.* http://bwnt.businessweek.com/interactive_reports/career_ launch_2009/ (accessed January 18, 2010); Model employer. 2009. http://www.deloitte.com/view/en_US/us/ About/Womens-Initiative/article/c7aa98bbcf084210VgnVCM100000ba42f00aRCRD.htm (accessed January 18, 2010). Shriver Report: A woman's nation changes everything. 2009. http://awom ansnation.com (accessed January 18, 2010).

THE LEADERSHIP QUESTION—REVISITED

The GLOBE research tells us that while not all cultures have the same ideals of leadership, there are some universal factors. Diversity research also points to differences in what different groups and individual may need and expect from their leader. However, the one factor that stands out regardless of national or group culture is integrity. To be effective, leaders, no matter where they are and who their followers are, must demonstrate integrity, honesty, and trustworthiness.

More often than not, obstacles that women and minority face are not immediately apparent, are often not illegal, and are unwritten and unofficial policy, which is one reason why the term *glass* is used to describe such obstacles—they are invisible. They are part of the organizational culture and are therefore difficult to identify and even more difficult to change. Although there are some differences, all members of nondominant groups face similar challenges. Changes in how individual leaders think and how organizations manage their employees are essential to creating a multicultural and diverse organization. We consider individual and organizational aspects of becoming a more diverse organization next.

DEVELOPING A CULTURAL MINDSET

From an organizational point of view, and aside from the fairness and social justice perspective, developing talented leaders, regardless of their culture, race, gender, or any other non-performance-related factor, is essential. The key to success in intercultural contact and interaction is cultivating a *cultural mindset* which is a way of thinking and an outlook where culture is taken into consideration in deliberations, decisions, and behaviors. For many years, organizations have emphasized the concept of cultural and linguistic competence, which is a set of behaviors, attitudes, and policies that are integrated to help deal with cross-cultural situations (Cross et al., 1989). The Georgetown National Center for Cultural Competence suggests that it includes awareness, attitudes, knowledge, and skills (Georgetown National Center, 2013). This competence is essential for today's leaders. However, a cultural mindset is the starting point; it includes and goes beyond skills and competence. It focuses on a way of thinking.

In order for organizations to truly become diverse and multicultural, leaders must think, not simply act, about culture. Action without cognition is not likely to last and cognition without action will not be effective. While it is close to impossible for anyone to acquire in-depth knowledge about all the cultures he or she might encounter, or learn all the necessary behaviors, it is possible to have a cultural mindset that allows one to understand cultural differences and their impact on behavior, and to take that knowledge into consideration when interacting with or leading others. That cultural mindset then allows for the development of appropriate skills and competencies.

Characteristics of a Cultural Mindset

A cultural mindset is a way of thinking that allows the individual to be aware of and open to culture and how it impacts his own and others' thinking and behaviors. It involves how one thinks, and how one behaves, as well as specific skills. It starts at the individual level and expand throughout an organization.

Figure 2-5 summarizes some of these key cognitions, behaviors, and skills. Cultural mindfulness starts with awareness of your own culture and how it influences how you perceive the world and what you do. Awareness of the role of culture is essential because culture is stable and hard to change and because some of the assumptions are not fully conscious. In addition to

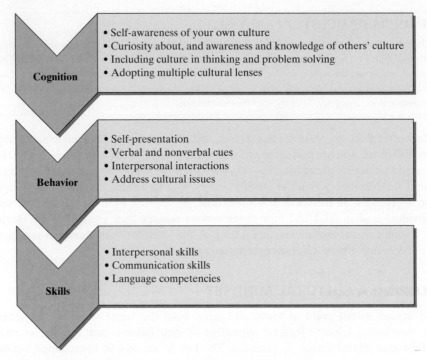

FIGURE 2-5   The Cultural Mindset

self-awareness, a cultural mindset requires knowing how culture may impact others. It further involves a degree of curiosity and inquisitiveness about how and why other people do what they do and appreciation and respect for differences. A culturally mindful person knows that the visible parts of culture are only a small part and seeks to uncover the hidden parts. He or she looks for cultural indicators, signs, and symbols that make people unique and values the diversity and potential strength culture can bring to interpersonal or organizational settings. Another component of a cultural mindset is curiosity about and knowledge of others' cultures. It includes the willingness to share your culture and learn from those who are different. A culturally mindful leader sees himself or herself as part of the world and uses the knowledge he or she acquires to improve his or her decisions and effectiveness. A final and key aspect of cognition is thinking about cultural issues when evaluating and addressing problems and looking at the world through multiple cultural lenses.

While a cultural mindset is first a way of thinking, how we think influences what we do, so it also becomes a way of acting. Behavior starts with self-presentation and using appropriate verbal and nonverbal messages and cues, such as level of formality, directness, or focus on relationships. For example, when a team with members from different cultures is formed, one of the issues that the culturally mindful manager includes in team training is knowledge of cultural factors and how to address cultural conflicts. These behaviors can result from developing various skills in managing interpersonal relations, communication, and other factors that can help intercultural interaction.

Although it is close to impossible for anyone to acquire in-depth knowledge about all the cultures he or she might encounter, it is possible to have a cultural mindset that allows one to understand cultural differences and their impact on behavior and to take that knowledge into consideration when interacting with and leading others. Such a cultural mindset engenders an awareness of and openness to culture and how it affects our own and others' thinking and behavior. A cultural mindset allows for a multicultural approach, which aims at inclusiveness, social justice, affirmation, mutual respect, and harmony in a pluralistic world (Fowers and Davidov, 2006). Rather than being viewed as an issue of quotas and percentages, diversity and multiculturalism refer to building a culture of openness and inclusiveness.

The Multicultural Organization

The fundamental solution to addressing cultural challenges is to make organizational climates hospitable to diverse groups with diverse needs (Solomon, 2010; Valerio, 2009). One of the key challenges that leaders face is how to keep people engaged. Having an organization that addresses the needs of individuals, which includes taking culture into account, is essential. The Gallup Survey, a regularly conducted survey about the workplace, finds that "the best managers recognize and understand the fundamental differences among their team members and think about the implications for the workplace. These managers are energized by the potential these diverse individuals bring to the table" (Gallup—State of the American Workplace, 2013). Gallup finds generational and gender differences in satisfaction and engagement and squarely puts the responsibility for motivating and engaging a diverse workforce on leaders. It also finds that the benefits of building a multicultural organization with a cultural mindset go beyond women and other minority groups; they extend to all employees. One of their surveys shows that organizations where diversity is valued have the most satisfied employees and better retention (Wilson, 2006).

Organizational leaders play a critical role in encouraging a cultural mindset in organizations. Leaders demonstrate through their words and actions the value of maintaining a multicultural organization where discrimination is not tolerated and where cultural differences are fully considered as part of all decision making (Figure 2-6). The Gallup survey's linking diversity to satisfaction further indicates that organizational leaders' commitment to diversity is linked to overall employee satisfaction (Wilson, 2006).

The case of Deloitte offers one example of building a multicultural organization. Another is Sodexo, the global, $20 billion food service and facility management company. Through a strong commitment from the top leadership, a managerial reward system based partially on achieving diversity objectives, extensive diversity training and mentoring, numerous diversity-focused partnerships and relationships including cooperation with historically black colleges and universities, work life programs, and sponsorship of diversity-focused groups and events, Sodexo keeps diversity in the forefront of its activities. A high-touch culture with an orientation toward action is responsible for the implementation of various diversity initiatives, says Betsy Silva Hernandez, senior director for corporate diversity and inclusion. A diversity leadership council, in place since 2002, and a committee of operation leaders are tasked with implementation and oversight of various policies through managers and employee groups (Inside diversity structure at Sodexo, 2013). Close to 90 percent of Sodexo managers participate in various employee resource groups that are instrumental in implementing diversity initiatives (Inside diversity structure, 2013). The company president and CEO, George Chavel, says: "Our diversity expertise helps us be more agile and responsive to customers and differentiates us from our competitors, and therefore directly contributes to our long-term business success" (Sodexo ranked number one company for diversity by DiversityInc., 2010). Rohini Anand, Sodexo's

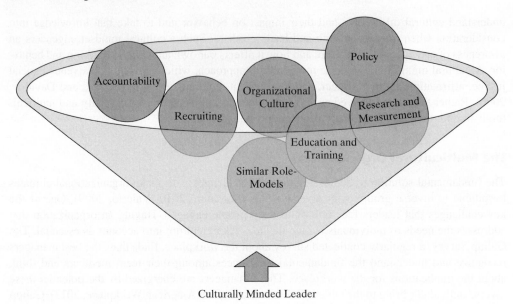

FIGURE 2-6   Organizational Factors in Becoming a Multicultural Organization

chief diversity officer, states: "Sodexo considers diversity and inclusion a business imperative as well as a social and ethical responsibility grounded in core values of team spirit, service spirit, and spirit of progress" (Reed, 2013). Sodexo's success in diversity is all the more impressive because, just a few years ago in 2006, the company settled a $80 million discrimination class action lawsuit (Reed, 2013).

The examples of Sodexo and Deloitte demonstrate the importance of leaders. The leader not only is a powerful decision maker but also exercises considerable influence through formal and informal communication, recruiting, role modeling, and the setting of various organizational policies. The message the leader sends through words and actions about the importance and role of culture, diversity, and multiculturalism in an organization is one of the most important factors in diversity (for a discussion on the influence process used by top leaders, see Chapter 7). Changing the culture of an organization to address discriminatory practices, behaviors, and symbols is another powerful tool. It is also one of the most difficult and lengthy processes any organization can undertake. However, without a cultural change toward addressing informal discriminatory practices and attitudes, other improvements are not likely to be as effective.

The presence of diverse role models throughout an organization is another part of the solution. By having diverse people in leadership positions and recruiting a diverse group of employees, an organization "walks the talk" and can demonstrate its commitment to diversity. Training and education can help people become aware of their biases, understand their own and others' cultural point of view, and better accept differences. For example, when the consulting firm of Bain & Company transfers its consultants from one part of the world to another, it not only provides them with information about living in the new country but also arms them with cultural knowledge specific to the country to allow them to function more effectively (Holland, 2007). Other companies such as Procter & Gamble (P&G) value and encourage the development of cultural knowledge in their employees and leaders. The company's motto of "everyone valued, everyone included, everyone Performing at their Peak" is more than words (Diversity and Inclusion, 2012). Linda Clement-Holmes, P&G's diversity officer and senior vice president for business services, says: "the more the employees can reflect the consumers, the better we do as a company" (Diversity and Inclusion, 2012: 6).

Toyota U.S.A., like many other successful multicultural organizations, builds the diversity of its workforce through a well-articulated strategy, a diversity advisory board, and various policies and actions such as supporting diverse groups, recruitment, and accountability (Toyota's Twenty-First Century Diversity Strategy, 2013). Many traditional organizational policies such as those on family leave can hinder people's chances of advancement. Similarly, performance evaluation criteria that may emphasize the stereotypical male and Western characteristics associated with leaders as the basis for success may undermine the ability of people who have other diverse characteristics and skills to rise to leadership positions. Finally, successfully encouraging diversity requires careful measurement and monitoring. Organizations must have baseline information about the hard facts about the actual numbers of women and minorities in leadership and about the softer data related to satisfaction, attitudes, and the less-visible obstacles that may be in place. Keeping track of changes and holding decision makers accountable, as do Deloitte, Sodexo, and others, are essential to solidifying any improvement that may take place. For example, another indicator of Toyota's commitment to a diverse and inclusive workforce is its quick action after one of its top executives was accused of sexual harassment. Not only did the executive leave his position, but the company also created a task force to enhance training of its executives and put in place better procedures for responding to allegations and complaints (Wiscombe, 2007).

The importance and key role of a leader who is culturally minded cannot be overemphasized. Building a diverse and multicultural organization where employees from diverse groups and cultures are welcome is an ethical and moral obligation in the global environment, and it is a sound business practice.

WHAT DO YOU DO?

Your company is growing fast and you need to hire many new employees and managers quickly. Several of your managers suggest that instead of going through a lengthy posting of jobs, you should simply encourage all your managers to personally recruit people they know and trust. Others say that your current management lacks diversity and is not likely to bring in a diverse pool of applicants. What do you do?

Summary and Conclusions

Culture is one of the factors that influence how people think and behave. It also affects whom we consider to be an effective leader and what we expect of our leaders. Several models have been proposed to increase our understanding of culture. Hall's cultural context focuses on the communication context. People from high-context cultures rely on the environment, nonverbal cues, situational factors, and subtle signals to communicate with others. Those from low-context cultures focus on specific written or oral messages. Hofstede's cultural values suggest that culture can be understood using the five dimensions of power distance, uncertainty avoidance, individualism, masculinity, and time orientation. Additionally, whether a culture is tight, with many rules and regulations, or loose, with fewer prescriptions for behavior, further affects how people behave. Trompenaars further refines our understanding of culture by considering nine dimensions and providing models for cross-cultural organizational cultures. The most recent and most comprehensive model for culture, the Global Leadership and Organizational Behavior Effectiveness (GLOBE), suggests that culture impacts, but does not predict, leadership behavior through culturally endorsed theory of leadership (CLT), and that leaders who behave according to their cultures' expectations tend to be most effective.

In addition to national culture, group culture, particularly as it relates to gender, plays a role in the leadership of organizations. Although women have active roles in organizations in the West and many other parts of the world, clearly they do not have access to the same power and leadership roles as men do. While gender inequality has many causes, consistent stereotypes and discrimination continues to prevent women from full progress in organizations. The development of a cultural mindset, whereby culture is at the forefront of leader's cognitions and behaviors, is the first step toward the development of multicultural organizations. Support from leadership, a supportive culture, appropriate policies, and accountability are among the factors that help build a diverse and multicultural organization.

Review and Discussion Questions

1. What are the four models of culture, and how do they affect leadership?
2. How could power distance and masculinity affect leadership?
3. How would the definitions of leaders and effectiveness differ based on the different cultural values presented by Hofstede, Trompenaars, and the GLOBE findings?
4. How does group membership affect leaders and leadership?

5. What is the glass ceiling? Could any of Hofstede's cultural dimensions contribute to its existence?
6. What are the elements of a cultural mindset?
7. How can individuals develop a more cultural mindset? How can leaders contribute to this process?
8. Why are leaders so important in that process?

Leadership Challenge: Juggling Cultures

Culture, gender, and leadership are closely related. In most cultures, even Western cultures, leadership is associated with males. This association is even stronger in many Arab Muslim countries, where women typically play a limited role in public and business life.

As a leader of an organization, you face the choice of selecting the leader of a negotiation team to draft a new deal with a potential Saudi Arabian client. By far, your best, most experienced, and most skilled negotiator is one of your female executives. She has, for many years, successfully negotiated deals within the United States and in several other countries. Her second in command is a promising but relatively young male executive who still needs to develop his skills and experience.

1. Whom do you send to Saudi Arabia as head of your team?
2. What cultural factors do you need to consider?
3. What are the implications of your decision for your business and the message you send as a leader?

Exercise 2-1: World Map

On a blank sheet of paper, draw a map of the world that includes all seven continents (or as many as you can remember).

1. How many continents did you place correctly (generally correct location)?

2. Where did you start your map? What's the first place you drew?

3. What continent is in the center? Why?

4. What does your map tell you about your knowledge of the world?

Please wait for further instructions.

Exercise 2-2: Proverbs as a Window to Leadership

What do these proverbs tell us about the culture? What implications do they have for leadership in that culture?

United States (mainstream)

Proverb	Implications for Leadership
Actions speak louder than words.	
Strike while the iron is hot.	
Time is money.	
God helps those who help themselves.	

From Other Cultures

Proverb	Implications for Leadership
One does not make the wind, but is blown by it (Asian cultures).	
Order is half of life (Germany).	
When spider webs unite, they can tie up a lion (Ethiopia).	
We are all like well buckets, one goes up and the other comes down (Mexico).	
Sometimes you ride the horse; sometimes you carry the saddle (Iran).	
We will be known forever by the tracks we leave (Native American—Dakota).	
One finger cannot lift a pebble (Hopi).	
Force, no matter how concealed, begets resistance (Lakota).	

Exercise 2-3: Narian Bridges

The following exercise is a cross-cultural role-play designed to allow you to experience the challenges and opportunities of interacting with people from different cultures. The setting is the fictional country of Nari. You will be asked to play the role of either an American or a Narian. Read the exercise carefully; your instructor will provide you with further information.

BACKGROUND

Nari is a Middle Eastern country with an old history and a rich cultural heritage. Through judicious excavation of a number of minerals, the country has obtained considerable wealth, and the stable political and social climate has attracted many foreign investors. As a result, Nari launched a careful and well-planned development campaign in the past 20 years that allowed the country's economy to become the strongest in the region. The per capita income is the highest in the region with a literacy rate greater than 80 percent for the population under 30 (which comprises 53 percent of the population).

The political system is an authoritarian monarchy. The powers of the elected parliament are limited to its consultative role to the king. This political system has been in place for more than 1,000 years, and the current dynasty began its reign 400 years ago. As compared with many of its unstable neighbors, Nari has enjoyed a calm political climate. The Western press, however, is highly critical of the lack of democracy and the authoritarian nature of the government. The king has unceremoniously dismissed the charges as cultural colonialism and emphasizes the need to preserve the Narian culture while welcoming the West's and the East's help in economic development.

The culture is warm and welcoming of outsiders. The Narian focus on politeness and kindness is easily extended to foreigners, although Narians do not accept criticism of their culture as well and do not tolerate debate about the topic, particularly with outsiders. Many younger Narians seek higher education in other parts of the world, but most return eagerly to their country. The extended family remains the core of society, with the father being the unquestioned head. Narians take pride in their family and maintain considerable commitment to it. They demonstrate a similar commitment to the organizations to which they belong; employees take pride in the accomplishments of their organizations. Although some rumblings can be heard about opening up the political systems and allowing for more democratic participation, the authority of the family, of the community, and of the monarch, are rarely, if ever, questioned. Narians often mention the importance of individual sacrifice, social order, and stability and express dismay, with a smile, at how Westerners can get anything done when they behave in such unruly ways. They also contrast the inherent trust in their society, where a handshake and a person's word are as good as gold, with other countries' legalistic systems that require extensive contracts to get anything done.

Narian leaders hold total and absolute power. Although not viewed as having power derived from divine rights, leaders are assumed to be infallible. Narian leaders are confident in their complete knowledge of all that they come to face. They do not ask questions and do not seek advice, even from equals. Often autocratic, the Narian leader, however, is expected to take care of loyal followers under any circumstance. As followers owe unquestioning obedience, leaders owe them total devotion. The leaders are fully responsible for all that happens to their followers, in all aspects of their life. They are expected to help and guide them and come to their rescue when needed. Leaders are expected to be caring and fair. Their primary duty is to look out for their followers.

In return, Narian followers are expected to be loyal, obedient, dutiful, and subservient. They accept their leader's orders willingly and wholeheartedly; all Narians are taught from the youngest age that leaders are infallible and that the proper functioning of the social order hinges on obedience and loyalty to leaders and elders and on their fulfilling their responsibility as followers. Dissent and conflict are rarely expressed in the open. People value politeness and civility and go out of their way to be kind. When mistakes are made, regardless of where the fault lies, all individuals work on correcting it without assigning blame. If the leader makes a mistake, an event rarely, if ever, brought out in the open, one of the followers openly accepts the blame to protect the leader's face and the social harmony. The person accepting that responsibility is eventually rewarded for the demonstration of loyalty.

The role of women in Narian society remains puzzling to Western observers. For more than 30 years, women have had practically equal rights with men. They can vote, conduct any kind of business transactions, take advantage of educational opportunities, file for divorce, obtain custody of their children, work in any organization, and so forth. The literacy rate for women is equal to that of men, and although fewer of them pursue higher education, it appears that most women who are interested in working outside the home find easy employment in the booming Narian economy. The society, however, remains highly patriarchal in its traditions.

ROLE-PLAY SITUATION

A U.S. engineering and construction company has won its first major governmental contract for constructing two bridges in Nari. With general terms agreed on, the company is working closely with several U.S.-educated Narian engineers employed at the Narian Ministry of Urban Development (UD) to draft precise plans and timetables. The minister of UD, Mr. Dafti, is a well-respected civil engineer, educated in Austria in the 1950s. In addition to Narian, he speaks fluent German, English, and French. He played instrumental roles in the development of his country. Although a consummate politician and negotiator and an expert on his country's resources and economic situation, he has not practiced his engineering skills for many years.

Mr. Dafti has decided on the general location and structure of the two bridges to be built. One of the locations and designs contains serious flaws. His more junior Narian associates appear to be aware of the potential problems and have hinted at the difficulties and challenges in building in that location, but have not clearly voiced their concerns to the U.S. contractors, who find the design requirements unworkable.

The role-play is a meeting with Mr. Dafti, his Narian associates, and representatives of the U.S. engineering firm. The U.S. head engineer requested the meeting, and the request was granted quickly. The U.S. team is eager to start the project. The Narians also are ready to engage in the new business venture.

Please wait for further instructions.

Exercise 2-4: Leadership and Gender

This exercise is designed to explore the relationship between gender roles and leadership. Your instructor will assign you to one of three groups and ask you to develop a list of characteristics of a particular leader. Each group will present its list to the class. Discussion will focus on the similarities and differences between gender roles and leadership.

Now, list eight to ten characteristics associated with _____ (wait for your instructor's direction). You can use specific personality traits or behavioral descriptions.

1.

2.

3.

4.

5.

6.

7.

8.

9.

10.

Exercise 2-5: Is This Sexual Harassment?

For each of the following scenarios, state whether you believe sexual harassment has taken place. Explain your reasoning.

1. A teacher stipulates that your grade (or participation on a team, in a play, etc.) will be based on whether you submit to a relationship.

   Is it harassment?

   Why?

2. Mary and Todd dated for a while. Mary broke off their relationship and no longer wants to date Todd and has told him so. Todd, however, continually behaves as if they are still dating. He phones her for dates. In the halls at the university, he comes up and puts his arms around her shoulders.

   Is it harassment?

   Why?

3. During a discussion at work regarding gay rights, Ricardo strongly defended the right of gays to have partner benefits at work and be able to form a civil union. He got very emotional when talking about the sadness he observed when one of his friends was not allowed to visit his partner of many years on his deathbed in the hospital because they were not legally related. Since that day, his coworkers have been making comments such as "Mama's boy," "You're such a girl," "Are you going to cry now?" and insinuating that he is gay. Ricardo is heterosexual.

   Is it harassment?

   Why?

4. Tara Washington has been Peter Jacobs's assistant for over five years, and they have had an excellent working relationship. Tara just found out that her father has terminal cancer, and one day recently at the office, she broke down and started crying. Peter came up to her and gave her hug.

   Is it harassment?

   Why?

5. Julie and Antonio started working at the office a few days apart. They are both recent college graduates. They immediately hit it off and soon started dating. Their supervisor talked to both of them and warned them not to let their relationship interfere with their work or affect others in the workplace. They both said that they understood the potential problems and made a commitment to keep things professional. After a couple of months, Antonio broke off the relationship. Julie was heartbroken. Both were very uncomfortable working with each other. After a few weeks, Julie talked to her supervisor about Antonio avoiding her and her belief that this may constitute sexual harassment.

   Is it harassment?

   Why?

6. Nadine is a very attractive young employee in a government office. She has developed a warm, friendly, and professional relationship with her colleagues, many of whom are males. They often joke and laugh with her, and she receives many compliments from them regarding her looks.

   Is it harassment?

   Why?

7. Nicholas is a recent immigrant from Greece who is working in a high-technology firm in Massachusetts. He really enjoys his job and likes his colleagues. They often go out to lunch and for drinks after work and play sports on weekends. Nicholas is shocked when he finds out that one of his colleagues has accused him of sexual harassment for inappropriate physical contact.

Is it harassment?

Why?

8. Kim is a realtor who specializes in selling homes from large developers. She shows a lot of property in construction sites and has a very successful track record. Recently, she has become very uncomfortable with rude and suggestive comments from the construction workers at one of the sites, so much so that she is avoiding showing property in that location. She complained to her office manager about the problem, but she was told that they cannot really control the construction workers because they do not work for the same company.

Is it harassment?

Why?

9. Gary has taken one of his company's biggest clients to dinner. The client is considering expanding her business with Gary's company. During dinner, she very clearly comes on to Gary who politely refuses her advances. The client brushes him off and says she will try again. The next day, Gary tells his supervisor about the incident and how uncomfortable he felt. His supervisor informs him that the client has specifically asked for Gary to stay on the case and has indicated that she looks forward to expanding her business with the company.

Is it harassment?

Why?

Self-Assessment 2-1: What Is Your Primary Cultural Background?

Identify the culture that you consider to be your primary cultural background (recognizing that you may be from multiple backgrounds).

1. What do you think makes that culture unique?

2. What are some of its key teachings about what is important? What is right?

3. How did you learn these?

4. How much do you agree with them? Why or why not?

5. How often do you share these cultural elements with others?

6. How much of your behavior do you think is influenced by that culture?

Please wait for further instructions.

Self-Assessment 2-2: Do You Have a Cultural Mindset?

For each of the following items, please use the scale below to indicate your answer.

1	2	3	4
Strongly Disagree	Disagree	Agree	Strongly Agree

Item		Response			
1.	I know a lot about my own culture.	1	2	3	4
2.	I don't think much about how my culture impacts me.	1	2	3	4
3.	I can tell how my cultural background influences how I think and what I do.	1	2	3	4
4.	I enjoy asking people about their culture.	1	2	3	4
5.	I seek out various cultural experiences any chance I can (e.g., food, travel, festivals, music).	1	2	3	4
6.	I know a lot about how cultural differences impact the thinking and behavior of those I work with.	1	2	3	4
7.	I like sharing my culture and its customs and beliefs with those who don't know it.	1	2	3	4
8.	I often include culture as one of the factors I consider when I think about solving problems either in my personal or professional life.	1	2	3	4
9.	I am comfortable with people who are from different cultures.	1	2	3	4
10.	When people around me speak a different language, it often makes me uncomfortable.	1	2	3	4
11.	I think people are the same, no matter where they are from.	1	2	3	4
12.	Although I am from _____ (state your country), I often think of myself as a citizen of the world.	1	2	3	4
13.	People may have different views, but I believe that in the end there is always a right way and wrong way.	1	2	3	4
14.	I am good at adjusting my behavior to different situations.	1	2	3	4
15.	My own and other people's cultural background is important to me.	1	2	3	4

Scoring: Reverse the scoring for items 2, 10 11, 13 (1 = 4; 2 = 3; 3= 2; 4 =1). Then, add up your scores for all of the questions.

Total: _____

The range of scores is 15 to 60. A score in the upper third (60 to 45) indicates strong cultural mindfulness. A score in the bottom third (30 to 15) shows little awareness of culture. Review each of your responses and the material about diversity and a multicultural mindset in this chapter to identify your areas of strength and weakness and decide what you can do to strengthen your cultural awareness and ability to work across diverse cultures.

Self-Assessment 2-3: Exploring Views of Women

Briefly describe the cultural views and expectations of women in your family and your culture. What are your personal views of the role of women in the following?:

Relationships

Family

Business/work

Community

How would those views facilitate or present obstacles for women in the workplace?

LEADERSHIP IN ACTION

LEADERSHIP BASED ON ANCIENT PRINCIPLES

"Responsible, authentic and integral" with commitment to a triple bottom line of profits, people, and the planet are the principles behind Tata, India's largest corporation (Babu, 2012). The conglomerate is a $100 billion family-owned Indian industrial giant that includes anything from information systems, steel, energy, cars, consumer goods, hotels with operations in over 80 countries, and ownership in international brands such as Jaguar, Land Rover, and Daewoo Motors (What Cyrus Mistry inherits, 2013). Its business is a symbol of the success of modern Western-style capitalism; its leadership and management principles hale back to India's ancient culture and religion based on values of integrity, hospitality, humility, kindness, and selflessness all ideals from the family's Parsi religious background and their rural roots (Deshpande and Raina, 2011).

As a family-owned and -run business, Tata benefited from the leadership of Ratan Tata for 21 years until he handed the reins to Cyrus Mistry, also a family member, in December 2012. An executive who worked with Ratan Tata says: "The chairmanship did not change him or his manner of arriving at the most appropriate course of action...Ratan Tata is not the type of boss who is given to thumping the table. He softly mandates, and those to whom the message is addressed get the point very clearly. He thinks big and encourages others to do likewise. He does not discourage those who occasionally fail to deliver" (Irani, 2013). Tata is reputed to be a good listener while also able to express his own view convincingly and some attribute his success to his ability to think big and small at the same time (Radhakrishman-Swami et. al., 2010). While many executives around the world develop arrogance and hubris and seek attention as international superstars, Ratan Tata has remained a private, self-effacing, and humble man who advocated the importance of globalization ahead of his time.

Because a majority of the company's business comes from outside India and because of India's own cultural diversity, the company promotes broad cultural diversity. Alan Rosling, executive director at Tata Sons, says: "The successful organization of tomorrow will diffuse geographically, and draw its competitive edge from a creative intermingling of people from all over" (Rosling, 2009). He believes that India has a unique advantage in promoting diversity because the country itself is one of the most diverse in the world. Although cultural misunderstandings and tension are bound to happen, Rosling believes that: "Only by exposing people to colleagues internationally can theses issues be tackled, and the potential for consequent value turned to real competitive edge" (Rosling, 2009).

One example of the unique management style was evident in 2008 when the Taj Mahal Palace hotel in Mumbai, India, the crown jewel of Tata' hospitality group, came under terrorist attack. What ensued was unimaginable bloodshed that left dozens dead and hundred others wounded. The attack brought to light the exemplary and uniquely selfless conduct of the hotel's staff members who remained and helped many guests escape at great risk to their own safety. The leadership principles that guide the company are implemented in recruitment and training, where many of the hotel's staff came from villages and were brought up with traditional cultural values, which are further reinforced through training and reward systems (Deshpande and Raina, 2011).

Questions

1. What are the characteristics of Tata's leadership?
2. Which levels of culture would the Tata Corporation need to consider?
3. Can the management style be implemented elsewhere?

Sources: Babu, S. 2012. "Why Ratan Tata is a role model for India Inc.," *Yahoo Finance*, December 27. http://in.finance.yahoo.com/news/why-ratan-tata-is-a-role-model-for-india-inc-101918923.html (accessed April 1, 2013); Deshpande, R., and Raina, A. 2011. "The ordinary heroes of the Taj," *Harvard Business Review*, December. http://hbr.org/2011/12/the-ordinary-heroes-of-the-taj/ar/1 (accessed April 1, 2013); Irani, J. 2013. "He would never thump the table," *Business Today*, January 20. http://businesstoday.intoday.in/story/j.j.-irani-on-ratan-tata-leadership-style/1/191230.html (accessed April 1, 2013); Radhakrishnan-Swami, M., M. R. K. Pratap, M. E. Haque, and A. Shashidhar. 2010. "The Tatas without Ratan," *Outlook Business-India*, October 16. http://business.outlookindia.com/article_v3.aspx?artid=267429 (accessed July 11, 2013); Rosling, A. 2009. "Business blooms in diversity," *Tata—Leadership with Trust*. http://www.tata.com/careers/articles/inside.aspx?artid=IAECTN1VmjM= (accessed April 2, 2013);

What Cyrus Mistry inherits from Ratan Tata. 2013. *Business Today*, January 28. http://businesstoday.intoday.in/story/what-cyrus-mistry-inherits-from-ratan-tata/1/191081.html (accessed April 1, 2013).

3

The Foundations of Modern Leadership

After studying this chapter, you will be able to:

1. Identify the three major eras in the study of leadership and their contributions to modern leadership

2. Present and be able to evaluate the contributions of the early theories of leadership including the following:
   - Fiedler's Contingency Model
   - The Normative Decision Model
   - Path–Goal theory
   - Substitutes for leadership
   - Leader–Member Exchange

THE LEADERSHIP QUESTION

Do you think some people are born leaders and can rise to the top no matter what the situation? What key characteristics do they possess?

The roots of the modern study of leadership can be traced to the Western Industrial Revolution that took place at the end of the nineteenth century. Although many throughout history focused on leadership, the modern approach to leadership brings scientific rigor to the search for answers. Social and political scientists and management scholars tried, sometimes more successfully than other times, to measure leadership through a variety of means. This chapter reviews the history of modern leadership theory and research and presents the early theories that are the foundations of modern leadership.

A HISTORY OF MODERN LEADERSHIP THEORY: THREE ERAS

During the Industrial Revolution, the study of leadership, much like research in other aspects of organizations, became more rigorous. Instead of relying on intuition and a description of common practices, researchers used scientific methods to understand and predict leadership effectiveness by identifying and measuring leadership characteristics. The history of the modern scientific approach to leadership can be divided into three general eras or approaches: the trait era, the behavior era, and the contingency era. Each era has made distinct contributions to our understanding of leadership.

The Trait Era: Late 1800s to Mid-1940s

The belief that leaders are born rather than made dominated much of the late nineteenth century and the early part of the twentieth century. Thomas Carlyle's book *Heroes and Hero Worship* (1907), William James's writings (1880) about the great men of history, and Galton's study (1869) of the role of heredity were part of an era that can be characterized by a strong belief that innate qualities shape human personality and behavior. Consequently, it was commonly believed that leaders, by virtue of their birth, were endowed with special qualities that allowed them to lead others. These special characteristics were presumed to push them toward leadership, regardless of the context. The historical context and social structures of the period further reinforced such beliefs by providing limited opportunities for common people to become social, political, and industrial leaders. The belief in the power of personality and other innate characteristics strongly influenced leadership researchers and sent them on a massive hunt for leadership traits made possible by the advent of personality and individual characteristics testing such as IQ in the early twentieth century.

The major assumption guiding hundreds of studies about leadership traits was that if certain traits distinguish between leaders and followers, then existing political, industrial, and religious leaders should possess them (for a thorough review of the literature, see Bass, 1990). Based on this assumption, researchers identified and observed existing leaders and followers and collected detailed demographic and personality information about them. *More than 40 years of study provided little evidence to justify the assertion that leaders are born and that leadership can be explained through one or more traits.* Some traits do matter. For instance, much evidence indicates that, on average, leaders are more sociable, more aggressive, and more lively than other group members. In addition, leaders generally are original and popular and have a sense of humor. Which of the traits are most relevant, however, seems to depend on the requirements of the situation. In other words, being social, aggressive, lively, original, and popular or having any other combination of traits does not guarantee that a person will become a leader in all situations, let alone an effective one.

Because of weak and inconsistent findings, the commonly shared belief among many researchers in the late 1930s and early 1940s was that although traits play a role in determining leadership ability and effectiveness, their role is minimal and that leadership should be viewed as a group phenomenon that cannot be studied outside a given situation (Ackerson, 1942; Bird, 1940; Jenkins, 1947; Newstetter, Feldstein, and Newcomb, 1938; Stogdill, 1948). More recent studies in the 1960s and 1970s reinforced these findings by showing that factors such as intelligence (Bray and Grant, 1966) or assertiveness (Rychlak, 1963) are related to leadership effectiveness, but they alone cannot account for much of a leader's effectiveness.

Recent views of the role of traits and other individual characteristics, such as skills, refined our understanding of the role of individual characteristics in leadership (for an example and review, see Mumford et al., 2000a, b). Current interest in emotional intelligence has also yielded new research on the leader's individual characteristics; these are discussed in more detail in Chapter 4. The leader's personality, by limiting the leader's behavioral range or by making it more or less difficult to learn certain behaviors or undertake some actions, plays a key role in his or her effectiveness. However, it is by no means the only or even the dominant factor in effective leadership.

The Behavior Era: Mid-1940s to Early 1970s

Because the trait approach did not yield the expected results, and because the need to identify and train leaders became an urgent necessity during World War II, researchers turned to behaviors, rather than traits, as the source of leader effectiveness. The move to observable behaviors was triggered in part by the dominance of behaviorist theories during this period, particularly in the United States and Great Britain. *Instead of identifying who would be an effective leader, the behavior approach emphasizes what an effective leader does.* Focusing on behaviors provides several advantages over a trait approach:

- Behaviors can be observed readily.
- Behaviors can be consistently measured.
- Behaviors can be taught through a variety of methods.

These factors provided a clear benefit to the military and various other organizations with a practical interest in leadership. Instead of identifying leaders who had particular personality traits, they could focus on training people to perform effective leadership behaviors.

The early work of Lewin and his associates (Lewin and Lippit, 1938; Lewin, Lippit, and White, 1939) concerning democratic, autocratic, and laissez-faire leadership laid the foundation for the behavior approach to leadership. Democratic leaders were defined as those who consult their followers and allow them to participate in decision making; autocratic leaders as those who make decisions alone; and laissez-faire leaders as those who provide no direction and do not become involved with their followers. Although the three types of leadership style were clearly defined, the research failed to establish which style would be most effective or which situational factors would lead to the use of one or another style. Furthermore, each of the styles had different effects on subordinates. For example, laissez-faire leadership, which involved providing information but little guidance or evaluation, led to frustrated and disorganized groups that, in turn, produced low-quality work. On the other hand, autocratic leadership caused followers to become submissive, whereas groups led by democratic leaders were relaxed and became cohesive.

Armed with the results of Lewin's work and other studies, different groups of researchers set out to identify leader behaviors. Among the best-known behavioral approaches to leadership are the Ohio State Leadership Studies where a number of researchers developed a list of almost 2,000 leadership behaviors (Hemphill and Coons, 1957). After subsequent analyses (Fleishman, 1953; Halpin and Winer, 1957), a condensed list yielded several central leadership behaviors. Among them, task- and relationship-related behaviors were established as primary leadership behaviors. The Ohio State studies led to the development of the Leader Behavior Description Questionnaire (LBDQ), which continues to be used today.

Although the Ohio State research, along with other studies (e.g., Bowers and Seashore, 1966), identified a number of leader behaviors, the links between those behaviors and leadership effectiveness could not be consistently established. After many years of research, it did not become clear which behaviors are most effective. Evidence, although somewhat weak, shows that effective leadership requires both consideration and structuring behaviors (Fleishman and

Harris, 1962; House and Filley, 1971). These findings, however, have failed to receive overwhelming support. Nevertheless, researchers agree that considerate, supportive, people-oriented behaviors are associated with follower satisfaction, loyalty, and trust, whereas structuring behaviors are more closely related to job performance (for a review, see Judge, Piccolo, and Ilies, 2004). However, the leadership dimensions of initiation of structure and consideration do not describe leader's behavior adequately for cultures other than the United States where values might be less individualistic and people have different ideals of leadership (Ayman and Chemers, 1983; Chemers, 1969; Misumi and Peterson, 1985).

Similar to the trait approach, the behavior approach to leadership, by concentrating only on behaviors and disregarding powerful situational elements, provides a relatively simplistic view of a highly complex process and, therefore, fails to provide a thorough understanding of the leadership phenomenon. Yet, *the two general categories of task and relationship behaviors are well established as the primary leadership behaviors*. Researchers and practitioners continue to discuss what leaders do in these general terms.

The Contingency Era: Early 1960s to Present

Even before the behavior approach's lack of success in fully explaining and predicting leadership effectiveness became evident, a number of researchers were calling for a more comprehensive approach to understanding leadership (Stogdill, 1948). Specifically, researchers recommended that situational factors, such as the task and type of work group, be taken into consideration. However, it was not until the 1960s that this recommendation was applied. In the 1960s, spearheaded by Fred Fiedler, whose Contingency Model of leadership is discussed later in this chapter, leadership research moved from simplistic models based solely on the leader to more complex models that take a contingency point of view. Other models such as the Path-Goal Theory and the Normative Decision Model, also presented in this chapter, soon followed. *The primary assumption of the contingency view is that the personality, style, or behavior of effective leaders depends on the requirements of the situation in which the leaders find themselves.* Additionally, this approach suggests the following:

- There is no one best way to lead.
- The situation and the various relevant contextual factors determine which style or behavior is most effective.
- People can learn to become good leaders.
- Leadership makes a difference in the effectiveness of groups and organizations.
- Personal and situational characteristics affect leadership effectiveness.

Although the contingency approach to leadership continues to be well accepted, the most recent approach to leadership focuses on the relationship between leaders and followers and on various aspects of charismatic and visionary leadership. Some researchers have labeled this approach the neo-charismatic school (Antonakis, Cianciolo, and Sternberg, 2004). We will present this most recent view of leadership in detail in Chapter 6.

EARLY THEORIES

An effective leader must know how to use available resources and build a relationship with follower to achieve goals (Chemers, 1993). The early leadership theories of leadership addressed these two challenges in a variety of ways.

Fiedler's Contingency Model

Fred Fiedler was the first researcher to propose a contingency view of leadership. His Contingency Model is the oldest and most highly researched contingency approach to leadership (Fiedler, 1967). *Fiedler's basic premise is that leadership effectiveness is a function of the match between the leader's style and the leadership situation. If the leader's style matches the situation, the leader will be effective; otherwise, the leader will not be effective.* Fiedler considers how the leader uses available resources to make the group effective.

LEADER STYLE   To determine a leader's style, Fiedler uses the least-preferred coworker (LPC) scale, a measure that determines whether the leader is primarily motivated by task accomplishment or by maintaining relationships. Fiedler's research shows that people's perceptions and descriptions of their least-preferred coworker provide insight into their basic goals and priorities toward either accomplishing a task or maintaining relationships (see Self-Assessment 3-1).

According to Fiedler, people with low LPC scores—those who give a low rating to their least-preferred coworker (describing the person as incompetent, cold, untrustworthy, and quarrelsome)—are task motivated. They draw their self-esteem mostly from accomplishing their task well (Chemers and Skrzypek, 1972; Fiedler, 1967; Fiedler and Chemers, 1984; Rice, 1978a, b). When the task-motivated leaders or their groups fail, they tend to be harsh in judging their subordinates and are often highly punitive (Rice, 1978a, b). When the task is going well, however, the task-motivated leader is comfortable with details and with monitoring routine events (Fiedler and Chemers, 1984; Table 3-1). People who have high LPC scores rate their least-preferred coworker relatively positively (describing that person as loyal, sincere, warm, and accepting); they are relationship motivated and draw their self-esteem from having good relationships with others. For them, the least-preferred coworker is often someone who has been disloyal and unsupportive rather than incompetent (Rice, 1978a, b). Relationship-motivated persons are easily bored with details (Fiedler, 1978; Fiedler and Chemers, 1984) and focus on social interactions (Rice, 1978a, b; see Table 3-1). The task-motivated person's focus on tasks and the relationship-motivated person's concern for relationships are most obvious in times of crisis when the person is under pressure.

A comparison between Hillary Clinton and Barack Obama illustrates the differences between task- and relationship-oriented leaders. During the 2004 presidential campaign, H. Clinton very clearly stated that she considers the role of the president is not only to provide

TABLE 3-1	Differences between Task-Motivated and Relationship-Motivated Individuals
Task Motivated (Low LPC)	**Relationship Motivated (High LPC)**
• Draws self-esteem from completion of task	• Draws self-esteem from interpersonal relationships
• Focuses on the task first	• Focuses on people first
• Can be harsh with failing employees	• Likes to please others
• Considers competence of coworkers to be key trait	• Considers loyalty of coworkers to be key trait
• Enjoys details	• Gets bored with details

vision but also to control and direct the federal bureaucracy (O'Toole, 2008). Obama, on the other hand, announced that he believes the president's role is to provide vision and inspiration while delegating the responsibility of managing agencies (O'Toole, 2008). Although President Obama's leadership style also fits that charismatic leaders discussed in Chapter 6, his broader focus and less attention to detail indicate a relationship-oriented style. Other leaders demonstrate both styles. Brady W. Dougan—53-year-old CEO of Credit Suisse Group, a major global bank, and its youngest CEO to date—is detailed oriented and task motivated (Anderson, 2007). He gets to work around 5 AM. and is known to work out twice a day while he trains for marathons. He spent two months practicing to dance with a Broadway star to prepare for a charity event (Anderson, 2007). Marissa Peterson, former executive vice president of worldwide operations of Sun Microsystems, is also task motivated. Her strength is in clearly outlining what role every one of her 2,000-strong staff plays. Her focus is on "developing the strategy for achieving my operation's goals and then laying out that vision for my team" (Overholt, 2002: 125). Peterson sticks to a strict routine in managing her daily and weekly activities. Contrast these task-motivated leaders with Mort Meyerson, chairman and CEO of 2M Companies of Perot Systems, a computer firm based in Dallas, Texas, and Darlene Ryan, founder and CEO of PharmaFab, a pharmaceuticals manufacturer, also located in Texas. Meyerson believes, "To win in today's brave new world of business, you must be more in-tune with your people and customers.... You must re-examine if you are creating an environment for your people to succeed and what that means. You must ask yourself: Am I really accessible? Am I really listening?" (Meyerson, 2010). Darlene Ryan takes a similar approach. She runs her company like a family; she encourages dissent, delegates, and is a consensus builder. She is a great listener and is able to take her time when facing tough decisions (Black, 2004).

Individuals who fall in the middle of the scale have been labeled socio-independent. They tend to be less concerned with other people's opinions and may not actively seek leadership roles. Depending on how close their score is to the high or the low end of the scale, they might belong to either the task-motivated or relationship-motivated group (Fiedler and Chemers, 1984). Some research suggests that middle LPCs may be more effective than either high or low LPCs across all situations (Kennedy, 1982). A potential middle LPC is Colin Powell. Even though he has been in many leadership positions, he has shied away from the presidency, and he has proven himself an outstanding follower to several presidents.

Despite some problems with the validity of the LPC scale, it has received strong support from researchers and practitioners and has even translated well to other cultures for use in leadership research and training (Ayman and Chemers, 1983, 1991). *A key premise of the LPC concept is that because it is an indicator of primary motivation, leadership style is stable. Leaders, then, cannot simply change their style to match the situation.*

SITUATIONAL CONTROL   Because effectiveness depends on a match between the person and the situation, Fiedler uses three factors to describe a leadership situation. In order of importance, they are (1) the relationship between the leader and the followers, (2) the amount of structure of the task, and (3) the position power of the leader. The three elements combine to define the amount of control the leader has over the situation (see Self-Assessment 3-2).

According to Fiedler, *the most important element of any leadership situation is the quality of the relationship and the cohesion between the leader and the followers and among the followers* (Fiedler, 1978). Good leader–member relations (LMR) mean that the group is cohesive and supportive, providing leaders with a high degree of control to implement what they want. When the group is divided or has little respect or support for the leader, the leader's control is low.

Task structure (TS) is the second element of a leadership situation. It refers to the degree of clarity of a task. A highly structured task has clear goals and procedures, few paths to the correct solution, and one or few correct solutions and can be evaluated easily (Fiedler and Chemers, 1974). The degree of task structure affects the leader's control. Whereas the leader has considerable control when doing a structured task, an unstructured task provides little sense of control. One factor that moderates task structure is the leader's experience level (Fiedler and Chemers, 1984). On the one hand, if leaders have experience with a task, they will perceive the task as more structured. On the other hand, not having experience will make any task appear to be unstructured. The third and least influential element of the leadership situation is the leader's position power (PP), which refers to the leader's formal power and influence over subordinates to hire, fire, reward, or punish. The leader with a high amount of formal power feels more in control than one who has little power.

The combination of LMR, TS, and PP yields the amount of situational control (Sit Con) the leader has over the situation. At one end of the continuum, good leader–member relations, a highly structured task, and high position power provide the leader with high control over the situation where the leader's influence is well accepted. In the middle of the continuum are situations in which either the leader or the followers do not get along or the task is unstructured. In such situations, the leader does not have full control over the situation, and the leadership environment is more difficult. At the other end of the situational control continuum, the leader–member relations are poor, the task is unstructured, and the leader has little power. Such a situation is chaotic and unlikely to continue for a long period of time in an organization. Clearly, this crisis environment does not provide the leader with a sense of control or any ease of leadership (see Self-Assessment 3-2 for Sit Con).

PREDICTIONS OF THE CONTINGENCY MODEL   At the core of the Contingency Model is the concept of match. If the leader's style matches the situation, the group will be effective. Because Fiedler suggests that the leader's style is constant, a leader's effectiveness changes as the situation changes. *The Contingency Model predicts that low-LPC, task-motivated leaders will be effective in high- and low-situational control, whereas high-LPC, relationship-motivated leaders will be effective in moderate-situational control.* Figure 3-1 presents the predictions of the model.

In high-control situations (left side of the graph in Figure 3-1), task-motivated, low-LPC leaders feel at ease. The leader's basic source of self-esteem—getting the task done—is not threatened, so the leader can relax, take care of details, and help the followers perform. The same high-control situation leads to a different effect on relationship-motivated, high-LPC leaders. They are likely to be bored and feel either that there is nothing to do or that nobody needs them. Because the group is cohesive and the task is clear, the leader is needed mainly to get the group the resources it needs, take care of details, and remove obstacles—all activities that are not appealing to high LPCs, who might, therefore, start being overly controlling and interfere with the group's performance to demonstrate that they are needed (Chemers, 1997; Fiedler and Garcia, 1987a). See Table 3-2 for a summary of the leaders' behaviors in each situation.

Moderate-situational control (the middle of graph in Figure 3-1) stems from lack of cohesiveness or lack of task structure. In either case, the situation is ambiguous or uncertain, and task completion is in jeopardy. The relationship-motivated, high-LPC leader's skills at interpersonal relationships and participation are well suited for the situation. This type of leader seeks out followers' participation and focuses on resolving task and relationship conflicts. The high-LPC leader uses the group as a resource to accomplish the task. The same elements that make

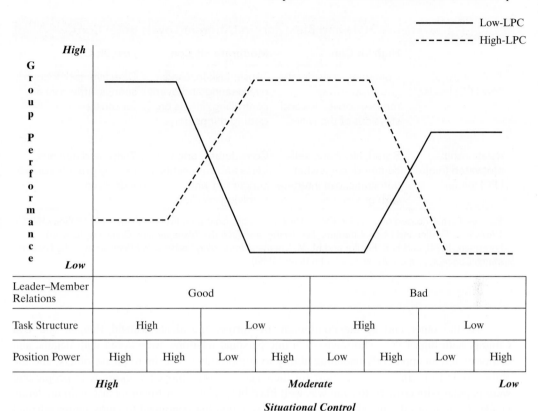

FIGURE 3-1 Fiedler's Contingency Model

moderate control attractive to relationship-motivated leaders make the situation threatening to the task-oriented, low-LPC leader. The lack of group support, the ambiguity of the task, or both make the low LPCs feel that the task might not be completed. The task-oriented leader becomes autocratic, ignores the task and relationship conflicts, and tries to simply complete the task to get a sense of accomplishment (Fiedler, 1993). The inappropriate use of resources is likely to worsen the group's lack of cohesion and prevent the exploration of creative solutions to an unstructured task. As a result, the task-motivated leader's group performs poorly in moderate control.

Consider the example of several U.S. presidents. Former presidents Richard Nixon and Jimmy Carter were task-motivated leaders. Both were highly intelligent, focused on the task, and able to analyze large amounts of detail. Both needed to stay in control, held uncompromising views and approaches to issues, and could be harsh toward failing subordinates. They performed well in high control. Nixon experienced considerable success in foreign policy, where he was respected, the task was clear, and he held power tightly. As his legitimate power and popularity decreased—leading to moderate control—he became controlling, punitive, and ineffective. Carter's effectiveness followed a similar pattern, although he never faced a high-control situation, a factor that might explain his overall poor effectiveness ratings as president. Almost immediately after being elected, he found himself in moderate control with poor relations with the U.S. Congress and an unstructured task exacerbated by his limited experience in foreign policy. His single-minded focus on human rights and his inability to compromise made him ineffective.

TABLE 3-2	Leader Style and Behaviors in Different Levels of Sit Con

	High Sit Con	Moderate Sit Con	Low Sit Con
Task-motivated (low-LPC) leader	Confident; considerate and supportive; removes obstacles and stays out of the way	Tense; task focused; overbearing and overly controlling; insists on getting things done	Directive; task focused; serious; little concern for others
Relationship-motivated (high-LPC) leader	Bored; aloof and self-centered; somewhat autocratic; can interfere with group	Considerate; open to ideas and suggestions; concerned with resolving conflicts	Tense and nervous; hurt by group's conflict; indecisive

Sources: Partially based on F. E. Fiedler. *A Theory of Leadership Effectiveness* (New York: McGraw-Hill, 1967); F. E. Fiedler and M. M. Chemers. *Leadership and Effective Management* (Glenview, IL: Scott-Foresman, 1974); and F. E. Fiedler and M. M. Chemers. *Improving Leadership Effectiveness: The Leader Match Concept,* 2nd ed. (New York: John Wiley, 1984).

At the other end of the continuum are former presidents Ronald Reagan and Bill Clinton, both high LPCs who focused on interpersonal relations, were bored with details, and demonstrated an apparently unending ability to compromise, a desire to please others, and the ability to perform and put on a show for their public. Both enjoyed working with people and were popular with crowds. Reagan was well liked but faced an unstructured task with moderate power. Clinton faced a novel and unstructured situation but continued to enjoy unprecedented support of the electorate. Both these relationship-motivated presidents were in moderate control where, by many accounts, they performed well.

As a situation becomes chaotic and reaches a crisis point with no group cohesion, no task structure, and no strong position power (the right side of the graph in Figure 3-1), the task-motivated, low-LPC leaders' need to complete the task pushes them to take over and make autocratic decisions without much concern for followers. As a result, although performance is not high and followers might not be satisfied, groups with a low-LPC leader get some work done. For the relationship-motivated, high-LPC leader, the low Sit Con environment is a nightmare. The group's lack of cohesion is further fueled by its inability to perform the task and makes efforts at reconciliation close to impossible. The high-LPC leader's efforts to gain support from the group, therefore, fall on deaf ears. In an attempt to protect their self-esteem, high-LPC leaders withdraw, leaving their group to fend for itself and causing low performance. The data for the socio-independent leaders are less clear. Fiedler (1978) suggests that they generally perform better in high-control situations, although more research is needed to predict and explain their performance.

EVALUATION AND APPLICATION   Although a large number of studies have supported the Contingency Model over the past 40 years, several researchers have voiced strong criticisms regarding the meaning and validity of the LPC scale (Schriesheim and Kerr, 1974), the predictive value of the model (Schriesheim, Tepper, and Tetrault, 1994; Vecchio, 1983), and the lack of research about the middle-LPC leaders (Kennedy, 1982). Forty years of research have addressed the majority, although not all, of the concerns. As a result, the Contingency Model continues to emerge as one of the most reliable and predictive models of leadership, with a number of research

APPLYING WHAT YOU LEARN
Putting the Contingency Model to Work

Fiedler's Contingency Model suggests that instead of focusing on changing their style, leaders should learn to understand and manage the situations in which they lead. Chances are however that most of the leadership training programs you may attend will focus on changing the leaders' style to adapt to different situations. Here's how you can take advantage of those training programs while following the Contingency Model's recommendations:

• Remember that learning will take place when you challenge yourself to undertake and master behaviors that do not come easily and therefore may be outside your comfort zone or primary motivation area.

• Regardless of your style, you can always learn new behaviors and expand your current range.

• All training, by design or default, will expose you to many new leadership situations. Take the opportunity to practice analyzing them to ascertain situational control.

• Do not expect miracles or even quick changes. Increasing your effectiveness as a leader is a long journey.

studies and meta-analyses supporting the hypotheses of the model (see Ayman, Chemers, and Fiedler, 1995; Chemers, 1997; Peters, Hartke, and Pohlmann, 1985; Strube and Garcia, 1981).

Importantly, a person's LPC is not the only or the strongest determinant of a leader's actions and beliefs. Although the focus has been on the description of stereotypical task-motivated and relationship-motivated leaders, a person's behavior is determined by many other internal and external factors. It would, therefore, be inappropriate to carry the task or relationship orientation considerably beyond its use in the Contingency Model. It is a reliable predictor of leadership effectiveness within the model, but not necessarily beyond it.

The Contingency Model has several practical implications for managers:

• Leaders must understand their style and the situation to predict how effective they will be.
• Leaders should focus on changing the situation to match their style instead of trying to change how they act.
• A good relationship with followers is important to a leader's ability to lead, and it can compensate for lack of power.
• Leaders can compensate for ambiguity of a task by getting training and experience.

Fiedler's focus on changing the situation rather than the leader is unique among leadership theories. Interestingly, Marcus Buckingham, a well-known leadership consultant, has suggested that leaders should focus on developing their strengths rather than trying to compensate for their weaknesses (Buckingham, 2005), advice that is consistent with Fiedler's approach. Other leaders also recognize the importance of the context. Drew Gilpin Faust, president of Harvard University, says, "I think the most important leadership lessons I've learned have to do with understanding the context in which you are leading" (Bryant, 2009m). As opposed to Fiedler, the Normative Decision Model considered next, along with many other leadership models, assumes that the leader can change styles depending on the situation.

The Normative Decision Model

Should a leader make decisions alone or involve followers? What factors can help a leader determine how to make decisions? Consider the case of Junki Yoshida, the Japanese-born, 58-year-old martial artist and founder and owner of Yoshida Group enterprises. In 2005, he was voted one of the 100 most respected Japanese in the world by the Japanese edition of *Newsweek* magazine. His company includes Mr. Yoshida Original Gourmet sauces and marinades and comprises 18 highly diverse companies that include Jones Golf bags, OIA Global Logistics, and a graphic design company (Yoshida Group, 2007). When he starts a new venture, Yoshida plays an active role in every aspect and stays close to every decision. Once the business takes off, however, he delegates to carefully selected specialists and lets them make many of the decisions. The way he makes decisions about his businesses changes as each business matures (Brant, 2004). The Normative Decision Model (NDM; also referred to as the Vroom–Yetton model), developed by researchers Victor Vroom, Philip Yetton, and Arthur Jago, addresses such situations and prescribes when the leader needs to involve followers in decision making (Vroom and Jago, 1988; Vroom and Yetton, 1973). It is called *normative* because it recommends that leaders adopt certain styles based on the prescriptions of the model. Like Fiedler, Vroom and his associates recommend matching the leader and the situational requirements. They, however, differ on several points. The Normative Decision Model is limited to decision making rather than general leadership, and it assumes that leaders can adopt different decision-making styles as needed.

The model relies on two well-established group dynamic principles: First are the research findings that groups are wasteful and inefficient, and second, that participation in decision making leads to commitment. *The NDM recommends that leaders adjust their decision style depending on the degree to which the quality of the decision is important and the likelihood that employees will accept the decision.*

LEADER'S DECISION STYLES   The NDM identifies four decision methods available to leaders (Vroom and Jago, 1988). The first method is autocratic (A), in which the leader makes a decision with little or no involvement from followers. The second decision method is consultation (C), which means that the leader consults with followers yet retains the final decision-making authority. The third decision method is group (G). Here, the leader relies on consensus building to solve a problem. The final method involves total delegation (D) of decision making to one employee. The decision styles and their subcategories are summarized in Table 3-3.

A leader must decide which style to use depending on the situation that the leader and the group face and on whether the problem involves a group or one individual. Individual problems affect only one person, whereas group problems can affect a group or individual. For example, deciding on raises for individual employees is an individual problem, whereas scheduling vacations is a group problem. Similarly, deciding on which employees should receive training or undertake overseas assignment is an individual problem, whereas moving a business to another state or cutting down a city service is a group problem. The distinction between the two is not always clear; individual problems can affect others, and group problems can have an impact on individuals.

CONTINGENCY FACTORS AND PREDICTIONS OF THE MODEL   The two central contingency factors for the Normative Decision Model are the *quality of the decision and the need for acceptance and commitment by followers.* Other contingency factors to consider are whether the leader has enough relevant information to make a sound decision, whether the problem is structured and clear, the likelihood that followers will accept the leader's decision, whether the employees agree with the organizational goals, whether employees are cohesive, and whether they have enough information to make a decision alone. Table 3-4 presents the eight contingency factors.

The NDM relies on a decision tree, as shown in Figure 3-2. Leaders ask a series of questions listed in Table 3-4; the questions relate to the contingency factors and should be asked sequentially. By responding "yes" or "no" to each question, managers can determine which decision style(s) is

TABLE 3-3	Decision Styles in the Normative Decision Model						
Decision Style	**AI**	**AII**	**CI**	**CII**	**GI**	**GII**	**DI**
Description	Unassisted decision	Ask for specific information but make decisions alone	Ask for specific information and ideas from each group member	Ask for information and ideas from whole group	Ask for one person's help; mutual exchange based on expertise	Group shares information and ideas and reaches consensus	Other person analyzes problem and makes decision
Who makes the decision	Leader	Leader	Leader	Leader with considerable group input	Leader and one other person	Group with leader input	Other person
Type of Problem	Group and individual	Group and individual	Group and individual	Group	Individual	Group	Individual

Note: Key: A = Autocratic, C = Consultative, G = Group

Sources: V. H. Vroom and A. G. Jago. *The New Leadership: Managing Participation in Organizations* (Upper Saddle River, NJ: Prentice Hall, 1988); and V. H. Vroom and P. W. Yetton. *Leadership and Decision Making* (Pittsburgh: University of Pittsburgh Press, 1973).

TABLE 3-4	Contingency Factors in the Normative Decision Model
Contingency Factor	**Question to Ask**
Quality requirement (QR)	How important is the quality of the decision?
Commitment requirement (CR)	How important is employee commitment to the implementation of the decision?
Leader information (LI)	Does the leader have enough information to make a high-quality decision?
Structure of the problem (ST)	Is the problem clear and well structured?
Commitment probability (CP)	How likely is employee commitment to the solution if the leader makes the decision alone?
Goal congruence (GC)	Do employees agree with and support organizational goals?
Employee conflict (CO)	Is there conflict among employees over a solution?
Subordinate information (SI)	Do employees have enough information to make a high-quality decision?

Sources: V. H. Vroom and A. G. Jago, *The New Leadership: Managing Participation in Organizations* (Upper Saddle River, NJ: Prentice Hall, 1988); and V. H. Vroom and P. W. Yetton, *Leadership and Decision Making* (Pittsburgh: University of Pittsburgh Press, 1973).

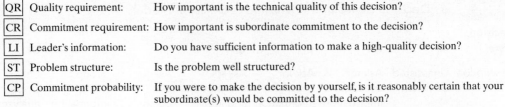

QR	Quality requirement:	How important is the technical quality of this decision?
CR	Commitment requirement:	How important is subordinate commitment to the decision?
LI	Leader's information:	Do you have sufficient information to make a high-quality decision?
ST	Problem structure:	Is the problem well structured?
CP	Commitment probability:	If you were to make the decision by yourself, is it reasonably certain that your subordinate(s) would be committed to the decision?
GC	Goal congruence:	Do subordinates share the organizational goals to be attained in solving this problem?
CO	Subordinate conflict:	Is conflict among subordinates over preferred solutions likely?
SI	Subordinate information:	Do subordinates have sufficient information to make a high-quality decision?

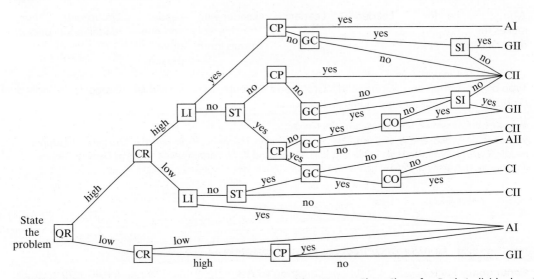

FIGURE 3-2 Normative Decision Model   *Source:* "Decision-Process Flow Chart for Both Individual and Group Problems" from *Leadership and Decision-Making* by Victor and Philip W. Yetton © 1973. All rights are controlled by the University of Pittsburgh Press. Pittsburgh, PA 15260. Used by permission of the University of Pittsburgh Press.

most appropriate for the problem they face. Figure 3-2 presents the most widely used Normative Decision Model and is labeled "time efficient," based on the assumption that consultation and participation require time and are not efficient (Vroom and Jago, 1988). Thus, whenever appropriate, the model leans toward more autocratic decision making. A second version of the model, labeled "time investment," focuses on the development of followers at the expense of efficiency. This version recommends more participative decision making whenever possible.

An autocratic decision-making style is appropriate in the following situations:

• When the leader has sufficient information to make a decision
• When the quality of the decision is not essential
• When employees do not agree with each other
• When employees do not agree with the goals of the organization

A consultative style of decision making is appropriate in the following situations:

- The leader has sufficient information, but the employees demand participation to implement the decision.
- The leader has insufficient information, and employee consultation will help the leader gather more information as well as develop commitment.
- Followers generally agree with the goals of the organization.

A group-oriented decision style should be used when the leader does not have all the information, quality is important, and employee commitment is essential. Delegation is used to assign the decision to a single individual who has the needed information, competence, and organizational commitment to make and implement it.

EVALUATION AND APPLICATION   Several research studies support the NDM in a variety of settings (Crouch and Yetton, 1987; Tjosvold, Wedley, and Field, 1986), including evaluating historical decisions (Duncan, LaFrance, and Ginter, 2003). The model has also been applied in not-for-profit settings with some success (Lawrence, Deagen, and Debbie, 2001), and recent research on sharing information with followers further support the contingency approach presented by the model (Vidal and Möller, 2007). The decision methods are clearly defined, and the contingency factors included are based on extensive research about group dynamics and participative management.

Some practitioners and theorists argue that the model is too complex to provide practical value. Few managers have the time to work their way through the decision tree. Furthermore, the assumption that leaders have the ability to use any of the decision styles equally well might be flawed. Not all leaders can be autocratic for one decision, consultative for another, and group oriented for still others. In addition, because the model relies on a manager's self-report, it may be subject to some bias (Parker, 1999).

The NDM, compared with Fiedler's Contingency Model, takes a narrower focus on leadership decision making. Within that limited focus, the model works well and can be a helpful tool for leaders. The model suggests several practical implications:

- Leaders must understand the situation and understand how and when to use the different decision methods.
- Participation is not always desirable as a leadership style.
- Leaders must pay particular attention to their followers' needs and reactions when making a decision.

In addition to Fiedler's and Vroom and Yetton's theories that focus on how leaders use their resources, three other contingency models hinge on how leaders manage their relationships with followers.

Path–Goal Theory

The Path–Goal Theory of leadership, developed in the early 1970s, proposes that the leader's role is to clear the paths subordinates use to accomplish goals (House, 1971; House and Dessler, 1974). By doing so, leaders allow subordinates to fulfill their needs, and as a result, leaders reach their own goals as well. The concept of exchange between leaders and subordinates, whether it is an implicit or explicit contract, is at the core of this model. The leader and followers establish a relationship that revolves around the exchange of guidance or support for productivity and satisfaction.

THE FRAMEWORK   The major conceptual basis for the Path–Goal Theory is the expectancy model of motivation (Vroom, 1964). Expectancy theory describes how individuals make rational choices about their behavior, based on their perceptions of the degree to which their effort and performance can lead to outcomes they value. The key to motivation, then, is to remove the various obstacles that weaken the linkages between effort and performance and between performance and outcomes. *The nature of the task and follower characteristics determine which leadership behavior contributes to subordinate satisfaction.* If the task is new and unclear, the followers are likely to waste their efforts due to a lack of knowledge and experience. They might feel frustrated and unmotivated, so the leader must provide instructions and training, thereby removing obstacles to followers' performance and allowing them to do their job. If a task is routine and subordinates performed it successfully a number of times, however, they might face an element of boredom, which would require the leader must show consideration, empathy, and understanding toward subordinates.

Behaviors the leader uses to motivate employees further depend on the employees themselves (Griffin, 1979; Stinson and Johnson, 1975). Some employees need guidance and clear instructions; others expect to be challenged and seek autonomy to do their own problem solving. The followers' need for autonomy and other personal characteristics, such as locus of control, are factors that the leader needs to consider before selecting an appropriate behavior. For example, a follower who likes challenges and needs autonomy will not need or want the leader to be directive even during an unstructured task. For that employee, leader directiveness can be irrelevant or even detrimental because it might reduce satisfaction.

EVALUATION AND APPLICATION   Despite several supportive research studies (e.g., House and Mitchell, 1974), the empirical support for the Path–Goal Theory remains mixed (Downey, Sheridan, and Slocum, 1975; Szilagyi and Sims, 1974). The model is generally underresearched, although researchers have proposed several new potential applications (Elkins and Keller, 2003). Notwithstanding contradictory findings, the *Path–Goal Theory contributes to our understanding of leadership by once more focusing attention on the behavior of providing guidance and support to followers.* It adds to other models, such as Fiedler's Contingency Model, by including followers' perceptions of the task and the role of the leader in removing blocks to task accomplishment. The Path–Goal Theory's use of employee satisfaction as a criterion for leadership effectiveness broadens our view of leadership. The model's suggestion that not all behaviors will be effective with all subordinates points to the importance of an employee's need for challenge and desire to be autonomous as a determinant of a leader's behavior. Interestingly, the role of the leader in the Path–Goal Theory is that of obstacle remover, which is similar to the role ascribed to team leaders (see Chapter 8) .

The next theory reviews a leadership model that focuses on how leaders interpret their followers' actions and use that information as the basis for their relationship with them.

Substitutes for Leadership

In some situations, a relationship between a leader and the followers is not needed to satisfy the followers' needs. Various aspects of the work environment provide enough resources and support to allow subordinates to achieve their goals without having to refer to their leader. For example, an experienced team of pharmaceutical salespeople, who spend a considerable amount of their time on the road and who have control over their commissions, are not likely to rely much on their manager. Their job provides them with challenges, and their experience allows them to make many decisions on their own. The office is not accessible, and they often rely on other salespeople for help and information. Similarly, skilled emergency room nurses and technicians

LEADING CHANGE
Jim Goodnight of SAS

Leading an organization that is consistently ranked as one of the best places to work in the world is not an easy feat (Crowley, 2013). However it's something that Jim Goodnight, CEO of SAS, has been able to do for over three decades. The company's culture of benevolence and respect yields high performance and employee loyalty. "Creativity is especially important to SAS because software is a product of the mind. As such, 95 percent of my assets drive out the gate every evening. It's my job to maintain a work environment that keeps those people coming back every morning. The creativity they bring to SAS is a competitive advantage for us" (Goodnight, 2010). That statement is one indicator of what Goodnight considers to be important in the success of his company. He states: "Employees don't leave companies, they leave managers" (Lauchlan, 2007). Goodnight cofounded SAS, the world's largest privately-held software company and, with John Sall, continues to fully own the company so that the two can think long term and do what it takes to take care of their employees and their customers. With a 98 percent customer renewal rate, global sales of $2.72 billion in 2012, and a turnover of around 4 percent compared to 20 percent in the industry (Goodnight, 2010), SAS is doing something right.

Goodnight is the public face of the company and deserves much credit for that success. SAS has kept its workforce happy by giving its employees challenging work, letting them enjoy a 35-hour workweek, free on-site day care, health care, an extensive fitness center, car detailing, and discounts to country club memberships; and free M&Ms one day a week (Goodnight-Employee benefits, 2012). Although the candy costs the company $45,000 a year, Goodnight believes it is a small price to show appreciation for his employees and is an indicator of the organization's friendly culture (Bisoux, 2004).

Goodnight believes that when the company removes day-to-day challenges, people can focus on their jobs. He tells his managers, "If you treat people like they make a difference, then they will make a difference" (Lauchlan, 2007). For him, it is about giving people a chance to prove themselves. Valuing employees is as important to him as keeping his customers happy. Goodnight states, "I simply wanted to create a company where I would want to work. Over the years, I've learned how employee loyalty leads to customer loyalty, increased innovation, and higher-quality software" (Faiola, 2006). He considers his employees and his customers the building blocks of the success of his organization (Goodnight, 2005). During his speech after being named as the year's top executive in 2005, Goodnight echoed this theme: "I simply facilitate a creative environment where people can create great software and foster long-term relationships with our customers" (Stevie, 2004). His formula for success is simple: "Keep your customers happy. Value your employees... while you may not grow your profits every quarter, you will grow your business over time" (Bisoux, 2004: 20).

Sources: Bisoux, T. 2004. "Corporate counterculture," *BizEd*, November–December: 16–20; Crowley, M.C. 2013. "How SAS became the world's best place to work," *Fast Company,* January 22. http://www.fastcompany.com/3004953/how-sas-became-worlds-best-place-work (accessed June 1, 2013); Faiola, A.M. 2006. Ask Jim Goodnight. Inc Magazine, June 1. Accessed at http://www.inc.com/magazine/20060601/handson-ask-the-bigwig.html on November 27, 2013. Goodnight-employee benefits. 2012. http://www.youtube.com/watch?v=T5O3L6UdIGw (accessed June 1, 2013); Goodnight, J. 2005. "Software 2005: Building blocks for success," http://www.sandhill.com/conferences/sw2005_proceedings/goodnight.pdf (accessed July 8, 2007); Goodnight, J. 2010. *SAS web site.* http://www.sas.com/presscenter/bios/jgoodnight.html (accessed January 20, 2010); Lauchlan, S. 2007. "Interview with Jim Goodnight," *MyCustomer.com,* May 22. http://www.mycustomer.com/cgi-bin/item.cgi?id=133019&d=101&h=817&f=816 (accessed July 8, 2007); and Stevie A. 2004. http://www.crm2day.com/news/crm/EpluuFlFFpWCyCGeTT.php (accessed July 8, 2007).

do not rely on a leader or manager to take care of their patients. In such circumstances, various situational factors replace the leader's functions of providing structure, guidelines, and support to subordinates.

Such situations led to the development of the Substitutes for Leadership Model (SLM; Kerr and Jermier, 1978). *SLM proposes that various organizational, task, and employee characteristics can provide substitutes for the traditional leadership behaviors of consideration and initiation of structure* (Table 3-5). In general, if information about the task and its requirements are clear and available to the subordinates through various means such as their own experience, their team, or through the organization, they are not likely to need the leader's structuring behaviors. Similarly, when support and empathy are not needed or are available through other sources such as coworkers, the subordinates will not seek the leader's consideration behaviors.

In addition to substituting for leadership, some situations can neutralize the effect of the leader. Most notably, the leader's lack of power to deliver outcomes to followers and an organization's rigid culture can prevent a leader's consideration and structuring behaviors from affecting subordinates. For example, a subordinate whose manager is in another state or is powerless to deliver on promises and reward or a subordinate who does not value the rewards provided by the manager is not likely to be affected by the leader's behaviors (see Table 3-5). The situation neutralizes the leader.

Consider how Ricardo Semler (featured in Leading Change in Chapter 5), president of the Brazilian firm Semco, author and proponent of open-book management, set up his company so that it runs with few managers so that they are free to do what they want and needs to be done (Semler Interview, 2013). Workers are trained carefully; provided with considerable information, including detailed financial data and salary information; and left to set their own hours,

TABLE 3-5 Leadership Substitutes and Neutralizers		
Substitutes or Neutralizers	**Consideration**	**Structuring**
Follower Characteristics		
1. Experience and training		Substitute
2. Professionalism	Substitute	Substitute
3. Lack of value for goals	Neutralizer	Neutralizer
Task Characteristics		
1. Unambiguous tasks		Substitute
2. Direct feedback from task		Substitute
3. Challenging task	Substitute	Substitute
Organizational Characteristics		
1. Cohesive team		Substitute
2. Leader's lack of power	Substitute	Neutralizer
3. Standardization and formalization	Neutralizer	Substitute
4. Organizational rigidity		Neutralizer
5. Physical distance between leaders and followers	Neutralizer	Neutralizer

Source: S. Kerr and J. M. Jermier. "Substitutes for leadership: Their meaning and measurement," *Organizational Behavior and Human Performance* 22 (1978): 375–403.

evaluate and vote for their managers, and make most of the decisions. The workers' training and experience allows the company to function with few senior managers. The structure, training, and teamwork at Semco act as substitutes for leadership.

WHAT DO YOU DO?

You have been promoted to a new managerial position and your team members are missing in action most of time. Their performance is by and large excellent, but getting them together is proving challenging. They are away on various jobs, and although friendly, don't seem to need you much. You feel like you should establish your authority. What do you do?

EVALUATION AND APPLICATION   The SLM has not been tested extensively and needs considerable clarification regarding the nature of the various substitutes and neutralizers and the situations to which they might apply. Because of inconsistent results, some researchers suggest that it suffers from methodological problems (Villa et al., 2003), and the few studies performed in non-U.S. cultural settings failed to yield support for the model (Farh, Podsakoff, and Cheng, 1987). Like the next model we will discuss, the Leader–Member exchange, however, the SLM is intuitively appealing and addresses processes not taken into account by other leadership models. In particular, it questions the need for leadership in certain situations and points to the difficulty of being an effective leader when many neutralizers are present. Furthermore, the model provides considerable potential for application. Depending on the culture, strategy, and goals of an organization and on a specific leader's personality, the leader might want to set up or remove leadership substitutes. For some control-oriented leaders or in organizations with traditional structures and hierarchies in place, the presence of substitutes could be perceived as a loss of control and authority.

Given the flattening of many organizations and the push toward empowerment and use of teams, judicious use of substitutes can free up the leader for other activities, such as strategic planning, and still allow the organization to achieve its objectives. The use of information technology tools that make information widely available and support work structures, such as telecommuting and outsourcing, further reduces the need for leadership in some situations (Howell, 1997). Consider the case of one of the oldest and one of the largest breweries in the United States (van der Pool, 2012). Despite its 175-year-old history, D.G. Yuengling & Son uses a modern, relatively flat structure that focuses on not becoming bureaucratic. Respect for the individual and a positive work environment are part of its core values (Yuengling, 2007). The company offers relatively high-paying jobs in an area where jobs are scarce and has developed a loyal following (Rubinkan, 2007). Like many other family operations, however, employees and managers found themselves relying too much on the owner, Dick Yuengling. Yuengling recognizes the need to set up substitutes for his hands-on leadership: "You've got to get people in the proper place" (Kurtz, 2004: 71). The company's chief operating officer, David Cainelli, along with Jennifer Yuengling, set up the structures that would allow for decision making to be decentralized and delegated to people closest to the products and markets (Kurtz, 2004).

Autonomous and self-managed teams provide an application of the SLM. The goal of such teams is to function without supervision. The team becomes a substitute for leadership. Extensive technical and team-building training, selection of team members with a professional orientation, intrinsically satisfying tasks for which team members are given considerable autonomy, and direct feedback can be used as substitutes for leadership structuring behaviors. Similarly, a cohesive team replaces the leader's supportive behaviors. The factors identified as substitutes can be used as a guide in setting up such autonomous work teams. One final implication of the SLM is leadership training. Based on this model, *leadership training might need to focus on teaching the leader to change the situation as much as it focuses on teaching effective leadership behaviors. Leaders can be taught how to set up substitutes and avoid neutralizers.* Such a recommendation is similar to those based on Fiedler's Contingency Model discussed earlier in this chapter.

The next model we consider focuses on the dyadic relationship between leaders and followers. Among the early leadership theories of leadership, it is the only one that continues to draw considerable interest and research.

Leader–Member Exchange

Many of us experience leadership, either as leaders or followers, as a personal relationship between a leader and a subordinate, rather than a group phenomenon. We interact daily with our managers and forge an individual relationship with them. As leaders, we do not experience the same relationship with all of our followers. Each dyadic relationship is different. A leader establishes a one-on-one relationship with each follower (Figure 3-3), and each relationship varies greatly in terms of the quality of the exchange. Some followers are part of in-group; some are in the out-group. These concepts are at the core of the Leader–Member Exchange (LMX) model, which was called the Vertical Dyad Linkage Model in its earlier versions (Dansereau, Graen, and Haga, 1975; Graen and Shiemann, 1978). *The LMX model focuses on the unique, relationship-based exchange between a leader and followers* (Graen and Uhl-Bien, 1995).

THE FRAMEWORK In each exchange, the leader and follower establish a role for the follower. The role can be based on long-term social exchange, or on a more market-based economic exchange (Kuvass et al., 2012; Walumbwa, Cropanzano, and Goldman, 2011). Those followers with a high-quality relationship are in the in-group. High-quality LMX involves mutual respect, anticipation of deepening trust, and expectations of continued and growing professional relationships and obligations. In-group followers enjoy their leader's attention, support, and confidence, and receive challenging and interesting assignments. The leader might overlook their errors

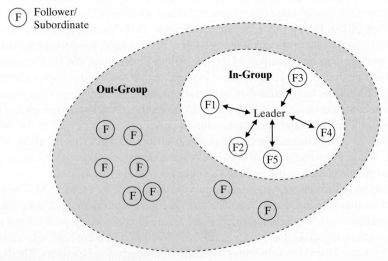

FIGURE 3-3 Leader–Member Exchange Model

(Duarte, Goodson, and Klich, 1994), attribute them to factors outside the followers' control, or recognize their contributions to a greater extent and reward them more (Burris et al., 2009). In exchange for the in-group status, the followers' role is to work hard, be loyal, and support the leader. They are likely to work beyond their formally prescribed job duties (Liden and Graen, 1980) and increase their commitment to their goals (Klein and Kim, 1998).

For the members of the in-group, such a high-quality exchange often becomes a self-fulfilling prophecy and leads to high performance, high satisfaction, and low stress. Studies extend the impact of a positive LMX to safety communication, commitment, and reduction of accidents (Hofmann and Morgeson, 1999), and creative work involvement especially when employees have some work autonomy (Volmer, Spurk, and Niessen, 2012). Other studies found that a positive LMX is related to higher frequency of communication, which in turn leads to more favorable job performance ratings (Kacmar et al., 2003), It also may lead to higher outputs in research and development teams (Elkins and Keller, 2003), encourage in-group members to participate more (Burris et al., 2009), and may impact complaints and organizational commitment (Cheng et al., 2012). Some research suggests that a high quality in-group LMX has the most positive impact when it is based on social rather than economic exchange (Kuvass et al., 2012). Conceptual extensions of the model suggest that the positive work relationship might even extend to social networks, whereby leaders sponsor members of their in-group into various social networks (Sparrowe and Liden, 1997). Research indicates that a positive exchange with a leader plays a role in the extent to which employees feel the organization supports them (Wayne, Shore, and Liden, 1997).

The followers in the out-group face a different situation. The leader might perceive them as less motivated or less competent, interact with them less, provide them with few opportunities to perform, and promote them less often (Wakabayashi et al., 1988). Their role tends to be limited to that defined by formal job descriptions, with little or no expectation of high performance, commitment, or loyalty. They often have to find ways of compensating for the low-quality relationship they have with their leader (Kacmar, Zivnuska, and White, 2007). Regardless of whether the leader's perception and expectations are accurate and fair, members of the out-group are likely to live up, or down, to them. As a result, out-group members who have a low-quality LMX will perform poorly and experience more stress. They also file for grievances more often (Cleyman, Jex, and Love, 1993), are more likely to take retaliatory actions against the organization (Townsend, Phillips, and Elkins, 2000), and may perceive more discrimination (Schaffer and Riordan, 2013).

The relationship between the leader and each follower forms early. The LMX model suggests that development of the leader–follower relationship takes place in stages summarized in Table 3-6. Additionally, leaders create positive relationships with three types of followers: those who are competent and show relevant skills, those whom they can trust, and those who are willing to assume more responsibility. Some research further suggests that followers can create a positive LMX by seeking feedback about their performance as long as the supervisor attributes the behavior to work rather than a desire to make a positive impression (Lam, Huang, and Snape, 2007). Culture can also play a key role in how in-group membership is assigned and which of these three factors is given more weight. In achievement-oriented cultures, such as the United States and Germany, individuals are evaluated based on their performance and achievement, rather than on their past or their membership in certain castes. Therefore, it is expected that leaders select their in-group members based on competence, performance, and commitment to the organization, rather than based on a personal relationship. Anything else would be called favoritism and nepotism. As a result, formal human resource policies and procedures, as well as

TABLE 3-6	Stages of Relationship Development between Leaders and Their Followers
Stage	**Description**
Testing and assessment	No relationship is yet formed. Leaders consider followers who do not yet belong to a group in terms of objective and subjective criteria for inclusion in either in-group or out-group. Followers' potential, ability, skills, and other psychological factors, such as loyalty, may be tested. Group assignments are made. The relationship with out-group followers does not progress beyond this stage.
Development of trust	This stage only exists for in-group members. Leader provides in-group followers with challenges and opportunities to perform that reinforce development of trust. In return, followers perform and demonstrate their loyalty to the leader.
Creation of emotional bond	In-group followers with a well-established relationship may move to this stage where the relationship and the bond between them become strong and emotional. Followers are highly committed to leader's vision.

Source: Partially based on information in Graen and Uhl-Bien, "The transformation of work group professionals into self-managing and partially self-designing contributors: Toward a theory of leadership-making," *Journal of Management Systems* 3(3) (1991): 33–48.

day-to-day personnel practices, in such cultures focus on fairness, equal opportunity, and hiring those who are most qualified for the jobs based on their personal competence.

In cultures such as many in the Middle East or France, where people are judged and evaluated more based on their group membership, rather than their individual achievement and performance, higher-quality exchange may depend more on the leader's ability to trust followers, which is likely to be based on issues such as social class and birth (Trompenaars and Hapden-tuner, 2012). The concepts of nepotism and inappropriate favoritism to one's in-group do not apply readily in ascriptive and collectivist cultures, where loyalty to one's village, clan, or family is the primary concern. In such cultures, managers hire those they know directly or who are recommended by others they know. Skills and competence are secondary to such personal recommendations. In Hong Kong, for example, leaders are obligated to take care of their own people first (Adler, 1991). Malaysians place a strong emphasis on loyalty and harmony in the work group (Kennedy, 2002). In many Middle Eastern countries, including Arab and non-Arab countries, such as Afghanistan and Iran, leaders surround themselves with family and clan members who can be trusted and who are loyal. Doing otherwise would be disloyal to one's community and even foolish. In such cultures, a wise leader does not allow strangers into the in-group, no matter how competent and qualified they are. Outsiders are hired to help, but access to the in-group is based on community factors. Recent studies further suggest that organizational culture may also affect the quality of the LMX, with better relationships in team-oriented cultures (Erdogan, Linden, and Kramer, 2006).

EVALUATION AND APPLICATION   Interest in LMX theory continues to be strong with many recent extensions and testing of its component and testing its application in various cultures.

Several areas require further clarification. Specifically, researchers question the adequacy of the theory, the multiple measures, and the methods used to test the concepts (for a detailed review, see Schriesheim, Castro, and Cogliser, 1999). In addition, despite continued research, the factors that lead to the development of an in-group versus an out-group relationship need more attention. Some research suggests that similarity in regard to personality (Nahrgang, Morgeson, and Ilies, 2009) or perceived identity (Jackson and Johnson, 2012) plays a key role early in the relationship, whereas performance matters more as time goes on (Bauer and Greene, 1996). More research needs to be conducted in other areas as well, including identifying factors that affect the development of the LMX, assessing the desirability of having the two groups, the conditions under which subordinates move from one group to the other, and exploring the cultural factors that are likely to affect the decision on who belongs to the in-group. The research on the impact of gender similarity on the development of LMX, for example, requires further clarification. The results of at least one study in Mexico, however, show gender similarity to be related to lower absenteeism, particularly with female leaders (Pelled and Xin, 1997) and higher trust (Pelled and Xin, 2000).

From a practitioner and application point of view, the LMX model is appealing. Anyone who has been part of an organization has experienced the feeling of being part of either the in-group or the out-group. Many have seen the departure of a well-liked manager, who is replaced with someone who has his own team. The quick movement from in-group to out-group is felt acutely. The concept of in-group and out-group also can be perceived as violating the norm of equality, which is highly valued in many Western cultures, including the United States. As leaders, most of us can identify our in-group (see Self-Assessment 3-3). Our in-group members are the people we trust. They are our right-hand assistants. We can give them any assignment with confidence. They will get the job done without us having to check up on them. We also know the members of our out-group. Toward some, we feel neutral; others we dislike and may try to get transferred. In both cases, those individuals do not get many chances to interact with us, and they are not provided with many opportunities to demonstrate their competence on visible and key projects.

The development of an individual exchange with others is a natural part of any interaction. Such a situation can be highly positive for an organization, allowing for the identification of competent individuals and ensuring that they achieve organizational goals. The creation of in-groups and out-groups, however, can also be highly detrimental, leading to feelings and accusations of unfair treatment (Scandura, 1999). Alan Canton, president of Adams-Blake Co., a software company in California, faced considerable obstacles in the development of a new software when three of the five-member team assigned to the task formed a friendship—a clique—and decided to exclude the other two members (Rich, 2005). Canton addressed the problem head-on to get rid of the unproductive in-group/out-group that formed. The key issue is the basis on which such relationships are formed. Researchers suggest that personal compatibility and employee ability are the basis for selection (Graen and Cashman, 1975). Unfortunately, organizational reality does not always match theory. Most of us can identify, or were part of, LMX relationships based on either positive or negative personal feelings, stereotypes, or interpersonal conflicts. Many highly competent and qualified employees are excluded from a leader's in-group based on personal dislike or organizational politics. After all, leaders are subject to human error just like the rest of us.

Abuse of power (discussed in Chapter 5) and membership of some top management teams (discussed in Chapter 7) are examples of the potential negative effects of in-groups. Being able to work with people, you trust and agree with and who share your vision for the organization sounds like an ideal situation for any leader, who would then not face unnecessary arguments and delays. Decisions would be made quickly and efficiently, and goals would be achieved. This ideal situation is exactly what many top-level executives attempt to set up when they select their top management team and the members of their board of directors. They pick people they trust and can work with. Executives rarely consciously and willingly pick members with whom they have major conflicts and differences. The goal is to create a workable team—a team made up of in-group members.

An example of the importance of being part of a team is the now-classic case of Michael Ovitz, who was hired to be Disney's president and was fired 14 months later, receiving a $140-million severance package for his short tenure. During the trial of a lawsuit filed by a Disney shareholder against CEO Michael Eisner for wasting company resources by hiring and then firing Michael Ovitz, Ovitz testified that from the first day, he was left out of decisions and undercut by the Disney management team, who did not report to him (Holson, 2004a). Eisner, for his part, testified that he had to spend too much time managing Ovitz (considered one of the most powerful and successful wheeler-dealers in Hollywood when he headed the Creative Artists Agency before coming to Disney): "Every day I was trying to manage Michael Ovitz. I did little else" (Holson, 2004b: C1). Eisner further accused Ovitz of "un-Disney-like" behavior and of not fitting in with the rest of management team. Eisner cited an example of Ovitz taking a limousine instead of a bus with other executives and states that Ovitz "was a little elitist for the egalitarian cast members" (Holson, 2004b: C12). Although the Ovitz–Eisner case is much more complex than an LMX relationship, the poor relationship and the fact that Ovitz either did not fit in or was not allowed to be part of the in-group clearly played a role in his firing from Disney, a factor that, in turn, was central to the shareholder lawsuit.

Research on friendship patterns and attraction to others indicates that people tend to associate with those who are like them, have similar backgrounds, and share their values and beliefs. To counteract this potential bias, Maggie Widerotter of Wink Communication makes a point of taking time to look for employees she does not see on a regular basis. She takes time to get out of her office and go on what she calls a "lion hunt" that gives her a chance to connect with employees.

Without a conscious effort to seek out new people, the in-group for most leaders includes people who are like them, with similar backgrounds and views. This homogeneity in top management teams and board membership caught the blame recently for many of the problems in U.S. businesses. Industrial giants such as General Motors, AT&T, and IBM suffered from the lack of initiative and creativity of their top management teams. The members worked well together and disregarded input from outsiders. As a result, they failed to foresee the problems and full consequences of their decisions or inaction. The same pursuit of homogeneity was also seen as a weakness in President George W. Bush's inner circle and administration and its decision making on highly complex issues such as the war in Iraq or the firing of U.S. attorneys. The ease, comfort, and efficiency of working with a cohesive in-group are usually because of the similarity of its members. These advantages, however, are sometimes offset by a lack of creativity and limited decision making. In an ideal case, no in-group or out-group should exist. All of a leader's subordinates should have equal access to the leader and to projects and resources. Those who do not perform well should be helped or moved out of the group altogether. Reality, however, is different, and avoiding the creation of in-groups and out-groups is difficult.

One of the key issues then becomes how members are selected to be in each group. For the individual relationship to be productive, leaders should follow some general principles in creating in-groups and out-groups and in selecting their membership. It is important to note that these guidelines apply mostly to achievement-oriented rather than ascriptive cultures:

- Pick in-group members based on competence and contribution to the organization.
- Periodically evaluate your criteria for in-group and out-group membership.
- Assign tasks to persons with the most applicable skills, regardless of group membership.
- Set clear, performance-related guidelines for in-group membership.
- Avoid highly differentiated in-groups and out-groups.
- Keep membership fluid to allow movement in and out of the groups.
- Maintain different in-groups for different activities.

The concept of exchange in the leadership interaction and the importance of the relationship between leaders and their followers continue to be of interest and are expanded and developed further in a more recent model of leadership, Transactional-Transformational Leadership, covered in more detail in Chapter 6.

THE LEADERSHIP QUESTION—REVISITED

Modern leadership theory has shown that being a leader is much more than a collection of traits. There may be some people who have a set of traits that can help in leadership, but leaders are not born. They are made from experience and from the interaction of individual and many contextual factors. While certain traits may make leadership difficult, there are no traits that guarantee that someone will be an effective leader. Most leaders succeed when they find themselves in the right situation that they can mold, or when they can adapt their style to the situation.

Summary and Conclusions

The scientific approach to understanding leadership that started at about the time of the industrial revolution added rigor and attempts at precise measurement to other already-existing views about leadership. The first modern approaches focused on the identification of traits that would distinguish leaders and followers. Although certain traits were found to be associated with leadership, no simple sets of traits consistently predicted who would be an effective leader. Because of inconclusive results, researchers turned their attention to leadership behaviors. The two major categories of initiation of structure and consideration were established as the central leadership behaviors. The switch from simple traits to simple behaviors still did not account for the complex leadership process and, therefore, did not allow researchers to make strong predictions about leadership effectiveness.

The early theories that are the foundation of modern leadership address either the way leaders use resources or the relationship between the leader and the follower. Fiedler's Contingency Model and the Normative Decision Model consider how the leader uses resources that are available and propose that the leader's style must be matched to the situation to achieve effectiveness. Whereas the Contingency Model assumes that the leader's style (LPC) is determined by internal traits and therefore difficult to change, the Normative Decision Model relies on decision-making styles that are assumed to be learnable. The two also differ on the criteria they use for leadership effectiveness. The Contingency Model looks at group performance; the Normative Decision Model focuses on decision quality. Perhaps their most interesting contribution to leadership application and training is that

TABLE 3-7	Comparison of the Early Contingency Models of Leadership				
	Leader Characteristic	Follower Characteristic	Task	Other Factors	Effectiveness Criteria
Fiedler's model	LPC based on motivation; not changeable	Group cohesion	Task structure	Position power	Group performance
Normative Decision Model	Decision-making style; can be changed	Group cohesion	Available information	Agreement with goals Time	Quality of the decision
Path–Goal theory	Leader behavior; can be changed	Individual follower need to grow	Clarity and routineness of task		Follower satisfaction and motivation
Substitutes	Leader behavior; can be changed	Group cohesion	Clarity of task; availability of information	Organization culture, structure, and processes	Need for leader
LMX					Quality of relationship with follower

both models involve a series of well-defined variables that can be used to improve leadership effectiveness.

The relationship-based theories focus on the relationship between the leader and the follower. The Path–Goal Theory proposes that the leader's main function is to remove obstacles in the subordinates' path to allow them to perform their jobs and to be motivated and satisfied. The Substitutes for Leadership Model (SLM) explores situations in which a relationship between the leader and subordinates is not needed and is replaced by individual, group, and organizational factors. Finally, the Leader–Member Exchange (LMX) Model focuses on the dyadic relationship between a leader and each follower and proposes the concept of in-groups and out-groups as the defining element of that relationship.

All the models use a contingency view of leadership, and in all of them, the leader's behavior or style depends on the requirements of the situation. Although the concept of task and relationship orientation continues to be dominant, several of the models consider other factors, thereby expanding our views of leadership. The structure and routine of the task continue to be key situational factors, although other variables such as follower independence and maturity are also introduced.

The contingency models of leadership presented here are the foundation of current theory in leadership and continue to dominate the field of leadership. The models differ in the factors they use to describe the leader's style or behavior and elements of the leadership situation that are considered (Table 3-7).

For each model, however, the focus is on the match between the leader and the situation. The extensive research about the various contingency models, although not always consistent and clear, led to the broad acceptance and establishment of the concept of contingency in leadership. Clearly, no one best way to lead exists. Effective leadership is a combination of and match between the leader and the leadership situation.

Review and Discussion Questions

1. What are the similarities and differences between the trait and behavior approaches to leadership?
2. What are the major assumptions of the contingency approach to leadership?
3. Define the leadership and situational factors included in Fiedler's Contingency Model. What are the primary predictions of the model?
4. After assessing your own style, interview several people with whom you worked to determine whether their perceptions match your score based on the LPC.
5. Provide examples for the situations in which each of the major decision styles of the Normative Decision Model would be appropriate.
6. What is the difference between Fiedler's model and later contingency models?
7. How does national culture affect relationships between leaders and followers?
8. How does the LMX Model differ from all the other contingency theories of leadership?
9. How can leaders use the LMX Model in improving their effectiveness?
10. What are the drawbacks of the Normative Decision Model?

Leadership Challenge: The In-Group Applicant

You are an expatriate manager sent to work in the Indian operation of your company. As you get settled in, one of your first decisions is to hire an assistant manager. Your efficient office manager, who has been extremely helpful to you already and has been with the company for many years, quickly suggests one of his relatives, who, he tells you, would be perfect for the job. According to him, his cousin just graduated from a top business school and, most important, is trustworthy, loyal, and eager to work and learn. Your office manager tells you that his cousin will be coming shortly to introduce himself. He tells you that you don't have to be inconvenienced any further and won't need to waste your time interviewing and checking references of strangers who could be unreliable.

1. How do you interpret and explain your office manager's actions?
2. Will you hire the "cousin"?
3. What factors do you need to consider before making your decision?

Exercise 3-1 The Toy Factory

The goal of this exercise is for each group to produce as many high-quality toy wolves as possible. Your instructor will assign you to a group, designate the leader, and provide you with a list of materials needed for making the toy wolves. Your team leader will give you instructions on how to make the toys. After a 15-minute production run, each group's productivity will be measured.

The Toy Factory Worksheet

1. How would you describe your team leader's style of leadership? Provide several specific behavioral examples.

2. How did you react to your leader's style? How satisfied were you?

3. What improvement suggestions (if any) could you offer your leader?

Exercise 3-2 Using the Normative Decision Model

This exercise is based on the concepts and principles presented in the Normative Decision Model of leadership. Use the contingency factors presented in Table 3-4 to analyze each case. Figure 3-2 along with Table 3-3 provides a guide to the appropriate decision styles for each case.

Case 1: Centralizing Purchasing

You are the western regional manager in charge of purchasing for a group of hospitals and clinics. Your territory includes eight western states. You recently joined the group but you brought with you nearly 10 years of experience in purchasing with one of the company's major competitors. One of your major achievements in the previous job was the implementation of a highly efficient companywide purchasing system. The health group oversees more than 30 associated health clinics and hospitals in your region alone. Each center operates somewhat independently without much control from the regional purchasing manager. Several of the clinics are cooperating under informal arrangements that allow them to get better prices from suppliers. The purchasing managers from the larger hospitals in your region, on the other hand, have almost no contact with one another or you. As a result, they are often competing for suppliers and fail to achieve economies of scale that would allow them to save considerable costs on their various purchases. In other cases, the managers rely on totally different suppliers and manage to obtain advantageous contracts.

With the pressure to cut health-care costs, the health group's board of directors and the group's president identified purchasing as one area where savings need to be achieved. You are charged with centralizing purchasing, and you are expected to reduce the costs of purchasing by at least 15 percent within a year.

You still need to meet many of the purchasing managers who are supposed to report to you. Your appointment was announced through a memo from the group's president. The memo also mentioned the need to cut costs in all areas and indicated the need to focus on purchasing as first step. The purchasing managers you did meet or contact were civil but not overly friendly. With only six months to show the first results, you need to start planning and implementing changes as soon as possible.

Analysis and Recommendation

Using the problem requirements, decision rules, and leadership styles of the Normative Decision Model, indicate which decision style(s) would be most appropriate.

1. What type of problem is it: group or individual?

2. Contingency Factors:
   Is there a quality requirement?

   Does the leader have enough information to make a high-quality decision?

   Is the problem clear and structured?

Is employee acceptance of the decision needed for its implementation?

Will subordinates accept the decision if the leader makes it by himself or herself?

Do subordinates share the organization's goals for the problem?

Is there conflict among subordinates (are they cohesive) regarding the problem?

3. What are acceptable decision styles? Why?

4. What are unacceptable decision styles? Why?

Case 2: Extraction of Natural Gas

You are the leader of a local council planning committee and you are aware that a planning application for fracking has recently been received. This involves the extraction of natural gas from under the ground using water pressure. You realize that allowing this project to go ahead could lead to the creation of many new local jobs but that the situation will require very careful handling because of the controversial nature of the process. Huge amounts of water are required on site to enable the process to work and there is also the possibility of chemical pollution, subsidence and even earth tremors.

You have to weigh up the economic benefits of allowing the application against the environmental concerns. There are eight other members in the committee, to assist you, but they have different opinions on the desirability of the project. Environmental protesters have already begun to arrive so you and your committee need to arrive at a speedy decision.

Analysis and Recommendation

Using the problem requirements, decision rules, and leadership styles of the Normative Decision Model, indicate which decision style(s) would be most appropriate.

1. What type of problem is it: group or individual?

2. Contingency factors:
Is there a quality requirement?

How important is the commitment of subordinates to the decision?

Does the leader have enough information to make a high-quality decision?

Is the problem clear and structured?

Is employee acceptance of the decision needed for its implementation?

Will subordinates accept the decision if the leader makes it by himself or herself?

Do subordinates share the organization's goals for the problem?

Is there conflict among subordinates (are they cohesive) regarding the problem?

3. What are acceptable decision styles? Why?

4. What are unacceptable decision styles? Why?

Case 3: Whether or not to keep a company open

You are in charge of a small engineering company that has been largely successful in recent years. Employees are motivated and content and share the goals and values of the organization. There is a trade union, but membership is quite low due to the stable nature of employment.

However, in the last few months your debtors have been delaying their payments. New business has been harder to obtain due to increased competition and recession. This has led to a serious cash flow problem. You feel that in these circumstances it would be difficult to carry on in the same way and are considering selling the business either in its present form or as individual assets. You have asked for advice on the future liquidity of the company from the chief accountant. The workforce naturally wants to see the company stay open or be taken over by another company. They also feel that they should be valued for their loyalty and commitment.

You value the commitment of the workforce and the economy is improving quite quickly, but with the company beginning to amass unpaid bills you need to decide if the company should continue to trade.

Analysis and Recommendation

Using the problem requirements, decision rules, and leadership styles of the Normative Decision Model, indicate which decision style(s) would be most appropriate.

1. What type of problem is it: group or individual?

2. Contingency factors:
   Is there a quality requirement?

   Does the leader have enough information to make a high-quality decision?

   Is the problem clear and structured?

   Is employee acceptance of the decision needed for its implementation?

   Will subordinates accept the decision if the leader makes it by himself or herself?

   Do subordinates share the organization's goals for the problem?

   Is there conflict among subordinates (are they cohesive) regarding the problem?

3. What are acceptable decision styles? Why?

4. What are unacceptable decision styles? Why?

Self-Assessment 3-1: Determining Your LPC

To fill out this scale, think of a person with whom you have had difficulty working. That person may be someone you work with now or someone you knew in the past. He or she does not have to be the person you like the least well, but should be the person with whom you experienced the most difficulty. Rate this person on the following scale.

			Score
Pleasant	8 7 6 5 4 3 2 1	Unpleasant	_____
Friendly	8 7 6 5 4 3 2 1	Unfriendly	_____
Rejecting	1 2 3 4 5 6 7 8	Accepting	_____
Tense	1 2 3 4 5 6 7 8	Relaxed	_____
Distant	1 2 3 4 5 6 7 8	Close	_____
Cold	1 2 3 4 5 6 7 8	Warm	_____
Supportive	8 7 6 5 4 3 2 1	Hostile	_____
Boring	1 2 3 4 5 6 7 8	Interesting	_____
Quarrelsome	1 2 3 4 5 6 7 8	Harmonious	_____
Gloomy	1 2 3 4 5 6 7 8	Cheerful	_____
Open	8 7 6 5 4 3 2 1	Guarded	_____
Backbiting	1 2 3 4 5 6 7 8	Loyal	_____
Untrustworthy	1 2 3 4 5 6 7 8	Trustworthy	_____
Considerate	8 7 6 5 4 3 2 1	Inconsiderate	_____
Nasty	1 2 3 4 5 6 7 8	Nice	_____
Agreeable	8 7 6 5 4 3 2 1	Disagreeable	_____
Insincere	1 2 3 4 5 6 7 8	Sincere	_____
Kind	8 7 6 5 4 3 2 1	Unkind	_____
		Total	_____

Scoring Key: A score of 64 or below indicates that you are task motivated or low-LPC. A score of 73 or higher indicates that you are relationship motivated or high-LPC. If your score falls between 65 and 72, you will need to determine for yourself in which category you belong.

Source: F. E. Fiedler and M. M. Chemers. *Improving Leadership Effectiveness: The Leaders Match Concept,* 2nd ed. (New York: Wiley, 1984). Adapted with permission.

Self-Assessment 3-2: Assessing a Leadership Situation

This assessment is based on Fiedler's Contingency Model and is designed to allow you to assess a situation you faced as a leader. To complete the questions in each category, think of a current or past situation at work, in sports, or in social or church events where you were the formal or informal leader of a group of people. You were either successful or not so successful. Rate the situation by circling one of the alternatives for each of the following questions; use the same situation to answer all the questions. You will evaluate your effectiveness, relationship with your followers, the structure of the task, and the power you had.

Self-Rating of Effectiveness

1. Considering the situation and task, how effective were you as a leader?

3	2	1
Very effective	Moderately effective	Not at all effective

2. How effective was your group in completing its task?

3	2	1
Very effective	Moderately effective	Not at all effective

3. How would you rate the overall performance of your group?

4	3	2	1
Very high performance	Moderately high performance	Somewhat low performance	Poor performance

Now add up the score of the three questions. The maximum score is 10; minimum is 3. A high-performance score would indicate effectiveness. A score between 7 and 10 indicates high performance; a score between 6 and 4 is moderate performance; score of 3 indicates poor performance.

Total Effectiveness score: _____

Leader–Member Relations (LMR) Scale

Write the number that best represents your response to each item using the following scale:

1 = Strongly agree

2 = Agree

3 = Neither agree nor disagree

4 = Disagree

5 = Strongly disagree.

_____ 1. The people I supervise have trouble getting along with each other.
_____ 2. My subordinates are reliable and trustworthy.
_____ 3. A friendly atmosphere exists among the people I supervise.
_____ 4. My subordinates always cooperate with me in getting the job done.
_____ 5. Friction is present between my subordinates and myself.
_____ 6. My subordinates give me a good deal of help and support in getting the job done.
_____ 7. The people I supervise work well together in getting the job done.
_____ 8. I experience good relations with the people I supervise.

Scoring: Add up your scores for all 8 questions.

Total LMR score: _____ *(Save to enter in Sit Con at the end)*

Task Structure Rating Scale—Part I (TS Part I)

Write the number that best describes your group's task using the following scale:

0 = Seldom true

1 = Sometimes true

2 = Usually true

Goal Clarity

_____ 1. A blueprint, picture, model, or detailed description of the finished product or service is available.

_____ 2. A person is available to advise and give a description of the finished product or service, or how the job should be done.

Goal–Path Multiplicity

_____ 3. A step-by-step procedure or a standard operating procedure indicates in detail the process that is to be followed.

_____ 4. A specific way to subdivide the task into separate parts or steps is provided.

_____ 5. Some ways for performing this task are clearly recognized as better than others.

Solution Specificity

_____ 6. It is obvious when the task is finished and the correct solution is found.

_____ 7. A book, manual, or job description indicates the best solution or the best outcome for the task.

Availability of Feedback

_____ 8. A generally agreed understanding is established about the standards the particular product or service must meet to be considered acceptable.

_____ 9. The evaluation of this task is generally made on some quantitative basis.

_____ 10. The leader and the group can find out how well the task was accomplished in enough time to improve future performance.

Add up your scores for all 10 questions. *Total for TS (Part I):* _____

Task Structure Rating Scale—Part II (TS Part II)

Only complete if your score on TS Part I is higher than 6.

Training and experience adjustment (circle a number for each of the following questions)

1. Compared to others in this or similar positions, how much training have you had?

3	2	1	0
No training at all	Very little training	A moderate amount of training	A great deal of training

2. Compared to others in this or similar positions, how much experience do you have?

6	4	2	0
No experience at all	Very little experience	A moderate amount of experience	A great deal of experience

Add the numbers you circled for the two questions. *Total TS (Part II):*

Scoring Task Structure

    Total from TS—Part I: _____

    Subtract Total from TS—Part II: _____

    Total TS score: _____ *(Save to enter in Sit Con at the end)*

Position Power (PP) Rating Scale

Circle the number that best describes your answer.

1. As the leader, I can directly or by recommendation administer rewards and punishments to my subordinates.

2	1	0
Can act directly or can recommend with high effectiveness	Can recommend but with mixed results	Cannot recommend

2. As the leader, I can directly or by recommendation affect the promotion, demotion, hiring, or firing of my subordinates.

2	1	0
Can act directly or can recommend with high effectiveness	Can recommend but with mixed results	Cannot recommend

3. As the leader, I have the knowledge necessary to assign tasks to subordinates and instruct them in task completion.

2	1	0
Yes, I have knowledge	Sometimes or in some aspects	No, I do not have knowledge

4. As the leader, it is my job to evaluate the performance of my subordinates.

2	1	0
Yes, I can evaluate	Sometimes or in some aspects	No, I cannot evaluate

5. As the leader, I have some official title of authority given by the organization (e.g., supervisor, department head, team leader).

    Yes = 2   No = 0

Scoring: Add your scores for the five PP questions.

    Total PP score: _____ *(Save to enter in Sit Con at the end)*

Situation Control (Sit Con) Score

Add up the scores of the LMR, TS, and PP scales.

$$\overline{}_{\text{LMR}} + \overline{}_{\text{TS}} + \overline{}_{\text{PP}} = \overline{}_{\text{Sit Con}}$$

Using the ranges provided, evaluate the situational control you have as the leader in the situation you described.

Total Score	51–70	31–50	10–30
Amount of Sit Con	High Control	Moderate control	Low control

Source: F. E. Fiedler and M. M. Chemers, *Improving Leadership Effectiveness: The Leaders Match Concept,* 2nd ed. (New York: Wiley, 1984). Adapted and used with permission.

Evaluation and Discussion

Self-Assessment 3-1 provided you with your LPC score; Self-Assessment 3-2 helped you assess the situational control you have as a leader. Fiedler's Contingency Model suggests that if you are a low-LPC task-motivated leader, you and your group will perform best in high- and low-situational control. If you are a high-LPC relationship-motivated leader, you and your group will perform best in moderate-situational control. If the leader is "in match," the group will perform best.

1. Were you "in match" with the situation you described?

2. To what extent did your level of effectiveness (refer to the self-rating at the beginning of this exercise) match Fiedler's predictions? Why or why not?

Self-Assessment 3-3: Identifying Your In-Group and Out-Group

This exercise is designed to help you identify the members of your in-group and out-group and your own behavior toward members of each group.

Step 1: Identify the Members

Make a list of the subordinates (or team members) whom you **trust**. Select people who work for you (or with you) and whom you like and respect, people who enjoy your confidence.

Make a list of the subordinates (or team members) who you **do not trust**. Select people who work for you (or with you) and whom you do not like or respect.

Step 2: Membership Factors

Reflect on the commonalties among the group members for each group. What are the factors that caused them to be in each group? Consider behaviors, personalities, and demographic factors, as well as any other relevant factors.

Step 3: How did You Treat Them?

Describe your own behavior as a leader toward each group and its members:

Leader Behaviors	In-Group	Out-Group
Amount of at-work interaction		
Type of interaction		
Type of assignments given		
How was feedback provided		
Amount of out-of-work		
Performance expectations		
Other factors: List		

Step 4: Self-Evaluation

1. What does it take for a person to move from your in-group to your out-group?

2. How does having two groups affect your group or department and the organization?

3. To what extent is group membership based on organizational versus personal factors?

4. What are the implications for you as a leader?

LEADERSHIP IN ACTION

THE CARING DICTATOR

By any measure, Jack Hartnett, the president of Texas-based D.L. Rogers Corp., is a successful man. D.L. Rogers owns 54 franchises of the Sonic roller-skating nostalgic hamburger chain, which generate $44 million in revenues for the company. Hartnett's restaurants make 18 percent more than the national average, and turnover is incredibly low for the fast-food industry, with a supervisor's average tenure at 12.4 years. He knows what he wants, how to keep his employees, and how to run his business for high profit.

In a management world where everyone will tell you that you need to be soft, be participative, be open to ideas, and empower employees, Jack Hartnett appears to be an anachronism. He runs his business on the Sinatra principle: "My Way!" He tolerates little deviation from what he wants, his instructions, and his training. He is absolutely sure he knows the best way, and more than one employee is scared of disagreeing with him. He likes keeping people a little off balance and a little queasy so that they will work harder to avoid his wrath. Hartnett even has his own Eight Commandments, and he will fire those who break any one of them twice. The last Hartnett commandment is, "I will only tell you one time." Interestingly, he believes that his style shows that he really cares about his people: "The success of our business is that we really care about our owner-operators—we don't have managers. Our No. 1 focus is to take care of our people" (Ruggless, 1998).

Hartnett restaurants run like clockwork. He does the top-level hiring himself and is reputed to spend as long as 10 grueling hours with prospective managers and their spouses. He wants to know about their personal lives and their financial health and looks for right responses and any signs of reticence to answer questions. Hartnett says, "I want them to understand this is not a job to me. This is a lifetime of working together. I want partners who are going to die with me" (Ballon, 1998: 67). If you are one of the selected few, you are expected to be loyal and obedient. Once a quarter, you can also expect a Hartnett "lock-in" meeting, where Jack will take you away along with other supervisors to a secret location with no chance of escape. You can expect to be blindfolded, put through survival exercises, and sleep in tents before you go to a luxury resort to discuss business.

For all their trouble and unquestioning obedience and loyalty, D.L. Rogers' employees and supervisors find a home, a family, a community, and a place to grow. If you have problems with your husband, like Sharon, the wife of one of the D.L. Rogers' supervisors, you can call Jack. He will listen to you, chew your spouse out, and send him home for a while. Hartnett says, "I don't want you to come to work unhappy, pissed off, upset, or mad about anything, because I don't think you can be totally focused on making money if you're worried" (Ballon, 1998: 63). He pays his employees considerably above national averages, plays golf with them, and gets involved with their personal lives. Hartnett wants to create a bond that lasts. A few years ago, he spent $200,000 to take 254 managers and their families to Cancun, Mexico, for four days. They got training on better time management and marketing techniques, and on how to be a better spouse.

Hartnett also likes to have fun. Practical jokes, including gluing supervisors' shoes to the floor, are common. But he also works hard. Eighty-hour weeks are common, and he starts his days earlier than most. He is not above taking on the most menial jobs in the restaurants and is willing to show the way, no matter what. His presence, his energy, and his unbending confidence in "his way" make converts. Hartnett has created an organization that is consistent and that simplifies everybody's life.

Questions

1. How would you describe Jack Hartnett's leadership style?
2. Why do you think some employees would find it difficult to work for him?

Sources: Ballon, M. "Extreme managing," *Inc.*, July 1998, 60–72. Ruggless. R. D. L. Rogers Group. 1998. *Nation's Restaurant News*, January. http://findarticles.com/p/articles/mi_m3190/is_n4_v32/ai_20199540/ (accessed January 20, 2010).

4

Individual Differences and Traits

After studying this chapter, you will be able to:

1. Explain the elements and impact of individual difference characteristics in leadership.
2. Discuss the role demographic characteristics play in leadership.
3. Identify the impact of values on leadership.
4. Present the relationship between abilities and skills and leadership including emotional intelligence and creativity.
5. Highlight the role of key personality traits relevant to leadership including the following:
   - The Big Five
   - The proactive personality
   - Type A
   - Self-monitoring
   - The dark triad
6. Be able to use individual characteristics appropriately.

THE LEADERSHIP QUESTION

You now know that leadership is more than just a set of traits. However, personal characteristics, including personality, do matter. What personal characteristics do you think matter most in leadership? Which ones detract from leadership effectiveness?

Even a quick reading of the history and mythology of any civilization indicates that leaders are considered special. Their physical characteristics are described in detail, their personalities dissected, and their actions celebrated. Long lists of traits and personal exploits are provided. The detailed information about leaders focuses our attention on the person. It echoes a common belief that leaders possess something out of the ordinary—something within them that makes them special and worthy of our attention. Many believe that good leaders have natural, inborn characteristics that set them apart from others. Most of us can produce a list of personal characteristics of effective leaders. Leaders are courageous; they show initiative and integrity; they communicate well; and they are intelligent, perceptive, goal-directed, and so forth. As discussed in Chapter 3 , the results of hundreds of studies do not yield a specific profile for leaders. Traits may matter, but one trait, or even a collection of traits, does not determine who will become a leader and whether that person will be effective. That said, there are certain individual characteristics that impact leadership and may affect leadership effectiveness. Jay Conger, renowned leadership scholar, once stated that the issue is not: "whether leaders are born or made. They are born and made" (Conger, 2004).

In recent years, the interest in understanding the individual characteristics and personalities of leaders has reemerged, with many studies linking personality and other stable individual characteristics to leadership (e.g., see Furnham et al., 2013; for reviews see Antonakis, Day, and Schyns, 2012; Judge, Piccolo, and Kosalka, 2009; and Zaccaro, 2007). Additionally, the neo-charismatic theories that we discuss in Chapter 6 include individual traits as a key factor in leadership effectiveness. The major difference between earlier approaches during the Trait Era and the recent ones is the researchers' more complex approach. The search is not simply for one individual trait or a combination of traits. Instead, modern theorists consider the complex interaction among traits, behaviors, and situational characteristics, such as expectations of followers. Within this framework, it is important to understand the role that several personal characteristics may play in determining leadership style and behavior. Additionally, self-awareness of one's strengths and weaknesses continues to be at the heart of leader development (see Chapter 10).

This chapter discusses the role of individual characteristics in leadership by considering demographic characteristics, values, abilities, skills, and several personality traits. These individual characteristics do not determine how effective a leader will be. They, however, do affect the way leaders think, behave, and approach problems, their preferences, and their interpersonal interactions.

ELEMENTS AND IMPACT OF INDIVIDUAL DIFFERENCE CHARACTERISTICS

What makes every person unique is a combination of many factors, including demographic, physical, psychological, and behavioral differences. They are at the core of who we are. Figure 4-1 shows a framework for understanding individual differences and their complex components. Heredity and environment are the two determinants of individual characteristics. The interactionist view suggests that, although experts debate the relative influence of each, these two determinants interact to influence the development of individual characteristics. Although genetic studies establish a link between heredity and some personality traits, research also shows that the environment strongly affects us. Influences include physical location, family, culture, religion, education, early experiences, and friends.

To understand individual differences, we must consider the interaction between heredity and the environment. Environmental and social conditions can reinforce genetic patterns to influence a leader's personality, as can cultural factors, the educational system, and parental upbringing. For instance, in the United States, the genetic traits typically associated with being male are further reinforced by social norms that encourage boys to be competitive and aggressive. Similarly, although female babies tend to develop language skills earlier than males, parents who speak more to their girls and schools that expect girls to be proficient in language reinforce their verbal skills. These genetic and environmental influences interact and are reflected later in life in leadership styles and behaviors.

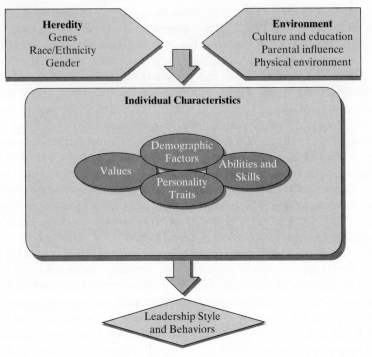

FIGURE 4-1 Individual Differences Framework

As shown in Figure 4-1, four major individual difference characteristics can affect leadership style: demographic factors, values, abilities and skills, and personality. *Demographic factors* such as age and ethnic background are individual difference characteristics that may affect individual behavior and to some extent leadership style. *Values* are stable, long-lasting beliefs and preferences about what is worthwhile and desirable. They are principles that guide behavior. *Ability*, or aptitude, is a natural talent for doing something mental or physical. This category includes things such as intelligence and creativity. A *skill* is an acquired talent that a person develops related to a specific task. Whereas ability is somewhat stable over time, skills change with training and experience and from one task to another. You cannot train leaders to develop an ability or aptitude, but you can train them in new leadership skills. *Personality* refers to a stable set of psychological characteristics that makes each person unique and constitutes a person's character and temperament.

Individual Characteristics Provide a Range

Although individual characteristics tend to be stable, that stability does not mean that people cannot behave in ways that are inconsistent with their personality, values, and attitudes. Instead, each characteristic provides a behavioral zone of comfort as presented in Figure 4-2. The zone of comfort includes a range of behaviors that come naturally and feel comfortable to perform because they reflect individual characteristics. Behaving outside that zone is difficult, takes practice, and in some cases might not be possible. Although we are at ease in our behavioral comfort zone, we learn and grow by moving to our zones of discomfort. The behaviors outside

For instance, the Japanese value and reward conformity to the group. Parents teach children not to stand out or draw attention to themselves. The Japanese proverb "the nail that stands out will be hammered down" reflects the value system of many Japanese who believe that they should sacrifice the self for the good of the collective. Leaders are similarly valued for their conformity to the social order as much as their uniqueness. Several Native American cultures, such as the Navajos, have similar cultural values. Navajos, who are a horizontal collectivistic culture, devalue individualism and standing out in one's community and, indeed, consider such behavior inappropriate. They appreciate leaders primarily for their contribution to their community. Hofstede's other cultural values of avoidance of uncertainty, power distance, and masculinity further influence an individual's value systems. For example research shows that different factors motivate managers in different cultures (Mathur, Zhang, and Meelankavil, 2001), and factors that determine commitment to work depend to some extent on cultural values (Andolsek and Stebe, 2004). When a culture emphasizes low power distance—such as in Sweden, which is individualistic but horizontal—leaders are likely to be cooperative and avoid status symbols and hierarchy. In masculine cultures, individuals are likely to emphasize honor and self-reliance. The concept of high and low context can further affect values. In high-context cultures, such as Mexico or Thailand, bending the truth to preserve relationships or protect feelings is much more accepted than in low-context cultures, such as Germany or the United States.

In addition to the impact of national culture, culture at the group level also affects values. For example, surveys consistently reveal what some people call the gender gap, a difference in the value systems of men and women. In the United States, women tend to place a higher value on family and social issues, whereas men focus more on economic problems. We discuss the impact of generational value systems next.

Generational Differences in Values

Research suggests that people from the older generation in the United States believe that the younger generation has worse moral values, less respect for others, and a lower work ethic than their parents (Taylor and Morin, 2009). However, the younger generation fears that older workers will not ever retire and leave younger workers stuck in middle management (Erickson, 2010). Other research has found generational differences in both the United States and several other countries such as Australia, France, Germany, and the United Kingdom. For example, in all those countries, Baby Boomers (born in the 1940s to the 1960s) tend to make fewer demands from their employers compared to Xers (those born in the 1970s and 1980s), who are more demanding in terms of salary and titles, while Millennials focus more on training, job perks, and flexible work hours (Hastings, 2012). Xers and Millennials have also been found to be generally less loyal to their companies, give work lower priority, something that is not unexpected, given that they grew up in times of lay-offs and economic crises (Dittman, 2005). They hop from one job to another, work odd shifts, rely on technology, work late into the night, and may not consider the traditional eight-hour workday appropriate.

Baby Boomers tend to consider work as central to their lives, sense of self-worth, and how they evaluate others (Gursoy et al., 2013). Interestingly, Gen Xers are more concerned than other generations about power and together with Millennials, seek work-life balance and recognition to a higher extent than previous generations (Gursoy et al., 2013). Younger generations are more accepting than older ones of social and technological changes, tend to view cultural diversity as a positive factor, and are more accepting of homosexuality (Millennials' Judgment, 2010). Table 4-1 presents some value differences based on age.

TABLE 4-1	Generation-Based Value Differences in the United States	
Generation	**Key Social and Historical Influences**	**Dominant Value System**
The Traditionalists; *GI generation*, 60+ (born in 1940s or before)	Raised by Depression-era parents in post–Depression period or around World War II; Big Band music	Hard work; frugality; patriotism; Protestant work ethic; respect for authority
Baby boomers, 50–65 (born between late 1940s and 1960s)	Raised by World War II parents; grew up during Korean and Vietnam wars; Kennedy assassination; moon landing; rock & roll and Woodstock; cold war energy crisis	Nonconformity; idealism; self-focus; distrust of establishment; happiness and peace; optimism; involvement
Baby Busters, 40–50 (born between the 1960s and 1970s)	Raised by the early hippies; post–Vietnam era; Watergate; the Beatles, Grateful Dead, Jimmy Hendrix	The Yuppies; "me" generation; ambitious; material comfort; success driven; stressed out
Generation Xers, 30–40 (born between 1970s and 1980s)	Peaceful era; fall of communism; Iran hostage crisis; recession and economic changes; Bill Clinton; AIDS; MTV; The Eagles, Michael Jackson	Enjoyment of life; jaded; latchkey kids; single-parent family; desire for autonomy and flexibility; self-reliance; spirituality; diversity; balance work and personal life
Millennials or Nexters under 30 (born after the mid-1980s)	A lot of parental focus; Oklahoma bombings; 9/11 World Trade Center attack; school shootings; globalization; threat of terrorism; first black president; Internet and media; tech savvy; Lady Gaga; Kanye West	Flexibility; choice; socially conscious; meaningful experiences and work; diversity; achievement; tolerance and openness

Sources: Partially based on N. A. Hira, "You raised them, now manage them," *Fortune*, May 28, 2007, 38–43; M. E. Massey, "The past: What you are is where you were when" (videorecording) (Schaumberg, IL: VideoPublishing House, 1986); D. J. Cherrington, S. J. Condies, and J. L. England, "Age and work values," *Academy of Management Journal*, September 1979, 617–623; and P. Taylor and R. Morin. 2009. Forty years after Woodstock: A gentler generation gap. *Pew Research Center: Social and Demographic Trends.* http://pewsocialtrends.org/pubs/739/woodstock-gentler-generation-gap-music-by-age (accessed February 21, 2010).

These generational differences have implications for leadership at two levels. First leaders from different generations are likely to have different values and therefore emphasize and value different things. Second, all leaders will be managing individuals from different generations with variability in their values and needs. Understanding these differences is essential to being able to lead diverse groups effectively. Giselle Kovary, managing partner of n-gen People Performance Inc, suggests that leaders working with Millennials need to point out their impact on their organization and team, while Xers may need to be reminded how their high performance will yield the rewards they seek (Hasting, 2012).

Values and Ethics

Ethics are a person's concept of right and wrong. Two general views of ethics are the relativist and universalist views. Individuals with a *relativist view* of ethics believe that what is right or wrong depends on the situation or the culture, while a *universalist view* would suggest that some things are right and wrong regardless of the context and situation. Research suggests that ethics is strongly influenced by culture (e.g., Hooker, 2009). An index collected by Transparency International, an organization that uses a complex set of data to monitor corruption around the world, shows distinct national differences in ethical behaviors. In their 2012 index, Denmark, Finland, and New Zealand were ranked as the least corrupt countries; Somalia, North Korea, and Afghanistan, Sudan, and Myanmar received the lowest scores (Corruption Index, 2013). The United States ranked 19 out of 180, behind Canada (#9), Germany (#13), Belgium, Japan, and the United Kingdom (16 to 18; Corruption Index, 2012). To illustrate, businesspeople in many places consider gifts, bribes, or kickbacks as acceptable behaviors in contract negotiations, although these activities are unethical and illegal based on U.S. values and laws. A person with a relativist view of ethics would take a "when in Rome, do as the Romans do" approach. That is, a U.S. manager who learns that it is generally accepted to bribe officials in Thailand to secure a contract would consider bribing a Thai official acceptable and ethical. Note that it is not possible for managers of U.S.-based companies to adopt a relativist view of ethics in business situations simply because U.S. laws forbid any form of bribery anywhere in the world. In contrast, a person with a universalist view of ethics believes that all activities should be judged by the same standards, regardless of the situation or culture. For example, a U.S. oil company manager would appoint a female manager to its Saudi operations, based on U.S. laws of equal opportunity and the principles of cultural diversity, despite the religious and cultural problems it might create in a traditional Muslim society.

The value and ethical issues facing leaders are highly complex. For example, research by Triandis and his associates (Triandis et al., 2001) indicates that collectivism tends to be related to greater use of deception in negotiation, as well as higher levels of guilt after using deception. Particularly, Koreans and Japanese feel considerable guilt and shame after using deception. Furthermore, based on what a culture values, individuals within that culture might lie for different reasons, such as protecting their privacy in the case of the United States or benefiting family members in the case of Samoans (Aune and Waters, 1994). Other research has found that people who are higher on collectivism and uncertainty avoidance, but low on masculinity and power distance reject ethically questionable practices to a higher extent than those low on collectivism and uncertainty avoidance and high on masculinity and power distance (Ziad, 2012).

Other research suggests that organizations from a low-power distance, long-term orientation, or highly individualistic cultures may be less likely to engage in giving bribes (Sanyal and Guvenli, 2009). When comparing U.S. and Hong Kong Chinese, some studies show cross-cultural differences in attitudes toward breach of contract (Kickul, Lester, and Belgio, 2004). U.S. employees responded more negatively to breaches of intrinsic contracts (e.g., autonomy) by displaying lower levels of job satisfaction and commitment. The Hong Kong Chinese are less accepting than U.S. workers of violations of extrinsic contract (e.g., salary or job training), but more tolerant of violations of intrinsic contract. The researchers attribute the differences to the Chinese Confucian value to preserve harmony compared with the U.S. value of individual success. Because of complex cross-cultural and individual differences in values, handling ethical and value-driven issues will continue to be a major part of every manager's job. Chapter 6 will review several new approaches that consider values to be at the core of leadership.

ABILITIES AND SKILLS

Much of the early research in leadership characteristics focused on establishing leadership abilities. Although leaders clearly must have some abilities, competencies, and skills, these characteristics do not have high correlations to leadership effectiveness (for a review of the early research, see Bass, 1990). Intelligence and creativity have been the primary focus in the area of abilities; technical, interpersonal, and cognitive skills are the focus in that area.

Intelligence

Intelligence is one of the most-often used characteristics to describe leaders and is often included in discussions of leadership. It is clear that the complex task of leading requires a person with a cognitive ability to remember, collect and integrate information, analyze problems, develop solutions, and evaluate alternatives, all of which are related to traditional definitions of intelligence. However, the actual link between intelligence and effectiveness is far from clear (Riggio, Murphy, and Pirozzolo 2002), as they are in other areas of success (Gladwell, 2008). Correlations vary, and many studies suggest that the link is relatively weak (for a review of past research, see Bass, 1990). To date, only one leadership theory, the Cognitive Resource Model (Fiedler, 2002; Fiedler and Garcia, 1987b), has used intelligence explicitly as a factor. Reviews of the link between general intelligence and leadership indicate that it is an important aspect of leadership; the relationship, however, may be moderated by many factors (Riggio et al., 2002). For example, when being competent is important, leaders who are more intelligent might do better, but in situations that require interpersonal skills, general intelligence might not be sufficient. The level of leadership also may be a factor. Particularly, intuition may be especially important for leaders at upper organizational levels. Furthermore, some early research shows that a curvilinear relationship may exist between intelligence and leadership (Ghiselli, 1963). Those individuals with either low or high scores are less likely to be effective and successful leaders. Both, for different reasons, might experience difficulty communicating with their followers and motivating them to achieve the task.

Consider Scott Rudin, producer of hit movies such as *The Girl with the Dragon Tattoo, It's Complicated, Social Network, and No Country for Old Men,* and more recently an investor in hit Broadway shows such as the *Book of Mormon*, and executive producer of television shows such as the *Newsroom*. Some of the people who work with him consider Rudin to be "one of the smartest and most clever and witty guys I have ever met" (Carvell, 1998: 201). He is bright and creative, and many admire his work. However, his intelligence and creativity are not his only well-known qualities. Rudin is famous for his fiery outbursts, throwing phones and office supplies, outrageous demands, and on-the-spot firing and rehiring of assistants—by some accounts 250 in a five-year period (Sutton, 2010). He has been ranked as one of the worst bosses in New York City (Gawker, 2007). As one of Rudin's ex-assistants states, "I think the people that work there—most of them hate him. Nobody likes him. Everybody's miserable" (Carvell, 1998: 201). Even his mentor, Edgar Scherick, referred to his protégé as "Scott Rude." As this example illustrates, being intelligent is not sufficient for being an effective leader. Many other characteristics play important roles. In Rudin's case, his high level of intelligence and creativity are not matched by his ability to relate to others.

Practical and Emotional Intelligence

In the past few years, other perspectives have been added to the concept of intelligence. Instead of primarily focusing on memory and analytical skills, several researchers have suggested that being able to work well with others or having the skills needed to succeed in life are important

TABLE 4-2	Components of Emotional Intelligence
Component	**Description**
Self-awareness	Being aware of and in touch with your own feelings and emotions
Self-regulation	Being able to manage various emotions and moods without denying or suppressing them
Self-motivation	Being able to remain positive and optimistic
Empathy for others	Being able to read others' emotions accurately and putting yourself in their place
Interpersonal and social skills	Having the skills to build and maintain positive relationships with others

Sources: Based on D. Goleman, "What makes a leader?" *Harvard Business Review* 82, no. 1 (2004): 82–91; and D. Goleman, R. E. Boyatzis, and A. McKee, *Primal Leadership: Realizing the Power of Emotional Intelligence* (Boston: Harvard Business School Press, 2002).

components of intelligence. Researcher Robert Sternberg and his colleagues introduced the concept of practical intelligence to address the types of abilities and attributes that people use to solve everyday challenges they may face (Hedlund et al., 2003; Sternberg, 2002a; Sternberg et al., 2000). People with this type of intelligence either change their behavior to adapt to the environment, manipulate the environment, or find a new environment in which to succeed (Sternberg, 2007). Sternberg further proposes a model of leadership, WICS, that integrates wisdom, intelligence, and creativity in a systems approach putting intelligence at the center of leadership traits (Sternberg, 2003).

Peter Salovey and John Mayer (1990) coined the term "emotional intelligence" (EI; or EQ for emotional quotient) to describe an ability to access and use emotions to promote growth (see Self-Assessment 4-2). Whereas intelligence generally is defined in terms of mental and cognitive abilities, some argue that the ability to relate interpersonally contributes another type of intelligence (see Goleman, 1995, 2004). The ability to interact well with followers, satisfy their emotional needs, and motivate and inspire them is central to effective leadership. Table 4-2 summarizes the five elements of EI/EQ.

Individuals with high EI/EQ are in touch with their emotions and demonstrate self-management in their ability to control their moods and feelings productively and in staying motivated and focused even when facing obstacles. They can calm themselves when angry and stay balanced. They also are able to read others' emotions, feel empathy for them, and put themselves in their place. The last component of EI/EQ is having the ability to develop productive and positive interpersonal relationships through understanding, conflict resolution, and negotiation (Goleman, 1998; see Self-Assessment 4-2). Goleman, whose model is both ability and skills-based, suggests that EI/EQ is important in leadership because of the increased use of teams, globalization, and the need to retain talented followers (Goleman, 1998). Many have explored the relationship between EI/EQ and transformational leadership; that topic is covered in Chapter 6. Some researchers suggest using EI in leader development (Sadri, 2012) as studies show that it is essential for effective leadership (Riggio and Reichard, 2008), can impact the development of visionary leadership (Boyatzis and Soler, 2012), and is linked to transformational leadership (Lopez-Zafra et al., 2012; Yitshaki, 2012). Others have found links to performance (Shahhosseini, Silong, and Ismaill, 2013) and the development of positive group norms (Koman and Wolff, 2008).

Daniel Goleman states, "The rules for work are changing, and we're all being judged by a new yardstick—not just how smart we are and what technical skills we have, which employers see as givens, but increasingly by how well we handle ourselves and one another" (Fisher, 1998: 293). Although competence and cognitive ability—namely, traditional intelligence—might be keys for success when working alone, leadership requires successful interaction with others and the ability to motivate them to accomplish goals. Therefore, EI/EQ is a central factor in several leadership processes, particularly in the development of charismatic and transformational leadership where the emotional bond between leaders and followers is imperative. Being able to empathize with followers can further allow a leader to develop followers and create a consensus. Some researchers suggest that emotional intelligence contributes to effective leadership because an emotionally intelligent leader focuses on followers, on inspiring them, and on developing enthusiasm (George, 2007). Whereas leaders with a high IQ lead with their head, leaders with a high EI/EQ lead with their heart and address their followers' emotional needs.

The role of emotions in leadership is increasingly being recognized. Ken Chenault, Chairman and CEO of American Express (AmEx), one of only a few African American leaders of *Fortune* 500 companies in the United States, is able to win his employees' trust and build cohesion partly through empathy and ability to express his emotions. He is described as understated, modest, and unassuming, with quiet warmth and a style that makes people want to be on his team (Schwartz, 2001). His skills at managing through crisis focus on communication. He states: "…you've got to communicate constantly…" (Colvin, 2009). He believes that although the rational aspects of leadership are essential, values are what make a leader. He states, "What I have seen in companies throughout my career is that if you are not clear on who you are, on what it is you stand for, and if you don't have strong values, you are going to run your career off a cliff" (*Knowledge@Wharton*, 2005). After AmEx was driven out of its Manhattan headquarters by the September 11 terrorist attacks, Chenault moved into a cramped windowless office with standard issue furniture. While addressing the AmEx employees during a company town hall meeting after September 11, he openly expressed his emotions, embraced grief-stricken employees, and stated, "I represent the best company and the best people in the world. In fact, you are my strength, and I love you" (Byrne and Timmons, 2001). Tom Ryder, who competed with Chenault for the top AmEx job, said, "If you work around him, you feel like you'd do anything for the guy" (Schwartz, 2001: 62). For Chenault, integrity, courage, being a team player, and developing people are foundations for becoming a leader; all are elements of emotional intelligence.

Because of the potential of EI/EQ to address an important aspect of leadership, many organizations are finding that developing their managers' EI can lead to higher performance. Consultants Louise Altman, cofounder of *Intentional Communication Consultants*, believes that awareness of emotions can make people more effective and that EI should be used more often. She states: "I think it's still viewed as slightly suspect in the average workplace. I'm kind of astonished on a regular basis at how little people really understand about human dynamics in the workplace" (Huppke, 2013). Danny Myers, who owns several highly successful restaurants in New York City, including the Union Square Café and Gramercy Tavern, and who has written a book about delivering first-class service (Myers, 2006), believes that the secret of his success is that he has surrounded himself with people who have higher EQs than IQs. He looks for people who have natural warmth, optimism, intelligence, and curiosity. Similarly, business education, which, for many years, emphasized analytical and numbers-oriented skills, is shifting attention to developing interpersonal skills. Former General Electric CEO turned management guru, Jack

Welch, who is known for his no-nonsense and hard hitting-approach says: "A leader's intelligence has to have a strong emotional component. He has to have high levels of self-awareness, maturity and self-control. He or she must be able to withstand the heat, handle setbacks, and, when those lucky moments arise, enjoy success with equal parts of joy and humility. No doubt emotional intelligence is more rare than book smarts, but my experience says it is actually more important in the making of a leader. You just can't ignore it" (Vise, 2011).

Creativity

According to a survey of 1,500 executives in 60 countries conducted by IBM in 2010, creativity is the most crucial factor for success in the future (IBM, 2010 Global CEO Study). CEOs participating in the survey believe that creative leaders make more changes, invite disruptive innovation, and are comfortable with ambiguity, all essential for leaders in today's complex organizations. *Creativity*—also known as divergent thinking or lateral thinking—*is the process of bringing into reality something novel and useful*. It is not just about doing something unusual and unexpected; it is about making things work better. It includes elements such as emotional stability, ambition, need for originality, and flexibility (Martinson, 2011). Lateral thinking focuses on moving away from the linear approach advocated by rational decision making (De Bono, 1992). Caterina Fake, cofounder of the photo-sharing site *Flickr*, likes to let her curiosity guide her. She states: "I work on whatever instinctively feels the right thing at the moment" (Buchanan, 2010: 69). David Rockwell, the architect who designed the 2009 Academy Award set and the Walt Disney Family Museum, says, "The key is to stay curious. As you have success in certain areas, you have to find ways to keep alive that sense of discovery, of not knowing all the answers" (Sacks, 2009: 133). Patrick Le Quément, French carmaker Renault's chief designer, is credited with many of the company's cutting-edge and highly unusual designs. He believes that being original is the key to his creativity, stating, "It's worth alienating most of your customers if you can make the rest love you" (Wylie, 2004a: 90).

Creativity is a necessary component of leadership because leaders are often expected to develop new ideas and directions that others will follow. Some research suggests that creative leaders can encourage creativity in employees (Collins and Cooke, 2013) and in their organizations (Mathisen, 2012). Creative leaders listen intently to all sources, especially to bad news, in order to know where the next problem is emerging. They value subjective as well as objective information. They turn facts, perceptions, gut feelings, and intuitions into reality by making bold and informed decisions. Other factors found to be important are modeling creative and unconventional behaviors, delegation, monitoring the process, and showing followers how their work affects the organization (Basadur, 2004). Creative leaders must not only be creative but also have considerable technical expertise to lead their followers through the challenges of creative decision making (Mumford and Licuanan, 2004). Creative leaders typically share four characteristics (Sternberg and Lubart, 1995):

1. *Perseverance in the face of obstacles and self-confidence.* Creative individuals persevere more in the face of problems and have strong beliefs in the correctness of their ideas.
2. *Willingness to take risks.* Creative individuals take moderate to high risks rather than extreme risks that have a strong chance of failing.
3. *Willingness to grow and openness to experience.* Creative individuals are open to experiences and are willing to try new methods.
4. *Tolerance of ambiguity.* Creative individuals tolerate lack of structure and not having clear answers.

TABLE 4-3	Leadership Skills
Skills Category	**Description**
Technical skills	Knowledge of the job processes, methods, tools, and techniques
Interpersonal skills	Knowledge of interpersonal relationships including communication, conflict management, negotiation, and team building
Conceptual skills	Knowledge of problem solving, logical thinking, decision making, creativity, and reasoning in general

As this list suggests, creative leaders tend to be confident in the paths they select and are willing to take risks when others give up. Creative people focus on learning and are willing to live with uncertainty to reach their goals. As with any other characteristic, the organizational setting can have a great impact on allowing creativity to flourish. Some suggest that creative people make a decision to be creative when facing challenging problems (Sternberg, 2002b). Interestingly, research suggests a link between a leader's EI and the ability to encourage followers to be creative (Zhou and George, 2003). Because creativity is an emotional process, managing emotions well can play a positive role in the creativity process. Teresa Amabile, head of the Entrepreneurial Management Unit at Harvard Business School, believes that creativity is not just the domain of creative people, but requires experience, talent, and motivation to push through problems. She also suggests that people are least creative when they feel time pressure, fear, or intense competitive pressures (Breen, 2004).

Skills

The research on leadership skills is considerably clearer and more conclusive than the research on leadership abilities. Leadership skills are divided into three categories: technical, interpersonal, and conceptual (Table 4-3).

As leaders and managers move up in their organization, they rely less on technical skills and increasingly more on interpersonal and conceptual skills. Company CEOs, school principals, or hospital administrators do not need to be able to perform various jobs in detail. They, however, should be able to negotiate successfully and effectively and manage various interpersonal relationships inside and outside the organization. Furthermore, top executives, more than lower-level leaders and managers, need to read and analyze their internal and external environments and make strategic decisions that require considerable problem-solving skills.

The impact of ability and skills on leadership depends to a great extent on the situation. Situational factors, such as the type of organization, level of leadership, ability and needs of followers, and type of task at hand, all influence what abilities and skills leaders will need to be effective. In addition, although skills can be learned and can affect a leader's behavior, research suggests that a lag time occurs between learning skills and translating them into actual behavior (Hirst et al., 2004).

PERSONALITY TRAITS THAT CONTRIBUTE TO LEADERSHIP

Although strong evidence of a consistent relationship between specific traits and leadership effectiveness is lacking, interest in understanding the personal characteristics of leaders continues. In 1974, a thorough review of traits by Stogdill, together with other findings, reestablished the validity of the trait approach, reviving research on the topic. In general, activity level and stamina, socioeconomic class, education, and intelligence, along with a variety of other traits, appear to characterize leaders, and especially effective leaders. The role of situational characteristics, however, is also recognized.

Kirkpatrick and Locke (1991) have proposed a modern approach to understanding the role of traits in leadership: Several key traits alone are not enough to make a leader, but they are a precondition for effective leadership. Kirkpatrick and Locke list a number of traits that facilitate a leader's acquisition of needed leadership skills. The key traits are as follows:

- Drive, which includes motivation and energy
- Desire and motivation to lead
- Honesty and integrity
- Self-confidence
- Intelligence
- Knowledge of the business

Some of the traits, namely intelligence and drive, cannot be acquired through training. Others, such as knowledge of the industry and self-confidence, can be acquired with time and appropriate experience. The trait of honesty is a simple choice. Studies of managers and leaders in other cultures found similar traits present in successful leaders. For example, successful Russian business leaders are characterized by "hard-driving ambition, boundless energy, and keen ability" (Puffer, 1994: 41). Chinese business leaders value hard work and an impeccable reputation for integrity. Being hard-driving to the point of being a workaholic is not an uncommon trait in U.S. business executives either. Surveys indicate that 60 percent of people in high-earning jobs work more than 50 hours a week; 35 percent more than 60 hours a week (Armour, 2007).

Consider how many business executives demonstrate the traits that Kirkpatrick and Locke propose. Kathy Wade, who runs a nonprofit organization called Learning through Art and is an accomplished jazz musician, considers passion and initiative to be key to leadership (BizEd, 2009). Similarly, Lisa Harper, CEO of Gymboree Corp., remembers the time when she took over the company with the task of turning it around: "I was passionate about the people, the product, and the customer…" (Canabou, 2003: 58). Small business owners succeed because of their extreme confidence in their own abilities (Wellner, 2004). Goran Lindahl, the former chief executive of the Swiss-Swedish engineering group ABB, was driven almost to the point of obsession to keep his company's stock prices high (Tomlinson, 2000). Other leaders develop knowledge of their business. Meg Whitman, former CEO of eBay, 2010 California gubernatorial candidate, and current CEO of Hewlett Packard made a point of traveling coach instead of taking the corporate jet. She wore an eBay T-shirt so that she could talk to people about their experience with her company and gather information (Dillon, 2004). Emilio Azcarraga Jean, chair of Grupo Televisa SA, the largest Spanish-language media company in the world, learned all the details of the family business when he took over from his ailing father (Kroll and Fass, 2007). Through his intense drive and motivation, he refocused his organization's culture from loyalty to performance to gain ground in the U.S. market.

Interestingly, integrity, or lack of it, is cited as a key factor in leadership. Many anecdotes about bad leadership contain elements of lack of trust, dishonesty, and unwillingness to be held accountable on the part of the leaders. The corporate scandals have increased and renewed focus on the importance of transparency and honesty. The GLOBE researchers have found that integrity is one of few culturally universal leadership characteristics (House et al., 2004).

Just as some traits are necessary for leadership, they can be detrimental when carried to an extreme (Kirkpatrick and Locke, 1991). A leader with too much drive might refuse to delegate tasks, and a desire for too much power can work against a leader's effectiveness (Bennis and Nanus, 1985). For example, Michael Eisner, the president of Disney, was not able to hold on to several talented executives because of his need for control and inability to delegate, which stemmed in part from his drive and motivation to lead. These characteristics were blamed for the high turnover on top. Eisner's tight hold on power also caused bitter disputes with several board members, triggered investor lawsuits, and was one of the factors that led to Eisner's resignation (Holson, 2004a). His replacement, Bob Iger, is known to be understated, calm, diplomatic, and collaborative, all characteristics that Eisner lacked (Steptoe, 2007). Small business owners who are highly driven face similar challenges when it comes to delegation. For example, Andrew Nadel, owner of Pride Products, a promotional and corporate gift company, does everything from calling customers to assembling new office chairs himself, even though he employs a staff to take care of many of these tasks (Wellner, 2004).

The current approach to understanding the role of leadership traits suggests that, as many of us believe, leaders are indeed gifted in at least some areas. Those gifts and talents alone, however, are not enough. Experience, correct choices, and exposure to the right situations are the keys to allowing those gifts to bloom.

Several traits play a role in leadership and can contribute to a leader's effectiveness in several ways (for a review, see Judge et al., 2009; Zaccaro, 2007).

- First, as discussed in Chapter 3 and earlier in this chapter, researchers have identified some traits that are consistently associated with leadership.
- Second, a leader's personality influences his or her preferences, style, and behavior.
- Third, personality may affect the ease with which a leader learns skills and is able to implement them.
- Fourth, being aware of key personality traits shown to affect work-related behaviors can help leaders develop their self-awareness and aid them in their learning and development.
- Finally, traits can be strong predictors of leadership when considered in an integrated system that includes several individual difference characteristics and situational and contextual variables.

The next section presents six personality traits with implications for leadership.

WHAT DO YOU DO?

A new employee is transferred to your department and you hear from several people around the organization that she is hard to manage. She has a reputation for questioning everything, challenging her boss, and refusing to give up when she wants something. Several of her previous team members tell you that she does not play well with others and is always second-guessing their actions and decisions. Your supervisor, however, thinks she is a star and believes that you are lucky to get her. How do you approach the situation?

The Big Five Personality Dimensions

Over time, psychologists and organizational behavior researchers have condensed countless personality traits into a list of five major personality dimensions, known as the *Big Five* (Barrick and Mount, 1991; Digman, 1990; Norman, 1963). Research shows that these five dimensions are consistent components of personality not only in the United States, but in several other cultures as well (e.g., Alessandri, 2011). Table 4-4 summarizes the key elements of the Big Five personality dimensions.

TABLE 4-4	Big Five Personality Dimensions
Personality Dimensions	**Description**
Conscientiousness	Degree to which a person is dependable, responsible, organized, and plans ahead
Extraversion/Introversion	Degree to which a person is sociable, talkative, assertive, active, and ambitious
Openness to experience	Degree to which a person is imaginative, broad minded, curious, and seeks new experiences
Emotional stability	Degree to which a person is anxious, depressed, angry, and insecure
Agreeableness	Degree to which a person is courteous, likable, good natured, and flexible

Sources: Based on descriptions provided by W. T. Norman, "Toward an adequate taxonomy of personality attributes: Replicated factor structure in peer nomination personality ratings," *Journal of Abnormal and Social Psychology* 66 (1963): 547–583; J. M. Digman, "Personality structure: Emergence of the five-factor model," *Annual Review of Psychology* 41 (1990): 417–440; and M. R. Barrick and M. Mount, "The five big personality dimensions and job performance: A meta-analysis," *Personnel Psychology* 44, no. 1 (1991): 1–76.

A number of the Big Five personality dimensions have links to work-relevant behaviors such as academic (Poropat, 2009) and career success (Seibert and Kraimer, 2001), the performance of managers who work abroad (Caligiuri, 2000), and use of different types of power (Karkoulian, Messarra, and Sidani, 2009). Additionally, conscientiousness, agreeableness, and emotional stability are found to be related to ethical leadership (Kalshoven, Den Hartog, and De Hoogh, 2011). However, none alone strongly predicts performance or leadership effectiveness.

Of the five dimensions, *conscientiousness* is the most strongly correlated to job performance. This connection makes sense: Individuals who are dependable, organized, and hard working tend to perform better in their job. *Extraversion* is the Big Five dimension with the second-highest correlation to job-related behaviors and is particularly important in jobs that rely on social interaction, such as management or sales (Anderson, Spataro, and Flynn, 2008). It is much less essential for employees working on an assembly line or as computer programmers. Unlike conscientiousness, which can apply to all job levels or occupations, extraversion is not an essential trait for every job, although it appears to be much celebrated in today's businesses. Susan Cain, author of the book "*Quiet: The Power of Introverts in a World That Can't Stop Talking*," believes that the United States has a bias for extroversion and the ideal person is considered to be extroverted. (2013). However, introverts can be highly effective. The ability to thoughtfully reflect and listen to others is a highly valuable trait in leaders. Lisa Petrilli, CEO of C-Level strategies, who considers herself to be an introvert, says: "We get our energy from what people refer to as our inner world. That's very powerful. Ideas really do run businesses" (Vanderkam, 2012).

Openness to experience can help performance in some instances, but not in others. For example, being open to new experiences can help employees and managers perform well in training because they will be motivated to explore fresh ideas and to learn (Goldstein, 1986), and it might help them to be more successful in overseas assignments (Ones and Viswesvaran, 1999). Neville Isdell, CEO of Coca-Cola until 2008 believes that openness to experience is key to leadership. He thinks that students should also learn about cultural differences through a variety of experiences including travel (Bisoux, 2008b). In describing the qualities he looks for in new Coca-Cola hires, he adds, "...they also must have a sense of curiosity. They must want to travel and discover new societies and see the world. Curious people are engaged." Ken Chenault, CEO of AmEx, suggests that being open to change and able to adapt to it are the most important characteristic today's leaders need to have: "It's not the strongest or the most intelligent who survive, but those most adaptive to change" (Chester, 2005). But the same eagerness to explore new ideas and ways of doing things can be an impediment to performance on jobs that require careful attention to existing processes and procedures.

As one would expect, *emotional stability* also is related to job behaviors and performance. At the extreme, individuals who are neurotic are not likely to be able to function in organizations. Some degree of anxiety and worrying, however, can help people perform well because it spurs them to excel. Andy Grove's (former executive at Intel) book *Only the Paranoid Survive: How to Exploit the Crisis That Challenges Every Company and Career* is an indication of the sense of anxiety he instilled at Intel to make sure employees perform and the organization excels. Finally, although *agreeableness* is a highly desirable personality trait in social situations, it generally is not associated with an individual's work-related behaviors or performance. Furthermore, some recent research suggests that leaders who are higher on emotional stability, extroversion, and agreeableness, while low on conscientiousness, have followers with higher job satisfaction and job commitment (Smith and Canger, 2004).

The most important managerial implication of the Big Five dimensions is that despite the reliability and robustness of the Big Five as measures of personality, no single trait is linked strongly to how well a leader or manager will perform in all types and levels of jobs. The links to leadership that do exist are relatively weak, and even a broad personality measure such as the Big Five alone cannot account for success or failure in the complex leadership process.

Proactive Personality

Do you know someone who routinely identifies opportunities, challenges the status quo, takes initiatives, and perseveres even when blocked by obstacles? No matter what happens, that person stays positive and keeps going. Chances are that the person has a *proactive personality* (see Self-Assessment 4-3). Proactives take control to influence events in their lives and attribute things that happen to them, particularly positive events, to their own efforts or abilities (Crant, 2000; see Figure 4-3). Such people focus on changing their environment rather than being constrained by it (Bateman and Crant, 1993). Research indicates that proactives have more job satisfaction and a more positive outlook about their career and life (Crant, 2000; Li, Liang, and Crant, 2010; Seibert, Crant, and Kraimer, 1999), have higher life satisfaction (Greguras and Diefendorff, 2010), and are more entrepreneurial (Becherer and Maurer, 1999). The construct has been linked to job performance to a higher extent than the Big Five dimensions (Fuller and Marler, 2009), and there is some cross-cultural research that indicates its applicability in cultures other than the United States

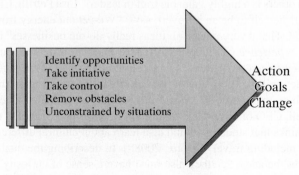

Identify opportunities
Take initiative
Take control
Remove obstacles
Unconstrained by situations

Action
Goals
Change

FIGURE 4-3   Characteristics of Proactives

and Britain (Joo and Ready, 2012; Kim, Hon, and Crant, 2009). Furthermore, proactivity involves both the setting of goals and the motivation to achieve them (Parker, Bindl, and Strauss, 2010).

Shelly Provost, a partner at the venture incubator Lamp Post Group, describes fearless entrepreneurs who are often considered proactives as people who speak up, inject energy and enthusiasm into their activities, and are positive, focused and hard working. She says: "The grittiest people don't just work longer and harder, although that is part of the equation. They keep a laser focus on their goal and say, 'no thanks,' to anything that gets in their way" (Haden, 2012). These are all qualities of proactive people. All these characteristics have implications for leadership especially during times when organizations are in need of change and revival. Being proactive is likely to help a leader identify opportunities, encourage followers toward action, and be more motivated to achieve goals, all important aspects of leadership.

Type A

We all know people who appear intense and in a hurry, always busy, and worried about getting things done. These are some of the characteristics of Type A individuals (see Self-Assessment 4-4). *Type As* are described as people who trying to do more and more in less and less time. As compared with Type Bs, they are involved in a whirlwind of activity. At the heart of the Type A construct is the need for control (Smith and Rhodewalt, 1986; Strube and Werner, 1985). Although the construct was developed in relations to coronary problems as a risk factor for coronary disease, it made its way to psychology and management as a personality factor with implications for work-related behaviors. Generally, when compared to Type Bs, who tend to have less need for control, Type A individuals show a high need for control, a factor that manifests itself in four general characteristics (Figure 4-4).

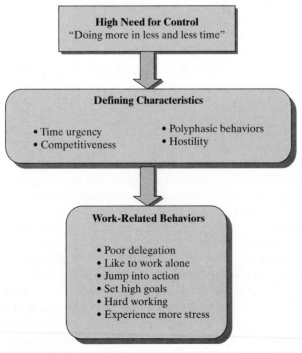

FIGURE 4-4 Type A Characteristics and Behaviors

The first Type A characteristic, time urgency, leads Type A individuals to be concerned with time. Being in a hurry, impatience with delays, and worries about time are aspects of time urgency. Jordan Zimmerman, CEO of Zimmerman Advertising, starts his day at 3:30 AM. with a three-hour exercise regimen that he believes gives him energy (Buchanan, 2010). Krissi Bar, founder of the consulting firm Barr Corporate Success, forces herself to work faster: "If I think something is going to take me an hour, I give myself 40 minutes. By shrinking your mental deadlines, you work faster and with greater focus" (Buchanan, 2010: 66). Carol Bartz, CEO of Yahoo until 2011, was known for her impatience, need for control, fiery temper, and secrecy (Kamer, 2011). She says she does not like to take too much time to think through issues: "This fits my impatient nature of 'doing' very well, and my belief that it's always worth spending energy on 'doing' something better" (Sellers, 2009). The second Type A characteristic is competitiveness. Type A individuals are generally highly competitive in work, social, and sport situations. They measure their outcomes against others and keep track of their performance; getting ahead and winning are major concerns. Legendary Boston Celtics basketball star Larry Bird demonstrated many of the Type A characteristics. When talking about playing against Magic Johnson and his relationship with the LA Lakers star, he states: "I had to have him there as someone I can compare myself to" (Heistand, 2010). The third characteristic, polyphasic behaviors, involves doing several things at once. Although everyone is likely to undertake several activities when pressured, Type As often do so even when not required to by work or other deadlines. For example, they might make a list of specific activities to undertake during a vacation. The last Type A characteristic is hostility. It is the only characteristic still found by researchers to be tied to coronary problems and other health problems (Alspach, 2004). It is manifested in explosive speech, diffused anger, intolerance for delays or mistakes, and a generally fiery, aggressive (Baron, Neuman, and Geddes, 1999), and sometimes malicious style of interaction (Strube et al., 1984). These four sets of characteristics are triggered by the Type A's need for control and are aimed at providing the Type A with a sense of control over the environment.

Type A characteristics are neither bad nor good. Type As and Type Bs possess certain traits and behaviors that can either be helpful or provide obstacles to being effective leaders; situational requirements are the key. The relationship of Type A to leadership has not been extensively studied, but a number of findings that link Type A behavior to work-related behaviors provide interesting insights. The results of one study suggest that being Type A affects the way CEOs approach organizational strategy (Nahavandi, Mizzi, and Malekzadeh, 1992). Type A executives see more threats in the environment of their organizations and set challenging strategies that still provide them with a sense of control. Furthermore, compared with Type Bs, Type As tend to be poor delegators and generally prefer to work alone (Miller, Lack, and Asroff, 1985). They like to maintain control over all aspects of their work. The lack of delegation can be damaging to a leader and often is considered a major pitfall of management. Furthermore, with the increasing focus on cooperation, use of teams, and empowerment as a leadership style, the inability to delegate can present an obstacle to successful leadership.

As can be seen in the example of Jeffrey Katzenberg, Type As tend to set high-performance goals and have high expectations for themselves and those around them. Such high expectations may lead to faster promotions at lower organizational levels (Stewart-Belle and Lust, 1999). When taken in a leadership context, such high expectations can lead to high performance and high quality, as well as to overload and burnout when carried to an extreme. The consistency of the findings that Type As like to maintain control, are active and hard working, and tend to be impatient with delays and with their coworkers, however, allows us to consider the potential implications for leadership. These behaviors are similar to the high energy and motivation that Kirkpatrick and Locke (1991) propose as central leadership traits. Type A leaders are likely to be

LEADING CHANGE
Jeffrey Katzenberg's Transformation

Jeffrey Katzenberg could be a poster child for the ambitious, impatient, competitive, angry, and highly successful Type A executive. He held top jobs at Paramount pictures and Disney, where he was responsible for hits such as *Aladdin* and *The Lion King*, before being publicly and unceremoniously fired from Disney in 1994. Katzenberg then teamed up with Steven Spielberg and David Geffen to start Dream Works Animation SKG, which has produced even bigger hits, including the Shrek movies and *Monsters vs. Aliens*. He recently extended his contract as CEO of DreamWorks Animation to 2017 with an annual base salary of $2.5 million (Sniderm, 2012). Aside from his amazing talent and continued success, Katzenberg had a reputation for being demanding, sometimes unreasonable, and having very public outbursts of anger, lashing out at colleagues and Hollywood stars. A Disney official states: "He was a screamer, and he was a shredder and a very tough force to be reckoned with" (Borden, 2009: 106).

Katzenberg seems to have changed, to a great extent as a result of his firing in 1994. He believes that the event was a wake up call that taught him to welcome change (Ten minutes, 2010). Katzenberg fully admits to his drive, which started early in his life. When describing some early leadership experiences he says: "The thing we all actually wished we had more of was time. I've never forgotten that. I'm always very punctual, and when I'm not, I have high, high anxiety" (Bryant, 2009l). But he has learned to temper his impatience, having become aware of its effects on followers. He uses what he calls a "five-second tape delay" to "self-edit" before he expresses his opinion and is careful to consider that others may not want to work at the same pace he does: "Something that I was kind of oblivious to for a long period of time is that I ended up setting a pace for everyone else, and they assumed if the boss is working 24/7, then we all must work 24/7. That's not such a good thing because not everyone loves it as much as I do, and it's not actually how you get the best out of people" (Bryant, 2009l). Although still not mellow by most people's standards, Katzenberg has altered his behavior to focus on valuing those who work for him and keeping some balance in his life and with his wife of 34 years. His biggest leadership lesson is to cultivate his followers: "I started to realize that if I wanted to stay surrounded by great people, I had to get out of their way and create the room and make sure they started to get the recognition and the credit and everything that goes with it. Honestly, it allowed me to stay around longer" (Bryant, 2009l).

Sources: Borden, M. 2010. The redemption of an ogre. *Fast Company* December/January: 104–108; Bryant, A. 2009l. The benefit of a boot out the door. *New York Times—Corner Office*, November 7. http://www.nytimes.com/2009/11/08/business/08corner.html?_r=1 (accessed on March 2, 2010); Ten minutes that mattered, 2010. *Forbes.com* February 5. http://www.forbes.com/2010/02/04/disney-dreamworks-shrek-intelligent-technology-katzenberg.html (accessed on March 2, 2010).

intense and demanding, set high-performance standards, and be intolerant of delays and excuses. They also might find it difficult to delegate tasks or work in a team environment. Some recent research suggests that Type As and Type Bs both prefer working in teams made up of others similar to them (Keinan and Koren, 2002). Other research indicates that Type As and Type Bs may be effective in different types of jobs (Rastogi and Dave, 2004). Yet, although some Type A characteristics appear to define effective leaders (i.e., drive, ambition, and energy) others aspects, such as impatience with delays and a tendency to jump into action, are characteristics that do not serve leaders well. One recent study found that Type A personality is related to depression and lower individual performance over time (Watson, 2006).

Self-Monitoring

When observing some leaders, we can identify their style and even personality traits easily. They seem to be an open book, and their behavior is consistent in many different situations. For example, Herb Kelleher, founder of Southwest Airlines, has a forceful but open style in all settings, whether he is dealing with the Southwest employees or stockholders or presenting at a business conference. Similarly, it was never hard for anyone to read Michael Eisner, the former CEO of Disney; he was highly aggressive and demanding in all settings with a take-no-prisoners approach (he was the one who fired Jeffrey Katzenberg described in the Leading Change case). Other leaders are harder to read, or their behaviors appear to change from one situation to another.

One reason it might be easy to read some people and establish their style but difficult to do so for others is self-monitoring. Developed by Snyder (1974), the *self-monitoring* scale identifies the degree to which people are capable of reading and using the cues from their environment to determine their behavior. High self-monitors (SM)—individuals who score high on the scale (see Self-Assessment 4-5)—are able to read environmental and social cues regarding what is appropriate behavior and use those cues to adjust their behaviors. They can present themselves, manage impressions (Turnley and Bolino, 2001), and are able to mirror and mimic others' behaviors better than low SMs (Estow, Jamieson, and Yates, 2007). Studies also find that high SMs are particularly good at getting along with others, may be more likely to emerge as leaders because of their ability to get ahead (Day and Schleicher, 2006), and that they may be more adaptive and innovative (Hutchinson and Skinner, 2007). Low SMs either do not read the cues or do not use them to change their behavior. For high SMs, behavior is likely to be the result of a perception of the environment and is therefore likely to change depending on the situation. Low SMs' behaviors are more internally determined and are likely to appear constant across different situations. This internal focus also seems to make them more accurate decision makers regarding performance ratings and personnel decisions (Jawahar, 2001).

Many leadership theories rely on the assumptions that leaders (1) have the ability to evaluate various situations and (2) can change their behaviors to match the requirements of the situation. In that context, being a high SM might become a key leadership trait. Being a high SM should help a leader better perceive and analyze a situation. Furthermore, given SMs' higher ability to adjust their behaviors, it is reasonable to suggest that, at least in situations that are ambiguous and difficult to read, they might be more effective leaders. Researchers have found that high SMs emerge as leaders more frequently than do low SMs, leading to the hypothesis that self-monitoring is a key variable in leadership and job performance (Day et al., 2002). The concept has also been linked to transformational leadership behaviors (discussed in Chapter 6).

Overall, self-monitoring presents interesting potential applications to leadership, many of which continue to remain unexplored (for a discussion of the potential impact of self-monitoring on leadership, see Bedeian and Day, 2004). Little doubt remains, however, that being a high SM can be a useful characteristic in helping leaders adjust their behaviors and perhaps even in learning new skills. High SMs may be better able to cope with cross-cultural experiences because such situations are ambiguous and require the ability to interpret environmental cues. Similarly, the changing leadership roles are making leadership situations considerably less routine and more uncertain than they were 20 years ago. Modern leaders must deal with diverse cultures and followers' demands for participation and autonomy, and they also need to understand an increasingly complex global environment. Self-monitoring might be a key characteristic in these new tasks.

The individual characteristics personality traits we have discussed so far either contribute positively to leadership or are "neutral." For instance, being conscientiousness, proactive, or a high self-monitor are desirable traits for leaders and being a Type A or Type B is related to certain behaviors that are neither inherently positive nor negative and, may play a role in how people lead or interact with others. We next consider personality traits that are detrimental to leadership and likely detract from a leader's effectiveness.

The Dark Triad: Machiavellian, Narcissistic, and Psychopathic Personality

Do you know a leader who is manipulative, callous, ruthless, emotionally cold, and self-centered? Have you worked with people who seem to get ahead without getting along with others? Have you had a supervisor who is self-promoting and aggressive? Do these characteristics and behaviors sound like some of the political and business leaders you have read about? Researchers Paulhus and Williams suggest the term "*Dark Triad*" (DT) to refer to the combination of three socially malevolent characteristics and behaviors that include Machiavellianism, subclinical narcissism, and subclinical psychopathy (Furnham, Richards, and Paulhus, 2012; 2002). The focus of leadership in recent years has been heavily on the positive nature of leaders, and some have even suggested that being positive and constructive is inherent to the definition of being a leader (e.g., Kellerman, 2004). Accordingly, destructive and evil leaders, for example Hitler, do not lead their followers; they simply rule them. However, many leaders who are toxic and abusive still achieve positive results. Many also are popular, at least initially, as was Hitler. Understanding these negative characteristics and traits and how they can contribute to destructive leadership is essential. The three elements of the Dark Triad have each been researched separately and specific characteristics have been identified (see Table 4-5 for a summary).

Machiavellian personality is based loosely on Niccolo Machiavelli's work, *The Prince* and suggests that some individuals are more willing than others to put their self-interests and preferences above the interests of the group. They are able and willing to manipulate others for personal gain (Christie and Geis, 1970; Jones and Paulhus, 2009). *Narcissism*, which, in its extreme form, is considered as a personality disorder, has a subclinical or "normal" form characterized by a sense of entitlement, superiority, and grandiosity, preoccupation with status, and insensitivity to others (Brown, Budzek, and Tamborski, 2009; Emons, 1987; Morf and Rhodewalt, 2001; Raskin and Hall, 1979). Recent research has linked the construct to leadership (Popper, 2002; Rosenthal and Pittinsky, 2006). Many narcissistic traits are related to characteristics of leaders, including desire to have power and influence over others and be in a leadership

TABLE 4-5	Machiavellian, Narcissistic, and Psychopathic Personality	
Machiavellianism	• Manipulative • Unscrupulous • Cunning	• Scheming and calculating • Low concern for others
Narcissism	• Entitled • Grandiose • Superior • Self-preoccupied	• Arrogant • Continual need for admiration • Exhibitionist
Psychopathy	• Impulsive and thrill seeker • Low anxiety • Skilled impression manager	• Low empathy for others • Lack of guilt, remorse, or shame

position (Brunell et al., 2008). Finally, the subclinical form of *psychopathy* is characterized by impulsivity, thrill seeking, low anxiety, and lack of concern for others or remorse (Babiak and Hare, 2006). The clinical form of psychopathy has extreme characteristics and behaviors and includes antisocial and violent behaviors that have been linked to criminal behavior (Hare, 1985). As is the case with narcissism, its nonclinical form is now considered a personality trait with implications for social interaction and organizational behavior (Levensen et al., 1995).

The three traits are correlated and share some common threads and themes, although they are not equivalent (Paulhus and Williams, 2002). All three entail malevolent, self-promoting, disagreeable, emotionally cold, and duplicitous characteristics; all three get ahead without establishing sincere connections with others (see Figure 4-5; Rauthman and Kolar, 2013a). Machiavellians and psychopaths use harder manipulation tactics such as threats (Janason, Slomski, and Partyka, 2012) and are less liked than the narcissists who are perceived as more friendly (Rauthman and Kolar, 2012; 2013b). Interestingly, men tend to score higher than women on all three constructs and are more aggressive and forceful in their manipulation (Janason, Slomski, and Partyka, 2012; Jonason and Webseter, 2012). However, in spite of the negative characteristics, the DT is, unfortunately, sometimes perceived as a positive leadership trait. The ability to handle and persuade people and play political games, and emotional detachment may appear beneficial in leadership situations (Boyle et al., 2012). More specifically, narcissism has been found to be associated with self-leadership (Furtner et al., 2011) and quicker promotions (Hogan and Kaiser, 2005) and some suggest that it may even be beneficial to organizations (Chatterjee and Hambrick, 2007).

Our popular press is full of examples of ruthless leaders from both the private and public sectors who wheel and deal their way to achieving their goals with considerable disregard for their subordinates. They bully their employees and can even be abusive, cruel, and threatening. One study reports that 45 percent of the 1,000 employees surveyed reported having worked with an abusive boss (Daniel, 2009). Some of these bosses are admired for what they can achieve; others are simply feared. Several publications regularly prepare lists of these tough bosses, and numerous websites are dedicated to describing power-hungry, controlling, and sometimes abusive bosses and helping employees deal with them (e.g., *Fortune* magazine and CNN.com, and bnet.com). In many cases, as long as the bottom line is healthy and key constituents, such as the board of directors or stockholders, are satisfied, the means used by these leaders are tolerated.

FIGURE 4-5   The Dark Triad

APPLYING WHAT YOU LEARN

Dealing with Abusive Bosses

Many of us have been faced with supervisors and bosses who appear to have strong narcissistic characteristics. Here are some suggestions in how to deal with them. These do not all work, and different ones work depending on the situation and the person you are dealing with:

- Keep your cool; do not react with an emotional response. Self-control is essential.
- Remain professional, even if the boss is not. You can't control his or her behavior; but you can control your reaction.
- Make sure you clearly understand and are able to describe the type of behavior you are facing (e.g., too much criticism, inaccurate feedback, yelling).
- Document everything! Keep careful notes of incidents.
- Make sure that your work and behavior are impeccable and beyond reproach.

- Keep track of any feedback from coworkers and customers that can be used to document your good performance.
- Do not get defensive; respond with level-headed comments without taking the abuse.
- Seek help from HR if that is available, especially if there are legal ramifications (e.g., discrimination, sexual harassment, or other ethical or legal violations).
- Maintain good working relationships and a strong network at work.
- Go up the chain of command as a last resort; provide facts and evidence—not just emotional reactions.
- Unless the situation is dangerous, don't make a quick decision about leaving; carefully plan for contingencies and an eventual exit.
- Plan an exit strategy; look for another position.
- Only you can determine when it's too much; with planning, you can leave on your own terms.

Well-known tyrants of history, such as Hitler and Stalin, exhibit one or more of the DT characteristics. So do other business leaders, including Michael Eisner and Scott Rudin, discussed earlier in this chapter, Steve Jobs of Apple, and many U.S. and world leaders, including presidents Carter, Clinton, and G.W. Bush (Rosenthal and Pittinsky, 2006). Leaders with DT traits self-promote, deceive and manipulate others, respond poorly to criticism and feedback, and blame others for their failures (Delbecq, 2001; Rosenthal and Pittinsky, 2006). However, they can also be charming and charismatic and may be well liked, at least initially (Back, Schmukle, and Egloff, 2010). Given the centrality of making a connection to followers in most conceptualization and definitions of leadership, it is easy to see that the DT would be a detriment to leaders. Leadership and social exchange require a fair and reciprocal give and take, mutual adherence to rules, respect for obligations, and commitment to others, all of which are lacking from the DT (Boyle et al., 2012).

Barbara Kellerman, the director of the Center for Public Leadership at Harvard University, suggests that we can learn as much from bad leaders as we can from good ones (2004). While we do not have clear list of characteristics that make a leader effective, we do know what ineffective leaders, those who fail and are derailed, do. Not surprisingly, many of the factors relate to the DT. A recent book about such failures (Gedmin, 2013) along with research by the Center for Creative Leadership (McCall and Lombardo, 1983), and many anecdotal accounts show clear patterns. Excessive greed, incompetence, rigidity, isolation from others, and lack of caring for others are just some of the characteristics of bad leaders. Others include not meeting objectives, poor interpersonal skills, hubris, stubbornness, and unethical behaviors. Lack of people skills and the inability to manage relationships are central causes of failure. Leaders who are good with followers and other constituents face a better chance of success. Pam Alexander, the CEO of Ogilvy Public Relations Worldwide, a public relations firm that concentrates on building relationships, states, "To build trust, invest in your relationships constantly. Don't sweat the ROI; help people, whether or not they can return the favor. Connect them to appropriate opportunities whenever you can" (Canabou and Overholt, 2001: 98–102).

THE LEADERSHIP QUESTION—REVISITED

How did your list match with the characteristics we reviewed? There is no one trait, or a set, that matters more although some can be very destructive. Given that leadership is about others and about connecting with followers to help them achieve goals, any characteristic that helps the leader make a connection with others is likely to be desirable for leadership. The key is self-awareness, building on existing strengths, and addressing areas of weakness through either personal development or through organizational support, such as other coworkers and pairing up with leaders with complementary characteristics.

USING INDIVIDUAL CHARACTERISTICS

Each of the preceding individual characteristics and traits plays a role in how leaders interact with others or make decisions. Any one trait alone, or even a combination, cannot explain or predict leadership effectiveness. These characteristics can be useful tools for self-awareness and understanding and can be used as guides for leadership development. The various individual characteristics presented in this chapter do not allow us to develop a clear leadership profile. But we do know that individual difference characteristics do affect leader behavior. The different traits discussed in this chapter are generally independent from one another. In other words, an individual might be proactive, a Type B, a high SM, and a narcissist. Although certain combinations are intuitively more likely to occur, each provides a unique perspective. Despite the validity of the constructs presented, it is important to limit their use for self-awareness and for the purpose for which they were developed. They are not selection tools and should not be used for promotional or other job-related decisions. They can help you develop self-awareness of your strengths and identify areas that you need to develop.

Summary and Conclusions

This chapter presents the current thinking on the role of individual characteristics in leadership effectiveness and identifies several individual differences and personality characteristics that affect a leader's style and approach. Although these individual differences do not dictate behavior, they establish a zone of comfort for certain behaviors and actions. Values are long-lasting beliefs about what is worthwhile. They are strongly influenced by culture and are one of the determinants of ethical conduct. Intelligence is one of the abilities that most affects leadership. On the one hand, even though being intelligent is related to leadership

to some extent, it is not a sufficient factor to predict effectiveness. On the other hand, research suggests that the concepts of emotional and social intelligence, which focuses on interpersonal rather than cognitive abilities, may link to leadership emergence effectiveness. Creativity is another ability that might play a role in leadership effectiveness, especially in situations that require novel approaches.

One of the most reliable measures of personality is the Big Five. Although the conscientiousness and extraversion dimensions in the Big Five show some links to work-related behavior, the traits are not linked directly to leadership. Several other individual traits do link to leadership. Proactiveness is an indicator of the degree to which individuals identify opportunities, take initiative and remove obstacles. Proactive people to be more satisfied with their work and career and more likely to initiate change, factors that may help leadership. Type A behavior focuses on the need for control as demonstrated through a person's time urgency, competitiveness, polyphasic behaviors, and hostility. The Type A's need for control makes it difficult to delegate tasks and pushes the individual toward short-term focus and selection of strategies that maximize control. Another relevant personality trait, self-monitoring, is the degree to which individuals read and use situational cues to adjust their behavior. High self-monitors possess a degree of flexibility that might be helpful in leadership situations. The Dark Triad (DT), which consists of Machiavellianism, and subclinical narcissism and psychopathy, describes a self-promoting, disagreeable, and emotionally cold pattern of traits and behaviors that are contrary to the emotional connection and fair and honest exchange that is essential to effective leadership.

All the concepts discussed in this chapter allow for better self-understanding and awareness, but none is a measure of leadership style and should not be used for personnel decisions.

Review and Discussion Questions

1. What is the impact of individual characteristics on behavior?
2. In what way do demographic characteristics affect the behavior of leaders?
3. How do emotional intelligence and general intelligence affect leadership?
4. What role does creativity play in leadership?
5. What are the implications of Type A characteristics for leadership styles? Differentiate Type A from key personality traits.
6. In your opinion (or based on your experience), do certain characteristics and traits have a greater impact than others on a person's leadership style? Explain your answer.
7. What are the limitations of the personality approach presented in this chapter, and how should the information about personal characteristics be used in leadership?
8. Why are Dark Triad (DT) characteristics tolerated or even encouraged in some organizations?

Leadership Challenge: Using Psychological Testing

Organizations are relying increasingly on psychological tests to select, evaluate, promote, and develop their employees and managers. Although many of the tests are reliable and valid, many others are not. In addition, tests developed in one culture do not always apply or have predictive validity in other cultures. However, such tests do provide a seemingly quick and efficient way to get to know people better.

As a department manager, you are faced with the selection of a new team of 10 members to run the marketing research and advertising campaign for a new product. The ideal employee profile includes intelligence, creativity, assertiveness, competitiveness, ability to persuade others and negotiate well, and ability to work with a team. Your human resources department conducted extensive testing of 50 inside and outside applicants for the new team. As you review the candidates' files, you notice that the majority of candidates who fit the profile best are young, Caucasian males; whereas women and minorities tend to have low scores, particularly on assertiveness and competitiveness.

1. How much weight do you give the psychological tests? What factors do you need to consider?
2. Who do you select for the team?

Exercise 4-1 Your Ideal Organization

This exercise is designed to help understand the way different individuals perceive and define organizations.

Part I: Individual Description

Think of working in the organization of your dreams. What would it look like? How would it be organized? How would people interact? Your assignment in this part of the exercise is to provide a description of your ideal organization. In doing so, consider the following organizational characteristics and elements.

1. What industry would it be?

2. What is the mission of your ideal organization?

3. What is the culture? What are the basic assumptions? What are the behavioral norms? Who are the heroes? How do people interact?

4. How would people be organized? What is the structure? Consider issues of centralization, hierarchy, formalization, specialization, span of control, departmentation, and so on.

5. What is the role of the leader? What is the role of followers?

6. Describe the physical location, office spaces, office decor, and so on.

7. Consider issues such as dress code, work schedules, and others that you think are important in describing your ideal organization.

Part II: Group Work

Your instructor will assign you to a group and provide you with further instructions.

Self-Assessment 4-1: Value Systems

Rank the values in each of the two categories from one (most important to you) to five (least important to you).

Rank	Instrumental Values	Rank	Terminal Values
_____	Ambition and hard work	_____	Contribution and a sense of accomplishment
_____	Honesty and integrity	_____	Happiness
_____	Love and affection	_____	Leisurely life
_____	Obedience and duty	_____	Wisdom and maturity
_____	Independence and self-sufficiency	_____	Individual dignity
_____	Humility	_____	Justice and fairness
_____	Doing good to others (Golden rule)	_____	Spiritual salvation

Scoring Key: The values that you rank highest in each group are the ones that are most important to you. Consider whether your actions, career choices, and so forth are consistent with your values.

Sources: Anderson, C. "Values-based management," *Academy of Management Executive* 11, no. 4 (1997): 25–46; Rokeach, M. *Beliefs, Attitudes, and Values* (San Francisco: Jossey-Bass, 1968).

Self-Assessment 4-2: Emotional Intelligence

Indicate whether each of the following statements is true or false for you.

Self-Awareness

_____ 1. I am aware of how I feel and why.
_____ 2. I understand how my feelings affect my behavior and my performance.
_____ 3. I have a good idea of my personal strengths and weaknesses.
_____ 4. I analyze things that happen to me and reflect on what happened.
_____ 5. I am open to feedback from others.
_____ 6. I look for opportunities to learn more about myself.
_____ 7. I put my mistakes in perspective.
_____ 8. I maintain a sense of humor and can laugh about my mistakes.

Managing Emotions and Self-Regulation

_____ 9. I can stay calm in times of crisis.
_____ 10. I think clearly and stay focused when under pressure.
_____ 11. I show integrity in all my actions.
_____ 12. People can depend on my word.
_____ 13. I readily admit my mistakes.
_____ 14. I confront the unethical actions of others.
_____ 15. I stand for what I believe in.
_____ 16. I handle change well and stay the course.
_____ 17. I can be flexible when facing obstacles.

Self-Motivation

_____ 18. I set challenging goals.
_____ 19. I take reasonable and measured risks to achieve my goals.
_____ 20. I am results oriented.
_____ 21. I look for information on how to achieve my goals and improve my performance.
_____ 22. I go above and beyond what is simply required of me.
_____ 23. I am always looking for opportunities to do new things.
_____ 24. I maintain a positive attitude even when I face obstacles and setbacks.
_____ 25. I focus on success rather than failure.
_____ 26. I don't take failure personally or blame myself too much.

Empathy for Others

_____ 27. I pay attention to how others feel and react.
_____ 28. I can see someone else's point of view, even when I don't agree with them.
_____ 29. I am sensitive to other people.
_____ 30. I offer feedback and try to help others achieve their goals.
_____ 31. I recognize and reward others for their accomplishments.
_____ 32. I am available to coach and mentor people.
_____ 33. I respect people from varied backgrounds.
_____ 34. I relate well to people who are different from me.
_____ 35. I challenge intolerance, bias, and discrimination in others.

Social Skills

_____ 36. I am skilled at persuading others.
_____ 37. I can communicate clearly and effectively.

_____ 38. I am a good listener.

_____ 39. I can accept bad as well as good news.

_____ 40. I can share my vision with others and inspire them to follow my lead.

_____ 41. I lead by example.

_____ 42. I challenge the status quo when necessary.

_____ 43. I can handle difficult people tactfully.

_____ 44. I encourage open and professional discussions when there are disagreements.

_____ 45. I look for win-win solutions.

_____ 46. I build and maintain relationships with others.

_____ 47. I help maintain a positive climate at work.

_____ 48. I model team qualities such as respect, helpfulness, and cooperation.

_____ 49. I encourage participation from everyone when I work in teams.

_____ 50. I understand political forces that operate in organizations.

Scoring Key: For each of the 50 items, give yourself a 1 if you marked "true" and 0 if you marked "false." Consider your total for each of the subscales and your overall total score:

Self-awareness:	_____	out of 8
Managing emotions and self-regulation:	_____	out of 9
Self-motivation:	_____	out of 9
Empathy for others:	_____	out of 9
Social skills:	_____	out of 15
Overall total:	_____	out of 50

Those with higher scores in each category, and overall, demonstrate more of the characteristics associated with high emotional intelligence. Some things you can keep in mind as you focus on developing your EQ:

- Keep a journal to track your behavior and progress.
- Seek help from friends, coworkers, and mentors.
- Work on controlling your temper and your moods; stay composed, positive, and tactful when facing difficult situations.
- Stay true to your words and commitments.
- Build relationships and a wide network.
- Practice active listening and pay attention to those around you.

Sources: Based on information in Goleman, D. *Working with Emotional Intelligence* (New York: Bantam Books, 1998); MOSAIC competencies for professional and administrative occupations (U.S. Office of Personnel Management); Rosier, R. H. (ed.), *The Competency Model Handbook*, Volumes One and Two (Boston: Linkage, 1994; 1995).

Self-Assessment 4-3: Proactivity

Using the scale below, indicate the extent to which each of the following statements describes you.

	Not at all like me	Not like me	Sounds like me	Sounds a lot like me
1. I am always looking for new opportunities.	1	2	3	4
2. I believe in leaving well enough alone.	1	2	3	4
3. Whenever I can, I take initiative in school or work projects.	1	2	3	4
4. I have a "can-do" approach.	1	2	3	4
5. I see change as an opportunity.	1	2	3	4
6. I focus on making things happen.	1	2	3	4
7. When I see that something works, I would rather leave it alone.	1	2	3	4
8. I like to advocate for others whenever I can.	1	2	3	4
9. Once I set my mind to do something, it gets done.	1	2	3	4
10. I see opportunity where many others see problems.	1	2	3	4
			Total	_____

Scoring Key: Reverse score items number 2 and 7 (1 = 4, 2= 3, 3 =2, 4 = 1), then add up your scores for the 10 items. The possible scores range from 10 to 40. If you have scored between 40 and 30, you have many of the characteristics of proactive people; if your score is between 10 and 20, you are less proactive. Scores in the middle indicate a moderate amount of proactiveness. Review each of the items to identify areas of strength.

Sources: Based on information in Becherer and Maurer, 1999; Crant, 2000; and Parker, Bindl, and Strauss, 2010.

Self-Assessment 4-4: Type A

Indicate whether each of the following items is true or false for you.

_____ 1. I am always in a hurry.

_____ 2. I have list of things I have to achieve on a daily or weekly basis.

_____ 3. I tend to take one problem or task at a time, finish, and then move to the next one.

_____ 4. I tend to take a break or quit when I get tired.

_____ 5. I am always doing several things at once both at work and in my personal life.

_____ 6. People who know me would describe my temper as hot and fiery.

_____ 7. I enjoy competitive activities.

_____ 8. I tend to be relaxed and easygoing.

_____ 9. Many things are more important to me than my job.

_____ 10. I really enjoy winning both at work and at play.

_____ 11. I tend to rush people along or finish their sentences for them when they are taking too long.

_____ 12. I enjoy "doing nothing" and just hanging out.

Scoring Key: Type A individuals tend to answer questions 1, 2, 5, 6, 7, 10, and 11 as true and questions 3, 4, 8, 9, and 12 as false. Type B individuals tend to answer in the reverse (1, 2, 5, etc. as false and 3, 4, etc. as true and so forth).

Self-Assessment 4-5: Self-Monitoring

Indicate the degree to which you think the following statements are true or false by writing the appropriate number. For example, if a statement is always true, you should write 5 next to that statement.

5 = Certainly always true

4 = Generally true

3 = Somewhat true, but with exceptions

2 = Somewhat false, but with exceptions

1 = Generally false

0 = Certainly always false

_____   1.   In social situations, I have the ability to alter my behavior if I feel that something else is called for.

_____   2.   I am often able to read people's true emotions correctly through their eyes.

_____   3.   I have the ability to control the way I come across to people, depending on the impression I wish to give them.

_____   4.   In conversations, I am sensitive to even the slightest change in the facial expression of the person I'm conversing with.

_____   5.   My powers of intuition are quite good when it comes to understanding others' emotions and motives.

_____   6.   I can usually tell when others consider a joke in bad taste, even though they may laugh convincingly.

_____   7.   I feel that the image I am portraying isn't working. I can readily change it to something that does.

_____   8.   I can usually tell when I've said something inappropriate by reading the listener's eyes.

_____   9.   I have trouble changing my behavior to suit different people and different situations.

_____ 10.   I have found that I can adjust my behavior to meet the requirements of any situation I find myself in.

_____ 11.   If someone is lying to me, I usually know it at once from the person's manner or expression.

_____ 12.   Even when it might be to my advantage, I have difficulty putting up a good front.

_____ 13.   Once I know what the situation calls for, it's easy for me to regulate my actions accordingly.

Scoring Key: To obtain your score, add up the numbers written, except reverse the scores for questions 9 and 12. On 9 and 12, 5 becomes 0, 4 becomes 1, and so forth. High self-monitors are defined as those with score of approximately 53 or higher.

Source: Lennox R. D., and Wolfe, R. N. "Revision of the self-monitoring scale," *Journal of Personality and Social Psychology*, June 1984: 1361. Copyright by the American Psychological Association. Reprinted with permission.

Self-Assessment 4-6: Narcissism

For each of the following statements, indicate the degree to which you think each describes you by writing the appropriate number. For example, if a statement fits you well and sounds a lot like you, you would write 4.

1 = Does not sound like me at all/does not fit me at all

2 = Does not sound like me

3 = Sounds like me

4 = Sounds a lot like me/fits me very well

_____ 1. I see myself as a good leader.

_____ 2. I know that I am good because everyone tells me so.

_____ 3. I can usually talk my way out of anything.

_____ 4. Everybody likes to hear my stories.

_____ 5. I expect a great from other people.

_____ 6. I am assertive.

_____ 7. I like to display my body.

_____ 8. I find it easy to manipulate other people to get what I want.

_____ 9. I don't need anyone to help me get things done.

_____ 10. I insist on getting the respect I deserve.

_____ 11. I like having authority over other people.

_____ 12. I enjoy showing off.

_____ 13. I can read people like a book.

_____ 14. I always know what I am doing.

_____ 15. I will not be satisfied until I get all that I deserve.

_____ 16. People always seem to recognize my authority.

_____ 17. I enjoy being the center of attention.

_____ 18. I can make anybody believe anything.

_____ 19. I seem to be better at most things than other people.

_____ 20. I get upset when people don't notice me or recognize my accomplishments.

_____ 21. I enjoy being in charge and telling people what to do.

_____ 22. I like to be complimented.

_____ 23. I can get my way in most situations.

_____ 24. I think I am a special person.

_____ 25. I deserve more than the average person because I am better than most people.

_____ 26. I have a natural talent for leadership.

_____ 27. I like to look at myself in the mirror.

_____ 28. I know how to get others to do what I want.

_____ 29. The world would be a better place if I was in charge.

_____ 30. I am going to be a great person.

Scoring Key:

Desire for power and leadership (L): Add up scores for items: 1, 6, 11, 16, 21, and 26:

Total: _____

Need for admiration and self-admiration (SA): Add up scores for items: 2, 7, 12, 17, 22, and 27.

Total: _____

Exploitiveness (EX): Add up scores for items: 3, 8, 13, 18, 23, and 28.

Total: _____

Arrogance and a sense of superiority (A): Add up scores for items: 4, 9, 14, 19, 24, and 29.

Total: _____

Sense of entitlement (ET): Add up scores for items: 5, 10, 15, 20, 25, and 30.

Total: _____

Add up the total for the five subscales: (30 lowest to 120 highest possible score).

Interpreting Your Score

The five subscales are the key factors in narcissism. The highest possible total in each subscale is 24, with highest possible total score of 120. The higher your scores, the more narcissistic characteristics you have. Some degree of narcissism is associated with healthy self-esteem and effective leadership.

Sources: Based on Emmons, 1987; Raskin and Terry, 1988; Rosenthal and Pittinsky, 2006.

LEADERSHIP IN ACTION

ZHANG XIN: THE HUMBLE CHINESE BILLIONAIRE

Close to half of the world's self-made female billionaires are Chinese (Forbes, 2013). This does not come as a surprise to Zhang Xin, who ranks fifth in that list. She believes: "China is so entrepreneurial…there are no glass ceilings" (Financial Times, 2011). "We all grew up with parents who both worked for equal pay. There was no such thing as a lady of leisure" (Foster, 2010).

Zhang's story is not unusual for her generation. Born to well-educated parents who were forced to work in the fields during Mao's revolution, Zhang is not a stranger to hardship and hard work. While working in factories and living in poverty with her mother in Hong Kong, she saved enough to buy a ticket to the United Kingdom where she attended Cambridge University. Her intelligence, hard work and perseverance landed her a job with Goldman Sachs. However, while quickly rising in the organization, she did not feel that she fit in: "I think investment banking environment was very competitive and cutthroat. I was always looking for opportunities to leave" (Stahl, 2013). She returned to China and married a budding entrepreneur, Pan Yishi, after a four-day courtship, and together they founded Soho China, the largest commercial real estate company in China. After a short stint as a stay-at-home mom to raise her two sons, Zhang quickly returned to the company to lead its international efforts.

Even with all her wealth, Zhang retains the values of thrift and humility that she learned as a child. She still does not fly first-class—"It's not about affordability, it's about conscience," she says – because she thinks about the hardships her family endured (Foster, 2013). Being named as one of the richest people in the world makes her "cringe," a feeling she also attributes to her upbringing. She wanted her 14-year-old son to work at McDonald's or KFC, and she tries to raise her children as normally as possible (Chiou, 2013). If being grounded and unpretentious are part of her, so are hard work and initiative. "I don't do evening business dinners and I don't do weekends" (Foster, 2013). She believes in cooperation. Talking about the challenges of working with her husband, she says: "When you have two people trying to figure out problems together, one brings out new things in the other and vice versa. Aren't human beings meant to be inspired in this way?" (Zhang, 2008).

Zhang is the first nonarchitect to be awarded the "Bold Personal Initiative" by the prestigious Italian organization *La Biennale di Venezia*, in recognition of her vision and creativity in the building of China, particularly Beijing (Li, 2006). Ingrid Li, who wrote a biography of Zhang, says: "What makes her stand out is her enormous drive to make a difference, her awareness of her strengths and competencies, and above all, her international outlook and unfailing vision for the coming of age of her homeland" (Li, 2006: xviii). Describing her vision, Zhang says "revitalizing Beijing's street culture is my job" (Li, 2006).

Questions

1. Why was working at Goldman Sachs not a suitable job for Zhang?

2. What role does culture play in who she is?

Sources: Chiou, P. 2013. "Richer than Trump or Oprah: Meet China's female property magnate," *CNN,* July 3 (accessed on July 12, 2013); Financial Times. 2011. *Women at the top.* http://www.ft.com/intl/cms/s/0/97c93ac0-0b42-11e1-ae56-00144feabdc0.html#axzz2YxgpAtmD (accessed on July 11, 2013); Forbes, 2013. "Self-made women billionaires of 2013," http://www.forbes.com/pictures/mel45ghjg/rosalia-mera/ (accessed on July 13, 2013); Foster, P. 2010. "Meet Zhang Xin, China's self-made billionaires," *Daily Telegraph,* June 27. http://www.telegraph.co.uk/news/worldnews/asia/china/7856265/Meet-Zhang-Xin-Chinas-self-made-billionairess.html (accessed on July 11, 2013); Li, I. 2006. *On the return to China.* New York: Pinto Books; Stahl, L. 2013. "China's real estate mogul," *60 minutes,* March 3, *2013.* http://www.cbsnews.com/8301-18560_162-57572175/zhang-xin-chinas-real-estate-mogul/ (accessed on July 13, 2013); Zhang, X. 2008. "The best advice I ever got," *CNN Money.* http://money.cnn.com/galleries/2008/fortune/0804/gallery.bestadvice.fortune/13.html (accessed on July 11, 2013).

Power

After studying this chapter, you will be able to:

1. Define power, its consequences, and its cultural roots.

2. Apply the different sources of individual and team power to achieve goals.

3. Explain the sources and process of power abuse, corruption, and destructive leadership and how to prevent them.

4. Analyze the changes in use of power and the development of empowerment, and explain their consequences for leadership.

THE LEADERSHIP QUESTION

Power is essential to leadership; but it can also be abused. How can leaders use power to get things done without becoming autocratic or abusive?

Power and leadership are inseparable. An integral part of the study of leadership is understanding power, how leaders use it, and its impact on leaders, followers, and organizations. Power is necessary and essential to effective leadership. Leaders need power to get things done. Without it, they cannot guide their followers to achieve their goals. Without power, things do not get done. We expect great things from our leaders and provide them with wide latitude and power to accomplish goals. They make decisions that have considerable financial and social impact on a wide range of stakeholders inside and outside their organizations. Using their power, department heads, CEOs, and city mayors implement strategies to achieve organizational goals. They influence those around them to take needed action, and they promote, hire, and fire their employees. None of these actions would be possible without power. Along with the power granted to leaders comes great privilege. In addition to high salaries and other financial incentives (some of the highest in the world in the case of U.S. business executives), leaders receive many benefits, such as stock options, company cars and planes, luxurious offices, generous expense accounts, and access to subsidized or free housing, just to name a few. The power and privilege are expected to encourage the leaders' sense of responsibility for the success of organizations and the well-being of followers.

We willingly grant our leaders power and privilege, even in a culture such as the United States, where power distance is relatively low. However, instances of power abuse and the development of new management philosophies such as teaming and empowerment are leading organizations to reexamine the need for centralized and concentrated power. As a result, we are changing the way we view power and how leaders use it. In addition, research concerning the potential of power to corrupt indicates the need to consider and use power with caution.

This chapter examines the various approaches to power and their implications for leadership. It presents the impact of power on leaders and followers, lists sources of power for individuals and groups, and discusses the potential detriments of excessive and concentrated power. As is the case throughout the book, we also consider the link of culture and power. Finally, the chapter analyzes current views of power and the changes in our management philosophies.

DEFINITIONS AND CONSEQUENCES

The words power, influence, and authority are often used interchangeably. In its most basic form, *power is the ability of one person to influence others or exercise control over them. Influence is the power to affect or sway the course of an action.* The two terms are almost synonymous, although influence refers to changing the course of an action or opinion. Clearly, power and influence are not exclusive to leaders and managers. Individuals at all levels inside an organization, as well as outsiders to an organization—namely, customers or suppliers—can influence the behavior and attitudes of others; they have power. *Authority is the power vested in a particular position,* such as that of a city mayor, CEO, or hospital administrator. Therefore, even though people at all levels of an organization may have power to influence others, only those holding formal positions have authority.

Consequences of Using Power

Power affects both those who exercise it and those who are subject to it. On the one hand, the person who has power changes in both positive and negative ways. On the other hand, being the target of power and influence also has consequences. Power changes people. Having the authority to influence others and being able to successfully do so transforms how one thinks about oneself and others and how one acts (see Figure 5-1). Those who have power tend to be more action oriented (Galinsky, Gruenfeld, and Magee, 2003), may show more interpersonal sensitivity toward others (Schmidt Mast, Jonas, and Hall, 2009), focus on rules rather than outcomes (Lammers and Stapel, 2009), and may become more generous (Seely Howard, Gardner, and Thompson, 2007). There may also be some negative consequences. Those with power may concentrate on retaining their power and acquiring more (Magee and Galinsky, 2008), may start believing that they are more in touch with the opinion of others than they actually are (Flynn and Wiltermuth, 2009), or may develop an addiction to power (Weidner and Purohit, 2009). A review by Magee and his colleagues (2005) provides evidence that those who are given power lose their ability to empathize with others and to see others' perspectives and that they are more likely to take credit for their followers' success. Similarly, members of majority groups with more power are more likely to negatively stereotype those in the minority (Keltner and Robinson, 1996). Another consequence

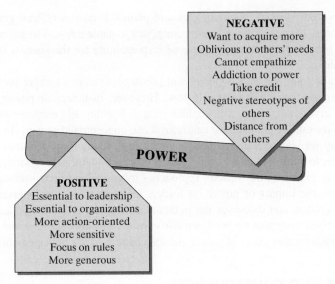

FIGURE 5-1   Impact of Power on Power Holder

of power, be it legitimate and appropriately used or excessive and abusive, is to increase the distance between leaders and followers. Power can remove leaders from the inner workings of their organizations. Such separation and distance can cause leaders to become uninformed and unrealistic and lead to unethical decision making, as we will discuss later in the chapter.

The consequences of power on followers depend to a great extent on the source and manner in which leaders use it. The three most typical reactions to use of power and attempts at influencing others are commitment, compliance, and resistance. *Commitment* happens when followers welcome the influence process and accept it as reasonable and legitimate. Consider the employees at Zingerman's Community of Business (ZCoB), a $45 million group of seven food-related businesses built around a delicatessen and a highly successful human resource training company, headquartered in Ann Arbor, Michigan (Zingerman's, 2013). The company was named one of the world's most democratic workplaces (WorldBlu, 2007); its management practices and food products continue to draw much praise. The founders, Ari Weinzweig and Paul Saginaw, pride themselves on being close to their community and customers, offering exceptional quality and building strong employee team spirit (Burlingham, 2003). In growing their business, they look for people who work with passion and take ownership. Weinzweig explains, "We wanted people who had vision of their own. Otherwise whatever we did would be mediocre" (Burlingham, 2003: 70). Todd Wickstrom, one of ZCoB's managing partners, who gave up his own business to join the company, says, "I would have come in as a dishwasher to be in this environment. Working here has never felt like a job to me. I'm constantly learning about managing, about food, and about myself" (66).

Another potential reaction to power is *compliance*. In this case, although followers accept the influence process and go along with the request, they do not feel any personal acceptance or deep commitment to carry out the order. Subordinates go along with their boss simply because they are supposed to. An example would be the imposition of unpopular new rules by a school administrator. Because of the administrator's authority, the faculty and staff are required to implement the rules. They, however, do so without any personal commitment; they simply comply.

The third possible reaction to power is *resistance*. The target in this case does not agree with the attempt at influence and either actively or passively resists it. Examples of resistance to a leader's authority abound in our institutions. The most dramatic ones occur in the labor–management disputes, when employees who typically either accept or comply with management's requests refuse to do so and take overt or covert action against management. The 2012–2013 National Hockey League lockout and the 2011 NBA dispute in the United States represent such overt action.

As a general rule, a leader's power increases when employees are personally committed and accept the leader's ideas and decisions, as is the case in ZCoB. Based on Fiedler's Contingency Theory that we reviewed in Chapter 3, power based on simple compliance does not really increase the leader's power. Similarly, some research shows that managers who lead with a firm hand may actually encourage deviant behaviors in their employees (Litzky, Eddleston, and Kidder, 2006). Despite much evidence supporting this assertion, leaders may come to rely excessively on compliance because it is easier and quicker to simply order people to do something rather than persuade them that they should do it. As you will read in this chapter, reliance on compliance alone can lead to dire consequences.

Distribution of Power

Traditional organizations typically concentrate power in a few positions. Authority is vested in formal titles and in managers, and all others are given limited power to make decisions. Their role is primarily implementing the leaders' decisions. Despite the vast amount of publicity about the use of empowerment and teams and their potential benefits, not many organizations around the world rely on such methods. Democracy, power sharing, and trust are even less common in business and other types of organizations than they are in political systems, despite research support for its benefits (Deutsch Salaman and Robinson, 2008; Harrison and Freeman, 2004). Interestingly, even before empowerment and teaming became a business trend in the late 1980s, research about the effect of the distribution of power in organizations suggested that concentrated power can be detrimental to organizational performance (Tannenbaum and Cooke, 1974). The more equal the power distribution is throughout the organization, the higher the performance of the organization. At the other extreme, much research indicates that being powerless has many negative consequences for both the individual and the organization (e.g., Bunker and Ball, 2009; Sweeney, 2007). When individuals feel powerless, they are likely to become resentful, may become passive-aggressive, and may even retaliate. Overall, research points to the need to distribute power as evenly as possible within organizations.

Power and Culture

Culture at the national, group, and even organizational level impacts our perception and use of power. For example, employees in the United States respond well to managers they like, but Bulgarian employees follow directions when their managers are vested with legitimate power or authority (Rahim et al., 2000). Nancy McKinstry, CEO of Wolters Kluwer, has learned that people in different countries react differently to their leaders. According to her, in the Netherlands you must "… invest a lot of time upfront to explain what you're trying to accomplish, get people's feedback, then when they do say yes, the time to implementation is really fast" (Bryant, 2009a). Other research suggests that because of cultural factors, delegation and power sharing may not be as effective in some Middle Eastern cultures (Pellegrini and Scandura, 2006).

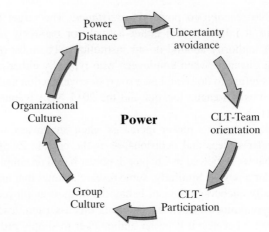

FIGURE 5-2   Culture and Power

Several cultural factors impact power (see Figure 5-2). First is power distance. For example, based on research we reviewed in Chapter 2 regarding different cultural values, the United States tends to be a low- to medium-power distance culture. The differential of power between the highest and lowest levels of the organization is not great (although the salary differential is one of the highest in the world). The low-power distance allows employees in the United States, and in other low-power distance cultures such as Australia, to call their bosses by their first name, interact with them freely, and express their disagreement with them. In such cultures, employees do not expect their managers and leaders to know all the answers and accept the fact that leaders, too, can make mistakes (Adler, 1991; Laurent, 1983). Low-power distance further facilitates the implementation of participative management and other power-sharing management techniques. In cultures with high-power distance, such as Thailand and Russia, employees have limited expectations for participation in decision making and assume leaders to be somewhat infallible (e.g., House et al., 2004; Pellegrini and Scandura, 2006).

Uncertainty avoidance is another cultural factor that may affect power. French, Italians, and Germans are relatively high on uncertainty avoidance, which may lead them to expect their managers to provide answers to questions and problems (Laurent, 1983). The Eiffel Tower model of organizational culture, used by the French as presented by Trompenaars, for example, concentrates power at the top of the organization. French managers report discomfort at not knowing who their boss is. They also place less emphasis on delegation of responsibility (Harris, Moran, and Moran, 2004). The need for a clear hierarchy is likely to make it more difficult for the French than for Swedes or North Americans to function in a leaderless, self-managed, team environment. In other countries such as Japan and Indonesia, people value clear hierarchy and authority. For example, Mexican workers may be less comfortable with taking responsibility for problem solving (Randolph and Sashkin, 2002). The Mexican culture, with a family type of organization culture, its strong paternalistic tradition, and the presence of the machismo principle, expects leaders to be strong, decisive, and powerful. Leaders, like powerful fathers, must provide answers, support the family, and discipline members who stray (Teagarden, Butler, and Von Glinow, 1992). The GLOBE CLTs (culturally endorsed leadership theory; see Chapter 2) further influence how power is viewed and used in organizations. Countries where team orientation and participation are valued, for example in the Nordic and Anglo clusters, power is distributed more evenly, employees expect to contribute to decisions, and consider such inclusion to be part of effective leadership.

Group and organizational culture further impact how people perceive and implement power. As we discussed in Chapter 2, research indicates that women are more participative than men. Additionally women are often perceived as having less power and, as a result, are limited in regards to the styles and tools they can use to influence their followers. Organizational culture also influences how leaders use power. In some organizations, power is centralized; in others, it is distributed more broadly. As we discussed earlier, Zingerman is reputed for being democratic and open. D.L Rogers Corp, presented in Chapter 3, is at the other extreme with the leader holding a great deal of power.

Understanding the culture, at any level, can help leaders use power appropriately and thereby be able to influence their followers. One aspect of appropriately using power is selecting a source of power, a topic discussed in the next section.

SOURCES OF POWER

Alan Greenspan, who was the chairman of the U.S. Federal Reserve (Fed) from 1987 to 2006 for an unprecedented 19 years, was considered one of the most powerful executives in the United States (Bligh and Hess, 2007). As chairman, Greenspan was able to set policies to sustain low to moderate economic growth, ensuring that the U.S. economy expanded but did not overheat, thereby avoiding high inflation. In a 1996 survey of 1,000 CEOs of the largest U.S. companies, 96 percent wanted him to be reappointed as the leader of the Fed (Walsh, 1996). Greenspan held considerable power with which to chart the course of the U.S. and world economies. He is a well-known economist, is a consummate relationship builder, and is described as low key and down to earth. He stated once that he learned to "mumble with great incoherence" (Church, 1997). Consider that Greenspan held no executive power, could not implement a single decision, and employed only a small staff. Nevertheless, he was powerful and had considerable authority. He was able to convince presidents, the Congress, other members of the Fed board, and the financial markets that his policies were devoid of politics and in the best interests of the United States. Where did Greenspan get his power? He relied on individual and organizational sources of power.

Sources of Power Related to Individuals

One of the most widely used approaches to understanding the sources of power comes from the classic research by French and Raven (1968). They propose five sources of power vested in the individual: legitimate power, reward power, coercive power, expert power, and referent power (see Table 5-1 for a summary). The first three sources of individual power—legitimate, reward, and coercive—are position powers. Although they are vested in individuals, the individuals' access to them depends on the position they hold. In the case of legitimate power, most managerial or even supervisory titles in organizations provide the ability to influence others. People with formal titles also typically have access to both rewards and punishments. They can give raises and assign perks, and demote or fire. All three of these sources of individual power depend on the organization that grants them, not the person who holds them. Once the access to title, rewards, or punishment is taken away by the organization, a leader or individual relying on such sources loses power.

The last two sources of power—expert and referent—are more personal; they are based on who the person is rather than the position he holds. Access to these two sources of power does not depend solely on the organization. A person does not need to have a formal title to

TABLE 5-1	French and Raven's Sources of Individual Power
Legitimate power	Based on a person holding a formal position. Others comply because they accept the legitimacy of the position of the power holder.
Reward power	Based on a person's access to rewards. Others comply because they want the rewards the power holder can offer.
Coercive power	Based on a person's ability to punish. Others comply because they fear punishment.
Expert power	Based on a person's expertise, competence, and information in a certain area. Others comply because they believe in the power holder's knowledge and competence.
Referent power	Based on a person's attractiveness to and friendship with others. Others comply because they respect and like the power holder.

be an expert. Additionally, he or she can be respected and liked by others, which provides power to influence others. In the case of expert power, people may influence others because of special expertise, knowledge, information, or skills that others need. We listen to the experts, follow their advice, and accept their recommendations. Alan Greenspan provides an excellent example of expert power. His knowledge, expertise, and an established record of success were the bases of his power. Although Greenspan also held legitimate power, in many other cases those with expert power might not hold official titles or have any legitimate power. Referent power operates in much the same way. Individuals with referent power can influence others because they are liked and respected. As with expert power, this power does not depend on the position or the organization. The person's power stems from being a role model for others. Greenspan was well liked for his ability to work with others. Employees at ZCoB respect Weinzweig and Saginaw for their vision and leadership style. The respect and friendship come on top of other considerable sources of power. Because these two sources of power are based on the person, not the position, they cannot be taken away and often provide the power holder with more influence.

Using different sources of individual power has different impact on followers (see Figure 5-3). When a legitimate authority source asks them to, people comply with requests and implement decisions (Yukl and Falbe, 1991). Similarly, we comply to receive rewards or avoid punishment. In the case of coercive power, repeated use may even lead people to resist either openly or passively. Conversely, when an expert or someone we admire makes a request, we will not only comply, we are likely to be committed to the decision. The use of expert and referent powers has been found to be related to higher follower satisfaction and performance (Yukl and Falbe, 1991). Given these possible reactions, it is critical for leaders to use all different sources of power and rely more heavily on the personal sources. If leaders overuse positional power, they are unlikely to obtain the commitment and buy-in that are necessary to pursue many goals in organizations.

USING INDIVIDUAL SOURCES OF POWER   Although power and influence are closely related, some research indicates that the two can be treated as separate concepts. A leader with power might not be able to influence subordinates' behaviors, or influence can occur without a specific source of power. Several researchers, most notably Kipnis and his colleagues (Kipnis, Schmidt,

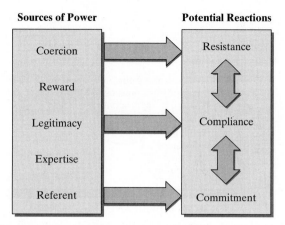

FIGURE 5-3 Potential Reactions to Individual Sources of Power

and Wilkinson, 1980) and Yukl along with several others (e.g., Yukl and Falbe, 1990, 1991), identified various influence tactics. The result of their work is the classification of influence tactics into nine categories (Table 5-2). Each tactic relies on one or more of the sources of power related to the individual. Each is appropriate in different situations and carries the potential for leading to commitment on the part of the person being influenced. For example, personal appeal relies on referent power and tends to be appropriate when used with colleagues; it is not likely to lead to a high degree of commitment. Inspirational appeal, which also relies on referent power, leads to high commitment. Rational persuasion relies on expert power and is appropriate to use when trying to influence superiors. The commitment tends to be moderate.

Although leaders must rely on all sources of power to guide and influence their followers and others in their organization, they often have to adjust how they use power, depending on

TABLE 5-2	Using Power: Influence Tactics and Their Consequences		
Influence Tactic	**Power Source**	**Appropriate to Use With...**	**Effectiveness and Commitment**
Rational persuasion	Expert and access to information	Supervisors	Moderate
Inspirational appeal	Referent	Subordinates and colleagues	High
Consultation	All	Subordinates and colleagues	High
Ingratiation	Referent	All levels	Moderate
Personal appeal	Referent	Colleagues	Moderate
Exchange	Reward and information	Subordinates and colleagues	Moderate
Coalition building	All	Subordinates and colleagues	Low
Legitimate tactics	Legitimate	Subordinates and colleagues	Low
Pressure	Coercive	Subordinates	Low

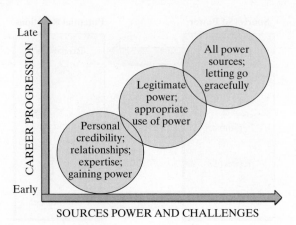

FIGURE 5-4   Power Sources and Career Stage

the context and throughout their career. For example, if the leader fits well with the organization, her influence is likely to increase (Anderson, Spataro, and Flynn, 2008). J. P. Kotter, a well-respected researcher on issues of leadership and managerial power, suggests that in the early stages of managers' careers, they must develop an adequate base of power (Kotter, 1985; Figure 5-4). Managers can be effective by relying on the various bases of personal power. In particular, young leaders must develop a broad network of interpersonal relationships and establish credibility through information and expertise. Other means involve becoming visible by volunteering for challenging and high-visibility projects.

The demonstration of competence and skills is central to the development of power in the early stages of a leader's career. In midcareer, most successful leaders already possess some degree of legitimacy through formal titles, along with other status symbols that demonstrate their power. Their early efforts are likely to have established their credibility and competence within a well-developed network of loyal subordinates, peers, and bosses (Kotter, 1985). Therefore, leaders in midcareer stage already hold considerable power. The challenge at this point is to use the accumulated power wisely and ethically to achieve organizational and personal goals.

Finally, leaders during the late-career stage must learn to let go of power gracefully. By the time they reach retirement age, successful leaders in thriving U.S. public and private organizations enjoy considerable power and influence. To use power well at this career stage, a leader needs to plan for its orderly transmission to others while simultaneously finding new personal sources of power and fulfillment.

Organizational Sources of Power: Power for Teams

The differences between organizational and individual sources of power are not always obvious. The structure of an organization provides sources of power to individuals and groups over and above those listed in Table 5-1. Although individuals can also rely on organizational sources of power, these sources are particularly important for teams. Aside from the expertise of their members or having people with titles and authority as members, teams have access to power in organizations mainly because of their control of resources and other things that are essential to the organization achieving its goals. These are called *strategic contingencies* (see Table 5-3).

TABLE 5-3	**Sources of Power for Teams: Strategic Contingencies**
Coping with uncertainty	Based on the ability to reduce uncertainty for others.
Centrality	Based on being central to how the organization achieves its mission and goals.
Dependency	Based on others depending on power holder to get their work done.
Substitutability	Based on providing a unique and irreplaceable service or product to others.

Source: Based on Hickson et al. "A strategic contingencies theory of intra-organizational power," *Administrative Science Quarterly* 16(1971): 216–229.

The concept of strategic contingencies was originally developed to understand the distribution of power across departments (Hickson et al., 1971; Salancik and Pfeffer, 1977b); however, it also applies well to teams. Strategic contingencies suggest that individuals, teams, or departments gain power based on their ability to address issues that are instrumental or strategic to reaching organizational goals.

COPING WITH UNCERTAINTY   The first source of power for teams is their ability to help others cope with uncertainty. With the increased competition and constant changes in the political and economic environments, having information about the changes and alternatives for dealing with them is essential to performance. For example, the leader and members of a cross-functional team designed to provide an organization with market information regarding future products and competitors will gain considerable influence by virtue of the fact that others need that information. The team's product or service reduces uncertainty. A case in point is governmental liaison teams and lobbyists in the United States in a time of change in the health care industry. These groups acquire particular power because they help others within the organization to reduce or manage the uncertainty they face.

Teams and their leaders can reduce uncertainty through three interrelated methods. First, they can obtain information that others need through market research, polls, contact with key constituents, focus groups, or reliance on external experts. The second method—uncertainty prevention—focuses on the prediction of upcoming changes. For example, a team might research and predict the moves of competitors. Public university administrators rely on their legislative liaison team to predict the mood of the legislature regarding funding of universities. Third, a team reduces uncertainty for others through absorption. In this situation, the team takes certain steps to prevent the change from affecting other teams or departments. The university administrator with information about the legislative mood might try to forestall budget cuts through lobbying. If the cuts happen anyway, various groups within the university might undertake less painful internal budget-reduction mechanisms, such as nonreplacement of retiring employees, thereby preventing more drastic measures from being imposed by outside sources and absorbing uncertainty. Through the use of these three methods, a team and its leader can reduce uncertainty for others and thus acquire power.

CENTRALITY   Another organizational source of power is the centrality to the production or service delivery process. This factor relates to how a team's activities contribute to the mission and goals of the organization. Teams closest to the customer, for example, will gain power.

Using the university example again, a recruiting team that is responsible for enrolling new students, who are a primary source of revenue for the university, is central to the survival of the organization. In another example, the librarian team at Highsmith reports directly to the company's executives about connections that can help make important business decisions—a factor that gives its members further power (Buchanan, 1999). Another case in point is the management of diversity in organizations. As was presented in Chapter 2, one of the recommendations for the successful implementation of diversity plans in organizations involves making diversity central to the organization and its leaders. The most successful programs put the individuals and teams in charge of diversity planning and implementation in strategic positions within organizations, reporting directly to the CEO.

DEPENDENCE AND SUBSTITUTABILITY   A final structural source of power available to teams and their leaders closely resembles the reward and expert power of individuals. This source of power depends on the extent to which others need a team's expertise. If employees depend on a team to provide them with information and resources, the team's power will increase. The larger the number of departments and individuals who depend on the team, the greater the team's power will be. In addition, if the tasks performed by the team are unique and not easily provided by others in the organization and if no substitutes are available, the dependence on the team and its power increases. If the team's collective expertise is duplicated in others and its function can be performed easily by another individual or group, however, the team will lack the influence necessary to obtain needed resources and implement its ideas. For example, despite the widespread use of personal computers and information technology tools, many individuals still require considerable assistance to use technology effectively. This factor allows information technology departments, for example, to gain power and obtain resources.

Interestingly, the major complaint from teams in many organizations is their lack of power to obtain resources or implement their ideas (Nahavandi and Aranda, 1994). In the new organizational structures, team leaders often do not have any of the formal powers traditionally assigned to managers. In the best of cases, team members respect their leader because of personal relationships or expertise. These individual sources of power, however, do not translate to power in the organization. As a result, many team leaders express anger and frustration at their lack of ability to get things done. Recommendations on how to make teams more effective often include making them central to the mission of the organization, assigning them to meaningful tasks, and providing them with access to decision makers (Katzenbach and Smith, 2003; Nahavandi and Aranda, 1994).

Special Power Sources of Top Executives

Top executives in any organization, public or private, hold considerable power. One obvious source of power is the legitimacy of their position. A number of symbols establish and reinforce that legitimacy: They have impressive formal titles and separate executive offices, they eat in separate dining facilities, and they are able to maintain privacy and distance from other employees (Hardy, 1985; Pfeffer, 1981). Pictures of past executives that hang in many organizations further signal their importance. Along with the sources of power we discussed earlier, top executives have four other sources of power:

- *Distribution of resources:* Top managers, either alone or in consultation with a top management team, are responsible for the distribution of resources throughout the organization. This access to resources is a key source of power.

APPLYING WHAT YOU LEARN

Managing Power When You Are a New Manager

Moving into a managerial position is an important step in any person's career. It comes with many opportunities and challenges. The change in actual and perceived power is one thing that any new manager must handle with care. There is fine balance between no longer being "one of the guys" and overusing one's new power. Here are some guidelines:

- *Know what you know and what you don't know.* Especially in the United States and other low-power-distance cultures, no one expects you to know everything.
- *Get help* from your boss, others at your level, and your reports. Asking questions is not a sign of weakness.
- *Rely on expert and referent power.* You have the legitimate power of a title and can punish and reward others. However, don't forget that other sources are more "powerful." And don't become bossy!
- *Empathize* with your reports about how they might feel. Put yourself in their shoes; the change is hard for them as well. But that does not mean that you will do everything they want or suggest, or continue to listen

to continuous complaints. Empathy shows that you care, but it does not always mean you have to act.

- *Set up new boundaries.* What you set up and how you set them up depends on each individual and may take some time. But you have to realize that things have changed, and you can't continue all the social contact and even work interaction you have had with your reports in the same manner. You won't be able to share as much information as you did in the past or speak as freely, and you are bound to make some unpopular decisions. All these need new sets of rules for interaction.
- *Set up meetings* with your new reports individually and as a team to discuss what they are doing, get their advice for what they can do, share ideas you have, and clarify expectations. This is the first step in establishing trust in the new relationship.
- *Keep your sense of humor* and give yourself time. Like anything else, it will take time for you to learn your new role; practice and be patient.

- *Control of decision criteria:* A unique power source available to executives is the control of decision criteria (Nahavandi and Malekzadeh, 1993a; Pettigrew, 1973). By setting the mission, overall strategy, and operational goals of organizations, top executives limit other managers' and employees' actions. For example, if a city mayor runs his or her campaign on the platform of fighting crime and improving education, the city's actions and decisions during that mayor's term will be influenced by that platform. Crime reduction will be one of the major criteria used to evaluate alternatives and make decisions. For instance, funding requests for increased police training or for building a neighborhood park will be evaluated based on the crime-fighting and education values of the proposals. If the requests address the decision criteria set by the mayor, they stand a better chance of passage, relying on the mayor's weight behind them. If they do not, such proposals might not even be brought up for consideration.
- *Centrality in organization:* Another source of executive power is a top manager's centrality to the organizational structure and information flow (Astley and Sachdeva, 1984). Whether the organization is a traditional hierarchical pyramid or a web, CEOs are strategically placed for access to information and resources. Indeed, new top managers often bring

with them a group of trusted colleagues who are placed in strategic locations throughout the organization to ensure their access to information.

- *Access:* Top executives' access to all levels of the organization assists in building alliances that further enhance their power. The most obvious example is the change in personnel in Washington with the election of a new president. Similar personnel changes occur on different scales in all organizations when a new leader is selected. University presidents bring with them several top assistants and create new positions to accommodate them. Other members of the top university administration are slowly replaced with those selected by the new leader. In the private sector, the changes designed to put key people in place are even more drastic and obvious. At General Electric, the selection of Immelt (see Leading Change in Chapter 9) to succeed Jack Welch as CEO led to the turnover of several top management team members who were contenders for the position. Whether new leaders force out several individuals to make room for their own team or whether the individuals leave on their own, the outcome of the personnel shuffle is to allow new leaders' access to trustworthy people and information.

In addition to their considerable power to achieve goals and benefit their various stakeholders, the case of many recent abuses indicates that top executives are not always accountable for their actions. This lack of accountability can lead to abuse and corruption, the topics considered next.

THE DARK SIDE OF POWER: ABUSE, CORRUPTION, AND DESTRUCTIVE LEADERSHIP

The very nature of leading, whether it is a business organization or a social movement, may require some disregard for norms and the possible consequences of violating them (Magee et al., 2005). After all, we do not often select leaders so that they can keep the status quo; we expect them to be innovative and change things. Innovation often requires behaving outside the norms and disregarding some rules. However, such disregard can also carry a negative side, as evidenced by the situations at Enron, Tyco, Goldman Sachs, and as some would suggest, even the G.W. Bush administration.

Power abuse and corruption are almost synonymous. *Abuse involves taking advantage of one's power for personal gain.* It includes unethical or illegal actions, taken while in a leadership position and in an official capacity, that affect organizational outcomes, followers, and other stakeholders negatively. It entails using one's title and position improperly to exploit situations and people. *Corruption is abusing one's power to benefit oneself or another person, or getting others to do something unethical or illegal.* Whereas power abuse is, unfortunately, not always illegal, corruption is both illegal and unethical. For example, during the 2008–2010 financial crisis and the $85 billion bailout of American Insure Group (AIG) by the U.S. taxpayers, the lavish executive AIG retreat that cost $440,000 was considered an abuse of power and unethical and immoral by many, although it was legal. The company's executives bonuses were also considered inappropriate and an abuse of power, but again not illegal or acts of corruption (Elliot, 2009).

Destructive or toxic leadership, which is defined as leadership that violates the interests of the organization and the well-being of followers (Einarsen, Aasland, and Skogstad, 2007), is one aspect of abuse and corruption. By its very nature, destructive leadership involves abuse of power and of followers, although it may not always involve corruption. In some cases, destructive leader may even make positive contributions to their organization (Padilla, Hogan, and Kaiser, 2007). Many organizations and followers experience toxic leadership. Some employees suffer in silence; others leave the organization. For example, by some accounts a third of military officers considered leaving the profession because of the way a supervisor treated them (Reed and Olsen, 2010).

The potential for abuse and corruption and the privilege associated with power and leadership have come under scrutiny (Block, 1993; Larcker and Tayan, 2012; Pfeffer, 2010). Interestingly, people often have a love–hate relationship with power. Particularly, in the United States, the framers of the Constitution were wary about concentrating power in the hands of one person or one group (Cronin, 1987). Power without accountability, together with greed, are blamed for many problems ranging from illegal actions and fraud to sexual harassment, favoritism, poor decision making, and financial waste. These problems appear to be widespread.

German Siemens AG executives were accused of bribing top Argentine officials to win government contracts; U.S. Halliburon, French Technip, Japanese JGC Corp, and Dutch Snamprogetti were all accused of paying brides to Nigerian officials; Swiss Panalpia World Transport was accused of bribing officials in several countries; and the list goes on (Goozner, 2011). Anders Eldrup, former CEO of Danish company Dong Energy resigned in 2012 after revelations that he abused his power by hiring and offering lucrative packages to employees without board approval and without any real responsibilities (Stanners, 2012). Conrad Black, CEO of Hollinger International, a newspaper company, billed $2,400 in handbags and the tab for his servants to his company, earning him the title of "kleptocrat" (Chandler, 2004). The old adage "Power corrupts" appears to be true. It is not difficult to see how the considerable power and privilege we grant our leaders can cause arrogance and hubris. Lloyd Blankfein, the CEO of Goldman Sachs, one of the most successful investment banks in the world, and one of the most criticized for its role the financial crisis of 2008–2010, perceives himself as much more than a very rich and thriving CEO. He says he is "doing God's work" (Arlidge, 2009).

The following sections consider the causes, consequences, and solutions to abuse of power.

Causes and Processes

It is easy to blame the leader's narcissism or simple greed and dishonesty for power abuse, corruption, and destruction. However, the leader's characteristics are only one of the factors that allow for problems to develop. One "bad apple" is necessary, but not sufficient. The characteristics of leaders and followers and organizational factors that contribute to power abuse and corruption are summarized in Table 5-4.

LEADER CHARACTERISTICS   The research about power abuse, corruption, and destructive leadership has heavily focused on the characteristics of the leader. Several researchers (e.g., Delbecq, 2001; Kets de Vries, 1993) have identified individual characteristics of leaders that make them likely to abuse power. The research on the Dark Triad also sheds light on characteristics that may make a leader more likely to disregard rules and step outside of acceptable boundaries of behaviors. Regardless of whether these managers are "evil" (Delbecq, 2001), tyrants (Ali, 2008), psychopaths (Babiak and Hare, 2006), or simply bullies (Hodson, Roscigno, and Lopez, 2006), they are willing to use their power to achieve their personal goals rather than for the good of followers and the organization. Often bright and initially likeable and sometimes perceived as capable and action oriented, they have an inflated view of themselves and are controlling, rigid, power hungry, and ruthless. They work well with supervisors and impress them, but they are uncaring and vicious with their subordinates. Their sense of entitlement and their belief that they

TABLE 5-4	Multiple Causes of Abuse and Corruption	
Leader Characteristics and Behavior	**Follower Characteristics and Behavior**	**Organizational Factors**
• Inflated view of self	• Fear	• Organizational culture
• Arrogant and controlling	• Silence	• Separation of leaders and followers
• Rigid and inflexible	• Agreement	• Hiring practices based on personal relationships rather than objective criteria
• Sense of entitlement	• Compliance	
• Willing to use and exploit others	• Inaction	
• Lack of empathy and caring for others	• Flattery	• Short-term-oriented reward system with limited criteria
	• Submissiveness	
• Disinhibited, vicious, ruthless	• Anxiety	• Centralized organizational structure
• Overly concerned with power	• Conformity	• High uncertainty and chaos
• The Dark Triad	• Collusion	• Highly unequal power distribution

deserve special treatment (Lubin, 2002) make them comfortable with abusing their power and their followers. Their world is divided into those who agree with them and can serve their purpose, and the rest, whom they at best ignore, or at worst, view with excessive suspicion and even paranoia. Those who are on their side are supported, at least temporarily; those who are not are denigrated, ridiculed, and eventually moved out.

Unfortunately, these types of managers are often able to climb the corporate ladder because others see their self-confidence as evidence of ability (see Chapter 4 regarding the Dark Triad). Once in power, they maintain it by surrounding themselves with weak followers, ruthlessly attacking those who disagree with them and managing their superiors so that they can continue their quest for power. Classic cases of evil, or destructive, narcissistic leaders include Al Dunlap (nicknamed "Chainsaw Al"), who ruthlessly cut jobs and abused followers in one job after another until he was fired as CEO of Sunbeam Corp. Philip Agee is another case. As CEO of Morrison Knudsen (MK), he not only abused and fired employees based on personal animosity, but is also accused of using company funds for his personal gain. When he was finally fired after much manipulation of board members, the company employees cheered in the parking lot (Lubin, 2002).

FOLLOWER CHARACTERISTICS   No matter how evil and manipulative leaders are, they cannot wreck havoc and abuse others without the compliance of followers. Dissent, which is often lacking, ignored, or punished in abuse situations, is considered by some researchers to be the essence of good followership (Reed, in print). Although followers rarely consider their contribution to the power abuse and corruption process, and they are not the starting point for corruption, they do play a significant role in two interrelated ways (Bardes and Piccolo, 2010; Carsten et al., 2010). First, their silence, agreement, and compliance send a clear message to the abusive and corrupt leader that they are either right or at least likely to get away with their actions. Those who comply may be simply conforming or even colluding with the leader (Thoroughgood et al., 2012). They may be afraid or respond to what they consider legitimate authority; or they may be seeking a quid pro quo from their leader. Second, there is evidence that some followers are more susceptible to abuse . Followers who have low self-esteem or those who are anxious have been found to be more susceptible to abusive bosses (Kant et al., 2013). In either case, follower compliance signals the abusive leader that followers are weak and incompetent and may deserve to be ruled with an iron fist.

ORGANIZATIONAL FACTORS   Finally, leaders could not abuse their power and manipulate even willing followers unless the organization implicitly or openly allows for such action. In some cases, the organizational culture and practices may even encourage power abuse. The most important determinant of power abuse is the culture of an organization. What is tolerated, accepted, encouraged, and rewarded determines whether a destructive leader can survive and thrive. Creating clear physical and psychological separation between leaders and others, while further isolating leaders from followers, is one indication that leaders are special and deserve exceptional treatment. Hiring practices, the characteristics and style of upper management, and the focus on short-term financial performance, without consideration for much else, all contribute to allowing a destructive leader to operate and even flourish. The more centralized and concentrated the power and hierarchy and the more closed the communication within an organization, the less likely that power abuses will be noticed or reported, further perpetuating the abuse. Centralized structures create distance between leaders and followers, allow them to make decisions without consultation and input, and may isolate the leader from others. Closed communication networks further reinforce the isolation and prevent followers from reporting abuses of power easily. Additionally, organizations where power is concentrated in the hands of a few and organizations that face uncertainty and chaos provide fertile grounds for power abuse (Hodson et al., 2006). When power is unequal or when there is high uncertainty, and rules are unclear, abuse can take place and go unnoticed.

The Cycle of Abuse, Corruption, and Destruction

Whether it is the leader who creates a corrupt organization or the organizational culture that creates the abusive leader is difficult to establish. Rather, individual leader characteristics, follower reactions, and organizational factors all combine to create an abuse and corruption cycle depicted in Figure 5-5. The leader's growing power, real or perceived, to act without accountability and with impunity leads to followers' compliance. Whether through voluntary compliance, fear, or because of their own personal characteristics, leaders dominate, manipulate, and abuse followers, creating a self-fulfilling prophecy where more compliance ensues, providing proof to the already arrogant abuser that followers are not deserving of better treatment and not capable of meaningful contribution, further reinforcing the cycle of abuse. Even when they express disagreement, followers do so in the softest, most roundabout ways, after praising the leader's ideas and painstakingly recognizing that the leaders are correct. Most of us have witnessed or even been party to such political behaviors, which are considered essential to obtaining needed resources. The insincere flattery, however, can further feed into a potentially destructive leader's sense of self-importance and entitlement and reinforce the devaluation of followers, thereby creating a self-fulfilling prophecy.

Even though the press and the public appear to value leaders such as Meg Whitman of Hewlett Packard, who worked in a cubicle and often took commercial flights instead of flying the corporate jet (Dillon, 2004), and despite changes made in many organizations, leaders still occupy offices on separate floors, park their cars in reserved areas, eat in executive dining rooms, and spend a great deal of their time with other power holders. All these symbols of power

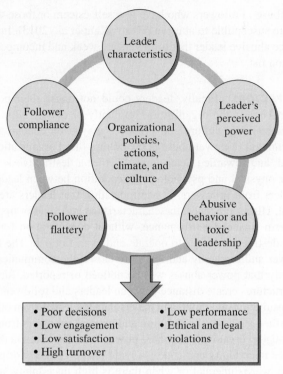

FIGURE 5-5 Power Abuse and Corruption Cycle

increase the legitimacy of leaders. The distance and separation can be justified based on the need to protect the leaders' valuable time and to allow them access to other power holders with whom they need to work to make decisions. These symbols, however, can also corrupt leaders by providing them with an overly inflated view of themselves.

An example of blatant abuse because of power without accountability is Richard Scrushy, former CEO of HealthSouth Corporation, a multibillion-dollar health-care company, who was famous for wielding tremendous power while in office. He intimidated his employees, going as far as sending them out of meetings if he did not like their clothing (Jones, 1998). He was ousted when accused of a $2.7 billion accounting fraud along with perjury, obstruction of justice, money laundering, and wire and securities fraud (Ryerson-Cruz, 2004) and was eventually sentenced to seven years in prison in 2007 (Carrns and Bauerlein, 2007). With more HealthSouth executives indicted for fraud, Scrushy's successor, Jay Grinney, CEO since 2004, states that the company was "managed from the top down" and that "those days are over" (Ryerson-Cruz, 2004).

Consequences of Abuse and Corruption

The excessive power and accompanying corruption of leaders can lead to serious consequences for an organization. Several studies show impact on organizational performance and the increase in deviant behaviors (Tepper et al., 2008; 2009). The most common consequences are poor decision making and miserable followers. Leaders' lack of relevant information and their distance from others in the organization puts them in the danger of poor decision making. Employees filter information, avoid giving bad news, and hide their mistakes, providing an overly rosy picture of the organization. As a result, leaders lose touch with their organization and its customers. Because of the compliance of followers, leaders might see their followers as dependent and incapable of autonomous behavior and decisions. Leaders then come to see themselves as the source of all events in the organization and consequently might rely less on persuasion and more on coercive methods to get followers to comply. Their style encourages followers to disengage and withdraw (Chi and Liang, 2013). A recent study of the impact of destructive leadership shows strong relationships to negative outcomes such as dislike for the leader, turnover, and counterproductive actions (Schyns and Schilling, 2013).

The development of a separate sense of morality based on all the other factors allows the leaders to easily fall into unethical decision making and actions. Such leaders come to believe that regular rules simply do not apply to them. Scrushy's actions, as well as those of many other executives who lie and steal from their company, are examples of such situations. Tyco's executives firmly believed that their outrageous salaries and bonuses were justified. The former CEO, L. Dennis Kozlowski, convicted in 2005 of misappropriation of funds, had no qualms about using and showing his power. "I worked my butt off and it was all based on my performance in Tyco's long-established pay-for-performance culture" (Maull, 2005: D5). There is little doubt that he used money from the company, but it is less clear whether he was authorized to do so. His $30 million apartment in New York City was reputed to have been paid for the company, as was a $2 million bill for his wife's birthday party (Top 10 crooked CEOs, 2009). In another example, James McDermott, Jr., former CEO of Keefe, Bruyette & Woods, was convicted of insider trading for providing secret information to his mistress about pending mergers in which his investment bank was involved. While disagreeing with his portrayal as a corrupt and arrogant executive, he stated: "I'm just an average person who's tried to work hard and to give back," a defense that played a part in the judge reducing his sentence from twenty-four to eight months. Referring to the success of the defense at convincing the judge, McDermott's attorney was overheard saying: "She bought it hook, line and sinker" (Top 10 crooked CEOs, 2009).

The power–corruption cycle, if not stopped, feeds on itself and can lead to dire consequences for any organization.

Solutions

Abuse and corruption result from the interaction of leader, follower, and organizational factors, therefore preventing them requires interventions at all three levels. Identifying individuals with a propensity for power abuse early is one obvious solution; however, it is not always possible or feasible. After all, many narcissists and psychopaths are charming and even liked initially (Back, Schmukle, and Egloff, 2010). There are no magic formulas that will prevent the rise of destructive managers and power abuses. Some solutions are presented in Table 5-5.

As organizations try to reduce, if not stop, power abuse and corruption, a clear message regarding the importance of ethical behavior and integrity is essential. The message that power abuse will not be tolerated accompanied by consistent practices demonstrating such stances are essential (Misangyi, Weaver, and Elms, 2008). Leaders who know that they will be held accountable for their actions are much more likely to consider the consequences of their actions and act thoughtfully (Rus, van Knippenberg, and Wisse, 2012). Although many mechanisms are in place to monitor the behavior of leaders in for-profit, not-for-profit, and governmental organizations, these mechanisms need to be implemented to hold leaders accountable. Maintaining checks and balances in the public sector and reinforcing the power of board of governors and directors in other organizations so that they can be independent from the leader are necessary steps toward holding

TABLE 5-5	Solutions to Corruption

- Clear message and consistency
- Accountability
- Reducing uncertainty
- Training for leaders and followers
- Protecting employees
- Open communication
- Leader involvement in day-to-day activities
- Reducing follower dependence on leader
- Empowerment
- Objective performance measures
- Involvement of outsiders
- Changing the organizational culture

leaders accountable. Organizations can further prevent abuse by reducing uncertainty whenever possible. When there are no clear rules of behavior, the leader with DT characteristics is more likely to exploit the situation and her followers (Hodson et al., 2006). Chaotic situations allow bullies to operate freely, so providing order and clear rules can address abuse and corruption.

Much research supports the effectiveness of providing ethics training to employees as a way of decreasing the occurrence of ethical violations. The same has been recommended in trying to address power abuse (Uhl-Bien and Carsten, 2007). Employees who are able to recognize abuse and know what actions may be effective in combatting it are more likely to resist their leader's abuse. In addition to training in ethics, organizations must be ready to act decisively to protect those who are abused and the employees who stand up to their abusive leaders (Hodson et al., 2006). The more followers and others are able to provide feedback both to the leader and to other powerful members of the organization, the more likely it is that destructive leaders will be detected and power abuses stopped. A recent study suggests that the presence of intranets and other technology-based communication tools encourages flexible control and empowerment equalizing power in an organization (Denton, 2007). Additionally, open communication and transparency regarding financial information further increases the leader's accountability (Welch and Welch, 2007).

The closer the leader is to the day-to-day activities of followers and to the organization's customers, the less likely is leader corruption (Block, 1993; Prendergast, 1993). In addition, the more independent the followers are, the less likely they are to contribute—intentionally or unintentionally—to the corruption cycle. If a person's pay, promotion, and career depend entirely on the manager's subjective opinion and rating, a person is more likely to comply with that manager (Prendergast, 1993). Training followers on how to develop and use personal sources of power can help reduce power abuse by leaders (Uhl-Bein and Carsten, 2007). Followers who have their own sources of power can better resist their leader's bullying. Instituting objective measures of performance, either through precise measurement or based on direct feedback from relevant constituents, is one way to curtail the excessive power of the leader and ensure proper and accurate flow of information. The subordinate can act for the benefit of the customers with feedback from them, rather than for the benefit of the boss.

By opening up the decision-making process to outsiders, an organization can get an objective view and prevent inbreeding. Outsiders can bring a fresh perspective that can break the corruption cycle. For example, the presence of outsiders on a company board of directors contributes to keeping executive salaries more in line with company performance (Conyon and Peck, 1998). Finally, the most difficult and most effective solution to preventing power corruption is a change in the culture and structure of organizations (Delbecq, 2001). The change should focus on performance, productivity, and customer service, rather than on satisfying the leaders.

Partly because of many abuses of power and partly because of philosophical and structural organization changes, the face of power is changing in many organizations.

EMPOWERMENT: THE CHANGING FACE OF POWER

One of the major forces for cultural and structural changes in organizations comes from the empowerment movement. *Empowerment* involves sharing power with subordinates and pushing decision making and implementation power to the lowest possible level. Its goal is to increase the power and autonomy of all employees in organizations. Its roots lie in perceptions of Japanese management, the quality circle efforts of the 1970s and the quality of work life (QWL) approach (Lawler and Mohrman, 1987), and the psychological concept of self-efficacy (Bandura, 1977). The underlying theme of empowerment is the giving away to and sharing of power with those who need it to perform their job functions. Such power sharing provides people with confidence in their abilities and enhances their sense of effectiveness. Research on the distribution of power (Tannenbaum and Cooke, 1974) and anecdotal and case evidence (Bennis and Nanus, 1985; Block, 1987) strongly suggest that equal power sharing contributes to an organization's effectiveness.

Empowerment of employees can be a powerful motivational tool because it provides them with control and a sense of accomplishment. Business organizations of all sizes, organizations in the nonprofit sector, as well as schools and governmental agencies have all implemented various aspects of empowerment (e.g., see Klidas, van den Berg, and Wilderom, 2007; Marshall, Talbott, and Bukovinsky, 2006; Silver, Randolph, and Seibert, 2006). Empowerment involves giving employees control over how they perform their work and over their work environment and building a sense of self-efficacy or competence by providing them with opportunities to succeed. In addition, encouraging participation in goal setting helps followers internalize the goals and builds commitment to them, an important factor in producing a feeling of empowerment (Menon, 2001). The continued emphasis on teams, flexibility, and quick response to environmental change further make empowerment an effective tool for organizations. When Linda Ellerbee, television reporter and CEO of Lucky Duck Productions, an award-winning television production company, learned of her cancer diagnosis, she gave up the reins of her company to her employees. Although she previously involved herself in every aspect of her company, she found out that "I had hired really good people who were good at their job, and what they needed was for me to get out of their way. The company continued to thrive in my absence. I never tried to micromanage again" (Ellerbee, 1999: 81).

Requirements of Empowerment

Once managers and leaders decide to adopt and implement empowerment as a management technique, they must adjust the culture and structure of their organization. Many managers talk about empowerment, but few fully accept the concept and implement it completely. Several leadership and organizational steps must be taken to implement empowerment (Table 5-6).

TABLE 5-6 Leadership and Organizational Factors in Empowerment	
Leadership Factors	**Organizational Factors**
• Creating a positive emotional atmosphere	• Decentralized structure
• Setting high performance standards	• Appropriate selection and training of leaders and employees
• Encouraging initiative and responsibility	• Removing bureaucratic constraints
• Rewarding openly and personally	• Rewarding empowering behaviors
• Practicing equity and collaboration	• Expressing confidence in subordinates
• Careful monitoring and measurement	• Fair and open organizational policies

The style of leadership has considerable impact on followers' perception of being empowered and on how effective teams can be (Srivastava, Bartol, and Lock, 2006). When empowering employees, the role of the leader is to provide a supportive and trusting atmosphere that encourages followers to share ideas, participate in decision making, collaborate with one another, and take risks. The leader can achieve empowerment through various means, such as role modeling, openness to others, and enthusiasm. Leaders who want to implement empowerment successfully must "walk the talk," be aware of their verbal and nonverbal signals, and believe in the empowerment process. They must encourage experimentation and tolerate mistakes. Leaders can further encourage an atmosphere of openness by increasing their informal interaction with subordinates in and out of the workplace. High work and productivity standards, clarification of organizational missions and goals, and clear and equitable rewards for proper behaviors and proper productivity outcomes must accompany the positive atmosphere the leader creates. Empowerment does not mean a lack of performance or standards. Rather, it involves providing employees with many opportunities to set high goals, seeking out resources they need, supporting them in their decisions and actions, and rewarding them when the goals are achieved. The leader needs to convey high expectations and express confidence in the followers' ability to deliver high performance.

Roy Vagelos, former CEO of Merck and currently chair of Regeneron Pharmaceuticals, insisted on the impossible when he set out to eradicate river blindness, a disease that had long gone without a cure. The price of the project was an apparently unmanageable $200 million for a drug whose customers were unlikely to be able to afford it. Vagelos forged ahead and continued to expect that the project would succeed. His high expectations paid off when the drug was developed and distributed to reach 19 million people (Labarre, 1998).

WHAT DO YOU DO?

You are comfortable with empowering your team members and allowing much freedom, input, and flexibility in how the work gets done, and you don't tend to "pull rank." The majority of your team members responds well and accepts responsibility. However, a couple of them are taking advantage of the situation and not pulling their weight. What do you do?

THE ORGANIZATIONAL REQUIREMENTS   In addition to the leader's role in empowerment, the organization also needs to take steps to empower employees (see Table 5-5). First and foremost, the structure of the organization must encourage power sharing by breaking down formal and rigid hierarchies and by decentralizing decision making (Menon and Hartmann, 2002). It is difficult for a leader to empower employees to make decisions when the organizational structure does not recognize the empowerment. The traditional lines of authority and responsibility do not lend themselves well to the empowerment process, so before new techniques can be implemented, organizations must evaluate their structure with an eye for removing bureaucratic barriers. In many cases, the physical office space must be changed to accommodate the new way people will be working. Formal offices and cubicles indicate hierarchy and individual work, so encouraging interaction will require a different work space that promotes flexibility and cooperation. Several organizations found that changing their office layout was the key to better performance (Goldstein, 2000).

Another organizational step is the selection of leaders and employees who are willing to share power. The change in structure and empowerment can be difficult for leaders and followers who are not comfortable with such a process (Frey, 1993). Along with proper selection, appropriate training can introduce the new behaviors of collaboration, encouragement, participation, and openness.

Setting high standards is a requirement for success of empowerment. Equally necessary, however, is the ability to monitor and measure performance and improvement. McDonald's, like many other retailers, has implemented elements of empowerment to engage and motivate employees with the belief that such programs improve morale of the frontline and the quality of service they deliver to customers. To keep track of its efforts and monitor performance, in addition to regular profit and quality measures, the company uses employee surveys and welcomes outsiders who are interested in studying its operations, thereby allowing itself to get feedback about climate and performance (Blundell, 2007).

Finally, just as leaders have to "walk the empowerment talk," so do organizations, by implementing appropriate reward structures and fair policies that allow for experimentation, initiative, making mistakes, and collaboration. Intense focus on the short-term financial outcomes can be deadly to an empowerment process that needs time to take hold. One of the ways organizations can start the process of empowerment is by recognizing and identifying the potential blocks to empowerment. Some consultants and academics even recommend that organizations and employees be encouraged to reject authority outright. Overall, empowering employees requires sharing information, creating autonomy, and holding employees accountable (Seibert, Silver, and Randolph, 2004).

Impact of Empowerment

Empowering employees is a difficult process, but it continues to be recognized as a key factor in today's new structures and a requirement for leaders (Harrison and Freeman, 2004). Leaders in large and small organizations are encouraged to give up power to their followers and rely on democratic practices. Many case examples and anecdotes illustrate that empowerment can be a motivational tool and lead to increased performance. It might even be that empowerment (or its opposite, too much control) can create a self-fulfilling prophecy (Davis, Schoorman, and Donaldson, 1997). On the one hand, the less a leader controls employees, the more likely they are to accept control and responsibility. On the other hand, increased control can cause followers to become passive and, in the extreme, can lead to corruption. The idea of self-leadership, discussed in Chapter 7, is partially based on the concept of empowerment.

There appears to be a resurgence in interest in empowerment (for a recent review, see Seibert, Wang, and Courtright, 2011), with many recent studies evaluating its impact, application, and effectiveness in a number of settings both in the United States and in others countries

LEADING CHANGE
Sharing Power and Reaping Profits

"As long as we know what each member of staff agrees to deliver in a period of time, their working hours or where they work are no longer important" (Glamorgan, 2006). Such a statement is typical of Ricardo Semler, CEO of Semco, a Brazilian company that produces marine and food processing equipment. He is used to being called a maverick. He actually wrote a book on the topic (Semler, 1993). One of the early proponents of open-book management, a method based on sharing financial information with employees and training them to interpret and use it to set and achieve performance goals, Semler believes in sharing information and power. He proposes that people who make far-reaching and complex decisions in their own lives every day are fully capable of managing themselves at work. He believes, "Freedom is the prime driver of performance" (Shinn, 2004: 18). He also believes that even though most people want democracy as a political system, most organizations do not run democratically. At Semco, employees not only pick the color of their uniforms and their work hours but also vote on adopting new products and undertaking new ventures. Semler states, "At Semco, employees decide where they work and what needs to be done" (Fisher, 2005). The company has set up hammocks in offices to allow employees to relax, so that they can be more creative. Employees can also take sabbaticals and "Retire-A-Little" time, where they can take time off to do what they would do when they retire.

All the freedom and participation are coupled with high-performance expectations. Employees who cannot work in the culture or who do not perform do not survive. The company has grown 900 percent under Semler's leadership, is either number one or number two in all the markets in which it competes, and has grown 27.5 percent a year for 14 years (Fisher, 2005). Semler succeeded in creating a culture where performance matters and people have freedom to do what they think is right and have the power to do it without asking their boss. He suggests that his management philosophy is not easy to implement everywhere because managers have a tough time giving up control (Fisher, 2005).

Sources: Colvin, G. 2001. "The anti-control freak," *Fortune*, November 26: 60; Fisher, L. M. 2005. "Ricardo Semler won't take control," *Strategy and Business*, Winter. http://www.strategy-business.com/media/file/sb41_05408.pdf (accessed July 13, 2007); Glamorgan University international business speaker, September 2, 2006. http://news.glam.ac.uk/news/2006/sep/07/international-business-speaker-glamorgan/ (accessed June 23, 2007); Shinn, S. 2004. "The Maverick CEO," *BizEd*, January/February: 16–21.

(e.g., Sarvar and Khalid, 2011; Singh, 2006). Despite the reported positive benefits of empowerment, however, research on the subject remains relatively scarce and mixed. Research conducted on the benefits for high-involvement organizations that use empowerment and employee participation to various degrees is increasing, but still includes few director empirical tests (Konrad, 2006; Lawler, Mohrman, and Ledford, 1995). Nevertheless, despite the many obstacles and difficulties and the limited empirical evidence, empowerment is a permanent feature of many organizations in the United States and many other Western countries (Randolph and Sashkin, 2002). When applied well and in culturally compatible institutions, empowerment can powerfully affect a leader's and an organization's effectiveness.

THE LEADERSHIP QUESTION—REVISITED

Using power well is all about balance and moderation. It has to be just right. Leaders should use all sources of power and influence available to them based on who their followers are and what the situation is. There is no one best way. Winning the hearts and minds is a long-term solution, but sometimes you have to push to get things done. In all cases, the exercise of power must be aimed at achieving organizational goals ethically. Leaders must demonstrate integrity and care for followers as they take action to achieve goals.

Summary and Conclusions

This chapter focuses on the link between power and leadership. A leader's power to influence others is the key to achieving goals and to being effective. In this influence process, a leader accesses a number of personal and organizational sources of power. Power changes people. The effect on those who hold power ranges from becoming more generous to abusing their power to exploit others. Those who are subject to it can commit to what is being asked of them or resist passively or actively. In either case, equal distribution of power tends to have positive effects in organizations. The more leaders rely on power sources vested in themselves, such as expertise or a relationship, the more likely it is that subordinates will commit to the leader's decisions and actions. Reliance on organizational sources of power, such as legitimacy, reward, or punishment, at best leads to temporary employee commitment and at worst to resentment and resistance. Given the increasing use of teams in many organizations, it is also important for teams and their leaders to develop sources of power by coping with uncertainty, becoming central to their organization's mission and goals, and providing unique products or services that make them indispensable to others in their organization.

Although power is necessary to accomplish organizational goals, power also leads to abuse and corruption and is one of the factors in destructive leadership. Excessive power can cause leaders to develop inflated views of themselves due to compliance of the followers, flattery and compliments, the separation of leaders from their subordinates, and their access to too many resources without much accountability. In addition to the ethical consequences, such excessive power can impair the leader's ability to make good decision making, increase their reliance on authoritarian leadership, engender adversarial interactions, and ultimately, cause subordinates to resist their leader's requests. Careful selection of leaders and implementation of an organizational culture based on integrity and openness are key to preventing abuse and corruption.

The face of power is changing in many organizations. The key aspect of this change is the sharing of power to allow subordinates to participate in decision making, thereby leading to higher-quality decisions and subordinates' sense of accomplishment. The success of empowerment depends on the leader and the organization creating a positive atmosphere in which structures are decentralized and employees are encouraged to experiment and innovate; employees also must be well trained and supported. In addition, high-performance standards need to be set, with rewards tied clearly and fairly to performance. Despite the bad press the abuse of power received recently, the proper application of power in organizations is essential to a leader's effectiveness. Power is at the core of leadership.

Review and Discussion Questions

1. How does power impact the power holders and those who are subject to it?
2. What is the difference between commitment and compliance?
3. Provide scenarios for the appropriate use of each source of power.
4. Provide examples of the use of different influence tactics.
5. Provide examples of how teams can use the sources of power available to them.
6. How are the team sources of power different from those available to individuals?
7. What are the factors that contribute to abuse, corruption, and destructive leadership?
8. What can be done to prevent or eliminate abuse of power and corruption?
9. What are the key roles of a leader in implementing empowerment?
10. Power is at the core of leadership. Could empowerment lead to powerless leaders? Why, or why not?

Leadership Challenge: How Much Is Enough

Business executives, particularly in the United States, commandeer incredibly high salaries and compensation packages. The numbers are approaching and surpassing the $100 million mark without including many other perks and bonuses, in some cases in companies that are performing poorly. A number of arguments explain the rise in compensation packages, including market forces and competition for the few talented executives. Where do you draw the line? If you were offered an outrageous compensation package to join a company that is laying off employees, declaring bankruptcy, and performing poorly overall, would you take it?

1. What factors contribute to high-compensation packages?
2. What are the personal and organizational implications of your decision?

Exercise 5-1 Words of Wisdom

Following are quotes by historical figures, scholars, and world leaders about power and its impact.

1. Be the chief, but never the lord. (Lao Tzu)
2. There is danger from all men. The only maxim of a free government ought to be to trust no man living with power to endanger the public liberty. (John Adams)
3. I know of no safe repository of the ultimate power of society but people. And if we think them not enlightened enough, the remedy is not to take the power from them, but to inform them by education. (Thomas Jefferson)
4. Justice without force is powerless; force without justice is tyrannical. (Blaise Pascal)
5. Knowledge is power. (Francis Bacon)
6. Power tends to corrupt, and absolute power corrupts absolutely. Great men are almost always bad men. (Lord Acton)
7. Power consists in one's capacity to link his will with the purpose of others, to lead by reason and a gift of cooperation. (Woodrow Wilson)
8. I suppose leadership at one time meant muscles; but today it means getting along with people. (Gandhi)
9. The problem of power is how to achieve its responsible use rather than its irresponsible and indulgent use—of how to get men of power to live for the public rather than off the public. (John F. Kennedy)
10. Those who seek absolute power, even though they seek it to do what they regard as good, are simply demanding the right to enforce their own version of heaven on earth. And let me remind you, they are the very ones who always create the most hellish tyrannies. Absolute power does corrupt, and those who seek it must be suspect and must be opposed. (Barry Goldwater)
11. The first principle of nonviolent action is that of noncooperation with everything humiliating. (Cesar Chavez)
12. Authority doesn't work without prestige, or prestige without distance. (Charles De Gaulle)
13. Power is the ultimate aphrodisiac. (Henry Kissinger)
14. If you can, help others; if you cannot do that, at least do not harm them. (Dalai Lama)
15. One of the saddest lessons of history is this: If we've been bamboozled long enough, we tend to reject any evidence of the bamboozle. The bamboozle has captured us. Once you give a charlatan power over you, you almost never get it back. (Carl Sagan)

Step 1: Individually

Select two of your favorite quotes. Briefly jot down the reasons why they appeal to you. Consider what their implications would be for organizational leadership.

   For example, Napoleon Bonaparte said: "A soldier will fight long and hard for a bit of colored ribbon." Based on this approach, it is important to have goals and rewards, even if not very significant, and leaders must clarify the rewards associated with achieving the goals. As a leader, being encouraging is essential and using reward power is important. This may appeal to you because you like having concrete and clear goals and work best when you have external rewards.

1. _____

2. _____

Step 2: In Groups

Review all the members' favorite quotes and select two that the group agrees on. For each, discuss the potential consequences for organizations and the reasons why your group has selected the quotes. Be ready to make a two- to three-minute presentation to the class.

1. _____

2. _____

Exercise 5-2 Who Holds Power in Your Team/Organization?

You have learned about various sources of power available to individual and groups. The goal of this exercise is for you to consider individuals in your team or organization who are powerful—able to influence others—and analyze their sources of power.

Step 1: Select People

Select three to five individuals from your team, department, or organization and identify which sources of power and influence they use and the impact it has on others. Provide an example for each.

Individual (First Name)	Source of Power	Most used Influence Tactic	Impact on Others	Example
1.				
2.				
3.				
4.				
5.				

Step 2: Evaluate Impact and Lessons Learned

Next, consider whether these individuals are effective in their use of power and influence. What do they do well? What could they do differently? What lessons can you take away from studying them?

Self-Assessment 5-1: Understanding Your Sources of Power and Influence

For each of the following items, please select the rating that best describes **what you actually do**, rather than what you would like to do. *"Organization" refers to your coworkers, team, department, or whole organization depending on which level you are.*

1 = Strongly disagree

2 = Somewhat disagree

3 = Neither agree nor disagree

4 = Somewhat agree

5 = Strongly agree

_____ 1. I strive to be friendly and supportive.

_____ 2. I include as many people as I can in decisions I make.

_____ 3. I strive to be positive.

_____ 4. I am an expert in my area.

_____ 5. I actively build my networks inside the organization.

_____ 6. I have access to resources that other people need or want.

_____ 7. I work hard on staying in my superiors' good graces.

_____ 8. I have a formal title.

_____ 9. I can, directly or indirectly, punish my coworkers (e.g., bad evaluation, not promoting, firing).

_____ 10. I work on building relationships with people at all levels.

_____ 11. I prefer to make decisions in a group.

_____ 12. I am a cheerleader for my coworkers and employees.

_____ 13. I try to convince people with facts and figures.

_____ 14. I do favors whenever I can so people owe me.

_____ 15. I can directly or indirectly help people get what they want (e.g., money, resources, perks, promotions).

_____ 16. I take care of what my superiors' need.

_____ 17. I am comfortable pulling rank to get people to do things.

_____ 18. I put pressure on people until they do what I want.

_____ 19. I manage to do something nice to thank people who help me or my team members.

_____ 20. I like to involve people in the decisions that affect them.

_____ 21. I am good at focusing people's attention on the mission of the organization.

_____ 22. I am known for my creativity and ability to solve problems.

_____ 23   I am good at compromising with others to get what I need.

_____ 24. I do many favors so that others owe me if I need something.

_____25.   I do my best to agree with people who have power over me, to keep them on my side.

_____26.   I make the final decision because that is my responsibility as a leader.

_____27.   I am comfortable threatening people to get them to do what I want.

_____28.   I am friendly and approachable.

_____29   I almost always get information from my coworkers before I make a decision.

_____30.   People often come to me when they need to regain their motivation.

_____31.   My skills and knowledge are at the cutting edge of my field.

_____32.   When I need something done, I go around and seek support ahead of time.

_____33.   I have information that others need.

_____34.   I make sure that my superiors are aware of my accomplishments.

_____35.   I rely on the chain of command and the organizational hierarchy to get things done.

_____36.   People know that being on my bad side can have bad consequences.

Scoring: To calculate your score, add the items as follows:

Items 1, 10, 19, and 28 = Total: _____ _Personal Appeal_

Items 2, 11, 20, and 29 = Total: _____ _Consultation_

Items 3, 12, 21, and 30 = Total: _____ _Inspiration_

Items 4, 13, 22, and 31 = Total: _____ _Rational persuasion_

Items 5, 14, 23, 32   = Total: _____ _Coalition building_

Items 6, 15, 24, 33   = Total: _____ _Exchange_

Items 7, 16, 25, 34   = Total: _____ _Ingratiation_

Items 8, 17, 26, 35   = Total: _____ _Legitimate tactics:_

Items 9, 18, 27, 36   = Total: _____ _Pressure_

Interpretation: Your total in each of the preceding nine categories indicates the extent to which you use each source of influence. Your score will range from 4 to 16 in each. A higher score in each indicates that you use that tactic more. A balanced score (approximately the same score in all categories) indicates that you tend to use all influence tactics to the same extent. If you have much higher scores in one or more category, consider why you prefer those methods, whether they are effective, and how you could expand your sources of power and influence.

Self-Assessment 5-2: Views of Power

This self-assessment is designed to provide you with insight into your attitude regarding power. Indicate your opinion on each question, using the following scale:

1 = Strongly disagree

2 = Somewhat disagree

3 = Neither agree nor disagree

4 = Somewhat agree

5 = Strongly agree

_____ 1. It is important for a leader to use all power and status symbols that the organization provides to be able to get his or her job done.

_____ 2. Unfortunately, for many employees, the only thing that really works is threats and punitive actions.

_____ 3. To be effective, a leader needs to have access to many resources to reward subordinates when they do their job well.

_____ 4. Having excellent interpersonal relations with subordinates is essential to effective leadership.

_____ 5. One of the keys to a leader's influence is access to information.

_____ 6. Being friends with subordinates often increases a leader's ability to influence them and control their actions.

_____ 7. Leaders who are reluctant to punish their employees often lose their credibility.

_____ 8. It is difficult for a leader to be effective without a formal title and position within an organization.

_____ 9. Rewarding subordinates with raises, bonuses, and resources is the best way to obtain their cooperation.

_____10. To be effective, a leader needs to become an expert in the area in which he or she is leading.

_____11. Organizations need to ensure that a leader's formal evaluation of subordinates is actively used in making decisions about them.

_____12. Even in most enlightened organizations, a leader's ability to punish subordinates needs to be well preserved.

_____13. The dismantling of formal hierarchies and the removal of many of the symbols of leadership and status caused many leaders to lose their ability to influence their subordinates.

_____14. A leader needs to take particular care to be perceived as an expert in his or her area.

_____15. It is essential for a leader to develop subordinates' loyalty.

Scoring: Add your scores on each items as follows:

Legitimate power: Add items 1, 8, and 13. Total: _____

Reward power: Add items 3, 9, and 11. Total: _____

Coercive power: Add items 2, 7, and 12. Total: _____

Referent power: Add items 4, 6, and 15. Total: _____

Expert power: Add items 5, 10, and 14. Total: _____

Interpretation: Your total in each of the preceding five categories indicates your belief and attitude toward each of the personal power sources available to leaders.

Self-Assessment 5-3: Recognizing Blocks to Empowerment

This exercise is designed to help you recognize organizational readiness for empowerment and the potential blocks to its implementation. For each question, think about the current state of your organization or department and check the appropriate box.

Questions	Yes	No
1. Is your organization undergoing major change and transition?	❏	❏
2. Is your organization a start-up or new venture?	❏	❏
3. Is your organization facing increasing competitive pressures?	❏	❏
4. Is your organization a hierarchical bureaucracy?	❏	❏
5. Is the predominant leadership in your organization authoritarian and top down?	❏	❏
6. Is there a great deal of negativism, rehashing, and focus on failures?	❏	❏
7. Are employees provided with reasons for the organization's decisions and actions?	❏	❏
8. Are performance expectations and goals clearly stated?	❏	❏
9. Are goals realistic and achievable?	❏	❏
10. Are rewards clearly tied to performance or the accomplishment of organizational goals and mission?	❏	❏
11. Are rewards based on competence and accomplishments?	❏	❏
12. Is innovation encouraged and rewarded?	❏	❏
13. Are there many opportunities for participation?	❏	❏
14. Are resources generally appropriate for performing the tasks?	❏	❏
15. Are most tasks routine and repetitive?	❏	❏
16. Are opportunities for interaction with senior management limited?	❏	❏

Scoring: For items 1 through 6 and 14 and 16, give a score of 1 if you have marked Yes, 0 if you have checked No. For items 7 through 14, reverse scoring, giving a 0 to Yes and 1 to No.

> *Interpretation:* The maximum possible score is 16. The closer you have rated your organization to that maximum score, the less ready it is for implementation of empowerment. An analysis of individual items can point to specific blocks to the implementation of empowerment.

LEADERSHIP IN ACTION

THE LAST CEO OF LEHMAN BROTHERS: RICHARD FULD

Among the most dramatic stories of the 2008–2010 global financial crisis was the sudden and unexpected demise of the Lehman Brothers, a financial services firm founded in 1850, in September 2008. After many years of success, the company was brought down by an accounting scheme, dubbed Repo 105, that allowed it to shuffle and hide its risks and bad assets (Johnson, 2010). Its downfall in September 2008 was one of the primary triggers of the global crisis.

Leading the company since 1994 and through is bankruptcy was the flamboyant Richard Fuld, who by most accounts was and still is a force to be reckoned with (Kim, 2013). Although he accepted responsibility for the demise of his company, he steadfastly had refused to admit any wrongdoing or any mistakes (NYT, March 12, 2010) and even denied having knowledge of the shady transactions (Gallu and Scheer, 2010). A serious and intense man who was considered one of the best traders at Lehman's, he seemed to have had the ability to make others want to follow him (NYT, March 12, 2010). He also brought considerable profitability to the company.

Those working with Fuld gave him the nickname of "Gorilla" for his habit of grunting instead of talking and his intimidating presence (Plumb and Wilchins, 2008). He quickly warmed up to the label and kept a life-size toy gorilla in his office (Fishman, 2008). One financial analyst states: "He had the typical hubris that any long-term CEO has: 'I built this thing, and it's got more value than the marketplace understands' " (Plumb and Wilchins, 2008). Several years before the collapse, Fuld refused several offers that could have saved his company, against the advice of many advisors, because he did not agree with them. He then was outraged that the U.S. government did not bail his company out and believes he is being used as a scapegoat because people need someone to blame, although some of his associates believe that Fuld was fully aware of what was going on in his company (Clark, 2010a). During the last days before the company went bankrupt, Fuld used all his political connections, calling U.S. Treasury Secretary Paulson, Jeb Bush (the president's brother), and others to pressure both the U.S. and British governments to intervene on behalf of his company (Clark, 2010b); his charm and pressure did not work.

While CEO, Fuld was not shy about using his power. He once berated one of his employees for wearing the wrong-colored suit and is reputed to have fired another for using an "appalling" shade of lipstick (Pressler, 2010). Describing an interaction with Fuld, one of Lehman's former executives states: "… he made it seem like [a situation] will lead to physical violence if you didn't relent" (Fishman, 2008). He approached his job as CEO with a strong "us vs. them" philosophy, adopting some of his mentor's (and previous Lehman's CEO, Glucksman) working-class suspicion of Wall Street and paranoia about his company being under attack (Fishman, 2008). His intimidating take-no-prisoners approach and sometimes explosive behavior—he once knocked down the papers from an executive's desk—was balanced with generosity to those he liked and those who performed well (Fishman, 2008). Fuld surrounded himself with highly skilled, often non–Ivy league performers—an unusual occurrence in Wall Street—who received some of the highest incentives in the industry for high performance.

With a new report out about the process and causes of the company's downfall and Lehman's in bankruptcy, Fuld spends his time in an office in the Time Life building in New

York City, a space that once served as overflow for the company, wrapping up what is left of the company, continuing to replay how things went so wrong, and worrying about the possibility of charges brought against him (Fishman, 2008; Ray, 2010). A few years after the collapse of his company, a milder Fuld is showing some remorse and some doubt about what could have been done to prevent it (Craig, 2011). However, in spite of his continued networking, Fuld remains difficult and risky to hire (Winkler, 2013).

Questions

1. What are the sources of Dick Fuld's power? How would you feel working for him?
2. What elements of power corruption are present in this case?

Sources: Clark, A. 2010a. "Could Lehman's Dick Fuld end up behind bars," *Guardian.com.* March 12 (accessed on March 24, 2010); Clark, A. 2010b. "Lehman Brothers bosses could face court over accounting gimmicks," *The Guardian,* March 12. http://www.guardian.co.uk/business/2010/mar/12/lehman-brothers-gimmicks-legal-claims (accessed on March 18, 2010); Craig, S. 2011. "In former CEO's words, the last days of Lehman Brothers," *Dealbook,* February 14. http://dealbook.nytimes.com/2011/02/14/a-different-side-to-dick-fuld/ (accessed on July 15, 2013); Fishman, S. 2008. "Burning down his house," *New York Magazine,* November 30. http://nymag.com/news/business/52603/ (accessed on July 15, 2013); Gallu, J. and D. Scheer. 2010. "Lehman's hidden leverage 'Shenanigans' may haunt Fuld," *Bloomberg.com,* March 13. http://www.bloomberg.com/apps/news?pid=newsarchive&sid=aQSvfN5gUfoE (accessed on July 15, 2013); Johnson, F. 2010. SEC concedes Lehman shortcomings. *The Wall Street Journal*, March 18. (accessed at on March 10, 2010); Kim, J. 2013. Richard Fuld in the news again. *Fierce Finance,* June 24. http://www.fiercefinance.com/story/richard-fuld-news-again/2013-06-24 (accessed on July 15, 2013); New York Times (NYT). 2010. Richard Fuld, Jr., *New York Times,* March 12, http://topics.nytimes.com/top/reference/timestopics/people/f/richard_s_fuld_jr/index.html (accessed March 18, 2010); Plumb, C. and D. Wilchins. 2008. Lehman CEO Fuld's hubris contributed to meltdown. *Reuters,* September 14, http://www.reuters.com/article/idUSN1341059120080914 (accessed on March 18, 2010); Pressler, J. 2010. "Former Lehman Brothers CEO Richard Fuld has a passion for fashion," *New York Magazine*, March 1 (accessed on March 18, 2010); Ray T. 2010. Lehman: "Colorable claims" against Dick Fuld. *Barron's* March 11. http://blogs.barrons.com/stockstowatchtoday/2010/03/11/lehman-colorable-claims-against-dick-fuld/ (accessed on March 24, 2010); Winkler, R. 2013. "Fuld disclosure," *Wall Street Journal-Overheard*, March 25. http://blogs.wsj.com/overheard/2013/03/25/fuld-disclosure/ (accessed on July 15, 2013).

II

Contemporary Concepts

Part II presents the recent views of leadership, including several approaches based on charisma and inspiration and other leadership perspectives such as upper echelon and the leadership of nonprofit organizations. After studying Part II, you will be familiar with the most current views of leadership, the importance of inspiration, the essential role of the relationship between leaders and their followers, and use of positive approaches in leading. You will also understand the differences between upper-echelon leadership and leadership at other levels of the organization, appreciate the challenges top-level leaders face, and explore the challenges of leadership of nonprofit organizations.

The considerable upsurge in the interest in leadership is partly the result of the need and the challenge to lead organizations effectively in highly complex times. The models presented in this second part of the book consider the type of leadership necessary to navigate organizations through change and address the deep needs followers have for leadership that goes beyond an exchange of direction or consideration for productivity and rewards.

Chapter 6 presents the most-current approaches to leadership that are focused on inspiration and connection to followers. A major difference with previous theories presented in Part I is the absence of a contingency approach. In addition, the concepts address both small-group and department-level leadership and upper-echelon leadership. Chapter 7 looks at two different perspectives in leadership: the view from the top levels of organizations and the characteristics of leading a nonprofit organization, both of which share some elements with other types of leadership we have considered, while presenting unique complexities and challenges.

6

Current Era in Leadership

Inspiration and Connection to Followers

After studying this chapter, you will be able to:

1. Discuss the distinguishing elements of the new era in leadership research and practice.

2. Understand charismatic leadership, explain the leader, follower, cultural, and situational characteristics that contribute to its development, and discuss its positive and negative implications.

3. Distinguish between transactional and transformational leadership and explain factors that contribute to transformational leadership.

4. Describe the value-based approaches to leadership, including servant, authentic, and positive leadership.

THE LEADERSHIP QUESTION

Charisma is considered a positive trait for a leader, and charismatic leaders are sought after. Are charismatic leaders always effective and desirable? Is it a necessary element of leadership?

For many people, the concept of leadership conjures up images of political or organizational leaders who accomplish seemingly impossible feats. When asked to name leaders, people mention the likes of John F. Kennedy, Mahatma Gandhi, Nelson Mandela, and Barack Obama. These leaders and others like them are passionate and generate strong emotional responses in their followers. They change their followers, organizations, and society and even alter the course of history. They have a relationship with followers that goes beyond simply setting goals, motivating them, allocating resources, and monitoring results. The concepts presented in this chapter are the most-current approaches to leadership that focus on leaders who create special and long-lasting relationships or deep emotional bonds with their followers and, through such bonds, are able to implement change and, in some cases, achieve extraordinary results.

NEW ERA IN LEADERSHIP RESEARCH

The theories presented in this chapter constitute the newest era in our understanding of leadership (following trait, behavior, and contingency; see Chapter 3). They were introduced in the late 1970s and currently dominate both academic and practitioner approaches to leadership. They have brought much-needed new life and enthusiasm to the field, which around the 1970s and 1980s was criticized for being irrelevant, trivial, and inconsequential (see McCall and Lombardo, 1978). Max Weber introduced the concept of charisma in the 1920s, and social historian James McGregor Burns presented transformational leadership, which has a charismatic component (1978). Bernard Bass (Bass, 1985) proposed a business-oriented version of transformational leadership, launching decades of empirical-based investigations. Since then, researchers have developed the concept of charisma for application to organizational contexts and proposed models of leadership that emphasize vision and large-scale change in organizations. The focus on values and a more spiritual aspect of leadership was also introduced in the 1970 with Greenleaf's work and has extended to authentic leadership. The newest developments borrow from positive psychology, a concept with roots in the humanistic approach of the 1960s and proposed in the 1980s (Seligman, 2002) and positive organizational behavior, its application to organizational behavior (Cameron, Dutton, and Quinn, 2003).

The approaches provide several advantages over other views of leadership presented in this book:

- They allow us to look at a different aspect of leaders and their role as inspirational visionaries and builders of organizational cultures (Hunt, 1999).
- They highlight the importance of followers' emotional reactions (Chemers, 1997).
- They focus on leaders at top levels who are the subject of study in strategic leadership (covered in Chapter 7), thereby allowing for a potential integration of upper-echelon research with transformational and charismatic leadership.
- They address the "heart" as well as the "mind" emphasizing the affective and the cognitive aspects of leadership.

Although the models have many differences, their common themes are inspiration, vision, and focus on the relationship and emotional connection between leaders and followers. Addressing the relationship with followers relates them to the exchange and relationship development models presented in Chapter 3. The current models, however, go beyond the study of that relationship by highlighting inspiration and vision and therefore are applicable at all levels of leadership. As opposed to previous concepts, these models do not rely on the principles of contingency and prescribe a one "best" approach to leading others, a factor that may limit their applicability.

CHARISMATIC LEADERSHIP: A RELATIONSHIP BETWEEN LEADERS AND FOLLOWERS

The word *charisma* means "an inspired and divine gift." Those who have the gift are divinely endowed with grace and charm. Charismatic leaders capture our imagination and inspire their followers' devotion and allegiance. We describe political and religious leaders as charismatic, but leaders in business organizations can also be gifted. Charismatic leaders are those who have a profound emotional effect on their followers (House, 1977). Followers see them not merely as bosses but as role models and heroes who are larger than life.

Consider the case of President Barack Obama who presents many of the elements of a charismatic leader. The large number of volunteers who engaged in his presidential campaigns and supported him felt a strong emotional connection to him, as witnessed by the many people who attended his events and the high level of emotion they exhibited. The expressions "Yes we can" and "This is our time" and other powerful messages during his acceptance speech in 2008, such as "If there is anyone out there who still doubts that America is a place where all things are possible, who still wonder if the dream of our founders is alive in our time, who still questions the power of our democracy, tonight is your answer" (Gibbs, 2008: 34) inspired his followers. Obama's optimism and perceived sincerity connected with the majority of the U.S. electorate and many around the world, for example in Germany, where 200,000 people turned out to see candidate Obama. He became the symbol of change and hope for many who, even without knowing much about him, felt a connection to him.

Charismatic leaders inspire followers who are devoted and loyal to them and their vision. The relationship involves an intense bond between leaders and their followers and goes beyond a simple exchange. The case of Obama and many other charismatic leaders also show that charisma is clearly in the eye of the beholder; followers make the charismatic leader. The charismatic bond is far from typical of leadership situations and neither essential nor sufficient for effective leadership. The following sections consider the three required elements for the development of charismatic leadership: leader characteristics, follower characteristics, and the leadership situation (Figure 6-1).

Characteristics of Charismatic Leaders

Charismatic leaders share several common personality and behavioral characteristics and traits (Table 6-1). Although many of the traits—such as self-confidence, energy, and the ability to communicate well—are related to all types of leadership, their combination and the presence of followers and a crisis are what set charismatic leaders apart. First and foremost, charismatic

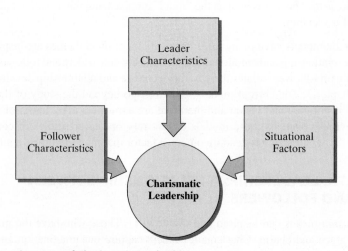

FIGURE 6-1   Requirements of Charismatic Leadership

TABLE 6-1	Characteristics of Charismatic Leaders

- High degree of self-confidence
- Strong conviction about ideas
- High energy and enthusiasm
- Expressiveness and excellent communication skills
- Active image building, role modeling, and impression management

leaders exude self-confidence in their own abilities and a strong conviction about their ideas along with a sense of moral righteousness of their beliefs and actions (Bass, 1985; Sashkin, 2004). Mahatma Gandhi's unwavering beliefs about the need for change in India and Martin Luther King Jr.'s single-minded focus on civil rights are examples of this trait. Their high level of confidence motivates their followers and creates a self-fulfilling prophecy. The more confident the leader is, the more motivated the followers are, which further emboldens the leader and encourages the followers to carry out the leader's wishes wholeheartedly. Additionally, charismatic leader's high energy and enthusiasm further boosts followers' positive moods, which increase the attraction to the leader and his or her effectiveness (Bono and Ilies, 2006). Positive expressions, motivation, and hard work increase the chances of success, which provides proof of the correctness of leader's vision.

Steve Case, chairman of the Start-up America Partnership (aimed at the growth of innovative firms in the United States; Start-up America, 2011) and the highly confident founder of Revolution, a company dedicated to increasing consumer power in health decisions, and former CEO of America Online (AOL), made others believe in his vision of connecting everyone through the Internet. Case believes that three things are most important in success: people, passion, and perseverance (Case, 2009). One of Case's former associates explains, "In a little company everybody's got to believe. But there needs to be somebody who believes no matter what. That was Steve. Steve believed from the first day that this was going to be a big deal" (Gunther, 1998: 71). Even though the merger of AOL with Time Warner was unsuccessful and led to a $135 billion loss, Case put the failure behind him and poured his energy and resources into several new ventures, including Revolution and a free health and medical information website, RevolutionHealth. Case's advice to potential entrepreneurs is, "If you feel passionate about a particular business and have the fortitude to break down barriers and redirect when needed, you can do great things" (Edelhauser, 2007).

Many examples of the charismatic leader's self-confidence can be found in political leaders. President Obama's simple message "Yes we can" is an example of the expression of confidence from a charismatic leader. Fidel Castro withstood considerable pressure over 50 years until his retirement in 2011 and has remained undaunted in his approach. Aung San Suu Kyi, the leader of the political resistance in Burma and 1991 Nobel Peace Prize recipient, who was under house arrest from 1989 to 2010, but persisted in proclaiming her agenda for democratic reform. President Gamal Abdul Nasser of Egypt galvanized Arab pride in the 1950s and 1960s, and his view of a united Arab world dominated the psyche and dreams of millions in the Middle East. Other destructive charismatic leaders use their "gift" to abuse and exploit followers; we discuss them in a later section.

Charismatic leaders are typically highly expressive with excellent communication skills and able to use nonverbal cues and dramatic symbols to lend dramatic support to their well-crafted verbal message. Their exceptional articulation skills, which help them express their excitement and communicate the content of their ideas to their followers, are a primary tool in persuading followers to join in their vision. Obama's considerable oratory skills provide an example, as do J. F. Kennedy's, Hitler's, and Fidel Castro's. The communication skills allow the charismatic leaders to define and frame the mission of the organization or the group in a way that makes it meaningful and relevant to followers. In addition, they appeal to their followers' emotion through the use of language, symbols, and imagery. Examples of all of these can be found in President Obama's first inaugural speech (Obama's Inaugural speech, 2009).

Finally, charismatic leaders present a carefully crafted image as role models to their followers and use active impression management to support that image (Conger and Kanungo, 1998). They "walk the talk," whether it is through the self-sacrifice that they make and demand of their followers or the self-control they demonstrate. House and Shamir (1993) note that a large number of charismatic political leaders spent time in prison, a sacrifice that demonstrates their willingness to put up with hardship to achieve their vision. For example, Gandhi and Nelson Mandela were imprisoned for defending their beliefs. Other charismatic leaders, such as Martin Luther King, Jr., who role modeled the peaceful resistance he advocated, demonstrate through their actions what they expect of their followers. James E. Rogers, chairman and CEO of Duke Energy believes leaders need to be closely involved and role model the behaviors they want followers to demonstrate (Bryant, 2009b). Overall, the characteristics of charismatic leaders are not in dispute; however, they are not the only factor. The next step is describing the development of followers who are devoted to the leader.

Characteristics of Followers

Because charismatic leadership results from a relationship between a leader and followers, the followers of such leaders demonstrate certain characteristics. Take away the frenzied followers and Hitler would not have been considered charismatic. The same is true for many cult leaders. Even for positive and constructive charismatic leaders such as Gandhi, followers demonstrate particular traits and behaviors (Table 6-2). Followers of charismatic leaders feel an intense emotional bond to the leader. Consider the reaction of employees of Russ Berrie and Co. when the toymaker's founder and namesake died suddenly. Berrie had established a close family bond with his employees. He was the best man at some of their weddings, and one company executive continued to visit his grave regularly because he felt a spiritual bond with the deceased leader (Marchetti, 2005). Additionally, charismatic followers respect and like their leader. They are strongly devoted to him or her and have a strong sense of loyalty. They admire their leader, and emulate his or her behaviors and mannerisms, including talking, dressing, and acting like the leader. They identify with him, a process that further helps followers internalize the

TABLE 6-2 Characteristics of Followers of Charismatic Leaders
• Intense emotional bond
• High degree of respect, affection, and esteem for the leader
• Loyalty and devotion to the leader
• Identification with the leader
• High confidence in leader
• High-performance expectations
• Unquestioning obedience

leader's values and aspirations as their own. In addition to the emotional component, charismatic followers have high confidence in their leader's ability and high-performance expectations. They believe their leader will change the world, or at least their community or their organization. All these characteristics are likely to lead followers to obey calls to actions without question, a factor that can have dire consequences if the leader is abusive or unethical (Samnani and Singh, 2013).

Researchers suggest that charismatic leaders change the followers' perception of the nature of what needs to be done and create a positive mood contagion (Bono and Ilies, 2006). Leaders offer an appealing vision of the future, develop a common identity, and heighten the followers' self-esteem and sense of self-efficacy (for a review, see Conger, 1998). In addition, one of the key components of the emergence of charismatic leaders is for the followers to perceive a need for change because the current state is unacceptable and because they believe that a crisis either is imminent or already exists (Shamir, 1991). The case of the 2008 election of Barack Obama presents all these elements. His supporters enthusiastically believed in his vision and their ability to create change to correct a situation they considered unacceptable.

The Charismatic Situation

President Obama's case provides yet one more element of charismatic leadership: a sense of crisis and need for change (see Table 6-3). Perception of crisis leads followers to look for new directions and solutions and prepares them to accept change. If an individual is able to capture and represent the group's needs and aspirations, that individual is likely to become the leader. In addition, individuals who demonstrate competence and loyalty to a group and its goals are provided with "credit" that they can spend to assume leadership roles. This *idiosyncrasy credit* allows certain individuals to emerge as leaders and change the direction of the group (Hollander, 1979). Because of the strong emotional impact of charismatic leaders, followers provide them with tremendous leeway (credit) to lead the group into new territory.

EXTERNAL CRISIS AND TURBULENCE   At the heart of charismatic leadership is how certain individuals either emerge as leaders in leaderless groups or replace an appointed leader. Many charismatic revolutionary leaders achieve their status without any formal designation. In organizations, their followers recognize them as leaders before a formal appointment, the last step in their rise to power, typically during a time of crisis. Popular political and religious leaders, such as Martin Luther King, Jr., Ronald Reagan, or Barack Obama won the hearts and minds of their followers, who then carried them into formal positions.

Although not all researchers believe that a situation of crisis is necessary for the emergence of charismatic leadership, many suggest that a *sense* of distress or crisis is (Davis and Gardner, 2012; Shamir and Howell, 1999). Research by Roberts and Bradley (1988) suggests that situations of crisis provide more latitude for leader initiative such that the person can demonstrate leadership abilities. Others link resilience and tolerance for ambiguity to charisma and

TABLE 6-3	Elements of Charismatic Situations

- Perceived need for change
- Sense of real or imminent crisis
- Opportunity to articulate ideological goal
- Availability of dramatic symbols
- Opportunity to clearly articulate followers' role in managing the crisis

its importance in crisis situations (Hunter, 2006), where followers believe that charismatic leaders are the only ones who can resolve the crisis. Therefore, charismatic leaders emerge in situations where a change and a new ideological vision need to be articulated and when followers are ready to be saved or more simply moved in a different direction. They use dramatic symbols to illustrate their goals and point to clear and specific roles that their followers can play in resolving the crisis. As a result, followers are convinced that the charismatic leader is the only one who can help, and the leader helps followers becoming aware of how they can contribute individually.

Historical charismatic leaders emerge in a time of real or perceived crisis. Cyrus the Great of Persia united warring tribes in 1500 B.C.; Napoléon galvanized a fractured postrevolutionary France; the fascist dictators of modern Europe took power during economic and social crises; in the United States, charismatic civil rights leaders of the 1960s rode on the wave of a cultural and civil unrest; and, recently, a sense of crisis and need for change led to the election of Obama to the presidency. These leaders brought a new vision of the future to their eager followers. As a matter of fact, many charismatic leaders fuel the sense of crisis, either sincerely or as a means of manipulation, as one of the reasons why followers need to select them. For example, the Tea Party movement in the United States has portrayed the Obama presidency and the Democratic majority as a symbol of the end of American democracy, enticing voters to the polls. In all cases, the crises and the perceived need for change set the stage for the charismatic leaders' skills and provide the leader with an opportunity to present a vision or solution.

INTERNAL ORGANIZATIONAL CONDITIONS   Researchers suggest that in addition to a sense of external crisis, several internal organizational conditions also facilitate charismatic leadership (Shamir and Howell, 1999).

- *Organizational life cycle.* Charismatic leaders are more likely to emerge and be effective in the early and late stages of an organization's life cycle, when either no set direction is established or change and revival are needed.
- *Type of task and reward structure.* Complex, challenging, and ambiguous tasks that require initiative and creativity and where external rewards cannot be clearly tied to performance can be ideal situations for charismatic leaders.
- *Organizational structure and culture.* Flexible and organic structures and nonbureaucratic organizational cultures are likely to encourage charismatic leadership.

Although some evidence is available to support these propositions, empirical testing is needed before they are established fully as conditions for the emergence of charismatic leadership.

Culture and Charisma

As you have read throughout this book, culture strongly affects what behaviors and styles are considered appropriate and effective for leaders. Based on the nature and processes involved in charismatic leadership, it would stand to reason that cultures with a strong tradition for prophetic salvation, in particular, would be more amenable to charismatic leadership. For example, the Judeo-Christian beliefs in the coming of the savior create fertile ground for charismatic leaders to emerge and be accepted. Prophets by definition are charismatic saviors. Israel, for example, has this type of strong tradition. Another case in point is the recent rise of Islamic fundamentalism, which typically is tied to a prophetic spiritual leader, as is the case in Sudan and Iran.

In cultures without such prophetic traditions, few charismatic figures are likely to emerge. For example, although China has experienced periods of crisis and change, the relationship between leader and followers is based more on the social hierarchy and need for order, as is prescribed in the Confucian tradition, rather than on the intense emotional charismatic bonds that exist in Judeo-Christian religions. This appears to be the case even for one of the few charismatic Chinese leaders, Mao Zedong. Furthermore, the factors that create the charismatic relationship may differ from one culture to another. The development of a charismatic relationship in a culture such as Japan relies on the leader's development of an image of competence and moral courage, and the securing of respect from followers (Tsurumi, 1982). By contrast, in India, charismatic leadership is associated with a religious, almost supernatural, state (Singer, 1969). In the United States, charisma is assertive and direct, whereas in other cultures it may be more quiet and nonassertive (Scandura and Dorfman, 2004). In any case, even if the concept of charisma is present within a culture, its manifestations may be widely different.

The GLOBE research, discussed in Chapter 2, has studied charismatic leadership in 60 countries (Den Hartog et al., 1999). The basic assumption of the research project is that "charismatic leadership will be universally reported as facilitating 'outstanding' leadership" (Den Hartog et al., 1999: 230). The researchers found that although some attributes are universally endorsed and some are universally negative, several attributes are culturally contingent. It is important to note that although some of the behaviors associated with charismatic leadership are universally associated with effectiveness, the term *charisma* evokes mixed reactions in different cultures. In other words, being charismatic is seen as both positive and negative.

In addition to characteristics typically associated with charismatic leadership (e.g., positive and dynamic), there are other characteristics (e.g., being a team builder and being intelligent) that are not part of charisma. Interestingly, although having a vision is universally associated with leadership, how it is expressed and communicated differs greatly across cultures. For example, Chinese leaders are seen as effective if they communicate their vision in a nonaggressive and soft-spoken manner, whereas Indians prefer bold and assertive leaders (Den Hartog et al., 1999). Similarly, followers universally value communication, but the communication style (e.g., level of directness, tone of voice) that is considered desirable is highly culture specific. For example, Cambodians expressed considerable enthusiasm at the ascendance of their new king Norodom Sihamoni in October 2004, even though he lacked any political experience, partly because they valued his extremely modest and soft-spoken demeanor (Sullivan, 2004). Furthermore, self-sacrifice and risk taking, important components of charismatic leadership in the United States, do not contribute to outstanding leadership in all other cultures (Martinez and Dorfman, 1998).

The Dark Side of Charisma

Given the charismatic leaders' strong emotional hold on followers, they can abuse that power easily and apply it toward inappropriate ends (e.g., Samnani and Singh, 2013). Along with Gandhi, Presidents Kennedy and Mandela, and Dr. King, the list of charismatic leaders unfortunately includes Hitler and Jim Jones (the cult leader who convinced thousands of his followers to commit suicide). The destructive charismatic leaders resemble the positive ones in some dimensions, but several characteristics distinguish them from one another (Table 6-4; Conger, 1990; Howell, 1988; and Howell and Avolio, 1992).

The major difference between ethical and *unethical charismatic* leaders is the unethical leaders' focus on personal goals rather than organizational goals. Unethical leaders use their gift and special relationship with followers to advance their personal vision and to exploit followers; they follow an internal and personal orientation, behaviors that are similar to those

TABLE 6-4	Ethical and Unethical Charisma
Ethical—Socialized Charisma	**Unethical—Personal Charisma**
• Focus on organizational goals	• Focus on personal goals
• Message built on common goals	• Message built on leader's goals
• Encourage and seek divergent view	• Censors, discourages, or punishes divergent views
• Open and two-way communication	• One-way, top–down communication
• Accepting of criticism	• Closed to criticism
• Impression management used to energize and motivate followers	• Impression management used to deceive followers
• Describe the actual need for change	• Create or exaggerate the sense of crisis

presented in the Dark Triad. The unethical charismatic leader censors opposing views and engages in one-way communication, whereas the ethical one accepts criticism and remains open to communication from followers. Given the considerable power of some charismatic leaders and their intense bond with their followers, it is easy to see how the line between ethical and unethical behaviors can be blurred. Leaders who are convinced of their vision do not doubt its righteousness, and leaders who have the ability to persuade often will do so without concern for others. The characteristics of self-confidence and skillful role modeling and persuasion that make a charismatic leader effective can also be the sources of highly destructive outcomes.

Distinguishing between the two types of charismatic leadership further helps explain how negative leadership can develop. Howell (1988) contrasts socialized and personalized charismatic leaders. Socialized leaders focus on satisfying their followers' goals and on developing a message that is congruent with shared values and needs and may be a factor in reducing deviance in their group (Brown and Treviño, 2006). Personalized leaders rely on getting followers to identify and agree with their personal values and beliefs. Both examples include all the characteristics of charismatic leaders, their followers, and the situation. Personalized leadership situations, however, are more prone to abuse.

In addition to the potential for power abuse and corruption, charismatic leaders also might present other liabilities ranging from a flawed vision that is self-serving to unrealistic estimates of the environment (Conger and Kanungo, 1998). The charismatic leader's skills at impression management and influence can become a liability when leaders mislead their followers with exaggerated estimates of their own or their followers' abilities and the chances for success. The unethical charismatic leader's journey becomes all about the leader. For the ethical one, it is about achieving a common goal. In many cases, the unethical charismatic leader will exaggerate the crisis and fan followers' sense of impending disaster and doom to demonstrate the need for his or her leadership. Other potential liabilities of charismatic leadership include failure to manage details, failure to develop successors, creation of disruptive in- and out-groups, and engaging in disruptive and unconventional behaviors (Conger and Kanungo, 1998). It is important to note that whereas followers often see their charismatic leader as ethical and their savior, detractors perceive him or her as unethical and even evil, both demonstrating very strong emotions. The emotion created by charismatic leaders leaves little room for moderation.

Evaluation and Application

The considerable changes in many organizations in recent years have created a sense of crisis and resulted in a perceived need for revitalization and change. Therefore, it is no coincidence that the concept of charismatic leadership dominates academic and popular views of leadership. The need to revitalize industrial, educational, health-care, and governmental institutions creates one of the essential elements for charismatic leadership; many perceive that we are in a time of turbulent change, if not crisis. We make many demands on our leaders to provide us with revolutionary ideas and are often disappointed when they cannot fulfill those expectations. In fact, our expectations are so high that we are bound to be disappointed.

Researchers have developed a number of different approaches to explain charismatic leadership, ranging from an attributional perspective, whereby the leader's behavior and the situation persuade followers to attribute charismatic characteristics to the leader (Conger and Kanungo, 1987), to self-concept views that focus on explaining how charismatic leaders can influence and motivate their followers (Shamir, House, and Arthur, 1993), to psychoanalytic perspectives (Kets de Vries, 1993), and self-presentational views (Sosik, Avolio, and Jung, 2002). Various studies have tested the elements of the different views of charismatic leadership; the results are not always consistent (e.g., see Shamir et al., 1998). Continued research, however, provides strong support for the existence and importance of understanding charismatic relationships and how such leaders affect their followers and their organizations. For example, charismatic leadership may lower burnout (De Hoogh and Den Hartog, 2009), facilitate team performance (Nohe et al., 2013), or engender positive affect in followers (Erez et al., 2008). Charismatic leaders seem to increase followers' efforts and citizenship behaviors (Sosik, 2005) and have been suggested to have a positive impact on external organizational stakeholders as well as immediate followers (Fanelli and Misangyi, 2006).

The charismatic relationship is a powerful and undeniable part of the most celebrated leadership situations, particularly in Western cultures. Charismatic leaders and their followers can achieve incredible feats. Such leadership, however, is not required for an organization to be successful. Indeed, it can be destructive, as is the case of unethical or personal charismatic leadership or even when a charismatic leader is simply wrong and drives the organization to failure. Charismatic leaders can also be powerful agents of change, but an equally powerful obstacle to change (Levay, 2010). In addition, because it is difficult, if not impossible, to train someone to be a charismatic leader (Trice and Beyer, 1993), the phenomenon depends on one individual rather than on stable organizational processes that can be put in place once the leader is gone. Finally, it is important to remember that charismatic leadership is not a cure-all. With all its potential benefits, charismatic leadership is a double-edged sword that requires careful monitoring to avert abuse. Although charismatic leadership holds a potentially negative side as demonstrated by many destructive charismatic historical figures, transformational leadership, which is presented next, relies on charisma as one element but concentrates on the positive role of leadership in change.

THE LEADERSHIP QUESTION—REVISITED

Charisma is clearly seen as a positive trait for leaders in many cultures. Research shows its many positive aspects and points to its destructive potential. But even in the case of positive charisma, emotionally connecting with followers and firing them up is not, in and of itself, enough for effective leadership. The emotional high must be followed by action, implementation and results. Lofty speeches and emotional highs do not run organizations. They do not replace the hard work of actually getting things done. Charisma can bring an emotional high, but it does not necessarily lead to effective leadership.

TRANSACTIONAL AND TRANSFORMATIONAL LEADERSHIP

How do leaders create and sustain revolutionary change in organizations? What style of leadership is needed to motivate followers to undertake organizational transformations? Several research-ers proposed transformational leadership concepts to answer these questions and to describe and explain how leaders succeed in achieving large-scale change in organizations. Originally developed by Burns (1978) who proposed it as a moral form of leadership, transformational leadership was introduced to organizational behavior to suggest that some leaders, through their personal traits and their relationships with followers, go beyond a simple exchange of resources and productivity.

The leadership models presented in previous chapters focused on the transaction and exchange between leaders and followers. For example, in Path–Goal Theory (see Chapter 3), the leader clears obstacles in exchange for follower motivation by providing structure to the task or by being considerate. Such basic exchanges, sometimes labeled transactional leadership, are considered an essential part of leadership, and leaders must understand and manage them well. To create change, however, they must supplement exchange with transformational leadership. Transformational leadership theory and observation of many leaders suggest that leaders use behaviors that are more complex than initiation of structure and consideration to establish a connection with their followers and transform organizations.

Transactional Leadership

Transactional leadership is based on the concept of exchange between leaders and followers. The leader provides followers with resources and rewards in exchange for motivation, productiv-ity, and effective task accomplishment. This exchange and the concept of providing contingent rewards are at the heart of motivation, leadership, and management theory and practice and is an essential component of effective leadership (e.g., Clarke, 2013; Wang et al., 2011). Two styles of transactional leadership are Contingent Reward (CR) and Management by Exception (MBE).

CONTINGENT REWARD   Through the use of *contingent reward*, leaders provide followers with promised rewards when followers fulfill their agreed-upon goals. When well managed, contingent rewards are highly satisfying and beneficial to the leader, the followers, and the organization. The informal and formal performance contracts that result are desirable and effective in manag-ing performance (Bass, 1985). Some research indicates that transactional leadership can provide structure and lead to positive outcomes (Walker, 2006) and that individualistic cultures may react more positively to transactional leadership than collectivistic cultures (Walumbwa, Lawler, and Avolio, 2007), whereas other studies (e.g., Rank et al., 2009) indicate that transactional leadership may impede innovation. CR is part of most leadership training whereby leaders are taught to reinforce appropriate behaviors, discourage inappropriate ones, and provide rewards for achieved goals. It is a necessary component of effective leadership and management. For example, transactional leadership successfully motivated remaining employees to decontaminate and tear down the infamous Rocky Flats nuclear site in Colorado. The Environmental Protection Agency certified the nuclear weapons site "clean" in June 2007 after years of mismanagement, accidents, and extensive cleanup. Denny Ferrara, whose whole family worked at the plant, was in charge of getting employees to work themselves out of a job. He accomplished this task by setting clear goals, communicating extensively, allowing employees to provide input into how to do the work, and encouraging them with recognition and generous rewards, which in some cases topped $80,000 a year (McGregor, 2004).

MANAGEMENT BY EXCEPTION   *Management by Exception* (*MBE*) is a leadership style whereby the leader interacts little with followers, provides limited or no direction, and only intervenes when things go wrong. In one type of MBE, labeled "active MBE," leaders monitor follower activities and correct mistakes as they happen (Bass and Avolio, 1990). In another type, labeled laissez-faire or omission, leaders are passive and indifferent toward followers and their task (Hinkin and Schriesheim, 2008). In both cases, little positive reinforcement or encouragement are given; instead the leader relies almost exclusively on discipline and punishment. Some managers confuse using MBE with empowering followers. After all, it does appear that followers have freedom to do as they please, as long as they do not make a mistake. Such comparisons, however, are not warranted. Encouragement and creating a supportive and positive environment in which risk-taking is encouraged, which are at the heart of empowerment, are clearly absent when a manager relies on MBE. Even though CR can yield positive effects, using MBE, particularly laissez-faire, as a primary leadership style has a negative impact on follower's performance and satisfaction.

Despite the success of some transactional relationships in achieving performance, an exclusive focus on such exchanges and transactions with followers is blamed for low expectations of followers and minimal performance in organizations (Zaleznik, 1990). Transactional contracts do not inspire followers to aim for excellence; rather, they focus on short-term and immediate outcomes. Long-term inspiration requires transformational leadership.

Transformational Leadership

Leadership scholars and practitioners suggest that today's organizations need leadership that inspires followers and enables them to enact revolutionary change. Transformational CEOs from the business and nonprofit sectors are credited with having dramatically changed their organizations and are also celebrated. *Transformational leadership* includes three factors—charisma and inspiration, intellectual stimulation, and individual consideration—that, when combined, allow a leader to achieve large-scale change (Figure 6-2).

ELEMENTS OF TRANSFORMATIONAL LEADERSHIP   *Charisma and inspiration* are one of the three central elements of transformational leadership (Bass, 1985; Bass and Avolio, 1993). The charismatic leadership relationship creates the intense emotional bond between leaders and

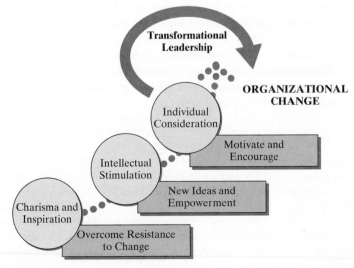

FIGURE 6-2 Transformational Leadership Factors

followers. The result is loyalty and trust in, as well as emulation of, the leader. Followers are inspired to implement the leader's vision. The strong loyalty and respect that define a charismatic relationship pave the way for undertaking major change by reducing resistance. The second factor is *intellectual stimulation*, which is the leader's ability to motivate followers to solve problems by challenging them intellectually and empowering them to innovate and develop creative solutions. The leaders and the group question existing values and assumptions and search for new answers (Shin and Zhou, 2003). By encouraging them to look at problems in new ways, requiring new solutions, and by triggering controversial discussions and debates, the leader pushes followers to perform beyond what they previously considered possible (Boerner, Eisenbeiss, and Griesser, 2007). Shantanu Narayen, CEO of Adobe Systems, when focusing on what leadership styles matter, states, "Challenging individual by setting goals and then letting them use their ingenuity to accomplish them is something that I hope I can pass on as part of my leadership style. If you set a common vision and then get really scary-smart people, they do things that amaze you" (Bryant, 2009b). The charismatic bond provides support and encouragement in this endeavor and prevents followers from feeling isolated. Intellectual stimulation includes a strong empowerment component, which assures followers of their abilities and capabilities and enables them to search out new solutions. Transformational leadership has been shown to create empowerment that, in turn, increases team effectiveness (Kark, Shamir, and Chen, 2003).

The last factor of transformational leadership is *individual consideration*, which leads to the development of a personal relationship with each follower. This factor is closely related to the Leader–Member Exchange (LMX) Model presented in Chapter 3. The leader treats each follower differently but equitably, providing everyone with individual attention. As a result, followers feel special, encouraged, motivated, and developed, and they perform better (Dvir et al., 2002). The leader's individual consideration further allows for matching each follower's skills and abilities to the needs of the organization. Anne Mulcahy, chairwoman and chief executive of Xerox, brought the company back from the brink of bankruptcy. She believes the most important leadership lesson is followership, "…I think it's a lot more about followership—that your employees are volunteers and they can choose to wait things out if they don't believe. And that can be very damaging in a big company. So it is absolutely this essence of creating followership that becomes the most important thing that you can do as a leader" (Bryant, 2009e).

The three factors—charisma and inspiration, intellectual stimulation, and individual consideration—combine to allow the leader to undertake the necessary changes in an organization. Referring back to the definition of leadership effectiveness presented in Chapter 1, we see that transformational leadership allows for external adaptation, whereas transactional leadership behaviors support the maintenance of the routine aspects of the organization necessary to maintain internal health. Some research suggest that the two go hand in glove, one building on the other to make leaders effective (Wang et al., 2011).

WHAT DO YOU DO?

You have been at your company for close to five years and have had excellent reviews. You are at a mid-level management position and you like your job. It's challenging and satisfying; you like your boss and your coworkers; your employees are great; and you have had satisfied customers and steady growth. Nothing spectacular; but things are going very well. A new CEO has just joined the company and she has announced major changes: restructuring, moving people around, new departments and teams, a push for new products and services, new technology, several young top managers from the outside, office redesign to make things open, and much more. Your comfortable, safe, and successful routine is being shaken up and everyone, including you, is stressed out. What do you do?

Evaluation and Application

Transformational leadership is one of the most popular and currently heavily researched theories of leadership. The theory has moved from the development of basic concepts to the stage where the concepts are critically reviewed and various moderating variables are identified (Antonakis, Avolio, and Sivasubramaniam, 2003). Therefore, considerable research about the various aspects of transformational leadership is available, several extensions of the model have been proposed (e.g., Rafferty and Griffin, 2004), and applications to broader organizational contexts, such as educational settings (Leithwood and Sun, 2012), the military (Hardy et al., 2010), and the public sector (Denhardt and Campbell, 2006) have been tested. Research shows that transformational leadership can increase employee proactivity by enhancing their commitment to the organization (Strauss, Griffin, and Rafferty, 2009). It is further linked to performance (Braun et al., 2013), particularly in smaller organizations (Ling et al., 2008), and employee engagement (Tims, Bakker, and Xanthopoulou, 2011). Other studies suggest that there is a positive relationship between transformational leadership, organizational climate, and innovation (Eisenbeiss, Knippenberg, and Boerner, 2008) and that perception of transformational leadership is linked to positive emotions in employees (Liang and Chi, 2013).

Several studies consider transformational leadership theory across gender and cultures. For example, female transformational leaders form a unique relationship with each of their followers, suggesting that women favor an interpersonal-oriented style of leadership (Yammarino et al., 1997). Women leaders often exhibit concern for others, expressiveness, and cooperation (Eagly, Karau, and Makhijani, 1995), traits that are associated with transformational leadership. Some research also suggests a link between being androgynous (blend of male and female behaviors) and transformational leadership (Kark, Waismel-Manor, and Shamir, 2012). From a national cross-cultural perspective, it appears that ideal leadership characteristics across many countries—such as Canada, South Africa, Israel, Mexico, Sweden, and Singapore—include some transformational leadership elements (Bass, 1997). The concept has been applied to non-Western cultures such as Israel (Dunn, Dastoor, and Sims, 2012), Pakistan (Tipu, Ryan, and Fantazy, 2012), and Turkey (Karakitapoğlu-Aygün and Gumusluoglu, 2012) and has shown predicted results. Additionally, research indicates that individuals from collectivistic cultures in particular, may be receptive to transformational leadership (Jung, Bass, and Sosik, 1995; Walumbwa and Lawler, 2003; and Walumbwa et al., 2007).

In spite of extensive research, transformational theories present some shortcomings. First, it is clear that many of the transformational behaviors include dispositional, trait-like elements that are reported to develop early in life (Bass, 1985). As such, it may be difficult to train leaders to become transformational. For example, although it might be easy to instruct a leader how to provide contingent rewards, teaching the leader to inspire and intellectually stimulate followers may not be as simple. Second, as is the case with charismatic leadership, the tendency is to propose transformational leadership as a panacea may be problematic. However, research regarding conditions under which transformational leadership may or may not be effective is lacking. A stronger contingency approach would identify various contextual organizational variables that might contribute to the effectiveness of transformational leadership (Pawar and Eastman, 1997). For example, not all organizations are in need of transformation and some may require effective maintenance of the status quo. There is little research about how transformational leadership may fare in those settings. Some researchers further suggest that the transformational leadership theory could benefit from clarification of the difference between charismatic and transformational leadership and the mediating processes and situational variables that lead to transformational leadership (Sashkin, 2004; Yukl, 1999). Finally, there is limited research about the potential negative consequences of transformational leadership. As is the case with charismatic leadership, transformational leadership involves the potential of leading to followers' excessive dependency (Eisenbeiß and Boerner, 2013; Kark et al., 2003) and negative and unethical behavior (Price, 2003); further research in that area would enhance the model.

Transformational leadership concepts apply widely to organizational effectiveness and leadership training. Connecting with followers and inspiring them would help most, if not all, leaders and their organizations become more effective. Recommendations for leaders based on transformational leadership models include the following:

- Project confidence and optimism about the goals and followers' ability
- Provide a clear vision
- Encourage creativity through empowerment, reward experimentation, and tolerate mistakes
- Set high expectations and create a supportive environment
- Establish personal relationships with followers

LEADING CHANGE
The Unconventional Sir Richard Branson

"Entrepreneurship isn't about selling things—it's about finding innovative ways to improve people's lives" says Sir Richard Branson, the fourth richest man in the United Kingdom, founder and CEO of the Virgin Group, and a daredevil entrepreneur (Branson, 2013a). The Virgin Group family of 400 companies with over 50,000 employees in 34 countries has been, for many years, a household name in Europe. From record stores to cell phones and airlines, to a commercial spaceport in New Mexico opened in 2011, Virgin is a formidable brand now exploring areas such as galactic travel and banking. Sir Richard Branson built his empire by breaking rules and successfully taking on challenges that everyone told him would fail. Running his business from his house on the private Caribbean island of Necker, and taking phone calls while resting in a hammock between tennis games, he claims he has never worked in an office a day in his life (Larson, 2013). Branson considers profits to be secondary: "The bottom line has never been a reason for doing anything. It's much more the satisfaction of creating things that you're proud of and making a difference" (Deutschman, 2004: 95).

Most often mentioned for his keen marketing skills and his ability in attracting attention through his daredevil endeavors such as hot-air balloon trips across the Atlantic, indulging in outrageous behaviors such as dressing as a bride or a pirate, or being photographed nude for his biography, Branson focuses on ventures he feels passionate about, and he cares deeply about the culture and people in his many companies (Hawn, 2006). With his businesses well established and considerable name recognition, he has turned his attention to social and environmental issues such as climate change, search for clean fuels, helping social entrepreneurs around the world, and even creating a group called the Elders—with Nelson Mandela as a founding elder—a rapid reaction force that brings together senior world leaders to address peace and human rights issues (http://www.theelders.org, 2013).

Branson believes, "You can't be a good leader unless you generally like people. That is how you bring out the best in them" (*Workforce*, 2004). He believes, "It's extremely important to respond to people, and to give them encouragement if you're a leader. And if you're actually turning people down ... take the time to do it yourself" (Branson, 2007). About flexible work policies at the Virgin Group, he says: "We like to give people the freedom to work where they want, safe in the knowledge that they have the drive and expertise to perform excellently, whether they at their desk or in their kitchen" (Larson, 2013). Encouraging people through lavish praise so they can flourish, allowing them to figure out their mistakes instead of picking on them, and moving employees around to help them to find a job that allows them to excel are all part of Branson's leadership philosophy. He suggests that most employees leave companies when they are frustrated because they are not heard.

Although often considered a control freak for keeping a hand in all his companies, Sir Richard has learned to delegate and develop the people who work for him. He describes the process: "I come up with the original idea, spend the first three months immersed in the business so I know the ins and outs and then give chief executives a stake in the company and ask them to run it as if it's their own" (*Workforce*, 2004). Branson wants to make sure that whatever he builds or takes part in is something that he can be proud of. He admits, "I made and learned from lots of mistakes. In the end, the key is will power" (Hawn, 2006). He also willingly admits that he is not a typical business person: "I have never been one for conventional thinking, and entrepreneurs launching startups always need to improvise quick, creative solutions to the obstacles they encounter" (Branson, 2013b). His description of Virgin Group's mission statement—"Ipsum sine timore, consector," or "Screw it, let's do it!"—is further testimony to his unique approach (Branson, 2013c).

Sources: Branson, R. 2006. "How to succeed in 2007," *CNN Money.com*. http://money.cnn.com/popups/2006/biz2/howtosucceed/4.html (accessed August 14, 2007); Branson, R. 2013a. "Richard Branson social entrepreneurship," *Entrepreneur*, June 17. http://www.entrepreneur.com/article/227044 (accessed July 29, 2013); Branson, R. 2013b. "How Richard Branson decides where to set up shop," *Entrepreneur*, July 15. http://www.entrepreneur.com/article/227415#ixzz2aSJ9l800 (accessed July 29, 2013); Branson, R. 2013c. "Richard Branson on crafting your mission statement," *Entrepreneur*, July 22. http://www.entrepreneur.com/article/227507#ixzz2aS6wGYVq (accessed July 29, 2013); Deutschman, A. 2004. "The Gonzo way of branding," *Fast Company*, October 91–96; Hawn, C. 2006. "Branson's next big bet," *CNN Money.com*, October 2. http://money.cnn.com/magazines/business2/business2_archive/2006/08/01/8382250/ (accessed August 12, 2007); Larson, L. 2013." Richard Branson brands Marissa Mayer's ban on Yahoo! Employees working from home 'perplexing and backwards,'|" *MailOnline*, February 25, http://www.dailymail.co.uk/news/article-2284540/Richard-Branson-criticizes-Marissa-Mayers-perplexing-backwards-ban-Yahoo-employees-working-home.html#ixzz2aSFVcPgD (accessed July 29, 2013); and Branso. 2004. "The importance of being Richard Branson," *Workforce*, December. www.workforce.com/archive/article/23/91/47.php (accessed January 30, 2005).

VALUE-BASED LEADERSHIP: SERVANT, AUTHENTIC, AND POSITIVE APPROACHES

Leadership is more than a series of behaviors and actions. For some, the leadership process is spiritual (Chen and Li, 2013; Fry, 2003; Fry et al., 2011), highly emotional and personal, and based on fundamental values such as integrity, caring for, and service to others (Greenleaf, 1998). Such concepts have found their way into leadership theory and research, and some approaches now take into consideration values, emotions, and optimism as primary aspects of leadership. Several different leadership approaches where the focus is broader than organizational performance and includes followers, culture, and other stakeholders are increasingly part of the research and practice of leadership (for a review, see Avolio, Walumba, and Weber, 2009). In talking about communicating with employees Gordon Bethune, the former CEO of Continental Airlines insists that integrity is an absolute requirement so that leaders can establish and maintain their credibility (Bryant, 2010a).

Servant Leadership

Many of the companies rated at best places to work in the U.S. name *servant leadership* as a core value (Hunter et al., 2013). The concept was first proposed by Robert Greenleaf who based leadership on service to followers, and effectiveness on whether followers were healthy, free, and autonomous and the extent to which those with less privilege were being taken care of (Greenleaf, 1977). Greenleaf's conception of servant leadership, though powerful, does not provide a clear definition; however, later work has helped refine the concept. At the heart of servant leadership, and the factor that distinguishes it most clearly from other leadership theories, is the focus on followers rather than the organization or the leader (for a review see van Dierendonck, 2011). Service to followers and their development and effectiveness, rather than organizational effectiveness, is essential to servant leaders.

Over 40 different traits and behaviors have been suggested to be related to servant leadership (van Dierendonck, 2011) with several key identifying characteristics (see Figure 6-3). When compared to other leadership approaches, some of these are unique to servant leadership, while others are not. For example, being first among equals, motivated by service and humility are not typically part of Western conceptions of organizational leadership. However, empathy for others is an element of emotional intelligence considered key to leadership. Similarly, authenticity, empowerment, and accountability are often considered to be leadership factors.

Servant leadership is a relatively new approach and needs considerably more empirical testing and development. However, the importance and significance of several of its components can be gleaned from other related research, and initial findings show considerable promise.

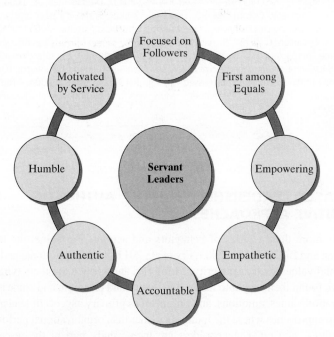

FIGURE 6-3   Key Characteristics of Servant Leaders

For example, a high-quality leader–member exchange (LMX, see Chapter 3) includes many of the elements of trust, respect, and cooperation with a focus on follower development that are part of servant leadership (van Dierendonck, 2011). Similarly, research on organizational citizenship behavior (OCB) shows that employees whose leaders have a strong service focus engage in more extra-role behaviors at work (Ng, Koh, and Goh, 2008), and servant leadership is related to team effectiveness in some settings (Irving and Longbotham, 2007). Other research shows links to follower commitment and satisfaction (Schneider and George, 2009), hopefulness (Searle, 2010), and engagement (Hunter et al., 2013). Furthermore, many of the servant leadership concepts are part of leadership in other cultures (see Mittal and Dorfman, 2012). For example, the themes of humility, accountability, and focus on followers are central to leadership ideals found in Iran and in other Indo-European cultures (Nahavandi, 2012).

Authentic leadership is another value-based leadership model that has received attention in recent years.

Authentic Leadership

Authentic leadership emphasizes the importance of leader's self-awareness and being true to his or her own values. "To be a great leader, you need to be yourself," states Padmasree Warrior, chief technology officer at Cisco Systems (Warrior, 2010). Hatim Tyabji, executive at Bytemobile, Inc., a wireless infrastructure provider and a world-renowned innovation expert, agrees that authenticity is essential to leadership. He believes the employees pay attention to what leaders do more than what they say, so it is essential that actions match the words (Tyabji, 1997). *Authentic leaders* (AL) are people who know themselves well and remain true to their values and beliefs. They have strong values and a sense of purpose that guide their decisions and actions (George, 2003). Bill George, the former CEO of Medtronics and one of the strongest proponents of AL, believes that the most effective leaders, those who have the most long-lasting impact on their followers and their organizations, are those who have a moral compass and have found their "true north" (George, 2007). The key to AL is understanding personal strengths and developing them. Consultant Marcus Bukingham recommends that leaders identify their strengths and build on them rather than try to address their weaknesses (Buckingham, 2005).

DEFINITION AND KEY ELEMENTS   The idea of authenticity as a primary factor in leadership is part of the new era in leadership research with many studies focusing on defining and measuring the construct and many others linking it to other leadership construct such as transformational leadership and to organizational outcomes (for a review, see Gardner, et al., 2011). The roots of AL can be traced back as far as Rogers' and Maslow's concept of self-actualization and more recently to the positive psychology movement (Seligman, 2002; Seligman and Csikszentmihalyi, 2000), the concept of positive organizational behavior (Cameron et al., 2003), and optimal self-esteem (Kernis, 2003; Kernis and Goldman, 2005). The basis for all the definitions of the concept is *awareness of one's values and self-knowledge* and acting according to that information. However, various conceptions of authenticity include other traits such as hopefulness, having enduring relationships, confidence, and behaving ethically. Authenticity is considered highly complex and includes traits, emotions, behaviors, and attributions (Avolio and Gardner, 2005; Cooper, Scandura, and Schriesheim, 2005; Ladkin and Taylor, 2010). Further, authenticity is differentiated from sincerity, which involves accurate self-presentations rather than being true to oneself (Avolio and Gardner, 2005). Table 6-5 summarizes the four key elements of AL.

Some have proposed that AL is the basis for many other leadership concepts such as charismatic, transformational, and servant leadership (Avolio and Gardner, 2005) and have related

TABLE 6-5	Components of Authentic Leadership (AL)
Components	**Description**
Self-awareness	Being aware of and trusting one's emotions, motives, complexities, abilities, and potential inner conflicts.
Unbiased or balanced processing	Ability to consider, within reasonable limits, multiple perspectives and inputs and assess information in a balanced manner in regard to information about both the self and others.
Behaviors are true to self and motivated by personal convictions	Focused by own convictions; unencumbered by others' expectations or desire to please others; decisions and behaviors guided by personal values.
Relational authenticity or transparency	Ability to disclose and share information about self appropriately and openly to relate to others; achieving openness and truthfulness in close relationships.

Source: Based on information in Avolio, B. J., and W. L. Gardner. 2005. Authentic leadership development: Getting to the root of positive forms of leadership. *The Leadership Quarterly*, 16:315–338; Gardner, W.L., G.C. Coglier, K.M. Davis, and M.P. Dickens. 2011. Authentic leadership: A review of the literature and research agenda. *The Leadership Quarterly*, 22: 1120–1145; and Kernis, M. H. 2003. Toward a conceptualization of optimal self-esteem. *Psychological Inquiry*, 14:1–26; Kernis, M.H., and B.M. Goldman. 2005. From thought and experience to behavior and interpersonal relationships: A multicomponent conceptualization of authenticity. In A. Tesser, J.V. Wood, and D.A. Stapel (Eds.), *On building, defending, and regulating the self: A psychological perspective* (31–52). New York: Psychology Press.

it to the positive leadership approach that we review in the next section (Luthans and Avolio, 2003). Researchers (e.g., Avolio et al., 2004) further consider AL to be a continuum where at one end a leader is either unaware of his or her values or does not follow them, and at the other end, the person is able to articulate values clearly and use them to guide his or her behavior (Figure 6-4).

AL is focused on the leader and on his or her self-awareness. It also carries a strong ethical and moral component that is similar to the servant leadership. Authentic leaders rely on their values to behave ethically and develop the genuine relationships with followers. Howard Schulltz, cofounder and CEO of Starbucks, has created an organization based on what matters most to him (see Leading Change in Chapter 10). As a child, Schulltz watched his family struggle without health benefits after his father lost his job because of an injury. Those experiences

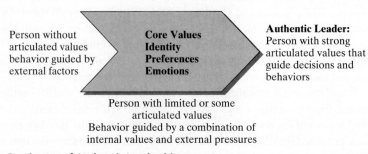

FIGURE 6-4 Continuum of Authentic Leadership

left an indelible mark on Schulltz, who made taking care of employees, providing health benefits, and not leaving anyone behind the core of Starbucks' culture. Schulltz' actions as a leader stem from his beliefs and values, which are the source of his success as a leader. Bill George suggests that Wendy Kopp, founder of Teach For America, is another example of an authentic leader (2007). With a strong desire to change the world and improve K–12 education, she organized conferences that included students and business leaders while she was a senior at Princeton University. Her isolated background from a middle-class family, her consideration of a teaching career, and her passion to make a difference led her to create Teach for America and lead the organization through many turbulent years before it established itself as a model for community engagement (George, 2007). Other leaders who believe that facing a major crisis allows people to find out who they are and what is truly important include John Chambers, the CEO of Cisco Systems. Chambers says: "People think of us as a product of our successes. I'd actually argue that we're a product of the challenges we face in life. And how we handled those challenges probably had more to do with what we accomplish in life" (Bryant, 2009d).

APPLICATION AND EVALUATION AL is still a new theory that requires much research. Consistent findings link it to positive organizational outcomes (see Gardner et al., 2011 for a review). For example, it has been linked to performance (Peterson et al., 2012), group ethical conduct (Zhu et al., 2011), team virtuousness (Rego et al., 2013), employee satisfaction and organizational commitment (Jensen and Luthans, 2006), and empowerment, engagement, and citizenship (Walumbwa et al., 2010). However, research about cross-cultural applications is still limited and the model and its applications and extensions continue to be developed. For example, researchers have suggested that authenticity should include not only awareness of strengths but also recognition of weaknesses (Diddams and Chang, 2012). Others have started considering various mediating, contextual and situational factors that may affect AL (Algera and Lips-Wiersma, 2012).

Positive Leadership

Several psychologists have recommended shifting the focus of how we look at both social and clinical situations from a negative—fix the problems, to a positive approach that focuses on elevating situations through having an affirmative bias that emphasizes strengths, capabilities, and possibilities, rather than weaknesses and problems (Seligman and Csikszentmihalyi, 2000; Snyder, Lopez, and Pedrotti, 2011). This *positive psychology* has in turn given rise to *positive organizational behavior* (POB; Cameron, Dutton, and Quinn, 2003) and *positive leadership* (PL). Much like spiritual and authentic leadership, POB and PL have roots in the concepts of self-actualization and the 1960s management approaches of Chris Argyris and Douglas McGregor, who focused on human growth and potential. PL includes a long list of traits, cognitions, and behaviors presented in Figure 6-5. At the core is the emphasis on *individual strengths* and helping people achieve their highest potential and what some researchers have called the psychological capital (PsyCap). *PsychCap* involves positive psychological states, confidence, positive attributions, perseverance, and resilience (Youssef-Morgan and Luthans, 2013). The various characteristics of positive leaders all operate together to allow them to function in their optimal range, something that is referred to as flourishing (Youseff and Luthans, 2012).

"What I've learned over time is that optimism is a very, very important part of leadership. However, you need a dose of realism with it. People don't like to follow pessimists," says Robert

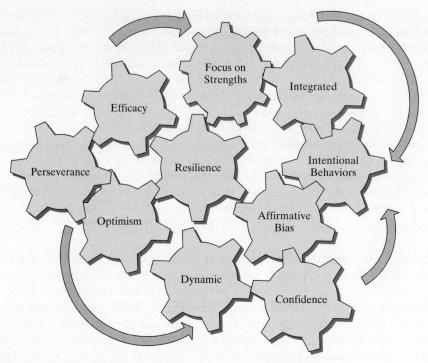

FIGURE 6-5   Characteristics of Positive Leaders

Iger, CEO of Disney (Bryant, 2009h). Author Carmine Gallo further states, "Inspiring leaders have an abundance of passion for what they do. You cannot inspire unless you're inspired yourself (Gallo, 2007). Tachi Yamada, the president of the Bill and Melinda Gates Foundation, echoes their thoughts, "If I spend my time focusing on everything that's bad, I'd get nothing done.... If you can bring out the best in everybody, then you can have a great organization" (Bryant, 2010b). These executives practice positive leadership, which includes (Cameron, 2008; Snyder et al, 2011) the following:

- *Being optimistic:* looking at the glass as half full; considering the positive side of events while remaining realistic
- *Encouraging positive deviance:* by promoting outstanding results that change the way things are for the better
- *Focusing on strengths:* having an affirmative bias that promotes what is going well instead of trying to correct what is wrong
- *Creating a positive climate:* where you give people the benefit of the doubt; foster compassion, forgiveness, and gratitude; and celebrate successes
- *Maintaining positive relationships:* with followers and advancing kindness, cooperation, support, and forgiveness in your team
- *Having positive communications:* with affirmative language, open and honest feedback geared toward building on and supporting strengths.
- *Dealing with negativity quickly:* addressing those who behave negatively and sap the energy of the team in a constructive manner.

APPLYING WHAT YOU LEARN
Balancing a Positive Approach with Realism

Positive leadership involves a way of thinking and a way of acting. Although both may have roots in personality, many of the actions of positive leaders can be developed and implemented with practice. However, positivity needs to be balanced with a healthy dose of realism. Some practical tips include the following:

- *Optimism is infectious*—most people respond to and are persuaded better with an optimistic message. Positivity engenders enthusiasm and motivation.
- *Stay data and fact-driven* when analyzing problems. Your analysis of issues should be based on as much objective information and facts as you and your team can find. So, temper your optimism when analyzing issues and take a hard, cold look at alternatives and options.
- *Be aware that we all overestimate our strengths.* Remain hopeful and positive, but be aware of this potential bias.

- *Positivity belongs in implementation.* When you have reached a decision, use your enthusiasm and optimism to cheer on your team. They need your encouragement, trust, and cheerleading at this stage.
- *Deal with negativity, but...* be careful not to shut down legitimate criticism and well-founded skepticism. Disagreement does not mean disloyalty, and you need to listen to dissenting voices.
- *Work hard at getting all sides.* The more power the leader has and the higher up she is, the less likely it is that followers will give bad news and voice dissent. You have to actively seek out their input.
- *Be aware of the power of a well-liked leader.* The more your followers like and respect you, the less likely they are to criticize you. Don't let their admiration and respect go to your head! You are never as good as you admirers say or as bad as your detractors think!

Evaluation and Application

The somewhat limited research about the impact of PL indicates that the leader's positivity, enthusiasm, and optimism can have many positive outcomes including higher performance (e.g., Avey, Avolio, and Luthans, 2011) and employee well-being (Kelloway et al., 2013). Some researchers have also suggested that PL can provide significant benefits when working across cultures (Youssef and Luthans, 2012). Positive leadership offers a fresh approach where the focus is more on how a leader thinks and less on what he or she is—charismatic, value based, or authentic, for example. Owing to its roots in psychology, positive leadership has a cognitive approach that emphasizes the perspective leaders choose to take, how they analyze and interpret the situation, and how those processes determine their behavior. Specifically, positive leaders take on positive perspective that guides their approach to leading themselves and others.

The concepts of value-based, authentic, and positive leadership share common elements with other approaches to leadership presented in this chapter. All focus on the relationship between leaders and followers and on the sharing of a vision for the group. Some researchers suggest that authentic leadership is at the root of the other concepts (Avolio and Gardner, 2005). Although charismatic, transformational, spiritual, and positive leaders all have to have some degree of authenticity, authentic leaders do not necessarily need to be charismatic, transformational, spiritual, or positive. In addition, authentic leaders may lead by being task or relationship oriented or by involving and empowering followers to various degrees. For charismatic and transformational leaders, the connection with followers comes from inspirational appeal, impression management, or focusing on the followers' needs. In the case of authentic leaders, a focus on followers and on attempts to win them over through arguments and rhetoric is usually absent (Avolio and Gardner, 2003). Instead, the authentic leader wins over followers by the strength of his or her own beliefs. The authentic leader does not focus on others' expectations.

As research topics, servant, authentic, and positive leadership present opportunities and challenges. The concepts add considerable richness to the study of leadership by introducing and considering the role of emotions in the leadership process. In addition, the introduction of hope and optimism, which is the basis of all three concepts, to understanding leadership is a significant contribution (Avolio et al., 2004). At this point in time, however, much of the information about value-based and authentic leadership theories is based either on case studies or on anecdotal accounts. Although the information is rich and provides many avenues for further study, empirical research about the topic is still scarce.

A Critical Look at Value-Based Models

While there is little doubt that the optimism, enthusiasm, and taking care of followers that are part of the value-based approaches can lend many benefits to organizations, some have sounded a note of caution regarding excessive positivity and misplaced optimism. Specifically, based on extensive research about perceptual and attributional biases, Lovallo and Kahneman point that leaders, as well as other people, have a tendency to overestimate their strengths, exaggerate their talents, and take credit for and overrate their control over positive events (2003). These researchers indicate that we tend to fall prey to *delusional optimism*, which makes us unrealistically optimistic about the success of our endeavors. Additionally, others have suggested that positive, or "Prozac," leadership (Collinson, 2012) and excessive optimism and "brightsideness" (Ehrenreich, 2009) can have dire consequences in organizational and political leadership. For example, business leaders' relentless optimism and their overconfidence may have played a role in the financial crisis of 2008 (Lewis, 2010).

Equating leadership with being positive, as is the hallmark of charismatic, transformational, and value-based models, may prevent us for dealing with the complex and multilayered issues that leadership presents (Collinson, 2012) and undermine the importance of followers, critical thinking and dissent (Banks, 2008). For example, can a leader be fully self-aware, but unethical? Or, when does a positive leader become dictatorial or even abusive in dealing with negative thinkers? Furthermore, while some researchers suggest that positive leaders are better suited to address cross-cultural challenges, there are few studies that apply the value-based leadership contexts outside of United States, where Barbara Ehrenreich, *New York Times'* bestselling author, says people have an obsession and a culturally based bias for positivity (2009). Finally, as is the case with charismatic and transformational leadership, the assumption that value-based leadership works in all situations and all contexts needs careful consideration.

Summary and Conclusions

This chapter presents the new era in leadership research and presents charismatic, transformational, and value-based models that currently dominate the field. Although the notion of charisma has been a central element of leadership for many years, recent scientific approaches allow for more-thorough descriptions of the process. In particular, current concepts view charismatic leadership as a relationship between leaders and followers, rather than as a combination of leadership traits and behaviors. For the charismatic leadership relationship to occur, leaders need certain traits and behaviors, followers must demonstrate particular traits and frames of mind, and the situation requires an element of crisis. The combination of these three factors allows for the emergence of charismatic leadership.

Charismatic leadership is one of the elements in the transformational leadership model. The model suggests that the transactional views of leadership, which focus on developing an exchange and transaction contract between leaders and followers, must be supplemented with behaviors that lead to organizational transformation. Transformational leaders provide vision and inspiration and engender the intense emotions required to enact such large-scale changes in organizations. Value-based models include servant, authentic, and positive leadership. Servant leadership is one of the few models that place follower's well-being at the center. AL emphasizes the leader's self-awareness as the source of effective leadership, and PL considers how a leader choosing to take a positive and optimistic perspective can encourage high performance.

Charismatic, transformational, value-based leadership have a broad appeal and provide an intuitive understanding of leadership that is applicable to large-scale leadership situations. They are also responsible for a resurgence in the interest in leadership. Because of their relatively recent development, the concepts still require much refinement, and their use in training leaders needs further refinement, particularly with regard to identification of various situations under which these models might be more appropriate and more effective.

Review and Discussion Questions

1. What are the factors that gave rise to the development of neo-charismatic leadership theories?
2. How do unethical charismatic leaders maintain their power?
3. What are the cultural constraints on the development of charismatic leadership?
4. Describe the elements of transactional leadership.
5. How is management by exception different from empowerment?

6. Describe the elements of transformational leadership and its role in enacting organizational change.
7. Differentiate servant leadership, authentic leadership and positive leadership.
8. What are the major contributions and shortcomings of the neo-charismatic approaches to our understanding of leadership?

Leadership Challenge: Standing Up to a Charismatic but Unethical Leader

You are one of the lucky people who work with a leader who has considerable personal charisma. She holds a grand vision of the future, communicates with passion, inspires her followers, and makes them feel special. Because of prior knowledge and experience with her, however, you are one of the few people who is aware that she is disingenuous, focused on her personal agenda and career, would not hesitate to sacrifice her followers for her own benefit, and is ruthless with those who disagree with her. You know that it is only a matter of time before her followers suffer because of her lack of concern and extreme self-interest.

1. What can you do?
2. Should you share your concerns with other department members? With her supervisor?
3. If you decide to act, what are some productive actions you could take?
4. What are the consequences of your action or inaction?

Exercise 6-1: Do You Know a Charismatic Leader?

Identify a leader you consider to be highly effective. This person may be in your work organization or a leader in your civic, sports, educational, or religious organization.

Step 1: Describe the Leader

Rate the leader you selected on the following items using the following scale.

1 = Never

2 = Occasionally

3 = Often

4 = Always

_____ 1. The leader shows a high degree of self-confidence.

_____ 2. The leader does not show any doubt about his or her ideas.

_____ 3. The leader has a clear, well-articulated vision.

_____ 4. The leader has a high-energy level.

_____ 5. The leader shows a lot of enthusiasm about the work to be done.

_____ 6. The leader is emotionally expressive.

_____ 7. The leader expresses his or her ideas well.

_____ 8. The leader is articulate.

_____ 9. The leader does all that he or she requires of followers.

_____10. The leader role models the desired behaviors and "walks the talk."

Scoring Key: Add up your scores for all 10 items. The maximum possible score is 40. The higher your leader's score, the more he or she demonstrates charismatic characteristics.

Total: _____

Step 2: Describe Followers' Reactions and Behaviors

Rate the leader's followers (including yourself) on the following items, using the following scale.

1 = Never

2 = Occasionally

3 = Often

4 = Always

_____ 1. The followers respect the leader.

_____ 2. The followers hold the leader in high esteem.

_____ 3. The followers are loyal and devoted to the leader.

_____ 4. The followers like the leader.

_____ 5. The followers believe in their own capability for exceptional performance.

_____ 6. The followers are enthusiastic about the work to be done.

_____ 7. The followers follow the leader's directions eagerly.

Scoring: Add up your rating for all seven items. The maximum possible score is 28. The higher the followers' scores, the more they demonstrate the characteristics of followers of charismatic leaders.

Total: _____

Step 3: Describe the Situation

Consider the situation that the leader and follower face in their day-to-day activities. Rate the situation on the following items using the following scale.

1 = Never

2 = Occasionally

3 = Often

4 = Always

_____1. Our team/organization needs to change.

_____2. We seem to go from crisis to crisis.

_____3. We could do many things better around here.

_____4. We do not seem to know what we are all about.

_____5. We have not yet explored many opportunities.

_____6. Many of us are not performing to our fullest potential.

Scoring: Add up your rating for all six items. The maximum possible score is 24. The higher your group's score, the more you are ready for change and face a crisis situation.

*Total:*_____

Step 4: Putting It All Together

Using the scores from the three previous measures, consider whether

1. Your leader has the personal characteristics of a charismatic leader.

2. The group exhibits the behaviors typically associated with charismatic leadership.

3. The group faces a crisis situation that involves a perceived need for change.

Based on these three questions, to what extent is the leader you selected charismatic?

1 = Not at all

2 = Has some, but not all elements

3 = To a great extent

Step 5: Discussion

1. What are the factors that explain your leader's effectiveness?

2. What do you foresee for the future if the situation changes?

Exercise 6-2: Charismatic Speech

One of the characteristics of charismatic leaders is their ability to articulate their ideas and vision in an inspiring manner. These articulation skills may come easier to some than to others, but they can be learned if practiced.

Two techniques are key to an inspiring message: (1) proper framing of ideas to give them a powerful context and (2) use of various rhetorical techniques to support the message.

Elements of Framing

Amplify values and beliefs.

Bring out the importance of the mission.

Clarify the need to accomplish the mission.

Focus on the efficacy of the mission.

Rhetorical Techniques

Use of metaphors, analogies, and brief stories

Gearing language to the audience

Repetition

Rhythm

Alliteration

Nonverbal message

Write a short speech that presents your goals (personal or for your team or organization). Revise and practice the message using charismatic speech methods listed above.

Source: This exercise is based on concepts developed by Conger (1989).

Exercise 6-3: Analyzing a Charismatic Speech

Charisma has been a much-talked-about topic in the United States and around the world in the past few years partly due to the election of President Barack Obama. One of the qualities often attributed to him is charisma, which is most evident during his speeches.

[Alternative exercise: Select a leader that you find charismatic and complete the exercise using that person to answer the questions.]

Step 1: Analyzing President Obama's Speeches

Using one of President Obama's speeches, analyze the charismatic qualities of his speeches. Examples of speeches you could use are as follows:

"Yes we can" (Nashua New Hampshire; January 9, 2008);

"A more perfect union" (Philadelphia, Pennsylvania; March 18, 2008);

"Victory speech" (Chicago, Illinois; November 4, 2008); and

"Keynote at DNC" (Boston, Massachusetts; August 18, 2004).

To what extent did the leader use each of the following?

	Elements of Framing	Not at All	To Some Extent	To a Large Extent
1.	Amplify values and beliefs.	1	2	3
2.	Bring out the importance of the mission.	1	2	3
3.	Clarify the need to accomplish the mission.	1	2	3
4.	Focus on the efficacy of the mission.	1	2	3
	Rhetorical Techniques			
5.	Use of metaphors, analogies, and brief stories	1	2	3
6.	Gearing language to the audience	1	2	3
7.	Repetition	1	2	3
8.	Rhythm	1	2	3
9.	Alliteration	1	2	3
10.	Nonverbal messages	1	2	3

Step 2: Other Noncharismatic Leaders

Consider other leaders, who may or may not be effective, but are generally not considered charismatic. For example, neither President G.H. Bush nor President G.W. Bush was considered a charismatic speaker, nor was Senator Hilary Clinton in most of her speeches.

Using the same scale, evaluate what elements of the charismatic speech are lacking from the way these leaders communicate.

Elements Of Framing	**Not at All**	**To Some Extent**	**To a Large Extent**
1. Amplify values and beliefs.	1	2	3
2. Bring out the importance of the mission.	1	2	3
3. Clarify the need to accomplish the mission.	1	2	3
4. Focus on the efficacy of the mission.	1	2	3
Rhetorical Techniques			
5. Use of metaphors, analogies, and brief stories	1	2	3
6. Gearing language to the audience	1	2	3
7. Repetition	1	2	3
8. Rhythm	1	2	3
9. Alliteration	1	2	3
10. Nonverbal messages	1	2	3

What other factors detract from these leaders' charisma?

Self-Assessment 6-1: Authentic Leadership

Being an authentic leader consists of several different elements. For each of the following items indicate to what extent the statement is descriptive of you, by using the following scale:

1 = Strongly disagree (does not sound at all like me)

2 = Disagree (I rarely behave this way)

3 = Agree (I often behave this way)

4 = Strongly agree (describes me very well)

_____ 1. I am aware of who I truly am.

_____ 2. I know what matters to me most.

_____ 3. I make my decisions based on my own principles, rather than what others think.

_____ 4. I have trouble handling my weaknesses and faults.

_____ 5. I have trouble opening up to others.

_____ 6. When I am in groups, I like to share as much information as possible with everyone.

_____ 7. Although I respect others' opinions, I tend to stick to things I believe in.

_____ 8. When I get conflicting advice, I have trouble deciding what the best course of action may be for me.

_____ 9. I am skilled at listening to and understanding many different points of view.

_____10. I like to hear information from all sides before I make up my mind.

_____11. Most people don't really know who I am.

_____12. I can tell when I am not being true to myself.

_____13. I ask for feedback from others to improve myself

_____14. I am able to clearly tell others how I feel and what I want.

_____15. In groups, I encourage discussion of various perspectives.

_____16. My actions and behaviors are consistent with each other.

Scoring: 1. Add up items 1, 2, 12, and 13 = ***Total:*** _____ *Self-awareness*

2. Reverse score for item 4 (1 = 4, 2 = 3, 3 = 2, 1 = 4) and add up items 4, 9, 10, and 15.
Total: _____ *Balanced perception*

3. Reverse score for item 8 (1 = 4, 2 = 3, 3 = 2, 1 = 4) and add up items 3, 7, 8, and 16.
Total: _____ *Value-based behavior*

4. Reverse score for items 5 and 11 (1 = 4, 2 = 3, 3 = 2, 1 = 4) and add up items 5, 6, 11, and 14.
Total: _____ *Relational Transparency*

5. Add up the total for the four subscales.
Grand Total: _____ *Authentic Leadership*

Interpretation. The range for the total scale is between 16 and 64. The closer you are to 64, the more elements of authentic leadership you have. Consider each of the subscales (scores range from 4 to 16) for areas where your score may be lower.

Source: This self-assessment is based on work by Avolio and Gardner (2005); Kernis (2003); and Neider and Schriesheim (2011).

Self-Assessment 6-2: Positive Leadership

Being a positive leader consists of several different elements. For each of the following items indicate to what extent the statement is descriptive of you, by using the following scale:

1 = Strongly disagree (does not sound at all like me)

2 = Disagree (I rarely behave this way)

3 = Agree (I often behave this way)

4 = Strongly agree (describes me very well)

_____ 1. I am an optimistic person.

_____ 2. Regardless of how bad things are, I generally tend to focus on the positive side of things.

_____ 3. I encourage my team members to look for novel solutions to reach the best results.

_____ 4. I expect the best from my team members.

_____ 5. When I give feedback, I focus most on people's strengths and developing strategies to build on them.

_____ 6. I look for ways to provide my team members with what they need to do their best.

_____ 7. I role model treating people well and with kindness.

_____ 8. I emphasize cooperation among my team and throughout the organization.

_____ 9. I behave kindly and with compassion.

_____10. When things go wrong, I focus my group on forgiveness and support.

_____11. I share information openly and provide honest feedback.

_____12. I encourage team members to communicate often and constructively.

_____13. I manage team members who do not stay positive.

_____14. I quickly address team members who are negative.

Scoring: Add up your rating for all 14 items. Your score can range between 14 and 56. A higher score indicates a more positive approach to leadership. For a finer analysis consider your score in each of the subcategories (refer to information in the section on Positive Leadership on pp. 200–202)

Optimism: Items 1 and 2

Positive deviance: Items 3 and 4

Focus on strengths: Items 5 and 6

Positive climate: Items 7 and 8

Positive relationships: Items 9 and 10

Positive communications: Items 11 and 12

Managing negativity: Items 13 and 14

Interpretation: Positive leadership is not considered a trait; rather it refers to way of interpreting events and a choice one makes to take on an affirmative perspective. A high score overall (higher than 40) indicates a generally positive approach. However, consider each of the subcategories to identify your strengths.

Source: This self-assessment is based on work by Cameron (2008), Luthans and Avolio 2003 (1992), and Snyder et al. (2011).

LEADERSHIP IN ACTION

ANDREA JUNG'S RISE AND FALL AT AVON

Andrea Jung was Avon's first female CEO until she left under a cloud of poor performance and legal troubles in 2011 (Nuyten, 2012). While CEO, Jung was an energetic and tireless spokesperson for her company, and with her outstanding retails credentials, her winning personality, and her big smile, she was the darling of the media throughout her tenure as CEO. Avon has been a global company for longer than many other companies have been in existence. It has served and employed women before diversity became an issue; and it was customer focused before the concept became an organizational mantra.

For more than 10 years, Jung successfully undertook the daunting task of reinventing a whole organization and moving a traditional, door-to-door sales company to the high-tech Internet world without alienating its loyal sales force—the "Avon Ladies" (Sellers, 2000b). In the process, Jung reinvented herself by rethinking what her role was and what was most important to her customers and stakeholders. Referring to the 2008 recession, she stated: "Leaders on the offense, not the defense, will come through this recessionary period" (Jones, 2009a). Jung undertook the makeover of Avon by pouring money into research and development, expanding the overseas markets, and focusing on jazzy marketing that included celebrities such as Salma Hayek. "Jung practically reinvented the company. She united its disconnected international operations into what she called a global 'company for women'" (Global Influentials, 2001). Her strategies paid off. Soon after she took over leadership, Avon's sales jumped from $5.7 billion to over $10 billion in 2009 (Forbes, 2010). She also increased Avon's visibility and credential as a responsible corporate citizen by raising millions of dollars for causes such as the children affected by the September 11, 2001, attacks; "Race for the Cure"; and by joining the campaign to end violence against women with Reese Witherspoon as its global ambassador. Helping women advance was one of Jung's personal passions. She believed that women were the answer to many economic and social challenges. She was also proud that during her leadership, Avon had more women in management than any other *Fortune* 500 company and that almost half of the company's board are women (Reilly, 2009).

Jung bet on the 5.5 million independent Avon Ladies and demonstrated her commitment to them by increasing the number of and incentives for the direct sales representatives and providing free training online and gas money. She involved them in the decision making rather than forcing the necessary changes from the top (Menkes, 2006). Kurt Schansinger, a financial analyst, described Jung as having a "strong vision, high standards, deep knowledge of the business, and enough confidence to delegate key tasks" (Brady, 2002). Birdie Jarworski, an Avon representative who met Jung at a company convention, described her as "the rock star of Avon"(Chandra, 2004). Allan Mottus, editor of a cosmetics newsletter, states that Avon "needed a person with charisma and Jung has that" (Chandra, 2004).

Born into a highly educated Chinese immigrant family— her father is an architect and her mother was Canada's first female chemical engineer—Jung always was expected to succeed. She received a Princeton education, graduating magna cum laude, and speaks fluent Mandarin and Cantonese as well as some French. When she joined Bloomingdale's, her parents did not originally approve of their daughter lowering herself to become a retailer, although her current position is winning their applause (Executive Sweet, 2005: 1). After Bloomingdale's, Jung followed her mentor Vass to I. Magnin and later to Neiman Marcus. Jung credits Vass with teaching her the art of tactful aggression, a style that matches her cultural roots (Executive Sweet, 2005: 2). Jung joined Avon partly because of the corporate culture and partly because women being a quarter of the company's board of directors appealed to her. She left an immediate connection to Avon, its employees and customers (Executive Sweet, 2005: 3). Her constant smile and upbeat approach and attitude set the tone for her company and sent a message of confidence and success. She believes that leading from the heart and flexibility are key to success (Executive Sweet, 2005: 3). Facing new challenges, Jung recommended, "Reinvent yourself before you reinvent your company" (Jones, 2009a).

Jung was able to achieve impressive results through dogged determination and unwavering confidence in her strategy, which involved the slow introduction of the Internet and other retail sales and a gradual blending of new retail methods with the traditional direct sales. However, in spite of all her efforts and persistence, an outdated supply system, increasing competition, poor marketing, and challenges in some of its global markets continued to challenge the company (Morrissey, 2013). Jung, who was named one of the most powerful women in business on several occasions and celebrated for her actions just a few years prior, was ranked third on Forbe's 2012 list of CEO screw-ups for rejecting a potentially lucrative merger offer from Coty cosmetics, not grooming a successor, and being under investigation by the Securities and Exchange Commission for a possible bribery case in China (Nuyten, 2012). In spite of all her efforts, Jung was not able to reinvent herself. Avon continues to be in need of a massive makeover, a task that now falls to its new CEO, Sherilyn McCoy, who took over in April 2012.

Questions

1. What are the key elements of Andrea Jung's leadership style? Consider the various models presented in this chapter.
2. What characteristics did Andrea Jung have that made her an ethical leader?

Sources: Chandra, S. 2004. "Avon's Andrea Jung Pins Hopes on China as Sales in U.S. Fade." *Bloomberg.com*, December 27. http://www.bloomberg.com/apps/news?pid=10000080&sid=aBrmvGQAml1c&refer=asia# (accessed January 31, 2005); "Executive Sweet," 2005. *Goldsea: Asian American*. http://goldsea.com/WW/Jungandrea/jungandrea.html (accessed January 31, 2005); Forbes. 2010. *Avon Products*. http://finapps.forbes.com/finapps/jsp/finance/compinfo/CIAtAGlance.jsp?tkr=AVP (accessed April 5, 2010); Global Influentials. 2001. *Time.com*. www.time.com/time/2001/influentials/ybjung.html (accessed January 31, 2005); Jones, D. 2009a. Avon's Andrea Jung: CEOs need to reinvent themselves. *USAToday,* June 15. http://www.usatoday.com/money/companies/management/advice/2009-06-14-jung-ceo-avon_N.htm (accessed March 24, 2010); Menkes, J. *Executive Intelligence* (New York: Harper Collins, 2006); Morrissey, J. (2013). Wall St. is pounding on Avon's Door. *The New York Times*. February 2. http://www.nytimes.com/2013/02/03/business/avon-tries-a-new-turnaround-plan-and-wall-st-is-anxious.html?ref=andreajung (accessed April 2, 2013); Nuyten, T. (2012). Avon—Andrea Jung, Nr. 3 in the Forbes worst CEO screw-ups of 2012. *Business for Home*, December 31, 2012. http://www.businessforhome.org/2012/12/avon-andrea-jung-nr-3-in-the-forbes-worst-ceo-screw-ups-of-2012/ (accessed April 2, 2013); Reilly N. 2009. Women: The answer. *Newsweek,* September 12. http://www.newsweek.com/id/215305 (accessed March 24, 2010); Sellers, P. 2000a. "The 50 most powerful women in business," *Fortune*, October 16: 131–160.

7

Other Leadership Perspectives
Upper Echelon and Leadership of Nonprofits

After studying this chapter, you will be able to:

1. Differentiate between micro and upper-echelon leadership and describe the domain and roles of strategic leaders.

2. List the individual characteristics of strategic leaders and consider the role of culture.

3. Explain how top-level managers affect their organization.

4. Analyze the unique challenges of leadership in nonprofit organizations.

THE LEADERSHIP QUESTION

Do you think there is a difference between leaders at different levels of the organization and in different organizations? Besides size and number of people who report to you, is leadership fundamentally different at top and lower levels or in different organizations?

When we talk about leadership, we are likely to refer to people who are at the top of their organizations; CEOs, city mayors, school principals, community leaders, and so forth. Based on the amount of attention given to top executives, one can deduce that we clearly believe the top leader of an organization is important. However, the academic research about top leaders' impact on organizational elements such as performance, culture, strategy, and structure is relatively new. With the exception of some of the leadership models discussed in Chapter 6, none of the leadership theories presented so far directly addresses the role and impact of upper-echelon leaders; most apply to supervisors, team leaders, and mid-level managers who lead smaller groups and departments. This chapter will explore the differences between mid-level (micro) and upper-echelon (macro) strategic leadership and consider the individual characteristics of strategic leaders and the processes through which they affect their organization. We will also address the special characteristics of nonprofit organizations and some of the challenges their leaders face.

DEFINITION AND ROLE OF UPPER-ECHELON LEADERS

Leadership in many organizations has become highly centralized with considerable power concentrated in the hands of top-level or upper-echelon (UP) leaders (Pearce and Manz, 2011). It is therefore important to gain an understanding of the particular characteristics and impact that UP leaders can have. We call UP leaders strategic leaders because they shape the whole organization. *Strategic leadership* involves a leader's ability to consider and anticipate external and internal events and maintain flexibility and a long-term perspective in order to guide the organization.

Research shows that CEOs impact the direction an organization takes, its strategy, and its performance (see Finkelstein and Hambrick, 1996; Hambrick, 2007; and Hambrick and Mason, 1984). For example, CEO's style can impact firm performance directly (Carmeli, Schaubroeck, and Tishler, 2011; Mackey, 2008) or indirectly through employee attitude (Wang et al., 2011), or affect the adoption of diversity strategies (Ng and Sears, 2012). CEOs can also play a key role in corruption and power abuse (Ashford and Anand, 2003), and the link between CEO narcissism and firm strategy and performance has also been explored (Chatterjee and Hambrick, 2007). Many of the leadership concepts and processes presented in previous chapters operate regardless of the level of the leader. For example, the basic definition of leadership and leadership effectiveness can be transferred from small groups to upper echelons with only minor adjustments. UP leaders are still the people who guide others in goal achievement, and their effectiveness depends on maintaining internal health and external adaptability. Therefore, the major differences between micro and macro leadership are not in the nature of the process, but rather in the level and scope of leadership (see Table 7-1 for a summary).

One of the first differences between micro and strategic leadership involves identifying who the leader is. In the case of micro leadership, the person leading the group, team, or department is clearly the leader. In the case of UP leadership the issue is not that simple (O'Reilly et al.,

TABLE 7-1	Differences Between Micro and Strategic Leadership	
	Micro (Group)	**Upper-Echelon—Strategic**
Who is the leader?	One person heading a group, team, or department	A person heading a whole organization with a variety of titles (president, CEO, COO); top management team (TMT); governance body such as board of directors
What is the scope?	Small group, team, or department	Entire organization
Where is the primary focus?	Internal	Internal and external
What are the effectiveness criteria?	Productivity; quality; employee satisfaction and motivation; turnover; absenteeism	Stock prices and other financial measures; overall performance; stakeholder satisfaction

2010). The leader of a business organization might be the president, chief executive officer (CEO), or chief operating officer (COO), or a top management team (TMT) made up of division heads and vice presidents. In some cases, such as nonprofits, the relevant strategic leadership may be a governance body such as the board of directors, board of regents, or supervisors. Any of these individuals or groups might be the senior executives who make strategic choices for the organization.

A second difference in leadership at the two levels is the scope of the leader's impact. Whereas most micro leaders are concerned with small groups, departments, or teams, upper-echelon leaders have jurisdiction over entire organizations that include many smaller groups and departments. Because of this broader scope, UP leaders have discretion and power over many decisions. Alan Mulally, president and CEO of Ford Motor, describes his job as a top-level leader as one where he has to connect talented people to the bigger purpose of the organization and encourage them to achieve their goals (Bryant, 2009f). James E. Rogers, CEO of Duke Energy, similarly believes that top leaders should have awareness of what all employees are going through so that they can tell the story regarding what the organization is doing (Bryant, 2009h).

A third difference between the two groups is their focus. The micro leaders' focus is typically internal to the organization and includes factors that affect their teams or departments. Part of their job may involve dealing with external constituents, as may be the case with a customer representative or a sales manager, or they might be under pressure to take on a more strategic view, even in their small department. They, however, generally do not need an external view to perform their job. In comparison, the job of the upper-echelon leader requires almost equal attention to internal and external factors. Dealing with outside constituents, whether they are stockholders, governmental agencies and officials, or customers and clients, is central to the function of executives. Alan Mulally of Ford says, "The more senior your management position is, the more important it is to connect the organization or the project to the outside world" (Bryant, 2009f).

The effectiveness criteria are also different for the two groups. Although, in a general sense, they are both effective when they achieve their goals, micro leaders focus on department productivity, quality of products and services, and employee morale. Effectiveness for the upper-echelon leader is measured by overall organizational performance, stock prices, and satisfaction of outside constituents. The hospital administrator has to integrate internal productivity issues with overall performance. The CEO of a major corporation does not focus on turnover of employees as a measure of effectiveness. Instead, the criteria are likely to be return on investment and the corporation's growth.

Strategic Forces

The six strategic forces depicted in Figure 7-1 are the primary domain of strategic leadership (Malekzadeh, 1995). *Culture* is defined as a common set of beliefs and assumptions shared by members of an organization (Schein, 2010). *Structure* comprises the basic design dimensions (centralization, formalization, integration, and span of control) that organize the human resources of an organization (Pugh et al., 1968). *Strategy* addresses how the organization will get where it wants to go—how it will achieve its goals. The *environment* includes all the outside forces that may potentially shape the organization. *Technology* is the process by which inputs are transformed into outputs, and *leadership* includes managers and supervisors at all levels.

FIGURE 7-1   The Domain of Strategic Leaders: The Six Strategic Forces

Any strategic effort requires the UP leaders to understand each of forces and how they are interrelated and to create a balance and fit among them. They must know their external environment and understand culture at all levels; they must know the leadership of their organization and its structure and technology and devise or implement strategies that accomplish their goals. When leaders understand the forces and create a good fit, the organization has a greater potential to be effective (Nahavandi and Malekzadeh, 1999). Consider the example of Jagged Edge Mountain Gear (JEMG), a Colorado-based company that specializes in fashionable mountaineering clothing and has become a fixture in the small mountain community of Telluride (Jagged Edge Story, 2013). Twin sisters Margaret and Paula Quenemoen founded the company in 1993 based on the Asian philosophy that focused on the journey and process (Nahavandi and Malekzadeh, 1999: 108–109). JEMG's goal was to become a nationally recognized competitor in their industry. As the Quenemoens state, however, "We are our own competition. We do what we think is right" (Nahavandi and Malekzadeh, 1999: 108). To achieve their goal, the sisters attracted a group of passionate mountain enthusiasts who perform the many business functions while remaining dedicated to cold-weather, extreme sports. The JEMG owners, managers, and employees worked together and played together. The culture of the organization was informal and exuded the members' passion for their sports. The structure, although formally stated, remained informal, with a heavy reliance on participation and empowerment. In addition, because of the company's relative isolation in Telluride, everybody depended on information technology to stay in touch with the marketing division located in Salt Lake City and their suppliers in Massachusetts, Tennessee, and China. The Quenemoens ran JEMG successfully by creating a fit among the six strategic forces.

The simultaneous management of the six forces is the essence of strategic management (Malekzadeh, 1995). The UP leader's role is to balance these various factors and set the direction for the organization. Once a direction is selected, internal forces (e.g., culture, structure, and leadership) come into play once more to move the organization toward its selected path.

Role of Strategic Leaders

Strategic leaders (CEO or the TMT) are the ones in charge of setting and changing the environment, culture, strategy, structure, leadership, and technology of an organization and motivating employees to implement the decisions. Their role is to devise or formulate the vision and strategy for their organization and to implement those strategies; they play the dual role of strategy formulator and implementer (Nahavandi and Malekzadeh, 1993a). If an organization has not drafted a strategy or is looking for major changes and strategic redirection, the UP leaders formulate the direction of the organization based on their reading of the environment. If the organization has a well-established, successful strategy already in place, the leaders' role is to implement that strategy. The dual role of strategic leaders is depicted in Figure 7-2.

Although UP leaders play a central role in creating and maintaining major organizational elements, their influence often is moderated by a number of organizational and environmental factors. The next section considers these factors.

Factors That Moderate the Power of Leaders

Upper-echelon leaders do not have unlimited power to impact their organization. The research about the limits of their power comes under the label of managerial or executive discretion and is the subject of considerable research in strategic management (Finkelstein and Hambrick, 1996). Table 7-2 presents the factors that moderate a leader's discretion. They are divided into external environmental and internal organizational factors. Both sets operate to limit the direct or indirect impact of senior executives on their organization.

EXTERNAL ENVIRONMENTAL FACTORS   Several researchers suggest that the leader's role becomes more prominent when organizations face an uncertain environment (Gupta, 1988; Hall, 1977; and Hambrick and Finkelstein, 1987). For example, in highly dynamic industries such as high tech or airlines, top managers must scan and interpret their environment actively and make

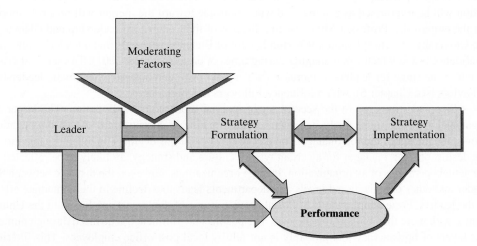

FIGURE 7-2   Dual Role of Strategic Leaders

TABLE 7-2	Moderators of Executive Discretion
External environmental factors	Environment uncertainty
	Type of industry
	Market growth
	Legal constraints
Internal organizational factors	Stability
	Size and structure
	Culture
	Stage of organizational development
	Presence, power, and makeup of TMT

strategic decisions based on their interpretations. The interpretation and the leaders' actions are essential. Bill George, former CEO of Medtronics and professor of management at Harvard, believes that leadership failure was key to the 2008–2010 economic crisis and that without effective leadership no action can be effective (George, 2009a). External forces include market growth and legal constraints. In fast-growing markets, strategic leaders have considerable discretion to set and change the course of their organization (Haleblian and Finkelstein, 1993). Legal constraints, such as environmental laws, health and safety regulations, and international trade barriers, however, limit the discretion of leaders. In such environments, many of their decisions already are made for them, leaving less room for action.

INTERNAL ORGANIZATIONAL FACTORS When organizations face internal uncertainty, organizational members question existing practices and decisions and rely more heavily on the leader to provide direction and guidance. In routine situations, organizational rules and regulations and a well-established culture in effect become substitutes for leadership (Kerr and Jermier, 1978). One example of a situation in which leaders are heavily relied on would be during a threatened or actual merger. The employees are likely to seek direction from their CEO, whose every word and action will be interpreted as a signal and whose attitude toward the merger will be a role model for the employees. Professor Mike Useem, director of the Center for Leadership and Change at the University of Pennsylvania's Wharton School of Business, suggests that a leader's calm and confidence is a key factor in managing during times of crisis (Maruca, 2001). The sense of crisis provides the stage for leaders to increase their impact or to demonstrate charismatic leadership behaviors (see Chapter 6), which influence followers to a high degree.

Size and structure are the second set of internal moderators of discretion. The larger an organization is, the more likely it is that decision making is decentralized. As an organization grows, the impact of the top managers on day-to-day operations declines. In small organizations, the desires of a top manager for a certain type of culture and strategy are likely to be reflected in the actual operations of an organization. In large organizations, however, the distance between the leader and other organizational levels and departments leads to a decline in the immediate effect of the leaders. For example, the U.S. Postal Service is one of the largest employers in the United States, with more than 650,000 employees. The postmaster's influence is diffused through numerous layers of bureaucracy and probably is not felt by local post office employees. This filtering also could be one reason it is difficult to change large organizations. Even the most charismatic, visionary leader might have trouble reaching all employees to establish a personal bond and energize them to seek and accept change.

One of the causes of internal and external uncertainty is the organization's life cycle or stage of development (Miller, 1987; Nahavandi and Malekzadeh, 1993a). When an organization is young and in its early stages of development, the impact of a leader's personality and decisions is pervasive. The personality and style of the leader/entrepreneur are reflected in all aspects of the organization. The younger an organization is, the more likely it is that its culture, strategies, and structure are a reflection of its leader's preferences. As the organization matures and grows, the leader's influence decreases and is replaced by the presence of a strong culture and a variety of well-established, successful routines. It is often at this stage that the founders of an organization leave and move on to new ventures. The leader's influence, however, becomes strong once again when the organization faces decline. The lack of success and the perceived need to revitalize the organization increase the reliance on the top managers. They once again have the opportunity to shape the organization. Ford CEO Alan Mulally's optimism and energy have had considerable impact on a very large organization that was facing decline. Mulally considers inspiring employees at all levels to be one of his top responsibilities. Bill Ford, the previous CEO of Ford who recruited Mulally, understood the power of a leader in times of crisis. He states: "We have good people. They just need a leader who can guide them and inspire them" (Gallo, 2012).

Mickey Drexler, current CEO at J. Crew and former chief executive of Gap, Inc., was credited with Gap's success in the late 1990s. Some even claim that he invented casual chic by providing fashionable clothes at a reasonable cost (Gordon, 2004). He is known for having considerable power. One former Gap employee states, "Mickey is omnipotent. There is nobody who is his equal. There is nobody who is near his equal" (Munk, 1998). Both at Gap and J. Crew, Drexler exercises considerable control over his organization. He believes in paying attention to every detail of the clothing his company sells and says: "I'm very proud to be a micro manager" (Sacks, 2013). Because the Gap was relatively new at the time and was experiencing a revival, Drexler's influence was pervasive. Another example of the leader's impact in the early stages of an organization's life is Oprah Winfrey—the first African American and the third woman to own a television and film production studio with more than $300 million in annual revenue; she runs an organization that reflects her high-energy, supportive style. She states: "It's all about attracting good people. I've always tried to surround myself not only with people who are smart but with people who are smarter in ways I am not" (Howard, 2006).

The last moderator of power and influence of top managers of an organization is the presence, power, and composition of a TMT and the board of directors (for a review, see Carpenter, Geletkanycz, and Sanders, 2004). As noted at the beginning of the chapter, upper-echelon leadership often involves working within a team; the presence of the team and how it interacts with the CEO has a strong impact on an organization. If an organization does not have a TMT or if it is weak, the impact of its CEO is likely to be more direct. If, on the other hand, the organization is managed by a powerful TMT, such a team will moderate the power and discretion of the individual leader (see the Section "Leadership in Action" case at the end of the chapter for an interesting example).

An example of a functioning partnership that increases a leader's power is the case of Oracle. Part of the success of the company is due to a strong relationship and match between its CEO, Larry Ellison, president, Safra Catz (one of the highest paid business women in 2013), and newly appointed copresident, Mark Hurd. Ellison is techy, extraverted, easily distracted, and a media celebrity. Catz and Hurd are both financial people with considerable knowledge of how to run a company (Lashinsky, 2010). Hurd is also a board member. Describing their relationship, one executive says that Safra seldom checks with Ellision on decisions and still follows him to impact the company (Lashinsky, 2009).

An interesting twist on the role and power of the TMT is the degree to which the members are similar to the leader and the diversity of the board. In many organizations, the UP leader both selects the members of the boards and often chairs the board (Pearce and Manz, 2011), a factor that makes it unlikely that the board members will either have approaches that are different than that of the CEO or challenge the CEO. Diversity in the board can have both good and bad consequences and has an impact on how the company makes decisions (e.g., Jansen and Kristof-Brown, 2006). Many organizations take into account the importance of heterogeneity in the makeup of the TMT or board of directors. Bill Kling, founder and president emeritus of the American Public Media Group, says: "I think every C.E.O. needs an executive team to be balanced to fit their strengths. The key elements, such as strategy, innovation, management, finance, don't need to be in any single position—but they need to be there in the executive team. It's terrific if you can walk through the halls and say hello by name to every employee. I can't. It's terrific if you can stand up at a staff meeting and do it in a way that people feel really good about your company. I can do that. But you never have all the pieces" (Bryant, 2012a).

These external and internal moderating factors limit the power and discretion of strategic leaders and can prevent the leader from making a direct impact on the organization. The next section considers the key relevant, individual characteristics of upper-echelon leaders.

APPLYING WHAT YOU LEARN
Managing in Times of Crisis

Leaders at all organizational levels have to manage difficult or crisis situations. No book knowledge replaces experience, but knowing what to do and having some guidelines makes handling crises a bit easier. The first step is to take a hard look and gain as good an understanding of the situation as possible. Here are some additional guidelines for handling crisis situations:

- *Be realistic* about how serious the situation is. Some people tend to sugarcoat too much and avoid problems; others tend to see everything as a crisis. Do a reality check.
- *Face the situation;* do not postpone or avoid dealing with the crisis.
- *Do your research and gather facts and information;* it is easier to make a hard decision when you have solid facts to back you up.
- *Seek help and support* from your supervisor if you can, or mentors and colleagues around the organization.

- *Be a role model;* make sure that you do what you are asking others to do; walk the talk.
- *Tell the truth;* communicate honestly and behave with integrity. If you have information you cannot share, simply say so; do not lie or make up what you don't know.
- *Remain calm and professional;* followers will react to your emotions and behaviors; be very deliberate about the tone of your verbal and nonverbal messages and how you behave.
- *Practice kindness* and give people the benefit of the doubt and support when you can.
- *Listen to concerns and have empathy;* put yourself in other people's shoes. You do not have to agree with or address everything you followers need, but you can listen to them.
- *Act!* As a leader you must decide and do something. It does not have to be spectacular and solve everything, but you cannot sit idle and avoid dealing with the crisis.

CHARACTERISTICS OF UPPER-ECHELON LEADERS

What impact do executives' personality and other individual characteristics have on their style and the way they run the organization? Are some characteristics or combinations of characteristics more relevant for upper-echelon leadership? Information about upper-echelon leadership characteristics is somewhat disjointed. Research about micro leadership presented throughout this book identified several important dimensions in predicting and understanding small-group leadership; the task and relationship dimensions, in particular, have dominated much of leadership theory for the past 40 to 50 years. These dimensions do not necessarily have predictive value when dealing with upper-echelon leadership (Day and Lord, 1988).

Demographic and Personality Traits

Older CEOs are generally more risk averse (Alluto and Hrebeniak, 1975), and insider CEOs (as opposed to those who are brought in from outside) attempt to maintain the status quo and are, therefore, less likely to change the organization (Kotin and Sharaf, 1976; Pfeffer, 1983). Researchers also considered the impact of an upper manager's functional background on an organization's strategic choices (Song, 1982), and a body of research explored the various personality characteristics with a recent focus on the impact of charismatic and transformational leadership (e.g., Hemsworth, Muterera, and Baragheh, 2013; Leithwood and Sun, 2012), emotions (e.g., Kisfalvi and Pitcher, 2003), emotional intelligence (e.g., Scott-Ladd and Chan, 2004), and the impact of negative traits such as those in the Dark Triad (e.g., Chatterjee and Hambrick, 2007).

Most of the leader's personal characteristics studied have some impact on organizational decision making, although the effect is not always strong. Two common themes run through the research about individual characteristics of strategic leaders. They are the degree to which they seek challenge and their need for control (Nahavandi and Malekzadeh, 1993a).

CHALLENGE SEEKING A number of researchers considered the upper-echelon leader's openness to change to be an important factor of strategic leadership. Upper-echelon management's entrepreneurship (Simsek, Heavy, and Veiga, 2010), openness to change and innovation, futuricity (Miller and Freisen, 1982), risk taking (Khandwalla, 1976), transformational and charismatic leadership, and even narcissism are all part of this theme. The common thread among these constructs is the degree to which leaders seek challenge. How much is the leader willing to take risks? How much will the leader be willing to swim in uncharted waters? How much does the leader lean toward tried-and-true strategies and procedures? A more challenge-seeking person is likely to engage in risky strategies and undertake new and original endeavors (Nahavandi and Malekzadeh, 1993a). A leader who does not seek challenges will be risk averse and stick with well-established and previously proven methods. The challenge-seeking dimension is most relevant in the way a leader formulates strategy. For example, one leader might pursue a highly risky product and a design strategy that will help produce and market such a product by accepting a high level of failure risk.

Challenge-seeking executives are celebrated in the current climate of crisis in many institutions. Richard Branson's willingness to take risks (see Leading Change in Chapter 6) has been key to his success and his fame. David Rockwell, the visionary behind many of New York's trendiest restaurants, is in high demand because of his creativity and his ability to harness the energy of 90 designers who work for him (Breen, 2002). Monica Luechtefeld, who now serves as a consultant to Office Depot and was the company's e-commerce vice president, is one of the "fearless mavericks" of e-commerce (Tischler, 2002: 124). She attributes her willingness to take on tasks that others shun to her parents' constant messages of "You can do anything" and "Figure it out," an approach she passed on to her son, who was raised hearing "Why not?" from her (Tischler, 2002).

NEED FOR CONTROL   The second theme in research about CEO characteristics is the leader's need for control, which refers to how willing the leader is to give up control. The degree of need for control is reflected in the extent of delegation and follower participation in decision making and implementation of strategy. Other indicators are the degree of centralization and formalization or encouragement and the degree of tolerance for diversity of opinion and procedures. Issues such as the degree of focus on process and interpersonal orientation (Gupta, 1984), tolerance for and encouragement of participation and openness, and what one researcher has called "organicity," which generally refers to openness and flexibility (Khandwalla, 1976), are all part of this theme.

The leader with a high need for control is likely to create an organization that is centralized, with low delegation and low focus on process (Nahavandi and Malekzadeh, 1993a, b). The culture will be tight, and focus will be on uniformity and conformity. The leader with a low need for control decentralizes the organization and delegates decision-making responsibilities. Such a leader encourages an open and adaptable culture, with a focus on the integration of diverse ideas rather than conformity to a common idea. The culture will encourage employee involvement and tolerance for diversity of thought and styles (Nahavandi and Malekzadeh, 1993a).

No apparent pattern emerges regarding how controlling the upper echelons of successful organizations are, despite the empowerment trends. In some cases, such as the CEO and TMT of Johnson & Johnson, decentralization and autonomy of various units are built into the credo of the organization and are central to the success of the company (Barrett, 2003). In other cases, such as Mickey Drexler, the CEO controls most of the decisions (Sacks, 2013).

Strategic Leadership Types

The two themes of challenge seeking and need for control affect leaders' decision-making and managerial styles and the way they manage the various strategic forces (Nahavandi and Malekzadeh, 1993a, b). First, the upper-echelon leader must understand and interpret the environment of the organization. Second, as the primary decision maker, the leader selects the strategy for the organization. Third, the leader plays a crucial role in the implementation of the chosen strategy through the creation and encouragement of a certain culture and structure and the selection of leaders and managers throughout the organization.

Challenge seeking and need for control combine to yield four strategic leadership types (Figure 7-3). Each type represents an extreme case of strategic management style, and each handles the strategic forces in a manner consistent with his or her basic tendencies and preferences. Given the pressure toward empowerment, employee participation, and the perceived need by many to be unconventional and innovative in all aspects of an organization, it might appear that some types of leaders are more desirable than others. The participative innovator (PI), in particular, could be perceived as ideal. Such an assumption, however, is inaccurate; different leadership styles fit different organizations based on their long-term strategic needs.

STRATEGIC LEADERSHIP TYPES AND THEIR IMPACT ON ORGANIZATIONS   The first strategic type is the high-control innovator (HCI). The HCI leader is a challenge seeker who likes to maintain tight control over organizational functioning. This type of leader sees opportunities in the environment and is willing to use technological advancements to achieve goals. HCIs look for risky and innovative strategies at the corporate and business levels that involve navigating

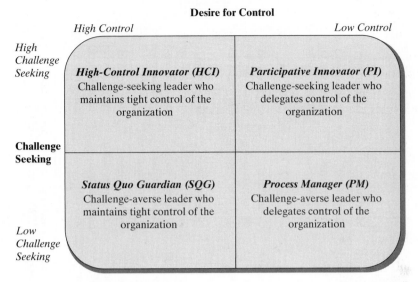

Desire for Control

FIGURE 7-3 Four Strategic Leadership Types

uncharted territories and entering new markets or new industries. (See Table 7-3 for a summary of leaders' impact on an organization and how they perceive and manage the six strategic forces.)

As opposed to the need for innovation when concerned with external factors, HCIs tend to be conservative in the management of their organization. The HCI leader has a high need for control that leads to the creation of a highly controlled culture in which adherence to common goals and procedures is encouraged and rewarded. Decision making is likely to be centralized, with the leader delegating few, if any, of the major decisions. The ideal organization for an HCI leader is one that is innovative and focused. The employees share a strong common bond and believe in "their way" of managing. Mickey Drexler, discussed previously, provides an example of an HCI. He has been described as a "visionary *and* a control freak" (Gordon, 2004). Although innovative and a risk taker in his strategies and marketing, he keeps a tight control over his organization. Drexler is a relentless "store walker," who picks on every detail (Kiviat, 2007). A Gap manager noted, "Nothing gets by Mickey. His attention to detail is extraordinary. He looks at threads, buttons, everything. He's difficult and very demanding. He can attack" (Munk, 1998: 71). He is also well known for his creativity, which he considers to be at heart of his success: "Most people underestimate the importance of creativity. Too many people overlook the importance of a beautiful product. Creativity drives growth in any business" (Sherman, 2013). Both at the Gap and in his new leadership role at J. Crew, Drexler is known for his knowledge and control of every detail. He admits, "I spot details quickly" (Gordon, 2004). Another example of a HCI is Jeffrey Katzenberg, CEO of DreamWorks Animation SKG, discussed in Chapter 4.

Unlike the HCI, the status quo guardian (SQG) does not seek challenge; however, like the HCI, SQGs want to maintain control (see Figure 7-3). This type of leader needs control over the internal functioning of the organization and is risk averse. SQGs perceive their environment as threatening and tend to want to protect their organization from its impact. They do not seek new and innovative strategies, but rather stick to tried and well-tested strategies (Nahavandi and Malekzadeh, 1993b). The organization run by an SQG leader is not likely to be an industry leader in new-product development and innovation. It, however, might be known for efficiency and low cost.

TABLE 7-3 The Impact of Strategic Leadership Types on the Six Strategic Forces

Leader	Perception of Environment	Technology	Strategy	Culture	Structure	Leadership
HCI	Presence of many opportunities for growth and threats from others	Innovation and use of high technology	High risk; product innovation; stick to core	Strong dominant culture with few subcultures	Centralized decision making by a few people	Leaders and managers with similar styles and views
SQG	Many threats; desire to protect organization from outsiders	Little focus on innovation unless it helps control	Low risk; few innovations; focus on efficiency	Strong dominant culture; low tolerance for diversity	Centralized decision making by a few people	Leaders and managers with similar styles and views
PI	Many opportunities; tendency to open organization to outside	Encouragement of experimentation; wide use of technology	High risk; product innovation; open to new areas	Fluid main culture; many subcultures; high tolerance for diversity	Decentralized decision making to lowest levels: empowerment and participation	Leaders and managers with many diverse styles and views
PM	Threats and tendency to protect organization from outside	Moderate use of technological innovation	Low risk; few innovations; focus on efficiency	Fluid culture with focus on "no change"; tolerance for diversity	Decentralized decision making; participation	Leaders and managers with many diverse styles and views

Source: Partially based on information in Nahavandi, A., and A. R. Malekzadeh. 1993a. Leader style in strategy and organizational performance: An integrative framework. *Journal of Management Studies* 30 (3): 405–425; Nahavandi, A., and A. R. Malekzadeh. 1993b. *Organizational Culture in the Management of Mergers.* New York: Quorum Books.

The ideal organization for an SQG leader is highly focused and conservative with a tight, well-defined culture that expects employees and managers to conform to existing practices and procedures. Decision making is highly centralized, with the SQG leader keeping informed and involved in the majority of decisions. Janie and Victor Tsao, *Inc.*, magazine's 2004 entrepreneurs of the year, built their $500 million, 300-person company, Linksys, on frugality, hard work, and tight control of every operation and decision (Mount, 2004). Although they develop networking products and allow employees to run their own projects, the husband-and-wife team believes that their product is neither spectacular nor involves any particular genius—just a good business plan and tight execution. One of their employees described their style: "Victor and Janie really like to see people execute" (Mount, 2004: 68). Tootsie Roll Industries, Inc., is another company run by SQG leaders: Ellen Gordon, president, and her husband Melvin, chair of the board, along with four other executives, fully control all operations. Tootsie Roll is named repeatedly as one of the best-run small companies in the United States. Much of the credit for its success goes to the Gordons for their single-minded focus on their business and their benevolent, authority-oriented styles. Ellen states, "We encourage a lot of new ideas, we create teams and we invite challenges, but we always have to make sure we stay on our overall goals" (Murrill, 2007). The company has managed to focus on the candy-making business for 100 years and through a number of defensive moves, warded off acquisition attempts. With a narrow strategy and tight controls, the Gordons encourage openness and feedback from employees and continue to build a strong, conservative culture.

The participative innovator is diametrically opposed to the SQG. Whereas the SQG values control and low-risk strategies, the PI seeks challenge and innovation on the outside and creates a loose, open, and participative culture and structure inside the organization. PIs view the environment as offering many opportunities and are open to outside influences that could bring change in all areas, including technology. Similar to the HCI, the PI is a challenge seeker and is likely to select strategies that are high risk. An organization run by a PI is often known for being at the cutting edge of technology, management innovation, and creativity.

The ideal organization for a PI leader is open and decentralized, with many of the decisions made at the lowest possible level, because the leader's low need for control allows for delegation of many of the decisions. The culture is loose, with much tolerance for diversity of thought and practice. The only common defining element might be tolerance of diversity—a "*vive la différence*" mentality. Employees are encouraged to create their own procedures and are given much autonomy to implement their decisions. The key to PI leadership is allowing employees and managers to develop their own structure and come up with ideas that lead to innovative products, services, and processes.

Ricardo Semler (see Leading Change in Chapter 5) is celebrated for his willingness to give up control and empower his employees while implementing innovative management strategies. Not only is Roy Wetterstrom, an entrepreneur who created several businesses, a high-risk taker, but he also believes that "to make a big strategic shift, you'll need to take a breather from day-to-day stuff (Hofman, 2000: 58) and push responsibility down the chain of command." John Chambers, CEO of Cisco Systems since 1995, often introduces himself as the "corporate overhead," serves ice cream to his employees, is open to ideas, is willing to adapt, and relies heavily on others to make decisions. He does not believe that leading means controlling people and budgets; instead leaders at all levels must be able to make decisions without asking for permission (McKinsey conversation, 2009). One Cisco employee described the culture: "John has instilled a culture in which it's not a sign of weakness but a sign of strength to say, 'I can't do everything myself'" (Kupfer, 1998: 86).

The last type of strategic leader, the process manager (PM), has the internal elements of PI leadership and the external elements of SQG leadership. The PM leader prefers conservative strategies that stick to the tried and tested. PMs are likely to shy away from risky innovation. The PM's low need for control, however, is likely to engender diversity and openness within the organization. Employees are not required to adhere to common goals and culture. As such, they have autonomy, and day-to-day operations are not highly standardized; the basic condition for decision making is not to create undue risk for the organization.

Jon Brock, who was the CEO of the world's No. 1 beer maker until 2005, is a process manager. His company, InBev, is part Brazilian and part Belgian with headquarters in Louvain, Belgium. It produces the famous Belgian beer Stella Artois and the Brazilian beers Skol and Brahma. Brock is informal, easygoing, and relaxed and makes it clear that he does not want to be the world's biggest brewer, just the best. His strategy focuses on efficiency and increasing profits by cutting costs. He wants to avoid hornets: "We're not going head-to-head with Budweiser, Miller, and Coors. That would be suicidal" (Tomlinson, 2004: 240).

As the former president of American Express and RJR Nabisco and CEO of IBM from 1993 to 2002, Lou Gerstner has a well-established and enviable track record as a strategic leader. He joined IBM at a time when the company was facing one of the most serious crises of its history. Gerstner is a cautious leader. While at RJR Nabisco, he opened the way for reconsideration of many internal processes. He is intelligent and has exceptional analytical skills, but he is careful about change. He strongly believes that change cannot happen unless it is balanced with stabilization (Rogers, 1994), and he is particularly skilled at letting his expectations be known. His approach is to improve existing processes slowly. He changed some elements of IBM and is proud of the company's slow and steady progress. Some call him an incrementalist rather than a revolutionary who avoids big mistakes but is moving too slowly.

All types of successful and effective leaders can be found in organizations. The need to revitalize our organizations is likely to be the reason we are celebrating innovators. The health care industry's award to best administrators regularly goes to innovators. The most-admired business executives are those who push their businesses through change. Many uncelebrated SQG and PM leaders, however, are managing highly effective and efficient organizations. For example, the leaders of the much-publicized Lincoln Electric Company are consistently SQGs for PMs. Their organization is a model for using financial incentives in successfully managing performance. Our current tendency to appreciate only change could make us overlook some highly effective managers and leaders.

WHAT DO YOU DO?

You are fully aware that change is not your thing. You are highly successful at creating systems and putting effective structures in place. You like order and predictability and have a track record to show how good you are at your job. You join the leadership team of a small company that is also highly successful, but that operates very loosely. Everything is decentralized and the focus is on change and innovation. How can you contribute? What do you do to succeed?

Culture and Gender

Given the cross-cultural differences in micro-leadership style and the importance and impact of culture on leadership behaviors, one would expect that strategic leadership also differs across cultures to some extent. Cultural values, in particular, can be expected to influence a top manager's decisions and style. With little empirical research conducted about the direct effect of culture on executive style, considerable anecdotal evidence suggests both similarities and differences across cultures. As organizations become more global, their strategic leaders are also increasingly global, a factor that can attenuate cross-cultural differences. Consider that Lindsay Owen-Jones, who is Welsh, was the CEO of French cosmetics company L'Oreal until 2011. Nissan, which is owned by French carmaker Renault, is run by Carlos Ghosn, who was born in Brazil of Lebanese and French parents and was educated in France. Austrian Peter Brabeck-Lethmathe was CEO of Swiss Nestle and continues as its Chairman. Other companies actively seek to build diverse and multicultural TMTs. For example, half of the senior managers at Citibank and P&G are not from the United States.

Models of cultures, such as those proposed by the GLOBE research (House et al., 2004) and Trompenaars and Hampden-Turner (2012), suggest that patterns of leadership differ from one country or region to another. Particularly, the GLOBE's culturally endorsed leadership theories (CLTs) show that although most cultures value leaders who have a vision and are inspirational, Anglos, Latin Americans, Southern Asians, and Germanic and Nordic Europeans do so to a greater extent than Middle Easterners. Similarly, participation is seen as part of leadership by Anglos and Nordic Europeans, but not as much by Eastern Europeans, Southern Asians, and Middle Easterners (Dorfman et al., 2012). Columbians want leaders who are proactive and recognize accomplishment without being too proactive in terms of change (Matviuk, 2007). Middle Easterners, more than other cultural clusters, consider self-protection (including self-centeredness, status consciousness, and face-saving) to be part of leadership (Dorfman et al., 2004). Based on cross-cultural research and case studies, it is reasonable to suggest that upper-echelon leaders from different cultures will demonstrate different styles and approaches.

For example, being part of the "cadre" (French word for management) in France means having fairly distinct characteristics (Barsoux and Lawrence, 1997). In the United States, upper-echelon managers are from different social classes with many different skills and backgrounds, but the French upper-echelon leaders are much more homogeneous. In a high-power-distance culture, in which leaders are ascribed much authority and many powers, the cadre comes almost exclusively from the upper social classes. Nearly all have graduated from a few top technical universities (*GrandesÉcoles*), where entry depends as much on social standing as it does on intellectual superiority. These schools have a strong military influence and continue to be male dominated. Their goal is to train highly intellectual, highly disciplined students who develop close ties and support with one another well beyond their years in school. The French cadre is, therefore, characterized by intellectual brilliance, ability to analyze and synthesize problems, and excellent communication skills. Contrary to U.S. leaders, the cadre's focus is not on practical issues or the development of interpersonal skills. Cultures with high-power distance show little need to convince subordinates of the leadership's ideas (Laurent, 1983). The cadre is expected to be highly intelligent, and its decisions are not questioned.

Many of the members of French upper management have considerable experience in public and governmental sectors. This experience allows them to forge government–business relationships that do not exist in countries such as the United States. Interestingly, graduates of the *Grandes Écoles* would not consider working for those who received regular university education. This factor perpetuates the homogeneity of the cadre, which in turn creates a group of like-minded executives who agree on many industrial and political issues. By the same token, this like-mindedness can lead to lack of innovation and the focus on intellect at the expense of action can cause poor implementation.

Another area of interest is potential gender differences. Unfortunately, research is lacking on the topic of gender differences in strategic leadership. It is evident that many of the top-level female executives in traditional organizations succeed because their style mirrors that of their male counterparts. Eileen Collins, commander of the space shuttle *Discovery*, believes that women often try to do too much and that men are more willing to delegate (Juarez, Childress, and Hoffman, 2005), a sentiment echoed by Judith Rodin, former president of the University of Pennsylvania and president of the Rockefeller Foundation. She suggests that women should find their own voice rather than try to emulate men and be aggressive (Juarez et al., 2005). We reviewed these differences in Chapter 2 with much of the recent research and many accounts of female executives and business owners and their focus on openness, participation, and interactive leadership provide some basis to make deductions about gender differences. It appears that the feminine style of leadership is generally low control. Meg Whitman, former CEO of Hewlett Packard, who is consistently ranked among the most powerful women in business (#15 in Forbes 2012 list) states, "I don't actually think of myself as powerful"; instead she relies on relationship building, developing expertise and credibility, and enabling—one of her favorite words—her employees (Sellers, 2004: 161). Similarly, Parmount's Sherry Lansing, cofounder of Stand Up to Cancer foundation, is famous for her nurturing style, charm, and ability to show empathy (Sellers, 1998). Gail McGovern, former president of Fidelity Investments and president and CEO of the Red Cross since 2008, observes that "real power is influence. My observation is that women tend to be better in positions where they can be influential" (Sellers, 2000a: 148).

Many female leaders, however, play down the gender differences. Judith Shapiro, former president of Barnard College, suggests, "You need to be supportive of your people because leading is about serving. That's not a girly thing; it's what I believe a strong leader does" (Juarez et al., 2005). She attributes any gender differences to women's social experiences. Chairman of the advertising company Ogilvy & Mather from 1997 to 2011, and now chairman emeritus, Shelly Lazarus asserts that everybody has to find their own way (Lazarus, 2010). She states: "I don't really believe that men and women manage differently. There are as many different styles and approaches among women as there are among men" (Juarez et al., 2005). Whether they are challenge seekers or risk averse, many upper-echelon women leaders, such as those described in the research by Sally Helgesen (1995), encourage diversity of thought and employee empowerment. Their open and supportive style allows employees to contribute to decision making. In addition, the web structure that some women leaders are reputed to use is flat, with well-informed leaders at the center and without centralized decision making.

As is the case with micro leadership, the type of strategic leadership that is needed depends on the type of environment the organization faces, the industry to which it belongs, and the internal culture and structure that it currently has. Therefore, leaders define and influence strategic forces, and their style also needs to match existing ones. If an organization is in a highly stable industry with few competitors, the need for innovation and openness might not be as great. The appropriate focus in such circumstances would be on efficiency. For such an organization, a highly participative and innovative strategic leadership style might not be appropriate.

HOW DO EXECUTIVES AFFECT THEIR ORGANIZATION?

Regardless of the type of leadership at the top of an organization, the processes through which strategic leaders affect and influence the organization are similar. As the chief decision makers and the people in charge of providing general guidelines for implementation of the strategies, top executives influence their organizations in a variety of ways (Figure 7-4).

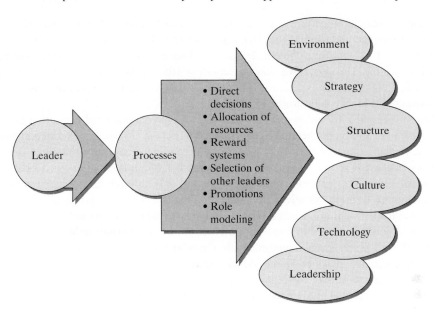

FIGURE 7-4 Processes Leaders Use to Impact their Organizations

Direct Decisions

Leaders' decisions regarding various aspects of the organization shape the course of their organization. The choices regarding the vision and mission for an organization influence all aspects of an organization's functioning. The vision and mission influence the culture of an organization by determining the basic assumptions, what is important, what needs to be attended to first, and what is considered less valuable. Similarly, the choice of strategy is considered to be the almost-exclusive domain of top management.

In addition to the vision, mission, culture, and strategy, the decisions to adopt a new structure, adjust an existing one, or make any changes in the formal interrelationship among employees of an organization rest primarily with top management (Miller and Droge, 1986; Nahavandi, 1993; and Yasai-Ardekani, 1986, 1989). The leader can determine the structure of the organization through direct decisions on the type of structure or indirectly through the way employees share and use information. Mickey Drexler of the Gap and J. Crew uses a public-address system to communicate with people in the office, leaves voice messages, and communicates face-to-face (Frieidman, 2011). A leader who consistently communicates only through formal reporting channels sets up a different structure than one who crosses hierarchical lines and encourages others to do so, as well.

Allocation of Resources and Control over the Reward System

In addition to direct decisions, one of the most powerful effects of top managers on their organization is through the allocation of resources and the control they have over the reward system. (Kerr and Slocum, 1987; Schein, 2010). A top executive is the final decision maker on allocation of resources to departments or individuals. If leaders want to encourage continued innovation and creativity, they might decide that the R&D and training departments of the organization will get the lion's share of the resources. Such allocations reinforce certain goals and actions, support a particular organizational culture and strategy, and create structures that facilitate desired outcomes and discourage undesirable ones (Kets de Vries and Miller, 1986; Miller, 1987). Consider that Jeff Bezos, CEO of Amazon.com, believes in focusing on customer satisfaction and not just the bottom line. He says: "We don't celebrate a 10% increase in the stock price like we celebrate excellent customer experience" (Yglesias, 2013). Given this approach, it is no surprise that Amazon ranks highly in customer satisfaction.

The formal and informal reward systems also can have a powerful impact on the culture of an organization and on the behavior of its members (Schein, 2010). For example, top managers can shape the culture of their organization by rewarding conformity to unique norms and standards of behavior at the expense of diversity of behaviors and opinions (Nahavandi and Malekzadeh, 1988). This process could take place not only through encouragement of certain behaviors but also through the selection of other top managers and the promotion of those who adhere to the leader's culture. Such a process is likely to take place regardless of the leader's style of strategic leadership. For instance, an HCI will be most comfortable with other HCIs, whereas a PI will prefer other managers with a similar style in key positions. A comparable process is likely to take place on an individual employee level. Employees whose actions fit the vision, mission, and culture of the organization are more likely to be rewarded. These processes create domino effects that further lead an organization to reflect the style and preferences of its leader.

Setting the Norms and Modeling

Rewarding certain types of behaviors and decisions is an overt action on the part of the leader; modeling behaviors and setting certain decision standards and norms, however, provide more indirect ways of affecting organizations. Alan Mulally of Ford Motor says, "I really focus on the values and standards of the organization. What are expected behaviors? How do we want to treat each other?" (Bryant, 2009g). In addition to making decisions, the top managers can set the parameters by which others make decisions. CEOs might tell their vice presidents that they will go along with their choice of a new product while also providing them with clear guidelines on which types of products are appropriate and which types of markets the organization should enter. By setting such standards, even without making a direct decision, the CEO still can be assured that the vice presidents will make the right decision.

Another subtle way in which leaders shape their organization is by the types of behavior they model (Nahavandi and Malekzadeh, 1993a; Schein, 2010). Mulally of Ford is the company's biggest cheerleader. Bryce Hoffman, who wrote a book about the Ford CEO, says: "Alan is all about evangelizing Ford through personal relationships" (Gallo, 2012). Irishman Feargal Quinn, founder and president of Superquinn, a chain of supermarkets, gained a reputation as the "pope of customer service." He focuses obsessively on making sure his customers come back—an obsession that he transfers to his employees (Customer service, 2007). James E. Rogers of Duke Energy, who was recently appointed to be on the presidential panel on energy policy, emphasizes walking the talk, "…as I've been CEO for over 20 years, it's really important to be on the front lines and to remember kind of the sound of the bullets whizzing by, to be on the ground" (Bryant, 2009h). Another area in which role modeling can have a powerful impact is in ethics. A. G. Lafley, CEO of P&G considers self-sacrifice and integrity to be essential traits of leadership (Jones, 2007). Similarly Gordon Bethune of Continental Airlines emphasizes the importance of integrity (Bryant, 2010a). Direct decisions, allocation of resources and rewards, setting of decision norms, and modeling are some of the ways through which a leader affects the organization. Through these various processes, leaders can make an organization the reflection of their style and preferences. They also provide strategic leaders with considerable power and influence. Such power requires some accountability, which is considered in the next section.

Strategic Leaders' Accountability

Chief executive officers and TMTs around the world have considerable power and influence over people's lives. Their actions affect the economic health of countries and citizens. For this burden, CEOs are well rewarded financially and achieve considerable status. The topic of executive compensation, another governance mechanism, continues to attract considerable attention and criticism. According to the AFLCIO, the U.S. CEO to worker pay ratio was 42:1 in 1982, 281:1 in 2002, and 354:1 in 2012, the highest in the world (Executive paywatch, 2013). In one case, for Ron Johnson of J.C. Penney, the ratio was 1,795:1 (Smith and Kuntz, 2013). The average salary of CEOs in Standard and Poor's top 500 companies in 2012 was $1.10 million, with perks averaging $273.154 (Executive pay watch, 2013). Such disparity has led many to call for mandatory disclosure of compensation packages and pay ratios, an action that stalled in the U.S. congress (Main, 2013).

Even ousted CEOs fare well. In 2011, ousting CEOs cost shareholders of Hewlett-Packard, Bank of New York Mellon, Burger King, and Yahoo $60 million (Flannery, 2011). Some estimate that CEO severance packages alone were over $1 billion in the United States in 2006 (Dash, 2007a). The list includes fired AOL CEO Randy Falco, who was paid $1 million in salary and $7.5 million in bonuses through 2010 (Carlson, 2009). Others include David Edmonston, who resigned from Radio Shack in 2006 after admitting lying on his resume ($1 million severance pay); Home Depot's Robert Nardelli, who is reputed to have refused to have his pay tied to the company performance and received an exit package of more than $200 million in 2007, despite poor stock performance and considerable controversy and criticism (Grow, 2007); Jay Sidhum, who resigned from Sovereign Bancorp amid criticism ($73.56 million that includes cash and stock options, five-year free health care, and consulting contract); and Douglas Pertz, who resigned from Harman International Industries after the stocks dropped during his four-month tenure and still earned $3.8 million in severance pay (Dash, 2007b). While the public outcry and political pressure have led to some changes such as more executive compensation packages being tied to company performance (Thurm, 2013), the income inequity in the United States continues compared to other nations. For example, in 2013, the pay ratio for CEO to worker was 206:1 in Canada, 104:1 in France, 93:1 in Australia, 84:1 in the United Kingdom, 89:1 in Sweden, and 48:1 in Denmark (Executive paywatch around the world, 2013).

The issue of executive compensation is highly complex. Theoretically, boards of directors determine CEO compensation relative to company performance; the better the financial performance of the company, the higher the CEO's compensation. Therefore, CEO's compensation can be an effective tool for motivating and controlling managers. In many cases, company leaders get fair compensation packages and perform well. The instances of lack of performance and high compensation, however, are hard to ignore. Many executives get pay raises that are considerably higher than their company's performance. For example, in 2008, profit at Archer Daniels Midland fell by 17 percent; CEO Patricia Woertz' salary was increased by close to 400 percent (The pay at the top, 2010). Similarly, while Boeing's profit dropped by 35 percent in 2008, CEO James McNemey got a 14 percent increase in his compensation (The pay at the top, 2010). After pulling Vioxx off the market, shares of Merck slumped 30 percent, but the company board gave the CEO, Ray Gilmartin, a $1.4 million bonus and stock options valued at $19.2 million (Strauss and Hansen, 2005).

TABLE 7-4	Determinants of Executive Compensation
Firm size	The larger the firm, the higher is the compensation.
Industry competition	Companies often outbid one another to hire top executives.
CEO power and discretion	The higher the power of the CEO, the higher is the compensation package.
Internationalization	Increased internationalization is related to higher executive pay.
High stress and instability	CEO jobs are considered high stress, requiring high compensation.

Based on these examples and the extensive research about CEO compensation (see O'Reilly and Main, 2007), company performance is not the only determinant of CEO compensation. So what determines an executive's worth? Table 7-4 gives a summary of factors that determine executive compensation. One factor that seems to explain the size of executive pay in the United States is the size of the organization (see Geiger and Cashen, 2007): The larger the organization, the larger the CEO's compensation package will be, regardless of performance. Another factor seems to be the competition for hiring CEOs: As organizations outbid one another, salaries continue to increase.

Organizations in which top managers have more discretion also tend to have higher pay (Cho and Shen, 2007). In addition, research shows that top management pay and company performance are more aligned when the company's board of directors is dominated by members from outside the organization (Conyon and Peck, 1998). Other research that considers the impact of internationalization found that increased internationalization is related to higher CEO pay (Sanders and Carpenter, 1998). The thought is that the high demands put on CEOs and the instability of their positions must be balanced with high salaries. These high salaries, now standard in U.S. industry, show no end in their upward trend, even during a time of economic crisis. The result is the creation of a new, powerful U.S. managerial class and a widening of the gap between high and low levels of organizations.

The highly paid top executives have become popular heroes whose names are part of our everyday life. Based on economic and organizational theory, environmental forces will push a nonperforming leader to be replaced. Ideally, elected federal, state, and city officials who do not perform are not reelected. Similarly, the board of directors replaces a CEO who does not manage well. The principal of a school with poor student academic performance and a high dropout rate would be fired by the school board. These ideal situations do not seem to be common, however. Many powerful leaders are not being held accountable for their actions. They continue to hold positions of power and influence regardless of their organization's poor performance, ethical abuses, and social irresponsibility. It is not common in the United States for a company CEO or public officials to resign when they fail to live up to the promises they made. When their organizations cause major disasters or commit illegal acts, the CEOs escape unscathed. The CEO of Exxon accepted none of the responsibility for the *Valdez* fiasco. After the Bhopal disaster, with several thousand dead and hundreds of thousands injured, the CEO of Union Carbide was not replaced. The public firing of the CEO of General Motors by the U.S. government in 2009 and the replacement of BP's CEO Tony Hayward in 2010 are the exception rather than the rule.

For the benefit of organizational and social functioning and well-being, it is essential that the tremendous power, influence, and status of CEOs be accompanied by accountability and responsibility to their various constituents. Such accountability exists on paper but is hardly ever executed. The power and impact of upper-echelon leaders are undeniable. Their credibility and ability to further affect their organizations, however, can increase only with more accountability.

UNIQUE CASE OF NONPROFIT ORGANIZATIONS

Nonprofit organizations are private organizations that cannot make a profit for its owners or members but can charge fees for services or membership. Other terms used to describe such agencies that are private, with a public purpose include voluntary, not-for-profit, philanthropic, and NGOs or nongovernmental organizations (Weiss and Gantt, 2004). Technically nonprofits are defined by their tax-exempt status, but they fit somewhere in between the public and private (business) organizations and the distinction among the various sectors is not always clear (Robichau, 2013). Their purpose is to create value by serving society and their clients (Drucker, 1990, Pynes, 2011).

Although many of the leadership and organizational principles that apply to business and other organizations are also relevant in nonprofit organizations, some of their distinguishing characteristics present them with unique leadership challenges, and nonprofit organizations have their own unique character (Ott and Dicke, 2012). The case of Public Allies in Leading Change in this chapter provides an example of a nonprofit organization whose primary purpose is public good, and its source of funding is donations through grants, foundations, and individuals.

Characteristics of Nonprofit Organizations

Many of the characteristics that identify nonprofit organizations are related to tax status. Other characteristics include the following:

- *Operate without profit.* Although nonprofit organizations charge for services or membership and many generate and use considerable sums of money, all the funds are reinvested to support the operations of the organization. Many nonprofits are highly "profitable"; however, all excess funds are reinvested to achieve their mission.
- *Public service mission.* The primary mission of a nonprofit organization is to serve the public good, whether it is health care (hospitals), education (schools and universities), churches, community improvement, or foundations with a broad purpose.
- *Governed by voluntary board of directors.* As opposed to business organizations that have paid board of directors, the governing boards of nonprofits are staffed by volunteers with a stake or interest in the mission of the organization.
- *Funded through contributions.* Whereas charging fees is a source of revenue for many nonprofit organizations, their primary sources of funding are contributions, grants, and donations from individuals, government agencies, and other foundations.

There are many organizations around the world that fit into the nonprofit category. Examples in the United States include the American Cancer Society, National Geographic Society, the Metropolitan Museum of Art, Stanford University, Planned Parenthood, the Ford and Rockefeller Foundations, the National Association for the Advancement of Colored People (NAACP), and the YMCA and YWCA. Around the world, NGOs make considerable contributions to improving social, human, political, economic, and ecological conditions. Organizations such as Doctors without Border (*Médecins sans Frontières*); OXFAM, an international relief agency; the International Red Cross; and the World Wildlife Fund are just a few that encourage development and support communities in crisis around the world. These organizations survive and achieve their goals by using funds they obtain through various means. For example, physicians volunteer their time through Doctors without Borders and provide health care in remote areas of the world; OXFAM provides funds and resources to combat global poverty and social injustice.

LEADING CHANGE
Public Allies: Building Leadership in the Community

"Leadership is an action-not a position," "Leadership is about taking responsibility," and "Leadership is about the practice of values" are the principles behind a unique and dynamic community organization called Public Allies (Schmitz, 2012). The organization is grounded in the belief that young members of a community have the capacity to lead others when given opportunity, support, and training, and that they can have a positive impact in their own backyard. Through a variety of programs, Public Allies aims at developing the next generation of leaders who will continue to change the world (Public Allies-Our Mission, 2013).

The organization was founded in 1992 in Washington D.C. by two young community activists, Vanessa Kirsch and Katrina Browne, who brought together 14 passionate members using grants from several organizations such as the MacArthur and Surdna Foundations. Public Allies quickly became one of the first organizations funded by the new Commission on National and Community Service created by President G.H. Bush and one of the first funded by the newly formed Americorps under President Clinton. By 1993, the organization had 500 graduates; in 2013, 4,000 Allies served in over 20 cities where they partnered with universities and nonprofit organizations to serve their communities. Making the right connections is at the heart of the organization's success. Kirsch followed the recommendation of several people and happened to connect with a community organizer in Chicago in the early 1990s named Barack Obama, convinced him to join her board, and listened to his recommendation to interview his wife Michelle, 28 at the time and working for Chicago mayor Richard Daley, to run the Chicago office in 1993 (Perry, 2008). Kirsch and Browne also connected with the first lady of Arkansas, Hilary Clinton, who promised to host an event in the White House, if her husband won his race to the presidency (Schmitz, 2012).

Passion, hard work, strategic thinking, proven results, and luck have all contributed to the rise of Public Allies. Aside from serving various communities, the organization provides an opportunity for young people, 18 to 30, to lead. Its CEO, Paul Schmitz, says: "There are so many talented people who just don't have knowledge of a path or access to a path to take their passions and skills and turn them into a viable career." He says, "That's what we're about, trying to build the pipeline" (Perry, 2008: 2). The pipeline of leaders is built through the Public Allies program, which places members to work in a local charity four days a week and in intensive leadership training on the fifth day. The training provides cutting edge leadership development curriculum, coaching, reflection, feedback, and team-based projects that connect the work of members in the community with the training. One of the graduates, Paul Griffin, who founded City at Peace, an organization that now operates in several U.S. cities as well as in Israel and South Africa, and that brings together youth to write and perform musicals about their lives, says that he learned how to lead from Public Allies. He believes they answered his basic questions: "How do you do it effectively? Who are your stakeholders? How do you develop a group of people to achieve these goals? (Perry, 2008: 3).

CEO Paul Schmitz says he often gets the question of how can everyone lead and what does it mean if no one follows. His response is that Public Allies is "reframing the idea of leadership, moving from an emphasis on the noun *leader* to an emphasis on the verb *to lead*" (Schmitz, 2012: xv).

By redefining leadership and building community capacity through engagement of citizens, providing services, and collaboration with many other organizations, Public Allies has been able to show striking results. While the large majority of nonprofit organizations serve diverse communities and many of their volunteers and members are women, they are primarily led by white males. Public Allies are 67 percent people of color and 60 percent women with the majority of members having a college education (Schmitz, 2012). The groups that host the Allies are highly satisfied with them; the organization is able to recruit large number of volunteers to support projects, over 20,000 in 2010 alone; and it creates thousands of connections among various organizations to support local communities. The graduates have been able to accomplish goals such as funding schools in a Chicago neighborhood (program headed by Public Ally Jose Rico), creating a youth academy in Washington D.C. (headed by Nigel Okumbi), supporting a youth program called Urban Underground in Milwaukee (headed by Reggie Moore and Sharlen Bowen Moore), among many others (Schmitz, 2012). All of the projects are based on a strict code of ethics that emphasizes collaboration, diversity and inclusion, community-based asset development, continuous learning, and integrity (Public Allies-Code of Ethics, 2010).

Sources: Perry, S. 2008. "Fired up and ready to go," http://www.publicallies.org/atf/cf/{FBE0137A-2CA6-4E0D-B229-54D5A098332C}/Chronicle%20Articles%20April%2014%202008.pdf (accessed July 20, 2013); Public Allies-Code of Ethics. 2010. http://www.publicallies.org/site/c.liKUL3PNLvF/b.4167361/k.B6B3/NEWS/apps/s/link.asp (accessed July 21, 2013); Public Allies-Our Mission. 2013. http://www.publicallies.org/site/c.liKUL3PNLvF/b.2775807/k.C8B5/About_Us.htm (accessed July 20, 2013); Schmitz, P. *Everyone leads: Building leadership from the community up* (San Francisco: Wiley, 2012).

Leadership Challenges of Nonprofits

The leadership of nonprofit organizations involves the same principles as other organizations. Their leaders must help individuals and groups set goals and guide them in the achievement of those goals. The public-good mission of nonprofits, along with the voluntary participation of many of their employees, contributors, and other stakeholders, creates a particular burden on leaders of such organizations to lead through a collaborative and trust-based style (Thomson and Perry, 2010). In most cases, individual donors, except for tax benefits when applicable, do not get tangible benefits from their donation, and the resources they contribute do not always stay in their community. The nonprofit is based to a great extent on the principles of altruism and selfless contribution.

As much as integrity, trustworthiness, and self-sacrifice are elements for all leadership situations, they are even more so in the nonprofit organizations. Without the profit motive, which legitimately guides business organizations and the rewarding of its leaders (e.g., top leaders being compensated with company shares), nonprofit organizations are likely to attract leaders with a stronger focus on civic contribution. The role of leaders in nonprofit organizations is that of an intermediary (Butler and Wilson, 1990). The leader guides the organization to allocate the resources, such as donations or grants, to various receivers turning the resources that are trusted to the organization into social good (Figure 7-5). In his commencement address at the University of Maryland, Brian Gallagher—president and CEO of the United Way, the $5billion umbrella organization for large number of charities—emphasized the importance of service to the community and stated that his organization "improves lives by mobilizing the caring power of communities" (Gallagher, 2006: 6). Luis A Ubiñas, president of the Ford Foundation, the second largest philanthropy in the United States that defines itself as a resource for innovative

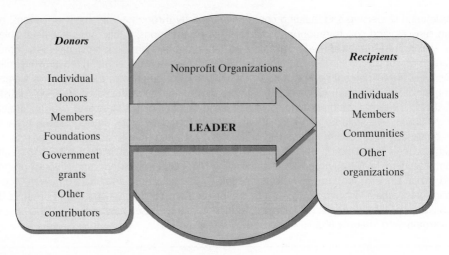

FIGURE 7-5 Role of Leaders in Nonprofit Organizations

people and institutions worldwide, leads an organization that has as its mission to support vision-ary leaders and organizations on the frontlines of social change worldwide with the goals to strengthen democratic values, reduce poverty, promote international cooperation, and advance human achievement (Ford Foundation Mission, 2013). The organization aims to achieve these goals by providing grants to qualified groups and organizations.

One of the major challenges that leaders of nonprofit organizations face is how to recruit, retain, and motivate employees, many of whom are volunteers, without having access to sub-stantial monetary rewards (Cryer, 2004). Even in the case of paid employees, salaries are often lower than comparable positions in business organizations. The leaders of nonprofits, therefore, require considerable skills in motivating and inspiring their followers. In many cases, followers have joined the organization because they are passionate about its mission; however, passion alone does not always lead to effectiveness. An additional factor is that the structure of many nonprofits is relatively flat, with few employees and few layers of management. Effective lead-ership requires empowerment; use of all available resources, often by harnessing the power of teams; and participation to creatively solve problems without many resources.

According to recent studies, nonprofit organizations are facing a leadership crisis because of a significant shortfall of qualified leaders (Tierney, 2006). As more nonprofit organizations are created and step in to address growing social challenges not addressed by government or busi-ness organizations, the need for effective leadership increases. The Bridgespan Group's study indicates that the total number of nonprofit organization has tripled over the past 20 years, with a 30 percent increase from 1999 to 2009 (National Center for Charitable Statistics, 2010). However, because of demographic shifts, retirement, and lack of active recruitment and development, the supply of potential leaders has not kept up (Tierney, 2006). One of the challenges leaders of nonprofits, therefore, face is the recruitment, retention, and development of future leaders. Such a task is much simpler in a business organization, where considerable resources are dedicated to recruitment and development and access to a pool of leaders from competitors is much greater.

Although many of the processes involved in leading nonprofit organizations are similar to those used in a business organization, leaders of nonprofits need a particular emphasis on build-ing relationships and trust and on the development of future leaders.

THE LEADERSHIP QUESTION—REVISITED

At some level, leading is leading; whether you lead a team or a large organization, you need to take care of the task and take care of people. However, leading at higher levels requires different skills, a heavier reliance on cognitive and interpersonal skills, and the ability to juggle many complex factors at a strategic level. Nonprofits face another challenge of both working with volunteers and having little access to typical rewards for their employees. Regardless of the organization and the level, connecting with followers is at the heart of leadership; competence and knowledge of the task or the business matter—there is no compromise on these issues at any level. But each leadership situation is also unique and being effective requires preparation, knowledge, experience, and styles and behaviors that fit the situation.

Summary and Conclusions

Upper-echelon or strategic leadership has many commonalities with leadership at lower levels of organizations. UP leadership, however, adds a new level of complexity to the process by focusing the leader on a whole organization rather than a small group or department and by giving the leader discretion with far-reaching influence over decisions. In addition, upper-echelon leaders focus on external constituencies as well as the internal environment and in so doing are required to lead with a team of other executives.

An integrated approach to upper-echelon leadership considers the leader to be a formulator and implementer of strategy. Therefore, in addition to considering the need to match the leader to existing strategy and other organizational elements, the integrated approach also considers the role of the leader's individual characteristics and style in the selection of various organizational elements and the implementation of decisions. The matching concept, which views the CEO primarily as an implementer of existing strategy, is also useful when selecting a leader to implement a newly charted course.

Two major themes run through the diverse research about top management characteristics. The first theme is the leader's degree of challenge seeking and preference for risk and innovation. The second is the leader's need for control over the organization. The combination of these two themes yields four types of strategic leaders: HCI, SQG, PI, and PM. These four types each exhibit different preferences for the direction and management of their organization. They exert their influence through direct decisions, allocation of resources and rewards, and the setting of norms and the modeling of desired behaviors. Through these processes, strategic leaders gain considerable power and influence. Such power is accompanied by generous compensation packages. Accountability for the actions of top executives, however, is still limited.

Although many of the processes involved in leading nonprofit organizations are similar to those used in business organization, leaders of nonprofits need a particular emphasis on building relationships and trust and on the development of future leaders. Overall, the area of strategic leadership, whether in business or nonprofit organizations, provides a different and important perspective to the study of leadership. Strategic leaders face many challenges that micro leaders do not. The study of strategic leaders is also a fertile area for integrative research linking micro and macro factors.

Review and Discussion Questions

1. What are the differences between micro and macro leadership?
2. What are the strategic forces that affect strategic leadership in organizations?
3. To what extent does the leader's need for control affect the structure and culture of an organization?
4. How do French upper echelon managers differ from their counterparts in the United States?
5. What are the major themes that are used to describe upper-echelon leaders?
6. Describe each of the four strategic leadership types. Provide examples of each type.
7. How do culture and gender affect strategic leadership?
8. Describe each of the processes used by leaders to influence strategic forces in their organizations. Which of the processes is most important? Why?
9. What is the upper echelon's responsibility in organizational actions and performance?
10. Why do chief executives sometimes receive substantial pay increases when the performance of their company has declined?

Leadership Challenge: The Board of Directors (BOD) and CEOs

Public corporations are led by CEOs and other upper-echelon leaders who, in turn, report to shareholders and boards of directors (BODs). Interestingly, even though the board oversees the CEOs, decides on terms of employment and salaries, and monitors their performance, the CEOs are, more often than not, the people who nominate board members. The justification is that CEOs are well placed to know what type of expertise they need on the board and should have a BOD they can work with. The relationship between BOD and CEO is a complex and interesting one.

1. What are the potential ethical and conflict-of-interest issues arising from CEO involvement in the selection of board members?
2. How can these issues be addressed?

Exercise 7-1: Understanding Strategic Forces

This exercise is designed to help you understand the role of leaders in managing the six strategic forces of environment, strategy, culture, structure, technology, and leadership presented in the chapter.

The Scenario

You are a member of a school board for a medium-sized middle (junior high) school in a major western city. The city has experienced tremendous growth in the past five years, and as a result, the student body increased by 20 percent without much change in facilities and relatively limited increases in funding. The classrooms are overcrowded, much of the equipment is old, teachers have limited resources to enrich the curriculum, and the sense of direction is unclear. During the same time period, the school slowly developed one of the poorest records for student academic performance and dropout rate.

Earlier to the past few years, however, the school held a well-established reputation as one of the most creative and academically sound schools in the city. Traditionally, parent involvement and interest in the school varied greatly. Similarly, the faculty are diverse in their approach, tenure, and backgrounds, but the majority demonstrate dedication to their students and are committed to the improvement of the school.

Because of a number of recent threats of lawsuits from parents over equal opportunity issues, several violent incidents among the students, and the poor academic performance, the principal was asked to resign. Many parents, teachers, and board members blame her for a laissez-faire attitude and what appears to be a total lack of direction and focus. Problems and complaints were simply not addressed, and no plan was articulated for dealing with the changes that the school was experiencing.

After a two-month multistate regional search and interviews with a number of finalists, the school board narrowed its search for the new principal to two candidates.

The Candidates

J. B. Davison is 55 years old, with a doctorate in education administration and BA and MA degrees in education. He previously served as principal at two other schools, where he was successful in focusing on basic academic skills, traditional approaches, discipline, and encouragement of success. Before moving to school administration, he was a history and social studies teacher. The board is impressed with his clear-headedness and no-nonsense approach to education. He readily admits that he is conservative and traditional and considers himself to be a father figure to the students. He runs a tight ship and is involved in every aspect of his school.

Jerry Popovich is 40 years old. She holds MA and PhD degrees in education administration with an undergraduate degree in computer science. She worked in the computer industry several years before teaching science and math. She worked as assistant principal in one other school and is currently the principal of an urban middle school on the West Coast. She successfully involved many business and community members in her current school. The board is impressed with her creativity and her ability to find novel approaches. She considers one of her major strengths to be the ability to involve many constituents in decision making. She describes herself as a facilitator in the education process.

Understanding Strategic Forces Worksheet: Comparing the Candidates

In helping you decide on which person to recommend, consider how each would handle and balance the six strategic management forces of environment, strategy, culture, structure, technology, and leadership.

Strategic Forces	J. B. Davison	Jerry Popovich
Environment		
Strategy		
Culture		
Structure		
Technology		
Leadership		

Discussion Items

How are the two candidates different?

What explains the differences between them?

Your Choice

Who would you recommend for the job? Why?

Exercise 7-2: Your Organization

This exercise is designed to illustrate the potential impact of an upper-echelon leader on the organization. Before starting this exercise, clearly define the department, team, or organization that you are rating. Your instructor may also provide you with several vignettes to use in your evaluation.

Rate your organization or team on the following items, using the following scale:

1 = Strongly disagree

2 = Somewhat disagree

3 = Neither agree nor disagree

4 = Somewhat agree

5 = Strongly agree

_____ 1. Decision making in my organization is centralized.
_____ 2. A strong, thick culture exists in my organization.
_____ 3. We are always coming up with new ways of doing things.
_____ 4. A few people make most of the important decisions.
_____ 5. The organization consists of many subgroups and cliques.
_____ 6. Our primary concern is efficiency.
_____ 7. We are known for our ability to innovate.
_____ 8. We are open to differing points of views.
_____ 9. Employees are empowered to make many decisions without checking with management.
_____10. We have not changed our course much in the past few years.
_____11. We take many risks.
_____12. Many rules and procedures are established for our tasks.
_____13. People are encouraged to do their own thing.

Scoring: Reverse score for items 5, 6, 8, 9, and 13 (1 = 5, 2 = 4, 3 = 3, 4 = 2, 5 = 1).

Organizational structure: Add items 1, 4, 9, and 12. Maximum score is 20. A higher score indicates a more centralized, control-oriented structure.

Total: _____

Organizational culture: Add items 2, 5, 8, and 13. Maximum score is 20. A higher score indicates a unicultural organization where diversity is not encouraged.

Total: _____

Strategy: Add items 3, 6, 7, 10, and 11. Maximum score is 25. A higher score indicates risk taking and innovation.

Total: _____

Discussion Issues

Based on your organization's score on the structure, culture, and strategy scales, what would you predict the organization leaders' strategic leadership style to be?

Exercise 7-3: Influence Processes

This exercise is designed to help you identify the processes that upper-echelon leaders use to influence their organization and most particularly its culture. After reading each of the following scenarios, identify the processes that the leaders and TMT are using to influence the organization.

Brain Toys Executives

Stanley Wang, the CEO of Brain Toys, joined the organization a few years before the founder, J. C. Green, decided to retire. It became clear early on that Stanley was destined to rise fast. With a BS degree in engineering and graphic design, an MBA, and several years of experience in computer software design, he fit right into the Brain Toys culture. He was bright, witty, analytical, and competitive. J. C. took a liking to him and put him in charge of several high-visibility projects with potential for high impact and big budgets. Stanley performed every time. Within the first two years, Stanley won all the internal awards that Brain Toys gives its managers. Several of his peers maliciously credited Stanley's love of running rather than his technical and managerial competence as the cause of his success. Stanley ran with the boss every day before work, and they trained for many races together.

The Soft-Touch Leader

Leslie Marks was proud of her accomplishments as one of the few executives in the male-dominated information technology field. As the president of Uniform Data Link, she describes herself as a "soft-touch" leader. "I just don't believe in heavy-handed leadership. People have to be able to express themselves and that is when you get the best out of them. Our best ideas come from all levels." She keeps an open door for all employees and has moved her office from the third floor to the first. She often comes to work in jeans and spends a lot of time with the engineers brainstorming on technical problems. She changed many of the evaluation and promotion procedures and asked several less-educated but highly experienced employees to work with her on important projects.

The Law Firm Senior Partner

James Bingham has recently been promoted to senior partner in Finlay's Law Firm after years of hard work. His advice is well respected by his portfolio of affluent clients and colleagues alike. He takes pride in making himself available to clients at all times. Having had a personal secretary he has been used to delegating administrative tasks. However, as a senior partner he is expected to take part in formulating overall strategy and managing junior lawyers. Since he was not expecting any major changes at the company he preferred to communicate through informal channels. He was however anxious to create partners in his own image and reward those that emulated his methods. There was considerable scope for this as compensation packages were agreed upon privately on an individual basis and rigid pay scales were nonexistent. James does not however have a say in the promotion of other partners. This is decided only by the founder of the firm, who is also a longstanding senior partner.

Influence Process Worksheet

Influence Method	Stanley Wang	Leslie Marks	James Bingham
Direct decisions			
Allocation of resources			
Reward system			
Selection and promotion of other leaders			
Role modeling			

Self-Assessment 7-1: What Is Your Strategic Leadership Type?

This exercise is a self-rating based on the four strategic leadership types presented in the chapter. You can also use the scale to rate your organizational leaders. For each of the items listed, please rate yourself using the following scale. (You can also use the items to rate a leader in your organization.)

0 = Never
1 = Sometimes
2 = Often
3 = Always

_____ 1. I enjoy working on routine tasks.
_____ 2. I am always looking for new ways of doing things.
_____ 3. I have trouble delegating tasks to my subordinates.
_____ 4. I like my subordinates to share the same values and beliefs.
_____ 5. Change makes me uncomfortable.
_____ 6. I encourage my subordinates to participate in decision making.
_____ 7. It is difficult for me to get things done in situations with many contrasting opinions.
_____ 8. I enjoy working on new tasks.
_____ 9. I feel comfortable giving power away to my subordinates.
_____10. I consider myself to be a risk taker.

Scoring: Reverse scores for items 1, 5, 6, 7, and 9 (0 = 3, 1 = 2, 2 = 1, 3 = 0).

Challenge-seeking score: Add items 1, 2, 5, 8, and 10. Your score will be between 0 and 15. Transfer the score to challenge-seeking line (vertical line) on the following grid.

Total: _____.

Need-for-control score: Add items 3, 4, 6, 7, and 9. Your score will be between 0 and 15. Transfer the score to control line (horizontal line) on the following grid.

Total: _____.

What Is Your Strategic Leadership Type?

Where do your two scores intersect? For example, if you have a score of 5 on control and 10 on challenge seeking, your scores indicate that you are a participative innovator.

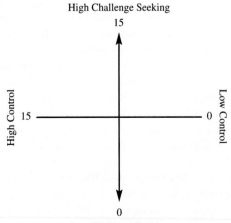

LEADERSHIP IN ACTION

LEADERSHIP MUSICAL CHAIRS AT P&G

The venerable consumer goods company Procter & Gamble (P&G) was founded in 1837 and is known globally for its products primarily directed at women, with brand such as Tide, Ivory, Pampers, Crest, Clairol, Cover Girl, and Pantene, just to name a few. Despite its history and well-known brands, P&G faced turbulent times in the 1990s, which some people attributed to a focus on internal promotions and sets of guidelines called "Current Best Approaches" that informed employees on how to do most everything. The company would have joined other disappearing business dinosaurs had it not been for the turnaround orchestrated by 20-year company insider A.G. Lafley in the first decade of 2000. Lafley retired in 2009 in accordance to the company tradition of retiring executives at age 65. Through a carefully orchestrated succession plan, he handed the company to another insider Bob McDonald. In 2013, P&G faced yet another crisis that caused the board to call Lafley out of retirement to become CEO once again. The appointment of a former CEO, rather than a new one, was a big surprise for a company that was known to have an excellent leadership and succession plan (Rosenbaum, 2013).

During his first tenure, Lafley quietly and effectively changed the P&G culture and the performance of the company. His actions were deceptively simple with what he called "Sesame Street language" to "make things simple because the difficulty is making sure everybody knows what the goal is and how to get there" (Markels, 2006). He consistently and patiently repeated those same messages any chance he got. In a highly symbolic, practical, and well-publicized move, he transformed the executive offices in the top floor of the company's headquarters into a leadership training center and moved the senior executives to the same floors as their staff. He created open offices, including one for himself and a couple of other executives. Lafley believed that the arrangement was not only symbolic of the new openness in the company and showed the importance of learning at P&G, but it also was conducive to collaboration, creativity, and flexibility, "I wanted an environment that would be more collaborative, more in touch, more designed to bring human beings together…. I wanted a place that was low tech and high touch" (Corporate Design Foundation, 2004).

Lafley's ability to transform P&G is even more surprising, given his quiet leadership, or maybe precisely because his style seems to so well fit the family culture at the company. He states, "I'm a low-ego guy. I don't have problems putting the greater good of the company or the P&G brands way ahead of my personal aspirations or achievements" (Jones, 2007). Words such as *quiet*, *soft-spoken*, *affable*, *calm*, and *consensual* are often used to describe Lafley along with mentions of his sharp focus and unbending resolve. Describing himself, he says, "I'm not a screamer, not a yeller. But don't get confused by my style. I am very decisive" (Berner, 2003). Regarding power, he believes, "The measure of a powerful person is that their circle of influence is greater than their circle of control" (Sellers, 2004: 162). After he was reappointed as CEO, Lafley was characteristically understated: "Out of the hat came my name and I said yes. Duty called" (Coolidge, 2013).

Bob McDonald, who succeeded Lafley in 2009, was considered Lafley's protégé and was the winner of a thorough and exhaustive leadership development program based on 360-degree feedback and evaluation (Reingold, 2009). He inherited a company in the midst of a global economic downturn and actually managed to deliver reasonable performance. Like his mentor, he was known to be understated and dedicated to the company and its leadership. He carried with him a list of ten leadership lessons that include, "Everyone wants to succeed," "Success is contagious," "Character is the most important trait of a leader," and "Organizations must renew themselves" (Dana, 2007). However, his understated message of "purpose-inspired growth" failed to inspire employees, the board, or investors (Lublin, Byron, and Glazer, 2013).

While not projected to stay on the job for more than a couple of years, Lafley is expected to once again revive the company, rebuild the leadership team that was depleted because of many executive defections when McDonald was appointed, and find the next CEO (Lublin et al., 2013). To accomplish all these challenging tasks, he must work with a P&G board of directors that is considered to be one of the most powerful boards in the world, with six top CEOs from other companies, including Boeing, Hewlett Packard, American Express, and Macy's, and a former Mexican president among its twelve members (Kerber, Damouni, and Wohl, 2013). However, working with such powerful people, several of whom face upheaval and crisis in their own company and may not have time to dedicate to the oversight of P&G, and having them look over your shoulder, may be a challenge for any CEO (Pichler, 2013).

Questions

1. What strategic forces affect P&G? Consider internal and external factors
2. What are the factors that affect the leaders' discretion?
3. What are key elements of Lafley's style?

Sources: Berner, R. 2003. "P&G: New and improved," *Business Week Online,* July 7. www.businessweek.com/magazine/content/03_27/b3840001_mz001.htm (accessed December 7, 2007); Coolidge, A. 2013. "P&G hands reins of power back to A.G. Lafley," *USA Today,* May 26. http://www.usatoday.com/story/money/business/2013/05/24/procter-gamble-ceo-lafley/2357141/ (accessed July 21, 2013); "Corporate design foundation: Procter & Gamble's A.G. Lafley on design," @*Issue: The Journal of Business and Design,* 9, no. 1 (2004). www.cdf.org/9_1_index/lafley/lafley.html (accessed February 8, 2005); Dana, D. 2007. "Bob McDonald CEO of P&G, on value-based leadership," *The Harbus,* October 15. http://media.www.harbus.org/media/storage/paper343/news/2007/10/15/News/Bob-Mcdonald.Coo.Of.Procter.Gamble.On.valuesBased.Leadership-3028093.shtml (accessed April 8, 2010); Jones, D. 2007. "P&G CEO wields high expectations but no whip," *USA Today*, February 19. http://www.usatoday.com/money/companies/management/2007-02-19-exec-pandg-usat_x.htm (accessed July 25, 2007); Kerber, R., N. Damouni, and J. Wohl. 2013. "Analysis: P&G all-star board's oversight questioned as CEO departs," *Reuters,* May 29. http://www.reuters.com/article/2013/05/29/us-proctergamble-ceo-board-analysis-idUSBRE94S05U20130529 (accessed July 21, 2013); Lublin, J.S., E. Byron, and E. Glazer. 2013. "P&G's Lafley begins new hunt," *The Wall Street Journal,* May 24. evernote:///view/28354196/s232/db4b3ba0-c657-4bde-94db-4910e495e72b/db4b3ba0-c657-4bde-94db-4910e495e72b/ (accessed July 21, 2013); Markels, A. 2006. "Turning the tide at P&G," *U.S. New and World Reports,* October 22. http://www.usnews.com/usnews/news/articles/061022/30lafley.htm (accessed July 25, 2007); Pichler, J. 2013. "Years of crises for P&G board," Cincinnati.com, June 1. http://news.cincinnati.com/article/20130602/BIZ01/306020023/Year-crises-P-G-board (accessed July 21, 2013); Reingold, J. 2009. "CEO Swap: the $79 billion plan," *CNN Money,* November 20. http://money.cnn.com/2009/11/19/news/companies/procter_gamble_lafley.fortune/ (accessed July 20, 2013); Rosenbaum, S. 2013. "Rinse and repeat: What's behind the encore succession at P&G," *Chief* Executive.net, June 6. http://chiefexecutive.net/rinse-and-repeat-what's-behind-the-encore-succession-at-pg (accessed July 21, 2013); Sellers, P. 2004. "eBay's secret," *Fortune,* October 18: 160–178.

Leading

Part III focuses on the practical business of leading groups and organizations, including participative management and leading teams, leading change, and developing leaders. After studying Part III, you will understand the challenges of leading teams and organizations through change and the approaches, methods, and tools available for developing leaders.

Organizations have changed considerably in recent years. The pressure for faster decision making, increased flexibility, managing diversity, and addressing global challenges represent just a few of the changes. To be successful and remain competitive, leaders must be able to respond quickly to increasing environmental pressures. The use of teams and increased employee involvement and participation in decision making are central themes in organizations' attempts to stay agile in the face of these demands and remain effective. One of the biggest challenges facing leaders and organizations is how to navigate the constant change they face. The often-used cliché that "the only constant is change" has never been more accurate. The leaders' ability to guide others through what some people call the "permanent white water" environment of today's organization is crucial. Our highly dynamic organizations must also find ways to help their leaders renew themselves and develop to be ready to address the many unknown challenges they will face.

Chapter 8 focuses on leading teams and participative management. Chapter 9 completes the discussions we started in Chapter 6 regarding the change-oriented theories of leadership by considering how leaders manage change. Finally, Chapter 10 explores the various ways in which leaders can improve and develop their skills and renew themselves to be able to continue being effective.

8

Leading Teams

After studying this chapter, you will be able to:

1. Understand when and why participation should be used to improve leadership effectiveness.
2. Explain the benefits of and provide guidelines for delegation.
3. Apply the use of various types of teams and self-leadership.
4. Lead teams effectively and manage and avoid team dysfunctions.

THE LEADERSHIP QUESTION

What are the factors that make the implementation of teams so challenging for many leaders? What can be done to improve the situation?

Teams and employee participation have been a central issue in organizations for many years. Almost all our past and current models of management and leadership address this issue in some form. For example, Theory Y recommends a higher level of employee participation than Theory X does. The Theory Y manager allows employees to set the direction for their development and provides them with support, whereas the Theory X manager controls employees and does not involve them in decision making. Likewise, the initiation-of-structure construct from the behavioral approach assumes that the leader is the one who provides the structure; no mention is made of subordinate participation in the development of the structure. The consideration behaviors in the same model include a stronger participation component. Fiedler's task-motivated leader makes decisions alone; the relationship-motivated leader involves the group. Finally, the degree of follower participation in decision making is the pivotal concept for the Normative Decision Model.

     This chapter focuses on the concept of participative management and leading teams. It discusses the use of participation and delegation and the challenges they present for leaders, it considers the special characteristics of teams and the importance of self-leadership, and provides guidelines on how to manage teams better and how to avoid dysfunction in teams.

PARTICIPATION AND TEAMS: BENEFITS AND CRITERIA FOR USE

Use of team and participative management occurs along a continuum. On one end, the leader retains all control and makes all decisions without any consultation or even information from the subordinates; on the other end, the leader delegates all decision making to followers and allows them the final say. Few leaders use extreme autocratic or delegation styles; rather, most rely on a style that falls somewhere in between. Similarly, few organizations are either entirely team based or make no use of teams at all. Most fall near the middle of the continuum, with a combination of teams and traditional hierarchical structures (Figure 8-1).

Benefits of Participation and Teams

Kevin O'Connor, cofounder of Doubleclick and CEO of Findthebest, a data comparison engine, believes that: "Having a great idea isn't enough to build a great company. what it really takes is teams of talented people, organized in ways that truly let them shine" (O'Connor, 2012). Many organizations apply the ideas that O'Connor proposes. For example, although still maintaining many elements of traditional structures, Ford Motor Company relies on teams for many tasks. Nancy Gioia, director of Global Electrification (all vehicles with electric drive; Voelcker, 2010) at Ford Motor Company, states, "As a director I'm very participative and hands-on when my team needs me to be. Ford's hybrid team has some of best and brightest minds around. I have complete confidence in their technical breadth and depth" (Peterson, 2005). Space X, the space transport company that is the first private company to take payload to the international space station, relies heavily on participation (Klotz, 2013). Founder and CEO Elon Musk, who is also the cofounder of PayPal, CEO of Tesla Motors, and who was *Inc.* magazine's 2007 entrepreneur of the year, depends on small groups of smart, motivated people to provide the creativity and innovation essential to the company. With a horizontal structure, no organizational charts, no red tape, and a culture that values teamwork and intelligence, employees are required to work together. Musk states, "I think it's really unacceptable here for anyone to bear a grudge" (Reingold, 2005: 78). Novartis, the drug manufacturer, similarly uses teams where members

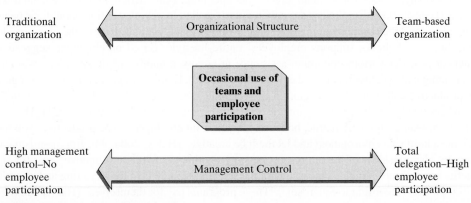

FIGURE 8-1 Continuum of Participation

work in spaces without walls or cubicles. The employees can also instantly connect with other teams around the world (Salter and Westly, 2010).

Longitudinal research about employee involvement conducted by researchers at the University of Southern California indicates that organizations can reap many benefits from employee participation and involvement initiatives, which include such methods as information sharing, group decision making, the use of teams, empowerment, profit sharing, and stock option plans (Lawler, Mohrman, and Ledford, 1995). Studies show that the adoption of such programs results in clear, positive impact on performance, profitability, competitiveness, and employee satisfaction (Carson, Tesluk, and Marrone, 2007; Lawler et al., 1995). Other research suggests that using teams can create synergy in decision making (Guido, 2011), and can be used effectively in a number of different organizations including schools (San Antonio and Gamage, 2007), health care (e.g., Mosadegh-Rad and Yarmohammadian, 2006), and government (Repetti and Prélaz-Droux, 2003). Additionally, teams have been found to learn faster even when they do not receive feedback and the team experience can even help individuals make better decisions on their own (Maciejovski et al., 2013). A recent dramatic example from swim relay teams shows that weaker members do best when working in a team (Osborn et al., 2012).

Organizations of all sizes and from many different sectors rely on teams and participation. A recent survey indicates increasing cooperation and collaboration is a key concern for managers and that 46 percent of companies rely on virtual teams that work across time and space (Minton-Eversole, 2012). Clarence Otis, Jr., CEO of Darden Restaurants, describes how much his business relies on teams, "It's less and less about getting the work done and more and more about building the team—getting the right people in place who have the talent and capability to get the work done and then do it" (Bryant, 2009i). Royal Phillips Electronics, Europe's largest electronics outfit, is counting on cross-boundary cooperation and conversations and employee participation to revive the company. In his attempts to reenergize Phillips, former CEO Gerard Kleisterlee gathered people who wanted to make a contribution, regardless of rank and position in the company. Kleisterlee states that "these meetings result in very clear goals and much better cooperation between the different divisions" (Wylie, 2003: 45). Genencor International, a health-care products company with 1,200 employees located in Palo Alto, California, is another example of the use and benefits of employee participation. With turnover rates of 4 percent compared with the industry average of 18 percent, and growing sales, the company is an example of a successful business that relies on worker involvement and input. The employee participation started when the company built its headquarters in 1996 and offered employees the opportunity to give input into the physical design of the building. Research scientists' requests for windows in their labs as well as other employees' suggestions for a "main street" that encourages interaction were implemented with success (Haley, 2004). Employees are now regularly polled to get information about their benefit preferences, and the company emphasizes a philosophy that Cynthia Edwards, the vice president for technology, believes supports employees' entire lifestyle. Based on employee suggestions, Genencor provides various commuter assistance programs, a number of on-site services such as dry cleaning and eyeglass repair, and emergency childcare. Employees get to nominate exceptionally productive colleagues for recognition and celebrate their success during Friday afternoon parties, where they have the chance to mingle and get to know one another (Haley, 2004). The CEO until 2005, Jean-Jacques Bienaimé, believes, "If you want employees to be productive, you have to create a nurturing environment and let them be creative" (Haley, 2004: 98). Jim Sjoerdsma, the company vice president of human resources, suggests that the $700-per-employee cost for such benefits is a wise investment compared with the average $75,000 cost for recruiting and training a new employee. According to Sjoerdsma, "These programs pay for themselves" (Haley, 2004: 99).

Criteria for Participation

Despite its many potential benefits, participation and use of teams are not a cure-all. Their use is more appropriate in some situations than in others and should follow a contingency approach. After many years of debate and research about participative management in social sciences and management, clear criteria suggest when participative decision making would be most appropriate (Table 8-1).

Overall, if the organization, its leaders, and its employees are ready for participative management, if the task is complex and involves no strong time pressures, and if employee commitment is important, leaders should rely on participative decision making. If time pressure is genuine or the leader, followers, or organization are not ready, however, then participation is not likely to yield many benefits. If leaders show a high need for control and were previously successful in using an autocratic style of leadership, they are unlikely to be able to implement participation easily. Furthermore, when followers who show little need to participate or when they trust their leader to make decisions, participation might not be required or at least might not lead to better results than the leader making the decision alone. In addition, some organizational cultures are more supportive of participation than others, thereby making the use of participation more or less easy. Another factor in using participation is whether the task or the structure limits its use. If followers cannot interact easily with one another and with the leader, either because of task or because of geographic restrictions, participation might not be appropriate. In some instances, legal and confidentiality requirements, such as in personnel decisions, may preclude participation.

The classic case of Kiwi Airlines presents an example of the potential pitfalls of mismanaged participation (Bryant, 1995). When Kiwi Airlines was founded in 1992, it quickly became the symbol of all that is good about participative and egalitarian leadership. Created

TABLE 8-1	Criteria for Use of Participation
Criteria	**Description**
When the task is complex and multifaceted and quality is important	Complex tasks require input from people with different expertise; people with different points of view are more likely to deliver a quality decision.
When follower commitment is needed in successful implementation	Follower participation increases commitment and motivation.
When there is time	Using participation takes time; legitimate deadlines and time pressures preclude seeking extensive participation.
When the leader and followers are ready and the organizational culture is supportive	Participation can only succeed if both leader and followers agree to its benefits, are trained in how to use it, and are committed to its success. The organizational culture must encourage or at least tolerate employee participation.
When interaction between leader and followers is not restricted by the task, the structure, or the environment	Participation requires interaction between leaders and followers; such interaction is only possible if restrictions because of factors such as geographic location, structural elements, or task requirements are minimized.

by a group of former Eastern Airline pilots and other employees, Kiwi promised not to repeat any of Eastern's mistakes and aimed at creating a family atmosphere for all its employees. The employees were all owners with varying degrees of shares and the corresponding pride and desire for involvement, control, and commitment that come from ownership. All decisions were made with full participation. All employees, regardless of levels, pitched in to get the job done and deliver the quality service that soon earned Kiwi honors in surveys of airline quality. The airline quickly grew to more than 1,000 employees with more than 60 daily flights. One of the pilot-founders and then chairman of Kiwi, Robert W. Iverson, attributed the stunning growth and success to the employees' commitment and the organization's egalitarian culture. Kiwi was truly a symbol of the benefits of participation and involvement. In 1994, the bubble burst. Kiwi's board, which included fellow founders and owners, booted Iverson out of office. This event revealed serious management and organizational deficiencies within the airline. The dark side of participation was an amazing lack of concern for management decisions. Many employee-owners failed to follow management directives if they did not agree with them. Employees demanded input in every decision, a factor that led to stagnation in decision making and an inability to act to solve problems. Iverson admitted, "One of the stupidest things I ever did was call everybody owners. An owner is somebody who thinks he can exercise gratuitous control." The case of Kiwi Airlines demonstrates the ineffective use of participation. A few managers could have handled many of the decisions more effectively and efficiently than the employees did through participation. As is the case with many management tools, situational factors impact whether participation should be used and whether it is likely to provide better results.

The Role of Culture

An important issue when considering the use of participation is national cultural values. Factors such as collectivism and power distance (Hofstede, 2001), team-oriented, participative, and autonomous leadership, and CLTs in each culture (GLOBE; Dorfman et al., 2012), and cross-cultural organizational cultures (Trompenaars and Hampden-Turner, 2012) affect whether leaders can use participation successfully. Collectivistic cultures tend to emphasize cooperative team processes, compensation, and promotion that take into consideration the group (Gelfand et al., 2004). Furthermore, the more the power distance, the less likely it is that teams will be empowered (Carl, Gupta, and Javidan, 2004). Other GLOBE findings suggest that a humane orientation, which includes concern for others and responsibility for their well-being, may also be a factor supporting team-oriented and participative leadership (Kabasakal and Bodur, 2004).

For example, the Japanese culture, with its strong emphasis on conformity, consensus, and collectivity at the expense of individual goals, supports the use of participative management, despite its relatively high-power distance. Participation in Japan is a mix of group harmony and consensus, with elements of directive leadership (Dorfman et al., 1997). In this vertical collectivistic culture, individuals are expected to sacrifice their personal goals for the good of the group. In China, establishing cooperative goals and taking care of relationships help participative leadership (Chen and Tjosvold, 2006). Mexico, which is also relatively high on collectivism, power distance, and masculinity, has a well-established tradition of autocratic leadership without a history of participative leadership (Dorfman et al., 1997). Similar cultural patterns are found in Dominicans (Montesino, 2003). In such cultural contexts, neither the leader nor the followers expect participation or find it desirable. In addition, in the cross-cultural organizational cultures that Trompenaars labels the Eiffel Tower—France, for example—the focus is on performance through obedience and respect for legitimate authority. In this environment, a leader is ascribed great authority and is expected to know much; asking for subordinate participation may be perceived as weakness and as an indicator of lack of leadership ability.

Cultures such as the United States and Australia, with relatively egalitarian power distributions and vertical individualism, pose a different challenge. The low-power distance allows for participation, but the value placed on individual autonomy and individual contribution can be an obstacle to cooperation in a team environment. In horizontal individualist cultures such as Sweden, participation and team cooperation are much easier because all individuals are equal. Furthermore, appropriate team behaviors vary considerably from one culture to another (Kanter and Corn, 1993). An effective team member in Japan is above all courteous and cooperative; members avoid conflict and confrontation (Zander, 1983). In the United States, effective team members speak their mind, pull their weight by contributing equally, and participate actively, yet they expect to be recognized individually. German employees are taught early in their careers to seek technical excellence. In Afghanistan, team members are obligated to share their resources with others, making generosity an essential team behavior. In Israel, a horizontal collectivistic culture, values of hard work and contribution to the community drive kibbutz team members. The Swedes are comfortable with open arguments and will disagree publicly with one another and with their leader. Each culture expects and rewards different types of team behaviors.

These cross-cultural differences in team behavior create considerable challenges for leaders in culturally diverse teams. Success depends on accurate perceptions and careful reading of cross-cultural cues. Leaders must be flexible and patient and be willing not only to listen to others but also to question their own assumptions. In addition, they must keep in mind that many behavioral differences stem from individual rather than cultural sources. The only constant in the successful implementation of teams is the leader's sincere belief in the team's ability to contribute to the organization (Marsick, Turner, and Cederholm, 1989). Such belief is necessary regardless of the cultural setting.

THE ISSUE OF DELEGATION

"...The trick is to get truly world-class people working directly for you so you don't have to spend a lot of time managing them," says Critóbal Conde, president and CEO of SunGard, a software and technology services company (Bryant, 2010c). Gauri Nanda, entrepreneur and creator of Clocky, a robot alarm that rolls around the room, discusses something she would do differently if she could, "I would try to find more good help from the beginning. I tried to do a little too much myself, and while that's a great way to learn the process and every part of your business, Iwould have stopped and tried to find one good person to help" (Kessler, 2010). These leaders are addressing one of the basic principles of management: delegation. *Delegation* means appointing someone to as deputy or representative and entrusting that person with a task. It differs from participation in a number of ways, although many managers consider it an aspect of participation. For example, many leaders define themselves as participative managers if they delegate tasks to their subordinates. Although this practice might lead to more subordinate participation in decision making, the goal of delegation is not necessarily to develop employees or create more commitment. Neither does delegation always involve power sharing with employees. The goal of delegation can be as simple as helping a leader manage an excessive workload. In its most basic form, delegation is simply handing off a task to someone else; in a more complex form, delegation can resemble participative management.

Benefits of Delegation

Delegating tasks well to subordinates is gaining importance as managerial ranks are thinned and managers see their workloads increase. Production managers find themselves with twice as many subordinates to supervise; sales managers see their territories double in current attempts to develop leaner structures. Organizations undergoing restructuring are testing team-based approaches. Until such techniques are well accepted and implemented, however, judicial delegation is still a basic tool for a leader's success. The potential benefits of delegation include the following:

- Delegation frees up the leader's time for new tasks and strategic activities.
- Delegation provides employees with opportunities to learn and develop.
- Delegation allows employees to be involved in tasks.
- Delegation allows observation and evaluation of employees in new tasks.
- Delegation increases employee motivation and satisfaction.

Aside from being a time- and stress-management tool for leaders, delegation allows subordinates to try new tasks and learn new skills, thereby potentially enriching their jobs and increasing their satisfaction and motivation. When employees perform new tasks, the leader has the opportunity to observe them and gather performance-related information that can be used for further development, evaluation, and preparation of employees for promotions. As such, delegation can be one of the tools available to leaders for succession planning in their organizations. Employees who consistently perform well on new tasks and are willing to accept more responsibility could be the future leaders of the organization. Without the opportunity to grow outside their current job, no data are available for accurate forecasting of their performance in higher-level positions. Debra Dunsire, M.D., CEO of the Millennium: The Takeda Oncology company, talking delegation, says that she has learned to provide a safe environment and let her employees present work that is not perfect so that they can learn from their mistakes (Bryant, 2009j).

The final benefit of delegation is, as is the case with participation, increased employee involvement and commitment. Job enrichment and participative management research (Hackman and Oldham, 1980) indicates that employees who are interested in growth quickly feel stifled and unmotivated if they do not have the opportunity to participate in new and challenging tasks. Delegation of such tasks to them helps increase their motivation and commitment to the organization.

Guidelines for Good Delegation

As with any tool, misuse and misapplication of delegation can be disastrous. Leaders must take into account some relatively simple principles (see Table 8-2 for a summary). One of the major issues for leaders is to separate delegation from dumping. Leaders need to delegate a mix of easy, hard, pleasant, and unpleasant tasks to their subordinates. If only unpleasant, difficult, and unmanageable tasks are assigned consistently to subordinates, while leaders complete the high-profile, challenging, and interesting projects, delegation becomes dumping. One of the major complaints of subordinates regarding delegation is this exact issue. To reap the benefits of delegation, a variety of tasks should be delegated, and the leaders should pay particular attention that their delegation is viewed as balanced.

Effective delegation requires more than handing off a task. Leaders must be clear about their expectations and support their followers while they perform the task. The support might include informing department members and others outside the department that the task has been

TABLE 8-2	Guidelines for Good Delegation
Guideline	**Description**
Delegate, do not dump	Delegate both pleasant and unpleasant tasks; provide followers with a variety of experiences.
Clarify goals and expectations	Provide clear goals and guidelines regarding expectations and limitations.
Provide support and authority	As a task is delegated, provide necessary authority and resources such as time, training, and advice needed to complete the task.
Monitor and provide feedback	Keep track of progress and provide feedback during and after task completion at regular intervals.
Delegate to different followers	Delegate tasks to those who are most motivated to complete them as well as those who have potential but no clear track record of performance.
Create a safe environment	Encourage experimentation; tolerate honest mistakes and worthy efforts that may fail.
Develop your own coaching skills	Take workshops and training classes to ensure that you have the skills to delegate.

delegated. Another aspect of support involves providing training and other appropriate resources that allow the subordinate to learn the needed skills. It also might require regular monitoring and clarification of reporting expectations (Foster, 2004). It is easy for an eager subordinate to make decisions that are inconsistent with the leader's goals if the leader does not properly monitor the situation.

One area that cannot and should not be delegated is personnel issues. Unless an organization or department is moving toward self-managed teams (SMTs) that have feedback and performance-evaluation responsibility, the task of performance management remains the leader's responsibility. For example, it would be inappropriate for a manager to delegate the task of disciplining a tardy employee to a subordinate or to expect the latter to monitor and manage the performance of coworkers. The situation of SMTs often changes this guideline; such changes will be discussed later in the chapter.

Leaders must choose carefully the followers to whom they delegate. The easiest choice for most managers is to delegate to the few people they know will do the job well (the in-group). Although such a position is logical and effective, at least in the short run, a leader must be aware of the in-group/out-group issues presented in Chapter 3. Therefore, leaders must select individuals who, in addition to having shown potential, are also eager and motivated to take on new tasks and have the appropriate skills for the new challenge. A follower who is competent and eager but who failed recently on one assignment might also be a good choice but could be overlooked if leaders keep relying on their few trusted in-group members. Kevin Ryan, CEO of AlleyCorp a group of Internet start-ups, keeps a list of 35 to 40 of his employees. According to him, he always connects with the top ten people on his list, but he makes an effort to see the rest, "...there are always 30 or 40 people who are up-and-comers or one or two levels down, and I want them to know I'm paying attention" (Buchanan, 2010: 65). Delegation of tasks to a varied group of followers further provides leaders with a broad view of the performance capabilities and potential of their team or department. Finally, creating a climate that tolerates mistakes and encourages continued training for the leader is essential.

Why Do Leaders Fail to Delegate?

Certain circumstances justify a leader's unwillingness to delegate. In some cases, followers are not ready for delegation, are already overworked, or have such specialized jobs that they cannot be assigned new tasks. Such situations are rare, however, and the considerable benefits of delegation far outweigh many of the arguments typically presented against it. The most commonly used argument against delegation is "I will get it done better and faster myself." Table 8-3 presents the typical excuses and counterarguments for not delegating. The excuses for not delegating tasks may be valid in the short run. By taking a long-term view that considers the leader's personal effectiveness as well as the development of followers, however, many of the excuses are no longer valid. Not only does effective delegation require effort and resources such as training, but it also allows leaders to focus on higher-level strategic issues instead of day-to-day routines. One underlying factor that might stop many leaders from delegating is their personality style, their need for control, and their fear of losing it. For example, as discussed in Chapter 4, a Type A's need for control often leads to lack of delegation. Competitiveness also might lead Type A leaders to compete with their followers. Other personal needs, such as a need for power, also might cause leaders to want to maintain power over all activities, preventing them from delegating.

Although for many years management and leadership included participation and delegation, they recently took on a new form in team-based organizations with the introduction of empowerment and concepts such as self-leadership, which are considered next.

TABLE 8-3	Excuses for Not Delegating	
Excuses	**Counterarguments**
My followers are not ready.	The leader's job is to get followers prepared to take on new tasks.
My subordinates do not have the necessary skills and knowledge.	The leader's responsibility is to train followers and prepare them for new challenges.
I feel uncomfortable asking my followers to do many of my tasks.	Only a few tasks cannot be delegated. Balancing delegation of pleasant and unpleasant tasks is appropriate.
I can do the job quicker myself.	Taking time to train followers frees up time in the long run.
Followers are too busy.	Leaders and followers must learn to manage their workload by setting priorities.
If my followers make a mistake, I am responsible.	Encouraging experimentation and tolerating mistakes are essential to learning and development.
My own manager may think I am not working hard.	Doing busy work is not an appropriate use of a leader's time. Delegation allows time to focus on strategic and higher-level activities.

EVOLUTION OF PARTICIPATIVE MANAGEMENT: TEAMS AND SELF-LEADERSHIP

In many organizations that have made teams a permanent feature, if not a cornerstone, of their structures, teams create a formal structure through which participation in decision making can be achieved. The use of teams in United States and other Western organizations was triggered to a great extent by Japan's economic success and its reliance on teams and participative management (Nahavandi and Aranda, 1994). Although teams are not uniformly successful and they often pose considerable challenges for organizations (for research about teams and their potential problems, see Allen and Hecht, 2004; Salas, Stagl, and Burke, 2004), a large number of organizations continue to use them as a technique to increase creativity, innovation, and quality. The example of Google in the Leading Change case shows that making teams successful takes considerable effort. In Google's case, everything in the organization is focused on collaboration and engagement, factors that are key to the successful implementation of teams. Simply putting, for people to work in teams is clearly not enough.

LEADING CHANGE

Google: The Happiest Workplace on Earth?

It may be a leading technology company and a verb as well as a noun, but Google is also fast acquiring the label of the happiest or at least the best place to work. In a statement that is uncharacteristic of corporate America, Google spokesman Jordan Newman says the company's goal is: "to create the happiest, most productive workplace in the world" (Stewart, 2013).

If that statement appear too "touchy-feely" for you, consider that extensive data collection and clear purpose that drive everything Google does. The company believes in and depends on employee engagement and collaboration according to Craig Nevill-Manning Google's engineering director, so its management, its physical settings, and its structure are all focused on making interaction easy and on removing any barriers that may prevent collaboration (Stewart, 2013). This collaboration is an essential part of achieving what Larry Page, cofounder and CEO, says is "a healthy disregard for the impossible" (Kelly, 2012).

To make sure it stays on track and knows the best way to keep employees engaged, Google measures everything (Fernholz, 2013). Its analytics have told Google that culture matters and that the right workplace can help people be more productive. So Google added the title "chief culture officer" to the head of the HR's job title (Dubois, 2012), and it provides a worplace where employees can freely interact, play, and work. In its California headquarters, play areas, coffee shops, kitchens, indoor terraces and treehouses, a yellow brick road, volley ball courts, massage chairs, nap pods, and access to free gourmet food all day long are some of the things that keep employees at work and allow them to spend time together. Each location draws from local flavor to deliver a comfortable atmosphere. For example, the Zurich office complex has ski gondolas (Johansson, 2013).

CEO Larry Page says: "My job as a leader is to make sure everybody in the company has great opportunities, and that they feel they're having meaningful impact and are contributing to the good of society" (Chatterjee, 2012). The "Googley" culture, intense focus on creativity and productivity and use of teams are the heart of the company's success. There are few single offices, teams members work and play together, and healthy competition between teams motivates employees and keeps them focused. A company spokesman states: "We believe in having a collaborative, vibrant culture where people work really hard, but they still like to have fun as well. We are a serious company, but we don't take ourselves too seriously…" (Lee, 2013). With a flat structure, a limited number of middle managers, an hands-on top leadership that is committed to engagement and participation, and extensive use of teams that have considerable autonomy and authority, Google continues to deliver results that are the envy of many others. Kevin Ryan, a vice president at SearchEngineWatch.com, states: "The Google culture is probably one of the most positive, influential, all-encompassing, productivity-inducing environments the world has ever seen" (Johansson, 2013).

Sources: DuBois, S. 2012. "The rise of the chief culture officer," *CNN Money,* July 30. http://management. fortune.cnn.com/2012/07/30/chief-culture-officers (accessed July 23, 2013); Chatterjee, S. 2012. "Top 5 reasons why Google is the best company to work for," *IBTimes,* January 20. http://www.ibtimes.com/top-5-reasons-why-google-best-company-work-553844 (accessed July 22, 2013); Fernholz, T. 2013. "Inside Google's culture of relentless self-surveying," *Quartz,* June 26. http://qz.com/97731/inside-googles-culture-of-relentless-self-surveying/ (accessed July 22, 2013); Johansson, G. 2013, "Google: The World's Most Successful Corporate Culture," *Suite 101,* March 25. http://suite101.com/article/google-the-worlds-most-successful-corporate-culture-a242303 (accessed July 22, 2013); Kelly, C. 2012. "O.K., Google, take a deep breath," *The New York Times,* April 28. http://www.nytimes.com/2012/04/29/technology/google-course-asks-employees-to-take-a-deep-breath.html?pagewanted=all&_r=0 (accessed July 22, 2013); Lee. A. 2013. "How to build a culture like Google: 7 practical ideas from 'The Internship,'" *"Entrepreneur,* June 7. http://www.entrepreneur. com/article/226948 (accessed July 22, 2013); and Stewart, J.B. 2013. "Looking for a lesion in Google's Perks," *The New York Times,* March 15. http://www.nytimes.com/2013/03/16/business/at-google-a-place-to-work-and-play.html?pagewanted=all (accessed July 22, 2013).

Characteristics of Teams

Although groups and teams both involve people working together toward a goal, they differ along several dimensions outlined in Table 8-4. The first distinguishing characteristic of a team is full commitment of its members to a common goal and approach that they often develop themselves. Members must agree that the team goal is worthwhile and agree on a general approach for meeting that goal. Such agreement provides the vision and motivation for team members to perform. The second characteristic is mutual accountability. To succeed as a team, members must feel and be accountable to one another and to the organization for the process and outcome of their work. Whereas group members report to the leader or their manager and are accountable to this person, team members take on responsibility and perform because of their commitment to the team.

The third characteristic of a team is a team culture based on trust and collaboration. Whereas group members share norms, team members have a shared culture. Team members are willing to compromise, cooperate, and collaborate to reach their common purpose. A collaborative climate does not mean the absence of conflict. Conflict can enhance team creativity and performance if handled constructively (Behfar et al., 2008). Related to the team culture is shared leadership. Whereas groups have one assigned leader, teams differ by sharing leadership among all members. Although this shared leadership is essential, leaders continue to play an important role in the success of teams. Particularly, leaders can help encourage a culture of collaboration (Taggar and Ellis, 2007) and help team learning by empowering members (Burke et al., 2006).

Finally, teams develop synergy. Synergy means that team members together achieve more than each individual is capable of doing. Whereas group members combine their efforts to

TABLE 8-4 Groups and Teams	
Groups	**Teams**
Members work on a common goal.	Members are fully committed to common goals and a mission they developed.
Members are accountable to manager.	Members are mutually accountable to one another.
Members do not have clear stable culture, and conflict is frequent.	Members trust one another, and team enjoys a collaborative culture.
Leadership is assigned to single person.	Members all share in leadership.
Groups may accomplish their goals.	Teams achieve synergy: 2 + 2 = 5.

Sources: Hackman, J. R. 1900. *Groups That Work (and Those That Don't)*. San Francisco, CA: Jossey-Bass; Katzenbach, J. R., and D. K. Smith. 2003. *The Wisdom of Teams: Creating the High Performance Organization*. New York: Harper Business.

achieve their goal, teams reach higher-performance levels. As groups become teams and reach their peak level of performance potential, they may provide their organizations with benefits such as cost reduction because of less need for supervision, higher employee commitment, enhanced learning, and greater flexibility (Cordery, 2004).

Self-Managed Teams

While some teams still rely on an external leader, *self-managed teams* (SMTs), which are teams of employees with full managerial control over their own work. Numerous organizations, such as Toyota, General Foods, and P&G, have used SMTs successfully for decades. In fact, P&G once claimed its SMTs were one of the company's trade secrets (Fisher, 1993). Kevin O'Connor, cofounder of Doubleclick and CEO of Findthebest, says managers forget how important it is to empower teams. He states: "If you have a smart team, you should empower each person to make decisions that apply to their own groups and roles. In addition to speeding up decisions and helping shape current team members into future managers, this will also instill a sense of ownership throughout your entire team" (O'Connor, 2012). The teams at Google (see Leading Change case in this chapter) are given both authority and autonomy to make many of their decisions. SMTs exhibit the following characteristics:

- *Power to manage their work.* SMTs can set goals, plan, staff, schedule, monitor quality, and implement decisions.
- *Members with different expertise and functional experience.* Team members can be from marketing, finance, production, design, and so on. Without a broad range of experience, the team cannot manage all aspects of its work.
- *Absence of an outside manager.* The team does not report to an outside manager. Team members manage themselves, their budget, and their task through shared leadership.
- *The power to implement decisions.* Team members have the power and the resources necessary to implement their decisions.
- *Coordination and cooperation with other teams and individuals affected by the teams' decisions.* Because each team is independent and does not formally report to a manager,

the teams themselves rather than managers must coordinate their tasks and activities to assure integration.

- *Team leadership based on facilitation.* Leadership often rotates among members depending on each member's expertise in handling a specific situation. Instead of a leader who tells others what to do, sets goals, or monitors achievement, team leaders remove obstacles for the team and make sure that the team has the resources it needs. The primary role of the team leader is to facilitate rather than control. Facilitation means that the leader focuses on freeing the team from obstacles to allow it to reach the goals it has set.

The success of the team depends on a number of key factors. First, the members of a team have to be selected carefully for their complementary skills and expertise (for some examples of research findings, see Kang, Yang, and Rowley, 2006; Van der Vegt, Bunderson, and Oosterhof, 2006). The interdependence among the members makes creation of the "right" combination critical. The right combination depends as much on interpersonal skills as on technical skills. Second, the team members need to focus on and be committed to the team goal. For example, individuals from different functional departments such as marketing or production, although selected because of their expertise in particular areas, need to leave the department mind-set behind and focus on the task of the team. When hiring new employees, Susan Lyne, CEO of the Gilt Groupe, a company that provides its customers with access to luxury goods at a discounted price, looks for team players who can work across the company (Bryant, 2009k). Third, the team task must be appropriately complex, and the team must have the critical resources it needs to perform the task. Finally, the team needs enough power and authority to accomplish its task and implement its ideas.

Building an effective team is a time-consuming process that requires interpersonal team-building skills and extensive technical support. The development of trust, a common vision, and the ability to work well together all depend on appropriate interpersonal skills. Once the trust and goals are established, tackling complex tasks requires timely technical training. Many of these interpersonal and technical functions traditionally fall on the leader's shoulders. Leadership in teams, however, is often diffused, a factor that puts further pressure on individual team members to take on new tasks and challenges.

APPLYING WHAT YOU LEARN
Using a Sports Team Model in Management

Organizational behavior expert and Harvard professor Nancy Katz suggests that managers can learn from sports teams how to make teams more effective (Katz, 2001). Here are some guidelines based on her work:

- Encourage cooperation and competition. The first leads to cohesion; the second energizes team members to do their best.
- Provide some early wins by assigning smaller, short-term, clearer tasks. Early successes build the team's confidence and create a success spiral.

- Break out of losing streaks through positive thinking, challenging the team to succeed, and focusing team members on external rather than internal causes for failure.
- Take time to practice; during practice the focus should be on learning and experimentation rather than success.
- Keep the membership stable to develop cohesion and give members time to learn to work together.
- Review performance, particularly mistakes and failures; analyze problems, and learn from them.

Self-Leadership

An extension of participative leadership is the concept of self-leadership. Whereas in both traditional and participation-based leaderships the source of leadership is external to followers and it resides with the leader, in self-leadership, the follower leads himself or herself (Neck and Manz, 2012). Charles Manz and Henry Sims first proposed a model for leadership that involves self-leadership and self-management by each team member (1991). *Self-leadership* is the process of influencing oneself (Neck and Manz, 2012). The concept is based on social cognitive theory that recognizes that people can manage and control their behavior and on intrinsic motivation theory that suggests that natural internal rewards can be a powerful motivators (Neck and Manz, 2012). As we empower individual employees and provide them with training in various areas of business, we expect them to make increasingly independent decisions. These changes shift the focus of attention away from the leader to followers. Self-leadership suggests that instead of leaders who rely on fear (the "strong man"), focus on narrow exchange relationships (the "transactor"), or inspire commitment while discouraging thinking (the "visionary hero"), leaders and followers must focus on leading themselves. As a result, team members must be taught and encouraged to make their own decisions and accept responsibility to the point where they no longer need leaders. Self-leadership within teams means that all team members set goals and observe, evaluate, critique, reinforce, and reward one another and themselves. In such an environment, the need for one leader is reduced; team members set goals and decide how to achieve them. Increased use of technology, the information revolution, and the preponderance of knowledge workers all support the need for self-leadership, which involves a focus on behaviors, providing natural rewards, and engaging in constructive thought patterns (for a detailed discussion, see Neck and Manz, 2012). Specifically, self-leaders:

- *Develop positive and motivating thought patterns.* Individuals and teams seek and develop environments that provide positive cues and a supportive and motivating environment.
- *Set personal goals.* Individuals and teams set their own performance goals and performance expectations.
- *Observe their behavior and self-evaluate.* Team members observe their own and other team members' behaviors and provide feedback and critique and evaluate one another's performance.
- *Self-reinforce.* Team members provide rewards and support to one another.

The role of formal leaders is, therefore, primarily to lead others to lead themselves or "to facilitate the self-leadership energy" within each subordinate (Manz and Sims, 1991: 18). Contrary to views of heroic leadership, whereby the leader is expected to provide answers to all questions and to guide, protect, and save subordinates, the concept of self-leadership suggests that leaders must get their subordinates to the point where they do not need their leader much. In effect, through the use of job-design techniques, the development of a team culture, proper performance management, and the modeling of self-leadership, the leader sets up internal and external substitutes for leadership. The right job design and the team are the external substitutes (see Chapter 3). The employees' developing skills and internal motivation serve as internal substitutes for the presence and guidance of a leader (see Exercise 8-2). Some of the strategies for the development for self-leaders include the following:

- Listen more; talk less.
- Ask questions rather than provide answers.
- Share information rather than hoard it.

- Encourage independent thinking rather than compliant followership.
- Encourage creativity rather than conformity.

Research on self-leadership continues to show support for the model (for a recent example of the link between self-leadership and entrepreneurship, see, D'Intino et al., 2007). The dimensions of self-leadership are valid and distinct from other personality variables (Houghton and Neck, 2002; and Houghton et al., 2004), and some research suggests that the practice of self-leadership can be beneficial to an organization (VanSandt and Neck, 2003). Some research also considers the applicability of the concept in other cultures (e.g., Alves et al., 2006; Ho and Nesbit, 2009). The concepts provide considerable appeal for the development of leaders and help establish workable leadership roles in organizations that rely on teams and empowerment.

In 2002, when Sam Palmisano, IBM's CEO, presented the initiative that was to jump-start the venerable company, Donna Riley, the company's vice president of global talent, had to work on reinventing its leadership (Tischler, 2004). With help from outside consultants, she set out to identify the set of skills, behaviors, and competencies that IBM leaders needed to help the company survive. The leadership traits they developed included trust and personal responsibility, developing people, enabling growth, collaboration, informed judgment, and building client partnerships. "In a highly complex world, where multiple groups might need to unite to solve a client's problems, old-style command-and-control leadership doesn't work" (Tischler, 2004: 113). The leadership characteristics used by IBM to shape its future were similar to those proposed by Manz and his colleagues.

To be successful, participative management and self-leadership require the empowerment of employees (see Chapter 5) and the changing of an organization's culture. One of the key components of the cultural change is redefining the concepts of leadership and followership. Employees who become self-leaders do not require organizing, controlling, and monitoring from their leaders. Such redefinition requires a reconsideration of many current definitions of leadership, including the one presented in Chapter 1. We next consider some methods and tools leaders can use to make teams effective.

LEADING TEAMS EFFECTIVELY

How do leaders handle some of the challenges that teams present? What can they do to help their teams become effective?

Size of the Team

One mistake many leaders make is try to include too many people either to provide representation or they think that more people would provide more ideas. While these are important issues, groups should be small enough for members to work closely together and interact easily. Research shows that many people underestimate how much more time is actually required to get things done when groups become large (Staats, Milkman, and Fox, 2012). Lily Kanter, cofounder and chief executive of Serena & Lily, a home décor company, believes that small groups work the best: "Ideally no more than four. It depends on the project, but somebody's got to own it. Two to four people on an innovative project is more than plenty. After all, how many companies get started with more than that? Small working groups are very efficient. It's about making sure people understand where decisions lie" (Bryant, 2013c). While there is no ideal group size, groups larger than eight to twelve members are less likely to function smoothly. Additionally, having an odd number of members may protect against deadlocks in case of disagreement. Generally, as size increases, individuals do not have the opportunity to participate and are less likely to take responsibility for their actions and the team outcomes. Additionally, as groups get larger, subgroups form to deal with different issues or to take on different parts of the task. While the formation of subgroups is not, in and of itself, a negative factor, subgroups have the potential to lose touch with one another and the result can lead to poor coordination of activities.

Composition of the Team

The other basic issue team leaders must address is the *membership or group composition* (see Figure 8-2). One of the key considerations is obviously the nature and requirements of the task. Additionally, extensive research suggests that groups that have *homogeneous members,* meaning members who have similar backgrounds, achieve higher cohesion (e.g., Dunlop and Beauchamp, 2011) and often can reach decisions more quickly (Civettini, 2007). Homogeneous groups, because of the similarity of perspective, are likely to achieve cohesion faster, agree on processes and alternatives, thereby reducing conflict and providing members with validation, and a sense of being right and of unanimity. However, too much similarity can cause several problems. The higher cohesion, and sometimes false belief in the rightness of the group, is one of the key contributing factors to Groupthink (a factor we discuss later in this chapter). Second, homogeneous groups tend to lose their creativity. Particularly, diverse perspectives have been found to be important when facing complex situations particularly when the group is facing ethical and moral dilemas (Kujala and Pietilainen, 2007; Mello and Ruckes, 2006) Diverse groups consider a wider range of alternatives and can generate higher quality decisions and a diverse group is more likely to integrate information that can improve their decision making (Rink and Ellemers, 2010; Woolley and Malone, 2011). Additionally, conflict, when managed well, can be highly beneficial to teams and their creativity (de Rond, 2012). In selecting members, team leaders need to balance the need for easy, comfortable interaction with the importance of creative and productive group processes.

Role of Leaders in a Team Environment

The role of the leader changes in a team environment, but it does not altogether disappear (see Figure 8-3). The leaders are not in charge and are not meant to command and control; team leadership must be less hands-on (Hackman, 2005). For this reason, many refer to team leaders as

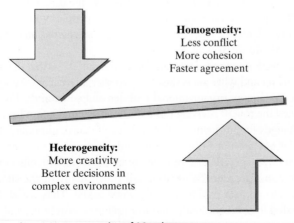

Homogeneity:
Less conflict
More cohesion
Faster agreement

Heterogeneity:
More creativity
Better decisions in
complex environments

FIGURE 8-2   Homogeneity vs. Heterogeneity of Members

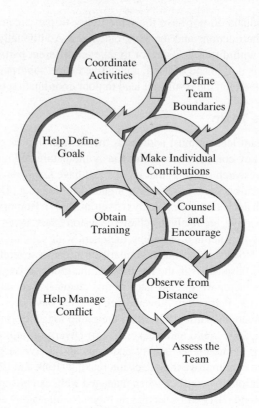

FIGURE 8-3   Roles for Leaders in a Team Environment

facilitators and coaches. One of the essential functions of leaders is to assure that members coordinate their activities and integrate actions and contributions. This coordination is the factor that contributes to the effectiveness of a team: effective teams coordinate and integrate their contributions; ineffective ones are a collection of activities and sometimes a simple collection of stars. Pulling people together is therefore essential. David Brock, the director of the NeuroLeadership Institute, suggests: "If you can create shared goals among people, you can create quite a strong 'in' group quite quickly... Unless a leader creates shared goals across an organization, an organization will be a series of silos" (Bryant, 2013a).

Leaders help teams define their goals and their boundaries, so that the team members know what they should focus on and what areas they need to stay away from. Many teams fail because they take on too much or ignore organizational realities and constraints. For example, a team of schoolteachers assigned the role of revising the social studies curriculum for fourth and fifth graders might propose changes that influence other parts of the curriculum and then be disappointed when its recommendations are not fully implemented. The role of the team leader would be to keep the team focused on its specific task or to integrate the team with others who can help it with its wider recommendations. Leaders/facilitators still fulfill many of the functions of traditional leaders, but they do so to a lesser extent and only when asked. They assist the teams by obtaining the resources needed to solve problems and to implement solutions, and only interfere when needed. The leader's central activities, therefore, become assessing the team's abilities and skills and helping them develop necessary skills, which often includes getting the right type of training. Even though strategies to make individuals more competent and effective will affect a team's overall ability to be productive, teams often need specialized support and interventions to develop synergy. Possible team-training activities include the following (Day, Gronn, and Salas, 2004):

- *Team building* to clarify team goals and member roles and set patterns for acceptable interaction
- *Cross training* to ensure that team members understand one another's tasks
- *Coordination training* to allow the team to work together by improving communication and coordination
- *Self-guided correction* to teach team members to monitor, assess, and correct their behavior in the team
- *Assertiveness training* to help team members express themselves appropriately when making requests, providing feedback, and other interactions among themselves

The team leaders also play the role of conflict and relationship manager while they continue doing real work themselves.

WHAT DO YOU DO?

You have been assigned to put together a team to support a high-profile client with a new product your company has developed. Your boss has given you the pick of any one you would like, but she is suggesting that you pick the best and the brightest performers to assure that the client gets top-notch service. What factors do you consider to create your team?

Managing Dysfunction in Teams

Although teams can provide considerable benefits to organizations, they can also provide challenges to their leaders. Not all teams function well; some fall prey to various problems that cause them to spend more time in conflict than in performing activities necessary to achieve their goals. Table 8-5 summarizes the typical problems that may occur in teams.

GROUPTHINK   Being cohesive is a valued goal for any team. Team members strive to get along, reduce conflict, and keep their membership in the group. Smaller groups with clear norms and members who share similar characteristics and a history of success are more likely to develop cohesion. Such cohesion can provide many benefits such as a supportive environment for learning and potential for high performance. However, it can also present one major problem: Groupthink. The concept of *Groupthink* was first proposed by Irvin Janis (1982) to describe

TABLE 8-5	Typical Team Problems
Groupthink	Poor decision making that results from too much cohesion and directive leadership
Free Riders	Unequal contribution to the team
Negativity—Bad Apples	Negative thinking from one or more members
Lack of cooperation	Inability to coordinate activities and poor interpersonal relations

dysfunctional group processes that can occur when group members focus on being cohesive, do not express disagreement or think critically, and as a result, make bad decisions. The process of Groupthink is presented in Figure 8-4. When cohesive groups face a complex situation, they insulate themselves from outsiders and fail to consider alternatives, instead reaching for quick agreement that protects the group sense of cohesion. A key antecedent of Groupthink is directive leadership that further encourages quick agreement. Once these conditions are in place, groups that fall prey to Groupthink show a number of symptoms, including the illusion of invulnerability and unanimity, collective rationalization, self-censorship and pressure on dissenters. As a result, alternatives are not evaluated, the group strives toward quick agreement, and the group fails to develop contingency plans, all leading to poor decision making. Janis used several historical examples such as the Bay of Pigs and Cuban Missile crises to illustrate the Groupthink process. Other examples where Groupthink can be applied to explain poor decisions include the space shuttle *Challenger* disaster and the decision for the United States to invade Iraq.

Many researchers believe that autocratic and directive leadership play a critical role in the development of Groupthink (e.g., Chapman, 2006; Hackman, 2009). In addition to encouraging dissent, building diverse membership, and bringing outsiders to the group, one of the primary solutions to avoiding Groupthink is for the leader to avoid pushing the group to reach a consensus, to assign members to be critical evaluators, and in some cases, even to stay away from the group as it considers alternatives and deliberates.

FREE RIDERS One of the common complaints people have when working in teams is the presence of people who do not contribute fully but still benefit from the work of the team (Taggar and Neubert, 2008). Often called free-riders, these individuals appear to be more common in individualistic cultures. In collectivistic cultures, the sense of group and the need to be part of the group often prevents people from free-riding. In individualistic cultures, the focus on individual contribution reinforces the need to have equal and similar contributions from all team members, causing them to feel a sense of unfair advantage when facing potential free-riders. The actual or perceived presence of free-riders can be highly detrimental to team effectiveness, potentially leading other members to reduce their input and contribution for fear of being taken advantage of or even looking to punish

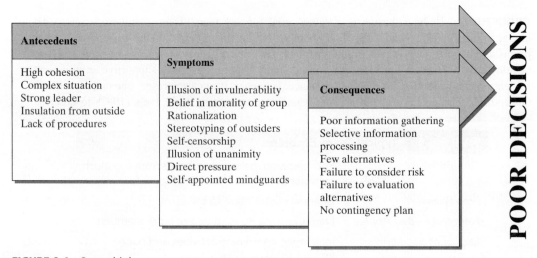

FIGURE 8-4 Groupthink

the free-rider, which can backfire and further damage the group's effectiveness (Hopfensitz and Reuben, 2009). Dealing with free-riders quickly is an essential role for team leaders.

NEGATIVITY AND BAD APPLES   Dinesh C. Paliwal, the chairman, president and chief executive of Harman International Industries, an audio and infotainment equipment company, believes that if leaders don't step in to stop negativity and political gamesmanship quickly, they are likely to encourage such behavior (Bryant, 2012b). Angies Hicks, founder of Angie's List, agrees that even one team member with a bad attitude can greatly impact the culture of an organization (Bryant, 2012b). As is the case of with positive behavior and attitudes, negativity can quickly spread and damage the cohesion, effectiveness, or even lead to unethical behavior (Kish-Gephart, Harrison, and Treviño, 2010) of a team. One unhappy and unmotivated team member can have a disproportionate negative effect on her team (Felps, Mitchell, and Byington, 2006; Myatt and Wallace, 2008). The "bad apples" are often focused on their own goals, uncooperative or domineering, and unwilling to contribute. Their constant complaining and lack of motivation draw the group down and prevent other team members for achieving the group's goals.

LACK OF COOPERATION   Peter Swinburn, president and CEO of Molson Coors Brewing Company, believes that the primary reason teams fail is because team members are not really team players (Swinburn, 2012). An effective team is one in which members trust one another to work toward a common goal. Cooperation depends heavily on the presence of trust and a resulting sense of safety within the team, both of which allow group members to experiment, learn, and make mistakes without fear of ridicule and retribution (Bret et al., 2012).

Helping Teams Become Effective

There are many recommendations for how to help teams become effective (for an example, see Frontiera and Leidl, 2012). Specifically, membership in teams should be voluntary and their objective and purpose must be clear (e.g. Xin, 2010). Team leaders must be ready to provide appropriate training and manage conflict while encouraging constructive dissent (Govindarajan and Terwilliger, 2012). One of the key roles of a team leader is to monitor the team and continuously assess its health and effectiveness. If the group develops any dysfunctional characteristics, it is essential for the leader step in to prevent further problems. In the case of Groupthink, the leader must often remove himself or herself from the group to avoid too much influence. In the case of free-riders or bad apples, the leader must take an active role in enforcing team norms, helping other members take leadership to stop the problem, or remove the noncontributing members. Even in a self-managed team environment where leaders are facilitators, it is important that they take action to address problems quickly.

One of the important roles of leaders in helping teams become effective is to support the group to develop trust. Trust requires a number of factors as presented in Figure 8-5. To build trust, team members must demonstrate integrity, hard work, and mutual respect. They must reward cooperation rather than competition, be fair to one another, celebrate success team and individual success, and communicate openly. Angie Hicks, founder of Angie's list, observes: "I've realized you just have to take extra care and make time to talk to people. I've realized that you need to over-communicate. When you're working with people, even if you think you've said something, maybe you need to say it two or three more times" (Bryant, 2012b).

They, further, must believe that their leaders—inside and outside the team—are predictable, have their best interests at heart, and will treat them fairly (Cunningham and MacGregor, 2000). Finally, celebrating small and big success and progress further builds cohesion and trust essential to team effectiveness. Ken Rees, president and chief executive of Think Finance, a

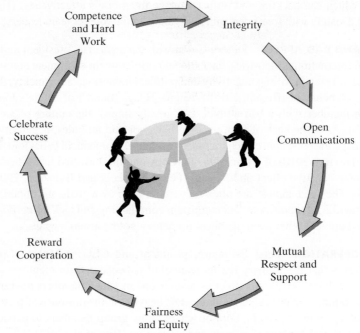

FIGURE 8-5 Building Trust

developer of financial products, says: "It's easy to get focused on the fact that you're not where you want to be, as opposed to all that you've accomplished. So taking a moment to talk about good news just keeps things more upbeat than they otherwise would be. For a lot of C.E.O.'s, I think, we're so focused on where we need to be that we don't necessarily have the fun we need to have along the way (Bryant, 2013b).

THE LEADERSHIP QUESTION—REVISITED

While teams can be very productive, they are sometimes overused and they are not easy to implement. In many individualistic cultures, working in teams is challenging. Additionally, organizations often reward individual stars and individual performance, factors that make the implementation of teams more difficult. To succeed, team should be used only when they can actually contribute more than individuals could. In those situations where teams are appropriate, members and leaders should receive training on issues such as culture, cooperative decision making, and conflict management. When they use teams, leaders must be prepared to delegate well and help them clarify the boundaries of their tasks and responsibilities. Teams are not a cure-all, but rather one of the tools available to leaders.

Summary and Conclusions

This chapter presents the concepts of participative management and its extension and application to the use of teams in organizations. Although many benefits can be drawn from the use of participative management, its success depends on appropriate application. Cultural and organizational factors should determine the use of participation as a management tool. A basic application of participation is the use of delegation by a leader.

Delegation must be implemented carefully and judiciously to ensure fair application; leaders must consider which tasks they should and can delegate and the individuals to whom they are delegating. Thorough feedback and monitoring are also important.

Many organizations formalize the use of participation through the creation of teams. The successful implementation of SMTs and self-leadership demonstrates the role of teams in revitalizing organizations. As teams continue to be used, their nature and role change, as does the role of leadership in a team environment. Despite the need for a contingency view in the use of participative management and teams, teams provide a basic management

tool in many parts of the world. More-focused attention on cultural factors, along with a continued analysis of the success of participative management and teams, should lead to continued evolution of the concepts.

The role of leaders often changes in a team environment to that of facilitator or coach, but the leader must continue to closely monitor the team to avoid dysfunctions such as Groupthink, the presence of free-riders or negative members, and the erosion of trust that is essential to effectiveness of teams. The team leader must also help members gain the right training to allow them to self-manage and self-lead in a team environment.

Review and Discussion Questions

1. What are the factors that determine the use of participation and what are the potential benefits and disadvantages of participation?
2. How should leaders approach the task of leading a culturally diverse team?
3. What organizational strategies can be used to help leaders delegate more often and more effectively?
4. Compare and contrast groups and teams. Provide an example of an effective team. What are the elements that contribute to its success?

5. What is the difference between delegation and implementation of self-managed teams?
6. What is the ideal size for a team and what problems can occur if a team is too large?
7. What is the main cause of groupthink and how is team performance negatively affected? What are some other typical dysfunctions that teams may face?
8. How can leaders contribute to team effectiveness?

Leadership Challenge: Who Gets the Project?

Your department includes 15 members, all of whom have been with you for at least a year. Although the department is generally cohesive and performs well, you are grooming four "stars" for promotion because you believe they are the best performers. You just landed a new account with a lot of potential, a tight deadline, and the need for considerable grooming and development. The success not only will give the person in charge of the project a lot of visibility but also could affect your career in the company. Everyone in the department is aware of the importance of the project, and several people, including your four stars, volunteered to take it on. In particular, one of the members with

the most tenure and experience (but not one of the four stars) is pushing to get the project. Given the project's importance, you want it to be handled well and without too much direction from you.

As you are about to delegate the project to your top star, you receive a call from the human resources director telling you that one of the department members filed an informal complaint against you, accusing you of favoritism. The director can't tell you the name, but wanted you to be aware of potential problems and that HR would be conducting informal fact-finding interviews.

1. Who will you assign to the project?
2. Consider the implications of your decision.

Exercise 8-1: To Delegate or Not to Delegate?

This role play is designed to provide you with an opportunity to experience the challenges of delegation either as a leader or as a follower. Read the following situation and description of team members.

Situation

You are a team manager in the public relations and marketing department at a major resort, Sunshine, Inc. Your organization specializes in all-inclusive package vacations and has a reputation for excellent customer service. As a team manager, you are responsible for the supervision and development of four account managers in the corporate area. Your team's role is sales and service to corporate clients.

Your manager, the marketing director, just handed you a new account that she inherited from another of the resort's partners. The client has been problematic in terms of payment and somewhat unreasonable demands, but it has a lot of potential. It is an entrepreneurial firm that your manager referred to as "spoiled brats." However, successful handling of this client, you are told, is important. "We don't want to lose them; in fact, we really want them to be happy! Nobody seems to have figured out how, but I'm sure you will come up with something."

You have four people in your team:

Fran Smith: Fran has been with Sunshine for four years. She recently obtained a bachelor's degree in marketing from a major state university. Her prior work experience was with a restaurant supplier, where she was a good performer with a lot of ambition, creativity, and motivation. You previously assigned many different tasks to her, and they were all done well. Fran is one of your in-group people, and you trust her a lot. You have had many discussions about future promotions, and she has followed your advice well. Fran seemed to be in a slump for the past three months but has not talked to you about it, and you let it go, assuming it may be a personal issue. Performance is still there, but some of the enthusiasm is gone.

Gerry Narden: Gerry has been with Sunshine for 10 years. He has an AA degree in business and got his first job as a desk clerk at the resort. Gerry has worked in many different parts of the resort and started in corporate sales only six months ago. He transferred in with outstanding evaluations from all his previous bosses. Gerry is the newest member of the team and has experienced some ups and downs in sales. One of them almost caused the loss of a major client. You intervened and managed to save the account. He seemed to learn from the experience and has done well in the past two months. You have not, however, given him any major accounts since, although he repeatedly asked for more challenge.

Terry Chan: Terry has been with your team for five years. Terry has a master's in communication and is a good performer. Her more than 10 years of work experience, most of which were in sales and customer relations within Sunshine, show her knack for working with "big" clients who keep coming back to her. She usually does not ask for assignments and is good at bringing her own. Terry needs little help or management from you and seems to do her own thing successfully.

Jim Johnson: Jim has been with your team for a year. He is intelligent, creative and well qualified. When in the mood for it he can cultivate client relationships with his calm and reassuring manner. However, his previous manager commented on a lack of enthusiasm that might be due to an absence of motivation and a laid back, relaxed approach that is really at odds with the demands of a sales and service role. There is no doubt that he has the ability but you wonder if the drive is lacking or whether in fact a different role may suit him better.

Role Play

After reading the scenario, please wait for further information from your instructor.

To Delegate or Not to Delegate: Worksheet for Managers

1. Who would you select to manage the account? What are your reasons?

2. Plan the meeting during which you will delegate the task. What do you need to say? What areas do you need to cover? How are you addressing your employees' needs?

To Delegate or Not to Delegate: Worksheet for Employees

1. What do you need to do a good job?

2. Has your manager provided you with clear information about the task and expectations? What is done correctly? What is missing? Do you feel ready and motivated to take on the task?

Exercise 8-2: Strategies for Becoming a Self-Leader

Changing Behaviors

1. Observe yourself
   Identify specific behaviors that are related to becoming a self-leader. (List at least three.)

   →

   →

   →

   Set specific goals for yourself for each behavior. (List at least three.)

   →

   →

   →

   Include a time line for each goal.

   →

   →

   →

   How will you measure your goals?

2. Set up opportunities for rehearsal.
Identify settings where you can practice the new behaviors. (List at least three.)

→

→

→

Identify and work with individuals who can help you rehearse.

3. Establish reminders.
Establish reminders in your work environment to encourage the new behaviors. (List at least three.)

→

→

→

List individuals who can help you. (List at least three.)

→

→

→

4. Set up reward and "punishments."

List rewards that would encourage you to use self-leadership behaviors. (List at least three.)

→

→

→

Clarify when each should be used.

List things that would stop unwanted behaviors. (List at least three.) Clarify when each should be used.

→

→

→

Changing Cognitive Patterns

1. Focus on natural rewards in tasks.

List aspects of your job that can naturally encourage self-leadership behaviors. (List at least three.)

→

→

→

2. Establish constructive thought patterns.
   Look for opportunities rather than obstacles. List your opportunities

3. Use positive mental imagery.
   Reevaluate your priorities, beliefs, and assumptions.

Source: Based on self-leadership concepts developed by Manz and Sims (1991); and Neck and Manz (2012).

Self-Assessment 8-1: Delegation Scale

Using the following scale, indicate how much you agree with the following items.

1 = Strongly disagree

2 = Somewhat disagree

3 = Neither agree nor disagree

4 = Somewhat agree

5 = Strongly agree

_____ 1. I can do most jobs better and faster than my subordinates.

_____ 2. Most of my tasks cannot be delegated to my subordinates.

_____ 3. Most of my subordinates do not have the appropriate level of skills to do the tasks that I could delegate to them.

_____ 4. I feel uncomfortable delegating many of my tasks to my subordinates.

_____ 5. I am responsible for my subordinates' mistakes, so I might as well do the task myself.

_____ 6. If my subordinates do too many of my tasks, I may not be needed any longer.

_____ 7. Explaining things to subordinates and training them often takes too much time.

_____ 8. My subordinates already have too much work to do; they can't handle any more.

_____ 9. If my subordinates do the tasks, I will lose touch and be out of the loop.

_____10. I need to know all the details of a task before I can delegate to my subordinates.

Scoring Key: Your total score will be between 10 and 50. The higher your score, the less inclined you are to delegate, and you agree with many of the common excuses used by managers not to delegate tasks to their subordinates.

Total: _____

Self-Assessment 8-2: Are You a Team Leader?

Rate yourself on each of the following items using the scale provided here:

1 = Strongly disagree

2 = Somewhat disagree

3 = Neither agree nor disagree

4 = Somewhat agree

5 = Strongly agree

_____ 1. I enjoy helping others get their job done.

_____ 2. Managing others is a full-time job in and of itself.

_____ 3. I am good at negotiating for resources.

_____ 4. People often come to me to help them with interpersonal conflicts.

_____ 5. I tend to be uncomfortable when I am not fully involved in the task that my group is doing.

_____ 6. It is hard for me to provide people with positive feedback.

_____ 7. I understand organizational politics well.

_____ 8. I get nervous when I do not have expertise at a task that my group is performing.

_____ 9. An effective leader needs to have full involvement with all his or her team's activities.

_____10. I am skilled at goal setting.

Scoring Key: Reverse score for items 2, 5, 6, 8, and 9 (e.g., 1 = 5, 5 = 1). Add your score on all items. Maximum possible score is 50. The higher the score, the more team leadership skills you have.

Total: _____

LEADERSHIP IN ACTION

JOHN MACKEY OF WHOLE FOODS

"I am now 53 years old and I have reached a place in my life where I no longer want to work for money…. Beginning January 1, 2007, my salary will be reduced to $1, and I will no longer take any other cash compensation" (Mackey, 2007). The statement is part of a letter John Mackey, the founder and CEO of Whole Foods, wrote to his employees when the sales were below expectations and the stock prices dropped. Mackey says: "We're trying to do good. And we're trying to make money. The more money we make, the more good we can do."

His company and a highly unique management style are a model of innovation and customer service around the world. He considers his company and his over 50,000 employees to be his children, says he does things for fun, and is considered by some to be a "right-wing hippy" (Paumgarten, 2010). His views, which he calls conscious capitalism, see business as having a higher purpose; he states: "We're trying to do good. And we're trying to make money. The more money we make, the more good we can do" (Paumgarten, 2010).

Although he says that his views and those of his company do not always match, he believes that: "We're changing the experience (of shopping) so that people enjoy it" (Sechler, 2004: 1). With bright facilities, wide aisles, rich colorful displays, expert employees, and lots of help and information for customers, Whole Foods has changed the way many people shop for food. John Mackey started the company in 1980 in Austin, Texas, with the first organic food store; it now numbers more than 150 stores with earnings of nearly $3 billion and is making a move to become a global company with the first store opening up in the United Kingdom (Duff, 2005).

"Mackey is hardly a manager at all …he's an anarchist" is how a former Whole Foods executive describes the company president (Fishman, 2004: 73). The CEO, who is now in his 50s, visits his stores in shorts and hiking boots and is equally as passionate about egalitarianism and democracy in the workplace and the humane treatment of animals as he is in his opposition to the new U.S. health-care plan (Mackey, 2009). He interacts freely with employees and is eager to learn from them and from his customers. Wendy Steinberg, who has worked at Whole Foods since 1992, describes him as an "observer" (Fishman, 2004: 76). A vegan, who changed his vegetarian diet to exclude all animal by-products after working with a group devoted to improving living conditions for farm animals, he still flies commercial airplanes, rents the cheapest cars, and is a shrewd and disciplined businessman leading his company and employees to considerable success (Fishman, 2004). Much of that success is attributed to Whole Foods' team-based culture that empowers employees and involves them in all aspects of decision making while demanding performance and customer service.

The basic decision-making power at Whole Foods rests with the teams that run each department (e.g., bakery, produce, seafood) in each store. The teams decide whom to hire, whether to retain members, what products to carry, how to allocate raises, and so forth. All teams together also make strategic decisions, such as the type of health insurance the company will offer. The National Leadership Team of the company makes the overall decision based on majority vote. Mackey says, "I don't overrule the National Leadership Team…. I've done it maybe once or twice in all these years" (Fishman, 2004: 74). He admits making some top–down decisions, but only when time to consult is not available.

Whole Foods has a "Declaration of Interdependence" that affirms the interdependence of all stakeholders and clearly states the goals of satisfying and delighting customers and of team-member happiness and excellence (Whole Foods, 2013). Building healthy relationships with team members, getting rid of the "us versus them" management mentality, and a deep-seated belief in employee participation are also highlighted. The core values regarding working at Whole Foods include the following (Whole Foods, 2013):

- Self-directed teams that meet to solve problems and appreciate members
- Increased communication through open-book management and "no secrets" management that allow employees access to financial data, salary and raise information, and so forth
- Profit- and gain-sharing to provide team members incentives to perform and build the team through shared fate (nonexecutive employees hold 94 percent of the company's stock options); a salary cap that limits the salary of any team member to times the average total compensation of all full-time team members
- Employee happiness through fun and friendship at work with liberal dress codes, ability to do volunteer work on company time, full health benefits, and emphasis on taking responsibility for successes and failures and celebration and encouragement of employees
- Continuous learning for employees about the products they sell and the job they do
- Promotion from within to appreciate and encourage employee talent and development and a strong equal opportunity policy

Although the positive work culture, fun, and friendship are key to the company's ongoing success, competition and focus on performance are not lost. Because individual raises are tied to their team's performance, team members want good workers on their team. Mackey, who wants his company to be based on love rather than fear, is also clearly in charge and in the forefront representing his company in the community. As he battles the animal rights groups that continue to criticize Whole Foods for being hypocritical and counterculture groups that accuse him of having become too corporate, or defending against the antiunion charges leveled at the company. Mackey responds, "We're in the business of selling whole foods, not holy foods" (Overfelt, 2003). The corporate side of the CEO became clearly evident when he had to apologize for having assumed an online alias "Rahobdeb" (an anagram of his wife's name) to bash his competitor Wild Oats Markets for years (Kesmodel, 2007; Stewart, 2007).

Questions

1. How does John Mackey use delegation in the operation of Whole Foods?
2. What makes the teams at Whole Foods effective?

Sources: Duff, M., "The perils of the imperial reach," *DSN Retailing Today* 44, no. 1 (2005): 10; Fishman, C., 2004. "The anarchist's cookbook," *Fast Company*, July: 70–78; Kesmodel, D., 2007 "Whole Foods sets probe as CEO apologizes," *The Wall Street Journal*, July 18: A3; Mackey, J., 2007 "I no longer work for money," *Fast Company*, February, 112; Mackey, J., 2009. " The Whole foods alternative to ObamaCare," *The Wall Street Journal*, August 11. http://online.wsj.com/article/SB1000142405297020 4251404574342170072865070.html (accessed April 16, 2010); Overfelt, M., 2003. "The next big thing: Whole food market," *Fortune,* June 2. http://www.fortune.com/fortune/print/0,15935,456063,00.html (accessed January 27, 2005); Paumgarten, N., 2010. "The food fighter," *The New Yorker*, January 4. http://www.newyorker.com/reporting/2010/01/04/100104fa_fact_paumgarten (accessed on July 13, 2013); Sechler, B., 2004. "Whole Foods picks up the pace of its expansion," *Wall Street Journal,* September 29: 1; Whole Foods Declaration of Interdependence. 2013. http://www.wholefoodsmarket.com/mission-values/core-values/declaration-interdependence (accessed on July 13, 2013); Stewart, J. B., 2007. "Whole Foods chief disappoints by sowing wild oats online," *The Wall Street Journal*, July 18: D5.

9

Leading Change

After studying this chapter, you will be able to:

1. Identify forces for change and the role of culture in change.
2. Describe types of change; apply Lewin's change model and explain the change process.
3. Summarize the reasons for resistance to change and apply possible solutions.
4. Present the practices necessary to lead change including the following:
   - Creativity and innovation
   - Changing the organizational culture
   - The role of vision and exemplary leadership
   - Creating learning organizations

THE LEADERSHIP QUESTION

Change is hard and most people will resist it. Given this, should leaders simply push change through (get it over with) or should they take time, introduce things slowly and give followers time to adjust?

"Permanent white water" and "turbulent" are some of the terms used to describe the environment that today's organizations face. Their environment is changing at a rapid pace, leading to the need for flexibility, innovation, and nimbleness. The effectiveness and very survival of our organizations depend on their ability to successfully adapt to environmental changes while still maintaining internal health. Leading change is therefore one of the leader's most challenging and vital responsibilities. Whether implementing new technology, updating existing products or services, launching new ones, or putting in place new administrative and management systems, leaders must guide their followers through change, which is more often than not perceived as painful, often resisted, and difficult to implement. Whereas managing change well is essential to the survival of the organization, various studies indicate that 60 to 70 percent of organizational change efforts fail (Cheese, 2013; McKinsey, 2013). Additionally, many organizational leaders are not satisfied with how well their organizations can innovate and adapt to change, and they fully realize that implementing change is a long-term process with many risks of failure (McGregor, 2007).

This chapter looks at the change process and the role that leaders play in leading and implementing change in their organizations.

FORCES FOR CHANGE

Change is the transformation or adaptation to a new way of doings things. *Innovation* is the use of resources and skills to create an idea, product, process, or service that is new to the organization or its stakeholders.

Internal and External Forces

When do organizations change? What makes leaders decide to implement change? Forces for change are both external and internal (see Figure 9-1). Environmental forces include factors such as social trends, cultural and demographic changes, political shifts, the economy, and technological advances. For example, in the United States and in many other parts of the world, demographic diversity related to both ethnic groups and age forces organizations to consider new ways of addressing their constituents' needs. The case of Avon (Leadership in Action in Chapter 6) shows how the company had to change because, in part, demographic and social changes led many women to work outside of the home, disrupting the home-based distribution of the company's products. As a result, Avon focused on introducing new distribution and marketing methods, changing how employees think about the products, and had to work on getting them to accept the changes. Similarly, the public interest in sustainability and demand for ecologically safe products have triggered the growth of organizations such as Ecover, the Belgian-based company, which is now the world's largest producer of ecological household cleaners and products. The success of Ecover, in turn, has forced changes in other consumer-good companies. Changes in the local and global political environments compel organizations to look for innovative ways of dealing with new problems. JetBlue (Leadership in Action in Chapter 1) was one of the first airlines to install reinforced doors to their planes' cockpits in

FIGURE 9-1 Forces for Change

response to the terrorist attacks of 2001. To take advantage of the Internet to connect with young voters, political candidates all over the world actively use social networking tools to campaign, pushing their political organizations to change.

The internal forces for change closely follow external forces. For example, Apple's iPhone has forced all other cell phone companies to change how they design and produce their phones. Amazon has redefined online customer service. A new service from one hospital will push others to consider changing their offerings and how they recruit and train employee. Wide uses of new technology such as the Web, or poor economic conditions, may lead city and state governments to expand their online services, requiring new hires, training, and new management processes. One of the most common forces for change inside organizations is the *performance gap*—the difference between expected and actual performance. Another potent internal force for change is new leadership at any level. Therefore, not only do leaders guide organizations through change, but they are also frequently the cause of change (see the Best Buy case in Leadership in Action at the end of this chapter).

Consider the forces that pushed the U.S. Federal Bureau of Investigation (FBI) to undergo extensive changes with varying degrees of success since the 9/11 attacks on the United States. The external forces for change were global politics, considerable political pressure in the United States, public demand for security, and changing technology among others. Internally, the FBI faced a performance gap (a glaring failure by some accounts), presence of old technology, antiquated management and administrative systems, and extensive employee dissatisfaction (Brazil, 2007). In addition, the agency has shifted its focus from reactive criminal investigations to proactive intelligence and greater emphasis on terrorism prevention, according to Thomas Harrington, the FBI's associate deputy director (St. Martin, 2011). Former U.S. Attorney Dick Thornburgh, who chaired a panel that reviewed the FBI, stated, "It's almost a total transformation of what the bureau does and how it does it. It's staggering" (Brazil, 2007). FBI Director Robert Mueller, a decorated ex-marine who took leadership a week before the 9/11 attacks and retired in 2013, was in charge of orchestrating the massive transformation. Talking about the challenges of transforming the organization, he stated: "I've come to find that one of the most difficult things one has to do is to bring an entity through the development of a change of business practices" (Ragavan, 2005). The case of the FBI illustrates the many forces that push organizations to change.

Culture and Change

As pressure for change increases from inside and outside organizations, not all leaders react and respond the same way. Some perceive the pressure as a threat; others see it as an opportunity. In addition to their personality, one factor that influences how leaders and their followers perceive pressures for change is culture, both at the national and organizational levels (we consider the importance of organizational culture later in this chapter). From a broader perspective, national cultural values of *tolerance of ambiguity* and *perception and use of time* can shape how leaders view change. In cultures such as Greece, Guatemala, Portugal, or Japan, where people do not easily tolerate uncertainty and ambiguity, change can be seen as a threat and is either ignored, resisted, or carefully planned and managed. A Japanese business leader is likely to manage change through extensive and detailed long-term planning and forecasting supported by governmental organizations such as the Ministry of International Trade and Industry (MITI). MITI targets certain industries for growth and supports them through various economic and political actions, thereby reducing the potential negative impact of change triggered by global competition. Similarly, in countries such as Malaysia and Thailand, with cultures that are risk averse, governmental centralized planning helps support business leaders reduce uncertainty and ambiguity. On the other end of the spectrum, in Sweden, the United States, and Canada, where change is tolerated and perceived as an opportunity, leaders deal with change by making quick changes to their organizations and implementing short-term strategies that address the immediate pressures relatively more quickly than in other cultures.

The perception of time further affects how leaders implement change. Leaders from present-oriented cultures, where time is linear, are likely to react fairly quickly to change and focus on short-term planning. The short-term orientation leads to a state of constant change that many U.S. organizations are experiencing. For example, when, in 2000, James McNerney became the first outsider to lead the 100-year-old 3M company, he immediately announced that he would change the DNA of the company. He implemented substantial changes that deeply affected 3M and left four years later to lead Boeing (Hindo, 2007). Leaders from past- and future-oriented cultures are less likely to react quickly to change, taking time to plan and to consider the long-term impact of their actions.

TYPES AND PROCESS OF CHANGE

Change is stressful and usually met with some resistance, as you will read later in this chapter. Different types of changes, however, affect people differently and require different types of leadership. Change that is sudden and drastic is more likely to cause stress and resistance, whereas gradual and programmed change is easier to implement.

Types of Change

In some cases, leaders can carefully plan and execute change; in others, leaders and followers are caught by surprise and have to react without specific preparation. Table 9-1 summarizes the different types of changes organizations face.

Even though many organizations carefully analyze their environment and internal conditions, through methods such as marketing intelligence, customer- and employee-satisfaction surveys or complex performance measures, in order to foresee changes and to plan their course of

TABLE 9-1	Types of Change
Type of Change	**Description**
Planned	Change that occurs when leaders or followers make a conscious effort to change in response to specific pressure or problem.
Unplanned	Change that occurs randomly and suddenly without the specific intention of addressing a problem.
Evolutionary	Gradual or incremental change.
Revolutionary or frame breaking	Change that is rapid and dramatic.

Sources: Partially based on M. S. Poole and A. H. Van de Ven (eds.). 2004. *Handbook of Organizational Change and Innovation.* Oxford, England: Oxford University Press; and by M. L. Tushman, M. L., W. H. Newman, and E. Romanelli, 1986. "Convergence and upheaval: Managing the unsteady pace of organizational evolution," *California Management Review*, Fall: 29–44.

action, they still face changes that they do not expect or are unable to anticipate. In addition, both planned and unplanned changes may happen, either gradually or rapidly, leading to dramatic impact on the organization. In the 3M example presented earlier, James McNerney planned the cultural and structural changes he wanted to implement to move the organization to improved efficiency through careful monitoring, measurement, and implementation of a process called Six Sigma, which relies on precision, consistency, and repetition (Hindo, 2007). The existing 3M culture, known worldwide for its ability to be creative and innovative, was based on experimentation and tolerance for trial and error, all factors that eventually led to innovative products and process (Winston, 2012). For example, all employees were encouraged to use 15 percent of their time to be creative (Goetz, 2011). McNerney moved to remove any variability from organizational processes, focusing instead on analysis, control, and efficiency. Although it was planned, the change was revolutionary and involved a complete cultural transformation (Hindo, 2007).

The different types of change may require different actions from leaders. For example, in the case of planned and evolutionary change, a leader's ability to structure tasks may be important. When facing unplanned and revolutionary change, charismatic, transformational, or positive leaders who make an emotional connection with followers and help them weather the change may become more central. In addition, based on the change process considered in the next section, the options that are available, and actions that are required from a leader may be different in each type of change.

Lewin's Model for Change

Understanding the process and course of change can help leaders plan and implement change more successfully. In the 1950s, social psychologist Kurt Lewin proposed a theory of organizational change that continues to influence current thinking (Lewin, 1951). Lewin's Force Field theory proposes that organizations face forces that drive change and forces that resist change see (Figure 9-2). When the two forces are balanced, the organization maintains its status quo. When the forces for change are stronger than those that resist change, leaders can overcome inertia and implement changes. If forces against change are stronger, the organization is not likely to implement change successfully. So, when implementing change, leaders must either increase and bolster the forces for change or reduce and neutralize the forces that resist change.

Lewin further suggests that change takes place in a three-stage process (see Figure 9-3). In the first, *unfreezing state*, the existing practices and behaviors are questioned and motivation to change develops. Unfreezing is likely to be easier when the forces for change, whether internal or external are strong and organizational members and leaders are aware of them. One of the major tasks of any leader is to help followers "unfreeze" and realize that there is a need for change. Consultant and executive coach Ray Williams argues that the key to successful organizational change is convincing thousands of employees to think differently about their job; they have to believe in the need for change. He says that employee: "to embrace change, must also engage in a process that changes how they think about themselves, not just their jobs (Williams, 2010). For example, when British Airways undertook a successful structural change that involved privatization and layoffs, the leadership of the organization made particular efforts to repeatedly communicate why the changes were essential (Faucheux, 2013). In the 3M case, the company's growth had slowed and the stock was performing poorly, prompting McNerney to implement drastic changes such as laying off 8,000 employees (11 percent of the workforce) and putting controls on the creative inventors (Hindo, 2007). The pressure for change may have been real, but based on all accounts, the employees never quite fully grasped the need for change; there had been no "unfreezing."

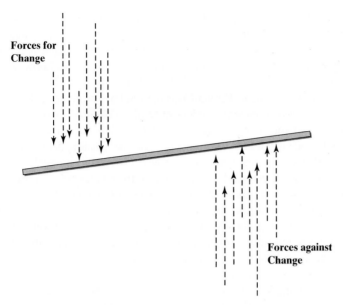

Forces for Change

Forces against Change

FIGURE 9-2   Force Field Model for Change

The second stage, according to Lewin, is the *change* itself, where new practices and policies are implemented and new behaviors and skills are learned. The change can involve technology, people, products, services, or management practices and administration. The leader's role continues to be essential, supporting followers, emphasizing the importance of the change, correcting course as needed, and so forth. Most organizations focus on this stage, making the change without paying enough attention to preparing the organization either for the change or to the last phase, *freezing*. In the last phase of change, the newly learned behaviors and freshly implemented practices are encouraged and supported to become part of the employees' routine activities. The leader's role in this stage is providing resources, coaching, training, and using appropriate reward systems to help solidify the changes that have been implemented.

All change takes time, but giving the organization time to settle down after a change is particularly important. Organizational researcher Kim Cameron believes that managing change requires fixed points without which organizations cannot steer (Cameron, 2011). He states,

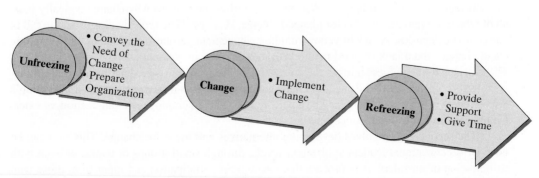

Unfreezing
- Convey the Need of Change
- Prepare Organization

Change
- Implement Change

Refreezing
- Provide Support
- Give Time

FIGURE 9-3   Lewin's Stages of Change

"Unfortunately, when everything is changing, change becomes impossible to manage. Without a stable, unchanging reference point, direction and processes are indeterminate" (Cameron, 2006: 317). Although change is essential to survival, constant change that is not given time to take hold is likely to be ineffective. It is important for employees to know what is not changing and to be allowed to practice the new behaviors long enough to learn them before something new is introduced. According to Harvard Business School professor John Kotter, a well-known authority on organizational change, leaders must also celebrate early successes and short-term progress to keep followers motivated (Brazil, 2007). In the case of the FBI, the ongoing transformation that took place had a negative impact on morale, causing heavy turnover (Brazil, 2007). For 3M, although the implementation of the new efficiency-oriented systems lasted for four years and stock prices did rebound, the architect of the change, McNerney, left, and most long-time employees did not fully adopt the change. The CEO who replaced McNerney was George Buckley, a soft-spoken company insider, who corrected course to refocus on the innovation process that 3M is so famous for. He said: "Perhaps one of the mistakes that we made as a company ... is that when you value sameness more than you value creativity, I think you potentially undermine the heart and soul of a company like 3M" (Hindo, 2007). He also made leadership training a priority, slowing the pace of moving top executives around and allowing them to savor their successes and learn from their mistakes before they were moved (Jones, 2009b). Inge Thulin, CEO since 2012, is following a similar strategy. He states: "I believe that what is driving this company in terms of return for us is the investment in research and development, and every time we do it we know that we have a competitive advantage" (Caruso-Cabrera, 2013).

Lewin's model of change has four implications for leaders:

1. Leaders must take time to prepare their followers for change and persuade them of the need for change.
2. No matter what the change, there will be resistance.
3. Leaders must invest resources to support the change and allow time for it to take hold.
4. Pacing change rather than piling one after another is likely to be more effective.

The typical model for implementing planned change and ways of managing unplanned change are presented next.

Process of Planned Change

Planned change follows a general process outlined in Figure 9-4. The process has six steps, each of which requires different types of resources and leadership skills. Peter Cheese who worked for over 30 years at the consulting firm Accenture identifies the reasons why change typically fails, all of which fall into the process for planned change. He says: "The typical culprits tend to fall in one of four categories: A lack of vision, middle management permafrost, a lack of understanding about change, and a lack of good methods to measure and implement change" (Cheese, 2013). The first step in the process mirrors the unfreezing phase of Lewin's model. Leaders and followers must become aware of the need for change and recognize its importance to the organization's effectiveness or survival. There may be a performance gap, or employee dissatisfaction, or external pressure from customers or competitors.

The second step involves developing alternatives and ideas for change. This step can be done by organizational leaders at different levels, through small groups or teams, or even with participation of outsiders. Any process that encourages participation and input from those who are affected most by the change is likely to facilitate the implementation process. For example,

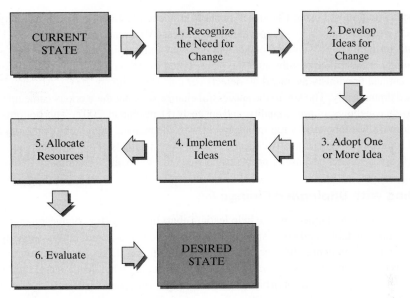

FIGURE 9-4   The Process of Planned Change

most municipalities systematically gather input from the public about projects such as parks, freeways, or other developments. Similarly, school boards ask for feedback from parents when planning changes. The use of team and empowerment in organizations can be one mechanism for allowing input into the development of alternatives. In addition, although there may not be a choice on whether or not to change, there are always many alternatives and paths to accomplish the goals; step two of the change process is an ideal opportunity to get involvement and buy-in.

The next two steps are adoption of ideas and implementation of the change plan. These two steps mirror Lewin's change phases. The fifth step is allocation of resources to support the change. Leaders have to either allocate new resources or shift current resources to help implement change and "freeze" the change. For example, FBI Director Mueller shifted resources from fighting crime to counterintelligence to support the new direction, and the FBI started training its executives through additional weeklong courses on leading strategic change (Brazil, 2007). The allocation of resources is a powerful message from leadership that the change matters and should be taken seriously. Finally, the last step in the process is evaluation of the change process and its outcomes. The process of planned change is a continuous and *dynamic loop*. After change is implemented, the organization must review and evaluate its effectiveness and assess whether the objectives are met. Did the performance gap narrow or close? Are various constituencies, including employees, more satisfied? Did the new products and services address stakeholders' needs? Are processes more efficient? Does the new technology work? If the goals are not achieved, the change process starts over with the recognition once again that change is needed.

The process of change either can take place in *top–down* manner with leaders initiating and driving the process or can be *bottom–up* with individuals and teams throughout the organization starting and implementing the process. A top–down change fits well with traditional, hierarchical, command-and-control organizations and tends to force rapid change. However, it also may engender more resistance. The bottom–up approach creates more involvement and participation, thereby reducing resistance. Yet, the risk of such an approach is not enlisting leadership support, which is essential to the success of any change. The case of Toyota taking over one of the lowest performing and most hostile Chevrolet plants from General Motors in Fremont, California, in the 1980s, is a case in point. No one expected much success. After renaming the plant New United Motor Manufacturing, Inc., or Nummi (sounds like *new me*) and keeping the same workers and the same technology, it took three months after the plant started to roll out cars again with almost no defects (the plant had previously averaged 40 defects per car; Deutschman, 2007). Absenteeism and costs dropped dramatically. The key to the successful change was that the workers came up with ideas on how to change things, improve quality, and cut costs (Deutschman, 2007). This bottom–up approach to change, fully supported by top management, was the magical ingredient. Although Nummi produced some of the highest quality cars and had the lowest defects of any Toyota plant, it was closed in 2010, some suspect because of problems between the union and the company (Gonzales, 2010).

Dealing with Unplanned Change

Whereas models of planned change help leaders chart the course for change, change is frequently sudden, unpredictable, and not planned. The economy changes, competitors come up with a new product, an environmental disaster happens, or unions go on strike. Managing unplanned change falls into the domain of *crisis management*. A crisis occurs when leaders and their organization substantially misread their environment or are caught off guard by events they could not have foreseen. Once crisis occurs, it is difficult to control. The cost to the organization, its employees, and its various stakeholders is likely to be high. Leaders can manage unplanned change to some extent by taking the following steps before a crisis develops (Mintzberg, Quinn, and Voyer, 1995; Starbuck, Greve, and Hedberg, 1978). As you will see, the steps have much in common with learning organizations, a topic we review at the end of this chapter.

- Avoid becoming too formal, hierarchical, rigid, and inflexible.
- Regularly infuse moderate amounts of uncertainty, unpredictability, and spontaneity into decisions to help prevent complacency.
- Stay on the offensive and be proactive with introducing new strategies, products, services, or processes.
- Replace and rotate leaders to bring in fresh ideas, methods, and visions.
- Experiment often with new methods, products, processes, structures, and so forth to help followers practice dealing with change.

Bill George, former CEO of Medtronics, further suggests that crises often present opportunities for organizations to change course for the better and for leaders to focus on their most important values (George, 2009). Whether planned or unplanned, and even with the most careful implementation, people are likely to resist change. The next section considers resistance to change, its solutions, and the role of leaders in the process.

RESISTANCE TO CHANGE AND SOLUTIONS

Change is one of the main causes of stress in our lives. Even positive changes such as receiving a promotion or getting married can create anxiety, lead to stress, and therefore engender resistance, which stops or slows the movement forward. Making major changes in one's life, for example changing your lifestyle after having a heart attack, are extremely difficult (Deutschman, 2007). Although people adjust to minor changes after a brief period of time, large-scale changes in life or work require long adaptation periods and much encouragement and support. Therefore, all changes, especially large-scale ones, meet with some resistance, especially when people do not feel ready for the change.

TABLE 9-2	Causes of Resistance to Change	
Organizational Causes	**Group Causes**	**Individual Causes**
Inertia	Group norms	Fear of the unknown
Culture	Group cohesion	Fear of failure
Structure	Leadership	Job security
Lack of rewards		Individual characteristics (personality; culture)
Poor timing		Previous experiences

Causes of Resistance

Three general causes explain resistance to change: organizational factors, group factors, and individual factors. (Table 9-2 presents the causes of resistance to change.) While planning and implementing change, leaders must consider all three causes. The primary organizational cause for resisting change is *inertia*, which is a tendency for an organization as a whole to resist change and want to maintain the status quo. Closely related to inertia are the culture and structure of the organization, which, if well established, are hard to change

In addition to inertia, culture, and structure, organizations can provide barriers to change by not rewarding people for change or implementing change at inappropriate times, for example when the previous change has not had time to "freeze." Other causes of resistance to change are related to group norms and cohesion. Cohesive groups with strong norms present many benefits. Members stick together, work well together, and can provide a supportive environment for learning. The same cohesive group can also be a formidable obstacle to change (Judson, 1991). In addition, the presence of strong leaders while a factor for change in some cases, can be a strong obstacle if the leaders do not support the change (Levay, 2010).

The final causes of resistance involve individual factors, such as fear of the unknown, of failure, and of job loss. Individual characteristics can also play a key role. For example, proactive individuals, those who are open to new experience, or are high self-monitors (see Chapter 4), are more likely to be comfortable with change and able to adapt to it more quickly. Similarly, entrepreneurs, who tend to be characterized by flexibility and willingness to try new ideas, are more comfortable with change. In addition, a person's culture, particularly the degree of tolerance of ambiguity, may play a role. Finally, the person's previous experience with change may be the cause of resistance. If an individual has experienced job loss or has been through other painful organizational changes in the past, he is more likely to be wary of implementing change in the future.

WHAT DO YOU DO?

You have the task of implementing a change in your team's work process. You have a very short deadline from your boss and you personally agree with the change. Half of your team is on board and ready to go. The other half is very skeptical about the change. What do you do?

Solutions

Steve Denning, author of *The leader's guide to radical management: Reinventing the workplace for the twenty-first century* (2010), suggests that organizations have three sets of tools available to them when managing change: leadership tools, management tools, and power tools. The leadership tools provide inspiration through persuasion, role modeling and support. The management tools provide information through training and various HR organizational processes. Finally, the power tools intimidate employees through coercion, threats, and punishments (Denning, 2011). The leader of an organization can do much to initiate change, inspire followers to implement it, and reduce resistance to change through inspiration, improvisation, creativity, and motivating followers. Overall, resistance can be reduced if employees learn to change their perception of change as negative and instead reframe it by seeing its potential benefits. Such change in perception can be encouraged by engaging employees in the change process and by rewarding behaviors and norms that support the change. Several specific methods for managing resistance are presented in Table 9-3.

TABLE 9-3	Methods of Dealing with Resistance to Change	
Methods	**Advantages**	**Disadvantages**
Leadership tools		
Vision, persuasion, and story telling	Helps in the unfreezing stage to explain need for change; provides a new frame to support the change	Time commitment from leader; requires communication skills
Role modeling	"Walk-the-talk" can inspire followers and build commitment to change	High time commitment and requires communication skills from leaders
Participation and employee involvement	Lead to commitment and can provide richer alternatives and ideas	Time consuming; risk of inappropriate change being implemented
Management Tools		
Facilitation and support	The only option when adjustment is the cause of resistance	Time consuming and high-risk of failure
Training and incentives	Easy to implement; part of ongoing organizational efforts	Can be costly and time consuming
Negotiation with key parties and agreements	Relatively easy to implement; only option when parties have equal power	Can be expensive, time consuming, and lead to continued and further negotiation
Power Tools		
Manipulation and cooptation	Relatively quick and inexpensive	Can lead to mistrust and resentment
Command and orders	Quick implementation; quick short-term results	Can lead to resentment and prevent long-term success; no employee buy-in
Explicit or implicit coercion and threats	Can be fast and effective in short term to end resistance	Can lead to resentment and morale problems; only effective in the short run

Sources: Based on J. P. Kotter and L. A. Schlesinger, 1979. "Choosing strategies for change," *Harvard Business Review,* March–April; and S. Denning, 2011. "How do you change an organizational culture," *Forbes,* July 23. http://www.forbes.com/sites/stevedenning/2011/07/23/how-do-you-change-an-organizational-culture/ (accessed August 3, 2011).

Leaders can prevent, manage, or reduce resistance to change by using a variety of these methods. The advantages of using leadership and management tools rather than power tools are very clear. A global survey conducted by McKinsey indicates that one of the keys to successful change is engaging employees to work collaboratively through the transformation (McKinsey, 2010). The next section focuses on the role of leaders in the successful implementation of change in organizations.

LEADING CHANGE: CREATIVITY, VISION, ORGANIZATIONAL LEARNING, AND ORGANIZATIONAL CULTURE

Change Track Research, an Australian organization that keeps a large database of organizational change, reports three key factors in successful organizational change: Change must be meaningful; trust in leadership is essential to success; and "one-size" does not fit all organizations (Three fundamentals of successful change, 2012). The role of leader in successfully implementing change is undeniable. Leaders must provide inspiration and vision for followers and put in place processes for changing organizational culture that successfully change their organizations.

Leaders are the guides as well as the role models for followers in implementing change. They must show followers through their own actions how change can be implemented and how it can successful.

Creativity

Creativity, also called *divergent* or *lateral thinking*, is the ability to link or combine ideas in novel ways (see Chapter 4). Creativity for leaders and followers is a key factor in organizational ability to innovate and change (see Self-Assessment 9-2). Creative people tend to be confident in the paths they select and are willing to take risks when others give up. They focus on learning and are willing to live with uncertainty to reach their goals. They are able to come up with new solutions to old problems. Kirthiga Reddy, director of Facebook online operation in India, and named the 4th most creative leader for 2013 by *Fast Company*, was able to grow the Indian Facebook users from 8 to 71 million in just two years. To achieve this, she used her deep knowledge of her culture and of Facebook, challenged the typical hierarchical Indian organizational culture, and encouraged her employees to be creative. She says: "You're not here to do just what you're told. You're here to see gaps and to act upon them." (Chu, 2013). Reddy was further able to reimagehow people use Facebook in India differently than those in the United States, often as a substititue for text or phone calls.

Creativity that allows people to think of new ways of addressing issues is at the heart of successful change. For P&G's cognitive science group, creativity sometimes means borrowing ideas from others. Pete Foley, the group's associate director, found some answers to challenges in the feminine products division in the San Diego Zoo by considering the biomimickry of geckos (Heath and Heath, 2009). Instead of inventing new solutions, this form of creativity involves looking for existing solution in other areas. Harvard professor Karin Lakhani says that people are not aware of other perspectives and being able to see things from a different point of view could make problems much easier to solve (Heath and Heath, 2009 : 83).

Leaders can put in place several processes to help their followers be more creative and accept change more readily:

1. *Leadership style.* Autocratic leaders who demand obedience impede the creative process and open exchange that encourage creativity.
2. *Flexible structure.* Less centralized and less hierarchical structures allow for free flow of ideas.
3. *Open organizational culture.* Being creative and seeking novel solutions is more likely in a culture that values change and constructive deviance rather than tradition and conformity.
4. *Questioning attitude.* Leaders can encourage and inspire followers to question assumptions and norms and look for novel alternatives instead of rewarding agreement and obedience.
5. *Tolerating mistakes.* By encouraging experimentation, tolerating, and even rewarding some mistakes, the leader can send a strong message about the importance of taking risks.

Many decision-making tools, such as brainstorming, can be used to enhance followers' creativity. In brainstorming (or brainsailing), team members are encouraged to generate a large number of ideas and alternatives without any censorship. Another method called *cooperative exploration* requires individuals to consider a problem by taking different positions and perspectives (de Bono, 1992; see Exercise 9.2). By using such techniques, leaders can encourage their followers to take broader perspectives and build a culture experimentation and creativity.

Max Levchin, entrepreneur cofounder of PayPal and CEO of Affirm, has been called the endless idea man. He has a process to encourage his companies and employees to be creative that includes talking to people at random, asking lots of questions, making lists of interesting ideas, following random leads, and finally, being aware that lists don't always work (Chafkin, 2013). The last item in his process refers to improvising when necessary.

Improvisation

Closely related to creativity is *improvisation*. According to researchers Robert and Janet Denhardt, authors of *The Dance of Leadership*, "improvisation is a vital leadership skill, one essential to the process of emotionally connecting with and energizing others" (2006: 109). These researchers liken leadership to art, particularly dance, focusing on the intuitive nature of leadership and the need to master its rhythms. "Improvisation," a term often used for artists rather than leaders, involves creation of something spontaneously and extemporaneously without specific preparation. Denhardt and Denhardt suggest that it occurs without a script and without perfect information and requires a combination of preplanned and unplanned activities and materials. Having expertise, knowledge, and perspective on the situation are also required, because without these elements, the leader is not likely to understand the leadership situation and environment enough to be able to lead. Improvisation is not "winging" a solution. It is based on deep preparation, self-knowledge, self-reflection, experience, and confidence, all also elements of authentic leadership. A musician states, "an ability to improvise … depends firstly on an understanding, developed from complete familiarity, of the musical context within which one improvises" (115).

Actor Bryan Cranston's prortrayal of Walter in the hit series *Breaking Bad*, required considerable creativity and improvision. While he carefully prepared for the role, did considerable research, and relied on a well-crafted script, he also used the element of surprise to deliver the scenes. He states that he enjoys not knowing what is going to happen and going with the flow (Laporte, 2013). The same elements of intense preparation and willingness to jump in are essential in using improvision when leading change in organization. To be able to change their organizations, leaders themselves must be able and willing to take risks. As do artists, leaders must hone their skills, practice often, develop competence, and be willing to work with their team of followers to experiment and transform themselves and their organization.

LEADING CHANGE

Mulally Takes on Ford

Ford Motor Company has faced the same challenges as other U.S. auto manufacturers in the past three decades and has made similar mistakes. However, it has been the healthiest among U.S. car manufacturers and has made a comeback, particularly in the United States. It owes a great deal of its success to the leadership of Alan Mulally, CEO since 2006, who has helped build the company's credibility back (Muller, 2012). Labeled as one of the few CEOs who actually puts the interest of shareholders and the public first, Mulally earns praise from many different circles for turning the company around, taking care of its employees, and being a responsible corporate citizen (Williams, 2013).

When Mulally joined Ford, the company provided a perfect example of inertia and the power of organizational culture, with entrenched management, fierce loyalties, and frequent turf battles (Taylor, 2009). The previous CEO and now chairman of the board, Bill Ford, Jr., gave up his job believing that an insider could no longer fix the problems and promising that the new CEO "knows how to shake the company to its foundations" (Kiley, 2007). Mulally, who had little experience in the car industry, faced what some considered Ford's dysfunctional and defeatist culture. To convince employees and leaders at Ford to change, he repeated the message: "We have been going out of business for 40 years" (Kiley, 2007). Ford's complacent culture, its highly rigid structure with a hierarchical pecking order that discouraged sharing ideas, and its well-established leadership-training practices that placed leaders in many jobs for short periods of time, all discouraged openness and cooperation and presented barriers to change. When Marc Fields joined the company in 1989, he was informed of group norms in the executive suites, which included making sure to get approval from his boss before he brought up any problems at meetings (Kiley, 2007).

Alan Mulally has been successful in slowly changing Ford by focusing heavily on communication to make sure everyone understands the extent of the problem, by setting a new mission, and printing it on cards that he distributed to employees. He believes that: "Everyone has to know the plan, its status, and areas that need special attention" (Taylor, 2009). He also made structural changes, "So I moved up and included every functional discipline on my team because everybody in this place had to be involved and had to know everything" (Taylor, 2009). Considering Mulally's effectiveness, Howard Schultz CEO of Starbucks states, "I've been studying the turnaround at Ford. The reason it has outpaced [GM and Chrysler] is because of the leadership and focus that Alan has brought" (Schultz, 2010). Mulally may be among a handful of U.S. CEOs who has a reputation for being effective as well as down to earth and a genuinely nice guy (Swisher, 2013).

He takes the time to make people feel important, engages with his employees, enjoys telling stories, and is reputed to be a good listener who takes the responsibility of leadership very seriously (Reed, 2012).

Sources: Kiley, D. 2007. "The new heat on Ford," *Bloomberg Business Week,* June 3. http://www.business week.com/stories/2007-06-03/the-new-heat-on-ford (accessed August 3, 2013); Muller, J. 2012. "Ford is worried, as it should be," *Forbes,* July 25. http://www.forbes.com/sites/joannmuller/2012/07/25/ford-is-worried-as-it-should-be/ (accessed August 3, 2013); Williams, S. 2013. "This is one incredible CEO," *Daily Financel,* June 13. http://www.dailyfinance.com/2013/06/13/this-is-one-incredible-ceo-30/?source=edddlftxt0860001 (accessed August 3, 2013); Reed, T. 2012. "6 leadership tips from Ford CEO Alan Mulally," *The Street,* April 12. http://www.thestreet.com/story/11480044/1/6-leadership-tips-from-ford-ceo-alan-mulally.html (accessed August 3, 2013); Swisher, K. 2013. "Ford's Mulally says he's shared 'business transformation' tips with Microsoft's Ballmer," *All Things D,* July 9. http://allthingsd.com/20130709/fords-mulally-says-hes-shared-business-transformation-tips-with-microsofts-ballmer/?refcat=news (accessed August 3, 2013); Schultz, H. 2010. "Who 9 CEOs admire most," *CnnMoney.com,* March 4. http://money.cnn.com/galleries/2010/fortune/1003/gallery.most_admired_executives.fortune/3.html (accessed April 21, 2010); and Taylor, A., III. 2009. *Fixing up Ford,* May 12. http://money.cnn.com/2009/05/11/news/companies/mulally_ford.fortune/index.htm?postversion=2009051212 (accessed April 21, 2010).

Vision and Inspiration

"You have to share the vision you want to accomplish and get everybody on board and enthusiastic about it. When you can get them to march in the same direction, you can really move mountains," states Carl-Henric Svanberg, CEO of the Swedish telecom giant Ericsoon (Bisoux, 2009). Svanberg, like many other leaders, knows that providing a vision and inspiring followers are the important functions of leaders during change. A clear vision provides followers with reasons for change. It further supports the actual change process by helping followers keep the goal in mind and helps them stay focused during refreezing. The inspiration that a leader can provide to his or her followers sustains the followers and helps reduce the resistance to change. Most historical leaders who were able to create change started with a vision that they, or their followers, translated into goals that they were able to achieve. John F. Kennedy envisioned space travel, which eventually culminated with the first man on the moon. Mahatma Gandhi had a vision of an India free of colonial Britain. Martin Luther King envisioned equality and civil rights in the United States and put in place the steps to achieve his vision. Wendy Kopp created Teach for America based on her vision of improving schools. Several themes emerge in the visionary leadership essential to change:

- *Importance of vision.* Successful and effective leaders provide a clear vision or help followers develop a common vision. Whether developed by the leader alone or with engagement with followers, vision is key to effectively leading change.
- *Empowerment and confidence in followers.* Visionary leaders empower followers to allow them to act autonomously and independently from the leader. This empowerment engages followers in the change, reducing resistance.
- *Flexibility and change.* The fast-changing environment requires leaders to develop and encourage flexibility and openness to change in their organization.

• *Teamwork and cooperation.* Successful leaders emphasize teamwork and, maybe more important, the development of shared responsibility, as well as the need for trust and cooperation between leaders and followers and among followers.

Some leaders communicate their vision and values through stories. Patrick Kelly, CEO of Physician Sales and Services (PSS), relies on his storytelling skills to remind employees what is important (Weil, 1998). Whenever he repeats one of his favorites, "PSS employees chuckle…. And they learn, or relearn, an important lesson: No matter how badly other people treat you, no matter how confident you get about your future, never burn your bridges" (38). Researcher Noel Tichy recommends that leaders develop three stories. The first one, the "Who I am" story, should tell who the leader is. The second story is about "Who we are." Finally, the leader must have a "Where we are going" story (Weil, 1998). Others agree that storytelling can be one of the most powerful ways for leaders to communicate their vision to their followers. According to Harvard professor Howard Gardner, "Stories of identity convey values, build esprit de corps, create role models, and reveal how things work around here" (Stewart, 1998: 165). For example, Howard Schulltz of Starbucks (see Leading Change in Chapter 10) is a master storyteller who relies on sharing his personal experiences as a way of explaining his vision for the company. Similar to the ideas proposed by charismatic, transformational, value-based, and spiritual leadership (see Chapter 6), the leader's vision is vital to creating change. A motivating vision is clear and understandable, challenging, idealistic yet achievable; it appeals to emotions and is forward looking. Having a forward-looking vision is essential for transforming organizations and enacting large-scale change.

Kouzes and Posner (2012) propose one of the most clearly developed models of *visionary leadership*. In addition to presenting the practices of what the researchers call exemplary leadership (Figure 9-5), the model considers the followers' points of view and their expectations of leaders. Leaders have to model the way, develop and inspire a shared vision, challenge the status quo, empower and enable their followers to act, and motivate and support them. Kouzes and Posner (2003, 2012) emphasize the importance of motivation, reward, and recognition—in their words "encouraging the heart"—as key aspects of empowerment, confidence in followers, and development of trust. They specifically suggest that to truly motivate and inspire followers, the leader must do the following:

1. *Set clear standards* for behavior and performance that are accepted by all followers.
2. *Expect the best* from followers through a genuine belief in their abilities. This strong belief creates a self-fulfilling prophecy in followers, who will, in turn, perform better.
3. *Pay attention* by being present, walking around, noticing followers, and caring about their behaviors, actions, and results.
4. *Personalize recognition* not only by considering each follower's needs and preferences but also by making them feel special in the process.
5. *Tell a story* about followers, events, and performances as a way to motivate and teach.
6. *Celebrate together.* Leaders must look for many opportunities to celebrate the team and the individual's success together.
7. *Role model* the preceding principles to gain credibility and reinforce the message.

To be exemplary and visionary, leaders need to commit themselves to continuously questioning old beliefs and assumptions. This process leads to the creation of a new common vision. Through empowerment, encouragement, and proper role modeling, leaders can motivate followers to implement the vision. The driving force behind a leader's ability to fulfill this

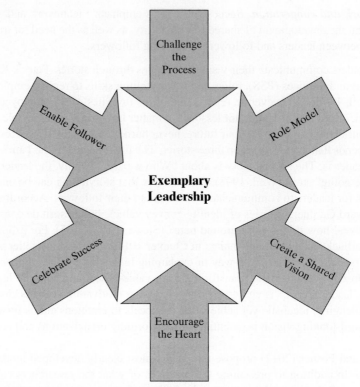

FIGURE 9-5 Practices of Exemplary and Visionary Leadership   *Sources:* Kouzes, J. M, and B. Z. Posner. 2003. *Encouraging the Heart: A Leader's Guide to Rewarding and Recognizing Others.* San Francisco: Jossey-Bass; and 2012. *The Leadership Challenge: How to Get Extraordinary Things Done in Organizations.* San Francisco: Jossey-Bass.

commitment is *credibility* (Kouzes and Posner, 1993). By asking followers about the characteristics they admire most and expect from their leaders, Kouzes and Posner suggest that honesty, the ability to be forward looking, and the capacity to be inspiring and competent are the pillars of a leader's credibility. Leaders' ability to change followers and the organization depends on their credibility (see Self-assessment 9-2).

When Rob Waldron became CEO of JumpStart in 2002, he took over a successful organization that was sending AmeriCorps volunteers and college students to teach Head Start programs in various cities to combat the rising trend of preschoolers in low-income communities entering school without the skills needed to succeed (Overholt, 2005). Waldron believes that growing the organization and leading the people have been one of the greatest challenges he has ever faced (Overholt, 2005). Waldron tackled the goals by decentralizing decision making, giving power to each center to encourage its employees to bring out their best ideas, and cutting staff at headquarters to raise everyone else's salary and attract fresh talent. His strategies paid off, and JumpStart grew 33 percent in 2003. Talking about his organization's achievement, Waldron said, "Our legacy is real social change. To have the joy of knowing your day-to-day struggles are turning into something that is life-changing.... I just wish everyone got to feel that way about their work" (55).

The visionary approach to leadership and change allows us talk about the leaders who everyone would agree are the real leaders—those who transform their organizations. It is clear that visionary leadership is needed in times of crisis and that it plays an essential role in implementing change. The effect of such leadership in times when consolidation and status quo are needed, however, is not as clear. Change-oriented leadership, by definition, works in times of change; the role of such a leader when change is not the focus is not clear. Anecdotes of the disastrous effects of change-oriented leaders in times when change is not needed are common and point to the limitations of visionary leadership. The current discussions of visionary leaders do not address these limitations. In addition, no research looks at the fate of organizations and employees who either do not buy into the leader's vision or buy into an inappropriate vision, as may have been the case at 3M. Many historical and political examples can be found, though. The extent to which similar events would occur in organizations needs to be explored.

Despite these shortcomings, visionary leadership provides guidelines for managing change. Accordingly, leaders must have passion, develop their credibility, develop and clarify their vision, share power with their followers, and—perhaps most important—role model all the attributes that they expect in their followers. To implement change successfully, most organizations must change their leadership and culture in fundamental ways. Although the various methods described earlier all support change, the most basic and essential steps to successful change is to design organizations that are built to change and have cultures that approach change positively (Worley and Lawler, 2006). The concept of learning organizations has been proposed to address the importance of flexibility and the ability to learn, adapt, and change continuously (Senge, 2006) and more recently, positive organizational behavior and leadership provide a fresh approach to leading organizational change.

Learning Organizations

Learning organizations are organizations in which people continually expand their capacity to create, where innovation and cooperation are nurtured, and where knowledge is transferred throughout the organization. Such an organization learns and creates faster than others, and this ability becomes a major factor in its survival and success. Learning organizations do not simply manage change; their goal is to become a place where creativity, flexibility, adaptation, and learning are integral parts of the culture and everyday processes.

The elements that make up the core of learning organizations are presented in Table 9-4. For organizations to learn and accept change as part of their routine, the leaders and members must have a shared vision of the current and future states. Charismatic, transformational, authentic, visionary, and positive leadership are all elements of building that vision. It is essential that leaders and followers understand how the organization functions as a system both internally and within its environment and be aware of the stated and unstated assumptions that make up the culture of their organizations. Without understanding how the organization truly functions, it is hard to implement change. The vision and the knowledge of the organization and its culture allow organizational members to identify what needs to be changed and the best ways to approach the transformation. Finally, successful change requires expertise and continuous development of new skills and competencies for individuals and for teams.

Figure 9-6 presents the factors that prevent organizations from learning. These factors are *organizational learning disabilities* of sorts. They are patterns of thinking and behavior that members have adopted that block change. According to Senge (2006), these blocks or

TABLE 9-4	Core Elements of Learning Organizations
Element	**Description**
Shared vision	Using cooperation and openness to build a shared vision through a common identity and a common goal of the future that leads to commitment
System thinking	Understanding interrelations and the invisible and visible bonds that connect people inside and outside the organization
Mental models	Being aware of stated and unstated assumptions and mental models that guide behaviors and decisions and developing new ones based on openness and cooperation
Personal mastery	Continually clarifying and developing personal visions and goals, and expanding skills sets and levels of proficiency
Team learning	Developing synergy and the ability to think and work together to question assumptions and build new processes

Sources: P. M. Senge. 2006. *The Fifth Discipline: The Art and Practice of Learning Organizations.* (New York: Doubleday; P. M. Senge. 1995. "Leading learning organizations," *Training and Development* 50, no.12: 36–37; P. M. Senge and J. D. Sterman. 1992. "System thinking and organizational learning: Acting locally and thinking globally in the organization of the future," *European Journal of Operations Research* 59, no.1: 137–140.

disabilities, stem from lack of system thinking and lead to looking at tasks, jobs, problems, and goals as separate and isolated from one another. In addition, leaders who are focused on large-scale change may fail to ignore the gradual and incremental change that may be occurring and likely to lead to the same outcome. They also may focus on specific events or causes of problems without considering the context in which they may be occurring or all the system-wide factors that may be contributing to them. The focus on events results in trying to find someone or

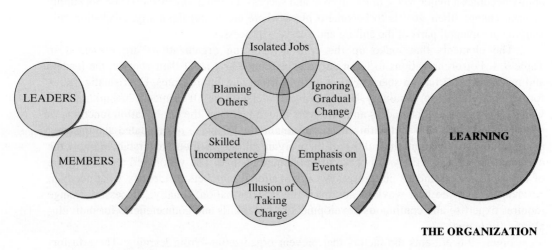

FIGURE 9-6   Blocks to Learning in Organizations

something to blame for the problems. Identifying these enemies detracts from fully considering the problems and focusing on solutions. Another organizational learning disability is skilled incompetence, which refers to relying on people with highly developed but narrow expertise who are celebrated and expected to provide answers. Because they are there to solve problems, they often cannot admit to lack of understanding or knowledge or to making mistakes. They, therefore, cannot learn and become incompetent despite their considerable skills. The situation becomes even more precarious if leaders are those who have skilled incompetence. Finally, another factor related to leadership is the illusion of taking charge and of one person being responsible to lead all others through the problem, instead of having shared leadership, empowerment, and cooperation.

To support their organizations in being change-ready and becoming learning organizations, leaders can take several actions to build an open and supportive culture that will support ongoing transformation. Actions include openness to new ideas, encouraging followers to develop local solutions rather than pushing standardization, providing time for learning and experimentation, and developing leaders who are open to participation and follower engagement.

The example of McNerney in 3M provides a case for obstacles and support for learning organizations. Based on its creativity and track record for innovation, 3M had many of the elements that encourage learning in organizations. Before McNerney took leadership, the organization focused on local solutions, open communication among inventors, and plenty of time and tolerance for learning and experimentation. In his search for efficiency, McNerney replaced many of the elements that made 3M a learning organization with factors that blocked learning. Implementation of a one-size-fits-all Six Sigma process, focus on specific events rather than looking for systemwide causes of problems, and an imposed vision from the top rather than a shared vision, all eroded the culture and 3M's ability to learn. Whereas the company continues to face challenges in maintaining its growth and profitability, the current leaders are reinstituting many of the elements that gave the company its innovative culture (Hindo, 2007).

Herman Miller, the office furniture maker, provides another example of a learning organization (Glaser, 2006; Herman Miller-things that matter to us, 2013). The company has been recognized as one of the best in its industry for its innovation and unique culture. It is known for its focus on its employees through flextime, telecommuting, and employee learning and ownership. It works with clients to develop distinctive solutions to their unique problems (Salter, 2000). But what makes the company truly a learning organization is the focus on curiosity and learning. Author Glaser describes the culture in her book *The DNA of Leadership*: "To encourage a wonderful sense of curiosity, leaders focus on helping Herman Miller employees experiment and take lessons from those experiments. This is such a strong part of the culture that's built into everything they do and say—it's embedded in their genetic code" (Glaser, 2006: 180).

Positive Approach

We have reviewed the positive organizational behavior and positive leadership approaches in Chapter 6. Many of their concepts and findings readily apply to leading change in organizations. While being positive is not in and of itself going to prevent resistance to change, the leader's positivity, optimism, and passion for change can be infectious. Followers look up to their leaders to role model appropriate emotions and behaviors. While positivity may not be important in the planning stages of change, it can make a significant impact in the implementation stages.

Best-selling authors and reporters Chip and Dan Heath consider the importance of positive thinking and positive role models in creating and sustaining change (Heath and Heath, 2010). They discuss the case of Jerry Sternin, who worked for Save the Children on improving child nutrition in third-world countries. When discussing how to change behavior, Sternin states: "Knowledge does not change behavior. We have all encountered crazy shrinks and obese doctors and divorced marriage counselors" (Heath and Heath, 2010 : 65). Instead, what works is having a role model of a positive outcome or event and understanding why things worked out and then trying to replicate them. This positive approach looks for "bright spots" that can be the guide of change in behavior.

Changing Organizational Culture

Chapter 7 presented the many ways in which top-level leaders can influence their organizations (see Figure 7-4 for a summary). In addition, Edgar Schein has identified several specific mechanisms that leaders use to shape the culture of their organization (2004). They include the following:

- *Communicate priorities.* By stating what is important, in terms of a general vision, specific issues that must be addressed, and ways in which they must be addressed, leaders make a powerful impact on their organization. For example, A. G. Lafley, CEO of P&G, is relentless about repeating the simple message of paying attention to customers (see Leadership in Action in Chapter 7).
- *Role model.* Although what the leader says is important, even more powerful is what the leader does. Leaders must be the change they want to see. Their actions demonstrate their values and what is truly important. For example, many historical charismatic leaders, including Mahatma Gandhi and Nelson Mandela, have gone to prison for their beliefs. A particular opportunity to role model desired behaviors occurs during times of crisis when the focus on and the need for leadership is increased. How a leader acts when facing unplanned change, what she pays attention to, and how her priorities may change all provide authoritative guides for followers.
- *Allocate resources and rewards.* A more practical and equally impacting action is how the leader allocates resources and rewards. By rewarding compliance and conformity, a leader who professes that she values innovation and experimentation shows what she truly values. Similarly, by promoting individuals who demonstrate the values and mission of the organization, the leader can make a clear impact on the culture of the organization.

Many other mechanisms that leaders use to shape their organizations are design of the structure and processes, setting design criteria, and even selection of the physical space (Schein, 2004), several of which are discussed in Chapter 7.

THE LEADERSHIP QUESTION—REVISITED

People will resist change, no matter what it is. Given that, some leaders just announce the change and implement it as fast as possible: Shock the system and "Rip the band aid off" as quickly as possible. While tempting, this approach is likely to, in most cases, cause more long-term resistance and cause the change effort to fail, something that is very common in organizations. Investing time and effort to prepare people, convince them of the need for change, and involve them in implementation options and ideas is time consuming, but likely to pay off in the long run.

APPLYING WHAT YOU LEARN

Change Agents and Peer Pressure

One of the key factors in the success of change is relying on change agents and positive examples as a way of encouraging others to adopt the change. This "peer pressure" can be a positive method of averting resistance to change. Here are some practical pointers on how to use peer pressure in leading change:

- *Don't approach the change alone.* Although leaders have responsibility and authority, successful change is a group effort. Carefully plan how to involve others to help you.

- *Find a few people who are excited about the change* and enlist their help in communicating with other employees.

- *Win over opinion leaders.* In every organization, there are opinion leaders who are respected. Winning them over and enlisting their support for the change will move implementation along much faster.

- *Set up a pilot that can show success.* People may know that the change will be good for them, but that knowledge does not translate into behavior. Seeing a successful example goes a long way to convince employees that things may actually work out.

- *Actions speak louder than words.* Provide concrete examples inside and outside the organization that show how things can work out.

Summary and Conclusions

Change has become the only constant in today's organizations. Internal and external forces pressure organizations to be flexible, adapt, and transform themselves. A leader's ability to guide and support followers through change is one of the key leadership roles and may vary depending on cultural factors such as tolerance for ambiguity and perception of time. Even though organizations would like to plan for change and implement change in gradual and incremental ways, many of them face unplanned change that is revolutionary and requires considerable transformation. Regardless of the type of change, leaders need to view change as a three-step process of unfreezing or preparing followers for change, the actual change, and refreezing, which involves providing resources and support to solidify new processes and behaviors.

Planned change often follows six steps from recognizing the need for change to developing, adopting, and implementing ideas; to allocation of resources; and finally evaluation.

In this process, leaders can implement the change from the top down, pushing the change faster or allow bottom–up input that helps to get commitment and reduces resistance to change. In addition, whereas unplanned change is by definition unpredictable, leaders can prepare their followers by supporting flexibility, introducing gradual change, and experimenting with new methods. Even with careful planning and preparation, resistance to change is likely to occur because of organizational factors such as inertia and culture, group factors such as group norms, and many individual factors such as fear and individual characteristics. Leaders can use several methods to manage resistance; however, at the core of all successful methods are supporting employees, engaging them in the change, and providing a culture that sustain change.

One of the essential roles of leaders in the change process is to develop a shared vision for the change to help support followers through the implementation phase. Other related roles for visionary leaders are challenging the process, motivating followers, role modeling, and empowerment, all of which can energize followers and establish a culture that can sustain change. Other leadership roles include role modeling and supporting creativity and improvisation. An organization that has flexible and open structures and cultures, where mistakes are tolerated and experimentation and a questioning attitude encouraged, can encourage creativity. Improvisation requires deep preparation, self-reflection, and

commitment, all of which are also elements of authentic leadership.

The leader's ability to support followers through organizational change ultimately depends on having an organizational culture that is built and ready for change and continuous learning. The leader plays a critical role in creating a learning organization and in developing followers' ability to think broadly, develop personal mastery, work as a team, and develop as shared vision to ensure that the organization as a whole is ready to learn and change.

Review and Discussion Questions

1. Describe the internal and external forces for change.
2. What role does culture play in how people perceive change?
3. How can leaders encourage creativity among their employees?
4. Explain Lewin's model for change and its implications for organizations.
5. Present the six steps in the process of planned change, and describe the role of leaders in each step.
6. What are the elements needed to build a learning organization? Which leadership styles would encourage this process?
7. Present the organizational, group, and individual causes of resistance to change.

8. Describe ways in which resistance to change can be reduced, and explain when each method can be used.
9. Provide a real life example each of a situation when planned change was appropriate and where unplanned change was suitable.
10. Which national cultures are more comfortable with planned change? Give reasons for your answer.
11. How can positive leadership support implementation of change?
12. What are the elements of an organizational culture that supports change, and what role do leaders play in developing that culture?

Leadership Challenge: Implementing Unpopular Change

Your supervisor has just informed you of a major restructuring in your area aimed at increasing efficiency. She is assigning you to implement the necessary changes. The plans are coming from headquarters and are not negotiable. In addition to losing a couple of positions, your department will be moved to a new less-desirable location across town and will have to share administrative support with another team. Upper management is further using the restructuring as an opportunity to implement a much-needed new Web-based customer relations system.

Your team of 15 people is cohesive, and you know that letting go of two of your members will be hard on everyone. In addition, the new location is farther for all of you, and your offices will not be

as nice. Although the new technology is welcome, there will be a great need for training and support before it can be fully implemented. On a personal level, you are very upset about the change. This is the second major change in as many years that you have had to implement without having a chance for input. You experienced considerable stress and are worried about your team's reaction and ability to pull this through. Yet, your career depends on implementing the change.

1. How should you approach your team?
2. How much of your personal feelings should you share?
3. What are some key actions you should take?

Exercise 9-1 Analyzing and Planning for Change

This exercise is designed to provide you with the experience of defining a problem and planning for the change. It follows the model presented in Figure 9-4.

Part I: Form Teams and Select a Problem

In teams of three to five members, select a problem (organizational or personal) that one team member faces that requires change. Potential examples include the following: the customer service team you work for feels that the deliveries section are making an excessive number of mistakes; the reception desk team are often unfriendly with customers; the payroll department frequently miscalculating the wages that are due to employees; two members of the sales team hardly speak to each other because of an argument they had a few weeks ago; the school governors are unable to agree on priorities for allocating resources in their school, and so on.

What problem will your group address?

Part II: Define the Problem

It is important for the team to have a clear idea about what the problem really is. As a team:

Restate the problem in as many different ways as you can.

Consider all the positive and negative aspects of the problem.

Consider all the related issues.

Agree on a final clear description of the problem.

Part III: Plan for Change

Instead of jumping into action and proposing solutions, your team must understand the problem and the process, consider many alternatives, and evaluate them before selecting a solution.

How will you help the organization understand the need for change? What steps will you take? What data do you need?

Identify as many alternative solutions as you can without evaluating each (brainstorm.)

Evaluate each solution carefully; consider the positive and negative aspects of each. Who is likely to be affected if the solutions are implemented? Who will resist? What are the costs? Do they fully address the problem?

Select one solution; it does not have to be perfect, just based on your team's analysis. Explain why it is the best solution.

How will you implement your solution? Consider people and resources, major obstacles, potential solutions, key people to be involved, training needs, timetable, costs, how you will measure success.

Part IV: Presentation

Each team will make a brief presentation of its plan for change.

Source: "Managing Change," in A. Nahavandi and A. R. Malekzadeh (eds.), *Organizational Behavior: The Person–Organization Fit* (Upper Saddle River, NJ: Prentice Hall, 1999).

Exercise 9-2: Creativity and Parallel Thinking—The Six Hats Method

International expert on creativity and lateral thinking Edward deBono suggests that arguing is often not constructive and that focusing on "what can be" can lead to much more creative and effective problem solving. He has proposed a technique called the "Six Hats" where instead of different people in a group each looking at different sides of an issue, all group members look at the same side at any one time, in a *parallel* fashion. To that end, the group members are all instructed to take a perspective at the same time by putting on imaginary (or real, if you want to be playful) different-colored hats.

White Hat: Neutral and objective: Focus on objectivity, facts and figures.

Red Hat: Anger (seeing red), rage, and emotions: Focus on the emotional view.

Black Hat: Somber, serious, and cautious: Focus on pointing out weaknesses and problems.

Yellow Hat: Sunny and positive: Focus on hope and positive thinking; look at the best possible outcome.

Green Hat: Abundance: Focus on creativity and new ideas.

Blue Hat: Sky view: Focus on control, integration, and putting together of ideas from a broad perspective.

A. *Select an issue or topic*

In your group, select a complex issue to discuss. It can be from your work, the college or department, your community, politics, or the business world. For example, you may want to discuss health care, foreign policy, increasing taxes, raising tuition and fees, or an interesting problem that one of your group members has encountered. It is best to stay away from highly emotionally charged and value-based issues such as abortion.

B. *Using the hats*

Once you have selected your topic, discuss the issue using the six hats method and by following these rules closely:

1. Designate a facilitator who will keep track of time, direct the group to switch hats, reiterate their function, and remind everyone of the rules. The facilitator will use language such as "now let's all put on our red hats" to transition from one hat to the other.
2. Always refer to the hat colors, not the function. For example, you can say "Let's put on our white hats" not "Let's look at the facts."
3. Begin and end with the blue hat. At the beginning, it allows you to address general issues and what you are doing (i.e., reviewing the rules and deciding the order of the hats). At the end, it allows you to review and sum up.
4. You may put the other hats on in any order your group wants.
5. Keep your "hat on" when you are in a color mode. For example, if the group is wearing the green hat and focusing on creativity, members cannot decide in the middle of the green period to put on their black hats and discuss the weaknesses of the ideas being proposed. You can only switch hats when time is up and the whole group wears a different hat.
6. You can also give each person a minute or two to think when you start and when you switch hats. With the hats "on," each member has about one minute to express his/her views under each color. The total amount of time will depend on the number of people in your group. For example, four people will take about 24 minutes to discuss an issue ($6 \times 4 = 24$) + an extra 4 minutes for the blue hat at the end + 6 minutes for reflection, for a total of 34 minutes (approximately).
7. Have fun!

C. *Review your process*

When you have completed your discussion, review your group process and consider the following questions:

1. What were the benefits and challenges of considering the various perspectives together rather than assigning them to each person?

2. What could you have done differently?

3. How can you use this in your personal and work life?

D. *Presentation*

Prepare a two-minute presentation to report on your experience to the class.

Source: Based on E. deBono,. *Six thinking hats.* (Great Britain: Penguin Books, 2000). *Adapted with permission.*

Self-Assessment 9-1: Building Credibility

One of the key elements to visionary leadership is the leader's credibility. Having credibility allows a leader to undertake the necessary changes with sincerity and with followers' trust. Following are the elements of credibility. Rate yourself on each of the items using the following scale:

1 = Never
2 = Occasionally
3 = Often
4 = Always

_____ 1. I state my position clearly.
_____ 2. My coworkers and subordinates always know where I stand.
_____ 3. I listen to other people's opinions carefully and respectfully.
_____ 4. I accept disagreement from my coworkers and followers.
_____ 5. I try to integrate my point of view with that of others.
_____ 6. I encourage and practice constructive feedback.
_____ 7. I encourage and practice cooperation.
_____ 8. I build consensus out of differing views.
_____ 9. I develop my coworkers' and subordinates' skills.
_____10. I provide frequent positive feedback and encouragement.
_____11. I hold myself and others accountable for actions.
_____12. I practice what I preach.

Scoring Key: Add up your rating for all 12 items. The maximum score is 48. A higher score indicates behaviors that build credibility.

Total: _____

Self-analysis and Action Plan

Which items have a low score? List those areas that you need to target to build your credibility.

What can you do about them? Focus on clear and specific behaviors. Develop short-term and long-term goals. When will you know that you have improved? How will you measure yourself?

Source: This self-assessment is partially based on concepts developed by Kouzes and Posner (1993; 2003).

Self-Assessment 9-2: Creativity

Being open to change is to some extent a function of being creative. Although creativity is partly a personality trait, individuals can enhance their personal creativity in several ways. Rate each statement according to how well it applies to you by using the following scale:

1 = Never
2 = Some of the time
3 = Always

_____ 1. My life is so hectic; I have no time to pay attention to anything new.
_____ 2. I set daily goals for myself and focus on getting them done.
_____ 3. I put considerable effort to do something well when I do it.
_____ 4. I have clear priorities about what is important to me and what is not. I look for ways to making things I enjoy more complex and challenging.
_____ 5. I know what I like and don't like in life.
_____ 6. I face problems head-on and look for solutions immediately.
_____ 7. I am disorganized and feel that my schedule is out of control.
_____ 8. I often surprise others with my unexpected actions or words.
_____ 9. My office/home is organized in a way that calms me and supports my activities.
_____10. I rarely follow through on things that spark my interest.
_____11. I keep routine things simple so that I have energy to focus on what is important.
_____12. I make time for relaxation and reflection.
_____13. I approach problems by trying to develop as many solutions as possible before I try to solve them.
_____14. I stop and look at unusual things, people, and events around me.

Scoring Key: Reverse score items 1, 7, and 10 (1 = 3, 2 = 2, 3 = 1). Total your score for the 14 items. The minimum is 14; the maximum is 42. A score above 30 indicates that you are undertaking many activities and managing your life in ways that enhance personal creativity.

Total: _____

SELF-ANALYSIS AND ACTION PLAN

Which items have a low score? List those areas that you need to target to improve your creativity. Which items have a high score? How can you build on them?

Source: Developed based on information in M. Csikszentmihalyi. *Creativity: Flow and the Psychology of Discovery and Invention* (New York: Harper Perennial, 1997).

LEADERSHIP IN ACTION

BEST BUY'S ALMOST TRANSFORMATION

You may know Best Buy as the mega store for electronics or the place you, or maybe your parents, used to buy CDs, but in the management and particularly human resource management world, Best Buy is also knows for the ROWE—Results Only Work Environment—program. Best Buy broke the mold of the 8-to-5, five-days-a-week workweek, a staple of the U.S. workplace, in 2005 and allowed its corporate employees to decide when and where they wanted to work and evaluated them on the results of their work, not the time they put in at the office (CultureRx, 2013). The program not only changed how people work, but it also changed the culture of the company, and yielded some significant performance improvement early on. Production improved by 35 percent, employees on ROWE processed 13 to 18 percent more orders than those not in the program (Conlin, 2006a), and it led to an 8 percent decrease in turnover, thereby reducing hiring costs. Then CEO Brian Dunn said: "The improvements in turnover were nationwide and at all levels" (Everitt, 2008).

No more. With less fanfare and less press coverage than a similar decision by Yahoo, Best Buy did away with ROWE in early 2013. New CEO Hubert Joly considered ROWE to be flawed from a leadership standpoint because it took away management control and used delegation as the only method of making decisions (Schafer, 2013). Matt Furman, the company public affairs officer, believes that organizations should focus on both the end results and the process by which things get done, which requires everyone to be around to connect and collaborate (Pepitone, 2013). Company spokesperson, Jeff Sherlman, further added that working from home used to be a right, but now it will be a discussion: "We believe in employee flexibility but it needs to come in the context of a conversation…about what the results are and how the work gets done" (Stuart, 2013).

The decision, although not officially linked to it, comes at the heels of several years of poor performance at Best Buy (Matthews, 2013). The change for Best Buy employees is as drastic as it was in 2005 when the program was instituted. While for most managers and corporate employees, the clock extends well beyond the 40-hour week and being seen, getting to the office before everyone else, being the last one to leave at night, and working on weekends are all considered a badge of honor and necessary to success in corporate America, Best Buy had bucked that trend, at least for a few years. Through the ROWE program, corporate employees of the Minnesota-based electronic store threw out the time clock, and set their own work schedule. "No one at Best Buy really knows where I am," said Steve Hance, Best Buy's employee relations manager (Kiger, 2006). This revolutionary approach focused on evaluating employees based on meeting their goals rather than worrying about how much face time they put in the office. The difference between ROWE and many innovative programs Best Buy instituted was that ROWE started somewhere in middle and lower management, was intentionally kept secret from upper management, tested in a few teams; and then presented to the leadership. The former CEO did not know about the program until two years after it had been implemented in some of the corporate offices with some success.

ROWE was the brainchild of two Best Buy HR employees, Jodi Thompson and Cali Ressler, who discovered they shared similar views about working in cubicles and how technology and wireless access could change how people work (Conlin, 2006a). They relied on the results of a 2001 survey that indicated widespread employee dissatisfaction and a perception of inability to balance work and life and developed the flexible work program (Kiger, 2006). The results were positive, and word got out about the new way to work. Those working under ROWE guarded their secret, fearing a reversal from upper management. Those who didn't convinced their managers to join the program, slowly spreading word about ROWE throughout Best Buy's corporate office. In the early days, Thompson and Ressler were viewed by some as subversives who were "infecting" the company (Conlin, 2006b). More traditional managers felt threatened that they are losing control and power. Others worried about employees never being able to get away from work. Those who were in the program and the company clearly benefited. But Thompson and Ressler left Best Buy and founded their own consulting firm CultureRx, have taken their ROWE concept outside Best Buy, and are working on spreading the unique work model to other organizations (CultureRx, 2013).

By all accounts, having employees spend more time at the office is not going to help Best Buy. Instead, analysts blame the leadership and the competition (Upbin, 2012) and the corporate culture of the company and suggest that cutting ROWE may actually negatively affect turnover, trust, and the company's ability to groom future leaders (Peterson, 2013).

Questions

1. What are the internal and external forces for change at Best Buy?
2. How were the two changes (ROWE and its removal) implemented?
3. What role did leaders play in each of the changes?

Sources: Conlin, M. 2006a. "Smashing the clock," *Business Week*, December 11. http://www.businessweek.com/stories/2006-12-10/smashing-the-clock (accessed August 5, 2013); Conlin, M. 2006b. "How to kill a meeting," *Business Week*, December 11. http://www.businessweek.com/stories/2006-12-10/online-extra-how-to-kill-meetings (accessed August 3, 2013); CultureRx. 2013. http://www.gorowe.com (accessed August 4, 2013); Kiger, P. J. 2006. "Throwing out the rules of work," *Workforce Management*, October 7. http://www.workforce.com/section/09/feature/24/54/28 (accessed April 25, 2010); Everitt, L. 2008. "How Best Buy slays the turnover beast," *Money Watch,* April 16. http://www.cbsnews.com/8301-505123_162-33340028/how-best-buy-slays-the-turnover-beast/ (accessed October 20, 2013); Matthews, C. 2013. "Best Buy's unlikely return from the dead," *Times Business and Money,* July 15. http://business.time.com/2013/07/15/best-buys-unlikely-return-from-the-dead/ (accessed August 3, 2013); Pepitone, J. 2013. Best Buy ends work-fro-home program. *CNN Money,* March 5. http://money.cnn.com/2013/03/05/technology/best-buy-work-from-home/index.html (accessed August 3, 2013); Peterson, G. 2013. "Cutting ROWE won't cure Best Buy," *Forbes,* March 12. http://www.forbes.com/sites/garypeterson/2013/03/12/cutting-rowe-wont-cure-best-buy/ (accessed August 3, 2013); Schafer, L. 2013. "Pitching in is the new rule at Best Buy," *Star Tribune,* February 16. http://www.startribune.com/business/191449391.html?refer=y (accessed August 3, 2013); Stuart, H. 2013. "Best Buy ends work-from-home program known as 'results only work environment'," *The Huffington Post,* March 6. http://www.huffingtonpost.com/2013/03/06/best-buy-ends-work-from-home-policy_n_2818422.html (accessed August 3, 2013); Upbin, B. 2012. "Why Best Buy CEO Brian Dunn had to quit," *Forbes,* April 10. http://www.forbes.com/sites/bruceupbin/2012/04/10/why-best-buy-ceo-brian-dunn-had-to-quit/ (accessed August 3, 2013).

10

Developing Leaders

After studying this chapter, you will be able to:

1. Define the elements of leader development.
2. Explain the factors involved in learning.
3. Review areas that are addressed in leader development.
4. Discuss the methods used in leader development and the benefits and disadvantages of each.
5. Consider the role of culture in leader development.
6. Summarize the role of the person and the organization in effective leader development.

THE LEADERSHIP QUESTION

How successful is leader development? What can we teach and can people really learn?

Leading is not a destination; it is a life-long trek. One of the fundamental premises of this book and modern leadership theory and practice is that leadership can be learned. Leaders are not born; they are made. Whereas our individual characteristics and traits may create barriers for some and make it easy for others to learn the art and practice of leadership, leadership scholars widely agree that leaders can improve and develop their leadership skills. The turbulent environment that organizations face and the need for flexibility make developing leaders and expanding their capabilities and skill set and their leadership "toolbox" even more important. It is, therefore, not surprising that organizations and individuals devote considerable resources to leader and leadership development. By some accounts, the large U.S. companies spent over $125 billion on employee learning and development in 2009 (Stern, 2011). In addition, extensive research is focused on leadership development and businesses are ranked on how well they develop leaders (e.g., *Fortune* magazine's Best companies for leaders). Unfortunately, many companies see the resources spent on development as a cost rather than an investment in the future and many do not perform a thorough evaluation of the effectiveness of the programs they use. In spite of these issues, developing leaders so that they are ready to address the changing needs of organizations and their stakeholders are a priority for many organizations. On a personal level, it is essential for leaders to plan for their own renewal and development regardless of what their organization offers.

Questions such as how do people learn, what are key elements of developing leaders, and what are the best methods for creating long-term behavioral change are integral parts of the discussion of leader development and the focus of this chapter. We address these questions in this chapter.

BASIC ELEMENTS OF LEADER DEVELOPMENT

Development is an ongoing, dynamic, long-term change or evolution that occurs because of various learning experiences (London and Maurer, 2004). More specifically, *leader development* is defined as the "expansion of a person's capacity to be effective in leadership roles and processes" (McCauley and Van Velsor, 2004: 2). It focuses on the individual and involves providing leaders with the tools they need to improve their effectiveness in the various roles they play. *Leadership development*, although related to leader development, is different in that it focuses on an organization's capability to get the work done through its many leaders (McCauley and Van Velsor, 2004). The differences are key as they each address different levels of development.

This chapter is primarily focused on leader development, although some of the methods described, when applied to the whole leadership of an organization, may affect its leadership development. In addition, although closely related and often using similar approaches, there are some differences between managerial, leader, leadership, and executive development (London and Maurer, 2004). They differ in terms of their *focus on the person or the organization* and the *degree to which they are customized* for individual participants (Figure 10-1). For example, managerial and supervisory development primarily focuses on education and teaching participants the skills to effectively conduct their day-to-day activities and take care of their employees. The focus is on developing skills for the organization, and the training programs are generic and often offered in classroom settings with many participants. Leader development focuses on developing the individual, taking a more holistic approach to increase self-awareness and provide skills. Such training may be either generic or customized. Leadership development is aimed at developing leadership ability across the organization. Finally, executive development targets developing leadership for the organization and frequently has a highly individualized nature, such as in executive coaching.

Factors in Learning

Learning involves a relatively permanent increase or change in behavior, knowledge, or skill that comes about as a result of experience. For leaders to develop, they must learn new skills and behaviors. Those changes must be relatively stable and last beyond the classroom or training setting. Whereas learning addresses the content of the change (Kegan and Lahey, 2001), development addresses the process. The two are therefore closely intertwined. Given that

LEADER DEVELOPMENT
PERSON

FIGURE 10-1   Types of Development

development and learning involve change, many of the concepts that we discussed in Chapter 9 regarding the models, processes, and resistance to change can apply to leader development as do theories of learning (e.g., Bandura, 1995). For individuals to learn and develop, they must first become aware of the need for change and accept it (unfreezing). Then, after change is implemented, it must be supported and sustained to result in the adoption and use of new behaviors, skills, or knowledge (freezing). Lasting change, which is at the heart of leader development, requires patience and persistence. As with any other change, it also is likely to be faced with resistance as the person may not be aware of the need to change, unwilling to make the necessary changes, or unable to sustain the newly learned behaviors because of lack of practice or support. Such potential resistance must be taken into account by both the person and the organization.

Several elements make up the core of learning. First, the person must be aware that learning and change are needed. She must have the willingness to learn, which requires both motivation and readiness (Figure 10-2). The awareness and motivational elements are related to the unfreezing step in change. Many of us have worked with leaders who are either un-aware of their areas of weakness or are unwilling to invest their time in changing. Without the recognition and willingness to learn and change, no development can take place. Recent focus of some leadership development research has been on the need for leaders to conduct deep exploration to understand their motives and sensitivities and identify potential obstacles to their growth (Kaiser and Kaplan, 2006). As we will discuss later in this chapter, increasing self-awareness and personal growth form a substantial portion of most leader development programs.

In addition to motivation to learn, the person must have the ability to learn through the right combination of intelligence and personality traits (Popper and Mayseless, 2007). Learning may come easier to some and be more challenging for others. For example, high cognitive

FIGURE 10-2   Factors in Learning

intelligence may help one participant grasp conceptual ideas quickly, whereas another who has high emotional intelligence will quickly learn social and interpersonal skills. Third, leaders must have access to developmental experiences and have the opportunity to practice and learn. For example, employees of smaller organizations are often exposed to diverse experiences, which are an excellent source of learning. In larger companies, jobs and duties are narrower and more specialized. Large companies, however, provide the benefit of extensive training and development resources, including educational benefits. For example, McKinsey has developed a special leadership training program called Centered Leadership that focuses on developing women (Barsh and Cranston, 2009).

Fourth, closely related to having opportunities is to encourage the development of self-efficacy, which is an individual's belief and capacity to learn as result of having positive and successful experiences (Bandura, 1995). If individuals are willing and able to learn and are exposed to challenging developmental experiences where they succeed, they can develop self-confidence related to the task and a sense of self-efficacy, which has been shown to be related to leadership effectiveness (Anderson, Spataro, Flynn, 2008). As opposed to simple self-confidence, *self-efficacy* is related to a specific context or task. In the case of leader development, providing successful opportunities for leaders in the context of their job can improve effectiveness (e.g., Baron and Morin, 2009; Moen and Allgood, 2009).

Finally, the organizational culture must support and sustain learning and development. This support comes not only in the form of training programs but also in the form of informal systems that value learning and tolerate experimentation and failure. The case study of Southwest Airlines at the end of this chapter provides an example of an organization that supports development. Mistakes are tolerated, and organizational leaders focus on developing leadership in others. Another factor in organizational support is supervision. Supervisors who support and encourage development are key to the development of leaders. Such support can be through formal assignments and training or through informal mentoring.

Learning requires consistent practice and persistence. Although many of us understand the need for practice and persistence when it comes to things such as learning a new sport, an instrument, or a new language, we tend to forget the importance of practice in the even more complex skills and behaviors required to lead others. Communicating well and clearly, motivating followers, coaching them in their development, and providing feedback are just some of the complex skills required to lead well. Learning any of them necessitates perseverance, making and learning from mistakes, and repetition.

What Is Developed: The Content

What do leader development programs address? What are the skills, knowledge, behaviors, and so forth that are developed? Table 10-1 summarizes the typical areas that are covered by leader development. The content is broad and complex, reflecting the richness and complexity of leadership, and the list is far from comprehensive. The content depends on the level of leader development such that basic knowledge and skills are typically aimed at supervisory and middle-level leaders, whereas strategic thinking is aimed at executives. Personal growth and self-awareness are included in most development programs with a more intense focus in top-level and executive leaders. In addition, the content areas, although presented in separate and distinct categories, are interrelated and integrated. For example, providing feedback, which is a basic supervisory skill, is related to communication, which is part of social skills. Similarly, strategic issues such as developing a vision rely on conceptual, communication, and interpersonal skills and require creativity.

Each of the content areas can be addressed through a number of different methods and tools reviewed later in the chapter.

TABLE 10-1	What Leader Development Addresses
Area	**Description**
Basic knowledge	Information about content of leadership; definitions; basic concepts such as communication, feedback, contingent rewards; typically through classroom education
Personal growth	Self-awareness and understanding strengths and weaknesses; leadership profile; getting in touch with personal values, dreams, and aspirations
Skills development: supervisory, managerial, and interpersonal skills	How to apply knowledge; includes supervisor and managerial skills such as planning, goal setting, and monitoring, as well as conceptual skills such as problem solving and decision making, and skills related to managing interpersonal relations; cross-cultural skills
Creativity	Expanding ability to think in novel and innovative ways and to think "outside the box"
Strategic issues	Developing mission; strategic planning

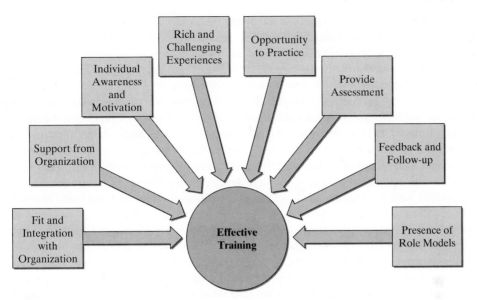

FIGURE 10-3   Required Element of Effective Training

REQUIRED ELEMENTS OF EFFECTIVE DEVELOPMENT PROGRAMS

Development programs have different goals, and each program provides a number of advantages and disadvantages. Several key elements are required for a development program to be effective (see Figure 10-3). Although all are not required, satisfying more of the requirements makes a program richer and more likely to lead to long-term change and learning. One of the first principles of an effective development program is that it provides participants with assessment data about their current strengths, weaknesses, performance, and some information about where they stand in regard to the goals of the program and their leadership ability (McCauley and Van Velsor, 2004). The availability of information about the self can encourage participants to improve and be a guidepost for their progress throughout the program. Many organizations recognize the importance of assessment. For example, Agilent, the maker of testing tools, spends considerable resources assessing its top 100 leaders through a comprehensive program (Frauenheim, 2007). The company has hired an outside consultant to implement a high-stakes assessment program to look at the potential for leadership. Leaders are evaluated based on business results, capabilities, and potential and a quarterly leadership audits completed by employees to indicate their confidence in their managers (Frauenheim, 2007).

The assessment data can help increase individual awareness, another principle of effective development programs. To learn, participants must be aware of the need for change and specific areas they should address so that they are ready to change. The awareness can result from formal data or from informal discussions with a supervisor, coworkers, a mentor, or a coach. In addition, an effective development program exposes participants to rich experiences that challenge them to step outside their zone of comfort, pushes them to experiment with skills, behaviors, and approaches (McCauley and Van Velsor, 2004), and allows them to develop self-efficacy. For example, being assigned to a new task or rotating to another department or team is likely to have the potential for rich experience. Whether through a new assignment or through a specific task, or even while conducting day-to-day activities, leaders must have the opportunity to practice the behaviors or skills they have learned.

One approach is to consider how artists use the studio system to integrate opportunity to practice with self-awareness and rich feedback from multiple sources (Denhardt and Denhardt, 2006). This artistic approach is gaining popularity in many areas of management (Adler, 2006). Without having the opportunity for practice, leaders cannot receive feedback about their performance, another criteria for effective development programs. As is the case with assessment, the feedback can be formal, for example when one's performance is reviewed or a 360-degree feedback is implemented, or informal through discussions with coworkers or a mentor. Anne Mulcahy, former CEO and chairman of Xerox, believes that her ability to handle criticism has been essential to her success. She also suggests that the higher up leaders go, the harder it becomes to get honest and open feedback because "people around you want to please" (Kharif, 2003). The last two requirements for effective development relate to the culture of the organization and how well it integrates its development programs with its strategic goals and with the needs of individual leaders. Supporting leaders to experiment with their new learning and providing them with training resources, opportunities for rich experiences, and feedback indicate the level of support from the organization and are a sign of the extent to which the organization as a whole supports learning. Finally, a key factor is the fit and integration of the person, the development program, and organizational goals (London and Maurer, 2004). At a very basic level, we learn and perform best when we love what we do and have passion for our work. L'Oreal's CEO, Jean-Paul Agon, recommends to students to "choose a job that is really exciting, a job that makes them want to get up from their beds every morning and feel happy about going to work" (Shinn, 2005: 23). The passion comes from a good fit between the person and the organization and the job. The same fit is essential for the effectiveness of leader development. From an organizational point of view, an effective program is based on strategic goals and support for those goals. It, therefore, has a relatively long-term focus rather than merely addressing the latest fads and trends, or what some call a "flavor-of-the-month" approach to training and development.

The criteria discussed are essential to the effectiveness of development programs; although not all are required to develop leaders, without most, the program may provide at best an entertaining experience with short-term benefits, but little long-term impact, as is the case with some popular programs we consider later in this chapter. Other specific conditions that help make any method for leader development more effective include the following:

- *Clear objectives* that are tied to organizational goals, the leader's personal goals, and the current of future challenges the leader may be facing. Such objectives must be stated ahead, and a means of assessing them before and after the program must be available.
- *Rewards* tied to learning and using the new behaviors, skills, and knowledge. Organizations must also allow for experimentation without punishing mistakes or failures, particularly while leaders are still learning.
- *Using a combination of tools and methods* that provide parallel learning environments and address different learning styles or reinforce one another. For example, classroom education may be combined with an assessment center, coaching, and new assignments.
- *Program assessment and follow-up* that measure change and support the new learning and ensure that new behaviors, skills, and styles are not forgotten or not used when the development program is over. Learning takes practice and persistence, and such opportunities should be present outside the training session.

The variety of training programs and methods available are considered next and evaluated in terms of how well they address the requirements for effective development presented in this section.

WHAT DO YOU DO?

You have a direct report you know is intelligent and who has an MBA. You would like to groom him for a management position, but he seems to lack in some areas such as teamwork, managing conflict, delegating, and generally "playing well with other." You have limited resources for training. What type of developmental experiences or training do you select for him?

METHODS OF LEADER DEVELOPMENT

There are many different approaches and methods to develop leaders, ranging from highly structured and formal programs to classroom education, to observation and hands-on experiences. Using a diversity of approaches can be key to effective development (Allen and Hartman, 2008) as can customizing the program to each leader as much as possible (Guillén and Ibarra, 2009). Each approach provides advantages and addresses particular aspects of leadership. Table 10-2 provides a comparison of the methods based on the criteria for effective development programs discussed earlier.

Self-Awareness

Self-awareness is considered the cornerstone of leader development; it is the starting point and basic building block. Sir Richard Branson, entrepreneur and founder and CEO of the Virgin Group, considers self-awareness to be a factor that can help leaders learn faster. He states: "I've found that knowing your business and yourself can also help you to know when to follow your instincts, so you can find the courage to move ahead and ignore the advice of naysayers…Self-awareness can also help you to persevere as you carry out your plan" (Branson, 2013b-June). Similarly, Anne Mulcahy of Xerox, who has been credited with bringing the company back from the brink of bankruptcy, believes that a good leader "will recognize what she does not know and be willing to learn all the time" (e.g., Anne Mulcahy, 2001). Anthony Tjan, CEO of the venture capital firm Cue Ball, further suggests that self-awareness is the one quality that trumps all others in leadership: "The best thing leaders can do to improve their effectiveness is to become more aware of what motivates them and their decision-making" (Tjan, 2012).

The academic research also emphasizes self-awareness. The concept of authentic leadership discussed in Chapter 6 also relies on leaders' having knowledge of his or her fundamental values (Gardner et al., 2011). The essential role of self-awareness in effective leadership is a theme throughout this book and in leadership practice and research (Kaiser and Kaplan, 2006). Personal reflection and getting feedback from others are necessary elements of developing self-awareness, a process labeled *double-loop learning* (Argyris, 1991). In addition, some studies show that a leader's self-awareness may be related to higher follower satisfaction and productivity (Moshavi, Brown, and Dodd, 2003).

Guidelines for increasing self-awareness include the following:

- *Clarify your values and priorities,* a process, which is a first step in self-awareness; the person must know what is important and what factors have priority.
- *Seek new experiences* that will challenge the leader to move outside the comfort zone and provide an opportunity to learn something about oneself; including opportunities to fail.
- *Observe your own behavior and reflect* by keeping a journal, reviewing your successes and mistakes, and reflecting on what works and does not work for you.
- *Seek feedback* through formal and informal channels as often as possible from as many diverse sources as possible. For example, the feedback from a customer regarding one set of behaviors may be very different, but equally relevant, as feedback from a supervisor regarding those same behaviors.

TABLE 10-2 Comparison of Development Methods

Criteria	Assessment	Individual Awareness	Rich Developmental Experience	Opportunity for Practice	Feedback on New Learning and Follow-up	Support from Organization	Fit and Integration
Self-awareness	✓	✓	—	—	?	—	—
Experience	?	✓	✓	✓	✓	✓	✓
Coaching	✓	✓	—	✓	✓	✓	✓
Mentoring	✓	✓	—	—	?	✓	✓
Feedback-intensive programs	✓	✓	—	?	—	?	?
Classroom education	?	✓	—	?	?	?	?
Outdoor challenges	—	?	—	—	—	?	?

✓: very Likely; integral part of the method; ?: possible, depending on situation and organizational conditions; __: highly unlikely; not part of the goal of the method

Being able to seek and accept information about oneself may, to some extent, depend on one's personality traits. For example, the person's openness to experience, one of the Big Five personality factors, may play a role (Chapter 4; Barrick and Mount, 1991). Other factors such as self-monitoring (Chapter 4: Snyder, 1974) may make leaders more perceptive and receptive to feedback from others and allow them to change their behaviors more easily. Even though self-awareness is the cornerstone of any development program and a requirement for getting the leader to be willing to change and learn, it is not enough. Leaders must also have the tools to change. Although assessment and individual awareness are integral to a development program based on self-awareness, they do not expose the leader to rich experiences, provide opportunity for practice, or demonstrate support from the organization. Therefore, by itself self-awareness does not satisfy most of the criteria for an effective development program (see Table 10-2).

Experience

If self-awareness is the cornerstone of development, then experience, or developmental experience, is its core. One does not learn to lead by knowing one's personality and values, sitting in a classroom, reading about leaders, or observing other leaders. Transmitting information through the classroom or observation is one thing; learning to exercise judgment, understand complex systems, and act on complex information requires hands-on practice (Thomas, 2008). A recent report by the Center for Creative Leadership finds that many leadership skills are primarily learned through experience in an appropriate context and setting (Wilson et al., 2011).

Although information and observation may result in an increase in a cognitive understanding of what leadership is and what leaders do, they do not develop leaders. The experience of actually leading others is one of the most effective ways to develop leaders (Conger, 2004; Day, 2010) and the core competencies essential to adaptability (Zaccaro and Banks, 2004). Having on-the-job experience is, in almost all organizations, essential to leadership. For example, Johnson & Johnson and P&G both consider developing leaders one of the company's critical leadership success factors. IBM puts special emphasis on providing broad experiences, particularly broad international experiences to their leaders. Samuel Palmisano, IBM CEO from 2000 to 2012, says, "Where the average company might offer several hundred employees an international opportunity for two or three years, IBM gives 'mobility assignments' to thousands for three to six months" (IBM, 2009). Similarly, 3M, under CEO George Buckley (2005–2012), refocused on leadership training allowing senior employees to stay in one job long enough to learn. Referring to moving people around from job to job, Buckley states, "I slowed the pace. They have to be in the job long enough, not only for their success to visit them, but for their failures to visit them" (Jones, 2009b). In many other organizations, such as small businesses or those that do not have resources to invest in formal development programs, varied job assignments and experiences are the primary development tool (Raskas and Hambrick, 1992).

For job experiences to be developmental, they need to stretch leaders and broaden their perspective by placing them in a novel and challenging situation (Ohlott, 2003). This can be achieved through increasing responsibility on a current job, a new task, working with a different or a new project team that is unfamiliar, rotating to a dissimilar job, international experiences, or even working with a difficult employee. All these experiences provide an environment in which the leaders have to assess and understand a novel environment and use unfamiliar styles and behaviors. Learning from practice can further build self-confidence and a sense of self-efficacy (Bandura, 1995).

Many methods for leader development based on hands-on practice have been developed, trying to approximate experience. For example, experience can be simulated by participants' involvement in small-group activities, games, role-plays, or simulations, or by following up critical events with discussion and reflection (Ernst and Martin, 2007). The U.S. Army, an organization with an ongoing focus on leader and leadership development, uses a method that combines self-awareness, values development, and knowledge and experience (Campbell and Dardis, 2004). The "Be, Know, Do" (BKD) model relies on a variety of development methods. Self-awareness is achieved through clarification of core values such as loyalty, duty, respect, and personal courage and development of mental, physical, and emotional attributes. The BKD model develops knowledge and skills in specific content areas such as technical and interpersonal skills. Finally, leaders are encouraged to "do" and develop familiarity with various aspects of their jobs at the personal, organizational, and strategic levels (Campbell and Dardis, 2004).

The U.S. Army develops its leaders by integrating many of the key factors of leader development and relying on experience and practice. All other methods can be combined with experience to provide an even more complete developmental experience (Kempster, 2006). For example, coaching can occur in the context of actual performance; classroom education can become more powerful when new knowledge is tested in an actual leadership situation. Real experience, through any means, satisfies almost all the criteria for effective development (see Table 10-2). It develops individual awareness, provides a rich experience and opportunity for practice and feedback, and when used in the context of development, requires support from the organization and integrates developmental goals with organizational goals. The only potential weakness may be assessment, which can easily be built in through formal programs or use of existing organizational performance tools.

Developmental Relationships: Coaching and Mentoring

"Throughout my life and career, I've had a number of people I'd call mentors, who passed along their principles to me … there are many people who have touched my life in different ways," says Cinta Putra, CEO of 3n (Bisoux, 2008a: 20). Similarly, the new CEO of Xerox, Ursula Burns, was mentored and coached by a number of people in the organization before she reached the highest level (Bryant, 2010d). Sir Richard Branson also believes in the importance of mentoring: "Whenever I am asked what is the missing link between a promising businessperson and a successful one, mentoring comes to mind. Giving people advice on how they can best achieve their goals is something that is often overlooked" (Branson, 2013a-May).

Coaching and mentoring are essential components of effective leader development. *Coaching* involves providing individualized and constructive feedback on someone's behavior and performance while focusing on future improvement. *Mentoring* provides similar individualized attention with a feedback and future orientation, but tends to be less task specific. Mentoring is a supportive long-term, formal or informal, professional relationship (McCauley and Douglas, 2004). Whereas mentoring can be informal, coaching tends to have a more structured and formal nature. Many of us have mentors and role models who provide us with advice and feedback. They are people we admire and with whom we build long-lasting relationships. Coaches are sought for specific situations and assigned by organizations. Coaching and mentoring are part of developmental relationships that can help leaders improve and grow personally and professionally. The success of all such relationships depends on establishing trust and rapport between the leader and the coach or mentor (Ting and Hart, 2004). Both coaches and mentors can be role models, demonstrating desired behaviors and thereby further enhancing learning through observation (Bandura, 1995).

COACHING   Coaching has been shown to be effective in many areas and settings (e.g., Nocks, 2007; Parker, Hall and Kram, 2008) and linked to increases in leader flexibility (Jones, Rafferty, and Griffin, 2006) and expatriate success (Abbott et al., 2006). Ros Taylor, a leadership coach, states the dire need for top-level leaders to get support: "When I am brought in to coach leadership teams … I frequently find that they are quite literally clinging on by their fingernails. They are on the brink of committing professional suicide because they don't know who to turn to" (Cooper, 2007: 24). Because of its many potential benefits, coaching is the focus of much of the leadership development practice and is beginning to become a topic of research (e.g., Joo, 2005). Sports coaches such as Duke University's basketball coach Mike Krzyzewski are considered leadership guru's for their ability to teach and motivate (McGregor, 2011). Coaching, whether the professional-executive kind, or the personal kind is also big business estimated to be over a $1-billion-a-year industry (Pagliarini, 2011).

Coaching can address existing problems in a real-life setting, thereby providing opportunity for feedback and practice, as well as demonstrating support from supervisors or coworkers. Because it is focused on specific behaviors, it narrows the scope of behavior, facilitating learning. Informal coaching is part of most effective supervisors' and leaders' repertoire in supporting their followers in learning new skills. Leadership-related coaching programs are most often used in executive development where either external consultants or successful current or past company executives provide individualized coaching to leaders. Executive coaches spend a substantial amount of time observing leaders, discussing behaviors, exploring options, and providing detailed feedback regarding all aspects of the leader's style, behavior, and performance. The individualized attention in the work setting can be a source of considerable development. If the coach is a person internal to the organization, the executive can further benefit from gaining a perspective on the organization. An external coach can bring fresh perspectives and approaches. Some reports indicate that coaching pays off very well as investment go, with companies reporting improvements in teamwork, relationship, and job satisfaction (Personal coach for CXOs, 2011).

Particularly when combined with other programs—for example, as a follow-up for an in-class training, used in combination with mentoring, or with assessment centers and 360-degree feedback—coaching can provide the benefits of general knowledge with specific application to day-to-day activities. Individually focused assessment takes place, there is a reasonable level of challenge, and the feedback is relevant and rich. In addition, the experiences that are observed and discussed are those that the leader finds challenging. The resources and expenses needed for formal coaching further demonstrate the organization's commitment to the person being coached and to developing leadership overall, all factors that have the potential to make coaching a highly effective development tool. Despite the fact that top executives get a lot of training before they are appointed to the leadership of organizations, many of them do not have the type of preparation they need to take on the complex job of upper-echelon leaders. Executive coach Ros Taylor notes, "New elected leaders are expected to run the race but have not been allowed to train for it" (Cooper, 2007: 24). Coaching can close that gap and support them in their success.

Table 10-3 presents the elements of effective coaching. As with other developmental programs, the leader's readiness is essential. Many successful executives may resist coaching because of their past success or because they receive filtered and only positive feedback that makes them believe they do not need development. As Bill Gates stated, "Success is a lousy teacher. It seduces smart people into thinking they can't lose" (21). An important point to note is that in addition to providing support and feedback to the individual, effective coaching requires integration with wider organizational goals and systems. As is the case with all other development programs, the success of coaching depends on integrating individual and organizational needs.

TABLE 10-3	Elements of Effective Coaching

- Individual readiness and willingness to be coached
- Consideration of wider organizational context and system
- Consideration of individual goals, values, and needs
- Focus on performance and work-related issues
- Sincere caring and concern
- Advocacy for self-awareness
- Meaningful feedback
- Supportive climate

MENTORING Professional connections are key to success, says John Hagel, cochairman of Deloitte's Center for the Edge: "These links are critical to individual development in a workplace culture where formal schooling and degrees give workers about five years' worth of usable skills" (Biro, 2012). Martinez Tucker, former CEO of the Hispanic Scholarship Fund and undersecretary of the Department of Education under the G. W. Bush administration, joined the nonprofit sector after working in business for many years; she believes that "Every boss is a learning opportunity—you either learn how to do things better or you learn how you never want to behave" (Shinn, 2006: 20). Throughout her career, she has learned from others who often were not similar to her. She believes that many people can be positive mentors if they understand where you are coming from.

Informal and formal mentoring is a powerful leader development tool and can lead to life-long supportive relationships between a mentor and a mentee. A more experienced leader provides guidance and advice to a less-experienced one. Formal mentors are assigned from within the organization, although many leaders establish mentoring relationships with individuals inside and outside their organization. As Sara Martinez Tucker suggests, one approach to mentoring is to consider learning from those who are poor, rather than good, role models. Even though there is no direct mentoring relationship, there can be considerable learning from observing other leaders inside and outside your organization who behave badly. One business writer suggests that even "antimentors" are reliable and consistent and therefore can be excellent sources of development (McFarland, 2007). Jeffrey Katzenberg of DreamWorks Animation SKG agrees: "I've had great bosses and I've had terrible bosses, and I have actually learned my greatest lessons and my most important lessons from my worst bosses" (Bryant, 2009j). Some research and anecdotal accounts suggest that formal mentoring may be less effective than informal kind. Because mentoring involves establishment of a personal professional relationship based on trust, forcing it through formal bureaucratic selection processes may reduce its effectiveness. A formal system, however, can be implemented to create relationships that may otherwise not develop, for example in the case of women and members of diverse groups, who often have trouble connecting with powerful mentors in traditional organizations (McCauley and Douglas, 2004).

Guidelines for establishment of productive mentoring relationships include (McCauley and Douglas, 2004) the following:

- *Find many mentors* instead of looking to one person for all guidance. Different mentors can support a leader with different perspectives and expertise.
- *Find mentors at different levels;* although typically mentors are more senior, peers, external people, and even followers can be great source of support and developmental advice.
- *Informal relationships* that provide casual support can be equally helpful.
- *Add mentors* as roles and responsibilities change or as leaders transition to new jobs.

Though mentoring can be a great source of support, it does not have the same strong development aspects of coaching. Because it is informal and more general in nature, the advice and feedback is typically less focused and less specific, and an opportunity to practice with quick and direct feedback is lacking (see Table 10-2).

Feedback-Intensive Programs

Currently one of the most popular methods of leader development at all levels is using intensive feedback program such as 360-degree feedback or other multisource and multimethod feedback programs (see Figure 10-4; for some reviews, see Lepsinger and Lucia, 1997; Tornow and London, 1998). The programs are used in a broad range of business, governmental, and nonprofit organizations. Their goal is to assess leaders' strengths and weaknesses and to identify development needs. Assessment is based on a combination of interviews, aptitude tests, personality tests, role-plays, simulations, and experiential exercises, as well as many other methods. Getting accurate feedback can be a highly developmental event and getting such feedback gets harder as leaders move up the organizational ladder. Addressing one of the lessons she learned when she ran human resources at Xerox, Anne Mulcahy says: "…you discover quickly how little honest feedback people get in companies, and how important it is for people to have a sense of candid assessment" (Bryant, 2009c).

In 360-degree and multisource feedback programs, the leaders are assessed by individuals around them, including direct reports, supervisors, peers, and in some cases, clients and other stakeholders who provide detailed feedback regarding their styles, behaviors, performance, strengths, and weaknesses (see Figure 10-4). In most situations, the leaders' self-rating on the same dimensions are also obtained, and trained facilitators review and analyze the data from different perspectives and help the leaders interpret the information, identify areas of strengths, and recognize targets for development (Chappelow, 2004).

The formal, official, and objective nature of multisource and multimethod feedback-intensive programs helps reduce the possible discomfort leaders may experience when receiving

FIGURE 10-4   360-Degree Feedback

negative feedback and neutralize some of the anxiety it typically produces. Because they can provide rich data from multiple perspectives, such programs are ideally suited for increasing individual awareness and providing a detailed evaluation of the leader. They are particularly effective when combined with coaching and mentoring (Thach, 2002); however, they do satisfy several of the criteria for development programs particularly in the areas of rich experiences, opportunity to practice new behaviors, and feedback (see Table 10-2).

Much research has been focused on 360-degree programs. Their effectiveness depends on several factors, including maturity of the organization and of its members to handle feedback openly and honestly (Reeves, 2006). Other factors that help their success are outlined in Table 10-4. Managers who have gone through a 360-degree feedback can greatly benefit from them; however, many complain about the lack of buy-in from their supervisors and the irrelevance or personal nature of the comments they receive (Jackson, 2012).

TABLE 10-4	Factors that Contribute to the Success of 360-Degree Feedback Programs
Factor	**Description**
Organizational buy-in and readiness	All levels of the organization must be well informed and prepared regarding process, content, and goals of program. Top management support is particularly essential.
Involve direct supervisors	While programs are run through HR, the involvement of director supervisors is essential.
Confidentiality and careful administration	Maintaining anonymity of the raters and confidentiality in the process ensures continued trust in the results and goals. Careful administration of surveys and handling of data are also essential.
Clear questions	The questions that participants get must be clear and specific.
Well-trained facilitator	Program success requires the skills of a well-trained, professional, internal or external facilitator to help interpret the information and deal with sensitive data and discomfort.
Focus on behaviors	The feedback should focus on specific behaviors that are related to job performance rather than general evaluative statements.
Avoid personal comments	Respondents should be trained and instructed to avoid personal statements and stick to work-related, actionable behaviors
Clear explanation of purpose and goals	Those providing feedback and the leader receiving the feedback should be very clear on the goal of the program and how data will be used.
Separate feedback from groups	Present the leader with separate feedback from each group or source to help clarity, interpretation, and understanding.
Follow-up	The initial step of increasing leaders' self-awareness must be followed up with action plans.
Combine with other developmental programs	The feedback increases awareness but without other developmental tools does not provide the leader with the means of changing behaviors.

Sources: Chappelow, C. T. 2004. 360-degree feedback. In The center for creative leadership handbook of leadership development, 2nd ed. C. D. McCauley and E. Van Velsor, 58–84. San Francisco, CA: Jossey-Bass; Lepsinger, R. and A. D. Lucia. 1997. The art and science of 360 degree feedback. San Francisco, CA: Jossey-Bass/Pfeiffer.

Classroom Education

By some accounts, 85 percent of U.S. corporations offer some sort of tuition assistance program (Bersin, 2009). Organizations provide their employees with some sort of educational benefit program to encourage them to develop and grow, and several have high-level executives in charge of learning, which includes leader and leadership development, or even whole "universities" dedicated to training and development (e.g., Motorola and Goldman Sachs). Even when companies are not providing support for education, however, the demand for executive education is growing. Because of increasing development needs and the desire to integrate such programs better with organizational goals, organizations are increasingly requesting customized programs such as MBAs with company-specific focus, and other training programs designed exclusively for the organization.

For example, Ingersoll-Rand, the global industrial manufacturing company, has partnered with Indiana University to offer a customized MBA program for its high-potential executives, where electives address the company's strategic priorities (Meister, 2006). Other companies, such as the Home Depot, have identified specific programs that address their needs. Leslie Joyce, the company's chief learning officer, states, "We decided to manage Home Depot tuition assistance programs as a strategic investment and apply the same rigor that we manage other vendor relationships" (Meister, 2006). Other examples include the many company-specific or generic executive development programs offered at a number of universities.

Classroom education is an efficient way of conveying information and knowledge to groups of people. It is used extensively in supervisory and mid-level management and leadership training programs. The primary goal of classroom education is to transfer knowledge. Depending on the content covered, such programs may also address individual awareness, but because of the setting, the ability to provide rich developmental experiences and opportunity for practice and feedback are relatively low (see Table 10-2). The classroom experience typically includes much more than lectures and discussion. Methods such as case studies, role-playing, exercises, debates, games, and simulations are all used to enrich the developmental experience (for an example, see Hess, 2007). Such methods involve practice and active involvement that enhance conceptual learning in classroom settings (Popper, 2005). The ability to practice new behaviors in the safe classroom environment, although limited, can provide a starting point for other developmental experiences.

Outdoor Challenges

A popular approach for leader and leadership development are outdoor challenge programs that put participants physically and mentally through increasingly difficult activities, such as obstacle courses, climbing, sport competitions, and games. Some suggest that sports in general, whether individual or teams, can be a good source for learning self-management, self-discipline, and teamwork (Wellner, 2007), and organizations are increasingly seeking innovative ways to both engage and entertain workshop and training participants through methods such as treasure hunts (Trucco, 2007). Many of the activities such as climbing poles, walking across rope bridges, and using trapezes are aimed at personal growth and increasing self-confidence by conquering fears and challenges. Other activities such as falling backward to be caught by teammates or going through an obstacle course blindfolded with the help of a partner focus on building trust and cooperation among members of existing departments, teams, organizations. Although frequently exhilarating and entertaining, the long-term impact of such programs on leader development is not well documented.

Using a combination of methods is key to successful and effective long-term development. Another factor that impacts the development is culture, which we consider next.

LEADING CHANGE
Howard Schultz Stirs Up Starbucks

"Profitability is a shallow goal if it doesn't have a real purpose and the purpose has to be share the profits with others" are the words of Howard Schultz CEO of Starbuck (Brodie, 2013). Starbucks tries to put these words into practice by being a good corporate citizen such as sponsoring its employees to complete hundreds of hours of community service (Fairchild, 2013) and also by developing employees and taking care of them. Taking care of people is a mantra in most companies these days, but few take it as seriously and as far as Starbucks, where all the employees are included in training, skill development, and the building of a unique culture. Howard Schultz, CEO of Starbucks, the now ubiquitous global coffeehouse, set out to create a different company from the moment he took charge. Motivated by a personal experience of family hardship when his father lost his job when he broke his leg, Schultz is committed to not leaving anybody behind, and he emphasizes that innovation and taking care of employees is key to the company's success (Berfield, 2009). He does not shy away from controversy and is not afraid to speak his mind on coffee and political issues (Baertlein, 2012). With more than 5,500 stores worldwide, 150,000 employees in over 50 countries, and over $11 billion in revenues, Starbuck is a well-established leader in its industry (Brain statistics, 2013). Health benefits, even for part-time workers, and a culture of caring are some of the ways Starbucks is committed to its employees. Although the company spends more on health care than it does on coffee, Schultz has repeatedly stated that "we will never turn our back on this benefit for our people" (Anderson, 2006).

Highly conscious about maintaining his company's culture, in April 2007, Schultz sent a memo to his management team that stated that the Starbucks experience has been watered down and that there was a need to go back to the roots and to maintain the "coffee *joie de vivre*" that the CEO had seen in Italian coffee bars (Helm, 2007). At the heart of the unique culture are the employees, who are trained in various programs such as the Coffee Master that teaches them the subtleties of various coffee flavors to graduate by receiving a special black apron and participating in a "cupping ceremony" where they appreciate the aroma of the coffee (Helm, 2007). The company baristas are trained to be considerate and are encouraged to be genuine. Schultz, who is sensitive, passionate, and a master storyteller, seeks to build connections among people and likes to remind everyone, "We're not in the business of filling bellies. We're in the business of filling souls" (Anderson, 2006).

Sources: Anderson, T. 2006. "Howard Schultz: The star of Starbucks," *CBS News*, April 23. http://www.cbsnews.com/stories/2006/04/21/60minutes/main1532246.shtml?source=search_story (accessed September 1, 2007); Baertlein, L. 2012. "Starbucks fiscal cliff cup campaign urges lawmakers to 'come together' on deal," *The Huffington Post,* December 26. http://www.huffingtonpost.com/2012/12/26/starbucks-fiscal-cliff-cup-campaign-2012_n_2364538.html (accessed August 5, 2013); Berfield, S. 2009. "Starbucks: Howard Schultz vs. Howard Schultz," *Bloomberg Business Week.* http://www.businessweek.com/magazine/content/09_33/b4143028813542.htm (accessed April 27, 2010); Brain Statistics. 2013. http://www.statisticbrain.com/starbucks-company-statistics/ (accessed August 5, 2013); Brodie, L. 2013. "Starbuck CEO: We're in early stages of growth," *CNBC-MadMoney,* June 27. http://www.cnbc.com/id/100850266 (accessed August 5, 2013); Helm, B. 2007. "Saving Starbucks' soul," *Business Week*, April 9. http://www.businessweek.com/magazine/content/07_15/b4029070.htm?chan=search (accessed September 1, 2007); Fairchild, C. 2013. "Starbucks CEO Howard Schultz: 'Profitability is a shallow goal,'" *The Huffington Post,* June 28. http://www.huffingtonpost.com/2013/06/28/starbucks-profitability-howard-schultz_n_3516065.html (accessed August 5, 2013).

DEVELOPMENT AND CULTURE

As in all other aspects of leadership, culture affects the process of leader development at both the national and subgroup (e.g., gender) levels. Culture shapes people's expectations of the learning context, the role of the facilitator, and what methods they prefer. For example, whereas people from the United States would comfortably and easily engage in a controversial case discussion and challenge their facilitator, many Middle Eastern or Asian participants may be more reluctant to do so. The French are taught throughout their education to question everything; so they are likely to want clear justification for the content and the methods of a program. Cultural values affect how the learning process is implemented, how feedback is provided, and the setting in which learning and development can be optimized. Leader development must therefore be considered within the cultural context (Hoppe, 2004). Table 10-5 outlines the cultural values that most affect development.

In a high-context and collectivist culture, such as Japan or Thailand, direct feedback, which is considered essential to learning in the United States and other Western countries such as Germany, would be poorly received and may be counterproductive, causing the participant to lose face. The information from feedback-intensive programs will have to be carefully considered and adjusted to preserve harmony and "face," particularly in cultures that are self-protective, such as many cultures in the Middle East or Asia (GLOBE; House et al., 2004). Another cultural value to consider is the degree of individualism or collectivism. Whereas in individualistic cultures such as the United States, the focus of leader development is on the individual and on getting the most talented person ready to lead, in collectivistic cultures, leadership resides with the group. Development must therefore target the group. Another factor often related to individualism is action orientation. The U.S. approach to development and training is hands-on, providing opportunities for practice, a factor that is one of the criteria for the effectiveness of a leader development program. In other cultures, the focus may be more on conceptual and holistic understanding and theoretical development. Tolerance of ambiguity may similarly

TABLE 10-5	Cultural Values and Leader Development
Cultural Value	**Potential Impact on Leader Development**
The communication context (high–low); directness	How information is communicated; how feedback is given; who provides feedback; directness of message in case of assessment and self-development
Individualism–collectivism	Focus of development on the individual leader or on the group; setting for development and training
Action–orientation	Content of development and training focused on practical matters and hands-on training or on theoretical understanding and conceptual development
Tolerance for ambiguity	Degree of exposure to new and challenging situations
Perception of time	Focus on quick and short-term results or on long-term development
Power distance and equality	Development provided to all or only individuals identified as high potential; implementation of 360-degree feedback and deciding who is included in feedback

influence the content of the development program. When individuals are relatively comfortable with change, such as in the United States, development places them in increasingly novel and challenging situations. When the cultural value is to avoid uncertainty, such as in Greece, development aimed at challenging that value is likely to face resistance and be counterproductive.

Many Western cultures focus on developing their employees for the short term or generally have a shorter time frame for planning and a focus on quick results. In long-term cultures, the scope of development may be on acquiring skills and knowledge in a much longer time frame spanning several years or even decades. An example is the case for the slow development of a martial arts master in some Asian cultures; organizations in such cultures may take years to groom leaders for their positions. Finally, position power and the degree of equality in a culture may affect leader development. In more egalitarian cultures such as Denmark or Sweden, development opportunities are made available to as many people as possible, and leaders may not feel comfortable being singled out (Derr, 1987). In more hierarchical and power-oriented cultures such as France, people deserving leader development are identified early through the educational system and singled out for special treatment (Barsoux and Lawrence, 1991; Belet, 2007).

The most effective development methods that are used extensively in the United States rely on intensive feedback and developmental relationships as their core. For example, the highly popular and effective method of 360-degree feedback relies on honest and direct feedback about a person's performance, style, and behavior from all levels of the organization. Interestingly, giving and receiving feedback is a highly culture-sensitive process (Hoppe, 2004). Hearing about weaknesses and mistakes directly, as is done as a result of assessment, would be highly inappropriate in some cultures, for example Thailand, where the person would be embarrassed, lose face, and perceive damage to his or her ability to lead effectively. Similarly, employees participating in providing feedback to their leader in high-power distance cultures such as Saudi Arabia or France might be uncomfortable, improper, and career threatening for both the leader and the followers. Even the concept of developmental relationships such as coaching and mentoring, which may be easier in collectivistic cultures, may pose some challenge when social relationships are highly prescribed and formal. Whereas a leader from a hierarchical and paternalistic culture may naturally feel a responsibility to take care of followers and develop them, such cultures may also have more rigid social structures that identify who should be developed and how negative information can be communicated. The considerable differences in cultural values and the lack of research in the applicability and generalizability of U.S. and other Western methods of leader development make their broad cross-cultural application risky. Much needs to be done to fully incorporate culture in leader development, as the large majority of our research and reviews of practices do not consider culture (e.g., Day, Zaccaro, and Halpin, 2004).

Gender and Diversity

Other cultural factors to consider in development are how to address the needs of diverse groups. Whereas all groups have the same training and development needs, one factor to consider is how to address the specific needs of women and members of underrepresented groups. Some research indicates that training programs have traditionally been developed with the white and male majority of organizational leaders in mind, a factor that can negatively affect the progress of diverse groups (Morrison and Von Glinow, 1990). Moreover, the presence of diversity programs in organizations for many years sometimes leads to the inaccurate perception that diversity issues have been resolved and that these programs, including those targeting leader development, are "color-blind" (Livers and Caver, 2004).

Differential opportunities for growth and limited exposure to developmental, high-visibility, high-stakes assignments and experiences, along with lack of connection to powerful and significant mentors, however, continue to be key reasons for differences between the advancement of men and members of diverse groups (for reviews, see Livers and Caver 2004; Ruderman, 2004). Women and minorities may face further challenges in leader development by being assessed and compared based on norms that are not always culturally appropriate. Some studies show that women often outperform their male counterparts on the results of 360-degree feedback (Posner and Kouzes, 1993), whereas other studies show that men are rated higher on some dimensions of leadership (Eagly, Makhijani, and Klonsky, 1992).

Potential solutions to the challenges that women and members of underrepresented groups face in leader development include the following:

- *Provide opportunity to participate in single-identity development programs* that reinforce validation, provide role models and networking, and can make available relevant content to address specific concerns (Ruderman, 2004).
- *Encourage developmental relationships* through formal and informal organizational programs to ensure that women and minorities have access to powerful coaches and mentors who are both similar to and different from them (Thomas, 2001).
- *Support development of networks* that can help women and minorities in their career development process (Ibarra, 1993).

Such actions, along with other diversity-oriented practices, several of which are presented in Chapter 2, can help address the unique challenges that women and minorities face in leader development.

EFFECTIVENESS OF DEVELOPMENT

Although highly popular and broadly implemented in many organizational settings, the effectiveness of all leader development programs is not always fully evaluated, and some researchers suggest that there is disconnect between the research on leadership and its application to the practice of leader and leadership development (Day, 2000). While many companies spend considerable amount of resources on development, they rarely know the actual return. Calhoon Wick, founder of Fort Hill company, a training consulting firm, says that companies are "focused on delivery of learning rather than on improved results" (Stern, 2011). When carefully examined, many of the existing methods and activities do not show consistent results in terms of increases in individual or organizational effectiveness. For example, although the highly trendy outward-bound experiences provide entertainment and are rated positively by participants, they do not always translate into long-term change in behavior. While some research suggests that such team activities may increase a team's cohesion, specific impact on leader effectiveness is not always well documented.

Despite lack of consistent research, the various methods of leader development do provide positive outcomes for leaders and their organization. For example, executive coaching is showing promising results (Neiminen et al., 2013), mentoring may help reduce intention to leave (Phornprapha and Chansrichawala, 2007), and even outdoor programs show positive results in terms of development of self-concept (Marsh, Richards, and Barnes, 1987). New leadership models are increasingly calling for the inclusion of learning and development as an integral part of our understanding of leadership (e.g., Day, Zaccaro, and Halpin, 2004; Uhl-Bien, Marion, and McKelvy, 2007), and changes in the global environment and technology call for continued leader and leadership development (Avolio, 2005; Suutari, 2002).

THE LEADERSHIP QUESTION—REVISITED

You can teach leaders a lot of things. Leader development can and does work. However, you cannot teach anything to someone who does not want to learn and people cannot learn without practice. It seems simple enough, but these are tough conditions. With proper support and the right experience, we can teach leaders a lot about being effective. But they have to be motivated to learn and the organization has to provide support and allow them to practice and occasionally fail.

Organizational and Personal Factors in Development

Based on the information presented in this chapter, it is clear that three factors can support leader development (Figure 10-5). First, the importance of individual leader's commitment to learning and growth cannot be overemphasized. To learn and grow, leaders must be dedicated to their own development. The ability to learn and self-regulate is not something that organizations can control; therefore, the leaders' readiness for change and commitment to it are essential. Second, organizational commitment is equally vital. No leader can sustain new behaviors without organizational support from supervisors and coworkers. The continuing trend in flatter organizations with fewer levels of supervision has increased the need for leaders to acquire new skills. Moreover, the use of teams puts pressure on many new behaviors (London, 2002). These and other organizational pressures must be matched with a focus on continuous learning and a culture that supports learning and change. The characteristics of learning organizations presented in Chapter 9 are some of the elements necessary to support development.

Finally, the effectiveness of development depends on integration of the program with overall organizational vision, mission, and strategic goals. It requires a reasonable fit between the needs of individual leaders and the organizational direction. Leader development, although aimed at increasing organizational effectiveness through increasing leaders' effectiveness, must also consider the personal effectiveness of the leader.

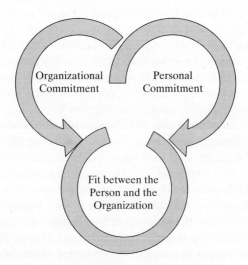

Organizational Commitment

Personal Commitment

Fit between the Person and the Organization

FIGURE 10-5 Three Keys to Successful Development

APPLYING WHAT YOU LEARN
Personal Development

In addition to formal programs, which may not be available to you, there are some steps you can take to develop your leadership skills:

- **Know yourself.** Seek any opportunity you can find to develop your self-awareness. Keep a journal; ask for feedback; fill out behavior and personality assessments; look for patterns, and so on. Not all information is equally valid and useful; however, the pursuit of self-awareness starts with you seeking information.
- **Be open to new experiences.** Seek new tasks, projects, classes, or experiences any chance you get. Although not all may be related directly to leadership, they provide a chance to expand your experience base.
- **Consider volunteer work.** Especially in early stages of one's career, volunteer work offers considerable "risk-free" opportunities for acquiring leadership skills. Students particularly can learn much from such experiences.
- **Seek feedback.** While working on projects, tell people you trust that you would like feedback about your behavior and performance. Not every piece of feedback you get will be helpful, but you may discern patterns in what people tell you.
- **Focus on understanding your strengths.** Instead of trying to fix your weaknesses, put your energy in developing your strengths.
- **Observe leaders around you.** You can learn by observing leaders around you. Both good and bad ones can teach you plenty about effective leadership that you can put into practice.
- **Be persistent and practice.** Change and learning take time. Be patient and persistent in practicing new behaviors until they become comfortable and part of your repertoire.

Summary and Conclusions

Developing leaders so that they can continue to address the changing needs of their organizations is essential to the survival and success of organizations. Organizations can focus on developing individual managers, leaders, and executives at various levels by providing them with increased skills and knowledge, or they can focus on developing the leadership capability of the organization. The process of development is akin to change in that it necessitates the person to recognize and accept the need for change and have the ability to learn. It then requires the opportunity to develop through exposure to appropriate and successful experiences that build the confidence and a sense of self-efficacy. Finally, the learning must be supported by the organization to solidify and reinforce new skills and behaviors.

Proper assessment, awareness, rich experiences that provide for opportunity for practice and feedback, support from supervisors and coworkers, good role models, and fit with the organization are all factors in an effective development programs. A variety of methods are available to develop leaders. Self-awareness is at the heart of any development; leaders must know their capabilities, strengths and weaknesses, and willingness and ability to learn. Actual leadership experiences are the most effectual method of development, whether through routine activities that are part of the job or through increasingly difficult tasks and assignments that challenge leaders to move outside their comfort zone. Coaching and mentoring can further enrich a leader's repertoire by providing relevant, task- and organizational-specific feedback and advice. Among other popular developmental activities are programs that rely on intensive feedback from multiple sources. Classroom education and its many different tools such as role modeling, case analysis, and games and simulations allow the leaders to increase their knowledge and practice new behaviors in a safe environment. Last, many other activities such as outward-bound and physical and team-building challenges address developmental needs.

Whereas the programs described in this chapter are commonly used in the United States and some other Western countries and show promising results, their applicability to other cultures is less certain. Culture must be considered when implementing any leader or leadership development program. The success and effectiveness of leader development depends first and foremost on the individual's commitment to learning and growth. Equally critical is organizational commitment to leader development. As a final point, effective leader development within organizations requires a fit and integration between the leader's individual values and needs and the vision, mission, and goals of the organization.

Review and Discussion Questions

1. What is the difference between leader and leadership development? Why is the distinction important?
2. What are the four factors in learning? What role do they play in leader development?
3. Describe the areas that are typically addressed in developing leaders.
4. What is the difference between managerial, leadership and executive development?
5. Compare and contrast the methods of leader development described in this chapter. What advantages or disadvantages do they each provide? When should they be used?
6. What are the core and cornerstone of development? How are they related?
7. How are coaching and mentoring similar and different?
8. What are the advantages of 360-degree feedback?
9. What role can classroom education play in leader development?
10. What is the role of culture in leader development? What cultural factors must be taken into account when implementing a program?
11. What are specific issues to consider when developing women and members of minority groups?
12. Enumerate the methods to develop leaders. Describe any two of them in detail.

Leadership Challenge: Finding the Right Fit

Your supervisor has just nominated you for a lengthy and complex leader development program that most of the top managers of your organization have completed. It is considered to be a program for high-potential employees and is likely to be key to a future promotion for you. Although you are flattered and the potential for a promotion and much better pay (maybe as much 50 percent more) is tempting, you are also concerned whether the organization is the right place for you. You value the balance between your personal life and your work and you are engaged in many sustainability efforts in your community, an activity that you personally value. The organization demands considerable time from you, and most evenings you do not get home before seven or eight. You have tried without much success to start a "green" program at the office and have brought up sustainability issues when making several decisions. Your supervisor thinks it's "cute" but has not shown any interest. Yet, you are still in the early stages of your career; the promotion would be very nice; the money even better. On the other hand, the training program will require even more time from you, time you could spend looking for other opportunities.

1. What are the factors that you should consider?
2. What would be the best decision for you? Why?

Exercise 10-1: Identifying Your Mentoring Needs and Potential Mentors

Mentoring is a personal professional relationship based on trust and common interests. Whereas mentors are often more senior and experienced than the people they support, many mentors can be at the same level, or even at lower organizational levels and with less experience than the mentee.

This exercise is designed to help you consider areas where you need help and identify a list of people you could approach to be your mentors.

Step 1: What Do You Need?

You can identify areas where you may need development through the following:

- Self-exploration and careful soul-searching
- Looking at your most recent performance reviews
- Considering the results of some assessment tools you have taken in school, or at work
- Identifying patterns in informal feedback you get from family members, friends, and coworkers

Based on your review of that information, what are the three areas that you would like to develop to further expertise and competence?

1.

2.

3.

Step 2: Who Do You Know?

Keeping those development needs in mind, who do you know with expertise in those areas? Start with a long list; include as many people as you can think of. Bosses, instructors, acquaintances, friends, and family members may all be able to help. Your peers are also likely to have many areas of expertise and some less-experienced and younger members of your organization may even have specialty or skills in the areas you are interested in.

Your long list:

Narrow your list based on the following criteria:

Those you trust to help you:

Those you feel comfortable with:

Step 3: Creating a Mentoring Relationship

You should now write down a few names for each of the areas you would like to target. You can approach each person and ask him or her for an informal meeting or to go to lunch or for coffee. If you feel comfortable, you can then ask them to help you in learning about the areas you are interested in. Most people are quite flattered to be asked to help and mentor someone, so they are not likely to turn you down. If they do, you may consider contacting them in the future.

A few things to keep in mind:

- Be very clear about how much help you need. Most of us are too busy to dedicate time to an involved process, so stick with a lunch or coffee once a month or so.
- Don't use your mentor as a "dumping" ground for all the problems you face at work or school; stay focused on learning about specific areas you think the person can help you with.
- Express your appreciation for their time and support, and send thank-you notes or e-mails after each meeting.
- Take the responsibility to keep the relationship going if you feel you are benefiting from it.

Although you may feel most comfortable with just one or two people, it is always helpful to have a broad network.

Self-Assessment 10-1: My Personal Mission Statement

One of the most important aspects of leadership development is self-knowledge and awareness of your priorities and values. You can use the information in Self-Assessment 4-1 to review your values and keep those in mind as you complete this exercise.

Step 1: What Do I Want to Be When I Grow Up?

What do I want to be known for?

If there was one thing I would like people to remember me for, what would that be?

What should my epitaph say about me? (a bit morbid, but give it a try)

When I retire, what I would like my most important accomplishment to be?

Step 2: My Personal Mission

Based on the results of the self-assessment about values in Chapter 4, and the answers to the preceding questions, write your personal mission statement. There is no right or wrong answer!

For information on how to write a mission statement, see: Levo League: http://www.levoleague.com/articles/career-advice/personal-mission-statement-three-easy-steps-defining-creating
Think Simple: http://thinksimplenow.com/happiness/life-on-purpose-15-questions-to-discover-your-personal-mission/ Franklin Covey: http://www.franklincovey.com/msb/

Once you have developed your mission statement, keep it accessible. It can guide you when you are having trouble making decisions and in setting the path for your development as a leader.

MY MISSION STATEMENT:

LEADERSHIP IN ACTION

DEVELOPING LEADERS AT SOUTHWEST AIRLINES

In the highly turbulent airline industry, Southwest Airlines (SWA) is one of the healthiest companies, continuing growth and profit in a climate that is threatening the survival of other airlines. Marketing strategist Micah Solomon believes the company's culture is the key to its success: "A consciously developed customer-centered culture is a business advantage that will serve you for years—and inoculate you against competitive inroads" (Solomon, 2012). SWA's special culture emphasizes individuality, taking care of people, and fun. "Learn from your mistakes; take the initiative; and listen to your heart" (The power of persistence, 2002) are simple and powerful words from Colleen Barrett, the former CEO of Southwest Airlines, who was with the airlines much of her career and as is the case with other members of the leadership team, including founder Herb Kelleher and current CEO Gary Kelly. David Ridley, the recently retired vice president of marketing and sales, talks with pride about Southwest's "warrior spirit," which focuses on caring, emotions, and putting employees first (Warrior Spirit, 2006). While Colleen Barrett headed the company, she also had the title of Queen of Hearts for sustaining a culture that is "fun, spirited, zesty, hard-working, and filled with love. Love is a word that isn't used too often in corporate America, but we've used it at Southwest from the beginning" (Shinn, 2004: 18).

In addition to a supportive culture, for which Kelleher and Barrett can take much credit, Southwest is deliberate about developing leaders and leadership. Talking about the company's HR practices, Barrett describes, "We are very, very disciplined about hiring and we're very, very disciplined about mentoring and coaching.... We're a very forgiving company in terms of good honest mistakes, but we're not forgiving about attitude and behavior and demeanor" (Fisher, 2007: 18). Barrett suggests that developing employees and maintaining the culture starts with the hiring process by carefully selecting people and being very clear about expectations and company culture (Sekula, 2007). Programs to develop leaders range from formal leadership training for everyone, including frontline employees, to presentation by outside consultants, leadership briefings, and communication about leadership in company bulletins. Managers and company leaders also make a point to include the topic of leadership in their regular interactions and strive to demonstrate the principles the company embraces (Shin, 2003). They also provide credible role models for others. For example, Kelleher works from a small windowless office and treats all employees regardless of their rank with care and respect (Warrior Spirit, 2006). The goal of training and development at Southwest is to perpetuate a culture and a leadership style that have been effective. Barrett says that they are not shy about closely monitoring their employees, getting rid of people who do not fit in, promoting those who represent the spirit of the company, and holding their leaders and managers accountable (Sekula, 2007). They are also not shy about standing up for employees who do their jobs well, even when customers complain (Warrior Spirit, 2006)

The concept of fit between the person and the company is central to Southwest's success. Through careful hiring and training, the company makes sure that those who do not fit well do not get hired or do not stay long. Caring about others, authenticity, and maybe most important, a sense of humor, are prerequisites for being successful at Southwest. Ridley says: "Our leaders have a genuine love for people. We don't want you in leadership if you don't. If it's all about

Chapter 10 • Developing Leaders 359

you we don't want you—there are no BS [Big Shot] leaders at Southwest" (Warrior Spirit, 2006). Barrett encouraged the culture by creating a Culture Committee, a group made up of a team of 100 employees who preach and teach the company's unique culture (Medley, 2006). In addition, local culture committee's members are further entrusted with the task for maintaining and strengthening the Southwest SPIRIT (always in capital letters). The culture even has its own language, which includes "Southwest Family," "Servant Leadership," and "New Hires," all used as proper nouns to indicate their importance to the company (Medley, 2006).

Although leaders play a key role in developing others, everyone at Southwest is in charge of that culture. Through strong training programs, promotions from within, the telling and retelling of many stories, for which the company cofounder and past CEO Herb Kelleher is famous, the culture is ever present. The company offices are decorated with memorabilia that further reinforce Southwest ideals. Kelleher ensured that current and upcoming leaderships are in place and guarantee "life after Herb" (Medley, 2006). Barrett played a further role in developing leaders, mentoring anyone who had "a passion for what he or she does or who has a desire to learn" (Shin, 2003), and she empowered her followers to do the same. She stated, "When New Hires ask me all the time, 'How are you going to keep the culture?' I say, 'I'm not. You are.'" (Medley, 2006). The new CEO, Gary Kelly, seems to be carrying on much of the tradition. He showed up dressed as Edna Turnball, the mom in the musical *Hairspray*, at a recent company Halloween party (Bailey, 2008).

Questions

1. How does Southwest develop its leaders?
2. What is the role of culture and fit in success of the company?

Sources: Bailey, J. 2008. "South by Southwest," *The New York Times,* February 13. http://www.nytimes.com/2008/02/13/business/13southwest.html (accessed April 27, 2010); Fisher, S. 2007. "Flying off into the sunset: An airline icon plans to slow down," *The Costco Connection,* September: 17–19; Medley, M. 2006. "The culture queen," *Motto.* http://www.whatsyourmotto.com/articles/culturequeen.aspx (accessed September 1, 2007); "The power of persistence," 2002. *Fast Company.* http://www.fastcompany.com/fast50_02/people/persistence/barrett.html (accessed April 27, 2010); Shin, S., 2003. "LUV Colleen," *BizEd,* March/April: 18–23; Sekula, R. D. 2007. "Air superiority," *Smart Business.* http://www.sbnonline.com/Local/Article/10596/71/0/Air_superiority.aspx (accessed April 27, 2010); Solomon, M. 2012. "What you can learn from Southwest Airlines' culture," *The Washington Post,* April 3. http://articles.washingtonpost.com/2012-04-03/business/35453344_1_culture-core-values-customers (accessed August 5, 2013); Warrior Spirit with a servant's hear: SWA's thriving culture of service. 2006. Knowledge: W. P. Carey, May 24. http://knowledge.wpcarey.asu.edu/article.cfm?articleid=125 (accessed April 27, 2010).

REFERENCES

5 influential CEOs weigh in what makes a good leader. 2013. *Entrepreneur,* February 25. http://www. entrepreneur.com/article/225804#devine (accessed October 6, 2013).

Abbott, G. N., B. W. Stening, P. W. B. Atkins, and A. M. Grant. 2006. Coaching expatriate managers for success: Adding value beyond training and mentoring. *Asia Pacific Journal of Human Resources* 44: 295–317.

Ackerson, L. 1942. *Children's behavior problems: Relative importance and intercorrelations among traits.* Chicago, IL: University of Chicago Press.

Adler, N. J. 1991. *International dimensions of organizational behavior.* 2nd ed. Boston: PWS-Kent.

———. 2006. The arts and leadership: Now that we can do anything, what will we do? *Academy of Management Learning and Education* 5: 486–499.

Alessandri, G. 2011. Three typologies and the Big Five Factors to study personality. *Giornale italiano Di psicologia* 2: 413–442.

Algera, P. M., and M. Lips-Wiersma. 2012. Radical authentic leadership: Co-creating the conditions under which all members of the organization can be authentic. *The Leadership Quarterly* 23: 118–131.

Ali, A. J. 2008. The tyrant executive. *Advances in Competitiveness Research* 16: i–iii.

Allen, N. J., and T. D. Hecht. 2004. The "romance of teams": Toward and understanding of its psychological underpinnings and implications. *Journal of Occupational Organisational Psychology* 77: 439–461.

Alluto, J. A., and L. G. Hrebeniak. 1975. Research on commitment to employing organizations: Preliminary findings on a study of managers graduating from engineering and MBA programs. Paper presented at the National Academy of Management Annual Conference, August, New Orleans.

Alridge, J. 2009. I'm doing "God's work." Meet Mr Goldman Sachs. *Sunday Times,* November 8. http://www.thesundaytimes.co.uk/sto/news/world_news/article189615.ece (accessed October 5, 2013).

Alspach, G. 2004. Wanna grow old? Then lose the attitude. *Critical Care Nurse* 24(1): 8–9.

Alves, J. C., K. J. Lovelace, C. C. Manz, D. Matsypura, F. Toyasaki, and K. Ke. 2006. A cross-cultural perspective of self-leadership. *Journal of Managerial Psychology* 21: 338–359.

Amanatullah, E. T., and M. W. Morris. 2010. Negotiating gender roles: Gender differences in assertive negotiating are mediated by women's fear of backlash and attenuated when negotiating on behalf of others. *Journal of Personality and Social Psychology* 98(1): 256–267.

Amble, B. 2006. Women still rare in Europe's boardrooms. *Management Issues*, June 20. http://www.management-issues.com/2006/8/24/research/women-still-rare-in-europes-boardrooms.asp (accessed June 19, 2007).

American Express Open. 2013. New OPEN reports shows phenomenal growth of women-owned business. https://www.openforum.com/articles/latest-trends-in-women-owned-businesses/ (accessed October 12, 2013).

America's highest paid chief executives. 2012. *Forbes.* http://www.forbes.com/lists/2012/12/ceo-compensation-12_rank.html (accessed June 19, 2013).

AmEx's Ken Chenault talks about leadership, integrity and the credit card business. 2005. *Knowledge@ Wharton*, April 20. http://knowledge. wharton.upenn.edu/article.cfm?articleid=1179 (accessed July 16, 2007).

Anderson, C. 1997. Values-based management. *Academy of Management Executive* 11(4): 25–46.

Anderson, C., S. E. Spataro, and F. J. Flynn. 2008. Personality and organizational culture as a determinant of influence. *Journal of Applied Psychology* 93(3): 702–710.

Anderson, J. 2007. Stepping lively at Credit Suisse; workaholic American named to lead Swiss financial services company. *New York Times*, February 16. http://query.nytimes.com/gst/fullpage.html?res=9B0DE4DE143EF935A25751C0A9619C8B63 (accessed January 8, 2008).

Andolsek, D. M., and J. Stebe. 2004. Multinational perspective on work values and commitment. *International Journal of Cross Cultural Management* 4(2): 181–209.

Anne M. Mulcahy. 2001. Leadership is about learning. *Knowledge@Wharton*, July 4. http//:knowledge. wharton.upenn.eduarticle.cfm?articleid389 (accessed September 8, 2007).

Antonakis, J., A. T. Cianciolo, and R. J. Sternberg. 2004. *The nature of leadership*. Thousand Oaks, CA: Sage.

Antonakis, J., B. J. Avolio, and H. Sivasubramaniam. 2003. Context and leadership: An examination of the nine-factor full-range leadership theory using the Multifactor Leadership Questionnaire. *The Leadership Quarterly* 14: 261–295.

Antonakis, J., D. V. Day, and B. Schyns. 2012. Leadership and individual differences: At the cusp of a renaissance. *Leadership Quarterly* 23(4): 643–650.

Arfken, D. E., S. L. Bellar, and M. M. Helms. 2004. The ultimate glass ceiling revisited: The presence of women on corporate boards. *Journal of Business Ethics* 50: 177–186.

Argyris, C. 1991. Teaching smart people how to learn. *Harvard Business Review* (May–June): 99–109.

Arlidge, J. 2009. I'm doing "God's work." Meet Mr. Goldman Sachs. *Timesonline,* November 8, http://www.timesonline.co.uk/tol/news/world/us_ and_americas/article6907681.ece (accessed March 24, 2010).

Armour, S. 2007. Hi, I'm Joan, and I'm a workaholic. *USA Today*, May 23, B1.

Ashford, B. E., and V. Anand. 2003. The normalization of corruption in organizations. In *Research in Organizational Behavior*, Vol. 25, ed. R. M. Kramer and B. M. Staw, 1–52. Amsterdam: Elsevier.

Astley, W. G., and P. S. Sachdeva. 1984. Structural sources of intraorganizational power: A theoretical synthesis. *Academy of Management Review* 9: 104–113.

Aune, R. K., and L. L. Waters. 1994. Cultural differences in deception: Motivation to deceive in Samoans and North Americans. *International Journal of Intercultural Relations* 18: 159–172.

Avey, J. B., B. J. Avolio, and F. Luthans. 2011. Experimentally analyzing the impact of leader positivity on follower positivity and performance. *The Leadership Quarterly* 22: 282–294.

Avolio, B. J. 2005. *Leadership development in balance: Made/born*. Mahwah, NJ: Lawrence Erlbaum.

Avolio, B. J., and W. L. Gardner. 2005. Authentic leadership development: Getting to the root of positive forms of leadership. *The Leadership Quarterly* 16: 315–338.

Avolio, B. J., W. L. Gardner, F. O. Walumbwa, F. Luthans, and D. R. May. 2004. Unlocking the mask: A look at the process by which authentic leaders impact follower attitudes and behaviors. *The Leadership Quarterly* 15: 801–823.

Avolio, B. J., F. O. Walumba, and T. J. Weber. 2009. Leadership: Current theories, research, and future directions. *Annual Review of Psychology* 60: 421–449.

Ayman, R., and M. M. Chemers. 1983. Relationship of supervisory behavior ratings to work group effectiveness and subordinate satisfaction. *Journal of Applied Psychology* 68: 338–341.

_____. 1991. The effect of leadership match on subordinate satisfaction in Mexican organizations: Some moderating influences of self-monitoring. *International Review of Applied Psychology* 40: 299–314.

Ayman, R., M. M. Chemers, and F. E. Fiedler. 1995. The contingency model of leadership effectiveness: Its levels of analysis. *The Leadership Quarterly* 6(2): 147–167.

Ayman-Nolley, S., R. Ayman, and J. Becker. 1993. Gender affects children's drawings of a leader. Paper presented at the annual meeting of the American Psychological Association, August, Chicago.

Babiak, P., and R. D. Hare. 2006. *Snakes in suits: When psychopaths go to work.* New York: Harper Collins Publishing.

Back, M. D., S. C. Schmukle, and B. Egloff. 2010. Why are narcissists so charming at first sight? Decoding the narcissism-popularity link at zero acquaintance. *Journal of Personality and Social Psychology* 98(1): 132–145.

Ballinger, G. A., and F. D. Schoorman. 2007. Individual reaction to leadership succession in workgroups. *Academy of Management Review* 32(1): 118–136.

Bandura, A. 1977. Self-efficacy: Toward a unifying theory of behavioral change. *Psychological Review* 84: 191–215.

_____, ed. 1995. *Self-efficacy in changing societies*. New York: Cambridge Press.

Banks, S. 2008. *Dissent and the failure of leadership*. Cheltenham, UK: Edward Elgar.

Bardes, M., and R. F. Piccolo. 2010. Goal setting as an antecedent of destructive leader behaviors. In *When leadership goes wrong: Destructive leadership, mistakes, and ethical failures*, ed. B. Schyns and T. Hansbrough, 3–22. Greenwich, CT: Information Age Publishing.

Baron, L., and L. Morin. 2009. The coach-coachee relationship in executive coaching: A field study. *Human Resources Development* 20(1): 85–106.

Baron, R. A., J. H. Neuman, and D. Geddes. 1999. Social and personal determinants of workplace aggression: Evidence for the impact of perceived injustice and the type A behavior pattern. *Aggressive Behavior* 25(4): 281–296.

Barrett, A. 2003. Staying on top. *Business Week*, May 5, 60–68.

Barrick, M. R., and M. Mount. 1991. The five big personality dimensions and job performance: A meta-analysis. *Personnel Psychology* 44(1): 1–76.

Barsh, J., and S. Cranston. 2009. *How remarkable women lead*. New York: Crown Business.

Barsoux, J. L., and P. Lawrence. 1997. *French Management: Elitism in action*. UK: Taylor and Francis.

Bartlett, C. A., and S. Ghoshal. 1992. Managing across borders: New organizational responses. *Sloan Management Review* 28(9): 3–13.

Basadur, M. 2004. Leading others to think innovatively together: Creative leadership. *The Leadership Quarterly* 15: 103–121.

Bass, B. M. 1960. *Leadership, psychology, and organizational behavior*. New York: Harper and Row.

_____. 1985. *Leadership and performance beyond expectations*. New York: Free Press.

_____. 1990. *Bass and Stogdill's handbook of leadership*. 3rd ed. New York: Free Press.

_____. 1997. Does the transactional-transformational leadership paradigm transcend organizational and national boundaries? *American Psychologist* 52(3): 130–139.

Bass, B. M., and B. J. Avolio. 1990. Developing transformational leadership: 1992 and beyond. *Journal of European Industrial Training* 14: 21–27.

_____. 1993. Transformational leadership: A response to critiques. In *Leadership theory and research: Perspectives and directions*, ed. M. M. Chemers and R. Ayman, 49–80. San Diego, CA: Academic Press.

Bauer, T. N., and S. G. Greene. 1996. Development of the leader-member exchange: A longitudinal test. *Academy of Management Journal* 39: 1538–1567.

Bedeian, A. G., and A. A. Armenakis. 1998. The cesspool syndrome: How dreck floats to the top of declining organizations. *Academy of Management Executive* 12(1): 58–63.

Bedeian, A. G., and D. V. Day. 2004. Can chameleons lead? *The Leadership Quarterly* 15: 687–718.

Behfar, K. J., R. S. Peterson, E. A. Mannix, and W. M. K. Trochim. 2008. The critical role of conflict resolution in teams: A close look at the links between conflict type, conflict management strategies, and team outcomes. *Journal of Applied Psychology* 93(1): 170–188.

Belet, D. 2007. Are "high potential" executives capable of building learning-oriented organisations? Reflections on the French case. *Journal of Workplace Learning* 19: 465–475.

Bennis, W. G. 2003. News analysis: It's the culture. *Fast Company*, August, 73. http://www.fastcompany.com/magazine/73/nyt.html (accessed September 30, 2004).

Bennis, W. G., and B. Nanus. 1985. *Leader: The strategies for taking charge*. New York: Harper and Row.

Bianchi, S. M. 2000. Maternal employment and time with children: Dramatic change or surprising continuity? *Demography* 37: 401–414.

Bird, C. 1940. *Social psychology*. New York: Appleton.

Biro, M. M. 2012. 5 methods for social leadership: Try reverse mentoring. *Forbes*, September 23. http://www.forbes.com/sites/meghanbiro/2012/09/23/5-methods-for-social-leadership-try-reverse-mentoring/ (accessed August 5, 2013).

Bisoux, T. 2008a. The instant messenger. *BizEd* (January–February): 16–20.

_____. 2008b. Good works. *BizEd* (May–June): 16–22.

_____. 2009. Making connections. *BizEd* (January–February): 16–22.

BizEd. 2009. *Tomorrow's Leaders* (September–October): 28–34.

Black, J. 2004. Always the optimist. *Inc.*, August, 95–98.

Bligh, M. C., and G. D. Hess. 2007. The power of leading subtly: Alan Greenspan, rhetorical leadership, and monetary policy. *The Leadership Quarterly* 18: 87–104.

Block, P. 1987. *The empowered manager.* San Francisco: Jossey-Bass.

_____. 1993. *Stewardship: Choosing service over self-interest.* San Francisco: Berrett-Koehler.

Blundell, M. 2007. How McDonald's tracks morale at the front line. *Strategic Communication Management* 11(4): 10.

Boerner, S., S. A. Eisenbeiss, and D. Griesser. 2007. Follower behavior and organizational performance: The impact of transformational leadership. *Journal of Leadership and Organizational Studies* 13: 15–26.

Boies, J. 2013. 6 ways Google builds company culture. *Sales Force,* June 14. http://blogs.salesforce.com/company/2013/06/google-company-culture.html (accessed June 22, 2013).

Bono, J. E., and R. Ilies. 2006. Charisma, positive emotion and mood contagion. *The Leadership Quarterly* 17: 317–334.

Bowers, D. G., and S. E. Seashore. 1966. Predicting organizational effectiveness with a four-factor theory of leadership. *Administrative Science Quarterly* 11: 238–263.

Boyatzis, R. E., and C. Soler. 2012. Vision, leadership and emotional intelligence transforming family business. *Journal of Family Business Management* 2(1): 23–30.

Brady, D. 2002. A makeover has Avon looking good. *BloombergBusisnessweek,* January 21. http://www.businessweek.com/stories/2002-01-21/a-makeover-has-avon-looking-good (accessed October 12, 2013).

Branson, R. 2007. Learn to say no. *CNNMoney.* http://money.cnn.com/popups/2006/biz2/howtosucceed_leader/ (accessed October 12, 2013).

Branson, R. 2013a. The importance of mentoring. *Virgin,* May 8. https://www.virgin.com/richard-branson/the-importance-of-mentoring (accessed August 5, 2013).

Branson, R. 2013b. Richard Branson on self-awareness for leadership growth. *Entrepreneur,* June 3. http://www.entrepreneur.com/article/226863#ixzz2b75J5cj9 (accessed August 5, 2013).

Brant, J. 2004. Lucky Junki. *Inc.*, October, 109–116.

Braun, S., C. Peus, S. Weisweiler, and D. Frey. 2013. Transformational leadership, job satisfaction and team performance: A multilevel mediation model of trust. *The Leadership Quarterly* 24: 270–283.

Bray, D. W., and D. L. Grant. 1966. The assessment center in the measurement of potential for business management. *Psychological Monographs* 80(17): 1–27.

Brazil, J. J. 2007. Mission: Impossible? *Fast Company,* March. http://www.fastcompany.com/magazine/114/features-mission-impossible.html (accessed August 21, 2007).

Breen, B. 2002. David Rockwell has a lot of nerve. *Fast Company,* November, 76–84.

_____. 2004. The six myths of creativity. *Fast Company,* December, 75–78.

Bret, B. H., B. E. Postlethwaite, A. C. Klotz, M. R. Hamdani, and K. G. Brown. 2012. Reaping the benefits of task conflict in teams: The critical role of team psychological safety climate. *Journal of Applied Psychology* 71(1): 151–158.

Brodsky, N. 2006. The one thing you can't delegate. *Inc.*, April, 61–62.

Brown, M. C. 1982. Administrative succession and organizational performance: The succession effect. *Administrative Science Quarterly* 29: 245–273.

Brown, M. E., and L. K. Treviño. 2006. Socialized charismatic leadership, values congruence, and deviance in work groups. *Journal of Applied Psychology* 91: 954–962.

Brown, R., K. Budzek, and M. Tamborski. 2009. On the meaning and measure of narcissism. *Personality and Social Psychology Bulletin* 35(7): 951–964.

Brunell, A., W. Gentry, W. Campbell, B. Hoffman, K. Kuhnert, and K. DeMaree. 2008. Leader emergence: The case of the narcissistic leader. *Personality and Social Psychology Bulletin* 34(12): 1663–1676. http://articles.moneycentral.msn.com/Investing/CompanyFocus/The5RichestPayoffsFor FiredCEOs.aspx (accessed March 16, 2010).

Bryant, A. 1995. Worker ownership was no paradise. *International Herald Tribune*, March 23, 16.

————. 2009a. Managing globally, and locally. *The New York Times*, December 13. http://www.nytimes.com/2009/12/13/business/13corner.html (accessed March 12, 2010).

————. 2009b. Connecting the dots isn't enough. *The New York Times,* July 19. http://www.nytimes.com/2009/07/19/business/19corner.html (accessed April 4, 2010).

————. 2009c. The keeper of the tapping pen. *The New York Times,* March 22, http://www.nytimes.com/2009/03/22/business/22corner.html (accessed April 4, 2010).

————. 2009d. In a near-death event, a corporate rite of passage. *The New York Times*, August 2. http://query.nytimes.com/gst/fullpage.html?res=9F04E6DD123CF931A3575BC0A96F9C8B63 (accessed April 4, 2010).

————. 2009e. He was promotable after all. *The New York Times*, May 3, http://www.nytimes.com/2009/05/03/business/03corner.html (accessed April 4, 2010).

————. 2009f. Imagine a world of no annual reviews. *The New York Times,* October 18. http://www.nytimes.com/2009/10/18/business/18corner.html (accessed April 4, 2010).

————. 2009g. Planes, cars and cathedrals. *The New York Times*, September 6. http://www.nytimes.com/2009/09/06/business/06corner.html (accessed April 7, 2010).

————. 2009h. The CEO as general (and scout). *The New York Times*, October 11, http://www.nytimes.com/2009/10/11/business/11corner.html (accessed April 7, 2010).

————. 2009i. Ensemble acting, in business. *The New York Times*, June 7, http://www.nytimes.com/2009/06/07/business/07corner.html (accessed April 12, 2010).

————. 2009j. Stepping out of the sandbox. *The New York Times*, August 30, http://www.nytimes.com/2009/08/30/business/30corner.html (accessed April 16, 2010).

————. 2009k. Want to talk to the chief? Book your half-hour. *The New York Times*, October 4. http://www.nytimes.com/2009/10/04/business/04corner.ready.html (accessed April 16, 2010).

————. 2009l. The benefit of a boot out the door. *The New York Times—Corner Office*, November 7. http://www.nytimes.com/2009/11/08/business/08corner.html?_r=1 (accessed March 2, 2010).

————. 2009m. No doubt women are better managers. *The New York Times*, July 26. http://www.nytimes.com/2009/07/26/business/26corner.html (accessed May 8, 2010).

————. 2010. The container store. *The New York Times,* March 12, http://www.nytimes.com/2010/03/14/business/14corners.html (accessed May 13, 2010).

————. 2010a. Remember to share the stage. *The New York Times,* January 3, http://www.nytimes.com/2010/01/03/business/03corner.html (accessed April 4, 2010).

————. 2010b. Talk to me. I'll turn off my phone. *The New York Times*, February 28. http://www.nytimes.com/2010/02/28/business/28corner.html (accessed April 4, 2010).

————. 2010c. Structure? The flatter, the better. *The New York Times*, January 17. http://www.nytimes.com/2010/01/17/business/17corner.html (accessed April 16, 2010).

————. 2010d. Xerox's new chief tries to redefine its culture. *The New York Times,* February 20. http://www.nytimes.com/2010/02/21/business/21xerox.html?pagewanted=all (accessed October 20, 2013).

————. 2012a. Sometimes, you need to blow the fuses. *The New York Times,* January 14. http://www.nytimes.com/2012/01/15/business/bill-kling-of-american-public-media-on-valuing-creativity.html (accessed July 22, 2013).

————. 2012b. Let everyone swim, but make sure you're in the pool. *The New York Times,* June. http://www.nytimes.com/2012/06/24/business/

angies-list-co-founder-reviews-management-style. html (accessed July 22, 2013).

_____. 2013a. A Boss's challenge: Have everyone join in the "in" group. *The New York Times,* March 23. http://www.nytimes.com/2013/03/24/ business/neuroleadership-institutes-chief-on-shared-goals.html?pagewanted=1 (accessed July 22, 2013).

_____. 2013b. How to become a bus driver, not a bulldozer. *The New York Times,* October 7. http:// www.nytimes.com/2012/10/07/business/ken-rees-of-think-finance-on-leading-a-growing-company. html (accessed July 22, 2013).

_____. 2013c. Shifting hats and working in small teams. *The New York Times,* February 23. http:// www.nytimes.com/2013/02/24/business/lily-kanter-on-working-in-small-entrepreneurial-groups.html (accessed July 22, 2013).

Buchanan, L. 1999. The smartest little company in America. *Inc.*, January, 43–54.

_____. 2001. Managing one-to-one. *Inc.*, October, 82–88.

_____. 2010. Productivity nation. *Inc.,* March, 62–73.

Buckingham, M. 2005. The Frankenleader fad. *Fast Company*, September, 93–94.

——. 2009. Why are women unhappier than they were 40 years ago? *Business Week,* October 16. http://www.businessweek.com/managing/content/ oct2009/ca20091016_302039.htm?chan=careers_ special+report+—+women+and+leadership_ special+report+-+women+and+leadership (accessed January 18, 2010).

Bunker, M., and A. D. Ball. 2009. Consequences of customer powerlessness: Secondary control. *Journal of Consumer Behavior* 8(5): 268–281.

Burke, C. S., K. C. Stagl, C. Klein, G. F. Goodwin, E. Salas, and S. M. Halpin. 2006. What type of leadership behaviors are functional in teams? A meta-analysis. *The Leadership Quarterly* 17: 288–307.

Burlingham, B. 2003. The coolest small company in America. *Inc.*, January, 65–74.

Burns, J. M. 1978. *Leadership.* New York: Harper and Row.

Burris, E., M. Rogers, E. Mannix, M. Hendron, and J. Oldroyd. 2009. Playing favorites: The influence of leaders' inner circle on group processes and

performance. *Personality and Social Psychology Bulletin* 35(9): 1244–1257.

Butler, R. J., and D. C. Wilson. 1990. *Managing voluntary and non-profit organizations: Strategy and structure.* London: Rutledge.

Byrne, J. A., and H. Timmons. 2001. Tough times for a new CEO: How Ken Chenault of AmEx is tested in ways few could have imagined. *Business Week*, October 29, 64–68.

Cain, S. 2013. *Quiet: The power of introverts in a world that can't stop talking.* New York: Random House.

Caligiuri, P. M. 2000. The Big Five personality characteristics as predictors of expatriate's desire to terminate the assignments and supervisor-rated performance. *Personnel Psychology* 53(1): 67–88.

Cameron, K. 2006. Good or bad: Standards and ethics in managing change. *Academy of Management Learning and Education* 5: 317–323.

_____. 2008. *Positive leadership.* San Francisco: Berrett-Koehler.

_____. 2011. Responsible leadership as virtuous leadership. *Journal of Business Ethics* 98: 25–35.

Cameron, K., J. E. Dutton, and R. E. Quinn, eds. 2003. *Positive organizational scholarship: Foundations of a new discipline.* San Francisco: Berrett-Koehler.

Campbell, D. J., and G. J. Dardis. 2004. The "Be, Know, Do" model of leader development. *Human Resource Planning* 27(2): 26–39.

Canabou, C. 2003. Fast talk. *Fast Company*, September 58.

Carl, D., V. Gupta, and M. Javidan. 2004. Power distance. In *Culture, leadership, and organizations: The GLOBE study of 62 countries*, ed. R. J. House, P. J. Hanges, M. Javidan, P. W. Dorfman, and V. Gupta, 513–563. Thousand Oaks, CA: Sage.

Carli, L. L. 1999. Gender, interpersonal power, and social influence. *Journal of Social Issues* 55: 81–99.

_____. 2001. Gender and social influence. *Journal of Social Issues* 57: 725–741.

Carlson, N. 2009. AOL will pay fired CEO Randy Falco $8.5 million through 2010. *Business Insider,* November 16. http://www.businessinsider.com/aol-will-pay-fired-ceo-randy-falco-85-million-through-2010-2009-11 (accessed April 8, 2010).

Carlyle, T. 1907. *Heroes and hero worship*. Boston: Adams.

Carmeli, A., Schaubroeck, J., and A. Tishler. 2011. How CEO empowering leadership shapes top management team processes: Implications for firm performance. *The Leadership Quarterly* 22(2): 399–411.

Carpenter, M. A., M. A. Geletkanycz, and W. G. Sanders. 2004. Upper echelons research revisited: Antecedents, elements, and consequences of top management team composition. *Journal of Management* 30: 749–778.

Carrns, A., and V. Bauerlein. 2007. Scrushy gets nearly 7 years in bribery case. *Wall Street Journal*, June 29, http://online.wsj.com/article/SB118307727806452313.html (accessed March 17, 2010).

Carson, J. B., P. E. Tesluk, and J. A. Marrone. 2007. Shared leadership in teams: An investiagaing of antecedent conditions and performance. *Academy of Management Journal* 50(5): 1217–1234.

Carsten, M. K., Uhl-Bien, M., West, B. J., Patera, J. L., and R. McGregor. 2010. Exploring social constructions of followership: A qualitative study. *The Leadership Quarterly* 21: 543–562.

Cartwright, D. C. 1965. Influence, leadership, control. In *Handbook of organizations*, ed. J. G. March, 1–47. Chicago: Rand McNally.

Caruso-Cabrera, M. 2013. 3M CEO: Research is "driving this company." *CNBC,* June 10. http://www.cnbc.com/id/100801531 (accessed August 1, 2013).

Carvell, T. 1998. By the way, your staff hates you. *Fortune* 138(6): 200–212.

Case, S. 2009. Graduation speech at George Mason University. *Case Foundation.* http://www.casefoundation.org/blog/steve-case-george-mason-university-commencement-speech (accessed March 25, 2010).

Chafkin, M. 2013. Most creative people 2013: 6. Max Levchin. *Fast Company,* May 13. http://www.fastcompany.com/3009197/most-creative-people-2013/6-max-levchin (accessed August 3, 2013).

Chandler, S. 2004. Execs take companies' cash as privilege. *Arizona Republic*, September 19, D1, D5.

Chapman, J. 2006. Anxiety and defective decision making: An elaboration of the groupthink model. *Management Decision* 44: 1391–1404.

Chappelow, C. T. 2004. 360-degree feedback. In *The Center for Creative Leadership: Handbook of leadership development*. 2nd ed. Ed. C. D. McCauley and E. Van Velsor, 58–84. San Francisco: Jossey-Bass.

Chatterjee, A., and D. C. Hambrick. 2007. It's all about me: Narcissistic chief executive officers and their effects on company strategy and performance. *Administrative Science Quarterly* 52(3): 351–386.

Chatterjee, S. 2012. Top 5 reasons why Google is the company to work for. *International Business Times,* January 20. http://www.ibtimes.com/top-5-reasons-why-google-best-company-work-553844 (accessed June 22, 2013).

Cheese, P. 2013. What's so hard about corporate change. *CNNMoney,* May 20. http://management.fortune.cnn.com/2013/05/20/corporations-change-failure/ (accessed August 1, 2013).

Chemers, M. M. 1969. Cross-cultural training as a means for improving situational favorableness. *Human Relations* 22: 531–546.

_____. 1993. An integrative theory of leadership. In *Leadership theory and research: Perspectives and directions*, ed. M. M. Chemers and R. Ayman, 293–320. New York: Academic Press.

_____. 1997. *An integrative theory of leadership*. Mahwah, NJ: Lawrence Erlbaum.

Chemers, M. M., and G. J. Skrzypek. 1972. An experimental test of the contingency model of leadership effectiveness. *Journal of Personality and Social Psychology* 24: 172–177.

Chen, C. Y., and C. I. Li. 2013. Assessing the spiritual leadership effectiveness: The contribution of follower's self-concept and preliminary tests for moderation of culture and managerial position. *The Leadership Quarterly* 24: 240–255.

Chen, Y. F., and D. Tjosvold. 2006. Participative leadership by American and Chinese managers in China: The role of relationships. *Journal of Management Studies* 43: 1727–1752.

Cheng, T, Huang, G., Lee, C., and X. Ren. 2012. Longitudinal effect of job insecurity on employee outcomes: The moderating role of emotional intelligence and the leader-member exchange. *Asia Pacific Journal of Management* 29(3): 709–728.

Cherrington, D. J., S. J. Condies, and J. L. England. 1979. Age and work values. *Academy of Management Journal* (September): 617–623.

Chester, A. 2005. Kenneth Chenault, AMEX CEO, speaks on leadership. *Wharton Journal*, March 28. http://media.www.whartonjournal.com/media/storage/paper201/news/2005/03/28/News/Kenneth.Chenault.Amex.Ceo.Speaks.On.Leadership-904135.shtml (accessed July 14, 2007).

Chi, S. C. S., and S. G. Liang. 2013. When do subordinates' emotion-regulation strategies matter? Abusive supervision, subordinates' emotional exhaustion, and work withdrawal. *The Leadership Quarterly* 24: 125–137.

Child, T. 2013. Workforce diversity: The bridge between the workplace and the marketplace. http://www.tedchilds.com/experience.html (accessed May 30, 2013).

Cho, T. S., and W. Shen. 2007. Changes in executive compensation following an environmental shift: The role of top management team turnover. *Strategic Management Journal* 28: 747–754.

Christie, R., and F. L. Geis. 1970. *Studies in Machiavellianism*. New York: Academic Press.

Chu, J. 2013. Most creative people 2013: 4. Kirthiga Reddy. *Fast Company,* May 13. http://www.fastcompany.com/3009243/most-creative-people-2013/4-kirthiga-reddy (accessed August 3, 2013).

Church, G. J. 1997/1998. Man of the year. *Time*, December 29–January 5. http://www.time.com/time/special/moy/grove/runnergreenspan.html (accessed December 29, 2004).

Civettini, N. H. W. 2007. Similarity and group performance. *Social Psychology Quarterly* 70(3): 262–271.

Clarke, S. 2013. Safety leadership: A meta-analytic review of transformational and transactional leadership styles as antecedents of safety behaviours. *Journal of Occupational and Organizational Psychology* 86: 22–49.

Cleyman, K. L., S. M. Jex, and K. G. Love. 1993. Employee grievances: An application of the leader-member exchange model. Paper presented at the 9th Annual Meeting of the Society of Industrial and Organizational Psychology, Nashville, TN.

Collins, J., and D. K. Cooke. 2013. Creative role models, personality and performance. *Journal of Management Development* 32(4): 336–350.

Collinson, D. 2012. Prozac leadership and the limits of positive thinking. *Leadership* 8(2): 87–107.

Colvin, G. 2001. The anti-control freak. *Fortune*, November 26, 60.

———. 2009. Crisis chief: Amex's Chenault. *Fortune.* October 15. http://money.cnn.com/2009/10/14/news/companies/american_express_chenault.fortune/index.htm (accessed March 1, 2010).

Conference board. 2012. Workers less miserable, but hardly happy. http://www.conference-board.org/press/pressdetail.cfm?pressid=4527 (accessed May 30, 2013).

Conger, J. A. 1989. *The charismatic leader: Behind the mystique of exceptional leadership*. San Francisco: Jossey-Bass.

———. 1990. The dark side of leadership. *Organizational Dynamics* 19: 44–55.

———. 1992. *Learning to lead: The art of transforming managers into leaders*. San Francisco: Jossey-Bass.

———. 2004. Developing leadership capability: What's inside the black box? *Academy of Management Executive* 18(3): 136–139.

Conger, J. A., and R. N. Kanungo. 1987. Toward a behavioral theory of charismatic leadership in organizational settings. *Academy of Management* 12: 637–647.

———. 1998. *Charismatic leadership in organizations*. Thousand Oaks, CA: Sage.

Containing Culture. 2007. *Chain Store Age* (April): 23–24.

Conyon, M. J., and S. I. Peck. 1998. Board control, remuneration committees, and top management compensation. *Academy of Management Journal* 41(2): 146–157.

Cooper, C. D., T. A. Scandura, and C. A. Schriesheim. 2005. Looking forward but learning from our past: Potential challenges to developing authentic leadership theory and authentic leaders. *The Leadership Quarterly* 16: 475–493.

Cooper, N. 2007. Looking after your leaders. *Personnel Today*, April 24, 24–26.

Cordery, J. 2004. Another case of the Emperor's new clothes? *Journal of Occupational and Organizational Psychology* 77: 481–484.

Corruption Index. 2013. http://www.transparency.org/research/cpi/overview (accessed October 11, 2013).

Crant, M. J. 2000. Proactive behavior in organiazations. *Journal of Management* 26(3): 435–462.

Cronin, E. T. 1987. Leadership and democracy. *Liberal Education* 73(2): 35–38.

Cross, T. L., Bazron, B. J., Dennis, K. W., and M. R. Isaacs. 1989. *Towards a culturally competent system of care: A monograph on effective services for minority children who are severely emotional disturbed,* Vol. 1. http://minorityhealth.hhs.gov/templates/browse.aspx?lvl=2&lvlID=11 (accessed June 21, 2013).

Crouch, A., and P. Yetton. 1987. Manager behavior, leadership style, and subordinate performance: An empirical extension of Vroom-Yetton conflict rule. *Organizational Behavior and Human Decision Processes* 39: 384–396.

Cryer, S. 2004. Recruiting and retaining the next generation of nonprofit sector leadership. *The Initiative for Nonprofit Sector Careers,* January. http://www.handsonnetwork.org/files/resources/AR_NextGenofNPSectorLeadership_2006_Scryer.pdf (accessed July 20, 2013).

Cummings, B. 2004. The best bosses: The Whipcracker. *Fortune Small Business*, October 1. http://www.fortune.com/fortune/print/0,15935,697855,00.html (accessed November 15, 2004).

Cunningham, J. B., and J. MacGregor. 2000. Trust and the design of work: Complementary constructs in satisfaction and performance. *Human Relations* 53: 1575–1591.

Customer service. 2007. http://www.superquinn.ie/Multi/default.asp?itemId=305 (accessed July 25, 2007).

Cyert, R. M., and J. G. March. 1963. *A behavioral theory of the firm*. Upper Saddle River, NJ: Prentice Hall.

Dana, J. A., and D. M. Bourisaw. 2006. Overlooked leaders. *American School Board Journal,* June, 27–30.

Daniel, T. 2009. Tough bosses or workplace bully. *HR Magazine,* June 2009. http://findarticles.com/p/articles/mi_m3495/is_6_54/ai_n32067231/ (accessed March 9, 2010).

Dansereau, F., Jr., G. B. Graen, and W. J. Haga. 1975. A vertical dyad linkage approach to leadership within formal organizations: A longitudinal investigation of the role making process. *Organizational Behavior and Human Performance* 13: 46–78.

Darla Moore Speech to Palmetto Center for Women. 2007. http://www.palmettoinstitute.org/.../darla%20moore%20speech%20to%20the%20twin%20awards%209%2007... (accessed January 11, 2010).

Dash, E. 2007a. Executive pay: A special report. http://www.nytimes.com/2007/04/08/business/yourmoney/08pay.html?ref=business (accessed January 8, 2008).

————. 2007b. Executive pay: Has the exit sign ever looked so good? *New York Times*, April 8. http://www.nytimes.com/2007/04/08/business/yourmoney/08axe.html?ref=businessspecial (accessed January 8, 2008).

Davidson, A. 2013. Workers of the world, sit tight. *The New York Times,* January 29. http://www.nytimes.com/2013/02/03/magazine/do-unions-have-a-shot-in-the-21st-century.html (accessed October 6, 2013).

Davis, J. H., F. D. Schoorman, and L. Donaldson. 1997. Toward a stewardship theory of management. *Academy of Management Review* 22: 20–47.

Davis, K. M., and W. L. Gardner. 2012. Charisma under crisis revisited: Presidential leadership, perceived leader effectiveness, and contextual influences. *The Leadership Quarterly* 23: 918–933.

Day, D. V. 2000. Leadership development: A review in context. *The Leadership Quarterly* 11: 581–613.

————. 2010. The difficulties of learning from experience and the need for deliberate practice. *Industrial and Organizational Psychology* 3(1): 41–44.

Day, D. V., and D. J. Schleicher. 2006. Self-monitoring at work: A motive-based perspective. *Journal of Personality* 74: 683–714.

Day, D. V., D. J. Schleicher, A. L. Unckless, and N. J. Hiller. 2002. Self-monitoring personality at work: A meta-analytic investigation of construct validity. *Journal of Applied Psychology* 87: 390–401.

Day, D. V., P. Gronn, and E. Salas. 2004. Leadership capacity in teams. *The Leadership Quarterly* 15: 857–880.

Day, D. V., and R. G. Lord. 1988. Executive leadership and organizational performance: Suggestions for a new theory and methodology. *Journal of Management* 14: 453–464.

Day, D. V., S. J. Zaccaro, and S. M. Halpin, eds. 2004. *Leader development for transforming organization:*

Growing leader for tomorrow. Mahwah, NJ: Lawrence Erlbaum.

De Bono, E. 1992. *Serious creativity: Using the power of lateral thinking to create new ideas.* New York: Harper Business.

De Hoogh, A. H. B, and D. N. Den Hartog. 2009. Neuroticism and locus of control as moderators of the relationship of charismatic and autocratic leadership with burnout. *Journal of Applied Psychology* 94(4): 1058–1067.

Delbecq, A. 2001. "Evil" manifested in destructive individual behavior: A senior leadership challenge. *Journal of Management Inquiry* 10: 221–226.

Denhardt, J. V., and K. B. Campbell. 2006. The role of democratic values in transformational leadership. *Administration and Society* 38: 556–573.

Denhardt, R. B., and J. V. Denhardt. 2006. *The dance of leadership.* Armonk, NJ: M. E. Sharpe.

Den Hartog, D. N., R. J. House, P. J. Hanges, S. A. Ruiz-Quintanilla, and P. W. Dorfman. 1999. Culture-specific and cross-culturally generalizable implicit leadership theories: Are attributes of charismatic/transformational leadership universally endorsed? *The Leadership Quarterly* 10: 219–256.

Denning, S. 2010. *The leader's guide to radical management: Reinventing the workplace for the 21st century.* San Francisco: Jossey-Bass.

————. 2011. How do you change an organizational culture. *Forbes,* July 23. http://www.forbes.com/sites/stevedenning/2011/07/23/how-do-you-change-an-organizational-culture/ (accessed August 3, 2013).

Denton, D. K. 2007. Using intranets as a training and empowerment tool. *Training and Development Methods* 21(1): 217–222.

De Pillis, E., R. Kernochan, O. Meilich, E. Prosser, and V. Whiting. 2008. Are managerial gender stereotypes universal? *Cross Cultural Management: An International Journal* 15: 94–102.

de Rond, M. 2012. Conflict keeps teams at the top of their game. *HBR Blog,* July 3. http://blogs.hbr.org/cs/2012/07/conflict_keeps_teams_at_the_to.html (accessed July 22, 2013).

Derr, C. B. 1987. Managing high potentials in Europe: Some cross-cultural findings. *European Management Journal* 5: 72–80.

Deshpande, R., and A. Raina. 2011. The ordinary heroes of the Taj. *Harvard Business Review,* December. http://hbr.org/2011/12/the-ordinary-heroes-of-the-taj/ar/1 (accessed February 21, 2012).

Deutsch Salaman, S., and S. L. Robinson. 2008. Trust that binds: The impact of collective felt trust on organizational performance. *Journal of Applied Psychology* 93(3): 593–601.

Deutschman, A. 2005. Change or die. *Fast Company,* May. http://www.fastcompany.com/magazine/94/open_change-or-die.html (accessed June 19, 2007).

————. 2007. The three keys to change. *Fast Company,* January. http://www.fastcompany.com/articles/2007/01/change-or-die.html (accessed August 22, 2007).

Diddams, M., and G. C. Chang. 2012. Only human: Exploring the nature of weakness in authentic leadership. *The Leadership Quarterly* 23: 593–603.

Digman, J. M. 1990. Personality structure: Emergence of the five-factor model. *Annual Review of Psychology* 41: 417–440.

Dillon, P. 2004. Perceptive, adaptable, and remarkably low-key, eBay chief executive Meg Whitman rides e-tail's hottest segment. *Christian Science Monitor,* March 10. http://www.csmonitor.com/2004/0310/p11s01-wmgn.htm (accessed July 12, 2007).

D'Intino, R. S., M. G. Goldsby, J. D. Houghton, and C. P. Neck. 2007. Self-leadership: A process of entrepreneurial success. *Journal of Leadership and Organizational Studies* 13: 105–120.

Diversity and inclusion: Unlocking global potential. 2012. *Forbes Insight,* January. http://www.forbes.com/forbesinsights/diversity_2012_pdf_download/ (accessed June 24, 2013).

Dorfman, P. W., J. P. Howell, S. Hibino, J. K. Lee, U. Tate, and A. Bautista. 1997. Leadership in Western and Asian countries: Commonalities and differences in effective leadership processes across cultures. *The Leadership Quarterly* 8(3): 233–274.

Dorfman, P., M. Javidan, P. Hanges, A. Dastmalchian, and R. House. 2012. GLOBE: A twenty year journey into the intriguing world of culture and leadership. *Journal of World Business* 47(4): 504–518.

Downey, H. K., J. E. Sheridan, and J. W. Slocum, Jr. 1975. Analysis of relationships among leader behavior, subordinate job performance and satisfaction: A path-goal approach. *Academy of Management Journal* 18: 253–262.

Drucker, P. F. 1990. *Managing the non-profit organization: Principles and practices.* New York: HarperCollins.

Drum, K. 2012. Digging into the pay gap. *Mother Jones*, May 3. http://www.motherjones.com/kevin-drum/2012/05/digging-pay-gap (accessed June 19, 2013).

Duarte, N. T., J. R. Goodson, and N. R. Klich. 1994. Effects of dyadic quality and duration on performance appraisal. *Academy of Management Journal* 37: 499–521.

Duncan, W. J., K. G. LaFrance, and P. M. Ginter. 2003. Leadership and decision making: A retrospective application and assessment. *Journal of Leadership and Organizational Studies* 9(4): 1–20.

Dunlop, W. L., and M. R. Beauchamp. 2011. Does similarity make a difference? predicting cohesion and attendance behaviors within exercise group settings. *Group Dynamics: Theory, Research, and Practice* 15(3): 258–266.

Dunn, M. W., B. Dastoor, and R. L. Sims. 2012. Transformational leadership and organizational commitment: A cross-cultural perspective. *Journal of Multidisciplinary Research* 4(1): 45–59.

Dvir, T., D. Eden, B. J. Avolio, and B. Shamir. 2002. Impact of transformational leadership on follower development and performance in a field experiment. *Academy of Management Journal* 45: 735–744.

Eagly, A. H., and L. L. Carli. 2004. Women and men as leaders. In *The nature of leadership*, ed. J. Antonakis, A. T. Cianciolo, and R. J. Sternberg, 279–301. Thousand Oaks, CA: Sage.

Eagly, A. H., M. C. Johannesen-Schmidt, and M. van Engen. 2003. Transformational, transactional, and laissez-faire leadership styles: A meta-analysis comparing women and men. *Psychological Bulletin* 95: 569–591.

Eagly, A. H., M. G. Makhijani, and B. G. Klonsky. 1992. Gender and the evaluation of leaders: A meta-analysis. *Psychological Bulletin* 111: 3–22.

Eagly, A. H., and S. J. Karau. 2002. Role congruity theory of prejudice toward female leaders. *Psychological Review* 109: 573–598.

Eagly, A. H., S. J. Karau, and M. G. Makhijani. 1995. Gender and the effectiveness of leaders: A meta-analysis. *Psychological Bulletin* 117: 125–145.

Edelhauser, K. 2007. Steve Case takes on health care. *Entrepreneur.com*, July 18. http://www.entrepreneur.com/ebusiness/article181860.html (accessed August 12, 2007).

EEOC Press release. 2013. *US Equal Employment Opportunity Commission*, January 18. http://www.eeoc.gov/eeoc/newsroom/release/1-28-13.cfm (accessed June 21, 2013).

Ehrenreich, B. 2009. *Bright-sided: How the relentless promotion of positive thinking has undermined America.* New York: Metropolitan Books.

Einarsen, S., Aasland, M. S., and A. Skogstad. 2007. Destructive leadership behavior: A definition and conceptual model. *The Leadership Quarterly* 18: 207–216.

Eisenbeiß, S. A., and S. Boerner. 2013. A double-edged sword: Transformational leadership and individual creativity. *British Journal of Management* 24(1): 54–68.

Elkins, T., and R. T. Keller. 2003. Leadership in research and development organizations: A literature review and conceptual framework. *The Leadership Quarterly* 14: 587–606.

Ellerbee, L. 1999. My biggest mistake. *Inc.*, January, 81.

Elliot, P. 2009. AIG bonuses: Scandal spurring government to rein in bail-out funds. *The Huffington Post*, March 16. http://www.huffingtonpost.com/2009/03/17/aig-bonuses-scandal-spurr_n_175634.html (accessed March 16, 2010).

Emmons, R. A. 1987. Narcissism: Theory and measurement. *Journal of Personality and Social Psychology* 52: 11–17.

Employees of big firms post lower job satisfaction. 2006. *Wall Street Journal*, November 13, 30.

Erdogan, B., R. C. Linden, and M. L. Kramer. 2006. Justice and leader-member exchange: The moderating role of organizational culture. *Academy of Management Journal* 49: 394–406.

Erez, A., V. F. Misangyi, D. E. Johnson, M. A. LePine, and K. C. Halverson. 2008. Stirring the hearts of followers: Charismatic leadership as the transferal of affect. *Journal of Applied Psychology* 93(3): 602–615.

Ernst, C., and A. Martin. 2007. Experience counts: Learning lessons from key events. *Leadership in Action* 26(6): 3.

Estow, S., J. P. Jamieson, and J. R. Yates. 2007. Self-monitoring and mimicry of positive and negative social behaviors. *Journal of Research in Personality* 41: 425–433.

Executive pay watch. 2013. CEO pay and you. *AFLCIO.* http://www.aflcio.org/Corporate-Watch/CEO-Pay-and-You (accessed July 20, 2013).

Executive paywatch around the world. 2013. http://www.aflcio.org/Corporate-Watch/CEO-Pay-and-You/CEO-to-Worker-Pay-Gap-in-the-United-States/Pay-Gaps-in-the-World (accessed July 20, 2013).

Fanelli, A., and V. F. Misangyi. 2006. Bringing out charisma: CEO charisma and external stakeholders. *Academy of Management Review* 31: 1049–1061.

Farh, J. L., P. M. Podsakoff, and B. S. Cheng. 1987. Culture-free leadership effectiveness versus moderators of leadership behavior: An extension and test of Kerr and Jermier's "substitutes for leadership" model in Taiwan. *Journal of International Business Studies* 18(3): 43–60.

Faucheux, M. 2013. Examples of change management plans that worked. *Bright Hub PM,* April 24. http://www.brighthubpm.com/change-management/55056-examples-of-change-management-plans-that-worked/ (accessed August 3, 2013).

Felps, W., T. R. Mitchell, and E. Byington. 2006. Now and when, and why bad apples spoil the barrel: Negative group members and dysfunctional groups. *Research in Organizational Behavior* 27: 175–222.

Fiedler, F. E. 1967. *A theory of leadership effectiveness.* New York: McGraw-Hill.

_____. 1978. The contingency model and the dynamics of the leadership process. In *Advances in experimental social psychology*, Vol. 2, ed. L. Berkowitz, 59–112. New York: Academic Press.

_____. 1993. The leadership situation and the black box in contingency theories. In *Leadership theory and research: Perspectives and directions*, ed. M. M. Chemers and R. Ayman, 2–28. New York: Academic Press.

———. 2002. The curious role of cognitive resources in leadership. In *Multiple intelligences and leadership.*

LEA's organization and management series. Ed. Riggio, Ronald E., Murphy, Susan E., and Pirozzolo, Francis J., 91–104. Mahwah, NJ, US: Lawrence Erlbaum Associates Publishers.

Fiedler, F. E., and M. M. Chemers. 1974. *Leadership and effective management.* Glenview, IL: Scott-Foresman.

_____. 1984. *Improving leadership effectiveness: The leader match concept.* 2nd ed. New York: John Wiley.

Fiedler, F. E., and J. E. Garcia. 1987a. *Improving leadership effectiveness: Cognitive resources and organizational performance.* New York: John Wiley.

_____. 1987b. *New approaches to leadership: Cognitive resources and organizational performance.* New York: John Wiley.

_____. 1996. *Strategic leadership: Top executives and their effects on organizations.* St. Paul, MN: West Publishing.

Fisher, A. 1998. Success secret: A high emotional IQ. *Fortune* 138(8): 293–298.

Fisher, K. 1993. *Leading self-directed work teams.* New York: McGraw-Hill.

Flannery, N. P. 2011. Paying for failure: The cost of firing America's top CEOs. *Forbes,* October 4. http://www.forbes.com/sites/nathanielparishflannery/2011/10/04/paying-for-failure-the-costs-of-firing-americas-top-ceos/ (accessed October 12, 2013).

Fleishman, E. A. 1953. The measurement of leadership attitudes in industry. *Journal of Applied Psychology* 37: 153–158.

Fleishman, E. A., and E. F. Harris. 1962. Patterns of leadership behavior related to employee grievance and turnover. *Personnel Psychology* 15: 43–56.

Flynn, F. J., and S. S. Wiltermuth. 2009. Who's with me? False consensus, advice networks, and ethical decision making in organizations. Working.

Ford. 2004. David Neeleman, CEO of JetBlue Airways, on people + strategy = growth. *Academy of Management Executive* 18(2): 139–143.

Ford Foundation. 2013. Our mission. http://www.fordfoundation.org/about-us/mission (accessed July 20, 2013).

Foster, T. 2004. Using delegation as a developmental tool: Methods and benefits. *Training Journal* (May): 28–32.

Fowers, B. J., and B. J. Davidov. 2006. The virtue of multiculturalism: Personal transformation, character, and openness to the other. *American Psychologist* 61: 581–594.

Frauenheim, E. 2007. Taking the measure of agilent. *Workforce Management*, January. http://www. workforce.com/section/10/feature/24/62/46/index. html (accessed January 8, 2008).

French, J. R. P., and B. H. Raven. 1968. The basis of social power. In *Group dynamics*. 3rd ed. Ed. D. Cartwright and A. Zander, 259–269. New York: Harper and Row.

Frey, R. 1993. Empowerment or else. *Harvard Business Review* (September–October): 80–94.

Friedman, V. 2011. Lunch with FT: Mickey Drexler. *Financial Times,* October 21. http://www.ft.com/intl/cms/s/2/bcf99a3e-fb01-11e0-bebe-00144feab49a. html#axzz2ZclR33J5 (accessed July 20, 2013).

Frontiera, J., and D. Leidl. 2012. *Team turnaround: A playbook for transforming underperforming teams.* San Francisco: Jossey Bass.

Fry, L. W. 2003. Toward a theory of spiritual leadership. *The Leadership Quarterly* 14: 693–727.

Fry, L. W., S. T. Hannah, M. Noel, and F. O. Walumba. 2011. Impact of spiritual leadership on unit performance. *The Leadership Quarterly* 22: 259–270.

Fulfilling the promise. 2012. *Statement by the policy and impact committee of the committee for economic development.* http://www.fwa.org/pdf/CED_WomenAdvancementonCorporateBoards.pdf (accessed June 19, 2013).

Fuller, B., and L. E. Marier. 2009. Change driven by nature: A meta-analytic review of the proactive personality literature. *Journal of Vocational Behavior* 75(3): 329–345.

Furnham, A., Richards, S. C., and D. L. Paulhus. 2012. The dark triad of personality: A 10 year review. *Social and Personality Psychology Compass* 7(3): 199–216.

Galinsky, A. D., D. H. Gruenfeld, and J. C. Magee. 2003. From power to action. *Journal of Personality and Social Psychology* 85: 453–466.

Gallagher, B. M. 2006. Commencement address at University of Maryland. http://national.unitedway. org/files/pdf/speeches/UniversityMaryland Commencement.pdf (accessed July 26, 2007).

Gallo, C. 2007. The seven secrets of inspiring leaders. *Business Week,* October 10. http://www. businessweek.com/smallbiz/content/oct2007/sb20071010_093227.htm (accessed April 5, 2010).

———. 2012. Alan Mulally, optimism, and the power of vision. *Forbes,* April 25. http://www. forbes.com/sites/carminegallo/2012/04/25/alan-mulully-optimism-and-the-power-of-vision/ (accessed July 20, 2013).

Galton, R. 1869. *Hereditary genius.* New York: Appleton.

Gallup—State of the American Workplace. 2013. http://www.gallup.com/strategicconsulting/163007/state-american-workplace.aspx (accessed June 25, 2013).

Gardner, W. L., G. C. Coglier, K. M. Davis, and M. P. Dickens. 2011. Authentic leadership: A review of the literature and research agenda. *The Leadership Quarterly* 22: 1120–1145.

Gawker. 2007. New York's worst bosses. http://gawker. com/243908/new-yorks-worst-bosses-scott-rudin (accessed March 1, 2010).

Geiger, S. W., and L. H. Cashen. 2007. Organizational size and CEO compensation: The moderating effect of diversification in downscoping organizations. *Journal of Managerial Issues* 19: 233–254.

Gelfand, M., D. P. S. Bhawuk, L. H. Nishii, and B. J. Bechtold. 2004. Individualism and collectivism. In *Culture, leadership, and organizations: The GLOBE study of 62 countries*, ed. R. J. House, P. J. Hanges, M. Javidan, P. W. Dorfman, and V. Gupta, 437–512. Thousand Oaks, CA: Sage.

George, B. 2003. *Authentic leadership.* San Francisco: Jossey-Bass.

———. 2007. *True north.* San Francisco: Jossey-Bass.

———. 2009. *Seven lessons for leading in crisis.* San Francisco: Jossey-Bass.

———. 2009a. S. Seven lessons for leading in crisis. *The Wall Street Journal*, March 5. http://online. wsj.com/article/SB123551729786163925.html (accessed April 8, 2010).

Georgetown National Center for Cultural Competence. 2013. http://www11.georgetown.edu/research/gucchd/nccc/foundations/frameworks.html#ccprinciples (accessed June 21, 2013).

Ghiselli, E. E. 1963. Intelligence and managerial success. *Psychological Reports* 12: 898.

Gibbs, N. 2008. This is our time. *Time Magazine*, November 17: 28–40.

Gladwell, M. 2008. *Outliers: The story of success.* New York: Little, Brown and Company.

Glaser, J. E. 2006. *The DNA of leadership.* Avon, MA: Platinum Press.

Goetz, K. 2011. How 3M gave everyone days off and created an innovation dynamo. *Fast Company,* February 1. http://www.fastcodesign.com/1663137/how-3m-gave-everyone-days-off-and-created-an-innovation-dynamo (accessed August 1, 2013).

Goldstein, I. L. 1986. *Training in organizations: Needs assessment, development, and evaluation.* Monterey, CA: Brooks/Cole.

Goldstein, L. 2000. Whatever space works for you. *Fortune*, July 10, 269–270.

Goleman, D. 1995. *Emotional intelligence: Why it can matter more than IQ.* New York: Bantam Books.

———. 1998. *Working with emotional intelligence.* New York: Bantam Books.

———. 2004. What makes a leader? *Harvard Business Review* 82(1): 82–91.

Goleman, D., R. E. Boyatzis, and A. McKee. 2002. *Primal leadership: Realizing the power of emotional intelligence.* Boston: Harvard Business School Press.

Goldsmith, S. 2008. *Denver's pre-kindergarten programme set up to benefit whole community.* http://www.citymayors.com/education/denver-pre-k.html (accessed January 4, 2010).

Gonzales, R. 2010. Nummi plant closure ends Toyota-GM venture. April 1. http://www.npr.org/templates/story/story.php?storyId=125430405 (accessed April 21, 2010).

Goozner, M. 2011, The 10 largest global business corruption cases. *Fiscal Times,* December 13. http://www.thefiscaltimes.com/Articles/2011/12/13/The-Ten-Largest-Global-Business-Corruption-Cases.aspx#page1 (accessed July 15, 2013).

Gordon, M. 2004. Mickey Drexler's redemption. *New York Magazine*, November 29. http://newyorkmetro.com/nymetro/news/bizfinance/biz/features/10489/index1.html (accessed February 7, 2005).

Govindarajan, V., and J. Terwilliger. 2012. Yes you can brainstorm without groupthink. *HBR BLOG,* July 25. http://blogs.hbr.org/cs/2012/07/yes_you_can_brainstorm_without.html (accessed July 22, 2013).

Graen, G. B. 2006. In the eye of the beholder: Cross-cultural lesson in leadership from Project GLOBE. *Academy of Management Perspectives* 20(4): 95–101.

Graen, G. B., and J. R. Cashman. 1975. A role-making model of leadership in formal organizations: A developmental approach. In *Leadership frontiers,* ed. J. G. Hunt and L. L. Larson, 143–165. Kent, OH: Kent State University Press.

Graen, G. B., and W. Shiemann. 1978. Leader-member agreement: A vertical dyad linkage approach. *Journal of Applied Psychology* 63: 206–212.

Graen, G. B., and M. Uhl-Bien. 1991. The transformation of work group professionals into self-managing and partially self-designing contributors: Toward a theory of leadership-making. *Journal of Management Systems* 3(3): 33–48.

———. 1995. Relationship-based approach to leadership: Development of leader-member exchange (LMX) theory of leadership over 25 years: Applying a multilevel-multidomain perspective. *The Leadership Quarterly* 6: 219–247.

Greenleaf, R. K. 1977. *Servant leadership: A journey into the nature of legitimate power an greatness.* New York: Pualist Press.

———. 1998. *The power of servant leadership.* San Francisco: Berrett-Koehler.

Greguras, G. J., and J. M. Diefendorf. 2010. Why does proactive personality predict employee life satisfaction and work behaviors? A field investigation of the mediating role of the self-concordance model. *Personnel Psychology* 63(3): 539–560.

Griffin, R. W. 1979. Task design determinants of effective leader behavior. *Academy of Management Review* 4: 215–224.

Grow, B. 2007. Out at Home Depot. *BusinessWeek. com.* January 9. http://www.msnbc.msn.com/id/16469224/ (accessed April 8, 2010).

Grzelakowski, M. 2005. *Mother leads best.* Chicago, IL: Dearborn Trade Publishing.

Guido, H. 2011. Synergetic effects in working in teams. *Journal of Managerial Psychology* 26(3): 176–184.

Gunther, M. 1998. The internet is Mr. Case's neighborhood. *Fortune* 137(6): 68–80.

Guillén, L., and Ibarra, H. 2009. Seasons of a leader's development: Beyond a one-size fits all approach to designing interventions. *Academy of Management Proceeding (*August 1): 1–6.

Gupta, A. K. 1984. Contingency linkages between strategy and general manager characteristics: A conceptual examination. *Academy of Management Review* 9(3): 399–412.

———. 1988. Contingency perspectives on strategic leadership: Current knowledge and future research directions. In *The executive effect: Concepts and methods for studying top managers,* ed. D. C. Hambrick, 141–178. Greenwich, CT: JAI Press.

Hackman, J. R., ed. 1990. *Groups that work (and those that don't): Creating conditions for effective teamwork.* San Francisco: Jossey-Bass.

———. 2005. Rethinking team leadership or team leaders are not music directors. In *The psychology of leadership: New perspectives and research,* ed. D. M. Messick and R. M. Kramer, 115–142. Mahwah, NJ: Lawrence Erlbaum.

———. 2009. Why teams don't work. *Harvard Business Review* 87(5): 98–105.

Hackman, J. R., and G. R. Oldham. 1980. *Work redesign.* Reading, MA: Addison-Wesley.

Haleblian, J., and S. Finkelstein. 1993. Top management team size, CEO dominance, and firm performance: The moderating roles of environmental turbulence and discretion. *Academy of Management Journal* 36: 844–863.

Haley, F. 2004. Mutual benefits. *Fast Company,* October, 98–99.

Hall, E. T. 1976. *Beyond culture.* Garden City, NY: Anchor Press, Doubleday.

Hall, E. T., and M. R. Hall. 1990. *Understanding cultural differences.* London: Nicholas Brealy Publishing.

Hall, R. N. 1977. *Organizations, structure, and process.* 2nd ed. Upper Saddle River, NJ: Prentice Hall.

Halpin, A. W., and B. J. Winer. 1957. A factorial study of the leader behavior descriptions. In *Leader behavior: Its description and measurement,* ed. R. M. Stogdill and A. E. Coons. Columbus: The Ohio State University, Bureau of Business Research.

Hambrick, D. C. 2007. Upper echelons theory: An update. *Academy of Management Review* 32(2): 334–343.

Hambrick, D. C., and S. Finkelstein. 1987. Managerial discretion: A bridge between polar views of organization. In *Research in organizational behavior,* Vol. 9, ed. L. L. Cummings and B. L. Staw, 349–406. Greenwich, CT: JAI Press.

Hambrick, D. C., and P. A. Mason. 1984. Upper echelon: The organization as a reflection of its top management. *Academy of Management Review* 9: 193–206.

Hammon, S. 2013. Bob Ladouceur steps down as De La Salle's head coach, ends historic era. *Mercury News. com,* January 4. http://www.mercurynews.com/high-school-sports/ci_22312816/bob-ladouceur-steps-down-de-la-salles-head (accessed May 30, 2013).

Hammond, K. H. 2004. GE smackdown. *Fast Company,* July, 32.

Hannan, M. T., and J. H. Freeman. 1977. The population ecology of organizations. *American Journal of Sociology* 82: 929–964.

Hardy, C. 1985. The nature of unobtrusive power. *Journal of Management Studies* 22: 384–399.

Hardy, L., C. A. Arthur, G. Jones, A. Shariff, K. Monnuch, I. Isaacs, and A. J. Allsopp. 2010. The relationship between transformation leadership behaviors, psychological, and training outcomes in elite military recruits. *The Leadership Quarterly* 21: 20–32.

Harris, P. R., R. T. Moran, and S. V. Moran. 2004. *Managing cultural differences.* 6th ed. Amsterdam: Elsevier.

Harrison, J. S., and R. E. Freeman. 2004. Democracy in and around organizations: Is organizational democracy worth the effort? *Academy of Management Executive* 18(3): 49–53.

Hastings, R. R. 2012. Generational differences exist, but beware stereotypes. *SHRM,* October 18. http://www.shrm.org/hrdisciplines/diversity/articles/pages/generational-differences-stereotypes.aspx (accessed October 11, 2013).

Heath, D., and C. Heath. 2009. Stop solving your problems. *Fast Company,* November, 82–83.

———. 2010. *Switch: How to change things when change is hard.* New York: Random House.

Hedlund, J., G. B. Forsythe, J. A. Horvath, W. M. Williams, S. Snook, and R. J. Sternberg. 2003. Identifying and assessing tacit knowledge: Understanding the practical intelligence of military leaders. *The Leadership Quarterly* 14: 117–140.

Helfat, C. E., D. Harris, and P. J. Wolfson. 2006. The pipeline to the top: Women and men in the top executive rank of U.S. corporations. *Academy of Management Perspectives* 20(4): 42–64.

Helgesen, S. 1995. *The female advantage: Women's way of leadership.* New York: Doubleday, Currency.

Hemphill, J. K., and A. E. Coons. 1957. Development of the leader behavior description questionnaire. In *Leader behavior: Its description and measurement,* ed. R. M. Stogdill and A. E. Coons. Columbus: The Ohio State University, Bureau of Business Research.

Hemsworth, D., J. Muterera, and A. Baragheh. 2013. Examining Bass's transformational leadership in public sector executives: A psychometric properties review. *Journal of Applied Business Research* 29: 853–862.

Herman Miller-things that matter to us. 2013. http://www.hermanmiller.com/about-us/things-that-matter-to-us.html (accessed August 3, 2013).

Hess, P. W. 2007. Enhancing leadership skills development by creating practice feedback opportunities in the classroom. *Journal of Management Education* 31: 195–213.

Hewlett, S. A. 2007. *Off-ramps and on-ramps.* Boston: Harvard Business School Press.

Hickson, D. J., C. R. Hinings, C. A. Lee, R. E. Scheneck, and J. M. Pennings. 1971. A strategic contingencies theory of intra-organizational power. *Administrative Science Quarterly* 16: 216–229.

Hindo, B. 2007. At 3M, a struggle between efficiency and creativity. *Business Week*, June 11, 8.

Hinkin, T. R., and C. A. Schriesheim. 2008. An examination of "nonleadership": From laissez-faire to leader reward omission and punishment omission. *Journal of Applied Psychology* 93(6): 1234–1248.

Hira, N. A. 2007. You raised them, now manage them. *Fortune*, May, 38–43.

Hirst, G., L. Mann, P. Bain, A. Pirola-Merlo, and A. Richter. 2004. Learning to lead: The development and testing of a model of leadership learning. *The Leadership Quarterly* 15: 311–327.

Ho, J., and P. L. Nesbit. 2009. A refinement and extension of the self-leadership scale for the Chinese context. *Journal of Managerial Psychology* 34(5): 450–459.

Hodson, R., V. J. Roscigno, and S. H. Lopez. 2006. Chaos and the abuse of power: Workplace bullying in organizational and interactional context. *Work and Occupation* 33(4): 382–416.

Hofman, M. 2000. The metamorphosis. *Inc.*, March 1, 53–60.

Hofmann, D. A., and F. P. Morgeson. 1999. Safety-related behavior as a social exchange: The role of perceived organizational support and leader-member exchange. *Journal of Applied Psychology* 84(2): 286–296.

Hofstede, G. 1992. *Culture and organizations.* London: McGraw-Hill.

———. 2001. *Culture's consequences: Comparing values, behaviors, institutions, and organizations across organizations.* Beverly Hills, CA: Sage.

Hofstede, G., G. J. Hofstede, and M. Minkov. 2010. *Culture and organizations: Software of the mind.* New York: McGraw-Hill.

Holland, K. 2007. How diversity makes a team click. *New York Times*, April 22. http://select.nytimes. com/search/restricted/article?res=F2 0D10FD3D5A0C718EDDAD0894DF404482 (accessed June 27, 2007).

Hollander, E. P. 1979. Leadership and social exchange processes. In *Social change: Advances in theory and research*, ed. K. Gergen, M. S. Greenberg, and R. H. Willis. New York: Winston-John Wiley.

Hollon, J. 2009. The last word: Calm, cool leadership. *Workforce Management,* October 19, 58.

Holson, L. M. 2004a. Eisner says Ovitz required oversight daily. *New York Times*, November 17, C1, C12.

———. 2004b. Ovitz testifies he was sabotaged at Disney. *New York Times*, October 27, C1, C4.

Homans, G. C. 1950. *The human group.* New York: Harcourt, Brace.

Hoobler, J. M, S. J. Wayne, and G. Lemmon. 2009. Bosses' perception of family–work conflict and women's promotability: Glass ceiling effects. *Academy of Management Journal* 52: 939–957.

Hooker, J. 2009. Corruption from a cross-cultural perspective. *Cross Cultural Management* 16(3): 251–267.

Hoppe, M. H. 2004. Cross-cultural issues in the development of leaders. In *The Center for Creative Leadership: Handbook of leadership development*. 2nd ed. Ed. C. D. McCauley and E. Van Velsor, 331–360. San Francisco: Jossey-Bass.

Hopfensitz, A., and E. Reuben, E. 2009. The importance of emotions for the effectiveness of social punishment. *The Economic Journal* 119(540): 1534.

Houghton, J. D., and C. P. Neck. 2002. The revised self-leadership questionnaire: Testing a hierarchical factor structure for self-leadership. *Journal of Managerial Psychology* 17: 672–691.

Houghton, J. D., T. W. Bonham, C. P. Neck, and K. Singh. 2004. The relationship between self-leadership and personality: A comparison of hierarchical factor structures. *Journal of Managerial Psychology* 19: 427–454.

House, R. J. 1971. A path-goal theory of leader effectiveness. *Administrative Science Quarterly* 16: 321–339.

———. 1977. A 1976 theory of charismatic leadership. In *Leadership: The cutting edge*, ed. J. G. Hunt and L. L. Larson, 189–204. Carbondale: Southern Illinois University Press.

House, R. J., and G. Dessler. 1974. The path-goal theory of leadership: Some post hoc and a priori tests. In *Contingency approaches to leadership*, ed. J. G. Hunt and L. L. Larson, 29–55. Carbondale, IL: Southern Illinois University Press.

House, R. J., and A. C. Filley. 1971. Leadership style, hierarchical influence, and the satisfaction of subordinate role expectations: A test of Likert's influence proposition. *Journal of Applied Psychology* 55: 422–432.

House, R. J., P. J. Hanges, M. Javidan, P. W. Dorfman, and V. Gupta. 2004. *Culture, leadership and organizations: The GLOBE study of 62 countries.* Thousand Oaks, CA: Sage.

House, R. J., M. Javidan, P. W. Dorfman, and M. S. De Luque. 2006. A failure of scholarship: Response to George Graen's critique of GLOBE. *Academy of Management Perspectives* 20(4): 102–114.

House, R. J., M. Javidan, P. Hanges, and P. Dorfman. 2002. Understanding cultures and implicit leadership theories across the globe: An introduction to project GLOBE. *Journal of World Business* 37: 3–10.

House, R. J., and T. R. Mitchell. 1974. Path-goal theory of leadership. *Contemporary Business* (Fall): 81–98.

House, R. J., and B. Shamir. 1993. Toward the integration of transformational, charismatic and visionary leadership. In *Leadership theory and research: Perspective and directions*, ed. M. M. Chemers and R. Ayman, 81–107. New York: Academic Press.

Howard, D. 2006. A case study on management style. *Management Style,* May 28. http://www.associatedcontent.com/article/35077/management_style_pg2.html?cat=4 (accessed April 8, 2010).

Howell, J. M. 1988. Two faces of charisma: Socialized and personalized leadership in organizations. In *Charismatic leadership: The illusive factor in organizational effectiveness*, ed. J. Conger and R. Kanungo, 213–236. San Francisco: Jossey-Bass.

Howell, J. M., and B. J. Avolio. 1992. The ethics of charismatic leadership: Submission or liberation. *Academy of Management Executive* 6(2): 43–54.

Howell, J. P. 1997. "Substitutes for leadership: Their meaning and measurement"—an historical assessment. *The Leadership Quarterly* 8(2): 113–116.

Humphrey, R. H. 2002. The many faces of emotional leadership. *Leadership Quarterly* 13(5): 493–504.

Hunt, J. G. 1999. Transformation/charismatic leadership's transformation of the field: An historical essay. *The Leadership Quarterly* 10: 129–144.

Hunter, D. 2006. Leadership resilience and tolerance of ambiguity in crisis situations. *Business Review* 5(1): 44–50.

Hunter, E. M., M. J. Neubert, S. J. Perry, L. A. Witt, L. M. Penney, and E. Weinberger. 2013. Servant leaders inspire servant followers: Antecedents and outcomes for employees and the organization. *The Leadership Quarterly* 24: 316–331.

Huppke, R. 2013. Do emotions have a place in the office? *Chicago Tribune,* January 14. http://articles. chicagotribune.com/2013-01-14/business/ct-biz-0114-work-advice-huppke-20130114_1_emotional-intelligence-new-workplace-average-workplace (accessed October 12, 2013).

Hutchinson, L. R., and N. F. Skinner. 2007. Self-awareness and cognitive style: Relationships among adaptation-innovation, self-monitoring, and self-consciousness. *Social Behavior and Personality* 35: 551–560.

Ibarra, H. 1993. Personal networks of women and minorities in management: A conceptual framework. *Academy of Management Review* 18: 56–87.

IBM. 2009. World's best company for leaders. *CNNMoney.com.*

———. 2010. Global CEO study. http://www-03.ibm. com/press/us/en/pressrelease/31670.wss (accessed October 12, 2013).

Inside diversity structure at Sodexo, Johnson & Johnson, and Rockwell Automation. 2013. *Diversity Best Practices*, January 29. http://www. diversitybestpractices.com/news-articles/inside-diversity-structure-sodexo-johnson-johnson-and-rockwell-automation (accessed June 18, 2013).

Irving, J. A., and G. J. Longbotham. 2007. Team effectiveness and six essential servant leadership themes: A regression model based on the items of the organizational leadership assessment. *International Journal of Leadership Studies* 2: 98–113.

Jackson, E. 2012. The 7 reasons why 360 degree feedback programs fail. *Forbes,* August 17. http://www. forbes.com/sites/ericjackson/2012/08/17/the-7-reasons-why-360-degree-feedback-programs-fail/ (accessed August 5, 2013).

Jackson, E. M., and R. E. Johnson. 2012. When opposites do (and do not) attract: Interplay of leader and follower self-identities and its consequences for leader-member exchange. *The Leadership Quarterly* 23(3): 488–501.

Jagged Edge Story. 2013. http://www.jagged-edge-telluride.com/jagged-edge-story/ (accessed July 20, 2013).

James, W. 1880. Great men, great thoughts, and their environment. *Atlantic Monthly* 46: 441–459.

Janis, I. L. 1982. *Groupthink*, 2nd ed. Boston: Houghton Mifflin.

Jansen, K. J., and A. Kristof-Brown. 2006. Toward a multidimensional theory of person-environment fit. *Journal of Management Issues* 18: 193–212.

Javidan, M., and R. J. House. 2001. Cultural acumen for the global manager: Lessons from project GLOBE. *Organizational Dynamics* 29: 289–305.

Jawahar, I. M. 2001. Attitudes, self-monitoring, and appraisal behavior. *Journal of Applied Psychology* 86(5): 875–883.

Jenkins, W. O. 1947. A review of leadership studies with particular reference to military problems. *Psychological Bulletin* 44: 54–79.

Jensen, S. M., and F. Luthans. 2006. Entrepreneurs as authentic leaders: Impact on employees' attitudes. *Leadership and Organization Development Journal* 27: 646.

Jones, D. 2007. P&G CEO wields high expectation but no whip. *USA Today,* February 19.

Jones. 2009a. Avon's Andrea Jung: CEOs need to reinvent themselves. *USAToday,* June 15. http://www. usatoday.com/money/companies/management/advice/2009-06-14-jung-ceo-avon_N.htm (accessed March 24, 2010).

———. 2009b. 3M CEO George Buckly focuses on leadership training. *USAToday,* May 17. http://www. usatoday.com/money/companies/management/advice/2009-05-17-buckley-3m-leadership_N.htm (accessed April 21, 2010).

Jones, R. A., A. E. Rafferty, and M. A. Griffin. 2006. The executive coaching trend: Toward more flexible executives. *Leadership and Organizational Development Journal* 27: 583.

Jones, S. 1998. Emergency surgery for MedPartners. *Business Week*, March 9, 81.

Joo, B. K. 2005. Executive coaching: A conceptual framework from an integrative review of practice and research. *Human Resource Development Review* 4(4): 462–488.

Joo, B. K., and K. J. Ready. 2012. Career satisfaction: The influences of proactive personality, performance goal orientation, organizational learning culture, and leader-member exchange quality. *Career Development International* 17(3): 276.

Juarez, V., S. Childress, and E. Hoffman. 2005. 12 women leaders on life. *Newsweek/MSNBC.com.* http://www.msnbc.msn.com/id/9712114/site/newsweek/page/0/ (accessed July 24, 2007).

Judge, P. C. 2001. Suddenly the world changes. *Fast Company*, December, 131–132.

Judge, T. A., and B. A. Livingston. 2008. Is the gap more than gender? A longitudinal analysis of gender, gender role orientation and earnings. *Journal of Applied Psychology* 93(5): 994–1012.

Judge, T. A., R. F. Piccolo, and R. Ilies. 2004. The forgotten ones? The validity of consideration and initiation of structure in leadership research. *Journal of Applied Psychology* 89(1): 36–51.

Judge, T. A., R. F. Piccolo, and T. Kosalka. 2009. The bright and dark sides of leader traits: A review and theoretical extension of the leader trait paradigm. *The Leadership Quarterly* 20: 855–875.

Judson, A. S. 1991. *Changing behavior in organizations: Minimizing resistance to change.* Cambridge, MA: Basil Blackwell.

Jung, D. I., B. M. Bass, and J. Sosik. 1995. Collectivism and transformational leadership. *Journal of Management Inquiry* 2: 3–18.

Kabasakal, H., and M. Bodur. 2004. Human orientation in societies, organizations, and leaders attributes. In *Culture, leadership, and organizations: The GLOBE study of 62 countries*, ed. R. J. House, P. J. Hanges, M. Javidan, P. W. Dorfman, and V. Gupta, 564–601. Thousand Oaks, CA: Sage.

Kacmar, K. M., L. A. Witt, S. Zivnuska, and S. M. Gully. 2003. The interactive effect of leader-member exchange and communication frequency on performance ratings. *Journal of Applied Psychology* 88: 764–772.

Kacmar, K. M., S. Zivnuska, and C. D. White. 2007. Control and exchange: The impact of work environment on the work effort of low relationship quality employees. *The Leadership Quarterly* 18: 69–84.

Kaiser, R. B., and R. B. Kaplan. 2006. The deeper work of executive development: Outgrowing sensitivities. *Academy of Management Learning and Education* 5: 463–483.

Kalshoven, K., Den Hartog, D. N., and A. H. B. De Hoogh. 2011. Ethical leadership at work questionnaire (ELW): Development and validation of a multidimensional measure. *Leadership Quarterly* 22(1): 51–69.

Kang, H. R., H. D. Yang, and C. Rowley. 2006. Factors in team effectiveness: Cognitive and demographic similarities of software development team members. *Human Relations* 59: 1681–1711.

Kant, L., A. Skogstad, T. Torsheim, and S. Einarsen. 2013. Beware the angry leader: Trait anger and trait anxiety as predictors of petty tyranny. *The Leadership Quarterly* 24: 106–124.

Kanter, R. M., and R. I. Corn. 1993. Do cultural differences make a business difference? Contextual factors affecting cross-cultural relationship success. *Journal of Management Development* 13(2): 5–23.

Karakitapoğlu-Aygün, Z, and L. Gumusluoglu. 2012. The bright and dark sides of leadership: Transformational vs. non-transformational leadership in a non-Western context. *Leadership* 9(1): 107–133.

Kark, R., B. Shamir, and G. Chen. 2003. The two faces of transformational leadership: Empowerment and dependency. *Journal of Applied Psychology* 88: 246–255.

Kark, R., R. Waismel-Manor, and B. Shamir. 2012. Does valuing androgyny and femininity lead to a female advantage? The relationship between gender-role, transformational leadership and identification. *The Leadership Quarterly* 23: 620–640.

Karkoulian, S., L. Messarra, and M. Sidani. 2009. Correlates of the bases of power and the Big Five personality traits: An empirical investigation. *Journal of Organizational Culture, Communications, and Conflict* 13(2): 71–82.

Katz, D., and R. L. Kahn. 1966. *The social psychology of organization.* New York: John Wiley.

Katz, N. 2001. Sports teams as a model for workplace teams: Lessons and liabilities. *Academy of Management Executive* 15(3): 56–67.

Katzenbach, J. R., and D. K. Smith. 2003. *The wisdom of teams: Creating the high-performance organization*. New York: Harper Business.

Kaufman, G., and P. Uhlenberg. 2000. The influence of parenthood on the work effort of married men and women. *Social Forces* 78: 931–949.

Kegan, R., and L. L. Lahey. 2001. *How the way we talk can change the way we work: Seven languages for transformation*. San Francisco: Jossey-Bass.

Keinan, G., and M. Koren. 2002. Team up type As and Bs: The effects of group composition on performance and satisfaction. *Applied Psychology: An International Review* 51(3): 425–445.

Kellerman, B. 2004. *Bad leadership: What it is, how it happens, why it matters*. Boston: Harvard Business School Press.

Kelloway, E. K., H. Wiegand, M. C. McKee, and H. Das. 2013. Positive leadership and employee well-being. *Journal of Leadership & Organizational Studies* 20(1): 107–117.

Keltner, D., and R. J. Robinson. 1996. Extremism, power and the imagined basis of social conflict. *Current Directions in Psychological Science* 5(4): 101–105.

Kempster, S. 2006. Leadership learning through lived experience: A process of apprenticeship? *Journal of Management and Organization* 12: 4–22.

Kennedy, J. C. 2002. Leadership in Malaysia. *Academy of Management Executive* 16(3): 15–26.

Kennedy, J. K., Jr. 1982. Middle LPC leaders and the contingency model of leadership effectiveness. *Organizational Behavior and Human Performance* 30: 1–14.

Kernis, M. H. 2003. Toward a conceptualization of optimal self-esteem. *Psychological Inquiry* 14: 1–26.

Kernis, M. H., and B. M. Goldman. 2005. From thought and experience to behavior and interpersonal relationships: A multicomponent conceptualization of authenticity. In *On building, defending, and regulating the self: A psychological perspective*, ed. A. Tesser, J. V. Wood, and D. A. Stapel, 31–52. New York: Psychology Press.

Kerr, J., and J. W. Slocum. 1987. Managing corporate culture through reward systems. *Academy of Management Executive* 1: 99–108.

Kerr, S., and J. M. Jermier. 1978. Substitutes for leadership: Their meaning and measurement. *Organizational Behavior and Human Performance* 22: 395–403.

Kessler, J. 2010. 6 CEOs share their biggest regrets. Inc.com. http:www.inc.comss6-ceos-share-their-biggest-regrets#0 (accessed April 16, 2010).

Kets de Vries, M. F. R. 1993. *Leaders, fools, and imposters: Essays on the psychology of leadership*. San Francisco: Jossey-Bass.

Kets de Vries, M. F. R., and D. Miller. 1986. Personality, culture, and organizations. *Academy of Management Review* 11: 266–279.

Khandwalla, P. N. 1976. Some top management styles, their context, and performance. *Organization and Administrative Science* 74: 21–52.

Kharif, O. 2003. Anne Mulcahy has Xerox by the horns. *Business Week*, May 29. http:www.businessweek.comtechnologycontentmay2003tc20030529_1642_tc111.htm?chansearch (accessed September 8, 2007).

Kickul, J., S. W. Lester, and W. Belgio. 2004. Attitudinal and behavioral outcomes of psychological contract breach: A cross-cultural comparison of the United States and Hong Kong Chinese. *International Journal of Cross-Cultural Management* 4(2): 229–252.

Kim, T. Y., A. H. Y. Hon, and M. J. Crant. 2009. Proactive personality, employee creativity, and newcomer outcomes: A longitudinal study. *Journal of Business Psychology* 24(1): 93–103.

Kipnis, D., S. M. Schmidt, and I. Wilkinson. 1980. Why do I like thee: Is it your performance or my orders? *Journal of Applied Psychology* 66: 324–328.

Kirkpatrick, S. A., and E. A. Locke. 1991. Leadership: Do traits matter? *Academy of Management Executive* 5(2): 48–60.

Kisfalvi, V., and P. Pitcher. 2003. Doing what feels right: The influence of CEO character and emotion on top management team dynamics. *Journal of Management Inquiry* 12: 42–66.

Kish-Gephart, J., D. Harrison, and L. Treviño. 2010. Bad apples, bad cases, and bad barrels: Meta-analytic evidence about sources of unethical decisions at work. *Journal of Applied Psychology* 95: 1–31.

Kiviat, B. 2007. A whole new crew. *Time-CNN*, March 15. http://www.time.com/time/magazine/article/ 0,9171,1599694,00.html (accessed July 25, 2007).

Klein, H. J., and J. S. Kim. 1998. A field study of the influence of situational constraints, leader-member exchange, and goal commitment on performance. *Academy of Management Journal* 41: 88–95.

Klidas, A., P. T. van den Berg, and C. P. M. Wilderom. 2007. Managing employee empowerment in luxury hotels in Europe. *International Journal of Service Industry Management* 18: 70–83.

Klotz, I. 2013. SpaceX dragon capsule returns from International Space Station. *NBCNews.com,* March 26. http://www.nbcnews.com/id/51336158/ns/technology_and_science-space/t/spacex-dragon-capsule-returns-international-space-station/#.Ue1-ihZLzow (accessed July 22, 2013).

Koman, E. S., and S. B. Wolff. 2008. Emotional intelligence competencies in the team and team leader. *Journal of Management Development* 27(1): 55–75.

Konrad, A. M. 2006. Engaging employees through high-involvement work practices. *Ivey Business Journal* (March–April): 1–6.

Kotin, J., and M. Sharaf. 1976. Management succession and administrative style. *Psychiatry* 30: 237–248.

Kotter, J. P. 1985. *Power and influence.* New York: Free Press.

_____. 1990. *A force for change: How leadership differs from management.* New York: Free Press.

_____. 1996. *Leading change.* Boston: Harvard Business School Press.

Kouzes, J. M., and B. Z. Posner. 1993. *Credibility: How leaders gain and lose it, why people demand it.* San Francisco: Jossey-Bass.

_____. 2003. *Encouraging the heart: A leader's guide to rewarding and recognizing others.* San Francisco: Jossey-Bass.

_____. 2012. *The leadership challenge: How to get extraordinary things done in organizations.* San Francisco: Jossey-Bass.

Kraemer, H. 2003. Keeping it simple. *Health Forum Journal* (Summer): 16–20.

Krech, D., and R. S. Crutchfield. 1948. *Theory and problems of social psychology.* New York: McGraw-Hill.

Kroll, L., and A. Fass. 2007. The world's billionaires. *Forbes.com*, March 8. http://www.forbes.com/2007/03/07/billionaires-worlds-richest_07billionaires_cz_lk_af_0308billie_land.html (accessed August 6, 2007).

Kujala, J., and T. Pietilainen. 2007. Developing moral principles and scenarios in the light of diversity: An extension to the multidimensional ethics scale. *Journal of Business Ethics* 70(2): 141–150.

Kupfer, A. 1998. The real king of the Internet. *Fortune* 138(5): 84–93.

Kurtz, D. L., L. E. Boone, and C. P. Fleenor. 1989. *CEO: Who gets to the top in America?* East Lansing: Michigan State University Press.

Kurtz, R. 2004. Knowing when to say when. *Inc.,* July, 65–71.

Kuvass, B., R. Buch, A. Dysvik, and T. Haerem. 2012. Economic and social leader-member exchange relationship and follower performance. *The Leadership Quarterly* 23(5): 756–765.

LaBarre, P. 1998. These leaders are having a moment. *Fast Company*, September, 86–88.

_____. 2001. Marcus Buckingham thinks your boss has an attitude problem. *Fast Company*, August, 88–98.

Labor force—Gender Statsitics. 2009. *Encyclopedia of the Nations.* http://www.nationsencyclopedia.com/WorldStats/Gender-statistics-labor-force-female2.html (accessed May 30, 2013).

Labor participation rate. 2013. *The World Bank.* http://data.worldbank.org/indicator/SL.TLF.CACT.FE.ZS (accessed June 24, 2013).

Ladkin, D., and S. S. Taylor. 2010 Enacting the "true self": Towards a theory of embodied authentic leadership. *The Leadership Quarterly* 21: 64–74.

LaGuarde, C. 2010. Women, power, and the challenge of financial crisis. *The New York Times*, May 10. http://www.nytimes.com/2010/05/11/opinion/11iht-edlagarde.html?_r=1 (accessed June 20, 2013).

Lam, W., S. Huang, and E. Snape. 2007. Feedback seeking behavior and leader-member exchange: Do supervisor-attributed motives matter? *Academy of Management Journal* 50(2): 348–363.

Lammers, J., and D. A. Stapel. 2009. How power influences moral thinking. *Journal of Personality and Social Psychology* 97(2): 279–289.

Laporte, N. 2013. Most creative people 2013: 8. Bryan Cranston. *Fast Company,* May 13. http://www.fastcompany.com/3009191/most-creative-people-2013/8-bryan-cranston (accessed August 3, 2013).

Larcker, D. F., and B. Tayan. 2012. Is a powerful CEO good or bad for shareholders. *Stanford Closer Look Series,* November 13. http://www.gsb.stanford.edu/sites/default/files/.../28_CEOpower_0.pdf (accessed July 15, 2013).

Lashinksly, A. 2009. Oracle's enforcer—Safra Catz. *CNNMoney.com.* October 10. http://money.cnn.com/2009/09/08/technology/oracle_safra_catz.fortune/index.htm (accessed April 8, 2010).

———. 2010. The Larry, Mark and Safra show at Oracle. *CNN Money,* September 7. http://tech.fortune.cnn.com/2010/09/07/the-larry-ellison-mark-hurd-and-safra-catz-show-at-oracle/ (accessed July 20, 2013).

Laurent, A. 1983. The cultural diversity of Western conceptions of management. *International Studies of Management and Organizations* 13(1–2): 75–96.

Lawler, E. E., III, and S. A. Mohrman. 1987. Quality circles: After the honeymoon. *Organizational Dynamics* 15(Spring): 42–54.

Lawler, E. E., III, S. A. Mohrman, and G. E. Ledford Jr. 1995. *Creating high performance organizations: Practices and results of employee involvement and total quality management in* Fortune *1000 companies.* San Francisco: Jossey-Bass.

Lawrence, R. L., D. A. Deagen, and A. Debbie. 2001. Choosing public participation methods for natural resources: A context specific guide. *Society and Natural Resources* 14: 57–872.

Lazarus, S. 2010. Authenticity, generosity, and passion in leadership: Womensphere. *Vimeo.* http://vimeo.com/18978904 (accessed July 20, 2013).

Leithwood, K., and J. Sun. 2012. The nature and effects of transformational school leadership: A meta-analytic review of unpublished research. *Educational Administration Quarterly* 48(3): 387–423.

Lennox, R. D., and R. N. Wolfe. 1984. Revision of the self-monitoring scale. *Journal of Personality and Social Psychology* 46(6): 1349–1364.

Lepsinger, R., and A. D. Lucia. 1997. *The art and science of 360 degree feedback.* San Francisco: Jossey-Bass/Pfeiffer.

Levay, C. 2010. Charismatic leadership in resistance to change. *The Leadership Quarterly* 21: 127–143.

Lewin, K. 1951. *Field theory in social science.* New York: Harper and Row.

Lewin, K., and R. Lippit. 1938. An experimental approach to the study of autocracy and democracy: A preliminary note. *Sociometry* 1: 292–300.

Lewin, K., R. Lippit, and R. K. White. 1939. Patterns of aggressive behavior in experimentally created social climates. *Journal of Social Psychology* 10: 271–301.

Lewis, M. 2010. *The big short.* London: Allen Lane.

Li, N., J. Liang, and J. M. Crant. 2010. The role of proactive personality in job satisfaction and organizational citizenship behavior: A relational perspective. *Journal of Applied Psychology* (March): 395–404.

Liden, R. C., and G. Graen. 1980. Generalizability of the vertical dyad linkage model of leadership. *Academy of Management Journal* 23: 451–465.

Lieberson, S., and J. F. O'Connor. 1972. Leadership and organization performance: A study of large corporations. *American Sociological Review* 37(2): 117–130.

Ling, Y., Z. Simsek, M. H. Lubatkin, J. F. Veiga. 2008. The impact of transformational CEOs on the performance of small-to-medium sized firms: Does organization context matter? *Journal of Applied Psychology* 93(4): 923–934.

Litzky, B. E., K. A. Eddleston, and D. L. Kidder. 2006. The good, the bad, and the misguided: How managers inadvertently encourage deviant behaviors. *Academy of Management Perspectives* 20(1): 91–103.

Livers, A. B., and K. A. Caver. 2004. Leader development across race. In *The Center for Creative Leadership: Handbook of leadership development.* 2nd ed. Ed. C. D. McCauley and E. Van Velsor, 304–330. San Francisco: Jossey-Bass.

London, M. 2002. *Leadership development: Paths to self-insight and professional growth.* Mahwah, NJ: Lawrence Erlbaum.

London, M., and T. J. Maurer. 2004. Leadership development: A diagnostic model for continuous learning in dynamic organizations. In *The nature of leadership*, ed. J. Antonakis, A. T. Cianciolo, and R. J. Sternberg, 222–245. Thousand Oaks, CA: Sage.

Lopez-Zafra, E., Garcia-Rentamero, R., and M. P. B. Martos. 2012. The relationship between transformational leadership and emotional intelligence from a gendered approach. *The Psychological Record* 62: 97–114.

Lovallo, D., and D. Kahneman. 2003. Delusions of success: How optimism undermines executive decisions. *Harvard Business Review,* July. http://hbr.org/2003/07/delusions-of-success-how-optimism-undermines-executives-decisions/ar/1 (accessed July 31, 2013).

Love, D. 2013. Former employee: "At Apple, they really are after you." *Business Insider,* January 9. http://www.businessinsider.com/apple-corporate-culture-2013-1 (accessed October 5, 2013).

Lubin, R. 2002. Long-term organizational impact of destructively narcissistic managers. *Academy of Management Executive* 16(1): 127–138.

Luthans, F. 1989. Successfull vs. effective real managers. *Academy of Management Executive* 2(2): 127–132.

Luthans, F., and B. J. Avolio. 2003. Authentic leadership: A positive developmental approach. In *Positive organizational scholarship*, ed. K. S. Cameron, J. E. Dutton, and R. E. Quinn, 241–261. San Francisco: Barrett-Koehler.

Maciejovsky, B., M. Sutter, D. V. Bedescu, and P. Bernau. 2013. Teams make you smarter: How exposure to teams improves individual decisions in probability and reasoning tasks. *Management Science* 59: 1255–1270.

Mackey, A. 2008. The effect of CEOs on firm performance. *Strategic Management Journal* 29(12): 1357–1367.

Magee, J. C., D. H. Gruenfeld, D. J. Keltner, and A. D. Galinsky. 2005. Leadership and the psychology of power. In *The psychology of leadership: New perspectives and research*, ed. D. M. Messick and R. M. Kramer, 275–293. Mahwah, NJ: Lawrence Erlbaum.

Magee, J. C., and A. D. Galinsky. 2008. Social hierarchy: The self-reinforcing nature of power and status. *The Academy of Management Annals* 2(1): 351–398.

Main, C. 2013. Solvency II costs: Compliance. *Bloomberg,* April 30. http://www.bloomberg.com/news/2013-05-01/ceo-worker-pay-ratio-boe-policy-solvency-ii-costs-compliance.html (accessed July 20, 2013).

Malekzadeh, A. 1995. How leaders manage the six strategic forces. Unpublished manuscript.

Manz, C. C., and H. P. Sims, Jr. 1991. Superleadership: Beyond the myth of heroic leadership. *Organizational Dynamics* 19(4): 18–35.

Marchetti, M. 2005. Stepping in for Superman. *Fast Company*, September. http://www.fastcompany.com/magazine/98/open_playbook.html (accessed August 12, 2007).

Marsh, H. W., G. E. Richards, and J. Barnes. 1987. A long-term follow-up of the effects of participation in an Outward Bound program. *Personality and Social Psychology Bulletin* 12: 475–492.

Marshall, L. 2009. Leadership is a choice: A conversation with Barbara Waugh of H-P's World E-Inclusion. http://www.linkageinc.com/thinking/linkageleader/Documents/Lisa_Marshall_ Leadership_Is_a_Choice_1005.pdf (accessed January 4, 2010).

Marshall, R., J. Talbott, and D. Bukovinsky. 2006. Employee empowerment works at small companies, too. *Strategic Finance* 88(3): 34–39.

Marsick, V. J., E. Turner, and L. Cederholm. 1989. International as a team. *Management Review* 78(3): 46–49.

Martin, R. 2013. Breaking into the business world with "women-friendly" model. *NPR-Weekend Edition Sunday,* June 23. http://www.npr.org/2013/06/23/194683800/breaking-into-the-business-world-with-woman-friendly-model (accessed June 24, 2013).

Martinez, S., and P. W. Dorfman. 1998. The Mexican entrepreneur: An ethnographic study of the Mexican empressario. *International Studies in Management and Organizations* 28(Summer): 97–123.

Martinson, L. 2011. *Creativity Research Journal* 23(3): 185–202.

Maruca, R. F. 2001. Masters of disaster. *Fast Company*, April, 81–96.

Massey, M. E. 1986. *The past: What you are is where you were when*. Schaumburg, IL: Video Publishing House.

Mathisen, G. E. 2012. Creative leaders promote creative organizations. *International Journal of Manpower* 33(4): 367–382.

Mathur, A., Y. Zhang, and J. P. Meelankavil. 2001. Critical managerial motivational factors: A cross-cultural analysis of four culturally divergent countries. *International Journal of Cross-Cultural Management* 1(2): 251–267.

Matviuk, S. 2007. A study of leadership prototypes in Colombia. *Business Review* 7: 14–19.

Maull, S. 2005. Tyco execs' trial to start with tight focus. *Arizona Republic*, January 18, D5.

Maune, D. J. 1999. The glass ceiling and the glass escalator: Occupational segregation and race and sex differences in managerial promotions. *Work and Occupations* 26: 483–509.

Mayo, A., and N. Nohria. 2006. *Paths to power: How insiders and outsiders shaped American business leadership*. Boston: Harvard Business School Publishing Corporation.

McCall, M. W., and M. M. Lombardo. 1978. *Leadership: Where else can we go?* Durham, NC: Duke University Press.

_____. 1983. Off the track: Why and how successful executives get derailed. Technical Report No. 21. Greensboro, NC: Center for Creative Leadership.

McCauley, C. D., and C. A. Douglas. 2004. Developmental relationships. In *The Center for Creative Leadership: Handbook of leadership development*. 2nd ed. Ed. C. D. McCauley and E. Van Velsor, 85–115. San Francisco: Jossey-Bass.

McCauley, C. D., and E. Van Velsor, eds. 2004. *The Center for Creative Leadership: Handbook of leadership development*. 2nd ed. San Francisco: Jossey-Bass.

McCauley, L. 2000. Unit of one: Don't burn out. *Fast Company*, May, 101–132.

McFarland, K. R. 2007. Lesson from the anti-mentor. *Business Week*, June 11, 86.

McGregor, J. 2004. Rocky Mountain High. *Fast Company*, July, 59–63. http://www.fastcompany.com/magazine/92/clear-leader-extra.html (accessed June 18, 2007), http://www.

fastcompany.com/magazine/91/gospels.html (accessed June 19, 2007).

McGregor, J. 2005. Competing on culture. *Fast Company*, March. http://www.fastcompany.com/magazine/92/clear-leader-extra.html (accessed June 18, 2007).

_____. 2007. The 25 most innovative companies: The leaders in nurturing culture of creativity. *Business Week*, May 14, 52.

_____. 2011. Coach K's leadership ABCs. *The Washington Post*, November 17. http://www.washingtonpost.com/blogs/post-leadership/post/coach-ks-leadership-abcs/2011/04/01/IQAkIpPUN_blog.html (accessed August 5, 2013).

McKinsey. 2010. *What successful transformations share: McKinsey global survey results*, March. http://www.mckinseyquarterly.com/Organization/Change_Management/What_successful_transformations_share_McKinsey_Global_Survey_results_2550 (accessed April 21, 2010).

McKinsey. 2013. *Transformational change*. http://www.mckinsey.com/client_service/organization/expertise/transformational_change (accessed August 1, 2013).

McKinsey conversation with global leaders: John Chambers of Cisco. 2009. *McKinsey Quarterly*, July. http://www.mckinsey.com/insights/high_tech_telecoms_internet/mckinsey_conversations_with_global_leaders_john_chambers_of_cisco (accessed July 20, 2013).

McMurray, A. J., M. Islam, J. C. Sarros, and A. Pirola-Merlo. 2012. The impact of leadership on work-group climate and performance in a non-profit organization. *Leadership & Organizational Development Journal* 33(6): 522–549.

Meindl, J. R., and S. B. Ehrlick. 1987. The romance of leadership and the evaluation of organizational performance. *Academy of Management Journal* 30: 90–109.

Meister, J. C. 2006. Grading executive education. *Workforce Management*, December 11, 1, 27.

Mello, A. S., and M. E. Ruckes. 2006. Team composition. *Journal of Business* 79(3): 1019–1039.

Menon, S. T. 2001. Employee empowerment: An integrative psychological approach. *Applied Psychology: An International Review* 50(1): 153–180.

Menon, S. T., and L. C. Hartmann. 2002. Generalizability of Menon's empowerment scale: Replication and extension with Australian data. *International Journal of Cross-Cultural Management* 2(2): 137–153.

Meyer, D. 2006. *Setting the table: The power of hospitality in restaurants, business, and life.* New York: HarperCollins.

Meyerson, M. 2010. Everything I thought I knew about leadership is wrong: Reinventing the leader in you. *Fast Company.* http://www.fastcompany.com/events/realtime/monterey/mentors/mmeyerson.html (accessed January 20, 2010).

Miller, D. M. 1987. The genesis of configuration. *Academy of Management Review* 12: 686–701.

Miller, D. M., and C. Droge. 1986. Psychological and traditional determinants of structure. *Administrative Science Quarterly* 31: 539–560.

Miller, D. M., and P. H. Freisen. 1982. Structural change and performance: Quantum vs. piecemeal-incremental approaches. *Academy of Management Journal* 25: 867–892.

Miller, D. M., E. R. Lack, and S. Asroff. 1985. Preference for control and the coronary-prone behavior pattern: "I'd rather do it myself." *Journal of Personality and Social Psychology* 49: 492–499.

Miner, J. B., and N. R. Smith. 1982. Decline and stabilization of managerial motivation over a 20-year period. *Journal of Applied Psychology* 67 (June): 298–305.

Minton-Eversole, C. 2012. Virtual teams used most by global organizations, survey says. *Society for Human Resource Management,* July 19. http://www.shrm.org/hrdisciplines/orgempdev/articles/Pages/VirtualTeamsUsedMostbyGlobalOrganizations,SurveySays.aspx (accessed July 22, 2013).

Mintzberg, H. 1973. *The nature of managerial work.* New York: Harper and Row.

_____. 2009. The best leadership is good management. *Business Week.* August 6. http://www.businessweek.com/magazine/content/09_33/b4143068890733.htm (accessed January 18, 2010).

Mintzberg, H., J. B. Quinn, and J. Voyer. 1995. *The strategy process.* Englewood Cliffs, NJ: Prentice Hall.

Misangyi, V. F., G. R. Weaver, and H. Elms. 2008. Ending corruption: the interplay among institutional logics, resources, and institutional entrepreneurs. *Academy of Management Review* 33(3): 750–770.

Mischel, W. 1973. Towards a cognitive social learning reconceptualization of personality. *Psychological Review* 80: 252–283.

Misumi, J., and M. F. Peterson. 1985. The performance-maintenance (PM) theory of leadership: Review of a Japanese research program. *Administrative Science Quarterly* 30: 198–223.

Mittal, R., and P. W. Dorfman. 2012. Servant leadership across cultures. *Journal of World Business* 47: 555–570.

Montesino, M. 2003. Leadership/followership between people in a developed and a developing country: The case of Dominicans in NYC and the Dominicans on the island. *Journal of Leadership and Organizational Studies* 10: 82–93.

Morf, C. C., and F. Rhodewalt. 2001. Unraveling the paradoxes of narcissism: A dynamic self-regulatory processing model. *Personality Inquiry* 12: 177–196.

Morrison, A. M., and M. A. Von Glinow. 1990. Women and minorities in management. *American Psychologist* 45: 200–208.

Mosadegh-Rad, A. M., and M. H. Yarmohammadian. 2006. A study of relationship between managers' leadership style and employees' job satisfaction. *Leadership in Health Service* 19(2): 11–28.

Moshavi, D., F. W. Brown, and N. G. Dodd. 2003. Leader self-awareness and its relationship to subordinate attitudes and performance. *Leadership and Organizational Development Journal* 24(7–8): 407–418.

Mount, I. 2004. Be fast, be frugal, be right. *Inc.,* January, 64–70.

Muio, A. 1999. Mint condition. *Fast Company,* December, 330.

Mumford, M. D., and B. Licuanan. 2004. Leading for innovation: Conclusions, issues, and directions. *The Leadership Quarterly* 15: 163–171.

Mumford, M. D., S. J. Zaccaro, M. S. Connelly, and M. A. Marks. 2000a. Leadership skills: Conclusions and future directions. *The Leadership Quarterly* 11: 155–170.

Mumford, M. D., S. J. Zaccaro, F. D. Harding, T. O. Jacobs, and E. A. Fleishman. 2000b. Leadership skills for a changing world: Solving complex problems. *The Leadership Quarterly* 11: 11–35.

Munk, N. 1998. Gap gets it. *Fortune* 138(3): 68–82.

Murrill, A. 2007. A friend to Kellogg and Northwestern, Tootsie Roll president Ellen Gordon creates value in the classroom and boardroom. *Kellogg World* (Summer). http://www.kellogg.northwestern.edu/kwo/sum07/features/gordon.htm (accessed April 8, 2010).

Myatt, D., and C. Wallace. 2008. When does one bad apple spoil the barrel? An evolutionary analysis of collective action. *The Review of Economic Studies* 75(2): 499–527.

Nahavandi, A. 1993. Integrating leadership and strategic management in organizational theory. *Canadian Journal of Administrative Sciences* 10(4): 297–307.

———. 2012. *Ancient leadership wisdom.* Shelbyville, KY: Wasteland Press.

Nahavandi, A., and E. Aranda. 1994. Restructuring teams for the re-engineered organization. *Academy of Management Executive* 8(4): 58–68.

Nahavandi, A., and A. R. Malekzadeh. 1988. Acculturation in mergers and acquisitions. *Academy of Management Review* 13: 79–90.

———. 1993a. Leader style in strategy and organizational performance: An integrative framework. *Journal of Management Studies* 30(3): 405–425.

———. 1993b. *Organizational culture in the management of mergers.* New York: Quorum Books.

———. 1999. *Organizational behavior: The person-organization fit.* Upper Saddle River, NJ: Prentice Hall.

Nahavandi, A., P. J. Mizzi, and A. R. Malekzadeh. 1992. Executives' type A personality as a determinant of environmental perception and firm strategy. *Journal of Social Psychology* 13(1): 59–68.

Nahrgang, J. D., F. P. Morgeson, and R. Ilies. 2009. The development of leader–member exchanges: Exploring how personality and performance influence leader and member relationships over time. *Organizational Behavior and Human Decision Processes* 109: 256–266.

National Center for Charitable Statistics. 2010. http://nccsdataweb.urban.org/PubApps/profile1.php (accessed July 20, 2013).

Neck, C., and C. C. Manz. 2012. *Mastering self-leadership: Empowering yourself for personal excellence.* 6th ed. Upper Saddle River, NJ: Prentice Hall.

Neider, L. L., and C. A. Schriesheim. 2011. The authentic leadership inventory (ALI): Development and empirical tests. *The Leadership Quarterly* 22(6): 1146–1164.

Neiminen, L. R. G., R. Smerek, L. Kotrba, and D. Denison. 2013. What does executive leadership coaching intervention add beyond facilitiated multisource feedback? Effect on leader self-ratings and perceived effectiveness. *Human Resource Development Quarterly* 24(2): 145–176.

Newstetter, W. I., M. J. Feldstein, and T. M. Newcomb. 1938. *Group adjustment.* Cleveland, OH: Western Reserve University Press.

Ng, E. S., and G. T. Sears. 2012. CEO leadership styles and the implementation of organizational diversity practices: Moderating effects of social values and age. *Journal of Business Ethics* 105: 41–52.

Ng, K. Y., C. S. -K. Koh, and H. -C. Goh. 2008. The heart of the servant leader: Leader's motivation-to-serve and its impact on LMX and subordinates' extra role behavior. In *Knowledge corporation-complex creative destruction*, ed. G. B. Graen and J. A. Graen, 125–144. Charlotte, NC: Information Age.

Nocks, J. 2007. Executive coaching: Who needs it? *Physician Executive* (March–April): 46–48.

Nohe, C., B. Michaelis, J. I. Menges, Z. Zhang, and K. Sonntag. 2013. Charisma and organizational change: A multilevel study of perceived charisma, commitment to change, and team performance. *The Leadership Quarterly* 24: 378–389.

Norman, W. T. 1963. Toward an adequate taxonomy of personality attributes: Replicated factor structure in peer nomination personality ratings. *Journal of Abnormal and Social Psychology* 66: 547–583.

Obama's inaugural speech. 2009. *CNNPolitics.com,* January 20. http://www.cnn.com/2009/POLITICS/01/20/obama.politics/index.html (accessed March 25, 2010).

O'Connor, K. 2012. 9 ways great companies organize their teams for success. *Fast Company,* August 21. http://www.fastcompany.com/3000584/9-ways-great-companies-organize-their-teams-success?utm_source=feedburner&utm_medium=feed&utm_campaign=Feed:+fastcompany/headlines+ (Fast+Company) (accessed July 22, 2013).

Ohlott, P. J. 2003. Answering the call: Job assignments that grow leaders. *Leadership in Action* 23(5): 19–21.

Ones, D. S., and C. Viswesvaran. 1999. Relative importance of personality dimensions of expatriate selection: A policy capturing study. *Human Performance* 12(3–4): 275–294.

O'Reilly, C. A., D. F. Caldwell, J. A. Chatman, M. Lapiz, and W. Self. 2010. How leadership matters: The effects of leaders' alignment on strategy implementation. *The Leadership Quarterly* 21: 104–113.

O'Reilly, C. A., III, and B. G. M. Main. 2007. Setting the CEO's pay: It's more than simple economics. *Organizational Dynamics* 36: 1–12.

Osborn, K. A., B. C. Irwin, N. J. Nikilaus, and D. L. Feltz. 2012. The Kohler effect: Motivation gains and losses in real sports groups. *Sport, Exercises, and Performance Psychology* 1(4): 242–253.

Osland, J. S., Bird, A., Delano, J., and M. Jacob. 2000. Beyond sophisticated stereotyping: Culture sensemaking in context. *Academy of Management Executive* 14(1): 65–79.

O'Toole, J. 2008. Obama vs. Clinton: Leadership styles. *Business Week*, February 8. http://www.businessweek.com/managing/content/feb2008/ca2008028_331189.htm (accessed January 20, 2010).

Ott, J. S., and Dicke, L. A. eds. 2012. *The nature of the nonprofit sector.* 2nd ed. Boulder, CO: Westview Press.

Overholt, A. 2001. Unit of one: Open to women. *Fast Company*, August, 66.

———. 2002. The art of multitasking. *Fast Company*, October, 118–125.

———. 2005. Jumpstart. *Fast Company*, January, 55.

Padilla, A., Hogan, R., and R. B. Kaiser. 2007. The toxic triangle: Destructive leaders, susceptible followers, and conducive environments. *The Leadership Quarterly* 18: 176–194.

Pagliarini, R. 2011. Top 10 professional life coaching myths. *CBS-Money Watch,* December 20. http://www.cbsnews.com/8301-505125_162-57345386/top-10-professional-life-coaching-myths/?pageNum=4 (accessed August 5, 2013).

Parker, C. P. 1999. The impact of leaders' implicit theory of employee participation on tests of the Vroom-Yetton model. *Journal of Social Behavior and Personality* 14(1): 45–62.

Parker, P., Hall, D. T., and K. E. Kram. 2008. Peer coaching: A relational process for accelerating career learning. *Academy of Management Learning and Education* 7(40): 487–503.

Pattison, K. 2010. How Herman Miller has designed employee loyalty. *FastCompany,* September 22. http://www.fastcompany.com/1689839/how-herman-miller-has-designed-employee-loyalty (accessed October 5, 2013).

Paulhus, D. L., and K. M. Williams. 2002. The dark triad of personality: Narcissism, Machiavellianism, and psychopathy. *Journal of Research in Personality* 36: 556–563.

Pawar, B. S., and K. K. Eastman. 1997. The nature and implications of contextual influences on transformational leadership: A conceptual examination. *Academy of Management Review* 22: 80–109.

The Pay at the Top. 2010. *The New York Times,* April 3. http://projects.nytimes.com/executive_compensation (accessed April 8, 2010).

Pearce, C. L., and C. C. Manz. 2011. Leadership centrality and corporate social ir-responsibility (CSIR): The potential ameliorating effects of self and shared leadership on CSIR. *Journal of Business Ehtics* 102: 563–579.

Pelled, L. H., and K. R. Xin. 1997. Birds of a feather: Leader-member demographic similarity and organizational attachment in Mexico. *The Leadership Quarterly* 8: 433–450.

———. 2000. Relationship demography and relationship quality in two cultures. *Organization Studies* 21(6): 1077–1094.

Pellegrini, E. K., and T. A. Scandura. 2006. Leader-member exchange (LMX), paternalism, and delegation in the Turkish business culture: An empirical investigation. *Journal of International Business Studies* 37: 264–279.

Pepitone, J. 2013. Best Buy ends work-from-home program. *CNN Money,* March 5. http://money.cnn.com/2013/03/05/technology/best-buy-work-from-home/ (accessed October 20, 2013).

Personal coach for CXOs. 2011. *The Economic Times,* August 23. http://economictimes.indiatimes.com/slideshows/management-leaders/a-personal-coach-for-cxos/taking-off/slideshow/9703084.cms (accessed August 5, 2013).

Pescosolido, A. T. 2002. Emergent leaders as managers of group emotion. *The Leadership Quarterly* 13: 583–599.

Peters, L. H., D. D. Hartke, and J. T. Pohlmann. 1985. Fiedler's contingency theory of leadership: An application of the meta-analysis procedure of Schmitt and Hunter. *Psychological Bulletin* 97: 274–285.

Peterson, G. 2005. Ford's Nancy Gioia: Hybrid Queen. *Vehicle Voice,* December 29. http://blog.vehiclevoice.com/2005/12/fords_nancy_gioia_hybrid_queen.html (accessed July 22, 2007).

Peterson, S. J., F. O. Walumbwa, B. J. Avolio, and S. T. Hannah. 2012. The relationship between authentic leadership and follower job performance: The mediating role of follower positivity in extreme contexts. *The Leadership Quarterly* 23: 502–516.

Pettigrew, A. 1973. *The politics of organizational decision making.* London: Tavistock.

Pfeffer, J. 1981. *Power in organizations.* Marshfield, MA: Pitman.

_____. 1983. Organizational demography. In *Research in organizational behavior,* ed. L. L. Cummings and B. W. Staw, 299–357. Greenwich, CT: JAI Press.

_____. 2010. *Power: Why Some People Have It—And Others Don't.* New York: HarperCollins Publishers.

Phomprapha, S., and S. Chansrichawla. 2007. Leadership-supported mentoring: The key to enhancing organisational commitment and retaining newcomers. *International Journal of Management and Decision Making* 8: 394.

Popper, M. 2002. Narcissism and attachment patterns of personalized and socialized charismatic leaders. *Journal of Social and Personal Relationships* 19: 797–809.

_____. 2005. Main principles and practices of leader development. *Leadership and Organization Development Journal* 26: 62–75.

Popper, M., and Mayseless, O. 2007. The building blocks of leader development: A psychological conceptual framework. *Leadership and Organizational Development Journal* 28(7): 664–684.

Poropat, A. E. 2009. A meta-analysis of the Five-Factor model of personality and academic performance. *Psychological Bulletin* 135(2): 322–338.

Posner, B., and J. Kouzes. 1993. Psychometric properties of leader practices inventory: Updated. *Educational and Psychological Measurement* 53: 191–199.

Powell, G. N., D. A. Butterfield, and J. D. Parent. 2002. Gender and managerial stereotypes: Have the times changed? *Journal of Management* 28: 177–193.

Prendergast, C. 1993. Theory of "Yes Men." *American Economic Review* 83(4): 757–770.

Price, T. L. 2003. The ethics of authentic transformational leadership. *The Leadership Quarterly* 14: 67–81.

Puffer, S. M. 1994. Understanding the bear: A portrait of Russian business leaders. *Academy of Management Executive* 8(1): 41–54.

Pugh, D. S., D. J. Hickson, C. R. Hinings, and C. Turner. 1968. Dimensions of organization structure. *Administrative Science Quarterly* 13: 65–105.

Pynes, J. E. 2011. *Effective nonprofit management: Context and environment.* Armonk, NY: M.E. Sharpe.

Rafferty, A. E,, and M. A. Griffin. 2004. Dimensions of transformational leadership: Conceptual and empirical extensions. *The Leadership Quarterly* 15: 329–354.

Ragavan, C. 2005. Fixing the FBI. *U.S. News &World Report* March 3. http://www.usnews.com/usnews/news/articles/050328/28fbi.htm (accessed April 19, 2010).

Rahim, M. A., D. Antonioni, K. Krumov, and S. Ilieva. 2000. Power, conflict, and effectiveness: A cross-cultural study in the United States and Bulgaria. *European Psychologist* 5(1): 28–33.

Randolph, W. A., and M. Sashkin. 2002. Can organizational empowerment work in multinational settings? *Academy of Management Executive* 16(1): 102–115.

Rank, J., N. E. Nelson, T. D. Allen, and X. Xu. 2009. Leadership predictors of innovation and task performance: Subordinate self-esteem and self-presentation as moderators. *Journal of Occupational and Organizational Psychology* 82(3): 465–470.

Raskas, D. F., and D. C. Hambrick. 1992. Multifunctional managerial development: A framework for evaluating the options. *Organizational Dynamics* 21(2): 5–17.

Raskin, R., and C. S. Hall. 1979. A narcissistic personality inventory. *Psychological Reports* 45: 590.

Rastogi, R., and V. Dave. 2004. Managerial effectiveness: A function of personality type and organisational components. *Singapore Management Review* 26(2): 79–87.

Reed, G. E. In print. Expressing Loyal Dissent: Moral Considerations from Literature on Followership. *Journal of Public Integrity*.

Reed, G. E., and R. A. Olsen. 2010. Toxic leadership: Part deux. *Military Review* (November–December): 58–64.

Reed, W. 2013. Diversity turnaround at Sodexo. *Louisiana Weekly,* March 4. http://www. louisianaweekly.com/diversity-turnaround-at-sodexo/ (accessed June 18, 2013).

Reeves, R. 2006. Our fetish for feedback. *Management Today*, June 25.

Rego, A., A. Vitória, A. Magalhães, N. Ribeiro, and M. Inan e Cunha. 2013. Are authentic leaders associated with more virtuous, committed and potent teams. *The Leadership Quarterly* 24: 61–79.

Reingold, J. 2003. Still angry after all these years. *Fast Company*, October, 89–94.

———. 2005. Hondas in space. *Fast Company*, February, 74–79.

Repetti, A., and R. Prélaz-Droux. 2003. An urban monitor as support for a participative management of developing cities. *Habitat International* 27(4): 653–662.

Rice, R. 1978a. Construct validity of the least preferred coworker. *Psychological Bulletin* 85: 1199–1237.

———. 1978b. Psychometric properties of the esteem for least preferred coworker (LPC) scale. *Academy of Management Review* 3: 106–118.

Rich, L. 2005. Hands-on managing: Playing well with others. *Inc.*, January, 29–32.

Rink, F., and N. Ellemers. 2010. Benefiting from deep-level diversity: how congruence between knowledge and decision rules improves team decision making and team perceptions. *Group Processes and Intergroup Relations* 13(3): 345–359.

Roberts, N. C., and R. T. Bradley. 1988. Transforming leadership: A process of collective action. *Human Relations* 38: 1023–1046.

Robichau, R. W. 2013. Between markets and government: Essays on nonprofitness and the institutional transformation of child welfare agencies. Unpublished dissertation, Arizona State University.

Rogers, A. 1994. Is he too cautious to save IBM? *Fortune* 130(7): 78–88.

Riggio, R. E., Murphy, S. E., and F. J. Priozzolo. 2002. *Multiple intelligences and leadership.* Mahwah, NJ, US: Lawrence Erlbaum Associates.

Riggio, R. E., and R. J. Reichard. 2008. The emotional and social intelligences of effective leadership: An emotional and social skill approach. *Journal of Managerial Psychology* 23(2): 169–185.

Rosenthal, S. A., and T. L. Pittinsky. 2006. Narcissistic leadership. *The Leadership Quarterly* 17: 617–633.

Rosier, R. H. 1994. *The competency model handbook*, Vol. 1. Boston: Linkage.

———. 1995. *The competency model handbook*, Vol. 2. Boston: Linkage.

Rubinkan, M. 2007. Teamsters still foaming over ejection by brewery Yuengling. *Philly.com*, May 29. http:www. phillyburbs.compb-dynnews103—05282007-1353974.html (accessed January 8, 2008).

Ruderman, M. N. 2004. Leader development across gender. In *The Center for Creative Leadership: Handbook of leadership development*. 2nd ed. Ed. C. D. McCauley and E. Van Velsor, 271–303. San Francisco: Jossey-Bass.

Rus, D., D. van Knippenberg, and B. Wisse. 2012. Leader power and self-serving behavior: The moderating role of accountability. *The Leadership Quarterly* 23: 13–26.

Ryan, M. K., and S. A. Haslam. 2007. The glass cliff: Exploring the dynamics surrounding the appointment of women to precarious leadership positions. *Academy of Management Review* 32: 549–572.

Rychlak, J. F. 1963. Personality correlates of leadership among first level managers. *Psychological Reports* 12: 43–52.

Ryerson-Cruz, G. 2004. Scrushy's successor at HealthSouth tries to pick up pieces. *Tennessean.com*, December 20. tennessean.com/business/archives/04/12/63085234.shtml?Element_ID = 63085234 (accessed December 28, 2004).

Sacks, D. 2009. Space man. *Fast Company*, October, 130–133.

_____. 2013. 10 creativity tips from J. Crew CEO Mickey Drexler. *Fast Company,* April 15. http://www.fastcompany.com/3007844/10-creativity-tips-jcrew-ceo-mickey-drexler (accessed July 20, 2013).

Sadri, G. 2012. Emotional intelligence and leadership development. *Public Personnel Management* 41: 535–548.

Salancik, G. R., and J. Pfeffer. 1977a. Constraints on administrator discretion: The limited influence of mayors in city budgets. *Urban Affairs Quarterly* 12(4): 475–496.

_____. 1977b. Who gets power and how they hold onto it: A strategic-contingency model of power. *Organizational Dynamics* 5(Winter): 3–21.

Salas, E., K. Stagl, and C. S. Burke. 2004. 25 years of team effective in organizations: Research themes and emerging needs. In *International review of industrial and organizational psychology*, Vol. 19, ed. C. L. Cooper and I. T. Robertson, 47–91. New York: John Wiley.

Salovey, P., and J. Mayer. 1990. Emotional intelligence. *Imagination, Cognition, and Personality* 9: 185–211.

Salter, C. 2000. What's your mission statement? *Fast Company*, July, 48–50.

Salter, C., 2004a. "And now the hard part," *Fast Company* 82. http://pf.fastcompany.com/magazine/82/jetblue.html (accessed October 1, 2004)

Salter, C., and E. Westly. 2010. Novartis. *Fast Company*, March, 65.

Samnani, A., and P. Singh. 2013. When leaders victimize: The role of charismatic leaders in facilitating group pressure. *The Leadership Quarterly* 24: 189–202.

San Antonio, D. M., and D. T. Gamage. 2007. PSALM for empower educational stakeholders: Participatory school administration, leadership, and management. *The International Journal of Education* 21: 254.

Sandberg, S. 2013. *Lean in: Women, work and the will to lead.* New York: Alfred Knopf.

Sanders, W. M. G., and M. A. Carpenter. 1998. Internationalization and firm governance: The roles of CEO compensation, top team composition, and board structure. *Academy of Management Journal* 41: 158–178.

Sankin, A. 2013. Bob Ladouceur, legendary De La Salle football coach retires after 34 years of stunning victories. *Huffington Post*, January 4. http://www.huffingtonpost.com/2013/01/04/bob-ladouceur_n_2412783.html (accessed May 30, 2013).

Sanyal, R., and T. Guvenli. 2009. The propensity to bribe in international business: The relevance of cultural variables. *Cross-Cultural Management* 16(3): 287–300.

Sarvar, A., and A. Khalid. 2011. Impact of employee empowerment on employee's job satisfaction and commitment with the organization. *Interdisciplinary Journal of Contemporary Research in Business* 3(2): 664–683.

Sashkin, M. 2004. Transformational leadership approaches. In *The nature of leadership*, ed. J. Antonakis, A. T. Cianciolo, and R. J. Sternberg, 171–196. Thousand Oaks, CA: Sage.

Scandura, T. 1999. Rethinking leader-member exchange: An organizational justice perspective. *The Leadership Quarterly* 10(1): 25–40.

Scandura, T., and P. Dorfman. 2004. Leadership research in an international and cross-cultural context. *The Leadership Quarterly* 15: 277–307.

Schaffer, B. S., and C. M. Riordan. 2013. Relational demography in supervisor-subordinate dyads: An examination of discrimination and exclusionary treatment. *Canadian Journal of Administrative Sciences* 31(1): 3–17.

Schein, E. H. 2004. *Organizational culture and leadership*. San Francisco: Jossey-Bass.

———. 2010. *Organizational culture and leadership.* San Francisco: Wiley & Sons-Jossey-Bass.

Schmid M. M., K. Jonas, and J. A. Hall. 2009. Give a person power and he or she will show interpersonal sensitivity: The phenomenon and its why and when. *Journal of Personality and Social Psychology* 97(5): 835–850.

Schmidt Mastm M., Jonas, K., and J. A. Hall. 2009. Give a person power and he or she will show interpersonal sensitivity: The phenomenon and its why and when. *Journal of Personality and Social Psychology* 97(5): 835–850.

Schneider, S. K., and W. M. George. 2009. Servant Leadership versus transformational leadership in voluntary service organizations. *Leadership and Organization Development Journal* 32(1): 60–77.

Schriesheim, C. A., S. L. Castro, and C. C. Cogliser. 1999. Leader-member exchange (LMX) research: A comprehensive review of theory, measurement, and data-analytic practices. *The Leadership Quarterly* 10(1): 63–113.

Schriesheim, C. A., and S. Kerr. 1974. Psychometric properties of the Ohio State University Leadership scales. *Psychological Bulletin* 81: 756–765.

Schriesheim, C. A., B. J. Tepper, and L. Tetrault. 1994. Least-preferred co-worker score, situational control and leadership effectiveness: A meta-analysis of contingency model performance predictions. *Journal of Applied Psychology* 79: 561–574.

Schwartz, N. D. 2001. What's in the cards for Amex? *Fortune*, January 22, 58–70.

Schyns. B., and J. Schilling. 2013. How bad are the effect of bad leaders? A meta-analysis of destructive leadership and its outcomes. *The Leadership Quarterly* 24: 138–158.

Scott-Ladd, B., and C. C. A. Chan. 2004. Emotional intelligence and participation in decision making: Strategies for promoting organizational learning and change. *Strategic Change* 13: 95–105.

Search for women. 2006. *Executive MBA Council.* http:www.emba.orgexchangeexpanded_web_may_2006feature_1.html#the_world_looks (accessed January 12, 2010).

Searle, T. P. 2010. Servant leadership, hope and organizational virtuousness: A framework exploring positive micro and macro behaviors and performance impact. *Journal of Leadership and Organizational Studies* 18(1): 107–117.

Seely Howard, E., W. L. Gardner, and L. Thompson. 2007. The role of the self-concept and the social context in determining the behavior of power holders: Self-construal in intergroup versus dyadic dispute resolution negotiations. *Journal of Personality and Social Psychology* 93(4): 614–631.

Seibert, S. E., J. M. Crant, and M. L. Kraimer. 1999. Proactive personality and career success. *Journal of Applied Psychology* 84(3) (June): 416–442.

Seibert, S. E., and M. L. Kraimer. 2001. The five-factor model of personality and career success. *Journal of Vocational Behavior* 58(1): 1–21.

Seibert, S. E., S. R. Silver, and W. A. Randolph. 2004. Taking empowerment to the next level: A multiple-level model of empowerment, performance, and satisfaction. *Academy of Management Journal* 47: 332–349.

Seibert, S. E., G. Wang, and S. H. Courtright. 2011. Antecedents and consequences of psychological and team empowerment in organizations: A meta-analytic review. *Journal of Applied Psychology* 96(5): 981–1003.

Seligman, M. E. P. 2002. *Authentic happiness: Using the new positive psychology to realize your potential for lasting fulfillment.* New York: Free Press.

Seligman, M. E. P., and M. Csikszentmihalyi. 2000. Positive psychology. *American Psychologist* 55: 5–14.

Sellers. 1998. The 50 most powerful women in American business. *Fortune* 138(7): 76–98.

———. 2000a. The 50 most powerful women in business. *Fortune*, October 16, 131–160.

———. 2000b. Big, hairy, audacious goals don't work—just ask P&G. *Fortune*, April 3, 39–44.

———. 2004. eBay's secret. *Fortune*, October 25, 161–178.

———. 2009. Gerry Laybourne reemerges, wisdom intact. *Fortune-Postcards.* http://postcards.blogs.fortune.cnn.com/2009/05/26/gerry-laybourne-reemerges-with-wisdom/ (accessed January 12, 2010).

Semler Interview. 1993. *Maverick! The success story behind the world's most unusual workplace.* London: Century.

_____. 2013. Interview with Ricardo Semler. *VPROBacklight,* February 5. http://www.youtube.com/watch?v=USC1RE8jE50 (accessed June 1, 2013).

Senge, P. M. 2006. *The fifth discipline: The art and practice of the learning organization.* New York: Doubleday.

Shahhosseini, M., A. D. Silong, and I. A. Ismaill. 2013. Relationship between transactional, transformational leadership styles, emotional intelligence and job performance. *Journal of Arts, Science and Commerce* 4(1). http://www.researchersworld.com/vol4/vol4_issue1_2/Paper_03.pdf.

Shamir, B. 1991. The charismatic relationship: Alternative explanations and predictions. *The Leadership Quarterly* 2: 81–104.

Shamir, B., R. J. House, and M. B. Arthur. 1993. The motivational effects of charismatic leadership: A self-concept-based theory. *Organization Science* 4: 1–17.

Shamir, B., and J. M. Howell. 1999. Organizational and contextual influence on the emergence and effectiveness of charismatic leadership. *The Leadership Quarterly* 10(2): 257–283.

Shamir, B., E. Zakay, E. Breinin, and M. Popper. 1998. Correlates of charismatic leaders' behavior in military units: Subordinates' attitudes, unit characteristics, and superiors' appraisals of leader performance. *Academy of Management Journal* 41: 387–409.

Sherman, L. 2013. J. Crew's Mickey Drexler on Secrets to his success. *Fashionista,* January 7. http://fashionista.com/2013/01/j-crew-mickey-drexler-wwd-ceo-summit/ (accessed July 20, 2013).

Shin, S. J., and J. Zhou. 2003. Transformational leadership, conservation, and creativity: Evidence from Korea. *Academy of Management Journal* 46: 703–714.

Shinn, S. 2004. The Maverick CEO. *BizEd* (January–February): 16–21.

_____. 2005. Beauty king. *BizED* (July–August): 20–23.

_____ 2006. *Profiting From Experience* (July–August): 16–20.

Silver, S., W. A. Randolph, and S. Seibert. 2006. Implementing and sustaining empowerment: Lesson learned from comparison of a for-profit and a non-profit organization. *Journal of Management Inquiry* 15: 47–58.

Simsek, Z., C. Heavy, and J. J. F. Veiga. 2010 The impact of CEO core selfevaluation on the firm entrepreneurial orientation. *Strategic Management Journal* 31(1): 110–119.

Singer, P. 1969. Toward a re-evaluation of the concept of charisma with reference to India. *Journal of Social Research* 12(2): 13–25.

Singh, J. 2006. Employee disempowerment in a small firm (SME): Implications for organizational social capital. *Organizational Development Journal* 24(1): 76–86.

Slaughter, A. M. 2012. Why women still can't have it all. *The Atlantic* (July–August). http://www.theatlantic.com/magazine/archive/2012/07/why-women-still-cant-have-it-all/309020/ (accessed June 19, 2013).

Smith, E. B., and P. Kuntz. 2013. CEO pay 1,795-to-1 multiple of wages skirts U.S. law. *Bloomberg,* April 29. http://www.bloomberg.com/news/2013-04-30/ceo-pay-1-795-to-1-multiple-of-workers-skirts-law-as-sec-delays.html (accessed July 20, 2013).

Smith, M. A., and J. M. Canger. 2004. Effects of supervisor "Big Five" personality on subordinate attitudes. *Journal of Business and Psychology* 18(4): 465–481.

Smith, P. B. 2002. Culture's consequences: Something old and something new. *Human Relations* 55: 119–135.

Smith, T. W., and F. Rhodewalt. 1986. On states, traits, and processes: A transactional alternative to the individual difference assumption in type A behavior and psychological reactivity. *Journal of Research in Personality* 20: 229–251.

Snyder, C. R., S. J. Lopez, and J. T. Pedrotti. 2011. *Positive psychology: The scientific and practical explorations of human strengths.* 2nd ed. Thousand Oaks, CA: Sage Publications.

Snyder, M. 1974. The self-monitoring of expressive behavior. *Journal of Personality and Social Psychology* 30: 526–537.

Sodexo ranked number one company for diversity by DiversityInc. 2010. *PRNewswire,* March 10. http://www.prnewswire.com/news-releases/sodexo-ranked-number-one-company-for-diversity-by-diversityinc-87219747.html (accessed June 18, 2013).

Solomon, N. 2010. In-house resource groups can help and harm. *NPR-Morning Edition,* January 13. http:www.npr.orgtemplatesstorystory. php?storyId122516577 (accessed January 18, 2010).

Song, J. H. 1982. Diversification strategies and the experience of top executives of large firms. *Strategic Management Journal* 3: 377–380.

Sosik, J. J. 2005. The role of personal values in the charismatic leadership of corporate managers: A model and preliminary field study. *The Leadership Quarterly* 16: 221–244.

Sosik, J. J., B. J. Avolio, and D. Jung. 2002. Examining the relationship of self-presentation attributes and impression management to charismatic leadership. *The Leadership Quarterly* 13: 217–242.

Sparrowe, R. T., and R. C. Liden. 1997. Process and structure in leader-member exchange. *Academy of Management Review* 22(2): 522–552.

Srivastava, A., K. M. Bartol, and E. A. Locke. 2006. Empower leadership in management teams: Effects on knowledge sharing, efficacy, and performance. *Academy of Management Journal* 49: 1239–1251.

Staats, B. R., K. L. Milkman, and C. R. Fox. 2012. The team scaling fallacy: Underestimating the declining efficiency of larger teams. *Organizational Behavior and Human Decision Processes* 118(2): 132–142.

Stanners, P. 2012. Abuse of power behind Dong CEO's dismissal. *The Copenhagen Post,* March 14. http://cphpost.dk/business/abuse-power-behind-dong-ceos-dismissal (accessed July 15, 2013).

Starbuck, W. H., A. Greve, and B. L. T. Hedberg. 1978. Responding to crisis. *Journal of Business Administration* 9(2): 111–127.

Start-up America Partnership. 2011. http://s.co/press-release/white-house-announces-startup-america-partnership-foster-innovative-high-growth-firms (accessed July 28, 2013).

Statistical overview of women in the workplace. 2013. *Catalyst,* March 13. http://www.catalyst.org/knowledge/statistical-overview-women-workplace (accessed June 24, 2013).

Steptoe, S. 2007. Building a better mouse. *Time. com,* June 14. http://www.time.com/time/globalbusiness/article/0,9171,1633077,00.html (accessed July 17, 2007).

Stern, G. M. 2011. Company training programs: What are they really worth? *CNN Money,* May 27. http://management.fortune.cnn.com/2011/05/27/company-training-programs-what-are-they-really-worth/ (accessed August 4, 2013).

Sternberg, R. J. 2002a. Creativity as a decision. *American Psychologist* 57: 376.

————, ed. 2002b. *Why smart people can be so stupid.* New Haven, CT: Yale University Press.

————. 2003. WICS: A model of leadership in organizations. *Academy of Management Learning and Education* 2(4): 386–401.

————. 2007. A systems model of leadership. *American Psychologist* 62: 34–42.

Sternberg, R. J., G. B. Forsythe, J. Hedlund, J. A. Horvath, R. K. Wagner, W. M. Williams, S. A. Snook, and E. Grigorenko. 2000. *Practical intelligence in everyday life.* New York: Cambridge University Press.

Sternberg, R. J., and T. I. Lubart. 1995. *Defying the crowd: Cultivating creativity in a culture of conformity.* New York: Free Press.

Stewart, J. B., 2007. "Whole Foods chief disappoints by sowing wild oats online," *The Wall Street Journal,* July 18: D5.

Stewart, J.B. 2013. Looking for a lesion in Google's Perks. *The New York Times,* March 15. Accessed at http://www.nytimes.com/2013/03/16/business/at-google-a-place-to-work-and-play.html?pagewanted=all on July 22, 2013.

Stewart, T. A. 1998. The cunning plots of leadership. *Fortune* 138(5): 165–166.

Stewart-Belle, S., and J. A. Lust. 1999. Career movement of female employees holding lower-level positions: An analysis of the impact of the type A behavior pattern. *Journal of Business and Psychology* 14(1): 187–197.

Stinson, J. E., and T. W. Johnson. 1975. The path-goal theory of leadership: A partial test and suggested refinement. *Academy of Management Journal* 18: 242–252.

St. Martin, G. Northeastern helps the FBI transform its culture. *Northeastern,* June 8. http://www.northeastern.edu/news/2011/06/executive_education/ (accessed August 1, 2013).

Stogdill, R. M. 1948. Personal factors associated with leadership: A survey of the literature. *Journal of Psychology* 25: 35–71.

Strauss, K., M. A. Griffin, and A. E. Rafferty. 2009. Proactivity directed toward the team and organization: The role of the leadership, commitment and role-breadth self-efficacy. *British Journal of Management* 20(3): 279–290.

Strauss, G., and B. Hansen. 2005. CEO pay "business as usual." *USA Today*, March 30. http:www.usatoday.commoneycompaniesmanagement2005—03-30-ceo-pay-2004-cover_x.htm (accessed July 26, 2007).

Strube, M. J., and J. E. Garcia. 1981. A meta-analytical investigation of Fiedler's contingency model of leadership effectiveness. *Psychological Bulletin* 90: 307–321.

Strube, M. J., C. W. Turner, D. Cerro, J. Stevens, and F. Hinchey. 1984. Interpersonal aggression and the type A coronary-prone behavior pattern: A theoretical distinction and practical implications. *Journal of Personality and Social Psychology* 47: 839–847.

Strube, M. J., and C. Werner. 1985. Relinquishment of control and the type A behavior pattern. *Journal of Personality and Social Psychology* 48: 688–701.

Su, R., J. Rounds, and P. I. Armstrong. 2009. Men and things, women and People: A meta-analysis of sex differences in interests. *Psychological Bulletin* 135(6): 859–884.

Sullivan, M. 2004. Cambodia's new king ascends the throne. *All Things Considered*, October 29. http://www.npr.orgtemplatesstorystory.php?storyId4133660 (accessed December 18, 2007).

Sutton, R. I. 2010. *Good boss, bad boss: How to be the best...and learn from the worst.* New York: Business Plus.

Suutari, V. 2002. Global leader development: An emerging research agenda. *Career Development Journal* 7: 218–233.

Swan, K. 2000. Difference is power. *Fast Company*, July, 258–266.

Sweeney P. 2007. Organizational Chaos and Relative Powerlessness: Breeding Ground for Bullies? *Academy of Management Perspectives* 21(2): 77–78.

Swinburn, P. 2012. Why do teams fail? *Fast Company,* October 24. http://www.fastcompany.com/3012311/30-second-mba/peter-swinburn-why-do-teams-fail (accessed July 22, 2013).

Szilagyi, A. D., and H. P. Sims. 1974. An exploration of the path-goal theory of leadership in a health care environment. *Academy of Management Journal* 17: 622–634.

Taggar, S., and R. Ellis. 2007. The role of leaders in shaping formal team norms. *The Leadership Quarterly* 18: 105–120.

Taggar, S., and M. J. A. Neubert. 2008. A cognitive (attributions)-emotion model of observer reaction to free-riding poor performers. *Journal of Business Psychology* 22: 167–177.

Tannen, D., ed. 1993. *Gender and conversational interaction.* Oxford: Oxford University Press.

Tannenbaum, A. S., and R. A. Cooke. 1974. Control and participation. *Journal of Contemporary Business* 3(4): 35–46.

Taylor, A., III. 2009. *Fixing up Ford.* May 12. http://money.cnn.com/2009/05/11/news/companies/mulally_ford.fortune/index.htm?postversion=2009051212 (accessed April 21, 2010).

Taylor, P., and R. Morin. 2009. Forty years after Woodstock: A gentler generation gap. *Pew Research Center: Social and Demographic Trends.* http://pewsocialtrends.org/pubs/739/woodstock-gentler-generation-gap-music-by-age (accessed February 21, 2010).

Teagarden, M. B., M. C. Butler, and M. A. Von Glinow. 1992. Mexico's Maquiladora industry: Where strategic human resource management makes a difference. *Organizational Dynamics* 20(3): 34–47.

Tepper, B. J, C. A. Henle, L. S. Lambert, R. A. Giacalone, and M. K. Duffy. 2008. Abusive supervision and subordinates' organization deviance. *Journal of Applied Psychology* 93(4): 721–732.

Tepper, B. J., J. C. Carr, D. M. Breaux, S. Geider, C. Hu, and W. Hua. 2009. Abusive supervision, intention to quit, and employees' workplace deviance: A power/dependence analysis. *Organizational Behavior and Human Decision Processes* 109: 156–167.

Thach, E. C. 2002. The impact of executive coaching and 360 feedback on leadership effectiveness. *Leadership and Organization Development Journal* 23: 205–214.

Thomas, A. B. 1988. Does leadership make a difference to organizational performance? *Administrative Science Quarterly* 33: 388–400.

Thomas, K. M. 2001. The truth about mentoring minorities: Race matters. *Harvard Business Review* 79: 98–112.

Thomson, A. M., and J. L. Perry. 2010. Collaboration processes: Inside the black box. In *The Jossey-Bass Reader on nonprofit and public leadership*, ed. J. L. Perry, 150–176. San Francisco: Jossey-Bass.

Thoroughgood, C. N., A. Padilla, S. T. Hunter, and B. W. Tate. 2012. The susceptible circle: A taxonomy of followers associated with destructive leadership. *The Leadership Quarterly* 23(5): 897–917.

Three fundamentals of successful change. 2012. *Track Change Research*, July 24. http://www.changetracking.com/insights/file/8-insight-0508-successfulchange (accessed August 3, 2013).

Thurm, S. 2013. "Pay for performance" no longer a punchline. *The Wall Street Journal*, March 20. http://online.wsj.com/article/SB10001424127887324373204578372444079319544.html (accessed July 20, 2013).

Tierney, T. J. 2006. *The non-profit sector's leadership deficit*. The Bridespan Group. http://www.bridgespangroup.org/kno_articles_leadershipdeficit.html (accessed July 26, 2007).

Tims, M., A. B. Bakker, and D. Xanthopoulou. 2011. Do transformational leaders enhance their followers' daily work engagement? *The Leadership Quarterly* 22: 121–131.

Ting, S., and E. W. Hart. 2004. Formal coaching. In *The Center for Creative Leadership: Handbook of leadership development*. 2nd ed. Ed. C. D. McCauley and E. Van Velsor, 116–150. San Francisco: Jossey-Bass.

Tipu, S. A. A., J. C. Ryan, and K. A. Fantazy. 2012. Transformational leadership in Pakistan: An examination of the relationship of transformational leadership to organizational culture and innovation propensity. *Journal of Management and Organization* 18(4): 461–480.

Tischler, L. 2002. Monica Luechtefeld makes the net click. *Fast Company*, November, 122–128.

_____. 2004. IBM's management makeover. *Fast Company*, November, 112–113.

Tjan, A. K. 2012. How leader become self-aware. *Harvard Business Review,* July 19. http://blogs.hbr.org/tjan/2012/07/how-leaders-become-self-aware.html (accessed August 5, 2013).

Tjosvold, D., W. C. Wedley, and R. H. G. Field. 1986. Constructive controversy: The Vroom-Yetton model and managerial decision making. *Journal of Occupational Behavior* 7: 125–138.

Tomlinson, R. 2000. Europe's new business elite. *Fortune*, April 3, 177–184.

_____. 2004. The new king of beers. *Fortune*, October 18, 233–238.

Top 10 crooked CEOs. 2009. *Time*. http://www.time.com/time/specials/packages/article/0,28804,1903155_1903156_1903152,00.html (accessed March 24, 2010).

Tornow, W. W., and M. London, eds. 1998. *Maximizing the value of 360 degree feedback: A process for successful individual and organizational development*. San Francisco: Jossey-Bass.

Townsend, J., J. S. Phillips, and T. J. Elkins. 2000. Employee retaliation: The neglected consequence of poor leader-member exchange relations. *Journal of Occupational Health Psychology* 5(4): 457–463.

Triandis, H. C. 1995. *Individualism and collectivism*. Boulder, CO: Westview Press.

_____. 2004. The many dimensions of culture. *Academy of Management Executive* 18(1): 88–93.

Triandis, H. C., P. Carnevale, M. Gelfand, C. Robert, S. A. Wasti, T. Probst, E. S. Kashima, et al. 2001. Culture and deception in business negotiations: A multilevel analysis. *International Journal of Cross-Cultural Management* 1(1): 73–90.

Trice, H. M., and J. M. Beyer. 1993. *The cultures of work organizations*. Upper Saddle River, NJ: Prentice Hall.

Trompenaars, A., and C. Hampden-Turner. 2012. *Riding the waves of culture: Understanding culture and diversity in business*. New York: McGraw-Hill.

Trucco, T. 2007. Meetings; rope climbing? Passé. Treasure hunts? Cool. *New York Times*, April 16. http://select.nytimes.com/search/restricted/article?es=F10813FC3A5B0C758D-DDAD0894DF404482 (accessed September 13, 2007).

Tsurumi, R. 1982. American origins of Japanese productivity: The Hawthorne experiment rejected. *Pacific Basin Quarterly* 7(Spring–Summer): 14–15.

Tuggle, K. 2007. Marathon man. *Fast Company*, February, 54.

Turnley, W. H., and M. C. Bolino. 2001. Achieving desired images while avoiding undesired images: Exploring the role of self-monitoring in impression management. *Journal of Applied Psychology* 86(2): 351–360.

Tyabji, H. 1997. What it means to lead. *Fast Company*, February–March, 98.

Uhl-Bien, M., and M. K. Carsten. 2007. Being ethical when the boss is not. *Organizational Dynamics* 36(2): 187–201.

Uhl-Bien, M., R. Marion, and B. McKelvey. 2007. Complexity leadership theory: Shifting leadership from the industrial age to knowledge era. *The Leadership Quarterly* 18: 298–318.

Useem, J. 2001. It's all yours Jeff. Now what? *Fortune*, September 17, 64–68.

Valerio, A. M. 2009. What companies need to develop women leaders. *Business Week*, October 16. http://www.businessweek.com/managing/content/oct2009/ca20091016_485645.htm (accessed January 18, 2010).

Vanderkam, L. 2012. Can introverts succeed in business. *CNN Money,* February 2. http://management.fortune.cnn.com/2012/02/02/can-introverts-succeed-in-business/ (accessed October 11, 2013). Producer Scott Rudin takes out NY Times ad and retaliates at NY Times writer.

van der Pool, L. 2012. Boston Beer company ties Yuenling for bragging rights. *Boston Business Journal*, February 27. http://boston.cbslocal.com/2012/02/27/boston-beer-company-tied-for-bragging-rights/ (accessed June 1, 2013).

van Dierendonck, D. 2011. Servant leadership: A review and synthesis. *Journal of Management* 37(4): 1228–1261.

Van der Vegt, G. S., J. S. Bunderson, and A. Oosterhof. 2006. Expertness diversity and interpersonal helping in teams: Why those who need the most help end up getting the least. *Academy of Management Journal* 49: 877–893.

VanSandt, C. V., and C. P. Neck. 2003. Bridging ethics and self-leadership: Overcoming ethical discrepancies between employee and organizational standards. *Journal of Business Ethics* 43: 363–388.

Vashdi, D. R., Vigoda-Gadot, E., and D. Shlomi. 2013. Assessing performance: The impact of organizational climate and politics on public schools' performance. *Public Administration* 91(1): 135–158.

Vecchio, R. P. 1983. Assessing the validity of Fiedler's contingency model of leadership effectiveness: A closer look at Strube and Garcia. *Psychological Bulletin* 93: 404–408.

Vidal, B. J., and M. Möller. 2007. When should leaders share information with their subordinates? *Journal of Economics and Management Strategy* 16: 251–283.

Villa, J. R., J. P. Howell, P. Dorfman, and D. L. Daniel. 2003. Problems with detecting moderators in leadership research using moderated multiple regression. *The Leadership Quarterly* 14: 3–23.

Vise, T. 2011. Business adVise: Emotional intelligence has effect on workplace. *North Jefferson News,* August 2011. http://www.njeffersonnews.com/business/x850291446/Business-AdVISE-Emotional-intelligence-has-effect-on-workplace/print (accessed October 12, 2013).

Voelcker, J. 2010. Five questions: Nancy Gioia., Ford Global Electrification director. *GreenCarReports.com* January 27. http://www.greencarreports.com/blog/1042040_five-questions-nancy-gioia-ford-global-electrification-director (accessed April 12, 2010).

Volmer, J., Spurk, D., and C. Niessen. 2012. Leader-member exchange (LMX), job autonomy, and creative work involvement. *The Leadership Quarterly* 23(3): 456–465.

Vroom, V. H. 1964. *Work and motivation.* New York: John Wiley.

Vroom, V. H., and A. G. Jago. 1988. *The new leadership: Managing participation in organizations.* Upper Saddle River, NJ: Prentice Hall.

Vroom, V. H., and P. W. Yetton. 1973. *Leadership and decision making.* Pittsburgh, PA: University of Pittsburgh Press.

Wakabayashi, M., G. B. Graen, M. R. Graen, and M. C. Graen. 1988. Japanese management progress: Mobility into middle management. *Journal of Applied Psychology* 73: 217–227.

Walker, M. C. 2006. Morality, self-interest, and leaders in international affairs. *The Leadership Quarterly* 17: 138–145.

Wallace, D. 2003. The soul of a sports machine. *Fast Company* 75(October): 100–104.

Walsh, J. 2012. Medtronic takes hunt for new technology to ends of the earth. *Star Tribune—Business.* September 23. http://www.startribune.com/business/170759356.html (accessed May 30, 2013).

Walsh, T. 1996. CEOs: Greenspan by a landslide. *Fortune* 133(5): 43.

Walters, J. 2006. Across the board innovator. *Governing*, November, 42.

Walumbwa, F. O., R. Cropanzano, and B. M. Goldman. 2011. How leader-member exchange influences effective work behaviors: Social exchange and internal efficacy perspectives. *Personnel Psychology* 64(3): 739–770.

Walumbwa, F. O., and J. J. Lawler. 2003. Building effective organization: Transformational leadership, collectivist orientation, work-related attitudes, and withdrawal behavior in three emerging economies. *International Journal of Human Resource Management* 14: 1083–1101.

Walumbwa, F. O., J. J. Lawler, and B. J. Avolio. 2007. Leadership, individual differences, and work-related attitudes: A cross-cultural investigation. *Applied Psychology* 56: 212–230.

Walumbwa, F. O., P. Wang, H. Wang, J. Schaubroeck, and B. J. Avolio. 2010. Psychological processes linking authentic leadership to follower behaviors. *The Leadership Quarterly* 21: 901–914.

Wang, G., I. S. Oh, S. H. Courtright, and A. E. Colbert. 2011. Transformational leadership and performance across criteria and levels: A meta-analytic review of 25 years of research. *Group and Organizational Management* 36(2): 223–270.

Warrior, P. 2010. Cisco's CTO's tips for a top career. *Fortune-Postcards,* March 8. http://postcards.blogs.fortune.cnn.com/2010/03/08/cisco-ctos-tips-for-a-top-career/ (accessed April 4, 2010).

Watson, W. E. 2006. Type A personality characteristics and the effect on individual and team academic performance. *Journal of Applied Social Psychology* 36: 1110–1128.

Wayne, S. J., M. Shore, and R. C. Liden. 1997. Perceived organizational support and leader-member exchange: A social exchange perspective. *Academy of Management Journal* 40(1): 82–111.

Weidner, C. K., and Y. S. Purohit. 2009. When power has leaders: Some indicator of power addiction among organizational leaders. *Journal Organizational Culture, Communication and Conflict* 13(1): 83–99.

Weil, E. 1998. Every leader tells a story. *Fast Company* (June–July), 38–40.

Weiner, N., and T. A. Mahoney. 1981. A model of corporate performance as a function of environment, organization, and leadership influences. *Academy of Management Journal* 24: 453–470.

Weiss, H. M., and S. Adler. 1984. Personality in organizational research. In *Research in organizational behavior*, Vol. 6, ed. B. Staw and L. Cummings, 1–50. Greenwich, CT: JAI Press.

Weiss, R. M., and V. W. Gantt. 2004. *Knowledge and skill development in non-profit organizations.* Peosta, IA: Eddie Bowers Publishing.

Welch, J., and S. Welch. 2007. When to talk, when to balk. *Business Week*, April 30, 102.

Wellner, A. S. 2004. Managing: Who can you trust? *Inc.*, October, 39–40.

_____. 2007. Eye on the prize. *Inc.*, January, 40–41.

Why I left Goldman Sachs. 2012. *USA Today,* October 22. http://www.usatoday.com/story/money/business/2012/10/22/greg-smith-goldman-sachs/1649643/ (accessed June 22, 2013).

Williams, R. 2010. Why change management fails in organizations. *Psychology Today.* September 28. http://www.psychologytoday.com/blog/wired-success/201009/why-change-management-fails-in-organizations (accessed August 3, 2013).

Wilson, D. C. 2006. When equal opportunity knocks. *Gallup Management Journal*, April 13.

Wilson, M. S., E. Van Velsor, N. A. Chandrasekar, and C. Criswell. 2011. *Grooming top leaders: Cultural perspectives from China, India, Singapore and the United States.* Center for Creative Leadership. http://www.ccl.org/leadership/pdf/research/GroomingTopLeaders.pdf (accessed August 5, 2013).

Winston, A. 2012. 3M's sustainability innovation machine. *Harvard Business Review,* May 15. http://blogs.hbr.org/winston/2012/05/3ms-sustainability-innovation.html (accessed August 1, 2013).

Wiscombe, J. 2007. What's behind the wheel at Toyota. *Workforce Management,* January. http://www.workforce.com/archive/feature/24/62/58/246260.php?ht=toyota%20toyota (accessed July 6, 2007).

Women CEOs in the Fortune 1000. 2013. *Catalyst—knowledge center,* June 18. http://www.catalyst.org/knowledge/women-ceos-fortune-1000 (accessed June 19, 2013).

Women in the Labor Force. 2010. *United States Department of Labor.* http://www.dol.gov/wb/factsheets/Qf-laborforce-10.htm (accessed October 6, 2013).

Women in the labor force: A databook. 2013. *Bureau of Labor Statistics,* February. http://www.bls.gov/cps/wlf-databook-2012.pdf (accessed June 24, 2013).

Woolley, A., and T. Malone. 2011. What makes a team smarter. *Harvard Business Review,* June.

World Fact Book: Malaysia. 2013. https://www.cia.gov/library/publications/the-world-factbook/geos/my.html (accessed May 30, 2013).

World Fact Book: Singapore. 2013. https://www.cia.gov/library/publications/the-world-factbook/geos/sn.html (accessed May 30, 2013).

WorldBlu list of most democratic places to work. 2007. http://www.worldblu.com/scorecard/list2007.php (accessed July 11, 2007).

Worley, C. G., and E. E. Lawler., III. 2006. Designing organizations that are built to change. *Sloan Management Review* 48(1): 19–23.

Wylie, I. 2003. Can Philips learn to walk the talk? *Fast Company,* January, 44–45.

_____. 2004. Please, displease me. *Fast Company,* December, 90–91.

Xin, J. 2010. How to motive people working in teams. *International Journal of Business and Management* 5(10): 223–229.

Yammarino, F. J., A. J. Dubinsky, L. B. Comer, and M. A. Jolson. 1997. Women and transformational and contingency reward leadership: A multiple-levels-of-analysis perspective. *Academy of Management Journal* 40: 205–222.

Yasai-Ardekani, M. 1986. Structural adaptations to environments. *Academy of Management Review* 11: 9–21.

_____. 1989. Effects of environmental scarcity and munificence on the relationship of context to organizational structure. *Academy of Management Journal* 32: 131–156.

Yglesias, M. 2013. Jeff Bezos explains Amazon's strategy for world domination. *Slate.com,* April 12. http://www.slate.com/blogs/moneybox/2013/04/12/amazon_as_corporate_charity_jeff_bezos_says_there_s_a_method_to_the_madness.html (accessed October 12, 2013).

Yitshaki, R. 2012. How do entrepreneurs' emotional intelligence and transformational leadership orientation impact new ventures' growth. *Journal of Small Business and Entrepreneurship* 25(3): 357–374.

Yoshida Group. 2007. http://www.yoshidagroup.com/index (accessed June 22, 2007).

Youssef, C. M., and F. Luthans. 2012. Positive global leadership. *Journal of World Business* 47: 539–547.

Youssef-Morgan, C. M., and F. Luthans. 2013. Positive leadership: Meaning and application across cultures. *Organizational Dynamics* 42(3): 198–208.

Yuengling, D. 2007. *Message from the president.* http:www.yuengling.commessage.htm#more (accessed June 22, 2007).

Yukl, G. 1999. An evaluation of conceptual weaknesses in transformational and charismatic leadership theories. *The Leadership Quarterly* 10(2): 285–305.

Yukl, G., and C. M. Falbe. 1990. Influence tactics in upward, downward, and lateral influence attempts. *Journal of Applied Psychology* 75: 132–140.

_____. 1991. The importance of different power sources in downward and lateral relations. *Journal of Applied Psychology* 76: 416–423.

Zaccaro, S. J. 2007. Trait-based perspectives of leadership. *American Psychologist* 62: 6–16.

Zaccaro, S. J., and D. Banks. 2004. Leader visioning and adaptability: Bridging the gap between research and practice on developing the ability to manage change. *Human Resource Management* 43: 367–380.

Zaleznik, A. 1990. The leadership gap. *Academy of Management Executive* 4(1): 7–22.

Zander, A. 1983. The value of belonging to a group in Japan. *Small Group Behavior* 14: 7–8.

Zhang, A., R. Ilies, and R. D. Arvey. 2009. Beyond genetic explanations for leadership: The moderating role of the social environment. *Organizational Behavior and Human Decision Processes* 110: 118–128.

Zhou, J., and J. M. George. 2001. When job dissatisfaction leads to creativity: Encouraging the expression of voice. *Academy of Management Journal* 44(4): 682–696.

_____. 2003. Awakening employee creativity: The role of leader emotional intelligence. *The Leadership Quarterly* 14: 545–568.

Zhu, W., B. J. Avolio, R. E. Riggio, and J. J. Sosik. 2011. The effect of authentic transformational leadership on follower and group ethics. *The Leadership Quarterly* 22: 801–817.

Ziad, S. 2012. Culture and consumer ethics. *Journal of Business Ethics* 108(2): 201–213.

Zingerman's. 2013. About us. http://www.zingermanscommunity.com/about-us/ (accessed July 14, 2013).

AUTHOR INDEX

A

Abbott, G. N., 343
Ackerson, L., 87
Adler, N., 106, 168, 338
Adler, S., 129
Alessandri, G., 140
Algera, P. M., 219
Ali, A. J., 177
Allen, N. J., 277
Alluto, J. A., 241
Alspach, G., 144
Alves, J. C., 282
Amanatullah, E. T., 64
Amble, B., 41, 63
Anders, G., 177
Anderson, C., 130, 141, 172
Anderson, J., 91
Anderson, T., 348
Andolsek, D. M., 131
Antonakis, J., 89, 127, 213
Arfken, D. E., 65
Argyris, C., 219, 339
Arlidge, J., 177
Armenakis, A. A., 30
Armour, S., 139
Armstrong, P. I., 64
Arthur, M. B., 209
Arvey, R. D., 129
Asroff, S., 144
Astley, W. G., 175
Aune, R. K., 133
Avey, J. B., 221
Avolio, B. J., 207, 209, 210,
    211, 213, 216, 217, 218,
    221, 222, 351
Ayman-Nolley, S., 42
Ayman, R., 42, 89, 91, 95

B

Babu, S., 84
Back, M. D., 149, 181
Baertlein, L., 348
Bakker, A. B., 213
Ball, A. D., 167
Ballinger, G. A., 29
Bandura, A., 183, 334, 335, 341

Banks, D., 222, 341
Baragheh, A., 241
Bardes, M., 178
Barnes, J., 351
Baron, R. A., 144, 335
Barrett, A., 242
Barrick, M. R., 140, 141, 341
Barsoux, J. L., 247, 350
Bartlett, C. A., 53
Bartol, K. M., 184
Basadur, M., 137
Bass, B. M., 25, 87, 134, 201,
    203, 210, 213
Bauerlein, V., 180
Bauer, T. N., 107
Beauchamp, M. R., 283
Becker, J., 42
Bedeian, A. G., 30, 146
Behfar, K. J., 278
Belet, D., 350
Belgio, W., 133
Bellar, S. L., 65
Bennis, W. G., 27, 140, 183
Beyer, J. M., 209
Bianchi, S. M., 63
Bird, C., 87
Biro, M. M., 344
Bisoux, T., 25, 63, 101, 141,
    314, 342
Black, J., 91
Bligh, M. C., 169
Bliss, J., 29
Block, P., 177, 182, 183
Blundell, M., 185
Bodur, M., 272
Boerner, S., 212, 213, 214
Boies, J., 52
Bolino, M. C., 146
Bono, J. E., 203, 205
Bowers, D. G., 88
Boyatzis, R. E., 135
Boyle, 148, 149
Boyle, M., 148, 149
Bradley, B. H., 205
Branson, R., 214, 215, 241,
    339, 342

Brant, J., 96
Braun, S., 213
Bray, D. W., 87
Brazil, J. J., 302, 306, 307
Breen, B., 138, 241
Bret, B. H., 287
Brodie, L., 348
Brodsky, N., 34
Brown, F. W., 339
Brown, M. C., 28
Brown, M. E., 208
Brown, R., 147
Brunell, A., 148
Bryant, A., 25, 27, 62, 95, 145,
    167, 204, 212, 216, 219, 220,
    235, 240, 250, 270, 271, 273,
    274, 280, 282, 284, 287, 288,
    342, 344, 345
Buchanan, L., 38, 137, 144,
    174, 275
Buckingham, M., 42, 63, 95
Budzek, K., 147
Bukovinsky, D., 183
Bunderson, J. S., 280
Bunker, M., 167
Burke, C. S., 277, 278
Burlingham, B., 166
Burns, J. M., 201, 210
Burris, E., 105
Butler, M. C., 168
Butler, R. J., 255
Butterfield, D. A., 65
Byrne, J. A., 136
Byron, E., 265

C

Caligiuri, P. M., 141
Cameron, D., 201
Cameron, J. E., 305
Cameron, K., 219, 305
Campbell, D. J., 342
Campbell, K. B., 217
Canabou, C., 139, 150
Canger, J. M., 142
Carl, D., 272
Carli, L. L., 52, 63, 65

Carlson, N., 251
Carmeli, A., 234
Carpenter, M. A., 239, 252
Carrns, A., 180
Carson, J. B., 270
Cartwright, D. C., 25
Caruso-Cabrera, M., 306
Carvell, T., 134
Case, S., 203
Cashen, L. H., 252
Cashman, J. R., 107
Castro, S. L., 107
Caver, K. A., 350, 351
Cederholm, L., 273
Chafkin, M., 312
Chambers, J., 219, 245
Chandler, S., 177
Chapman, J., 286
Chappelow, C. T., 345, 346
Chatterjee, S., 52, 277
Cheese, P., 301, 306
Chemers, M. M., 89, 90, 91, 92,
   95, 201
Chen, C. Y., 215
Chen, G., 212
Cheng, B. S., 103, 105
Cheng, T., 105
Chen, Y. F., 272
Cherrington, D. J., 132
Chester, A., 142
Childress, S., 248
Child, T., 41
Chiou, P., 162
Chi, S. C. S., 181, 213
Cho, T. S., 252
Christie, R., 147
Chu, J., 311
Church, G. J., 169
Cianciolo, A. T., 89
Clarke, S., 210
Cleyman, K. L., 105
Cogliser, C. C., 107
Collins, J., 137
Collinson, D., 222
Colvin, G., 136, 186
Condies, S. J., 132
Conger, J. A., 127, 204, 205, 207,
   208, 209, 226, 341
Conlin, M., 330–331
Conyon, M. J., 183, 252
Cooke, D. K., 137

Cooke, R. A., 167, 183
Coolidge, A., 264
Coons, A. E., 88
Cooper, C. D., 127
Cooper, N., 343
Cordery, J., 279
Corn, R. I., 273
Courtright, S. H., 185
Craig, S., 197
Crant, M. J., 142
Cronin, T. E., 177
Cropanzano, R., 104
Crouch, A., 99
Crowley, M. C., 101
Crutchfield, R. S., 25
Csikszentmihalyi, M., 217, 219
Cummings, B., 35
Cunningham, J. B., 287
Cyert, R. M., 28

D

Damouni, N., 265
Dana, D., 265
Dana, J. A., 65
Daniel, T., 148
Dansereau, F., Jr, 104
Dardis, G. J., 342
Dash, E., 251
Dastoor, B., 213
Dave, V., 145
Davidov, B. J., 69
Davidson, A., 39
Davis, J. H., 185
Davis, K. M., 205
Day, D. V., 29, 127, 146, 241, 285,
   341, 350, 351
Deagen, D. A., 99
Debbie, A., 99
De Bono, E., 137, 312
De Hoogh, A. H. B., 141, 209
Denhardt, J. V., 213, 312–313, 338
Denhardt, R. B., 312–313, 338
Den Hartog, D. N., 141, 207, 209
Denning, S., 310
Denton, D. K., 182
de Rond, M., 283
Derr, C. B, 350
Deshpande, R., 84–85
Deutschman, A., 42, 214, 215, 308
Deutsch Salaman, S., 167
Dicke, L. A., 253

Diddams, M., 219
Diefendorff, J. M., 142
Digman, J. M., 140
Dillon, P., 139, 179
D'Intino, R. S., 282
Dodd, N. G., 339
Donaldson, L., 185
Dorfman, P. W., 58, 207, 217,
   247, 272
Douglas, C. A., 342, 344
Downey, H. K., 100
Droge, C. D., 249
Drum, K., 62
Duarte, N. T., 105
Duff, C., 28, 298, 299
Duncan, W. J., 99
Dunlop, W. L., 283
Dunn, M. W., 213
Dutton, J. E., 201, 219
Dvir, T., 212

E

Eagly, A. H., 52, 63, 64, 65,
   213, 351
Eastman, K. K., 213
Eddleston, K. A., 167
Edelhauser, K., 203
Egloff, B., 149, 181
Ehrlick, S. B., 28
Eisenbeiss, S. A., 212, 213, 214
Elkins, T., 100, 105
Ellemers, N., 283
Ellerbee, L., 183
Elliot, P., 176
Ellis, R., 278
Elms, H., 181
Emmons, R. A., 161
England, J. L., 132
Erdogan, B., 106
Erez, A., 209
Erickson, R. J., 131
Ernst, C., 342
Estow, S., 146

F

Fairchild, C., 348
Falbe, C. M., 170, 171
Fanelli, A., 209
Fantazy, K. A., 213
Farh, J. L., 103
Faucheux, M., 304
Feldstein, M. J., 87

Felps, W., 287
Fernholz, T., 277
Fiedler, F. E., 25, 86, 89–96, 99–100, 109, 110, 111, 118, 134, 167, 268
Field, R. H. G., 99
Fields, M., 313
Finkelstein, S., 28, 234, 237, 238
Fisher, A., 136
Fisher, K., 279
Fisher, L. M., 186
Fishman, C., 298, 299
Fishman, S., 196, 197
Flannery, N. P., 251
Fleishman, E. A., 88–89
Flynn, F. J., 141, 165, 172
Foster, P., 162
Foster, T., 275
Fowers, B. J., 69
Fox, C. R., 282
Fox, L., 282
Frauenheim, E., 337
Freeman, J. H., 28
Freeman, R. E., 167, 185
Freisen, P. H., 241
Frey, R., 185
Frontiera, J., 287
Fry, L. W., 215
Furnham, A., 127, 147

G

Galinsky, A. D., 165
Gallagher, B. M., 255
Gallo, C., 220, 239, 250
Gamage, D. T., 270
Gantt, V. W., 253
Garcia, J. E., 92, 95, 134
Gardner, W. L., 165, 205, 217, 218, 219, 221, 222, 229, 339
Geddes, D., 144
Geiger, S. W., 252
Geis, F. L., 147
Geletkanycz, M. A., 239
Gelfand, M., 272
George, B., 25, 30, 34, 136, 217, 238, 306, 341
George, J. M., 138
George, W., 41, 219
Ghiselli, E. E., 134
Ghoshal, S., 53
Gibbs, N., 202
Ginter, P. M., 99

Gladwell, M., 134
Glaser, J. E., 265, 319
Goetz, K., 304
Goldman, B. M., 104
Goldsmith, S., 26
Goldstein, I. L., 141
Goldstein, L., 185
Goleman, D., 135, 136, 156
Gonzales, R., 308
Goodson, J. R., 105
Goozner, M., 177
Gordon, M., 239, 243, 245
Govindarajan, V., 287
Graen, G. B., 58, 104, 106
Grant, D. L., 87
Greene, S. G., 107
Greenleaf, R. K., 25, 215, 216
Greguras, G. J., 142
Greve, A., 308
Griesser, D., 212
Griffin, M. A., 213, 343
Griffin, R. W., 100, 341
Gronn, P., 285
Grow, B., 251
Gruenfeld, D. H., 165
Grzelakowski, M., 64
Guido, H.; 270
Gumusluoglu, L., 213
Gupta, A. K., 237, 242
Gupta, V., 272
Guvenli, T., 133

H

Hackman, J. R., 274, 279, 283, 286
Haga, W. J., 104
Haleblian, J., 238
Haley, F., 270
Hall, C. S., 147
Hall, E. T., 53
Hall, R. N., 237
Halpin, A. W., 88
Halpin, S. M., 350, 351
Hambrick, D. C., 28, 148, 234, 237, 241, 341
Hammonds, K. H., 38
Hammon, S., 35
Hampden-Turner, C., 56, 106, 247, 272
Hannan, M. T., 28
Hansen, B., 251
Hardy, C., 174

Hardy, L., 213
Harris, D., 63
Harris, E. F., 89
Harrison, D., 287
Harrison, J. S., 167, 185, 287
Harris, P. R., 168
Hart, E. W., 342
Hartke, D. D., 95
Hartmann, L. C., 185
Haslam, S. A., 65
Hastings, R., 131, 132
Heath, C., 311, 320
Heath, D., 311, 320
Heavy, C., 241
Hecht, T. D., 277
Hedberg, B. L. T., 308
Hedlund, J., 135
Helfat, C. E., 63
Helgesen, S., 33, 248
Helms, M. M., 65
Hemphill, J. K., 88
Hemsworth, D., 241
Hess, G. D., 169
Hess, P. W., 347
Hewlett, S. A., 63
Hickson, D. J., 173
Hindo, B., 303, 304, 306, 319
Hinkin, T. R., 211
Hira, N. A., 132
Hirst, G., 138
Hodson, R., 177, 179, 182
Hoffman, E., 250
Hofman, M., 248
Hofmann, D. A., 105
Hofstede, G., 54, 55, 272
Ho, J., 282
Hollander, E. P., 205
Holland, K., 70
Hollon, J., 26
Holson, L. M., 108, 140
Homans, G. C., 25
Hoobler, J. M, 65
Hooker, J., 133
Hopfensitz, A., 287
Hoppe, M. H., 349, 350
Houghton, J. D., 282
House, R. J., 58, 60, 89, 99, 100, 139, 168, 202, 204, 209, 247, 349
Howard, D., 239
Howell, J. M., 205, 206, 207, 208
Howell, J. P., 103, 274, 275

Hrebeniak, L. G., 241
Huang, X., 105
Hunter, D., 206
Hunter, E.M., 216–217
Hunt, J. G., 201
Huppke, R., 136
Hutchinson, L. R., 146

I

Ibarra, H., 339, 351
Ilies, R., 89, 107, 129, 203, 205
Irani, J., 84
Ismaill, I. A., 136

J

Jackson, E., 107, 346
Jago, A. G., 96, 97
Jamieson, J. P., 146
Janis, I. L., 285, 286
Jansen, K. J., 240
Javidan, M., 58, 272
Jawahar, I. M., 146
Jenkins, W. O., 87
Jensen, S. M., 219
Jermier, J. M., 102, 238
Jex, S. M., 105
Johannesen-Schmidt, M. C., 64
Johansson, G., 277, 278
Johnson, R. E., 107
Johnson, T. W., 100
Jones, D., 207, 231, 232, 250, 264
Jones, S., 180
Joo, B. K., 143, 343
Juarez, V., 248
Judge, T. A., 65, 89, 127, 136, 140
Jung, D., 209

K

Kabasakal, H., 272
Kacmar, K. M., 105
Kahn, J., 25
Kaiser, R. B., 148, 176, 334, 339
Kalshoven, K., 141
Kamer, 144
Kang, H. R., 280
Kanter, R. M., 273, 282
Kant, L., 179
Kaplan, R. B., 334, 339
Karakitapogˇ lu-Aygün, Z., 213
Karau, S. J., 65, 213
Karkoulian, S., 141
Kark, R., 212, 213, 214

Katz, D., 25
Katzenbach, J. R., 174, 279
Katz, N., 280
Kaufman, G., 63
Kegan, R., 333
Keinan, G., 145
Kellerman, B., 30, 147
Keller, R. T., 100, 105
Kelloway, E. K., 221
Kelly, C., 277
Keltner, D. J., 165
Kempster, S., 342
Kennedy, J. C., 106
Kennedy, J. K., Jr, 91, 94
Kerber, R., 265
Kernis, M. H., 217, 229
Kerr, J., 35, 249
Kerr, S., 94, 102, 238–239
Kessler, J., 273
Kets de Vries, M. F. R., 177, 209, 250
Khalid, A., 186
Khandwalla, P. N., 241, 242
Kharif, O., 338
Kickul, J., 133
Kidder, D. L., 167
Kiley, D., 313, 314
Kim, J., 196
Kim, J. S., 105
Kipnis, D., 170
Kirkpatrick, S. A., 139, 144
Kisfalvi, V., 241
Kish-Gephart, J., 287
Kiviat, B., 243
Klein, H. J., 29, 105
Klich, N. R., 105
Klidas, A., 183
Klonsky, B. G., 351
Klotz, I., 269
Koman, E. S., 136
Konrad, A. M., 186
Kopp, W., 219, 314
Koren, M., 145
Kosalka, T., 127
Kotin, J., 241
Kotter, J. P., 31, 42, 172, 306, 310
Kouzes, J. M., 315, 316, 328, 351
Kraemer, H., 38
Kraimer, M. L., 141, 142
Kramer, M. L., 106
Krech, D., 25
Kristof-Brown, A. L., 240

Kroll, L., 139
Kruse, K., 25, 31
Kuntz, P., 251
Kupfer, A., 245
Kurtz, D. L., 129
Kurtz, R., 103
Kuvass, B., 104, 105

L

LaBarre, P., 42, 184
Lack, E. R., 144
Ladkin, D., 217
LaFrance, K. G., 99
LaGuarde, C., 61
Lahey, L. L., 333
Lammers, J., 165
Lam, W., 105
Laporte, N., 313
Larcker, D. F., 177
Larson, L. L., 214, 215
Laurent, A., 168, 247
Lawler, E. E., III, 183, 186, 270, 317
Lawler, J. J., 210, 213
Lawrence, P., 247, 350
Lawrence, R. L., 99
Lazarus, S., 248
Ledford, G. E., 186, 270
Lee, C. A., 278
Leidl, D., 287
Leithwood, K., 213, 241
Lemmon, G., 65
Lennox, R. D., 159
Lepsinger, R., 345, 346
Lester, S. W., 133
Levay, C., 209, 309
Lewin, K., 88, 304, 305
Lewis, M., 222
Liang, J., 142, 181, 213
Licuanan, B., 137
Liden, R. C., 105
Lieberson, S., 28
Li, N., 142, 215
Linden, R. C., 106
Ling, Y. Z., 213
Lippit, R., 88
Lips- Wiersma, M., 219
Litzky, B. E., 167
Livers, A. B., 350
Locke, E. A., 139, 144
Lombardo, M. M., 149, 201
London, M., 333, 338, 345, 352

Lopez, S. J., 177, 219
Lopez-Zafra, E., 135
Lord, R. G., 29, 241
Love, D., 52
Love, K. G., 105
Lubart, T. I., 137
Lubin, R., 178
Lublin, J.S., 265
Lucia, A. D., 345, 346
Lust, J. A., 144
Luthans, F., 26, 42, 218, 219, 221

M

MacGregor, J., 287
Mackey, A., 29, 234
Magee, J. C., 165, 176
Mahoney, T. A., 28
Main, C., 251
Makhijani, M. G., 213, 351
Malekzadeh, A. R., 34, 144, 175, 235, 236, 237, 239, 241, 242, 243, 244, 250, 325
Malone, T., 283
Manning, J. E., 277
Manz, C. C., 234, 240, 281, 282
Manz, D., 234, 240
Marchetti, M., 204
Marion, R., 351
Markels, A., 264
Marrone, J. A., 270
Marshall, L., 26
Marshall, R., 183
Marsh, H. W., 351
Marsick, V. J., 273
Martin, A., 342
Martin, R., 62
Martinez, S., 207
Martinson, L., 137
Maruca, R. F., 238
Mason, P. A., 234
Massey, M. E., 132
Mathisen, G. E., 137
Mathur, A., 131
Matthews, C., 330
Matviuk, S., 247
Maull, S., 181
Maune, D. J., 65
Mayer, J., 135
Mayo, A., 130
McCall, M. W., 149, 201
McCauley, C. D., 333, 337, 342, 344, 346

McFarland, K. R., 344
McGregor, J., 27, 201, 210, 219, 301, 343
McKinsey, 311, 335
McMurray, A., 30
Meelankavil, J. P., 131
Meindl, J. R., 28
Meister, J. C., 347
Menon, S. T., 183, 185
Messarra, L., 141
Meyerson, M., 91
Milkman, K. L., 282
Miller, D. M., 144, 239, 241, 246, 249, 250, 253, 278
Miner, J. B., 37
Minkov, M., 54
Minton- Eversole, C., 270
Mintzberg, H., 32
Misangyi, V. F., 181, 209
Mischel, W., 129
Misumi, J., 89
Mittal, R., 217
Mohrman, S. A., 183, 186, 270
Möller, M., 99
Montesino, M., 272
Moran, R. T., 168
Morf, C. C., 147
Morgeson, F. P., 105, 107
Morin, R., 131, 132, 335
Morris, M. W., 64
Morrison, A. M., 350
Morrissey, J., 232
Mosadegh-Rad, A. M., 270
Moshavi, D., 339
Mount, I., 245
Mount, M., 140, 141, 341
Muio, A., 38
Muller, J., 313
Mumford, M. D., 88, 137
Munk, N., 239, 243
Murphy, S. E., 134
Murrill, A., 245
Muterera, J., 241
Myatt, D., 287
Myers, D., 136

N

Nahavandi, A., 34, 144, 174, 175, 210, 217, 236, 237, 239, 241, 242, 243, 244, 249, 277
Nahrgang, J. D., 107
Nanus, B., 140, 183

Neck, C. P., 281, 282
Neiminen, L. R. G., 351
Nesbit, P. L., 282
Neubert, M. J. A., 286
Neuman, J. H., 144
Newcomb, T. M., 87
Newstetter, W. I., 87
Ng, E. S., 234
Niessen, C., 105
Nocks, J., 343
Nohe, C., 209
Nohria, N., 130
Norman, W. T., 140
Nuyten, T., 231, 232

O

O'Connor, J. F., 28, 269, 279
Ohlott, P. J., 341
Oldham, G. R., 274
Olsen, R. A., 177
Ones, D. S., 141
Oosterhof, A., 280
O'Reilly, C. A., 234–235, 252
Osborn, K. A., 270
O'Toole, J., 91
Ott, J. S., 253
Overholt, A., 62, 91, 150, 316

P

Pagliarini, R., 343
Parent, J. D., 65
Parker, C. P., 99, 143, 157, 343
Partyka, 148
Pattison, K., 52
Paulhus, D. L., 147, 148
Paumgarten, N., 298
Pawar, B. S., 213
Pearce, C. L., 234, 240
Peck, S. I., 183, 252
Pedrotti, J. T., 219
Pelled, L. H., 107
Pellegrini, E. K., 167, 168
Pepitone, J., 330
Perry, J. L., 255
Pescosolido, A. T., 35
Peters, L. H., 95
Peterson, E., G., 331
Peterson, G., 269
Peterson, M. F., 89
Peterson, S. J., 219
Pettigrew, A., 175
Pfeffer, J., 28, 42, 173, 174, 177, 241

Phillips, J. S., 105
Piccolo, R. F., 89, 127, 178
Pichler, J., 265
Pitcher, P., 241
Podsakoff, P. M., 103
Pohlmann, J. T., 95
Popper, M., 147, 334, 347
Poropat, A. E., 141
Posner, B. Z., 315, 316
Powell, G. N., 65, 91
Prendergast, C., 182
Pressler, J., 196
Price, T. L., 214
Puffer, S. M., 139
Pugh, D. S., 235
Purohit, Y. S., 165
Pynes, J. E., 253

Q

Quinn, R. E., 201, 219, 250, 308

R

Radhakrishnan-Swami, 84
Rafferty, A. E., 213, 343
Rahim, M. A., 167
Raina, A., 84–85
Randolph, W. A., 168, 183, 185, 186
Rank, J., 210
Raskas, D. F., 341
Raskin, R., 147
Rastogi, R., 145
Raven, B. H., 169
Ray, 197
Ready, K. J., 143
Reed, G. E., 70, 177
Reed, T., 314
Reeves, R., 346
Rego, A., 219
Reichard, R. J., 135
Reingold, J., 42, 64, 264
Repetti, A., 270
Reuben, E., 287
Rhodewalt, F., 143, 147
Rice, R., 90
Richards, G. E., 351
Richards, S. C., 147
Rich, B. L., 107, 337, 340
Riggio, R. E., 134, 135
Rink, F., 283
Riordan, M., 105
Robert, C., 56, 135
Roberts, N. C., 205

Robichau, R. W., 253
Robinson, S. L., 165, 167
Rogers, A., 246
Rokeach, M., 154
Roscigno, V. J., 177
Rosenbaum, S., 264
Rosenthal, S. A., 147, 149
Rosier, R. H., 156
Rounds, J., 64
Rowley, C., 280
Rubinkan, M., 103
Ruderman, M. N., 351
Rus, D., 181
Ryan, M. K, 65, 213
Rychlak, J. F., 87
Ryerson-Cruz, G., 180

S

Sachdeva, P. S., 175
Sacks, D., 137, 239, 242
Sadri, G., 135
St. Martin, 302
Salancik, G. R., 28, 173
Salas, E., 277, 285
Salovey, P., 135
Salter, C., 48, 270, 319
Samnani, A., 205, 207
San Antonio, D. M., 270
Sandberg, S., 63, 64
Sanders, W. G., 239
Sankin, A., 35
Sanyal, R., 133
Sarvar, A., 186
Sashkin, M., 203, 214
Scandura, T., 107, 207, 217
Schafer, L., 330
Schaffer, B.S., 105
Schaubroeck, J., 234
Schein, E. H., 34, 52, 235, 249, 250, 320
Schilling, J., 181
Schleicher, D. J., 146
Schmukle, S. C., 149, 181
Schoorman, F. D., 29, 185
Schriesheim, C. A., 94, 107, 211, 217
Schultz, H., 313
Schwartz, N. D., 136
Schwartz, S. H., 136
Schyns, B., 127, 181
Searle, T. P., 217

Sears, G. T., 234
Seashore, S. E., 88
Seely Howard, E., 165
Seibert, S. E., 141, 183, 185
Seligman, M. E. P., 217, 219
Sellers, P., 62, 144, 248, 264
Semler, R., 186
Senge, P. M., 317, 318
Shahhosseini, M., 136
Shamir, B., 204, 205, 206, 209, 213
Sharaf, M., 241
Shen, W., 252
Sherman, L., 243
Shiemann, W., 104
Shinn, S., 358
Shin, S. J., 212
Shlomi, D., 30
Shore, M., 105
Sidani, M., 141
Silong, A. D., 136
Silver, S., 183, 185
Simsek, Z., 241
Sims, H. P., Jr, 100, 213, 241, 281
Singer, P., 207
Singh, J., 186, 205, 207
Sivasubramaniam, H., 213
Skinner, N. F., 146
Skrzypek, G. J., 90
Slaughter, A. M., 61
Slocum, J. W., 35, 249
Smith, D. K., 174, 279
Smith, E. B., 251
Smith, M., 142
Smith, N. R., 37
Smith, P. B., 63
Smith, T. W., 143
Snape, E., 105
Snyder, C. R., 219, 220
Snyder, M., 146, 341
Soler, C., 135
Solomon, M., 358
Solomon, N., 69
Song, J. H., 241
Sosik, J. J., 209
Sparrowe, R. T., 105
Spataro, S. E., 141, 172
Spurk, D., 105
Srivastava, A., 184

Staats, B. R., 282
Stagl, K., 277
Stagl, K. C., 277
Stahl, L., 162
Stanners, P., 177
Stapel, D. A., 165
Starbuck, W. H., 308
Steptoe, S., 140
Sternberg, R. J., 89, 135,
    137, 138
Stern, G. M., 332, 351
Stewart-Belle, S., 144
Stewart, J. B., 277
Stewart, T. A., 144, 315
Stinson, J. E., 100
Stogdill, R. M., 87, 89
Strauss, G., 251
Strauss, K., 143, 213
Strube, M. J., 95, 143, 144
Stuart, H., 330
Sullivan, M., 207
Su, R., 64
Sun, 213, 241
Sutton, R. I., 134
Suutari, V., 351
Swan, K., 41
Sweeney, P., 167
Swinburn, P., 287
Swisher, K., 313
Szilagyi, A. D., 100

T

Taggar, S., 278, 286
Talbott, J., 183
Tamborski, M., 147
Tannenbaum, A. S., 167, 183
Tannen, D., 64
Tayan, B., 177
Taylor, A., 217, 313, 314
Taylor, P., 131
Taylor, S. S., 217
Teagarden, M. B., 168
Tepper, B. J., 94, 180
Terwilliger, J., 287
Tesluk, P. E., 270
Tetrault, L., 94
Thach, E. C., 346
Thomas, A. B., 29
Thomas, K. M., 351
Thompson, L., 165
Thomson, A. M., 255

Thoroughgood, C. N., 178
Thurm, S., 251
Tierney, T. J., 256
Timmons, H., 136
Tims, M., 213
Ting, S., 342
Tipu, S. A. A., 213
Tischler, L., 241, 242, 282
Tishler, A., 234
Tjan, A. K., 339
Tjosvold, D., 99, 272
Tomlinson, R., 139
Tornow, W. W., 345
Townsend, J., 105
Treviño, L., 208, 287
Triandis, H. C., 55, 133
Trice, H. M., 209
Trompenaars, A., 56–57, 58, 61,
    106, 168, 247, 272
Trucco, T., 347
Tsurumi, R., 207
Tuggle, K., 26, 35
Turner, E., 273
Turnley, W. H., 146
Tyabji, H., 217

U

Uhl-Bien, M., 104, 182, 351
Uhlenberg, P., 63
Upbin, B., 331
Useem, J., 35

V

Valerio, A. M., 69
van den Berg, P. T., 183
Vanderkam, L., 141
van der Pool, L., 103
Van der Vegt, G. S., 280
van Dierendonck, D., 216, 217
van Engen, M., 64
van Knippenberg, D., 181
VanSandt, C. V., 282
Van Velsor, E., 333, 337
Vashdi, D. R., 30
Vecchio, R. P., 94
Veiga, J. F., 241
Vidal, B. J., 99
Villa, J. R., 103
Vise, T., 137
Viswesvaran, C., 141
Voelcker, J., 269
Volmer, J., 105

Von Glinow, M. A., 168, 350
Vroom, V. H., 96, 97, 98, 99

W

Waismel-Manor, R., 213
Wakabayashi, M., 105
Walker, M. C., 210
Wallace, C., 287
Wallace, D., 35
Walsh, J., 35
Walsh, T., 169
Walters, J., 38
Walumbwa, F. O., 210, 213, 219
Wang, H., 185, 210, 212, 234
Warner, R., 203
Warrior, P., 217
Waters, L. L., 133
Watson, W. E., 146
Wayne, S. J., 65, 105
Weaver, G. R., 181
Wedley, W. C., 99
Weidner, C. K., 165
Weil, E., 315
Weiner, N., 28
Weiss, H. M., 129
Weiss, R. M., 253
Welch, J., 182
Welch, S., 182
Wellner, A. S., 139, 140, 347
Werner, C., 143
Westly, E., 270
White, C. D., 105
White, R. K., 88
Wilderom, C. P. M., 183
Williams, R., 304
Williams, S., 313
Williams, W. M., 147
Wilson, D. C., 69, 255, 341
Wiltermuth, S. S., 165
Winer, B. J., 88
Winkler, R., 197
Winston, A., 304
Wiscombe, J., 71
Wisse, B., 181
Wohl, J., 265
Wolfe, R. N., 159
Wolff, S. B., 136
Wolfson, P. J., 63
Woolley, A., 283
Worley, C. G., 317
Wylie, I., 137, 270

X

Xanthopoulou, D., 213
Xin, J., 287
Xin, K. R., 107

Y

Yammarino, F. J., 213
Yang, H. D., 280
Yarmohammadian, M. H., 270
Yasai-Ardekani, M., 249
Yates, J. R., 146

Yetton, P., 96
Yglesias, M., 250
Yitshaki, R., 135
Youssef, C., 219, 221
Youssef-Morgan, C. M., 219
Yuengling, D., 103
Yukl, G., 170, 171, 214

Z

Zaccaro, S. J., 127, 140, 341,
 350, 351

Zaleznik, A., 31, 211
Zander, A., 273
Zhang, A., 129
Zhang, Y., 131
Zhou, J., 138, 212
Zhu, W., 219
Ziad, S., 133
Zivnuska, S., 105

SUBJECT INDEX

Note: The letter followed by 'b' refer to boxes

A

ABB, 139
Abel, Scot, 38
Abilities, 134–138
creativity, 137–138
emotional intelligence, 134–137
intelligence, 134–137
practical intelligence, 134–137
Abuse, 176–183
causes of, 177–179
leader characteristics, 177–178
organizational factors, 179
consequences of, 180–181
cycle, 179–180
solutions, 181–183
Access, 176
Accountability, 251–253
Adams-Blake Co., 107
Adobe Systems, 212
Agee, Philip, 178
Agilent, 337
Agon, Jean-Paul, 338
Agreeableness, 141
AIG. See American Insure
Group (AIG)
Alexander, Pam, 149–150
Allen, Scott, 339
AlleyCorp, 275
Amabile, Teresa, 138
Amazon.com, 250
Ambiguity, tolerance of, 302–303
American Express (AmEx),
130, 136
American Insure Group (AIG), 176
America Online (AOL), 203
AmeriCorps, 316
AOL. See America Online (AOL)
Apple, 31, 52, 149
Archer Daniels Midland, 251
Ascriptive cultures, 109
Assertivenes, 58, 87
AT&T, 108
Attributional approach to
leadership, 209

Authentic leadership, 217–219
components of, 218
continuum of, 218
definition and elements, 217–219
Authority, 165, 167
Autocratic decision-making, 98
Autocratic leadership, 88, 272
groupthink and, 285–286
Autonomous leaders, 59
Autonomous teams, 103
Avon, 231–232
Azul, 48–49

B

Baby boomers, 41, 131, 132
"Bad apples," 287
Bador, Nancy, 62
Bain & Company, 70
Bar, Krissi, 144
Barrett, Colleen, 358–359
Bartz, Carol, 144
Bass, Bernard, 201
Baxter, Harry, 38
Baxter Healthcare, 38
BDK. See "Be, Know, Do" (BDK)
model
"Be, Know, Do" (BDK) model, 342
Behavioral range, 129
Behavior era (mid-1940s to early
1970s), 88–89
Bennis, Warren, 140
Best Buy, 302, 330–331
Bethune, Gordon, 216, 250
BET network, 38
Bezos, Jeff, 250
Bienaimé, Jean-Jacques, 270
Big Five dimensions, in
personality, 140–142
agreeableness, 141
conscientiousness, 141
emotional stability, 141–142
extraversion, 141
openness to experience, 141
Bill and Melinda Gates
Foundation, 220

Bird, Larry, 144
Black, Conrad, 177
Blankfein, Lloyd, 177
Boards of directors, 251
Boone, Garrett, 29
BP (British Petroleum), 252
Brabeck-Lethmathe, Peter, 247
Brahma, 246
Branson, Sir Richard, 214–215
Brock, Jon, 246
Buckingham, Marcus, 42, 95
Buckley, George, 306, 341
Burns, Ursula, 342
Bush, George W., 53, 108, 149, 176

C

Cadre, 247
Cainelli, David, 103
Cameron, Kim, 305
Canton, Alan, 107
Carter, Jimmy, 93
Case, Steve, 203
Case studies. See Leadership
experiences
Castro, Fidel, 203–204
Catz, Safra, 239
Centered Leadership, 335
Centrality, in organizations, 173–174
Challenger, space shuttle, 286
Challenge-seeking executive, 241
Chambers, John, 219, 245
Change
agents, 321
forces of, 301
internal and external factors, 39
planned, 307
resistance to, 309, 310
types of, 303
Change-oriented leadership, 317
Charismatic leaders
characteristics of, 202–204
defined, 202
Charismatic leadership, 61
characteristics, 202–204
of followers, 204–205

Charismatic leadership (*continued*)
  in charismatic situations, 205
  culture and, 206–207
  ethical, 207–208
  evaluation and application, 209
  internal organizational conditions
    and, 206
  requirements of, 202
  unethical, 207–208
Chavel, George, 69
Chavez, Hugo, 27
Chenault, Ken, 136, 142
Childs, Ted, 41
Chinese culture, 206–207, 272
Cisco Systems, 217, 219, 245
Citibank, 247
Classroom education, for leadership
    development, 338, 347
C-Level strategies, 141
Clinton, Bill, 94
Clinton, Hilary, 254
Clocky, 273
Closed communication networks, 179
Coaching, 342–343
  elements of, 344
Coca-Cola, 141
Coercive power, 169–170, 181
Cognitive Resource Model, 134
Collaborative individualism, 282
Collectivism, 58, 133, 349
  deception and, 133
  dimensions of, 56
Collins, Eileen, 248
Commitment, 166, 171
Compensation, 251–252
Compliance, 166, 178
Conde, Critóbal, 273
Confucian cluster, 58
Confucian tradition, 207
Conscientiousness, 141
Consultative style of decision
    making, 98
Container Store, 25, 29
Content of leader development,
    336–337
Continental Airlines, 216, 250
Contingency era (early 1960s
    till date), 89
Contingent rewards, 210
Cooperative exploration, 312
Coping with uncertainty, 173

Corruption, 176–183
  causes of, 177–178
    leader characteristics, 177–178
    organizational factors, 179
  consequences of, 180–181
  cycle, 179–180
  solutions, 181–183
Corruption Index, 133
Creativity, 137–138, 311–312
Credit Suisse Group, 91
Crisis management
  guidelines, 240
  unplanned change, 308
Cross-cultural organizational
    cultures, 58–59
  Trompenaar's model, 57
Cue Ball, 339
Cultural mindset, 67–69
Culture
  ascriptive, 109
  characteristics, 51
  charismatic leadership and,
    206–207
  defined, 51
  family and Eiffel Tower, 57
  gender and leadership, 61–65
    causes of gender differences,
      63–66
    trends in leadership, 62–63
  group, 61–67
  guided missile, 56–57
  high-context *vs.* low-context,
    53–54
  incubator, 56–57
  and leader development,
    349–350
  levels of, 51–53
  loose, 55
  managing, 61
  national
    GLOBE, 58–61
    Hall's high-context and low
      context cultural framework,
      53–54
    Hofstede's five cultural
      dimensions, 54–55
    model of, 53–57
    Trompenaars's dimensions of
      culture, 56–57
  organizational. *See*
    Organizational culture

organizational change and, 301
participative management,
    271–272
power distribution and, 167–168
value system and, 130–131
Western *vs.* Eastern, 130–131
Cyrus the Great, 206

D

The Dance of Leadership, 312
Dark Triad personality, 147–150
Decision making, 180–181
  autocratic, 96, 98
  centralizing, 243, 244, 245
  consultative, 97, 98
  creativity and, 137–138
  decentralizing, 185, 316
  delegation of, 96
  group, 96
  Normative Decision Model, 95–96
  outsiders in, 182–183
  participative, 271, 272
  tools, 312
  unethical, 166, 181
360-degree feedback programs,
    345–346
  factors contributing to success
    of, 346
Delegation, 273–276
  benefits of, 274
  guidelines for, 274–276
  leaders' failure in, 276
Deloitte, 66
Demographic characteristics, of
    leaders, 138–140
Destructive narcissistic leaders,
    147, 178
Development
  defined, 333
  leadership. *See* Leadership,
    development
  personal, 353
Development programs, criteria for,
    337–338
  assessment and follow-up, 338
  assessment data of strength, 337
  clear objectives, 338
  organizational culture, 335–337
  rewards, 338
  self-awareness, 339–341
  tools and methods, 338

Devine, Ted, 38
D.G. Yuengling & Son, 103
Diehl, Philip, 38
Discrimination
    leadership, 64
    workplace, 64
Disney, 108
Divergent thinking. *See* Creativity
Diversity, cultural
    dimensions, 61
    as factor in leadership, 61
    solutions to, 69–71
D.L. Rogers Corp., 124–125
The DNA of Leadership, 319
Doctors without Border, 253, 254
Double-loop learning, 339
Dougan, Brady W., 91
Drexler, Mickey, 239, 242, 243
Duke Energy, 204, 235
Dunlap, Al, 41, 178
Dunn, Brian, 330
Dunsire, Debra, 274

E

eBay, 62
Ecover, 301
Edmonston, David, 251
Edwards, Cynthia, 270
EEOC. *See* Equal Employment
    Opportunity Commission
    (EEOC)
Effective leadership
    CEO of a company, 26
    definitions of, 27
    football coach, 26–27
    obstacles to, 30–31
    politicians, 26–27
    school principal, 27
Effectiveness, defined, 26–27
Eiffel Tower culture, 57
Eisner, Michael, 108, 140, 146
Eldrup, Anders, 177
Ellerbee, Linda, 183
Ellison, Larry, 239
Emotional intelligence, 134–138
Emotional stability, 141–142
Empowerment, 183–187
    impact of, 185–186
    leadership factors, 184
    organizational factors, 184–185
    steps to, 183–184

Enron, 176
Equal Employment Opportunity
    Commission (EEOC), 65
Ericsoon, 314
Ethics
    charismatic leadership and,
        207–208
    values and, 133
Executive discretion, 237–238
    moderators of
        external environmental factors,
            237–238
        internal organizational factors,
            238–240
Executive compensation, 252
Executive pay watch, 251
Experiences, for leader
    development, 341–342
Expert power, 169, 170–171
External adaptability, 27
Extraversion, 141
Exxon, 252

F

Facebook, 63, 64, 311
Falco, Randy, 251
Falk, Jonas, 25
Family culture, 57
Favoritism, 105, 106
FBI. *See* Federal Bureau of
    Investigation (FBI)
Federal Bureau of Investigation
    (FBI), 302, 306, 307
Feedback, for leadership
    development, 336–337
Feedback-intensive programs,
    345–346
    factors contributing to success
        of, 346
*The Female Advantage: Women's
    Way of Leadership,* 33
Fiedler, Fred, 25
Fiedler's Contingency Model
    compared, 110
    evaluations and application, 94–95
    leader style, 90–91
    predictions, 92–94
    recommendations, 95
    situation control, 91–92
    task-and relationship-motivated
        individuals, 90–91

5 influential CEOs, 38, 40
Foley, Pete, 311
Force Field theory, 304
        See also Lewin's model of
            change
Ford, Bill, Jr., 313
Ford Foundation, 255–256
Ford Motor Company, 62, 269,
    313–314
Fortune (magazine), 62
Fortune 500 companies, 136
Fox, Vincente, 53
Free-riders, 286
French cadre, 247
Friendship, 108
    patterns and attraction, 108
    sources of power, 170
Fuld, Richard, 196–197
Functions, of leaders, 32–36
Future orientation, 58, 342

G

Gallagher, Brian, 255
Gallup Organization, 42, 69
Gandhi, Mahathma, 203, 320
Gap Inc., 239
Gardner, Howard, 315
Gates, Bill, 343
Gender and leadership, 61
    causes of differences, 63–65
        discrimination, 64–65
        inequality, reasons for, 64
        solutions to
            challenges, 69–71
        stereotypes, 64–65
        trends, 63
Gender egalitarianism, 58, 59
Genencor International, 270
General Electric, 35, 38, 176
General Motors, 308
Generation-based value differences,
    131–132
    in United States, 132
Generation Xers, 131, 132
George, Bill, 41,
    219, 308
Georgetown National Center, 67
Gerstner, Lou, 246
Ghosn, Carlos, 247
Gilmartin, Ray, 251
Gilt Groupe, 280

Gioia, Nancy, 269
Global Leadership and
    Organizational Behavior
    Effectiveness Research
    (GLOBE), 58–61
  country clusters, 59
GLOBE. *See* Global Leadership
    and Organizational
    Behavior Effectiveness
    Research (GLOBE)
Goldman Sachs, 52, 347
Goleman, Daniel, 135, 136
Goodnight, Jim, 101
Google, 277–278
Gordon, Ellen, 243, 245
Gramercy Tavern, 136
Grandes Écoles, 247
Greenspan, Alan, 169
Grinney, Jay, 180
Grogan, Barbara, 62
Groups
  and teams, 279
Groupthink, 285–286
Grove, Andy, 142
Grundhofer, John, 41
Grupo Televisa SA, 139
Guided missile, 57
Gymboree Corp., 139

H

Hall's high-context and low context
    cultural framework, 53–54
Hance, Steve, 330
Harman International Industries, 251
Harper, Lisa, 139
Hartnett, Jack, 124–125
Hayward, Tony, 252
HCI. *See* High-control
    innovator (HCI)
Head Start, 316
HealthSouth Corporation, 180
Helgesen, Sally, 33, 248
Herman Miller, 52, 319
Heroes and Hero Worship, 87
Heroic leadership, 281
Hesselbein, Francis, 62
Hewertson, Roxan, 40
Hewlett-Packard, 251
Hewlett-Packard Laboratories, 26
Hickenlooper, John, 26
High-control innovator (HCI), 242,
    243, 245

Highland Consulting Group, 40
Hispanic Scholarship Fund, 344
Hitler, 147
Hoffman, Bryce, 250
Hoffman, Linda, 248, 250
Hofstede's five cultural
    dimensions, 54–56
Hollinger International, 177
Home Depot, 347
Homogeneity vs. heterogeneity,
    in teams, 283
Honesty, 139
Horizontal collectivistic (HC)
    culture, 55
Horizontal individualists (HV), 55
House, Robert, 25, 202

I

IBM, 41, 246, 282, 341
Iger, Bob, 140
Iger, Robert, 219–220
Immelt, Jeff, 35, 176
Immelt, Jeffrey, 38
Improvisation, 310–311
InBev, 246
Inc (magazine), 269
Incubator cultures, 56
Indiana University, 347
Individual characteristics
  behavioral range, 128–129
  elements of differences, 127–129
    abilities and skills, 128
    heredity and environment,
      127–128
    leadership traits, 127–129
    overview, 126–127
    personality traits. *See* Personality
      traits
    situation and, 129
Individualism, 54–56
  dimensions of, 56
Individual power
  consequences, 170–172
  French and Raven's sources
    of, 170
  potential reactions to, 171
  sources of, 170–172
  use, 170–172
Ingersoll-Rand, 347
In-groups and out-groups, 107, 108
Initiation-of-structure
    concept, 37, 268

Inspirational appeal, 171
Integrity, 139, 154
Intel, 142
Intelligence, 134–137
  emotional and practical, 134–137
Internet, 203
Isdell, E. Neville, 141
Islamic fundamentalism, 206
Israel, 206
Iverson, Robert W., 272

J

J. Crew, 239
Jagged Edge Mountain Gear
    (JEMG), 236
Japanese culture, 272–273
Jean, Emilio Azcarraga, 139
JEMG. *See* Jagged Edge Mountain
    Gear (JEMG)
JetBlue Airways, 48–49, 301
Job experiences, 341
Jobs, Steve, 52, 149
Johnson, Sheila, 38
Johnson, Magic, 144
Johnson & Johnson, 341
Jones Golf bags, 96
Joyce, Leslie, 347
Judeo-Christian beliefs, 206, 207
JumpStart, 316
Jung, Andrea, 231–232

K

Katzenberg, Jeffrey, 144, 145,
    146, 344
Keefe, Bruyette & Woods, 181
Kelleher, Herb, 146, 358–359
Kelly, Gary, 358–359
Kelly, Patrick, 315
Kennedy, J. F., 200, 207, 314
King, Martin Luther, Jr., 203, 205
Kiwi Airlines, 271
Kleisterlee, Gerard, 270
Kopp, Wendy, 219
Kotter, John, 42, 306
Kozlowski, L. Dennis, 181
Kyi, Aung San Suu, 203

L

Labor–management disputes, 167
Ladouceur, Bob, 35
Lafley, A. G., 264–265, 320
Laissez-faire leadership, 88, 211

Lakhani, Karin, 311
Lansing, Sherry, 248
Lateral thinking. *See* Creativity
Laybourne, Gerry, 62
Lazarus, Shelly, 248
LBDQ. *See* Leader Behavior
    Description Questionnaire
    (LBDQ)
Leader Behavior Description
    Questionnaire (LBDQ), 88
Leader–Member Exchange (LMX),
    104–109
  evaluation and application, 106–109
  framework, 104–106
Leader-member relations (LMR),
    91–92
Leaders
  autocratic, 88, 286, 312
  autonomous, 59
  changes in organizations and
    expectations of, 38–41
  charismatic leaders, 201–204.
    See also Charismatic
    leadership
  creative, 137–138
  cultural values, 349
  demographic characteristics of,
    138–140
  development methods, 337–346
    classroom education, 339–340
    coaching and mentoring,
      343–345
    comparison of, 340
    experience, 341–342
    feedback-intensive programs,
      345–346
    outdoor challenges, 347
    self-awareness, 341, 342
  and Hall's high-context and low
    context cultural framework,
    53–54
  followers, relationship with, 106
  of incubator cultures, 56
  managers and, 32
  micro, 234–235
  need for, 28
  position power (PP) of, 91–92
  positive narcissistic, 148
  processes, 249
  roles and functions of, 32–36
  self-monitoring style, 146–147
  in team environment, 283–285

Leadership
  abilities, 134–138
    creativity, 137–138
    emotional intelligence,
      134–138
    intelligence, 134
  authentic, 217–219
    components of, 218
    continuum of, 218
    definition and elements,
      217–219
  basics, 36
  born leaders, 86
  change, forces of, 300, 320
  charismatic, 59, 200, 209
    characteristics, 202–205
    in charismatic situations, 205
    culture and, 206–207
    ethical, 207–208
    evaluation and
      application, 209
    followers, 204–205
    internal organizational
      conditions and, 206
    requirements of, 202
    unethical, 207–208
  control vs result-oriented, 37
  cultural profiles, 60
  development, 332, 352
    criteria for effective program
      of, 337–339
    and culture, 349–350
    effectiveness, 351–353
    elements of, 333–337
    organizational and personal
      factors in, 352
  discrimination, 64
  gold standards, 50
  individual traits, 126
  laissez-faire, 88, 211
  and management, 31–32
  levels in organization, 233
  models
    Fiedler's contingency, 90–95
    LMX, 104–109
    normative decision, 95–99
    SLM, 102–103
    substitutes for leadership,
      100–103
    participative, 59
  neutralizers, 102
  personality traits, 138–150

    Big Five dimensions, 140–142
    Machiavellian personality,
      147–150
    narcissistic, 147–150
    self-monitoring, 146–147
    Type A personality, 143–146
    Type B personality, 143–146
  power, 164
  significance, 30
  skills, 138
  spiritual, 215, 221
  strategic leadership. *See*
    Strategic leadership
  substitutes, 102
  team-based, 60, 268, 288
  theories
    behavior era (mid-1940s to
      early 1970s), 88–89
    contingency era
      (early 1960s till date), 89
    path-goal, 99
    trait era (late 1800s to
      mid-1940s), 87–88
  transactional, 210
  transformational, 211–212
  value-based, 59, 215–216
Leadership experiences
  in Container Store, 29b
  at Deloitte (Accounting firm), 66b
  in Ford Motor Company, 313b
  Fuld, Richard on, 196b–197b
  at Google, 277
  Hartnett, Jack on, 124b–125b
  Joly, Hubert on, 330b–331b
  Jung, Andrea's, 231b–232b
  of Katzenberg, 145b
  Lafley, A.G. on 264b–265b
  Mackey, John's, 298b–299b
  Neeleman, David's, 48b–49b
  at Public Allies (community
    organization), 254b
  at SAS, 101b
  at Semco, 186b
  in Southwest Airlines, 358b–359b
  in Starbucks, 348b
  Tata, Ratan's, 84b–85b
  in Virgin Group, 214b
  Xin, Zhang's, 162b–163b
Leader to Leader institute, 62
Learning, and leadership
    development, 333–336
  elements of, 333–337

Learning, and leadership
   development (*continued*)
   emotional intelligence for, 335
   factors, 335, 352
   opportunity for, 335
   organizational culture in, 335
   practice and persistence in, 336
   self efficacy in, 335
   types, 334
Learning organizations, 317–319
   blocks to, 318
   elements of, 318
Learning through Art, 139
Least preferred coworker (LPC), 90
Legitimate power, 169, 170, 172
Lehman Brothers, 61, 196–197
Levchin, Max, 312
Le Quément, Patrick, 137
Lewin's model of change, 304–308
   changing, 305
   characteristics of, 306–307
   freezing, 305
   unfreezing, 305
Lincoln Electric Company, 246
Lindahl, Goran, 139
Linksys, 245
LMR. *See* Leader-member
   relations (LMR)
LMX. *See* Leader–Member
   Exchange (LMX)
Lombardo, Gian, 149, 201
Loose culture, 55
L'Oreal, 247
LPC. *See* Least preferred
   coworker (LPC)
Lucky Duck Productions, 183
Luechtefeld, Monica, 241
Luthans, Fred, 26
Lyne, Susan, 280

M
3M, 303, 304, 306
Machiavellian personality, 147–150
Mackey, John, 298–299
Management by Exception
   (MBE), 210
Managers
   power of top executives, 174–176
   successful, 26
Mandela, Nelson, 200, 204, 320
Mao Zedong, 207
Masculinity, 54, 55

MBE. *See* Management by
   Exception (MBE)
McDermott, James, Jr., 181
McDonald, Bob, 264–265
McDonald's, 162, 185
McGovern, Gail, 248
McKinsey, 301, 311
McKintry, Nancy, 27, 167
McNerney, James, 303, 304, 319
Medtronics, 34
Mentoring, 342–346
   formal and informal, 344
Merck, 184, 251
Mexico, 272
Meyerson, Mort, 91
Micro leaders, 234–235
Microsoft, 25
Middle Easterners, 247
Millennials, 131, 132
Millennium (Company), 274
Ministry of International Trade and
   Industry (MITI), 302
Mintzberg, Henry, 32, 33
MITI. *See* Ministry of International
   Trade and Industry (MITI)
Moore, Darla, 62
Morris Air, 48
Morrison Knudson (MK), 178
Motorola, 347
Mueller, Robert, 302, 307
Mulally, Alan, 235, 250, 313–314
Mulcahy, Anne, 338
Multiculturalism, 69, 70
Multicultural organization, 69–71
Musk, Elon, 269
Musser, Cherri, 62
Myers, Danny, 136

N
NAACP. *See* National Association
   for the Advancement of
   Colored People (NAACP)
Nadel, Andrew, 140
Nanda, Gauri, 273
Napoléon, 189, 206
Narayen, Shantanu, 212
Narcissistic personality, 147–150
   bosses with, 149
Nardelli, Robert, 251
NASA. *See* National Aeronautics
   and Space Administration
   (NASA)

Nasser, Gamal Abdul, 203
National Aeronautics and Space
   Administration (NASA), 57
National Association for the
   Advancement of Colored
   People (NAACP), 253
National culture
   GLOBE, 58–61
   Hall's high-context and
      lowcontext cultural
      framework, 53–54
   Hofstede's five cultural
      dimensions, 54–56
   model of, 53–57
   perception of time and, 303
   tolerance of ambiguity, 302
   Trompenaars's dimensions of
      culture, 56–57
National Hockey League, 167
National organizational heritage, 53
Navajos, 131
Neeleman, David, 34, 48–49
Negativity, in teams, 287
Nepotism, 105, 106
New United Motor Manufacturing
   Inc. (Nummi), 308
New York City Mutual.com, 38
New York Times, 27, 222
Nickelodeon, 62
Nissan Motors, 247
Nixon, Richard, 93
Nonprofit organizations, 253–255
   leadership of, 255–256
Normative decision model, 95–99
   contingency factors, 96–99
   evaluation and application, 99
   leader's decision styles, 95–97
Nummi. *See* New United Motor
   Manufacturing Inc.
   (Nummi)

O
Obama, Barak, 28, 90–91, 200,
   202–205, 254
O'Connor, Kevin, 269, 279
Oesterle, Stephen, 26, 34
Ogilvy & Mather, 248
Ogilvy Public Relations
   Worldwide, 150
Ohio State Leadership Studies, 88
OIA Global Logistics, 96
Openness to experience, 141

Optimal self-esteem, 217
Oracle, 239
OrganicLife, 25
Organizational change
  approaches, 319–320
  barriers to, 41–42
  creativity and, 311–312
  factors driving, 38–40
  forces for
    culture, 301–302
    internal and external, 301–302
  improvisation and, 312–313
  leaders in, 317–319
  model for, 304–306
  planned change, 306–308
  resistance to, 308–309
    solutions, 308–311
  roles for leaders, 36–37
  types of, 303–304
  unplanned change, 308
  vision and inspiration in, 314–317
Organizational culture, 51–53, 56–61
  creation and maintenance of,
    33–35
  in development programs, 336
  leader's function in, 34
  and learning, 333–336
Otis, Clarence, Jr., 270
Outdoor challenges programs, for
    leadership development,
    340, 347
Ovitz, Michael, 108
Owen-Jones, Lindsay, 247
OXFAM, 253, 254
Oxygen Media, 62

P
Page, Larry, 277–278
Palmisano, Samuel, 282, 341
Participative innovator (PI), 242,
    243, 245
Participative leadership, 59
Participative management
  concept of, 269–272
  continuum of, 269
  criteria for participation,
    271–272
  culture in, 272–273
  delegation, 273–275
    benefits of, 274
    guidelines for, 274–276
    leaders' failure in, 276

Path-Goal Theory, of leadership, 99
  evaluation and application, 100
  framework, 99–100
PayPal, 269, 312
Peer pressure, 321
Perception of time, 303
Performance orientation, 58, 59
Perot Systems, 91
Personality, defined, 128
Personality traits, 138–152
  Big Five dimensions, 140–142
  Machiavellian personality,
    147–150
  narcissistic, 147–150
  self-monitoring, 146–147
  Type A personality, 143–146
  Type B personality, 143–146
Pertz, Douglas, 251
Peters, Tom, 42, 64
Peterson, Marissa, 91
Petrilli, Lisa, 141
PharmaFab, 91
Physician Sales and Services
    (PSS), 315
PI. *See* Participative innovator (PI)
Planned change, process of,
    306–308
PM. *See* Process manager (PM)
Position power (PP), 91–92
Positive leadership
  approaches, 319–320
  characteristics, 220
  concept of, 219–220
  evaluation and application,
    221–222
  practical tips, 221
Positive narcissistic leaders, 148
Power, in organizations
  and abuse and corruption,
    176–183
    causes of, 177–178
    consequences of, 180–181
    cycle, 179–180
    solutions, 181–183
  career stage and sources of, 172
  consequences, 165–167
  definition of, 165
  distribution of, 167
  empowerment, 183–187
    impact of, 185
    leadership factors, 183–184

    organizational factors, 184–185
    steps to, 183–185
  managing, 175
  sources
    consequences, 171
    related to individuals, 170–172
    for teams, 172–173
    of top executives, 174–176
Power distance, 168
Power Holder, 166
Practical intelligence, 134–137
Pride Products, 140
The Prince, 147
Proactive personality, 142–143
Process manager (PM), 243, 246
Procter & Gamble, 35, 38, 264–265
PSS. *See* Physician Sales and
    Services (PSS)
Putra, Cinta, 63, 342

Q
Quenemoen, Margaret, 236
Quenemoen, Paula, 236
*Quiet: The Power of Introverts in
    a World That Can't Stop
    Talking* (Cain), 141
Quinn, Feargal, 250

R
Rainwater, Inc., 62
Reagan, Ronald, 94
Reddy, Kirthiga, 311
Referent power, 170–171
Regeneron Pharmaceuticals, 184
Relationship-motivated leaders
    vs task-motivated leaders, 90
Renault, 247
Resistance, 167
  to change, 308–311
    causes of, 309
    methods for managing,
      310–311
Ressler, Cali, 330–331
Results-Only Work Environment
    (ROWE), 330–331
Revolution (company), 203
RevolutionHealth, 203
Reward power, 169, 170
Reward system
  of CEO, 250
  formal and informal, 250
Ridley, David, 358–359

RJR Nabisco, 246
Rockwell, David, 137, 241
Rocky Flats nuclear site, 210
Rodin, Judith, 248
Rogers, James E., 204, 235, 250
Rogers' and Maslow's concept of
    self-actualization, 217
Role model, 315
ROWE. *See* Results-Only Work
    Environment (ROWE)
Royal Phillips Electronics, 270
Rudin, Scott, 134
Russ Berrie and Co., 204
Ryan, Darlene, 91
Ryan, Kevin, 275
Ryder, Tom, 136

S

Saginaw, Paul, 166, 170
Salary packages, 251–252
Sall, John, 101
Salzberg, Barry, 66
Sandberg, Sheryl, 63, 64
Sapio, Rick, 38
SAS, 101
Scherick, Edgar, 134
Schultz, Howard, 34, 313, 348
Scrushy, Richard, 180
Secure Works, 35
Self-awareness
    for effective development
        program, 339–341
    guidelines for, 339
    for leader development, 339–341
Self efficacy, 335
Self-leadership, 281–282
    development of, 281
Self-managed teams (SMT), 275,
    279–280
    characteristics, 279–280
Self-monitoring style, of leader(s),
    146–147
Semco, 186
Semler, Ricardo, 102, 186, 245
Servant leadership, 215–217
    key characteristics, 216
Sexual harassment, 65
Shapiro, Judith, 248
Shirley, Stephanie, 62
Sidhum, Jay, 251
Sihamoni, Norodom, 207
Sims, Ron, 38

Sit Con. *See* Situational control
Situational control, leader styles
    and behavior, 94
Six Sigma, 304, 319
Sjoerdsma, Jim, 270
Skills, for leadership, 138
Skol, 246
Smith, Carol, 62
Smith, Sarah, 52
Smooth internal processes, 27
SMT. *See* Self-managed teams (SMT)
Sodexo, 69
Soho-China, 162
Southwest Airlines, 48, 335,
    358–359
Sovereign Bancorp, 251
Space X, 269
Spice Works, 38
Spirituality, 130, 132
Spiritual leadership, 215, 219, 315
Stalin, 149
Stand Up to Cancer, 248
Starbucks, 34, 218, 313,
    315, 348
Status quo guardian (SQG), 243,
    244, 245
Stella Artois, 246
Sternin, Jerry, 320
Stock prices, 26, 139, 234
Strategic forces, 235–237, 242
Strategic leadership
    accountability of leaders,
        251–253
    culture and gender, 246–248
    domain and impact of, 235–236
    dual role of, 237
    impact and influence on
        organization, 248–249
        allocation of resources, 249–250
        direct decisions, 249
        norms and modeling
            behaviors, 250–251
        reward systems, 249, 250
    micro leadership *vs.*, 234–235
    types, 242–246
Substitutes for Leadership Model
    (SLM), 102
Successful managers, 26
Sunbeam Corporation, 41
SunGard, 273
Sun Microsystems, 91

Superquinn, 250
Svanberg, Carl-Henric, 314
Swinburn, Peter, 287
Swiss Nestlé, 247
Symond, Curtis, 38

T

Takeda Oncology company, 274
Task-motivated leaders, 92, 93–94
    relationship-motivated leaders
        vs, 90
Task structure (TS), 93
Taylor, Ros, 343
Teach for America, 219, 314
Team-based leadership, 60
Teams
    characterictics of, 278–279
    effectiveness, 287–288
    and groups, 279
    homogeneity vs. heterogeneity, 283
    leaders in, 283–285
    managing dysfunction in,
        285–286
    problems in, 285
    self-leadership, 281–282
    self-managed, 279–280
    sources of power for, 172–178
        centrality, 173–174
        coping with uncertainty, 173
        dependence and
            substituability, 174
        trust and collaboration culture,
            278, 288
    sports model, 280
Tesla Motors, 269
Thompson, Jodi, 330–331
Thompson, John, 331
Thulin, Inge, 306
Tichy, Noel, 315
Time efficient, normative
    model, 98
Time, perception of, 303
Time orientation, 54, 55
Tindell, Kip, 29
Tjan, Anthony, 339
Tolerance of ambiguity, 302
Tootsie Roll Industries Inc., 245
Torre, Joe, 26
Toyota, 38, 71, 279, 307–308
Toyota U.S.A., 71
    Twenty-First Century Diversity
        Strategy, 71

Trait Era (late 1800s to mid-1940s), 87–88
Transactional leadership, 213
  contingent reward (CR), 213
  MBE, 214
Transformational leadership
  charisma and inspiration, 211–212
  evaluation and application, 213–214
  factors, 211
  individual considerations in, 212
  intellectual stimulation, 212
Trompenaars's dimensions of culture, 56–57
TS. *See* Task structure (TS)
Tsao, Janie, 245
Tsao, Victor, 245
Tucker, Sara Martinez, 344
Tyabji, Hatim, 217
Tyco, 176, 181
Type A personality, 143–146
Type B personality, 143–146

U
Ubiñas, Luis A, 255–256
Uncertainty, coping with, 173
Uncertainty avoidance, 55, 58, 168
Union Carbide, 252
Union Square Café, 136
United Way, 255
University of Southern California, 270
Unplanned change, dealing with, 308
Upper-echelon leaders
  characteristics of, 241–248
  demographic and personality traits, 241
  dual role of, 237
  micro *vs.*, 234–235
  need for control, 242
  openness to change, 241
U.S. Army, leader development at, 342

U.S. demographic highlights and trends in workforce, 40–41
U.S. Federal Bureau of Investigation (FBI). *See* Federal Bureau of Investigation (FBI)
U.S. Mint, 38
U.S. National Aeronautics and Space Administration (NASA). *See* National Aeronautics and Space Administration (NASA)
U.S. Population, ethnic and demographic changes, 40
U.S. Postal Service, 238
U.S. presidents
  and national culture, 52–53
  as relationship-motivated leaders, 93–94
  as task-motivated leaders, 93, 94
Useem, Mike, 238

V
Vagelos, Roy, 184
Value-based leadership, 59, 215–216
Values, 130–132
  and ethics, 133
  generational differences, 131–133
  system and culture, 130–131
Vertical collectivistic (VC) culture, 55
Vertical Dyad Linkage Model. *See* Leader–Member Exchange (LMX)
Vertical individualist (VI), 55
Virgin Group, 214–215
Visionary leadership, 314–317
Vroom–Yetton model. *See* Normative decision model

W
Wade, Kathy, 139
Waldron, Rob, 316
Wallace, Mark, 287

Waugh, Barbara, 26
Weinzweig, Ari, 166, 170
Welch, Jack, 35, 38, 176
Wetterstrom, Roy, 245
Whitman, Meg, 62, 139, 179, 248
Whole Foods, 38, 298–299
Wickstrom, Todd, 166
Widerotter, Maggie, 108
Winfrey, Oprah, 239
Wink Communication, 108
Winkler, Tyler, 35
Woertz, Patricia, 251
Wolters Kluwer, 27
Women
  business owners in U.S, 130
  challenges in balancing family and work, 63–64
  discrimination against, 64–65
  in organizations, 62–63
Women in the Labor Force, 63
Working mothers, 63
Workplace discrimination, 64–65
World Fact Book, 39, 40

X
Xerox, 28, 212, 338, 339, 342
Xi, Zhang, 162–163

Y
Yahoo, 251, 330
Yamada, Tachi, 220
Yoshida, Junki, 95
Yoshida Group, 95–96
Yuengling, Dick, 103
Yuengling, Jennifer, 103

Z
Zander, Ed, 273
ZCoB. *See* Zingerman's Community of Business (ZCoB)
Zimmerman, Jordan, 144
Zingerman's Community of Business (ZCoB), 166, 167, 170